To Nin and ...

Thanks for the
kind words.

Joanne and Stephen McKinnon
Barrington
Oct. 2, 1988

Agnes Smedley

Agnes Smedley as a war reporter in China, circa 1939.
(Courtesy of Aino Taylor.)

Agnes Smedley

*The Life and Times
of an American Radical*

Janice R. MacKinnon
Stephen R. MacKinnon

UNIVERSITY OF CALIFORNIA PRESS
Berkeley · Los Angeles

Grateful acknowledgment is made to
Alfred A. Knopf, Inc., for permission to
reprint material from *Battle Hymn of
China* by Agnes Smedley, copyright 1943, 1970.

University of California Press
Berkeley and Los Angeles, California

Library of Congress Cataloging-in-Publication Data

MacKinnon, Janice R.
  Agnes Smedley, the life and times of an
American radical.

  Bibliography: p.
  Includes index.
  1. Smedley, Agnes, 1890–1950—Biography.
2. Authors, American—20th century—Biography.
3. Journalists—United States—Biography.
4. Radicals—United States—Biography.
I. MacKinnon, Stephen R.   II. Title.
PS3537.M16Z77   1988   818'.5209 [B]   87-10853
ISBN 0-520-05966-2 (alk. paper)

Printed in the United States of America
1 2 3 4 5 6 7 8 9

To our children
Rebecca and Cyrus

Contents

Preface

It did not take us long to discover why there have been no biographies of Agnes Smedley. Even the most ordinary facts about her life, including her birthdate, were a mystery. She wrote six books, which were not hard to find; but she also wrote hundreds of articles in publications scattered around the globe, and these had never been collected. Nor was there the usual corpus of personal letters and papers waiting for us in a comfortable academic library. As a result of the basic detective work required, it has taken us fourteen years to compile Smedley's writings, collect her letters, track down and interview her old friends and enemies, and scour intelligence files. The Bibliography at the back of the book presents a detailed summary of these sources. (Secondary sources are cited in the Notes.)

In our effort to view Smedley from every possible perspective, we have pursued traces of her throughout the United States and around the world—in Europe, India, and China. China presented special difficulties, especially in 1973, when we started our research. But after a number of trips and two years of residence in Beijing from 1979 to 1981, the Chinese pieces of the Smedley puzzle began to fall into place. By the end, we had interviewed thirty-two Chinese intellectuals and leaders who had been active in the 1930s—which we believe is the most intensive study of this group since 1976.

Under the circumstances, the debts we have accumulated are formidable. In terms of finding source material on Smedley, we have to begin by thanking all persons listed in the Bibliography as having been interviewed. Among them, Elinor and Thorberg Brundin, Florence Lennon, Aino Taylor, Elizabeth Smedley, Rewi Alley, Chen Hansheng, Toni Willison, Mildred Price Coy, and Ge Baochuan gave indispensable support. The initial encouragement supplied by Florence Howe, Paul Lauter, and the Feminist Press staff, as well as Marilyn Young, was also crucial. The American research institutions we wish to thank include the Library of Congress (Manuscript Division), the Firestone Library (Princeton), the Newberry Library (Chicago), the Hoover Institution (Stanford), Arizona State University's Inter-Library Loan Service, and the University of California's South and Southeast Asia Library (Berkeley). Our special thanks go to Albert Thomas for establishing the Smedley collection in the University Archives of Arizona State University, and to Oscar Berland for research assistance. We are grateful also to the following institutions overseas: the Nehru Memorial Library (Teen Mooti House, New Delhi), the National Archives (New Delhi), the Jawaharlal Nehru University (New Delhi), the Shanghai Municipal Library, the Chinese History Museum (Beijing), the Lu Xun Museums (Shanghai and Beijing), the Public Records Office (London), and Det Kongelige Bibliotek (Copenhagen). To facilitate a visit to South Asia, a Fulbright Research Scholar award to India during the fall and winter of 1977–78 was invaluable, as were two subsequent summer grants from the Arizona State University Faculty Grants-in-Aid program. For one month during the spring of 1978 the Chinese Peoples Friendship Association helped us by arranging the key interviews that truly launched the Chinese phase of our research; Zi Zhongyun and Zhang Kejiu were instrumental in the success of that visit.

As for the writing phase, we are especially grateful to the following for reading all or part of the manuscript at various stages: Joan Jensen, Beth Luey, Charlotte Furth, Eleanor Bidien, F. McCracken Fisher, Bill Powell, and Karen Leonard. Susan Chambers's and Linda Grove's excellent translations of Japanese materials overcame our weakness in that language. Without the intellectual and emotional support of Daniel C. Calhoun, the original 1500-page manuscript would have stayed in a desk drawer. Joan Jensen also gave us emotional support and shared her pioneering research on the Indian nationalist movement in the United States. Lorain and Frank Kadish provided us with working space, and Betty Parker with typing help, at a crucial point in the writing process. The final distillation of the manuscript benefited immeasurably from the editorial talents of Gene Tanke, whom we wish we could have discovered earlier. At the University of California Press, we give special thanks to Marilyn Schwartz, Jane-Ellen Long, and Sheila Levine. It should go without saying that none of the above are responsible for the views expressed in the book.

We should like to end this litany by thanking Helen and Cyrus Mac-Kinnon, whose aid to their grandchildren helped relieve parental guilt over their time-consuming and money-consuming Smedley habit. And finally, we thank our children, Rebecca and Cy, for enduring our endless talk about Agnes and our worldwide pursuit of Smedley's old friends.

NOTE ON ROMANIZATION OF CHINESE

Throughout the text the contemporary *pinyin* romanization system has been applied consistently to Chinese names, places, and terms. There are two notable exceptions: Sun Yat-sen and Chiang Kai-shek, two figures so well known by these spellings that to render them into *pinyin* would create undue confusion and relegate them to sudden obscurity.

Introduction

At the peak of her fame, in the late 1930s and early 1940s, Agnes Smedley was considered the John Reed of the Chinese revolution for her tireless advocacy of the Chinese Communist cause. But very little has been written about her other achievements. Although she was born into miserable poverty on a tenant farm in Missouri and raised in mining camps in Colorado, by 1918, at the age of twenty-six, she had gained entrée to liberal parlor rooms in New York City, where she fought for Margaret Sanger's birth control movement, wrote muckraking political journalism, and was jailed for helping organize the overseas Indian independence movement. She matured as an activist, feminist, and writer in Weimar Germany in the 1920s, in China in the 1930s, and in the United States in the 1940s. Her story ends abruptly and mysteriously in 1950 with her death in England under a cloud of suspicion as an accused Soviet spy.

Today, although she remains better known in China and Japan than in her native country, Agnes Smedley inspires socially concerned American writers like Alice Walker, Marie Hong Kingston, Tillie Olsen, and Marge Piercy, who have praised her ability to write with power and honesty about the lives of the poor. Unlike her contemporary Anna Louise Strong, with whom she is often confused, Agnes Smedley did not romanticize the poor. In *Daughter of Earth* (1929) she wrote about her own family as poor white trash engaged in a brutalizing struggle to overcome their environment.

But how did the poor white daughter of an uneducated Missouri tenant farmer end up operating at a global level, working with the likes of Zhou Enlai, Jawaharlal Nehru, Emma Goldman, Käthe Kollwitz, and General Joseph Stilwell? Or to put the question more politically, why did Smedley seem to turn her back on the struggles of the oppressed in her own country? Moreover, as a feminist, why did she enjoy the company of military men like Marshall Zhu De, Colonel Evans Carlson, General Stilwell, and others? And why, despite her many connections at such high levels, did she find herself at the end of her life alone and vulnerable? Finally, there is the apparent contradiction of her political loyalties: why did a woman so often called a Soviet spy or Comintern agent refuse to join the American, German, or Indian Communist Party, only to be denied membership in the Chinese Communist Party? These are some of the questions that have intrigued Smedley's readers and made her a difficult subject for a biography.

The underlying premise of this biography is the one that Smedley herself often argued: the interaction between environment and will power shapes character. Thus in tracing Smedley's development into a major American radical, we have tried to show how her growth took place simultaneously at the political, social, and psychological levels. As historians, we have tried to show how the historical setting, at any given time, acted as a catalyst for the interactions of all three levels. As writers, however, we have tried to do justice to the facts without becoming overly academic. Remembering Smedley's lifelong scorn for all forms of pretension, we have tried to be as plain-spoken as we can.

CHAPTER I

Bitter Roots, 1892–1912

Trains stopped running through Osgood, Missouri, years ago, and the United States Post Office no longer serves it. The handful of old-timers who remain are mostly widows, in their well-kept wood-frame houses where they've lived for decades. From their old Midwest-style porches, complete with rockers, hanging swings, or wicker chairs for "sitten a spell," they look out over deserted streets.[1] Across the railroad tracks on the east edge of town and down the country road about two miles is Campground, where the first white settlers arrived in the 1830s. Among those pioneers was Agnes Smedley's maternal great-grandfather, Morgan Ralls, whose mother, Naomi Ralls, was the daughter of Alexander Montgomery, a Revolutionary War patriot. Campground was part of the northern Missouri county of Sullivan in 1886, when the Chicago, Milwaukee, and St. Paul Railroad purchased forty acres of nearby land from another pioneer, Elbert McNabb. A depot and station supply house were erected, and the town was named Osgood after a company official. Thus Sullivan County's "thickly settled" population of approximately 17,000 had themselves a new town, which by 1900 encompassed six full and six partial blocks around a Main Street two blocks long. The first passenger train arrived in Osgood in 1888, changing rural America as profoundly as the westbound wagon had before it.[2]

Agnes Smedley's father, Charles, came to Campground from Kansas in 1879 at the age of sixteen, along with his older sister Mary, Mary's husband Jacob Armstrong, and their seven children. Charles and Mary

Smedley were of English stock, except for a grandmother who was a Cherokee Indian. In 1885, when she was seventeen, one of the Ralls girls, Sarah Lydia, ran away with her neighbor, Charles Smedley. Sarah's father, John Ralls, who believed "you could never trust Indians or foreigners," thought Charles's Indian blood made him shiftless and therefore unable to provide a secure future for his daughter. After getting married in a small town nearby, Charles and Sarah hid in the house of Charles's elder sister, Mary Smedley Armstrong, by then a widow. When John Ralls stormed over to retrieve his daughter, events took a curious turn: he fell in love with the widow, "Aunt Mary." In *Battle Hymn of China*, Agnes Smedley repeated the rumors that one still hears in Osgood: "John's wife was still alive, and to judge by faded tintype, very beautiful. But she died shortly after, following a long illness, and my grandfather [John] married Aunt Mary. In the small drab villages and isolated farmhouses of northern Missouri little rumours often grew to gargantuan proportions. The gossips specialized most of all in the gruesome, and more than one farm woman [talked] of strange things that were supposed to have happened in my grandfather's house—of evil widows and poor ailing wives . . . and poison" (p. 4).

Charles and Sarah Smedley eventually moved from "Aunt Mary's" to a windswept two-room cabin in a field about one mile south of Campground. At the edge of a grove of trees and surrounded by purple thistles, the cabin stood on a hill overlooking stony fields. In 1976 its occupants were cows. It was there, on February 23, 1892, that Agnes Smedley was born, the second of five children.[3]

Smedley later wrote about Campground in brutal yet lyrical terms. She recalled the earth—all its colors and odors, its demands and its harvests. She said that because the two-room cabin was so small, she was terrified at an early age by seeing her parents in the act of intercourse. She decided that her mother was accepting a terrible humiliation, and later claimed that she lost all real respect for her at that time. She remembered realizing that her father valued the birth of a son more than the arrival of a daughter. Her father she recalled as a singer of songs, a spinner of tales—a romantic figure full of life and full of dreams, a man desperate to blur the sharp edges of everyday reality. She remembered his chronic discontent and his talk of moving off the land and getting rich somehow. She recalled that she got much more attention when she was sick than when she was well. And she remembered that her mother beat her, more frequently as more children arrived and the arguments between mother and father escalated. She wrote that her mother never sang, that "her tears . . . embittered my life" (p. 37).*

In contrast, Smedley saw her grandmother, "Aunt Mary," as a strong and independent woman, who managed her farm and her husband efficiently. Significantly, Aunt Mary's favorite stepchild was Tillie, Sarah Lydia's beautiful and self-assertive sister. Tillie demanded the right to hire herself out as help on a nearby farm in order to support herself and buy pretty clothes. Her father objected, arguing that this would make it harder to marry her off into a respectable family. But John Ralls lost to his new wife, and Tillie was allowed to hire herself out for three dollars a month.

According to old-timers, women rarely farmed alone or hired themselves out, even if widowed. Spinsters were dependent on relatives to take them in. There were no women's organizations in the county until around 1910, when they sprang up out of church groups. Jobs were scarce in Osgood, because the town was new and most work was concentrated in small family businesses; it was still considered improper for a woman to take a job outside the family. The alternative open to the few prosperous families—sending their daughters away for a higher education—was not considered respectable either. The first local woman daring enough to go away to school for a teaching certificate did so around 1912. For the Smedley women, this was out of the question. As Agnes's father quipped, "Education is only for dudes."

Agnes's closest school friend from 1901 to 1903, when she was between nine and eleven, was Mamie Weston. Mamie recalled that Agnes had to walk a mile to Knob Hill School, where about twenty-five students of all ages recited lessons from readers and did lots of memorizing, math, and spelling. Agnes always did her lessons and recited them easily.

---

* Ruth Ralls Fisher, Osgood's town historian and a distant relative of Smedley's, has written: "[Smedley] also was a writer, and among her books was an autobiography which she called *Daughter of Earth*. This book completed the alienation of her Missouri kin, for in it, she dragged to view family skeletons she should have been ashamed to bare" (*This Small Town—Osgood* [Milan, Missouri, 1975], pp. 28–31). Smedley indeed bared many family skeletons, and this one—that Sarah Ralls Smedley beat her children—has been the most painful for the Rallses who remain. They insist that Sarah Lydia was a good woman—a good mother and gentle; that if Agnes became anything at all, it was because she had a good mother; and that if Sarah Lydia was willing to walk two miles barefoot to the well for water each day with heavy buckets, and if she was reluctant to share her husband's dreams, it was for the sake of her children. Even Agnes's close friend Mamie Weston, who shared a double desk with her at school when they were nine, ten, and eleven years old, remembers Agnes's mother as a gentle woman. (Interviews with Ruth Ralls Fisher and Mamie Weston McCullough.)

She disliked math, excelled in spelling. During recess they played bat and ball, with a homemade ball and a board for a bat. Mamie would sometimes walk over to visit Agnes at the Smedley cabin, which was built partly of logs and was poorly furnished; the family's prized possessions were a clock and a sewing machine. In the winter the girls played dominoes (Agnes had a doll but wouldn't make clothes for it), and in the summer they helped with outside chores or searched for wildflowers. Mamie recalled that Agnes's mother worked at other houses, canning, gardening, and picking fruit, in exchange for food. She remembered that Agnes's father, a short, stocky man, did odd jobs around the Campground area but little farming at home. The Smedleys had a small vegetable garden and some chickens, but no cow. Agnes's mother had to walk to a neighbor's place to get milk. Mamie went to Sunday school at Campground but didn't remember Agnes ever attending—"Just didn't have the clothes, I suppose." Though her mother and father had been orphans and were poor themselves, Mamie thought Agnes's family had a harder life, mainly because the father was seldom at home. In 1903 Mamie and her family moved to California because of her father's health. When she returned eighteen months later, the Smedleys had moved away.[4]

Charles Smedley deserted his wife and family in the autumn of 1903, saying he was going off to apprentice himself to a doctor. For the winter, grandfather Ralls moved Sarah Lydia and her children to a shack on the edge of Osgood. The yard had no trees, flowers, or grass, only baked yellow clay. The shack had no plaster on the inside; to prepare for winter, Sarah and the children papered the drafty board walls with newspapers soaked in flour and water. In the spring of 1904 Charles Smedley returned to his family, penniless and on foot. He never said what had happened. He had another dream now: to move his family to the West.

Within weeks of Charles's announcement, the Smedleys moved by train to the mining area of southeastern Colorado. To the twelve-year-old Agnes, raised in Campground, Missouri, their destination must have seemed like a city out of a fairy tale. Nestled among juniper-covered mountains, Trinidad, Colorado, stood at 6,000 feet beneath the crags of Fischer's Peak, with the snowcapped Rockies in the distance. A thriving cultural and commercial hub, Trinidad was surrounded by vast cattle ranches and tied to mining camps by various spur railroad lines. Since the arrival of the railroad in 1878, coal-mining had become Trinidad's most important industry. As early as the 1880s, the town boasted an elaborate, two-balconied opera house, a Catholic convent, one of the West's oldest and most active synagogues, beautiful Victorian homes, and a school that looked like a fortress. The school's annual photos and lists of graduates showed remarkable ethnic diversity: Blacks and Hispanics mixed with whites, whose numbers included many recent Slavic and Italian immigrants. During the time the Smedleys lived there, Trinidad's population of about 12,000 was served by fourteen churches and ten newspapers, three of which were in Spanish.[5]

Although Trinidad's public schools were integrated and open to everyone, southern Colorado was economically and politically a near-fiefdom of the coal companies; the Trinidad area was dominated by the Victor American Fuel Company and the Rockefeller-controlled Colorado Fuel and Iron Company. Conditions for the miners there were no better in 1904 than in 1915, when a federal commission reported: "Two entire counties of southern Colorado for years have been deprived of popular government, while large groups of their citizens have been stripped of their liberties, robbed of portions of their earnings, subjected to ruthless persecution and abuse, and reduced to a state of economic and political serfdom." [6]

The Smedleys pitched a tent on the banks of the Purgatory River across from Trinidad. Outside the tent Charles built a wooden shed for a kitchen, and then hired himself out with his newly acquired team for three dollars a day, hauling sand and bricks. At first, all went well for the family. Charles's three dollars a day was unheard-of wealth, and Sarah Lydia was happy because her children could now go to a proper school.

Sarah Lydia's excited letters soon brought Tillie, her independent-minded sister, to Colorado—even though she was engaged to marry the eldest son on the Missouri farm where she had been working. When Tillie arrived, Charles and Sarah urged her to hire out in a private home, because girls who took the better-paying outside jobs "went bad." Insisting that she could take care of herself, Tillie chose laundry work, where she could earn seven dollars a week on the mangle and work up to the stiff-shirt machine that paid eleven dollars. From the beginning she was a paying guest and gave most of her money to Sarah. As Agnes wrote in *Daughter of Earth,* "For years it was her money—earned in one way or another—that furnished us with most of the colorful and good clothing we had" (p. 49). Agnes worshipped Aunt Tillie. She noticed that economic independence gave her aunt equal status with her father, who couldn't boss her or hit her the way he did her mother. Also, Aunt Tillie would invariably step in to protect her sister in arguments with Charles.

Often she became so angry with him that words failed her: "She would whirl with a rapid movement and just before flinging out of the room would, with a flash of her hands, hoist her skirts to the waist in the back. My father was left speechless with rage. There seemed no answer to such an insult" (p. 50).[7]

The Smedleys' good fortune in Trinidad was short-lived. In the spring of 1904 a flash flood swept through the Purgatory riverbed area where their tent was pitched and they lost all they possessed—the clock and the sewing machine brought from Missouri, Tillie's beautiful clothes, everything. Charles then contracted for himself and his team to work around mines up in the hills, far from a town or schools. Sarah and the children followed, found a small house, and took in boarders. From May to November of 1905, Charles worked from sunrise to sunset. When the time came for him to be paid, Sarah Lydia prepared what the children considered a banquet for the mine owner, while the family ate the usual beans and bacon. After the mine owner finished his meal, he explained that the contract Charles had signed (without being able to read it) entitled him to next to nothing in payment for six months' work. Sarah Lydia's tears did not move him; he said he was only "stickin' to the contract."

After this, Charles set off to seek work in another mining town, Tercio, and Sarah and the children returned to Trinidad. With what money they had and some from Tillie, Sarah Lydia rented a house at 611 Cottonwood Street—on the other side of the tracks, by the banks of the Purgatory River—and opened what she called the Tin Can Boarding House. Agnes returned to school, proud of her mother. But Sarah Lydia had trouble getting boarders to pay their rent, and the enterprise soon failed.

The situation grew worse for the Smedleys as 1906 dragged on. Charles Smedley, away in Tercio, was drinking more and sending home less. For a while Tillie's earnings from the stiff-shirt machine kept the family going. When this amount could no longer be stretched far enough, Tillie turned to waitressing. Agnes's older sister, Nellie, now over sixteen, quit school to work in the laundry. She, too, became a paying guest and thus had her own room. Agnes, now turning fourteen, was sent to work after school in the homes of other people, and her small earnings went straight to her mother. Much of what she saw in these homes horrified her, and she concluded that for women, marriage meant nothing but imprisonment and humiliation. Before long, however, she lost her job as a domestic helper: she had been drinking the cream off the tops of the milk bottles each morning to ease her hunger pangs. On the day she was fired, Agnes took hours to return home, afraid that a beating awaited her. When she arrived, her recently returned father was throwing Tillie out of the house. In a rage, he accused her of being a whore and threatened to kill Sarah Lydia if she left the house with Tillie. Tillie shouted back that it was he who had made her what she was by sitting in saloons and not providing enough food and clothing for her sister and their children. His response was to get an axe and wait for her to leave. Tillie soon moved to Denver.*

With Tillie gone, the family's fortunes hit rock bottom in 1906–07. Charles bolted again, claiming to be outraged that Sarah Lydia had refused to tell him how she would vote in her first election. Sarah Lydia's only recourse was to hire herself out as a washerwoman for $1.30 a day—which meant 7:00 A.M. to 8:00 P.M. A frail-looking woman with big-veined hands and disheveled hair knotted at the nape of her neck, she worked in other people's homes in order to get "free" meals and thus save money. The children ate potatoes and flour gravy and kept themselves warm by burning coal they found along the railroad tracks or scrap wood they "snitched" from the lumberyard. Agnes took an after-school job in a tobacco store, stripping and rolling cigars. Later she recalled that union men there had good working conditions compared to the nonunion "girls" in the back room, who had bad lighting, worked longer hours, and were expected to work faster. When Agnes admitted to the owner that she read books, he advised her that too much reading would lead to daydreaming, and she was soon dismissed for being too slow. She now took a place by her mother's side at the washtub. As the winter wore on, she became increasingly bolder in her "snitching" and also lost interest in school, where she had once been at the head of her class. She took up bragging and swearing with the kids from the wrong side of the tracks, and she heard their version of "the facts of life."

Charles Smedley was in Ludlow, Colorado (a nearby mining camp), living with another woman. Early in the spring of 1907 he returned to Trinidad and tried to persuade Sarah Lydia to take him back. She threatened divorce and sent him away. But she desperately needed help. With the coming of good weather, people started doing their own wash again,

---

*Whether or not Aunt Tillie had become a prostitute depends on how one defines the term. Smedley's definition was a woman who slept with men for economic reasons. Calling her aunt a prostitute in *Daughter of Earth* (New York, 1929) deeply offended Tillie and other members of the family, who preferred to see Tillie's escapades, particularly her periods as a "mistress," as different from prostitution.

and she had to reduce her price for an increased amount of work. Agnes quit school to help out.

One day Sarah Lydia stayed home, too sick to move. But no one thought of calling a doctor. Doctors were only for rich people. As Agnes wrote: "We always just waited to get over a sickness. I heated hot bricks all day long and kept them against her back and the side of her head. And each day I cooked potatoes and made a flour-and-water gravy for us all" (p. 95). Then her father turned up again, and this time he wasn't sent away.

Aunt Tillie's Missouri fiancé, Leonard Hutchinson, also showed up in town. Having received a letter in which Tillie said she wouldn't marry him after all, he had followed her to Denver, where she refused him again—not because she didn't love him, as she told Agnes years later, but because once a woman marries, her husband starts bringing up her past. Mr. Hutchinson's response was to return to Trinidad and propose to Agnes's older sister, Nellie, who accepted. The family was about to leave for Delagua, another small mining camp up the canyon from Ludlow, where Charles and his team had a contract, and so the marriage ceremony was performed right away. Agnes was shocked: the idea of Nellie engaging in sex was repulsive to her. She never saw her sister again. The Smedley family Bible records that Nellie died in childbirth two years later in western Oklahoma.

Agnes's new home, Delagua, was entirely owned by the Victor American Fuel Company. The underpaid workers lived in company housing, bought necessities at marked-up prices at the company store (the only store in town), and drank at the company saloon. They were paid in company scrip, which had to be converted into U.S. dollars at a loss in the banks of larger towns like Trinidad. Of course, the company also hired the schoolteacher. Successive attempts to strike for better treatment culminated in the famous Ludlow massacre of 1914: six men, two women, and eleven children were killed when the National Guard attacked a strikers' tent colony.[8]

Fifteen years later, in *Daughter of Earth*, Smedley took pains to reconstruct the conditions of her life in Delagua: the tensions that preceded the Ludlow massacre, the unhealthy and dangerous conditions in the mines, the cheating by company officials, the blacklisting of miners, and the rape and abuse of poverty-stricken women by soldiers brought in to keep order. Husbands and fathers were too frightened to intervene: "no one would have dared touch a 'uniform' of the United States"

(p. 99). Since "nearly all native American [white] working men feared the mines," all but a fraction of the mine workers were foreigners, mostly Mexicans; 80 percent of the miners spoke no English. Charles Smedley and his "native American" or Anglo crew were in Delagua with a contract to do hauling work outside the mines. The Smedleys therefore had no place socially among the company people, and they chose not to associate with the foreign miners. They were poor, but in Delagua, at least, they were better off than most. The majority of miners and workers in the camps were men without their families who had come with the intention of making some quick money and then returning home. A few never returned, but sent instead for their families. What Smedley did not explain in *Daughter of Earth* was the important role the schools played in pacifying the inhabitants of the mining settlements. Along with the company stores, school buildings physically dominated the camps. In their memoirs and oral histories, former students, and their teachers, uniformly expressed gratitude to the coal companies for giving them the opportunity to go to school. Most of them were immigrants, and they knew they would have remained illiterate in their native countries.[9]

Working under Charles were eight teams of Anglo men and their horses, whose feeding and housing were looked after by Sarah Lydia, Agnes, and the younger children. Agnes later described these cowboys, who arrived with all their earthly possessions on their horses, as "courageous, kindly, trusting—and foul-mouthed. When they received their wages they spent it in one night in Trinidad, 'on the hill' where women sold themselves to men's desires. When they married, which was rare, they married only virgins. Women had nothing but virginity to trade for bed and food for the rest of their days. Fathers protected the virginity of their daughters as men guard their bank accounts; with a gun slung at the hips and a gleam of warning in the eye. But now I was growing up and my father let all men know that I was not to be trifled with" (p. 107). One of these men, a lanky twenty-nine-year-old up from a ranch in New Mexico, paid special attention to Agnes, who was now fifteen, but he didn't trifle with her. He gave her a gold watch-chain and promised her a pony, a good gun, and half his ranch back in New Mexico if she would marry him. The pony and the gun fired Agnes's imagination, and she was ready to accept. That evening her father and mother called her in and told her she was too young for marriage. Besides, her father continued, "there's things in marriage you don't know nothin' about . . .

there is dooties" (p. 110). Repulsed, Agnes announced that she would have nothing to do with that: "dooties be damned." The proposal was rejected and the cowboy left town the next morning.

In 1907 the fortunes of the Smedley family rose and fell, depending on the bids that Charles got and how much he was drinking and gambling. They stayed in Delagua only a few months and then went back to Trinidad. Sometime in late 1907 they moved to Tercio, another company town much like Delagua. Always in the background was the tension created by unorganized miners' strikes, which company officials dealt with heavy-handedly, using sheriffs and police to protect strikebreakers. This is how Smedley remembered her parents' response:

> My mother listened to all the news from the camp during the strike. She said little, especially when my father or the men who worked for him were about. I remember her instinctive and unhesitating sympathy for the miners. She hated rich or powerful people or institutions. Through the years she had been transformed from a poor farming woman into an unskilled proletarian. But my father was less clear. As a "native American" himself, with hopes of becoming an employer, he tried to identify himself with the sheriff and the officials of the camp against the strikers, who were foreigners. Still he was unclear; he had men working for him and yet he was an ignorant working man himself, and however hard he worked he seemed to remain miserably poor. He was too unknowing to understand how or why it all happened. But he, like my mother, had certainly come to know that those who work the most do not make the most money. It was the fault of the rich, it seemed, but just how he did not know. He drowned his unclearness and disappointment in drink, or let poker absorb his resentment. (p. 119)

Confirmation of this image of her father comes from a photograph of Charles Smedley in Trinidad posing proudly with six-guns and a sheriff's badge.[10]

It was in Tercio in early 1908 that Agnes Smedley got her first break, a chance to step out on her own. A red-haired grade-school teacher encouraged her to take a county teacher's examination in the neighboring state of New Mexico. She met the prerequisite, which was an eighth-grade education. Agnes borrowed the teacher's blouse and skirt and rode across the border to take the examination. Although her marks were mediocre, she passed and was assigned to a school. The pay was forty dollars a month.

In the summer of 1908 Agnes returned to Osgood, Missouri, with her mother and her younger sister, Myrtle, to attend the funeral of her grandfather, John Ralls. Not until 1943, in *Battle Hymn of China,* did she expose in print the town gossip she heard about her grandfather's last days. It was talk that in another century might have had Aunt Mary burned as a witch: "As he lay dying, rumor ran, he wanted to cleanse his soul of the sin of poisoning his first wife, but Mary had smothered his confession by placing her hand across his mouth" (p. 4). During this visit Agnes spent some time with her old friend and former classmate Mamie Weston. On the way to the train station on the day Agnes left, they exchanged mementos. Smedley gave Mamie the gold watch-chain that had been given her a year earlier along with a marriage proposal, and told her that the cowboy "didn't mean much to her now." [11]

After a brief visit to Tercio, Agnes resumed her teaching job. From the fall of 1908 to February, 1910, she taught primary school in and around Raton, a town of about 4,000 in Colfax County in northeastern New Mexico, which had been in need of schoolteachers since the railroad line and coal-mining had produced a boom at the turn of the century. [12] In *Daughter of Earth,* she recalled her schoolteaching years in New Mexico as a lonely but happy period in her life. She was the unmarried, white, "educated" virgin schoolteacher in the area, and this gave her status and protection. She spent many nights square dancing into the late hours or riding into the countryside and singing Western songs with the cowboys around a campfire. She taught mostly Spanish-speaking people who spoke little English outside her classroom (though, so far as is known, she made no attempt to learn Spanish). Some of the students were her own age. She sidestepped her weakness in math by calling on the older boys to do the harder problems at the blackboard. By answering an advertisement in a women's magazine she gained a male pen-pal from "back East" who sent her books. She admired his penmanship greatly, thinking that if she could only write like that, she would really be educated. Her social conscience was still relatively undeveloped; when attracted to a handsome Indian-Mexican student, she "felt ashamed." *

Smedley's carefree life as a schoolteacher around Raton came to an abrupt end one snowy day in February of 1910. A message brought to her classroom said that her mother was dying. She left immediately for Tercio, and for three days and three nights she sat by Sarah Lydia's bedside. A doctor treated her mother's abdominal pains with bicarbonate of soda. He said it was inevitable that a woman who lived on potatoes and

---

* A January 2, 1909, postcard to her younger brother Sam reflects the racial prejudices that were so much a part of Smedley's social milieu: "Dear old Droggle Tail: Was in Trinidad yesterday afternoon and until ten o'clock this morning. What resolutions did you make for the New Year? I resolved to beat Mexicans and Dagos—beat time out of them too!"

flour-and-water gravy should be sick; undernourishment and tuberculosis was his diagnosis. At the age of forty-two, Sarah Lydia had only
one tooth left in her mouth. As her mother lay dying, Agnes remembered initiating an embrace for the first time, and that her mother called
her "my daughter," a thing she had never said before, since "affection
between parents and children was never shown among my people"
(p. 135). Sarah Lydia died, of a ruptured appendix, in her daughter's
arms. Her husband's reaction was to rifle Sarah Lydia's trunk, take the
money hidden in it, and go out to get drunk.

Aunt Tillie came from Denver to help the family take Sarah Lydia's
body to western Oklahoma, where she was buried near the Hutchinson
homestead—beside her daughter Nellie, who had died in childbirth the
previous September. Upon returning to Tercio, Agnes, now eighteen
years old, quit her teaching job and for the spring took over sole responsibility for her sixteen-year-old sister Myrtle, her brothers John and Sam,
aged fourteen and twelve, and Nellie's infant son. But she had no more
success than her mother in keeping Charles Smedley sober and nonviolent. And so in about June, after an incident in which she managed to
stop Charles from horsewhipping one of her brothers, she took the baby
and fled to Aunt Tillie in Denver. Arrangements were made for Myrtle
to work for a family in New Mexico and for the two brothers to go to
Oklahoma to work on Leonard Hutchinson's farm. Throughout her life,
Smedley expressed guilt over becoming "hard" enough deliberately to
leave her family: "And my hardness called itself principle. I threw up
fortifications to protect myself from love and tenderness that menace
the freedom of women; I did not know then that one builds fortifications only where there is a weakness" (p. 156).

Since education seemed to be the only way to escape marriage and
the sort of life her parents had lived, Agnes pleaded with Aunt Tillie to
help her go to school. Tillie agreed to pay for a short stenography
course—not in Denver, but in Greeley, Colorado.* Returning to Denver
after a few weeks, she found that Leonard Hutchinson had come from
Oklahoma and taken his infant son away, much against Aunt Tillie's
wishes. (According to Agnes, Leonard called Tillie names at first and

* For reasons that are not entirely clear but probably related to her love life, Tillie did
not want Smedley living with her in Denver. Later, in a letter to Florence Lennon dated
June 17, 1924, Smedley recalled what crude and awkward country girls she and her
friends in Greeley were: "the girl with whom I went had her teeth all pulled out and solid
plated gold ones put in to attract attention because she was so unattractive. She was a sight
when she laughed."

then pleaded with her to marry him. She again refused, fearing that he would always hold her past against her.)

Tillie helped Agnes find a job in Denver as secretary to an elderly man who edited a local magazine. Within a few weeks he tried to seduce her and she quit. Tillie then found her a similar job with another magazine editor. For a while this man treated Agnes like a daughter and won her over as a friend; but then he started asking for more—love, he called it—and told her she needn't be afraid of having children. When she told him she was afraid of sex itself, he laughed and she dissolved into tears. In *Daughter of Earth* she admitted that she had seen this coming and hated herself for letting it happen—which she did because she wanted so much to learn to write for his magazine. Although this editor did not force the issue, Agnes was uncomfortable around his office, and so she asked him to put her "on the road" selling magazine subscriptions. Both Aunt Tillie and the editor tried to dissuade her, arguing that it was no life for a woman. But she insisted.

Smedley worked as a magazine agent for about six months in 1911, from early in the year until the beginning of summer, traveling mainly by train throughout Colorado and New Mexico. She quickly learned to avoid conventional homes with respectable housewives who rudely slammed doors in her face. She sold instead to newsstands and businessmen, making contacts through local newsboys. On trains, women who were friendly at first sometimes moved to other seats when they learned what kind of work she was doing. Men reacted differently, but often on the same assumption—that she was a loose woman.

Her career as a magazine agent ended dramatically in the dusty little Texas town of Tascosa, two dozen or so adobe buildings about a half-hour's walk up a canyon from the train depot. It had several saloons with gambling tables at the back, and from outside Agnes could hear the squeaking of a violin and the stomping of men's feet as they danced. Founded during buffalo-hunting days, the town was located halfway between the range lands of two warring cattle companies, and the graves in the local boot hill testified to the violence of their competition. When Smedley arrived, Tascosa was on the decline. The rough signboard on the Exchange Hotel where she stayed was riddled with bullet holes. Shortly after she lay down on her bed there, faint from hunger and completely broke, the hotel proprietor tried to rape her. After a struggle convinced him that she was a virgin, he became solicitous and proposed marriage—which Smedley of course refused.

The next day, in desperation Smedley wrote to Big Buck, a forty-two-year-old cowboy with a moustache running from ear to ear who had often worked for her father. When the cattle business began to decline, Buck had become a mechanic in the copper-mining town of Clifton, Arizona. In Colorado, Big Buck had taught Agnes to shoot, ride, lasso, and do tricks with a jackknife. She later wrote that he "had tried hard to blast out of me everything feminine," and that he was the one man she felt she could trust: "The memory of Big Buck is dear to me. . . . Was there ever a man closer to the spirit of the West than he, I wonder: a strain of ironic humor in all he did: generous in all material things he possessed or earned; very remote in thought and spirit; stubbornly convinced of the inferiority of Mexicans, Indians, Mormons, and men frail of body" (p. 169).

In reply to her letter, Big Buck sent Agnes the money for a train ticket from Tascosa to Clifton. He arranged for her to stay in his hotel and introduced her to all as his sister, telling Agnes she had better "let that stand put." He paid for her meals at the "Chink" restaurant across the street and convinced her to rest up for a month in order "to put some beef back on her bones." Smedley's intention was to find a stenography job after a month and repay Big Buck. While resting, she made friends with a young unmarried Mormon forest ranger, going on long rides with him in the surrounding countryside. This was the summer of 1911, when Congress passed a bill granting Arizona statehood. On the way to a celebration dance, Big Buck declared his jealousy of the Mormon and proposed to Agnes. She was startled; she had always thought of him as old. Gently, she replied that she didn't think she would ever want to get married. At the dance itself, held in a pool hall with Chinese lanterns strung up to illuminate the flags, Agnes happened to talk with a woman who said that she was leaving the next morning by train for a teachers training school at Tempe, just outside Phoenix. Agnes bragged that she had already been a teacher and a stenographer and had "finished [her] education long ago." The woman politely replied that she didn't see how that was possible, for at the school she attended one had to study for six years—four in high school and two in normal school—before becoming a teacher. Big Buck easily read Agnes's jealousy and her desire to go back to school. On the way home from the dance he offered to stake her to part of her school expenses for six months. After that, he said, he hoped she would return to Clifton and take him up on his marriage proposal.

Tempe, Arizona, was a quiet little town at a railroad and ferry junction on the Salt River a few miles southeast of Phoenix. Since the 1880s it had been the home of a small normal school (teachers college), the majority of whose students were Mormon girls from the surrounding area. Nearby Phoenix was the bustling capital of the new state, with a population of about 25,000; it had a Chinatown and a large Mexican-Indian community, and most of its civic leaders were Mormons. Just south of Tempe was the much older Yaqui Indian settlement of Guada-lupe, which Smedley described so lyrically in *Daughter of Earth*. And beyond that was the desert, serene and hot, inhabited by Papago and Pima Indians.

Agnes Smedley entered Tempe Normal School on September 11, 1911, as a special student because of lack of documentary proof of a high school degree. To questions about her family, she declared that they were all deceased; she gave her father's occupation as "doctor." She be-came a lab assistant for the school's popular biology and chemistry teacher, Frederick Irish, whose bachelor apartment near the campus served as headquarters for many of the school clubs in which Agnes was active. A group photograph shows her with the Kalakagthia Society, a Bible study group of twenty women who met in the dorm every Saturday night and studied scripture for two hours. Despite her poverty (she had two dresses to her name), unusual background, and special-student status, she was well liked by her classmates, who recalled that she loved literature and debate and was the founder of the campus Greeley Club.[13]

Agnes also joined the school weekly, the *Normal Student,* as a staff writer. After January 12, 1912, when she was elected chief reporter, her articles were signed, and on March 29, 1912, the *Normal Student* an-nounced her election as editor-in-chief.[14] In her first editorial Smedley urged her classmates to use their education to understand better those less fortunate than themselves. Despite its self-conscious and flowery language, this was her first statement of the role she saw for herself as a writer: to serve as an interpreter for the disadvantaged, a person who could explain what it is like to be "in the darkness of not-knowing . . . to be so far removed from the world of knowledge" that one cannot think but only react (p. 120). The March 29 issue included two other signed pieces of hers: a short story entitled "The Romance" and a book review of *The Mind of Primitive Man* by the pioneering anthropologist Franz Boas. Transparently autobiographical, "The Romance" demon-strated the liberating impact of Boas's study of racial prejudice and cul-tural differences, and it established a method of work that she would refine in later years: she would explain the implications of a scientific or academic study in the form of a story. In "Romance" a mother tells her children how she overcame her own racial prejudice in order to marry an Indian, and many of her emotions are clearly drawn from Smedley's attraction to a Mexican-Indian boy two years earlier in New Mexico. Shortly after this story appeared, Agnes publicly acknowledged her own Indian ancestry and asked to be called "Ayahoo."

Just as her first journalistic success was giving her a new sense of dignity and self-respect, Smedley's six-month support from Big Buck ran out. In a letter from Clifton, he said that he assumed she wasn't taking up his proposal, and that he was going off to join the Mexican Revolution (according to family lore, he died in it). Agnes never heard from him again, but among the personal papers she gave to a friend for safe-keeping in 1949 was a photograph of a cowboy named Big Buck. By April she was struggling to scrape together enough money to stay in school. She washed dishes in a restaurant and took on any kind of household work she could, putting off studying until late at night. After about a month of this, she decided she would have to leave school in order to support herself. She felt trapped and deeply depressed because she considered her prospects, even as a schoolteacher, extremely limited and unattractive. But just as she was deciding to quit school, she met two persons who set her life on a course she had never imagined.

CHAPTER II

The Dilemma of Marriage, 1912–1916

During the week of April 21, 1912, a state debating contest was held at Tempe Normal School. The first subject was, "Resolved: Woman's Suffrage Should Be Adopted in Arizona." Agnes led off, arguing in favor of suffrage against opposing arguments based on fundamentalist Bible positions. According to the *Normal Student,* she did well.[1] More important, during the week of the debates, the judges stayed in the women's dormitory with the students, and Agnes gave her room to Thorberg Brundin, a young Phoenix high school teacher with a bachelor's degree from Columbia University, who was to judge the next day's debate. The two met the night before the first debate, when Agnes returned to her room to fetch hair curlers ("more than one hundred, which she put in every night").

Thorberg Brundin, a New Yorker from a Swedish immigrant family, had recently arrived in Phoenix to teach school, see something of the West, and be near her brother Ernest. She was a strikingly beautiful and poised woman in her mid-twenties and certainly the most cosmopolitan person Agnes had ever met. For her part, Thorberg was astonished by Agnes—an outspoken, swashbuckling young woman of unusual intensity who swept in wearing a gun and a dagger and went by the Indian name of Ayahoo. Thorberg was further impressed by the quality of Ayahoo's performance in the debates.

After the week of the debates, Thorberg and Agnes began seeing each other every Friday night, when Thorberg would come over from Phoenix to meet her brother, who could leave his job in the mountains for weekends in Tempe. In long talks over chocolate sodas, for which both women had a passion, intimacy grew rapidly. Smedley talked about her ambition to become a journalist. She told Thorberg how disturbed she was by her mother's death, and vowed that she would never die that way. She was trying hard to dissociate herself from the crudeness of her past; she worked at correcting her accent and her grammar and expressed scorn for anyone who drank alcohol, denouncing the practice as vulgar and animalistic. Smedley also felt attracted to Ernest Brundin, Thorberg's brother.

Ernest was a tall, gaunt man who was about a year younger than his sister. After graduating from high school, he had worked for a year in a surveyor's office in New York City and then studied engineering for a year at the University of Maine. In Maine he came down with tuberculosis and spent a year recovering in a sanitarium. Then, after a short and frustrating attempt at chicken farming in New Jersey, he migrated to Tucson, Arizona, in 1910, where he haunted an engineering office until they gave him a job driving a team of horses. In 1911 he was assigned to a surveying job on the huge Roosevelt Dam project at the headwaters of the Salt River, in the Superstition Mountains to the east of Tempe. After Thorberg joined him, they made plans to take their savings and migrate to San Francisco, with hopes of entering the University of California at Berkeley. Beginning in May of 1912, Ernest spent most weekends with Agnes and Thorberg in Tempe.

Smedley envied the Brundins' education and sophistication, and after the school year ended she moved to Phoenix to look for work. When she expressed disappointment over being unable to continue with school, Thorberg and Ernest dismissed her feelings by saying that school didn't necessarily teach one anything really important—an attitude that Smedley resented ("from the heights they could afford to be critical").[2]

In retrospect, the political, social, and emotional impact of the Brundins on Agnes Smedley is difficult to overestimate. Both Thorberg and Ernest were strong Socialists. Although Agnes had already developed a sense of righteous indignation about the social evils she had seen around her, she had never met anyone who claimed to have an enlightened political solution for them. Moreover, although Ernest held firm convictions, he was a courteous, soft-spoken man, and he and his sister were extremely close. Theirs was the first relationship Agnes had seen in which a man and a woman shared obvious love, comradeship, and understanding. In *Daughter of Earth* she recalled that she had wondered: "Could human beings be tender and still not weak? Could there really be love free from danger and subjection for a woman?" (pp. 185–86). Could it be, she asked herself, that Ernest was really capable of respecting a free and independent woman?

One moonlit summer night, a wild ride with Ernest over the desert on a runaway horse led to a passionate embrace. Tearful goodbyes followed when Ernest and Thorberg left for San Francisco soon thereafter. A few weeks later a marriage proposal came in a letter from Ernest. Agnes quickly took a train to San Francisco, where she moved in with Ernest, Thorberg, and Thorberg's future husband, Robert Haberman, all of whom were sharing an apartment at 624 Octavia Street. Thorberg had a part-time job, and Agnes found full-time work as a secretary, but Ernest could find nothing that paid well until he was offered a job working on the American Canal project, which would bring Colorado River water to southern California. He accepted the offer, and on August 24, 1912, a few hours before he boarded the train for the Imperial Valley, Justice of the Peace A. T. Barnett at City Hall recorded the marriage of Ernest George Brundin, white, aged twenty-four, and Ayahoo Smedley, white, aged twenty.*

Tensions soon rose among the remaining three on Octavia Street. Thorberg became impatient with Agnes's lack of sophistication. For example, when they went to the theater, Agnes was bored if the play lacked music and dance. More important, Thorberg was appalled at the arrangement reached by her brother and Agnes: they had agreed not to have children, at least not until Agnes had saved enough money to get herself, her sister, and her two brothers through school. Much as she liked Agnes, Thorberg thought the pair were totally mismatched by temperament and told them so. She also knew how much Ernest wanted to have children. But most of all, she was stunned by Smedley's categorical hatred of sex and her naive belief that a marriage could survive on "romantic friendship." Thorberg even suspected that Smedley had married Ernest because she wanted to stay close to her.

Painful though all this was, Smedley found it even harder to cope with the hostility of Thorberg's future husband, Robert Haberman. Haberman was a volatile Rumanian-Jewish American who practiced pharmacy in San Raphael. He was a dedicated Socialist and often at-

---

*The casualness Agnes tried to adopt is revealed in a postcard she sent to her father from San Francisco a few days later, on September 6, 1912: "Dear Dad, As busy as a cranberry merchant. Fine health, however. Frisco is a rather nice town, but I don't care much for it." The marriage was not mentioned. On Smedley postcards see Chapter 1, note 7.

tended meetings and demonstrations held by the I.W.W. and other Socialist and radical groups. When Thorberg first met him, he was becoming increasingly involved in supporting the Mexican Revolution of 1911.
He insisted on taking Thorberg and Agnes to places like Playland, an
amusement park at the ocean end of Golden Gate Park, so they could
mingle with "the common man." When Agnes said she didn't want to associate with "vulgar, cheap, and ugly people," Haberman would shout
back that their vulgarity was the fault of the system—a retort that
would leave her quiet and sullen.

Smedley was struggling to come to terms with a new environment
and new ideas. In February of 1913 the *Tempe Normal Student* published an article entitled "The Yellow Man," sent in by A. Smedley-
Brundin. It was an impressionistic piece about San Francisco's Chinatown, in which Smedley tried to counter the racial prejudices against
Chinese that she knew to be rampant in Arizona. Her observations on
Chinese culture were naive, romanticized, and transparently escapist—
an early attempt to find an alternative to a white society that she personally found oppressive.

The situation in the Octavia Street apartment continued to irritate
her. She was jealous of Thorberg, who was successfully pursuing a Master's degree in zoology at the University of California in Berkeley.[3] She
also resented the fact that Thorberg continually shirked doing her share
of the cooking and cleaning. Agnes couldn't tolerate a messy place and
would clean the house "with a vengeance."

Ernest's visits were brief and infrequent. According to both Thorberg
and Ernest's second wife, Elinor, the marriage was completely devoid of
sex until April of 1913. At that time, to escape Octavia Street and be
closer to Ernest, Agnes moved to El Centro in the sun-parched Imperial
Valley of southern California. She hoped that by doing secretarial work
in this small town, where she could live cheaply, she could save enough
money to get back into school.

When Ernest visited in El Centro, sex was included in the marriage,
but Agnes continued to resist. It didn't help her attitude that after she
had found a secretarial job at a hotel, many of the land speculators arriving from Los Angeles crudely propositioned her. By the beginning of
June, with the onset of morning sickness, Agnes knew that what she had
dreaded had become fact: she was pregnant. The realization came when
Ernest was out of town, and she reacted with terror. She was convinced
that her equal relationship with her husband would soon vanish and

that the arrival of a child would make it impossible for her to go to school and thus become his intellectual equal. Already bitter about her poor rural background and envious of Ernest and Thorberg, she clung fiercely to her dream of someday becoming a successful journalist. Tortured by these fears and haunted by the memory of her mother's fate, she went to a druggist and bought poison that would induce an abortion.

Ernest arrived back in El Centro to find Agnes nearly dead. He took her, panic-stricken and hysterical, to the local doctor and insisted that he complete the abortion before Agnes killed herself. The doctor complied. Smedley wrote in *Daughter of Earth:* "When I came back to consciousness Ernest was sitting by my bedside, smiling. I lay gazing at him and hating the smile, hating it, hating it! How dared he smile when my body was an open wound, when I had stood before eternity. . . . How dared he smile when a child had been taken from my body and now my body and mind called for it. . . . How dared he smile . . . [he] a man who knew nothing, nothing, nothing" (pp. 198–99). Agnes refused to let Ernest pay for the abortion, saying that she would let no man pay for her body.

The Smedley-Brundin marriage had not been consummated until the eighth month. The physician who had attended Agnes told Ernest after the abortion that because of her deep-seated fear he doubted whether she would ever be able to enjoy sex or have an orgasm. For Ernest, this was too much. He wanted to be Agnes's friend, but he also wanted a wife and children.[4]

With financial and moral support from Ernest, Agnes S. Brundin left him in El Centro and registered as a student at San Diego Normal School on June 28, 1913. She entered with the academic self-confidence she had developed in Arizona, and her personal magnetism and energy are apparent even from the skimpy records left in the school archives. She helped found the school's weekly newspaper, *Normal News,* and during the paper's first year (November, 1913, to August, 1914) she was listed on the masthead as the business manager. Theater was emphasized on campus that year, and Smedley was heavily involved. The paper reported that Agnes, "known in our corridors as A. S. Brundin, played the part of Antonio in the court scene from *The Merchant of Venice* by 'Bill' Shakespeare." She also performed in *Scenes from Greek Plays* by Stephen Phillips and joined the party and dance held afterward. The *Normal News* listed A. S. Brundin among the class of 1914 that was to graduate at the close of the summer session. In June, 1914, Smedley was appointed faculty secretary and typing teacher for the Normal School's Intermediate School, positions she would retain through 1916, remaining associated with the *Normal News* as Alumni Editor.[5]

Since arriving in San Diego, Smedley had worried about her sister and two brothers. The brothers wrote that they were being mistreated by the farmer in Oklahoma to whom Charles Smedley had hired them out. Agnes could do nothing about that situation, but on November 12, 1914, the *Normal News* announced that Agnes's sister, Myrtle Smedley, had arrived on campus as a special student in woodwork and sewing. Agnes had made enough money to bring Myrtle out from New Mexico, where she had been working as a hired girl with a ranching family. According to family lore, Myrtle's first reaction was hostile; she thought that Agnes, with her "proper accent" and "corrected grammar," was putting on airs. But by March of 1915 Myrtle was enrolled as a regular student and was in charge of "outside circulation" for the *Normal News,* which reported that the two sisters spent their spring vacation in 1915 visiting Ernest.[6]

In the spring of 1915 a controversy arose on campus when a "Hindu reformer," Dr. Keshava D. Shastri, was allowed to speak only to the faculty (including Smedley, in her capacity as Supervisor of Intermediate School typing); the majority of faculty members considered him too anti-British in his views to be allowed to address the students. Their decision was made, in part, out of fear. San Diego still lived in the shadow of the violence that had erupted in 1912, when vigilante committees of merchants and citizens forcibly prevented the anarchist Emma Goldman from speaking, by tarring and feathering her manager (and lover) Ben Reitman. In response, thousands of I.W.W. members and their supporters descended on the town, and the jail could not hold all who were arrested. The controversy then spread throughout California. Tensions over the free-speech issue continued into 1915. Such was the political climate when Emma Goldman came to San Diego, one day before Dr. Shastri's lecture, to give a series of three public lectures off campus: one each on Ibsen, Nietzsche, and Margaret Sanger's birth control movement.[7]

The Shastri-Goldman episode was a political education for Smedley. Shastri awakened her to the global issue of British imperialism. Since she took pride in the fact that an ancestor of hers had fought the British during the American Revolution, Shastri's anticolonialism struck a major chord. Afterward she talked with Shastri and asked for more information about Lajpat Rai, a major Indian politician in exile in New

York, who had been mentioned in the lecture. Smedley also attended Emma Goldman's lectures, and what Goldman had to say in favor of birth control, especially for poor women, hit her hard. This experience also put her in touch with a new organization, the Open Forum, which had stepped in as a sponsor of the Goldman lecture after the Socialist Party backed down under pressure. The forum soon became an important focus of Smedley's political and social life. When she returned from summer vacation, she acted as its secretary.[8]

In June, 1915, Agnes and Myrtle left for Berkeley, where Ernest soon joined them. To Agnes, summer school at a university was a dream come true. Ernest, too, was hungry for more education. But the trauma of living together as husband and wife remained. Again the problem was sex, and once again Agnes became pregnant—which led to the same desperate reaction and another abortion. The following story became legendary in the Brundin family: returning home on the streetcar from the doctor's office after the abortion, Agnes lay down on the side seat in the back, doubled up, and began to moan. She evidently made no attempt to control the volume of her moaning. Some of the passengers started mumbling that she must be drunk, and others rushed back to see if she needed help. Ernest, a very proper person, was beside himself, thinking only of how to get her home without getting kicked off the streetcar. He spoke angrily to her: "Sit up! People are looking at you—do you want to make a scene in public?" He had never spoken to her in this way, and never did so again. But their dreams of an academically satisfying summer were shattered, as they struggled to control their emotions.

In the fall Agnes and Myrtle Smedley returned to San Diego for the academic year 1915–16. After Ernest rejoined her in January 1916, Smedley tried to save her marriage while at the same time becoming increasingly committed as a political activist and socialist. Ernest opened a gas station in San Diego and rented a house with Agnes near campus which became, according to the *Normal News,* a lively social center. Smedley's delight in entertaining with cowboy and folk songs was irrepressible. The couple also bought a car they named Wiggles, and Agnes soon became known as a "fearless" driver.[9]

As secretary of the Open Forum, Smedley handled arrangements for an impressive group of speakers whose impact on her personally appears to have been considerable. Most important was Upton Sinclair, the socialist and muckraker who inaugurated the forum's lecture series on January 17. He and Smedley struck up a personal acquaintance which endured into the 1930s; Sinclair recalled later, "She was a young school teacher, very pretty, and happy over meeting an author to whose ideas she was sympathetic." [10] In April, the best-known socialist politician in the nation, Eugene Debs, came to speak. Jane Addams was expected but could not come. There were also on-campus lectures on the Mexican Revolution, and Smedley was involved with arranging a dance at a Mexican settlement for fund-raising purposes.

By the spring of 1916, Smedley was a committed member of the Socialist Party. A central reason was the share of power the party gave women. Important women in the party included union organizer "Mother" Mary Harris Jones; Helen Keller; the editor and co-publisher of the popular paper *National Rip Saw,* and the party's vice-presidential candidate in 1916, Kate Richards O'Hare; the founder of the birth control movement in the United States, Margaret Sanger; and the general secretary of the National Consumers League and co-founder of the National Child Labor Committee, Florence Kelly. The party campaigned hard wherever the suffrage issue was at stake in an election. The party put women up for office and their elected officials appointed women to such public positions as that of the first woman judge in California in 1912. By 1910 women were sharing responsibilities at all levels of the party infrastructure, including its National Executive Committee. One of the latter's members in 1916, for example, was Anna Maley, who also managed Thomas Van Lear's successful campaign to be elected mayor of Minneapolis.

Many middle-class women who were active in religious social-reform organizations of the time also joined the Socialist Party, perceiving a Christian-like, service-oriented, and collectivist ethic as implicit in Socialist theory. One such was Francis Willard, president of the Women's Christian Temperance Union, who concluded her presidential address in 1897: "Beloved Comrades . . . socialism is the higher way; it enacts into everyday living the ethics of Christ's gospel. Nothing else will do." [11]

The West had its own regional variety of socialism. Many Western Socialists had an I.W.W. or anarchist-syndicalist orientation, which emphasized organizing unskilled migratory workers as "the genuine proletariat." By 1916 the I.W.W. had failed as an organized movement. The Socialist Party, however, remained strong.*

* Founded in 1905 as an offshoot of the Socialist movement, the Industrial Workers of the World (I.W.W.) aimed at a more transient and less stable constituency than mainstream Socialists, depreciating methodical practical programs and emphasizing "revolutionary" appeals and demands for higher wages, shorter hours, and improved working conditions. The leader and founder was William D. Haywood, whose political philosophy was a composite of Socialist and syndicalist ideas. Throughout the West, a socialist-syndi-

Like Aunt Mary and Tillie, Smedley was a survivor. Her political commitment sprang basically from personal rage over the indignities she and her family had suffered in the mining towns of the West. As a lower-class product of the harsh economic conditions and strong individualism of the West, Smedley might well have been more attracted to the I.W.W.'s anarchist brand of socialism than to the more middle-class orientation of the Socialist Party. But the particular way in which her personal rage interacted with the environment in San Diego led her to join the Socialist Party.

In 1916 Smedley's most immediate and pressing personal problem was sexuality. Recently acquired information on birth control gave her the means with which to deal with it physically. She channeled her personal anger in a political direction by blaming the state for keeping the liberating knowledge of birth control out of the hands of poor women. Her political consciousness was still shaped largely by Thorberg and Ernest Brundin, the two people she most admired and loved and who loved her in return. Moreover, her friends in San Diego came largely from the Open Forum, most of whose members were middle-class Socialists and liberals. Thus it was natural for her to join the Socialist movement with which they were associated. In short, Smedley joined the Socialist Party less for its theoretical insight or Socialist vision than to satisfy immediate emotional and social needs. She was attracted not by party meetings but by her personal relationships with leaders of the Socialist Party and the liberal Open Forum, as well as the forum's lecture series. As she wrote in *Daughter of Earth*:

> About me at that time—and it was in California—were small Socialist groups who knew little more than I did. We often met in a little dark room to discuss the war and to study various problems and Socialist ideas. The room was over a pool room and led into a larger square room with a splintery floor; in the corner stood a sad looking piano. In the little hall leading to it was a rack holding various Socialist or radical newspapers, tracts, and pamphlets in very small print and on very bad paper. The subjects treated were technical Marxist theories. Now and then some Party member would an-

---

calist press sprang up in small mining camps and in railroad yards located just outside towns. By 1910 the I.W.W. was strong in southern California, as well as integral to the Socialist movement there. Then in January, 1913, for using violent tactics in wildcat strikes, Haywood was expelled from the National Executive Committee of the Socialist Party (led by Eugene Debs). Although several thousand syndicalists followed Haywood out of the party, the majority, like Smedley's friends in San Diego, remained within the Socialist Party. See Melvyn Dubofsky, *We Shall Be All: A History of the I.W.W.* (New York, 1969), and James R. Green, *Grass-Roots Socialism: Radical Movements in the Southwest, 1895–1943* (Baton Rouge, 1978).

nounce a study circle, and I would join it, along with some ten or twelve working men and women.

I joined another circle and [the] leader gave us a little leaflet in very small print, asking us to read it carefully and then come prepared to ask questions. It was a technical Marxist subject and I did not understand it nor did I know what questions to ask.

Once or twice a month our Socialist local would announce a dance and try to draw young workers into it. Twenty or thirty of us would gather in the square, dingy room with splintery floor. The Socialist lawyer of the city came, with his wife and daughter. They were very intelligent and kindly people upon whose shoulders most of the Socialist work in town rested. The wife had baked a cake for the occasion and her daughter, a student, played a cornet. While the piano rattled away and the cornet blared, we circled about the room, trying to be gay. I danced with a middle-aged machinist and we said not a word during the dance. An elderly Single Taxer, who had come for the specific purpose of gaining converts for his ideas, was my second partner, talking Single Tax while we danced.

I attended a few such study circles and dances, but there was seldom enough interest or beauty in them to hold me. The leaders of the study circle did not know how to teach in a manner essential to such a subject. . . . [Myrtle] attended one class only and never went again. I recall them as sad and dreary affairs.

(pp. 147–48)

Smedley had come to accept the Socialist view that change for the working class as a whole was both possible and desirable. In this regard, she had altered her position drastically; in San Francisco in 1912 she had tried to avoid contact with people from her own background. In 1916 Smedley's sister Myrtle labored to suppress the reality of their family past in order to make good her escape into the American middle class. For the rest of their lives, the issue of how to react to their background would continue to divide the two sisters. Myrtle, for her part, thought that trying to make basic changes in the structure of society was foolish, romantic, and doomed to failure, and would perhaps cause even more misery. Agnes, for her part, could never understand why Myrtle did not condemn a system of government that tolerated great extremes of wealth, unequal opportunities for its citizens, and injustices perpetrated by big business. Why wasn't Myrtle as outraged as she that their own mother had suffered from malnutrition and overwork, and died from lack of adequate medical care?

Although the Smedley-Brundin marriage still limped along, by June, 1916, it was clear that Ernest Brundin was not making a go of the gas station. He decided to return to Fresno to a part-time job that paid well enough that he could attend classes on and off at the state college. Following her husband to Fresno for the summer, Smedley landed her first job with a commercial newspaper, the *Fresno Morning Republican.*

Although this was a conservative paper, highly critical of President Wilson, Smedley agreed with its stands on two issues. Like the largest newspaper chain in California, the Hearst papers, and public opinion in California as a whole, it maintained a strong anti-British position up to the eve of the United States' entry into World War I. Although not pro-German, its editorials stressed the need for the United States to remain neutral and it continued to be highly critical of the war-preparedness policies of the Wilson administration. Smedley agreed with this position. The other issue was women's suffrage, for the paper ran many pro-suffrage articles both before and after Smedley joined the staff. Exactly what work Smedley did for the paper is hard to assess, as very few articles were signed, but she did acknowledge one story that she covered. Fresno was the center of the Indian Sikh community in California, and it definitely was Smedley who was sent to cover a Hindu rally in September of 1916. The speaker was Ram Chandra, the editor of *Free Hindustan,* a San Francisco monthly supported primarily by the Sikh farmers near Fresno. (At this time there were about 10,000 immigrant Hindu men in the United States and a minuscule number of women, since female Hindus were excluded by law.) Chandra's aim that day was to report on the progress of the Indian nationalist movement and to raise money to support the overthrow of the British in India. The intent of his newspaper was to publicize the particulars of injustices stemming from British colonial rule, such as press censorship and widespread famine.[12]

Smedley was struck by the fact that the speaker seemed to be supported by a majority of the 500-plus rural Indian-American farmers present. She thus became aware that the Indian nationalist movement was well established in India and around the world and that it saw the war between England and Germany as a golden opportunity for the overthrow of the British in India. The Sikh farmers in California had formed the largest Indian political organization outside India, and they had named it the Ghadar, or "Mutiny," Party.

But aside from discovering the Indian nationalist movement and holding her first commercial newspaper job, Smedley continued to live in trauma. Her marriage was in crisis again, and Ernest finally initiated divorce proceedings.

Smedley returned alone to San Diego in the fall of 1916. The focus of her extracurricular activities continued to be the Open Forum, which hosted a parade of liberal to Socialist speakers, notably Allan L. Benson, the Socialist candidate for president in 1916; Rabinandrath Tagore, the Indian nationalist and poet; Lincoln Steffens, who spoke on the situation in Mexico; and Corneling Lehane, who gave an address on the "Irish Rebellion." [13]

Sometime in December, 1916, a major change in Smedley's life was provoked by a simple quirk of fate: she lost her purse. The purse was found by San Diego Normal School's president, Edward Hardy. When he opened it to determine the owner, he discovered a pink membership card of the Socialist Party bearing the name of Agnes Smedley Brundin. He called her in, dismissed her from her job, and suggested that she leave town immediately, for her sister's sake: Myrtle, after all, would be looking for a job as a teacher the following year, and it would be much harder for her to find one if Agnes Smedley Brundin was still in town. [14]

Smedley promptly left San Diego. Her announced destination was New York, but she headed first for Fresno, where Ernest was still in school. She pleaded with him to attempt another reconciliation, but to no avail. He was convinced that Smedley would never be happy as anyone's wife and that she had to find happiness in a career. Smedley herself had no lasting bitterness about her marriage to Ernest Brundin. As she later wrote in a letter: "I should so like to see Ernest and talk with him. He was the 'stufe' [sic] on which I stood while drawing myself out of a lower standard of thought, life, and culture. He was my one support. Had it not been for him I doubt if I would ever have known of another life. I have no regret; but I am sorry he was hurt, and that he loved me. But only a man who loved me enough to suffer could have helped me. I owe Ernest a debt greater than he can imagine." [15]

Smedley left California in 1916 feeling vulnerable and still emotionally dependent on Ernest Brundin. She stopped in Colorado to visit her Aunt Tillie. After leaving Colorado, she must have felt desperately lonely, for on the way to New York she stopped in a small midwestern town to look up her old pen pal from the New Mexico schoolteaching days. The man whose handwriting she had once admired was a short, God-fearing store clerk with very conservative ideas about women— hardly a fit companion for Agnes Smedley.

CHAPTER III

Finding a Cause, 1917–1918

Although Smedley was uneasy about their attitude toward her, it was to Ernest and Thorberg's parents in New York that she first went. "Mom" Brundin provided her with a hat and insisted that she wear gloves while interviewing for a job. The formula worked, and Smedley soon found work as a secretary. For a few months after arriving in New York, Agnes shared Thorberg Brundin's apartment in Greenwich Village, and it was basically among Thorberg's group of progressive friends that she first moved socially and politically. Thorberg herself had become a high school teacher and had joined the Socialist Party. Her local party organization had many intellectuals in it, and in their presence Smedley felt awkward, naive, and condescended to. Moreover, it galled her to hear them say that "life" and experience were more important than formal education. In *Daughter of Earth* she wrote: "They idealize the working class, and I feared they might not understand the things that grow in poverty and ignorance" (p. 242).

Thorberg's friends were the generation that first gave the Greenwich Village area a sense of community and an identity as a center for bohemian radicals. The Villagers of the prewar and war years were members of an intellectual community—mainly middle-class—dedicated to seeking new ways to implement social change in the larger society. Their intellectual quests, like those of many Americans prior to our entry into World War I, had a strong international thrust. For Smedley, their most impressive effort was the women's movement.

Whether the issue was suffrage, birth control, or opposing war and working for peace, women such as Jane Addams and Margaret Sanger always spoke in terms of an international sisterhood. They assumed that women, who struggled with the universal human problems of birth and death and raising a family, stood ethically above the politics of nationalism. This stance was consistent with Smedley's own position on suffrage (forged in the Normal School debate in Tempe in 1912) and also suited her distrust of male-dominated organizations. With the winning of the vote for women in New York state in 1917, the attention of suffragists was turning to other areas. Women novelists were advocating "equal opportunities" for sexual fulfillment. Women activists were becoming involved in the birth-control movement led by Margaret Sanger. And for several years before Smedley's arrival in New York, the New Feminist Alliance had been petitioning educational institutions, especially professional schools, to accept women students. The founder of the alliance, whom Smedley soon met through Thorberg, was the charismatic and flamboyant Henrietta Rodman, who wore sandals and loose-flowing gowns and, according to contemporaries, "invented Greenwich Village." Like the many other intellectuals in the village who were voraciously reading anthropology and studying the new theories of Freud, Rodman believed that sexual roles were not universally the same, but varied according to culture. In short, she and her friends were evolutionary socialists who hoped to create a new society through legislation and education.[1]

By the early spring of 1917, public concern about U.S. involvement in the war in Europe had become intense. Since the elections of 1916 a minority coalition of pacifists, Socialists, and intellectuals had been arguing vigorously that the United States should stay out of the war or should act only as a peace negotiator. Socialists, especially, thought that U.S. monopoly capitalism both supported the war and was leading the nation into it. But like others who joined them in the antiwar cause, they considered themselves patriotic Americans who were trying to persuade their fellow citizens by means of education and demonstration. By April, 1917, however, the majority of U.S. voters had become strongly pro-British. And after President Wilson signed the formal declaration of war, massive political witch-hunting soon destroyed the political potential of the Socialist Party. The practice of placing American civilians under domestic military surveillance was initiated, and with it the pursuit of Smedley by intelligence agents which would last for the rest of her life.[2]

The Socialist group to which Thorberg belonged was actively antiwar and participated in a coalition called the People's Council for Peace
and Democracy. In the summer of 1917 Smedley went with this group to
antiwar rallies and began to speak to workers outside factories. As a
speaker, she was shy and ineffectual. She recalled in *Daughter of Earth:*
"Working men stood outside a factory to hear us, and in one such gathering someone pushed me forward and told me to speak to them. . . .
I have often heard or read in novels how a man or woman suddenly
faced with great responsibility rises to the occasion; how eloquently and
magnificently they speak or act until the audience breaks into wild applause. It seems that their rise to fame begins from that moment. But I
was not a character in a novel, and I stood on the fender of the automobile, looking with astonishment into the up-turned faces of working
men. I realized how very ignorant, how very confused, I was. Uttering a
few empty sentences, I stepped down" (p. 250). But she felt strongly
about the issue. It seemed to her that the war was most vehemently supported by the middle and upper classes, and she could not forget that it
would be mostly poor young men, like her brothers, who, for want of a
steady job, would fight the war and die in it. She wrote later in *Daughter of Earth:* "[Myrtle] wrote that she was doing war work. I opposed it,
but she said one must do something for one's country. Whose country, I
asked her—the country that would let her starve as it had our mother,
become a prostitute as it had [Tillie], or be killed like a rat as was
[John]" (p. 252).

Not long after she arrived in New York, she had received a letter from
her brother John, now twenty-one years old and a day laborer in Oklahoma, in which he said only that he was in jail for stealing a horse.
Smedley felt ashamed of his behavior and could not tell her new middle-
class friends: "they would say my brother would have been justified had
he stolen bread, when hungry, but he shouldn't have stolen a horse. Even
I, who loved him dearly, felt this" (p. 242). But Smedley also felt partly
to blame for not helping him more. She sent him an angry letter but
enclosed money and said that he should have patience until she finished
helping finance his sister Myrtle's schooling, for then she could help her
brothers. The reply came in the form of a telegram from her youngest
brother, Sam: John was dead. She learned a few weeks later that he had
been killed on April 2, 1917, when the sewage ditch he was digging had
fallen in on him and broken his neck. He had been buried beside his
mother, and the company he worked for paid their father fifty dollars in
compensation. Sam bitterly condemned Agnes for her letter to John,

saying it was easy for her to criticize when she had a good job and would be entering a university again; he said he was tired of going hungry when he couldn't find work, and threatened to join the army if she didn't quickly send him enough money to enroll in a trade school. Overwhelmed by guilt, Smedley debated whether to give up her dream of a university education and take another job to help Sam. But Sam removed the dilemma by joining the army. Smedley felt caught. Because she was surrounded by a minority within the middle-class who, in their opposition to the war, romanticized the working class, she felt isolated. She knew that the men of her own family would support their country if they perceived a foreign threat. But she was more cynical about Myrtle's motivations; she believed her sister was responding in an acceptable middle-class way in order to make good her own escape into that class.

Because her main goals were to gain financial independence and success as a writer—which would require learning to translate her emotional reactions against racism and economic imperialism into convincing intellectual arguments—Smedley still felt she needed the background and polish of a university education. She began attending night classes at New York University, but in the classroom her inadequate background and relative inarticulateness only embarrassed her. She was also troubled by her feelings about sex. According to those who knew her during this period, she was a pretty, dynamic, sensual woman, and many men, intrigued by her frank curiosity and naïveté, saw her as part "noble savage" and part child of the working class. She started having affairs, but she was over her head emotionally. Still viewing the sexual act as animalistic, she felt guilty, vulnerable, and wary of the men around her.

It was in a mood of frustration and emotional isolation, therefore, that Smedley attended a lecture by the Indian leader Lajpat Rai at Columbia University on March 10, 1917. Rai finished his speech as follows: "You Americans—can you be at peace in your minds when your system, your leisure that created culture, rests upon the enslaved bodies of others? Is this law of the jungle the law of life to you? If so, you are machines without a soul, without a purpose. I have spoken to you of the freedom for which we Indians are working; can it be that you, like England, believe in freedom only for yourselves? Your war is for democracy, you say. I doubt it—your principles do not extend to Asia, although Asia is three-fourths of the human race" (p. 264). Deeply moved by this challenge, Smedley approached Rai after the lecture and asked if she might meet with him. When she called on him the next Sunday, they had a long talk, at the end of which she was won over to the idea of studying to become a teacher in India. Rai told her: "We need teachers in India—teachers who come as friends, not conquerors." As Smedley reflected in *Daughter of Earth:*

> Then a man came into my life. A lover—no. But it was not my fault that he was not. For I was a turmoil of vague yearnings and of confusion. He was a teacher and a wise man. A dark man with white in his hair, a man from India, ugly and severe. There was a scar down one side of his face and one eye was blind. He stood for a brief hour upon the threshold of my life, and I think he always had a touch of scorn for me. Why he concerned himself with me at all is still inexplicable. Perhaps he was lonely in exile, or perhaps my need for affection, for someone to love, for someone to take the place of a father, was strong, and when I found a person who seemed to promise this, I did not lightly release my grip. For I was as primitive as a weed.
>
> (p. 262)

The impact of this meeting was enormous. Within weeks Smedley quit her job. She moved out of Thorberg's apartment and took a small room near Rai's residence. She began working as a secretary for Rai in the morning, attending classes at New York University in the afternoon, and then returning to Rai's in the evening to be tutored by him or others on Indian history and culture. Rai drove Smedley hard in her studies, and she responded with total commitment. In *Daughter of Earth* she wrote:

> He worked with me although I was raw and ignorant of many things. I was not an interesting person to associate with and yet he worked with me and taught me, filling my life with meaning. He introduced me to the movement for the freedom of his people and showed me that it was not only an historic movement of itself, but it was a part of an international struggle for emancipation—that it was one of the chief pillars in this struggle. It was not a distant movement. Because I loved him as I might have loved my father, I learned more than I could have learned from any other source.
>
> Through him I touched for the first time a movement of unwavering principle and beauty—the struggle of a continent to be free.
>
> (pp. 278–279)

When Smedley first met Rai, she was feeling alienated from and socially inferior to Thorberg Brundin and her friends. But she was also defiantly determined to prove her worth. Meeting Lajpat Rai gave Smedley the chance to grow intellectually by studying Indian history, politics, and culture with a major intellectual of the time, in a nonthreatening environment. Of more importance, working with Rai offered her a way to assuage the guilt she felt for putting her own needs for emotional and intellectual survival above those of other members of her family. Choosing a large, principled cause allowed her to look forward with hope, not backward in despair, and gave her a new sense of energy and purpose.

Since Lajpat Rai was Smedley's window to a new future, an understanding of who he was and the background of the overseas Indian nationalist movement up to 1917 is crucial to an understanding of Smedley's role in that movement.

Lajpat Rai, known as the Lion of the Punjab, had a broad political base in India. An experienced worker in religious and educational reforms and famine relief, he understood the enormous burden of poverty and illiteracy that would be bequeathed to an independent India after generations of British colonial rule. From this and his assessment of the world situation, he had already concluded that if India were given complete independence immediately, it might well be swallowed up by another imperialist power. He therefore advocated Indian self-rule within the British Commonwealth system, so that India could at least control its own internal affairs, especially its fiscal policy and armed forces.

In 1913, Rai had been sent to England by the Twenty-ninth Karachi session of the Indian Congress Party to present their position to the British Parliament. Toward the end of 1914, he came to the United States with a letter of introduction from a British Fabian, Sidney Webb, to Professor E. R. A. Seligman of Columbia University. He had planned only a brief fact-finding visit, but wartime restrictions on travel imposed by the British authorities in both Britain and India forced him to remain in exile in the United States for almost five years. From his initial introduction to Seligman, Rai created a group within the liberal intelligentsia who became more familiar with and sympathetic toward the nationalist cause. Much of the credit for attracting Americans to the cause of Indian nationalism during this period belongs to Rai. He built his network on missionary and mainstream support for the Anti-Imperialist League, formed in the 1890s, which in turn had grown out of the deeply American-rooted anticolonial opposition to the U.S. acquisition of the Philippines.* Most of the initial spokesmen for the organization had earlier been active in the abolitionist movement. By the 1910s they had been joined by laissez-faire conservatives such as Andrew Carnegie,

---

* Not to be confused with the later League Against Imperialism, which was founded in Europe in 1928 and with which Smedley was involved (see Chapter 8).

who feared that American democracy would be threatened by the enlarged military and administrative forces that would be needed to control a colony. Their arguments stressed the principle of government by consent.

With the exception of a five-month trip to Japan, Rai spent most of 1915 in California, where he concentrated on publishing articles in liberal magazines to introduce his cause to American academics, of whom Professor Arthur Pope of the University of California, Berkeley, became the most helpful to him.[3]

In 1916 Rai made New York the base for his activities. Through his membership in the liberal Civic Club, he won the support of Irish Americans and their impassioned champion Francis Hackett, who broadened his dislike of British imperialism to become active in the Indian cause. Through Hackett, Rai met Oswald Garrison Villard, the publisher of *The Nation* and the *New York Evening Post*. A former member of the Anti-Imperialist League, Villard became an ardent supporter of the nationalist cause and opened *The Nation* to its spokesmen. The founder of the New Feminist Alliance, Henrietta Rodman, whom Smedley knew through Thorberg, also met Rai at the Civic Club. She soon took charge of the Civic Club's study sessions on India, and she remained an ardent advocate of the Indian nationalist cause until her death in the early 1920s.

In 1917 Rai helped to found the India Home Rule League of America. Supported by a majority of Indian nationalists in India, the Home Rule League urged all-out support for the British war effort but emphasized their expectation that self-government for India should soon be forthcoming. This position was undercut, however, by the activities of the much smaller Ghadar Party, which, encouraged by Germany, repudiated nonviolent agitation and sought to gain independence by revolution. Thus, despite the substantial wartime aid given to Britain, the Indian nationalist cause in America remained tainted by charges of conspiracy with Germany. Rai had met with members of the Ghadar Party in California in 1915, but he had refused to ally himself openly with them, because of their German connections and their willingness to use violence.

The majority of Ghadar Party members were hardworking Sikh farmers and laborers in California who felt provoked to their revolutionary position by the racism they had encountered as émigrés trying to become citizens in the United States and Canada around the turn of the century. After constant harassment they had turned to the British government to protect their rights, but they received no help. When World War I broke out in July of 1914, the Ghadars saw the war as an opportunity to foment rebellion, and began sending Indians and arms back to India to lead it. At the same time, the British clampdown on all dissidence in India during World War I drove an increasing number of young Indian nationalists abroad, creating a numerically small but worldwide network connecting India to Japan, Hong Kong, Shanghai, Singapore, Thailand, Turkey, Persia, Mexico, Germany, and the United States. But the techniques and propaganda of these overseas nationalists were so blatant, and the planning of what to do when they arrived back in India so naively left undone, that the British had little trouble in violently putting down an attempted uprising in the Punjab in February 1915. Until then, the Ghadars in California appear to have been financially independent, supported by donations from the overseas Indian community. But after the failure of the February effort, they began accepting financial aid and technical advice from the German government through a Berlin-based committee of Indian nationalists. Rai, however, had strenuously objected to this later policy of accepting aid from the Germans.

The leadership of the Ghadars was mostly in the hands of young and politically inexperienced students and intellectuals like Ram Chandra, whom Smedley had heard speak in Fresno, California, in 1916. With repeated failures in India and growing financial aid from Germany, factionalism was inevitable. Differences grew particularly sharp between the predominantly Sikh rank and file in California and the smaller group of mainly Bengali intellectuals centered in New York, who were in direct contact with the Germans and the Indians in Berlin.[4]

As the United States moved toward a declaration of war on Germany, emotional ties to Britain were increasingly stressed, contravening the Indian nationalist cause. By the time of Rai's talk at Columbia in March, 1917, the U.S. government was cooperating with the British in attempts to suppress the nationalist movement and arrest its radical spokesmen as participants in a German plot.[5] In fact, for weeks before Rai's lecture the British had been using informers to try to ensnare one Indian student who was thought to have received aid from the Germans for his conspiratorial activities. New York City policemen attended the lecture. At its conclusion, a plainclothesman singled out a young Bengali, M. N. Roy, his bride, Evelyn Trent, and Herambalal Gupta and pushed them into a waiting car. After several hours of investigation Trent and Roy still refused to say anything, but Gupta was more cooperative. All three were then released and put under surveillance. The next day, the *New*

York Evening World splashed "spy plot" headlines across its front page. Gupta had supposedly told police that a German had given him money to purchase arms in the United States and ship them back to India. "The easy carelessness of American tolerance has given way to a sternness befitting the time and danger," said the *New York Times*. It condemned the Indians and praised the New York police.[6]

British propaganda continued to portray Germans, radicals, and anarchists as the real masterminds behind the Indian nationalist movement, and by blurring the distinction between revolutionary and nationalist, it tried to discredit the nationalist movement as a whole. The British were also quick to publicize any information that connected Russian radical revolutionaries with the nationalists. On January 9, 1917, en route to New York, Leon Trotsky had reportedly said: "If we [Bolsheviks] were really logical we would declare war on England now for the sake of India, Egypt, and Ireland." Soon after his arrival in New York, Trotsky met in the Bronx Public Library with one of the Indian nationalists who were dealing with Berlin. On March 6, four days before the Rai lecture at Columbia, this same Indian's home was searched at the instigation of a British agent. The Indian was taken to New York police headquarters, where he admitted his ties with Germany. A grand jury indicted him on charges of conspiracy on March 9. Trotsky left New York at the end of March, but his boat was intercepted by the British around Nova Scotia; Trotsky was arrested and held for one month in a British prisoner-of-war camp.[7]

Publicity given to these arrests helped turn American opinion against the Indian nationalists. The public did not seem surprised, therefore, when on the morning of April 16, before President Wilson had signed the House resolution declaring war on Germany, the Justice Department ordered the arrest of Ghadar Party newspaper editor Ram Chandra and sixteen other Indians involved in the "German-Hindu conspiracy." Not until the afternoon of April 16 were seventy Germans arrested as dangerous to the security of the United States. The Indian nationalist movement was further discredited in the eyes of the public when a connection was drawn in the press between the leader of the Ghadar Party and two American anarchists, Emma Goldman and Alexander Berkman, arrested under the Espionage Act. Then on July 7, 1917, a San Francisco grand jury returned indictments for conspiracy against 105 men in the *Annie Larsen* gun-running case, and on July 12 it indicted 19 more. This was the same case that the Justice Department had refused to pursue earlier that spring, for lack of evidence. Now it was claimed that the

Hindu-German conspiracy had begun three years earlier, when Indians and Germans met to prepare a military expedition.[8] The Justice Department's arrest of Hindus in New York and Chicago—whom it considered agents of a worldwide Indo-German conspiracy against the United States' new wartime ally—was part of the growing political repression of the war period.

Working for Rai, Smedley met a number of the more radical nationalists who came to him, as a senior statesman, for advice and support. Rai pleaded for a moderate response to the growing repression. Two Bengalis, Sarindranath Ghose and M. N. Roy, along with Roy's wife, Evelyn Trent, fled to Mexico in May to avoid possible arrest.[9] Before their departure, they introduced Smedley to the more radical ideas advocated by the Ghadar Party in California.*

From Roy and Ghose, Smedley learned about the activities of Bengalis like Taraknath Das, a U.S. citizen who in the spring of 1917 was in Japan to expedite the smuggling of guns and men into India.[10] From Roy, Ghose, and others Smedley heard an exaggerated picture of the "revolutionary" potential of overthrowing the British in India. Moreover, most of the Ghadar rank and file whom Smedley had met earlier in California were Sikh farmers and working people with whom she could easily identify. As a countervailing force there was only her mentor, Lajpat Rai, who cautioned her repeatedly about the romanticism of the Ghadar movement. But increasingly, because Smedley had never been to India, she became persuaded by the Ghadar argument that Rai was representing only the viewpoint of the upper class and landowners of India.

By the fall of 1917, buoyed by news of the Russian Revolution in October, Smedley began to reject Rai's advice and embrace the more radical Ghadar movement and such leaders as Taraknath Das and Ghose. In November she began serving as a kind of New York agent in an elabo-

---

* Both Ghose and Roy were fresh from a bomb-throwing, Robin Hood–like nationalist movement in Bengal. They were revolutionary only in the sense that they advocated the violent overthrow of the British government in India. At this point, neither had much knowledge of Marxism. Ghose had joined the Bengal independence movement when he was a teenaged physics student and had been forced underground in 1915. Late in 1916, at the age of twenty-two, he was sent to the United States to improve contact between the Ghadar Party and the Bengal movement. Ghose went first to California, where he became a member of the Ghadar Party, and then, in mid-February of 1917, to New York, where he moved in with Roy and Trent. Roy was in touch with the Berlin Committee of nationalists who were cooperating with the Germans, and he had himself just arrived in New York via East Asia and California. (Samaren Roy, "M. N. Roy in America," *Radical Humanist* 47, no. 1 [March 1983]: 23–30; John P. Haithcox, *Communism and Nationalism in India* [Princeton, N.J., 1971], chapters 1 and 2.)

rate plot engineered by Ghose and Das in San Francisco to win recognition for the overseas independence movement.

In Mexico in mid-1917 Sarindranath Ghose had conceived the idea of establishing an internationally based Indian National Party. It was to act in a more radical and independent way than the Indian National Congress ever could in colonial India; it would represent Indian interests abroad; and ultimately it would become a government in exile. In those days Ghose was associating with Communists like Michael Borodin and was reading Marx for the first time; he found the Bolshevik Revolution of October 1917 exhilarating. By November, he was back in the United States, living secretly in San Francisco and working on the establishment of the Indian National Party. Das, too, had returned to San Francisco in November to stand trial on charges relating to the Indo-German conspiracy cases pending since the arrests of the previous spring and culminating in the San Francisco "Hindu conspiracy" trial of 1918. When Das was released on bail, he shared an apartment with Ghose.[11]

From November, 1917, to March, 1918, Smedley worked with Das and Ghose in a naive bid to win recognition for the Indian National Party. Special stationery marked "Diplomatic Correspondence" and a set of official-looking seals were purchased. The plan was to issue documents that fabricated the existence of such a party at the branch level both within and outside India, explained its purpose, and asked for recognition by foreign governments. These documents were written by Ghose and Das in San Francisco on stationery reading "Tagore Castle, Calcutta," then sent from New York to President Woodrow Wilson and diplomatic representatives of various countries in Washington, D.C. Cover letters were written and signed in New York by Pulin Behari Bose, special representative of the Indian National Party in the United States. Bose was, in fact, an assumed name; it was Agnes Smedley who wrote and signed the cover letters and sent the material to Washington. The mailing of letters and documents began in early December of 1917, with the majority sent the next month. Often embassies refused to accept the packets and returned them to Smedley's Waverly Place address in New York. (On occasion Smedley would sign such correspondence as "M. A. Rogers, Secretary to P. B. Bose"—a foreshadowing of Marie Rogers, the heroine of Smedley's *Daughter of Earth*.) At about this time, Das and Ghose sent a strongly worded appeal to Trotsky and the Bolsheviks in Moscow, seeking support for Indian independence and for Indian nationalists under arrest in the United States and elsewhere, but this they sent directly from San Francisco and not through Smedley in New York.

Ghose in particular wanted to go to Russia and make direct contacts, and Smedley offered to help through her connections with Robert Minor and other new pro-Bolshevik friends in New York. Indeed, Ghose was probably on his way to Moscow when he left San Francisco for New York early in March of 1918.[12]

By mid-April of 1918, Smedley had survived two traumatic events: one, of a very personal nature, would undermine her emotionally and its future disclosure would be used to discredit the political positions she represented; the other, of a public nature, would propel her career to a new stage of prominence and give her credibility on the left.

Smedley had carried her unresolved attitudes toward sex into her work with the Indian community of male nationalists. Besides having found a father figure in Lajpat Rai, Smedley felt that she had a "family" among men who agreed with her that sex was an evil to be controlled or suppressed for the higher ideals of the cause. Within the Hindu tradition, single women are looked upon as evil temptresses. A woman does not have a positive image or high status until she is married and has children. Single men or women who indulged in sex were considered morally weak and rendered powerless as leaders. After Smedley became involved with the Indian nationalists, it appears that she stopped having affairs. Although the Indian community provided a safe haven from the promiscuous atmosphere of Greenwich Village, total denial of her sexuality did not make Smedley any less vulnerable. Sometime in mid-February her defenses broke down.

The man's name was Herambalal Gupta.[13] He was a veteran Bengali nationalist in his late thirties who had been released on bail after his arrest on the night of Rai's lecture almost a year earlier. After reading the ambiguous accounts in the press, some Indians had expressed the fear that he had given the police the names of other Indians with German connections, and he was thought to be bitter about his loss of position within the movement after his arrest. He came late one night to Smedley's apartment on Waverly Place, seeking information on the whereabouts of Ghose and to say good-bye before leaving town. As Smedley reconstructed it in *Daughter of Earth:*

> I sat staring back and up at him hearing my jeering voice reply: "I am not interested in anything about you!"
>
> But something had weakened within me even as I jeered, and I was confused.
>
> His voice was close to my ear and it was saying, "Are you quite certain

you are not interested?" His hands closed softly, firmly, on my shoulders, and then slid gently down along my arm and caught my hands in a warm, trembling grip. . . .

"Why do you lie to me?" he whispered. "Why? . . . tell me the truth . . . Was [Ghose] here?"

I jerked. "No . . . let me go!"

Arising, he drew me firmly to my feet, holding me still in a vise-like grip from the back. . . .

"Tell me."

"Let me go! . . . Do you hear?" I jerked in blind fear, for I liked him and a yearning in my blood, long suppressed in shame, had begun to struggle with my mind. It grasped at the words that followed:

"Dear . . . you love me, don't you?" . . . The lips were very hot.

When I felt the trembling a blind panic seized me and something closed in upon my throat. Quickly he whirled me into his arms and his big shoulders crushed me. "Don't!" My voice was choking. "Don't . . . you see. . . ." My mind could no longer think. . . . I struggled, gasping for breath, about my waist a cold, fearful trembling, so cold it froze me. The room became a whirring, blurred image, then clear, then whirring. Terror . . . the shadow of dark outspread wings of a bird, swooping . . . he was carrying me in his arms . . . his lips were hot as fire . . . and his body had hurled itself upon me.

(pp. 279–81)

As he was about to leave her apartment, Gupta asked Smedley not to tell anyone. "It would ruin me in my work . . . you know how our men regard such things as this. Do you hear?" After he had gone, Smedley found fifty dollars on the table. Overwhelmed by guilt and shame and realizing that her own work was also compromised, she once again attempted suicide, this time by blowing out the flame on the gas jet. Her landlady smelled the gas and entered to find Smedley unconscious on her bed. She awoke in a hospital bed.

In spite of her secret worries that her work in the movement might be compromised if the incident with Gupta became known, a public event occurred in mid-March that deepened Smedley's commitment to the Indian nationalist cause and strengthened her position with the movement's leaders. Ironically, it would also begin the process of making her private life a matter of public record.

By March of 1918, Smedley was living quietly in her apartment on Waverly Place, trying to recover psychologically from Gupta's attack, doing mailings for the Indian National Party, and waiting for Ghose's arrival from San Francisco. She did not know that immigration authorities and representatives of the Justice Department had been monitoring Ghose's and Das's mail in San Francisco and intercepting their correspondence with her and others. On the morning of March 15, 1918, military intelligence officers and representatives of the Justice Department ransacked Smedley's apartment and brought her uptown for questioning. A stakeout at her apartment netted Ghose two days later, fresh from San Francisco.[14]

For two weeks Smedley was alternately interrogated and held in solitary confinement. Her moral indignation was fueled by the tone of police interrogations, and she recorded her feelings later in *Daughter of Earth:*

> An inner door at last opened and I was led down an inner hall and into a long room.
>
> I gave my name, parentage, nationality. No, I was not of German birth, nor were my parents. Very, very certain. My father was of Indian descent, my mother an old American also. Indians from India? No, American Indians.
>
> Other men entered, bearing everything from my room—my books, my clothing, even my soiled laundry. I watched them, speechless. They made a little pile of the books—in horror I saw the black notebook among them.
>
> (p. 301)

The notebook contained a sheet of paper with the names and addresses of Indian nationalists. Seeing it, Smedley quickly tried to shift the focus of attention to herself by demanding to see a lawyer. Her examiner claimed that this wasn't necessary because she wasn't formally under arrest. Since she was just being questioned, they said, she had no right to demand anything. They then tried to intimidate her by attacking her character.

> "Miss [Smedley]: do you smoke?"
>
> No answer.
>
> "Do you curse?—here is a letter in which you use the word 'damn' rather freely." He was reading through my private letters. They had been stealing my mail!
>
> "To what church do you belong? Oh—you are not a Christian? Then do you believe in God? No! What do you mean, young woman! What is your religion?—are you a yogi?"
>
> I glanced about the room—at the well-fed men, at the Englishman in the corner, at the thin-lipped examiner, and then at the black notebook on the table. I sat down again.
>
> "That's it, just take your time and talk," one of them said.
>
> I looked up. "Leave me in peace. I will have nothing to do with you."
>
> "Young woman—this is wartime and it is dangerous to play with the United States!"
>
> " 'The United States!' Well, I'm as much a part of the United States as you are—and more than that sausage in the corner with his English accent!"

"It will not go easier with you if you are fresh! I know you think you are being a grand person, protecting these yellow dogs you have been running around with."

"Yellow dogs!"

"Asiatics—you know what I mean!"

"What Asiatics?"

"Here is a letter you wrote to [Ghose] a few days ago telling him how to escape from the country! You knew he was a fugitive from justice! Your duty as a citizen was to notify the police. Where is the man?"

I watched the Englishman in the corner—my duty as a citizen indeed!

"I don't know what you are talking about," I replied.

"You are lying! We have no intention to fool about with a German spy!"

"Who are you calling a German spy, you! You dirty English spies, you!"

The men arose to their feet, and the examiner, red as if I had struck him, shouted: "We will arrest [Lajpat Rai] at once!"

(pp. 302–3)

When Smedley acknowledged that she knew Rai, they asked if he had given her money for her "services." They then threatened to tell the press some interesting facts about her personal life unless she cooperated. When she refused, they told her that hers was a "silly attempt to pose as a martyr" and then booked her as a federal prisoner and put her into solitary confinement. She wrote: "I lay trembling on the cold bars of the bed and closed my eyes . . . perhaps my body would warm the steel. The night wore on. How shivering cold it was—would the dawn never come? What would tomorrow bring? Suppose they found the notebook—and the men were jailed and their comrades would think I had betrayed them! A black notebook took form in my mind until it seemed my head itself was a black notebook" (p. 305).

Smedley's arrest was reported in the *New York Times* on Tuesday, March 19, 1918: "Important evidence bearing on a plot to cause uprisings in India against British rule has come into the possession of the Government as the result of the arrest yesterday of Miss Agnes Smedley, an American girl, also known as Agnes Brundin." Ghose was described as the "directing genius" of the plot. The article went on to emphasize the international contacts of Smedley and Ghose, especially to Leon Trotsky, and ended: "When Commissioner Shields suggested to Miss Smedley that she might aid her country by helping to expose the conspiracy, she repudiated the suggestion."

Learning of the arrest, Ernest Brundin in California dropped his studies, his job, and the courtship of his future bride Elinor and left immediately for New York to see what he could do to help Smedley. Firm in the face of physical abuse, threats, and promises of leniency in exchange for information, Smedley and Ghose were taken before Judge A. N. Hand on April 1, 1918, and indicted under the Espionage Act for attempting to stir up rebellion against British rule in India, thereby abetting the German enemy, and for representing themselves as diplomats; Smedley was also charged with violating a local ordinance against disseminating birth control information. Both were put into Manhattan's Tombs Prison; bail was set at $10,000 for Smedley and $20,000 for Ghose.[15]

Because of the birth control charge, Margaret Sanger rallied to Smedley's defense, along with other New York liberals and Socialists. The attempt to raise the required $10,000 bail was led by Sanger and a leading New York Unitarian clergyman, J. H. Holmes, known as the "patron saint" of Protestant pacifists and a founder of the N.A.A.C.P. The Socialist Party newspaper, the *Call*, ran a story after the indictments asking for contributions to a newly formed defense fund. One of the country's most prominent constitutional lawyers, Gilbert Roe, took the case for "whatever the defendants could afford to pay." Roe, a law partner of Senator La Follette and a friend of many prominent liberals such as Senator George Norris, had a reputation for defending the poor, liberals, and organized labor.[16]

On May 16 Congress passed the Sedition Act, which provided heavy penalties for those who hindered the war effort by making false statements, obstructing enlistment, or criticizing the production of war materials, the American form of government, the Constitution, or the flag. Enforcement was aimed against Socialists and pacifists.

One June 11, a second indictment against Smedley for violating the Espionage Act was filed in San Francisco. Ghose, Das, Bhagwan Singh, William and Marian Wotherspoon—a liberal lawyer and his wife—and Bluma Zalaznek, a young Russian woman, were included in the charges. By this time the newspapers were characterizing Zalaznek as the "reputed leader of the Bolshevik Party in San Francisco," but Smedley had never met or corresponded with either Zalaznek or the Wotherspoons.[17]

By the summer of 1918, bail was raised and Smedley was released into the custody of her counsel, Gilbert Roe. Margaret Sanger threw a party to celebrate her release and raise bail money for Ghose.[18]

The indictments against the Indian nationalists and Smedley should be viewed in the context of the war effort and the growing concern, in the wake of the Russian Revolution, about the "red menace." Another example of the government's escalating paranoia was the June 30 arrest of Socialist presidential candidate Eugene Debs on charges of interfering with military recruitment and his subsequent September 14 sentence of ten years' imprisonment.

At first, both the American and British governments thought the influence of the Revolution of 1917 was a madness that would pass. But Lenin's peace treaty with Germany, the Treaty of Brest-Litovsk, signed on March 3, 1918, just a few weeks before Smedley's arrest, gave cause for grave concern. In it, Bolshevik Russia renounced two hundred years of history and acknowledged the "independence" of Poland, the Ukraine, Finland, Estonia, Latvia, and Lithuania. Germany was at the height of its military success. Through puppets placed at the heads of new states, Germany now dominated eastern Europe. The naval blockade of food supplies was somewhat offset by shipments of foodstuffs from the Ukraine. It was no longer a two-front war, as much of the German army was shifted from the east for a massive blow to France, in an attempt to end the war.

Thus with the signing of the treaty Russia became the object of Allied hostility. Russian Czarist reactionaries, liberals, and various anti-Leninist Socialists including the Mensheviks scattered in all directions and began to organize resistance, receiving substantial aid from the Western Allies. In August the Allies, including the United States, launched a military expedition at Vladivostok against the Bolshevik menace. In war-weary Russia, the civil war increased in intensity and violence in reaction to the extreme scarcity of food.

In the spring months following Smedley's arrest, the Germans opened a final offensive, hoping to end the war before American participation, only a year old, could turn the balance. But by July the Germans were overextended. About 250,000 American troops were landing in France every month. In September, the Allied offensive opened and proved to be more than the Germans could withstand.

Unrest in India also continued. On March 21, the India Office in London announced that an uprising in the Baluchistans had been put down by air strikes which "on two occasions recently bombed tribal concentrations with effect." This first concentrated bombing of civilians from the air appears to have aroused no indignation from the general public in Allied countries.[19] It was in this atmosphere that, in August of 1918, the U.S. government summed up its case against the San Francisco "Hindu conspirators," labeling them tools of German agents and appealing to the jury to "hold the line for democracy."

The San Francisco Hindu conspiracy trial was sad but colorful, with testimony by undercover agents and informers taken out of six British prisons around the world. One informant went mad in his cell; one Indian, after killing Ram Chandra during the trial itself, was in turn shot dead by a marshal. The jury found all the defendants, with the exception of an American millionaire shipbuilder from Long Beach, guilty of conspiring to launch a military expedition.[20]

The growing arrests and publicity given to Indians, anarchists, and spies helped to create the climate in which a bill passed by Congress on October 16 provided for the deportation of alien anarchists.[21] On October 14, 1918, Smedley appeared in court; an unsuccessful attempt was made to extradite her to San Francisco. Legal wrangling continued throughout October as Roe fought to keep Smedley and Ghose in New York and out of prison and to have their arrests declared illegal. On the last day of October, Smedley was again in court, and this time she was sent back to jail.

The jail experience further alienated Smedley from establishment views, and her cellmates, despite differences in background, sharpened her political thinking and sense of commitment. The two fellow prisoners who made the greatest impression on her were Mollie Steimer and Kitty Marion. In addition to joking about rats, bed bugs, and cockroaches, she wrote to Margaret Sanger: "Kitty, Mollie Steimer, and I have wonderful meetings when we can dodge in some corner of the cell. Kitty is turning the place into a birth control branch. And she has held a meeting. And her friends are writing out demanding that their parents and friends vote Socialism!"

Steimer was a young follower of Emma Goldman serving a fifteen-year sentence for circulating leaflets in opposition to U.S. intervention in the Russian civil war. She was twenty-one years old and had come to New York from her native Ukraine five years earlier. Pasted in red on the walls of her cell was the slogan "Long Live the Social Revolution" and newspaper photographs of Karl Liebknecht, Eugene Debs, and John Reed. Steimer was totally dedicated to the cause of worker and class struggle. Every afternoon after the cell doors clanged shut, she would stand grasping the steel bars and speak in simple English. Smedley wrote:

> The three tiers would become silent and only an occasional question would interrupt her talk. . . . Mollie championed the cause of the prisoners—the one with venereal disease, the mother with diseased babies, the prostitute, the feeble-minded, the burglar, the murderer. To her they were but products of a diseased social system. She did not complain that even the most vicious of them were sentenced to no more than 5 or 7 years, while she herself was

facing 15 years in prison. She asked that the girl with venereal disease be taken to a hospital; the prison physician accused her of believing in free love and in Bolshevism. She asked that the vermin be cleaned from the cells of one of the girls; the matron ordered her to attend to her own affairs—that it was not *her* cell. "Lock me in," she replied to the matron; "I have nothing to lose but my chains." [22]

Kitty Marion was already a legend in Margaret Sanger's birth control movement. A veteran of Mrs. Pankhurst's suffragette wars in London, she was in the Tombs on a thirty-day sentence for giving a pamphlet on birth control to an agent of the notorious Association for Suppression of Vice. Kitty also knew how to turn a prison into a school for political education. In dealing with prison authorities and her cellmates, she rarely lost her focus on the birth control issue or her sense of humor. In Smedley's words, "Kitty came clattering down the stone corridors every morning with her scrub pail in her hand. 'Three cheers for birth control,' she greeted the prisoners and matrons. And 'three cheers for birth control,' the prisoners answered back." [23]

While in prison, Ghose and Smedley met Roger Baldwin, who later founded the American Civil Liberties Union. Baldwin spent three weeks in the Tombs at the beginning of a long jail term for his public support of conscientious objectors. Smedley could only wave to Baldwin through the window of the women's section, but Baldwin and Ghose had long talks about what could be done to arouse American support for Indian independence. Baldwin was an anticolonialist who supported Irish independence. According to him, the Irish at this time were making it very clear that they regarded continuing British rule of India as the biggest obstacle to the freedom of all colonial peoples, including themselves. Prison terms only reinforced the anticolonial views of all three: Ghose, Baldwin, and Smedley. [24]

On November 19 the fighting ended in Europe, but Smedley and Ghose remained in the Tombs. In the month that followed, Lajpat Rai and other moderate Indian nationalists managed to generate support among some American liberals to petition President Wilson for consideration of Indian independence at Versailles. Official Washington, however, had decided not to challenge the British Empire. Although the Labor Department was not confident it could use the new aliens bill to deport Indian nationalists, nevertheless, in December of 1918, immigration authorities appeared at Fort Leavenworth, Kansas, to interview Indians convicted during the war, with the intention of deporting them to India. [25]

Early in December, Smedley was released on bail provided by Henrietta Rodman, and Ghose was also let out on bail, which in the end was reduced to $6,000. The judge had ruled that neither of them could be extradited to San Francisco. Their attorney, Gilbert Roe, had argued that now, with the war over, to pursue the indictments would be interpreted as indicating America's intention to do away with its long-established right of political asylum. But although extradition attempts were dropped, the original indictments were not.

Building in the background was the Red scare arising out of the government's fear of the impact of the Russian Revolution on the American left. British intelligence was doing its part by continuing to emphasize to the American government the connections among American liberals, radical leftists, and Indian nationalists. Thus even moderate nationalists in New York, such as Lajpat Rai and his Home Rule League, became suspect.[26]

CHAPTER IV

Advocate Journalist, 1919–1920

Smedley's imprisonment, besides making her a celebrity in the New York left-liberal community, also brought her a job. Margaret Sanger was at this time preparing to go to California for several months to sort out personal problems, and soon after Smedley was released from jail, Sanger put her in charge of the day-to-day management of *Birth Control Review,* which was then the only reliable source of birth control information for many women around the country. The pay was small (the *Review* depended heavily on volunteer labor and donations), but Sanger was impressed by Smedley's commitment to the cause and knew that she had the secretarial skills to do the job. By February of 1919 Smedley was sending out business letters for Sanger's office, and she continued to manage the administrative and production work at least through September. During this period she was also on the street working with her recent cellmate Kitty Marion, who could be found almost every day passing out birth control literature in front of Macy's.[1]

Smedley had a job but no place to stay. Thorberg Brundin Haberman could not help; she had gone to Mexico to join her husband, Robert, who was then working on General Salvador Alvarado's plan to set up a series of cooperative stores throughout the Yucatán. She tried apartment-hunting, but whenever she made serious inquiries about renting, a government agent would turn up to question the landlord, and she would be refused. She decided that if she couldn't rent in her own name, she needed a roommate. So began her intimate friendship with Florence Lennon, which was to last for fifteen years.

When she met Smedley in 1919, Florence was only twenty years old, the daughter of a wealthy merchant family named Tannenbaum. She considered herself a budding poet and teacher and was translating letters by the Italian educational reformer Maria Montessori, which were then published in the Socialist Party paper, the *Call*. (She had left a Montessori teacher-training course after a year's work when the school's managers suggested to her that it would be hard for them to find a job for a Jew.) When Smedley's problem was described to her by Sarindranath Ghose at a Civic Club meeting organized by Henrietta Rodman, Florence agreed to rent to Agnes, for $10 a month, the living room of her apartment in an Italian tenement at 184 West Fourth Street (which cost her $75 at the time). Agnes put up a chintz curtain around the couch and it was here that she slept for over a year, with occasional absences when she was "keeping the steady company" of one man or another.*

Lennon was dazzled by Smedley's behavior: her antics on the subway ("trying to make the dead faces laugh"), her spontaneous folk-singing, her witty and bawdy talk, her exotic Indian friends, and her passionate engagement in the political causes that were sweeping the left-liberal and intellectual communities. A virgin who had undergone psychoanalysis off and on ever since she was eleven, Lennon was mesmerized by Smedley's stories of her hard-drinking father, her unsuccessful marriage, and her abortions; she was shocked by detailed descriptions of the "disgustingly messy" act of intercourse; and she was excited and intrigued when Smedley disappeared to spend the night with a man. But it was Smedley's serious dedication to her work that most impressed Florence.

In spite of the low rent Florence charged her, the pay at the *Birth Control Review* was not enough for Agnes to live on, so friends who had read early drafts of her short sketches of her cellmates arranged a job for her on the *Call,* the Socialist Party newspaper. Smedley had always seen the press as an instrument of social change. In her first articles for student newspapers in Arizona and California, she had expressed simple outrage at social injustice. On the *Call* she learned to

---

* Although her name changed with various marriages, Florence published under, and is known today by, the name Florence Lennon. The apartment building on West Fourth Street housed several other aspiring young women: Kathleen, the sister of Edna St. Vincent Millay; Ethel Leginskina, a concert pianist; and Gertrude Boyle, a sculptor who also worked on illustrations and layout for the *Birth Control Review*. Another friend Smedley met there was Ellen Kennan, a teacher of Latin and Greek, from Colorado, who after seventeen years had lost her job over the controversy surrounding her antiwar position and her association with Emma Goldman. Florence Lennon became a biographer of Lewis Carroll and a published poet. In a 1977 interview, once again a member of a synagogue, she joked about her youthful "hubris of wanting to be a man."

marshal evidence and write more convincingly in support of a political position. But she never tried to be "objective" or "neutral"; she was unabashedly opinionated and autobiographical in everything she wrote. In fact, she was simply working in a time-honored tradition that stretches back to Thomas Paine and forward to H. L. Mencken, Henry Luce, and William F. Buckley. It should be remembered that the personal and partisan approach that had dominated American journalism throughout the nineteenth century was still strong. Not until the turn of the century did the development of telecommunications and wire services require publishers of different political persuasions to pool resources to gather the news. This new arrangement, combined with the rise of schools of journalism, meant that "neutrality" or "objectivity" first became the professed goal of good news reporting in the 1920s. Smedley's models in 1919 were the newspaperman Horace Greeley, the muckraker Upton Sinclair, the novelist Jack London, and the polemicist Emma Goldman.[2]

It was an exciting time to begin writing political journalism. In 1919 the left and the right clashed politically around the world, and the United States was no exception: high unemployment and high inflation produced a period of unprecedented labor unrest punctuated by strikes, bombings, and riots. One strike shocked the nation and was generally interpreted by the press as having a radical political, not an economic, end. On January 21, 1919, some thirty-five thousand Seattle shipyard workers struck for shorter hours and better pay. On February 6, over sixty thousand workers from 110 local unions walked off their jobs in support of the strike, and the economic life of the city was virtually paralyzed. The mayor called in federal troops and refused to compromise. Realizing that a general strike, which was quickly labeled "un-American," had been a fatal mistake, on February 10 the conservative American Federation of Labor ordered the workers to stop the strike. During World War I, the government had implemented far-reaching measures to muzzle criticism of the war effort in the press. Now that the war had ended, some conservatives wanted to continue to censor what they considered to be "un-American" radical publications, most of which were supporting strikes. Such attempts also alienated liberals and accelerated polarization. During the war, the Socialist press had been labeled pro-German and un-American. It was now labeled "red" or Bolshevik and un-American.[3]

In New York, Smedley's friends were debating the meaning of the Russian Revolution of 1917. One of those whom Smedley most respected was Robert Minor, a political cartoonist for *Mother Earth* and

Masses. He was from Texas and one of the few persons in New York with whom she shared a lower-class Western background and an individualistic, "cowboy" approach to socialism. Minor had begun his political career as an I.W.W. activist in the West, and when he met Smedley in 1918 he still considered himself an anarchist of the type epitomized by Emma Goldman and Alexander Berkman. He left for Moscow as a special correspondent for the *Call* in early 1919, to evaluate the Russian Revolution in person, and Smedley followed his dispatches closely. At first he seemed ambivalent in his overall assessment, mixing praise with criticism of the new government ("there was too much law and order in Russia"—an oblique reference to the purge of anarchists by the Bolsheviks). But after a few months he seemed to move away from his anarchist-syndicalist position toward one that accepted the need for centralization of the revolutionary Soviet government in order to deal with the threat of foreign intervention and internal subversion. After leaving Russia, Minor sent reports from Germany on the abortive attempt by Rosa Luxemburg, Karl Liebknecht, and other left-wing members of the ruling German Social Democratic Party to establish a Bolshevik-style revolution in Germany in January of 1919. There Minor was arrested and put under detention pending an investigation of charges brought by the British, who said he had been spreading treasonous propaganda among British and American troops in Germany by condemning the Allied expedition against the new Bolshevik government in Russia.[4]

As Smedley struggled to understand the course of revolution in Europe and Russia, as well as the changing political positions of friends like Minor, she also noted with alarm the growing political activity on the American right and its effect on the Indian nationalist movement in the United States. When it became known that the majority of long-term resident aliens interned during the war had not been deported, a movement began in Congress to pass legislation that would ensure their deportation. By January 28, 1919, a House Committee reported favorably on such a bill, with Representative Albert Johnson of Washington State tacking on a provision for the direct deportation to India of all Indians convicted during the war. On February 5, Attorney General T. W. Gregory wrote to the Senate Committee on Immigration and Naturalization urging that the bill be passed. The Seattle general strike was still in progress, and press stories on the strike connected alien radicals and the I.W.W. to events and ideas originating in Russia. By mid-February a trainload of aliens from the Northwest arrived at Ellis Island for deportation. A government spokesman said on February 12 that it was the first opportunity in several years to deport "troublesome" radicals and predicted that many more would be deported during the next sixty days if transportation could be arranged. The Commissioner General of Immigration, Anthony J. Caminetti, denied that the majority were being deported for political reasons: "I should say that virtually ninety percent of these are being deported because they were insane," he quipped. Indian nationals were soon targeted. On February 23, 1919, the Labor Department arrested Gopal Singh, one of those convicted in the San Francisco Hindu conspiracy trial, as he walked out of prison. Its intention was to deport him.[5]

One of the first to challenge government officials about the deportation of Indians was the historian Charles Beard. In February, 1919, he wrote to various government officials to ask that discriminating attention be given to each individual deportation case. Like many liberal intellectuals, Beard was concerned about the mass of state and federal legislation on sedition and espionage that remained intact after the armistice of November, 1918.[6] This legislation formed a complicated web of ambiguously worded laws that allowed for great discretion by both local officials and immigration officers. On the federal level, the Justice Department was responsible for implementing the Espionage Act of 1917 and the Sedition Act of 1918. But the 1918 Alien Law was to be implemented by the Labor Department's Commissioner General of Immigration.*

Secretary of Labor William Wilson answered Beard on March 3, saying that there were no cases pending before the Labor Department charging Indians with advocating national independence and that in fact the department had no authority under law to deport an alien simply because he advocated political reforms or changes in his native country. The one case before him, Wilson said, involved the conviction of an Indian within five years of entry for a crime involving "moral tur-

---

*Deportation hearings involved no criminal proceedings, since deportation was not regarded as a punishment. No judge or jury was involved; cases were handled administratively by immigration officials. The Labor Department therefore was responsible for the rules governing the procedure of detainment of aliens for deportation hearings. Deportable aliens were not considered to have the protection of the ex post facto clause in the Constitution. An alien had two chances for reversing the administrative decision: the secretary of labor might personally review the record and reverse any deportation decision, or the alien might obtain a writ of habeas corpus, which would bring his case before a federal judge—but only if it could be shown that the deportation proceedings had been manifestly unfair. See Robert K. Murray, *The Red Scare: A Study in National Hysteria, 1919–1920* (Minneapolis, 1955), pp. 14, 211–12.

pitude." What he did not tell Beard was that Immigration had decided
that a conviction for "conspiracy to violate a neutrality law" could be
defined as "moral turpitude," and that the case before him was that of
Gopal Singh.[7]

Smedley and her American and Indian friends quickly mobilized a
counteroffensive. On March 6, 1919, they formed the Friends of Freedom for India, with Robert Morss Lovett as temporary president, the
Irish-American lawyers Dudley Field Malone and Frank P. Walsh as vice
presidents, Agnes Smedley as secretary, and Louis P. Louchner as trea-
surer. They opened an office at 92 Fifth Avenue, enlisted Gilbert Roe's
services as attorney, and began to coordinate the defense of all Indians
threatened with deportation. Of equal importance, they began a large-
scale educational campaign seeking the support of intellectuals and labor unions around the country.[8]

Robert Morss Lovett, a professor of English at the University of Chicago, was the editor of *Dial,* a distinguished publication of arts and
letters; and he now opened his magazine to a full discussion of the Indian nationalist cause. In a separate pamphlet he wrote that he had been
"irritated" to learn that Sir George Denham, the head of the British police in Calcutta, had been an active participant in the arrest and trial of
a U.S. citizen, Taraknath Das. According to Lovett, Denham had been
allowed by local authorities to search Das's apartment without a war-
rant and to send six convicts from British prisons around the world to
testify against Das at his trial in San Francisco. Furthermore, after the
trial ended in Das's conviction, the U.S. District Attorney had been
"brilliantly feted" by the British Empire Society. As Lovett noted, the
one element common to all Americans who supported Friends of Freedom for India was a sense of outrage over what they considered to be
direct and open British interference in the internal affairs of the United
States.

The British, for their part, were quick to react to the Friends of Freedom. One person who had joind the group while in Great Britain was
deported. Another, James Maurer, the chairman of the Pennsylvania
Federation of Labor, was stopped at the gangplank in New York harbor
as he prepared to cross the Atlantic to attend a meeting of British trade
unions. Through the 1920s at least, the British officially nurtured this
grudge. Lovett was never again granted a visa to Britain, and Margaret
Sanger was detained in both Hong Kong and Singapore in 1922 and
advised not to travel to India. Many other visa refusals were made for
the same reason: membership in Friends of Freedom for India.[9]

At the Central Opera House on April 11, the F.F.I. held its first mass meeting. Resolutions drafted by Lovett demanding political amnesty for those Indians still in jail were sent to President Wilson in Paris and to the departments of Labor and State. Lovett went to Washington to talk directly with senators who would be voting on the Johnson immigration bill. He reported that many were quite sympathetic, and some were even willing to declare that India had as much right to independence as the United States.[10]

At the time of the Opera House meeting, newspaper headlines across the nation warned of bomb plots by "reds" or anarchists. On April 13 the Socialist leader Eugene Debs began serving a ten-year prison term for violation of the Espionage Act. A year earlier he had been arrested in Canton, Ohio, for publicly exhorting Socialists to continue their opposition to the war. The Supreme Court had denied his appeal. On May 1, 1919, soldiers, sailors, and angry citizens broke up Socialist May Day parades in several cities and raided Socialist newspapers. Smedley's New York *Call* office was one of those broken into by a mob, and a number of bystanders were brutally beaten. Although the Wilson administration was issuing strong statements condemning violence by the left, it clearly sympathized with this particular kind of violence by the right. When the *Call* sent a telegram to Secretary of the Treasury Carter Glass asking him to investigate allegations that Victory Loan workers had incited the mob that had broken into the *Call* offices, he answered: "I am not prepared to say that the ultimate responsibility for the disorders to which you called attention rests with the sailors and soldiers, rather than those incendiary publications which they resent." On the evening of June 2, a bomb was tossed by unknown persons at the home of U.S. Attorney General A. Mitchell Palmer. His response was to ask Congress to appropriate half a million dollars to investigate the "criminal class"—in which he included political "radicals."[11]

At this time the general public was equating the Socialist Party with the Bolsheviks, perhaps because it had officially opposed the Allied expedition against the Soviet Union. This was ironic, for only a month earlier the National Executive Committee of the Socialist Party had expelled its own left wing, which had been calling for immediate revolution. The Socialist Party made it clear that it retained its belief in democratic, evolutionary action to achieve domestic goals. By September, the expelled left wing split into two groups both of which supported the principles of the March, 1919, International and declared that the world was in crisis and capitalism in the process of disintegration and collapse.

One group, made up of mainly native-born Americans, was the Communist Labor Party led by John Reed, Benjamin Gitlow, and William B. Lloyd. The American Communist Party was made up and led primarily by foreign-born radicals who looked directly to the Russian Revolution as a model to be followed in the United States.[12] On June 10, 1919, the Socialist Party paper, the *Call*, had warned on its front page: "He who dreams of a 'dictatorship of the proletariat' in a single state of this country, to say nothing of the whole, . . . invites all the powers of reaction and must eventually go underground." Although asked to join by both left-wing factions, Smedley took her political stand by continuing to work for the *Call*.

During the summer of 1919, besides working on the *Call*, Smedley was effectively coordinating various legal cases for the F.F.I. and organizing a nationwide campaign to gain resolutions of support from labor unions and progressive organizations. At a June national meeting of the American Federation of Labor in Atlanta, members voted tentative approval of an F.F.I. resolution and appointed an executive committee to make further investigations into the F.F.I.'s allegations. This committee was astonished to find that the British had spent over $2.5 million on the 1918 San Francisco conspiracy trial. Samuel Gompers, the head of the A.F. of L., sent a copy of the Atlanta resolution to Secretary of Labor Wilson in early July, and thereafter the Labor Department's mail began to be flooded with resolutions opposing the deportation of Indians. By July, when six Hindus were under arrest and facing deportation, the F.F.I. was also conducting a major campaign to publicize the British Rowlett Bill, passed earlier that spring, which authorized continued military rule in India. Its aim was to demonstrate the danger facing Indians who were scheduled for deportation back to India.[13]

Somewhat later, in an emotionally charged *Call* article of September 16, Smedley argued that India had made a significant contribution to Britain's war effort, and she mustered facts and figures in support of the view, held by the majority of the Indian nationalists at the time, that famines had actually increased in India under British rule. Like other American and British liberals, she argued that it was unconscionable of Britain to continue to extract so much wealth from an India plagued with poverty and starvation.

During the war the California-based Ghadar Party, the majority of whom were Sikh immigrants, had supported armed uprisings in India. With the backlash against all Indians after the San Francisco Hindu conspiracy trial, the organization now took a more defensive and moderate position. To fight deportation and confiscation of their land, the Ghadar Party joined with the F.F.I. to win support for Indian independence within the American political system.

Lajpat Rai's Home Rulers in New York were not directly involved in the movement to stop deportations. But they too became visibly more impatient with Britain as it became apparent that the extreme curtailments on freedom of speech and mass assembly were to be kept in place in India after the war ended. They continued their efforts to educate the American public about India, choosing not to focus on the political problems of Indians in the United States. Although they cooperated with the American members of the F.F.I. by sharing some facilities, they continued to dissociate themselves from the Ghadar Party, and Home Rule League President N. S. Hardiker publicly urged Indians to keep their distance from both organizations.

It was the policy of Friends of Freedom to support all Indians,[14] no matter what their politics, out of fear that siding with one faction on any issue could prove detrimental to the whole independence movement. From the correspondence it is clear that Lajpat Rai, Smedley, and other Americans helped to keep factionalism from surfacing during the first year. Many of the native-born who stepped forward to help the Indians were Irish-Americans who saw Ireland and India linked in a common cause. In a July 30 letter, Smedley encouraged the Irish-American organizer Ed Gammons in San Francisco: "The Hindus working for freedom not only have some of their own countrymen to fight, but they have a hostile world, a hostile white race. . . . And I hope that you will never be discouraged or disgusted with things that happen no matter what they are. India is bigger than the personality of a few men who appear to be cowardly or self-seeking. Had I been guided by personalities up to this time, I should have left the Indian movement long before this. But the ideal itself is so great, and the struggle of the men in this country so tremendous, that there is nothing left to wish for but to fight on."

By August the F.F.I. began to see their work pay off. The United Mine Workers of Pennsylvania, the International Ladies Garment Workers Union, the Brotherhood of Metal Workers, Carpenters, and Joiners, the Molders unions, and the Erie Central Labor Union were among the hundreds of groups and individuals that sent resolutions to the Department of Labor. The American Federation of Labor continued to cooperate and sent its secretary, Frank Morrison, to attend the August 25 hearing before Immigration Commissioner Caminetti on the Gopal Singh deportation case.[15]

For two weeks in September, Smedley took a vacation from her job as associate editor of the *Birth Control Review* to work in Washington with attorneys Roe and Walsh on the preparation of a brief on all the Hindu cases, to be mailed to senators and congressmen.[16] She and Ghose proved in Washington that they could be effective lobbyists. On September 28, in a letter to Roe concerning arrangements for the presentation of cases before Secretary of Labor Wilson, she reported that the briefs sent earlier had won the support of nine senators, including La Follette of Wisconsin, Norris of Nebraska, Gronna of North Dakota, Kenyon of Iowa, and Borah of Idaho. Privately, Smedley was somewhat taken aback by her own success: "Friday evening both Mr. Singh and I spoke before a gathering of some fifty men and women in the so-called Cooperative House here, occupied by a number of leading liberals in the city. [Frank] Walsh was down and attended our meeting Friday. At the close of the meeting, I noticed him sitting modestly in the back of the room. I must say I was somewhat shocked. We drank coffee and gossiped and carefully analyzed Englishmen afterward." [17]

Throughout the year Gilbert Roe had been working on dismissal of the San Francisco indictments against Smedley and Ghose. In an October, 1919, letter to Attorney General Palmer, he argued: "A mistaken patriotism, or a too fervent attachment to the cause of the oppressed people of other countries, is not an offense that we ordinarily have any reason to prosecute in time of peace." Assistant Attorney General Robert P. Stewart studied the case again and told Palmer in a memo that the charge seemed of a "manifestly political character and so subversive of the political ideals of this Government, and the spirit of its laws, [that] the United States should not be a party to further pressing this case." He argued that since the indictments against the Wotherspoons and Zalaznek had been dropped (see Chapter 3), those against Smedley and the other Indians should also be dismissed. Roe's argument and Stewart's conclusion were accepted by Solicitor General Alexander C. King, who commented in mid-October that the case "probably sprang out of the close relations between this Government and the English Government, and the supposed connection of these defendants with the effort to raise disturbances in India under German instigation." The San Francisco indictments were dismissed that October, but the original New York indictment against Smedley remained open, although not pursued, until 1923. The legal fight for the return of her personal property seized at the time of her 1918 arrest would last until May 20, 1920.[18]

On October 29, 1919, at Allaire's restaurant on Seventeenth Street and Third Avenue, a dinner was held by the Friends of Freedom to celebrate Taraknath Das's release from prison and the dropping of the San Francisco indictments against Ghose and Smedley. Professor Arthur Pope was toastmaster and the Socialist Rose Strunsky gave an address. According to the *Call*, Das, Ghose, and Gopal Singh promised to "continue their fight for the freedom of India until the 315 million Hindus were given an opportunity to regulate their own lives and stand side by side with the other nations of the world." Taraknath Das, an experienced organizer, immediately began working for the Friends of Freedom for India and helped expand its activities. His presence boosted Smedley's morale, and within months the two became close friends.[19]

In the middle of November Smedley went to Washington again, to lobby against passage of the alien deportation bill. She and Das urged Senator La Follette to offer an amendment that would exclude the deportation of Hindus, and they persuaded Upton Sinclair to publicize the planned deportations of Indians in his *Appeal to Reason*.[20] On November 28, nine days after the first failed Senate vote to ratify the Versailles Peace Treaty, Smedley organized a Friends of Freedom farewell banquet for Lajpat Rai at the Hotel des Artistes.* After five years, the British had finally granted Rai permission to return to his homeland. At the dinner, chairman Oswald Garrison Villard introduced such speakers as the lawyer Dudley Field Malone, and Souney Tsheng, a Chinese delegate to the Versailles Peace Conference. Also present were Egyptians and Irish, who, together with the Chinese and Indians, were displeased that the Versailles Treaty made no provision for the independence of the colonies of the Allies or for the return to the Chinese of territory in Shandong controlled by the Germans. The Indians had supplied soldiers, and the Chinese had sent over 140,000 coolies from China to work in labor corps in Europe, digging trenches and burying the dead for the English, French, and Americans. They now felt betrayed. Rai spoke of the harassment that had followed him during his years in the United States: "I have been arrested six times by the United States Department of Justice. My telephone has been tapped. But at no time have they ever found any-

---

* President Wilson, it will be recalled, had suffered a stroke that September in Pueblo, Colorado, while on a speaking tour to win support for the treaty. It is now generally recognized that from that day to the inauguration of Harding in March of 1921, Wilson was virtually incapacitated.

thing against me." He proclaimed that the Hindus, having seen their country "bled white" by the British, were determined to gain national independence for India. He ended by asking for the support of the American public.[21]

Smedley also helped arrange a mass labor rally in the Cooper Union on December 4. The chairman of the meeting, Edward I. Hannah, president of the Central Federated Union of New York, introduced such speakers as Andrew Furuseth, president of the International Seaman's Union; Dr. Abraham Lefkowitz of the Teacher's Union; Rose Schneiderman, president of the Woman's Trade Union League of New York; and Sasanta Koomar Roy of the Friends of Freedom for India. Two resolutions were passed by the rally. The first called on the United States to recognize the right of a British colony to revolt against oppression, and the second called on Washington to recognize the right of political asylum.[22]

Late in the year Smedley had her hands full with another F.F.I. project, the India News Service—a digest of news stories (not commentaries) from the Indian press, which was sent out weekly to over three hundred labor papers and one hundred magazines and daily newspapers throughout the United States. By December, 1919, the F.F.I.'s mailing list included over five thousand names, including those of senators and congressmen, and its publications, like the India News Service, were financed entirely by private donations.[23]

For Smedley and the Friends of Freedom, another important event occurred in December: several major U.S. newspapers reported the findings of Britain's Hunter Committee, which had been appointed to investigate the tragedy of the April, 1919, uprisings in the Punjab sparked by the killing of over five hundred unarmed Indians by British government troops.* It had taken the mainstream daily press in the United States

---

* Early in 1919, Gandhi had appealed for a passive resistance movement and a business boycott to protest the British government's Rowlett Act, which extended the life of repressive wartime regulations in India. Rabinandrath Tagore gave up his knighthood and supported noncooperation; with the help of the Home Rule League in India, the movement spread rapidly. But soon the protests became violent. On April 4, word of riots in Delhi reached the Sikh capital of Amritsar, in the Punjab, and rioting began there. On the evening of April 11, General Dyer arrived in Amritsar and issued an order prohibiting public meetings, saying that if any were held the participants "were liable to be fired upon straight away." On the evening of April 13, hearing that a mass meeting was in progress, Dyer immediately confronted it with a force consisting of twenty-five British rifles, twenty-five Indian rifles, forty Gurkha mercenaries, and two armored cars with machine guns. No order to disperse was given to the unarmed crowd of five thousand, and within seconds after arriving Dyer ordered his men to fire. They fired until they ran out of ammunition, 1,650 rounds altogether. It was estimated that over five hundred were killed and three times that number wounded.

almost eight months to publish the facts about this event, which the
Friends of Freedom had been publishing all along. Now that the British
report was getting some attention, Smedley and others tried to get
major newspapers to carry follow-up stories from India. But the response was cold, as this communication from the San Francisco *Examiner* suggests: "Mr. Coblentz suggests that when the matter comes
directly from headquarters, as in the case of the London dispatches
printed Sunday and today, it will be played up properly, but we do not
care to make a special feature of this stuff."[24] By and large, the American press relied on the British press for stories about India and refused
to consider other sources. Americans, except for liberals, intellectuals,
and labor leaders, were mostly indifferent to the Indian cause. In hundreds of labor unions, members approved resolutions of support for the
Indian cause, but in others the issue brought smoldering racist sentiments to the surface. For example, the International Brotherhood of
Electrical Workers, Local Union No. 207 in Stockton, California, sent
this resolution to the F.F.I.:

> Whereas the Hindus are brought to this Country to exploit against White
> Citizens of the laboring class, And will or do not become Naturalized Ameri-
> can Citizens But expect all the freedom and protection of the Country same
> as the Naturalized or Native born Citizens of the U.S.A.
> Whereas the deportations of all Hindus back to India will not only assist
> the Government but all other Governments of the White people, to uphold
> their Laws, protect their Lives and Property, Also their Traditions, Religion
> and Economic conditions of all White People.
> And be it Resolved that We assist in every way possible the British Govern-
> ment to Deport all Hindus back to India, even to the extent of giving them
> Financial Assistance.[25]

This political posture was not at all uncommon. Racism in America
was on the rise. Figures released by the U.S. government for the first ten
months of 1919 revealed that sixty-three persons, fifty-nine of them
Blacks, had been lynched, and that eleven Blacks had been burned alive.
The *Call* noted a rapid growth of the Ku Klux Klan throughout 1919
and 1920.[26]

Developments like these made Smedley, Das, and Roe worry that
popular support for the Indian cause was falling off just at the most crucial time. As Smedley wrote to Gopal Singh in San Francisco on December 18, 1919: "I feel a lessening in the tension of our friends; they
say the Hindus will not be deported. I think that [idea] is dangerous . . .
born of desire. I have been talking with Mr. Roe, your attorney here, and

he tells us that we must keep up the fight without fail. He is in Washington often and he feels that we need more support than we have been able to muster. Do not fail to strike this note in our letters of appreciation to other workers. Do not let them think that their work is finished." [27]

As the year 1919 came to a close, Smedley was depressed. One of her former cellmates, Mollie Steimer, had just lost her appeal to the Supreme Court and had been sentenced for espionage to fifteen years in prison at Jefferson City, Missouri, where Kate Richards O'Hare, the former candidate for vice president on the Socialist Party ticket, was still serving a term for the same charge. [28] On December 22, 1919, the U.S. transport ship *Buford* sailed for Europe with 249 radical deportees aboard, including Emma Goldman and Alexander Berkman. Smedley had already planned to celebrate Christmas of 1919 by picketing churches over the Allied blockade of Soviet Russia. On December 12, she wrote to Ed Gammons in San Francisco:

> This is Christmas time—a fine day for Christians. A woman was arrested yesterday for picketing against the Russian blockade. . . . Helen Todd is her name, and she led our other picket line against the blockade. On Christmas day, we are going to picket all the big Christian churches here with our hands manacled, demanding release of political and industrial prisoners. I suppose we will all go to jail. Why don't the women of San Francisco picket all the churches there on Christmas day? This damn Christian civilization gets on my nerves, if I may take the liberty of being profane. Hypocrisy all the way along. We are now, along with the British, well entitled to the title "perfidious."

The year 1920 opened on an ominous note for Smedley and her friends. It was a presidential election year, and one man serving in the Department of Justice had presidential ambitions. On January 2 the Justice Department, on the orders of Attorney General A. Mitchell Palmer, made one of the country's largest mass arrests ever: beginning on January 2, government agents carried out raids in thirty-three cities, arresting 2,500 supposed radicals and issuing deportation warrants for approximately 5,000 aliens. Later that year, in New York State officials of both the American Communist Party and the Communist Labor Party were imprisoned, and the state legislature expelled five of its elected Socialist members. Raids continued until May, when it finally became apparent that in the overwhelming majority of cases there was insufficient evidence to substantiate the charges. In that month the deportation cases against three Indians who had been involved in the San Francisco conspiracy trial were dropped. But just as the pressure of the "Red scare" was helping to split both the left and liberal communities (in the 1920 presidential election, a new Farmer-Labor Party joined the Socialist, Socialist-Labor, Democratic, Republican, and Prohibition parties on the ballot), the Indian independence movement began to splinter in public. Without Lajpat Rai to mediate disputes, schisms became more pronounced and bitter. Smedley herself seemed to come increasingly under the influence of Taraknath Das, who, although he never became a Marxist-Leninist, held pan-Asianist views and interpreted the Indian struggle for independence as the crucial fight in the global struggle for liberation of the colonial countries from the white imperialist powers, especially Britain. In February, in two articles for the *Call* and one for *Birth Control Review*, Smedley demonstrated more militance and embraced Das's pan-Asian thesis that Japan should play a major role in helping to bring down British imperialism.[29]

As the year progressed, Smedley was writing more and organizing less. She began to work full time on the *Call*, gradually giving to Das and Ghose major responsibility for the everyday organizational work of the Friends of Freedom. It was in the *Call*, between February 15 and March 14, that she published "Cell Mates," her most polished work to date. These four engaging and incisive portraits of fellow prisoners— Kitty Marion, Mollie Steimer, a prostitute, and a check forger—won the respect and future support of liberal editors at the *Nation* and the *New Republic*.

Early in the year Smedley was also working with Theresa S. Malkiel, the wife of the editor of the *Call*, to produce a special issue on February 29 in honor of International Women's Day. Like her fellow contributors—who included Margaret Sanger, the teacher Ellen Kennan, the sculptor Gertrude Boyle, the Socialist Kate Richards O'Hare, the I.W.W. activist Elizabeth Gurley Flynn, the women's trade-unionist leader Rose Schneiderman, and the journalist Louise Bryant—Smedley saw herself as an American who was demanding full implementation of the individual rights guaranteed in the Constitution; but, like most of the others, she also believed that a Socialist form of government would be more likely to provide equal opportunities for women and racial minorities. The majority of women in Smedley's Greenwich Village community welcomed the Russian Revolution primarily as a political victory that would free women and serfs from authoritarian and tyrannical rule. Throughout their careers, both Sanger and Smedley criticized any policy— whether advocated by a person, a party, or a government, and whether in Russia, China, India, or the United States—that did not serve the cause of equality and freedom for women. Sanger summarized their position in 1920: "We are interested in the freedom of women, not in the power of the state. Upon that freedom depends the power and endurance of the state, as well as the health of the women and children. Upon that freedom depends the revolutionizing of man's inherent attitude toward women, whether they be Russian men under the Soviets, or men in America. Without that freedom for women—not only economic, but personal freedom as well—the right kind of state cannot exist, and will not exist."

As Sanger pointed out in her article, however, there was a potential conflict between the Socialist women's movement and orthodox Marxism. After stating that the growth of the birth control movement had paralleled the growth of the Socialist movement throughout most of the world, Sanger condemned the British Socialists for opposing it. She summed up the conflict as follows: birth control advocates generally use the Malthusian argument that poverty is caused primarily by large families, whereas orthodox British Marxists insisted that poverty is caused primarily by the unequal distribution of wealth. Sanger went on to expose what she considered a possible contradiction in the Soviet government's position on this issue:

> The representative of the Soviet government to whom I spoke was a man. I cannot imagine, with the greatest stretching of the imagination, Russian women standing up and demanding as a new idea the privilege of "having as many children as they want." Nothing will ever keep women from having as many children as they want. What women desire is the knowledge which will enable them to have as few children as they themselves consider consistent with their health, their desires, their opportunities for development, their economic resources, their ability to rear and educate.
>
> Unless women understand this, they are likely to find themselves under a co-operative commonwealth, a Socialist republic or a Soviet government, being fatted and fed and kept in excellent condition for breeding purposes, in order to maintain a particular form of society for masculine needs. A recognition of this fact is the fundamental basis of the birth control movement today.[30]

Smedley accepted Sanger's general views about the relationship between the individual, the state, and political parties, and agreed with her about the need to educate and legislate for the liberation of the "new woman." But as the years passed, she developed her own perception of the complexity of implementing Sanger's ideas. Through her association with Indian nationalists, she had come to view U.S. policy toward colonial countries as a logical extension of the same forces of prejudice that had produced laws discriminating against women and racial minorities. According to this logic, to fight for one victim of discrimination was to fight for them all.

At the *Call* Smedley continued to be responsible for the frequent appearance of articles on India and deportation cases, including a special May issue featuring articles by Das and Ghose. With the Friends of Freedom, she marched up Fifth Avenue in a sari. As she wrote to the F.F.I.'s San Francisco office on March 1: "We are in the St. Patrick's Day parade. All the Hindus in the city, practically, will wear native costume and turbans and march. We had the Indian republic flag and banners demanding independence. Watch for the movies and you will see us big as life. If the flu doesn't take me again, I'll be there all dressed up with no place to go, hair blackened and all."

Journalism had now become a passion with Smedley. Her roommate Florence Lennon recalled that Agnes once dressed herself as an immigrant in order to investigate conditions on Ellis Island. And she was proud of exposing a scandalous local situation: eight scows of garbage had been anchored in the July heat for three weeks at the edge of one of the poorest and most congested sections of the city. Her story in the July 23 *Call* helped prod city officials into action.

By the summer of 1920 Smedley was thinking about going to Europe to see the unfolding world revolution for herself. One reason was uncertainty about what position to take amid the splintering left in New York. A major rift had occurred between the Socialist Party, the native-born Communists, and recent immigrant Communists. She had stayed in contact with Robert Minor, who had gone to Moscow as an anarchist and returned to join the new Communist movement. But when Earl Browder invited her to join the newly formed Communist Party, she turned down the offer. She wanted to go to Germany and Moscow and then make up her own mind. Based on her own experiences in the American West, she remained skeptical that capitalism was crumbling or that workers would support a revolutionary movement with foreign connections. To her and her family, the American dream had meant the chance to escape from the working class. Her goal now was to transform that class. Moreover, considering the repression being exerted in the United States, she saw Berlin as the future center of the overseas Indian nationalist movement. Finally, the challenge and adventure of such a trip appealed to her. She wanted to try her hand overseas as a journalist like her friend Thorberg Brundin, who had recently left for Mexico. And since Europe was where the next revolution was supposed to break out, she wanted to be there.

Three years earlier, when she arrived in New York, Smedley would have been too insecure to attempt such a trip alone. But since 1917 she had developed strong ties with several women associated with the *Birth Control Review,* notably Mary Knoblauch, Josephine Bennett, Ellen Kennan, Gertrude Boyle, and Florence Lennon. These women were from middle-class and upper-class backgrounds, and a few of them were independently wealthy. The sustenance Smedley drew from them was primarily psychological. By 1920 they had replaced the Brundins as her "family," and she would derive emotional and financial support from them in the years ahead.

During the summer of 1920, anticipating her departure, Smedley announced her intention of resigning as general secretary of the F.F.I. But in early August the deportation situation became urgent again. The number of Indians already deported had risen to around eighty. Over the next few weeks Smedley and Das led the fight to stop further deportations, and they succeeded in over forty cases. By the time she had organized a national convention for it on December 5, the Friends of Freedom for India was an established and effective organization. Lovett, Baldwin, Roe, and Norman Thomas were still serving on the executive board, and they were backed up by a national council of more than twenty-five prominent members, among them Upton Sinclair and W. E. B. Du Bois.[31]

In the fall of 1920, Smedley had declined a marriage proposal from Taraknath Das, and although she remained on friendly terms with him she felt uneasy about their relationship. Das may have felt the same way. At any rate, he and other Indian leaders of the Friends of Freedom for India were eager to see her go to Europe. They wanted better contact with Indian activists in Berlin, and they wanted to send a representative to the upcoming summit of Indian nationalists in Moscow during the summer of 1921. Smedley seemed the ideal choice: as a founder of the Friends she knew their thinking well, and as an American she would have less difficulty in returning to the United States than an Indian would.

Because the indictments in New York against her and Ghose were still pending, Smedley decided to leave without a passport. On December 17, 1920, she borrowed one hundred dollars and sailed for Europe as a stewardess on a Polish freighter. Das saw her off.[32]

Formative Years, 1892–1928

Smedley's birthplace and home at Campground near Osgood, Missouri. (In 1976; photo by authors.)

Charles and Sarah Lydia Smedley, in Trinidad, Colorado, circa 1903–04. (Courtesy of Elizabeth Smedley.)

Smedley family in 1899. Front, left to right: Myrtle, John, Sam; back, left to right: Charles, Agnes, Nellie, and Sarah Lydia. (Courtesy of Elizabeth Smedley.)

Smedley children, left to right: Nellie, John, Myrtle, Sam, and Agnes in Trinidad, Colorado, circa 1903–04. (Courtesy of Elizabeth Smedley.)

Delagua mining camp, five miles up the canyon from
Ludlow, Colorado, circa 1914. Note dominance of
Longfellow School, built and staffed by the Victor
American Fuel Company to draw miners to the camp.
(Courtesy of Altman Studio, Trinidad, Colorado.)

Aunt Tillie Ralls in Denver,
Colorado, circa 1909–10.
(Courtesy of Elizabeth
Smedley.)

Star Tobacco store where Smedley worked circa
1909, near the mining camp at Tercio, Colorado.
Figures unidentified. (Courtesy of Elizabeth
Smedley.)

Charles Smedley
(far left) and
working crew in
Trinidad, Colo-
rado, circa 1908–
09. Middle stand-
ing figure is Big
Buck. (Courtesy
of Elizabeth
Smedley.)

Big Buck in Clifton, Arizona, in 1911 staked
Smedley to tuition at Tempe Normal School.
Smedley carried this photo with her through-
out the rest of her life. (Smedley papers,
Arizona State University.)

Thorberg Brundin,
Ernest's older sister
and Smedley's close
friend, at M.A. de-
gree ceremony at the
University of Califor-
nia, Berkeley, 1913.
(Courtesy of Elinor
Brundin.)

Horace Greeley Club at Tempe Normal School in 1911.
Smedley is in front row, third from left. (Smedley papers,
Arizona State University.)

Smedley's first husband,
Ernest Brundin, circa
1912. (Courtesy of
Elinor Brundin.)

Agnes Smedley in San Diego,
October, 1914. (Courtesy of
Elinor Brundin.)

Smedley dressed in immi-
grant costume to report on
conditions at Ellis Island for
the *Call*, New York, 1920.
(Courtesy of Florence
Lennon.)

Agnes Smedley in sari, New York, circa 1919.
(Courtesy of Florence Lennon.)

Virendranath
Chattopadhyaya,
Smedley's common-
law husband, circa
1931.

Smedley with
Emma Goldman
in Germany, circa
1925. (Courtesy of
Florence Lennon.)

Smedley's patron, actress Tilla Durieux, in her
Eliza Doolittle costume, as painted by Auguste
Renoir in 1914. (Courtesy of The Metropolitan
Museum of Art, Bequest of Stephen C. Clark,
1960 [61.101.13].)

Agnes Smedley in Berlin, circa 1928. (Courtesy of Elinor Brundin.)

Smedley in Berlin hospital, spring of 1928. Etching by her friend Käthe Kollwitz. (Courtesy of Galerie Kornfeld.)

Cover of 1929 German edition of *Daughter of Earth* (title translates as *A Woman Alone*). (Lu Xun's inscribed copy, courtesy of Lu Xun Museum, Shanghai.)

CHAPTER V

Sexual Politics and Breakdown, 1921–1923

Armed with a typewriter and briefcase, Agnes Smedley jumped ship at Danzig in late December of 1920. Held up at customs because she had no passport and no visa, she telegrammed Virendranath Chattopadhyaya of the Berlin Indian Revolutionary Committee. The committee promptly contacted the German Foreign Office, which interceded with customs officials at Danzig and eased Smedley's way to Berlin.

For at least a decade, Berlin had been the vortex of the European Indian nationalist movement. During World War I, the Berlin committee had worked closely with the German Foreign Office on insurrectionary plots to overthrow the British in India. In the confusion of the postwar period, the committee retained a semblance of German protection. But as its financial backing was drying up, it was forced to consider adopting a new strategy more oriented toward Soviet Russia and the anti-imperialist position of Lenin.

Smedley's reputation as a successful organizer and propagandist had preceded her, and she was accepted immediately as a key member on the Berlin team of nationalists. Personally, however, she was feeling lonely and vulnerable. On January 17, only a week after her arrival in Berlin, she wrote to Florence Lennon:[1]

> Here I am—isolated—because I do not speak German. I am studying, and can say *Ich habe einen hund*, etc. . . . Brilliant progress after a week! I can fight but can not learn the "furren" language spoken by the "natives."
>
> I am mentally isolated. I subscribed to the *Call*, leaving a money order for $5.00 for Das before I left. . . . Kindly keep my presence here absolutely

quiet. I am here illegally and the German authorities fear disagreements with the land of the free. I fear I shall have to keep moving and write under the name I have given you [Alice Bird]. I have thought a lot of you since I left. Your love and eternal consideration all return to me now that you are not here. I think you are the only person whom I have ever known who tolerated my many faults and eccentricities. You are the only one who really understood. And I have marked Rabir's poem with you in mind in which he says: "Listen to me friend, he understands who loves."

Loneliness led her into an affair with Virendranath Chattopadhyaya, the seasoned Bengali nationalist who led the Berlin committee, and a remarkable man by any reckoning.* Chatto, as he was known to all, was more than twelve years older than Smedley. Her attraction to him

---

* Virendranath Chattopadhyaya (1880–1941), the eldest son of a scholarly Brahmin Bengali family, was a legendary father figure to young Indian nationalists arriving in Europe as students in the 1920s. Although a Bengali and a Hindu, he grew up in Hyderabad in southcentral India. His father, Agonerath Chattopadhyaya, was one of the earliest Western-educated Indians and the principal of a college in Hyderabad. He was also a pioneering nationalist in the Hyderabad area and was finally forced by the British authorities into early retirement and a kind of house arrest in exile in Calcutta, where he died around the turn of the century. His children were all remarkable and fervent nationalists. The oldest of Chatto's younger sisters, Sarojini Naidu, was and is the best known. She was a poetess and politician who became a leading figure in the Indian National Congress from the 1900s until her death in the 1950s, when she was governor of West Bengal. A younger brother, Hirendranath, was still alive in 1980 and active as a poet, actor, playwright, and movie director.

Having received a classical education in Hyderabad, Chatto left India in 1901 for Great Britain. After failing the Indian Civil Service examination (the quota for Indians then was extremely small), he took up legal studies and married an Englishwoman. By 1907 he had become a major activist in London's embryonic Indian nationalist movement, an editor of the journal *Indian Sociologist,* and a contact man for national revolutionary groups in Ireland, Egypt, Poland, and Paris. His legal studies ended in 1909, when he was expelled from school because of his political activities. In 1910 Chatto left his wife and moved to Paris to escape arrest. There he joined the French Socialist Party and, with Madame Cama, the veteran propagandist for Indian independence, he edited and wrote for *Bandemataram* as well as a new journal, *Talwar,* and contributed articles on Indian subjects for the French press, especially the Socialist paper *L'Humanité.* As before, he worked hard to establish links between the Indian independence movement and other anti-imperialist movements, such as the one in Egypt. In 1912 Chatto, now divorced, apparently gave up political activities and entered into a stormy marriage with a wealthy Irishwoman. The coming of World War I reawakened him politically. In April, 1914, anticipating arrest by the French, who were now allied with the British, he headed for Berlin. Chatto and the comrades he gathered around him saw the war as a golden opportunity to strike a blow against the British lion in India: Britain's enemy was India's friend. They seemed little concerned about the consequences of collaborating with another equally racist and imperialistic European power and unaware that such collaboration was unpopular with their countrymen in India. In August, 1914, Chatto met for the first time with German Foreign Office officials in Berlin. Within a week a document was worked out by which the Germans agreed to provide necessary aid for propaganda work and for sending arms and men to India. The United States was to be the staging ground, and emissaries were dispatched to Indian communities around the world. By the end of 1914, the Indo-German conspiracy was well underway, with Chatto as its coordinator and head of Berlin's Independence Committee. Chatto was also effectively single again; his Irish wife had retreated to a nunnery. The Indo-German conspiracy failed miserably: Britain stopped the

may well have been like her attraction in 1917 to the veteran Punjabi nationalist Lajpat Rai. Chatto, however, was not so fatherly in his treatment of her. Their relationship deepened rapidly, and within a month or two they were living together and calling themselves man and wife. Writing twenty years later, in *Battle Hymn of China*, Smedley recalled:

> Virendranath was the epitome of the secret Indian revolutionary movement, and perhaps its most brilliant protagonist abroad. He was nearly twenty [sic] years my senior, with a mind as sharp and ruthless as a saber. He was thin and dark, with a mass of black hair turning grey at the temples, and a face that had something fierce about it. He might easily have been taken for a southern European, a Turk, or a Persian. To me he seemed something like thunder, lightning, and rain; and wherever he had sojourned in Europe or England, he had been just about that to the British. His hatred for the islanders who had subjugated his country knew no bounds.
>
> The foundation of his emotional life had been laid in the feudal Mohammedan state of Hyderabad. To this he had added a quarter of a century of intellectual training in England, Europe, and the Near East. His was a famous Brahmin family abounding in poets, singers, educators, and scientists. Viren had been educated by his father, by Moslem scholars and English tutors. He grew up speaking Hindustani, English, a smattering of German, and the court language of the Moslem world, Persian. Throughout his childhood he had heard his mother—a poetess and an advocate of the emancipation of women—referred to with contempt by Moslems, and this had generated in him emotions which he had never been able to reconcile. This was only one of the many conflicts that went on within him and made his mind and emotional life remind me of one of those Hindu temples in south India—a repository of all the cultural movements of the ages.
>
> When Viren and I began life together, two eras and two cultures met. I was an American working woman, the product of a distorted commercial civilization, he a high-caste Indian with a cultivated, labyrinthine Brahmin mind and a British classical education. Though he hated everything British, he had an even deeper contempt for an American capitalism which judged all things by their money value. His mind was modern, but his emotional roots were in Hinduism and Islam.
>
> Whether or not I loved him I do not really know. Many years after I had

---

shipment of arms and, in 1915 and 1916, arrested and executed many of the insurgents. By the end of World War I Chatto was still in Berlin, looking for a new ally in his war with Britain; by 1920 the Soviet Union was the likeliest candidate. Sources on Chattopadhyaya and his family include M. P. Sarangapani, "Mrs. Sarojini Naidu," *Modern Review* 39, no. 1 (January 1926): 99–107; J. C. Kerr (of British intelligence), *Political Trouble in India, 1907–1917* (Delhi, 1973 reprint), pp. 198–214; A. C. Bose, *Indian Revolutionaries Abroad* (Patna, 1971), pp. 13–36; Padmini Sen Gupta, *Sarojini Naidu: A Biography* (Bombay, 1966); Bombay Government Records, *Source Material for a History of the Freedom Movement in India,* vol. 2 (London, 1920), pp. 499–518; G. Adhikari, ed., *Documents of the History of the Communist Party of India* (New Delhi, 1971), vol. 1, pp. 79–84; Chinmohan Sehanavis, "Pioneers among Indian Revolutionaries in Germany," *Mainstream* 13, no. 46 (July 19, 1975): 11–14.

left Viren I remember writing to an American friend that to my astonishment and resentment Viren remained the center of my emotional life, and if he were in danger I suppose I would walk barefoot around the world to help him. Yet I would not live with him for a day. That was long ago and time again proved the great healer. That he loved me there is no doubt. Neither I nor others understood why.

(pp. 12–15)

Smedley's "marriage" soon started to fall apart. The major causes of tension were political, but they were also rooted in personal jealousies within the Indian movement—which was almost entirely male—and in the kind of furtive underground life that she and Chatto were forced to lead as revolutionaries in exile. The troubles began in late March of 1921, when she joined a delegation of fourteen, led by Chatto, on a trip to Moscow to discuss the direction of the Indian nationalist movement with other Indians and Comintern figures.[2] The delegation set out in high spirits, but as soon as they arrived at the Moscow railroad station they were confronted by M. N. Roy and Abani Mukerjee, the leaders of the rival group that had just founded the Communist Party of India in Tashkent. The two groups clashed immediately over policy. By the time the special commission of the Comintern established to discuss the future of the Indian nationalist movement began its meetings, their differences had become irreconcilable.

The substantive issue dividing the two groups was one of priorities: which was to come first: the anti-British struggle, or Socialist revolution in India? Chatto and Smedley called for the organization of a united front of anti-imperialist groups, Communist and non-Communist, in the struggle against the British in India. Chatto, Smedley, and the others from Berlin were not Communists or Comintern members. They wanted national independence for India, and they were willing to seek it through a united effort with others. Roy, however, argued eloquently against such a united front and in favor of leadership being placed firmly in the hands of his embryonic Communist Party of India. He emphasized organizing the Indian proletariat in order to ensure the Socialist direction of the movement. Roy's faction eventually won the day.[3]

The struggle between the two camps soon became more personal than issue-oriented. As a non-Indian and a woman, Smedley was highly vulnerable, and from the beginning she became a chief target for attack. Roy, whom Smedley had met in New York in 1917, accused her of immorality—of being an "evil temptress" who was stirring up opposition to him and probably working as a spy for the British. Roy's real target, of course, was Chatto, whom he wished to discredit in the eyes of his followers. Smedley was furious and fought back. She accused the chairman of the Comintern commission investigating the Indian question, James Bell, who was British and siding with Roy, of being a British spy. She raged to Florence on October 3, "The Indians opposing our plan did such dirty work as to call me a British spy! Think of it—not even an American spy—but a British one!!! So I was under investigation! . . . If I had not been a member of a large delegation I suppose I would have been locked up."

Chatto's Berlin delegation spent much of its time waiting: waiting for the special commission of the Comintern to convene, and waiting to meet Lenin, which they never did, being effectively blocked by Roy.* As a result, Smedley spent much of her time at the Lux Hotel mixing with guests, most of whom were delegates from around the world who were gathering for the July meeting of the Third Congress of the Comintern (which Smedley did not attend). She summarized her impressions in an article for a New York Socialist journal, *The Liberator* (published in October, 1921). She was impressed by the gulf between the Western and Asian revolutionaries, and her sympathies were strongly with the Asians. Most reprehensible to her were the British Communists, whose views on Asian questions she considered imperialist. But she described all the Western delegates, especially the Americans, as naive and unrepresentative. In her letter to Florence of October 3, for example, she had this to say about the American delegates Ella Reeve Bloor and Earl Browder:

> In Moscow, amid great poverty, she (Mother Bloor) wore lace dresses over silk colored slips; also long strings of colored beads, rings, etc. . . . And she

---

* M. N. Roy had already impressed Lenin with the famous counterthesis on colonialism that he presented at the Second Congress of the Comintern in 1920; and before Chatto's delegation arrived in Berlin, he was also on good personal terms with such other leading Comintern figures as K. Radek, M. Borodin, N. Bukharin, A. Thalheimer, and J. Bell. Thus he was easily able to prevent Chatto's group from meeting Lenin and to cut off any chance of their gaining direct Comintern support. Roy's brief prominence in Comintern politics has led most Western writers to infer that he was the most influential leader of the Indian nationalist movement in European exile. In fact, the memoirs of Jawaharlal Nehru, Muhammad Ali Jinnah, Zakir Hussain, Sarojini Naidu, and Rabinandrath Tagore leave little doubt that during the 1920s it was Chatto who was the most widely respected Indian nationalist living in Europe. Roy was known as an arrogant man, very difficult to work with; when he was in Europe, he worked in relative isolation from the rest of the Indian community. Chatto, on the other hand, had connections and friends all over Europe, as well as a legendary reputation and a host of important family connections in India. By 1928 Roy had fallen out with the Comintern and been expelled from the Communist Party of India. Thus contemporary communist scholars in India consider Chatto (who joined the party in 1928), and not Roy, to be the central figure in the early decades of their movement. See, for example, Adhikari, ed., *Documents*, vol. 1, pp. 79–84, and Sehanavis, "Pioneers among Indian Revolutionaries in Germany."

lived with an idiot, Earl Browder, a young, dainty man of some 25 or 26 who bought (and wore) baby-blue silk Russian smocks in the market; and long black silk ribbons which he wore as belts. And then he, with his baby white skin and fair toothbrush moustache, posed in Moscow as the delegate from the Kansas *miners!* So help me gawd!! It was awful! I was so disgusted I couldn't even protest. I hate female men above all. And then to have them say they represent miners when I know they haven't been within a thousand miles of a mine. And Mother Bloor posed as the representative of five or six organizations, from the far West to Massachusetts!

Smedley was also disillusioned by the political climate in the Soviet Union, and she bitterly condemned the authoritarianism and irrationality of the new state. The Moscow house arrest of two of her heroes, the anarchists Emma Goldman and Alexander Berkman, shocked her deeply, and she made a point of going to visit them with Chatto. Late in 1921 (the letter is undated) she wrote to Florence in New York:

> Much that we read of Russia is imagination and desire only. And *no person* is safe from intrigues and the danger of prison. The prisons are jammed with anarchists and syndicalists *who fought in the revolution.* Emma Goldman and Berkman are out only because of their international reputations. And they are under house arrest; they expect to go to prison any day, and may be there now for all I know. Any Communist who excuses such things is a scoundrel and a blaggard. Yet they do excuse it—and *defend* it. . . . If I'm not expelled or locked up or something, I'll raise a small-sized hell. Everybody calls everybody a spy, secretly, in Russia, and everybody is under surveillance. You never feel safe.

She was also distressed, she said, by the misery and poverty of the ordinary people in Russia, particularly the gangs of homeless urchins she saw wandering the streets of Moscow: "People have reached the lowest level possible for human beings; beyond this stage they will die or return to the animal stage."

Emma Goldman appreciated Smedley's visit and the courage she displayed in doing so. It was the beginning of a friendship that helped to sustain Smedley through the next decade. In her autobiography, *Living My Life,* Goldman recalled her first impressions: "She was a striking girl, an earnest and true rebel, who seemed to have no interest in life except the cause of the oppressed people in India. Chatto was intellectual and witty, but he impressed me as a somewhat crafty individual. He called himself an anarchist, though it was evident that it was Hindu nationalism to which he devoted himself entirely" (p. 905).

Soon after Smedley and Chatto returned to Berlin, the German government, under pressure from Britain, began proceedings to deport both of them. Before this effort was abandoned, they were forced to live illegally in the city for several months, which meant moving frequently from hotel to hotel and house to house in order to escape police raids. It also meant constant surveillance and harassment by British secret service agents. On one occasion, British agents drugged and kidnapped Chatto; he was saved only by an alert border guard during an automobile search. When not on the run, Smedley, Chatto, and the others manned a new Indian News and Information Bureau, through which they hoped to step up their propaganda and organizational work for Indian independence. To start the bureau, they raised money by selling the furniture of Chatto's old wartime Berlin committee. Politically as well as financially, their situation was as difficult as it had been in Moscow.

Smedley's troubles were compounded by the appearance in Berlin of Herambalal Gupta, the man who had forcibly engaged in sex with her just before her arrest in New York in 1918. The two clashed initially at a meeting of the Berlin committee of nationalists just after her return to Berlin from Moscow. As Smedley recalled the scene in *Daughter of Earth* (she changed the names as follows: Gupta to Juan Diaz, Chatto to Anand, and Smedley to Marie Rogers):

> To the eyes of the other men present, it was an impersonal thing; to Juan Diaz and me it was not. Back of each word uttered by him lay a cynicism and a threat that was hateful. Once I caught Anand's eyes travelling from him to me, questioningly, and something within me quivered. He would find out— he was subtle enough to find out anything!
>
> "I am opposed to point four advanced here," I said, rising and speaking against a resolution advanced by Juan Diaz. Anand, listening, followed and supported my objections. When he had finished Juan Diaz sprang to his feet.
>
> "I object to foreigners influencing our movement. Not only am I opposed to foreigners, but I object to women and to wives influencing our members."
>
> I was on my feet livid with rage. "Foreigners! You do not object to foreigners who help save the lives of your men! Wives! Don't you insult me, Juan Diaz! I am not here as a wife, but as a comrade and a co-worker, and I demand to be treated as such!"
>
> Anand was also angry: "We speak of no wives here, Comrade Diaz; nor foreigners. I have been in our movement for years, and this is the first time any one has had the unmitigated audacity to suggest that I cannot think for myself. I oppose resolution four, as do other comrades here who are not married to Comrade Rogers. Unless you, Diaz, apologize for this insult, I withdraw from the conference. I make this demand not as a husband, but as a revolutionary."
>
> (pp. 384–85)

Gupta refused to apologize, and after the meeting broke up he spread the rumor that Smedley had had sexual relations with him. Within a matter of months, the resulting furor led Smedley to a nervous breakdown: in November she collapsed and entered a hospital for a month. For support, she reached back to her network of women friends in New York. In two letters to Florence Lennon (one undated, the other dated June 1, 1922), she wrote:

> The Indian work has completely ruined my health. Here it is a thousand times harder than in the U.S. Here I have *no* associates and no intellectual companionship such as in New York. The Indian work and my illness have prevented my learning German or anything else. The Indians here harbor harsh prejudices against women and against foreigners. As usual, they are inefficient in work and jealous of efficient persons. . . .
>
> There is a dirty man here who has gossiped without any foundation and it seems that every note I write to America is read by many people. I know the deep and sincere friendship of [Das] and I have a similar impersonal friendship to offer in return. But there are Indians who make it their business to gossip and make my life miserable. . . . I request that you burn all my letters after you have read them. There are men here to make it their business to collect "news" from American fellows and then to pervert it and circulate it broadcast. There is no way of meeting a half lie or rumor.

Smedley's problems were not simply personal. She was deeply depressed by conditions in Germany. Crowds of men and women with grim faces and angry eyes stood in the cold wind for hours waiting their turn to buy a bit of bread or fat or potatoes. Newspaper stories and headlines announced an alarming increase in suicides. Every church in Berlin, she said, seemed to hold a funeral a day. On December 31, 1921, she sent Florence a long letter describing her reactions:

> Germany is in terrible condition this year. This is particularly true of the working masses, who are so undernourished that tuberculosis is having a rich harvest, particularly of adolescent children. Gambling in the mark has been the great indoor sport of the capitalists for months, and consequently food has increased by 25 to 100 per cent. I have lived in the homes of workers; they live on boiled potatoes, black bread with lard spread on it instead of butter, and rotten beer. In one hotel, the maid who built the fire fainted in our room. Exhaustion was the cause. We talked with her later and learned that she worked 17 hours a day and makes 95 marks a *month*—about 50 cents. She lives in the hotel, sleeping in one room with all the other maids—a tiny, dirty little place. They receive their food also—clothing they buy themselves—out of the 95 marks a month! This means they all become prostitutes and haunt the streets whenever they have time. Or they pick up "clients" in the hotel.
>
> Of course, with Germany economically helpless, England has her own sweet way politically. It is very terrible to see the once independent Germany bending to every whim of England, or growing hopeful and happy everytime Lloyd George utters a word or a hint in favor of Germany against France.

There are prominent Germans here who say they wonder how long it will be until anti-English propaganda of any sort, whether carried on by Germans or by foreigners, will be forbidden. . . .

All hopes of a revolution are dwindling, and the German working class seems to be entering that phase of "India-ization" which leads to physical and intellectual slavery. For months it seemed that a revolution was certain. But instead, slavery seems more likely now. The working class no longer has the physical resistance for a revolution, and the Entente is too strong, and Russia is too weak. More and more do I see that only a successful revolution in India can break England's back forever and free Europe itself. It is not a national question concerning India any longer; it is purely international. . . .

When we returned to Germany, [Chatto] was ordered by the German Government to leave this country. The British Government demanded this of the German Government. Consequently, we have been living illegally for months—since September. Our house was raided by the honorable police, and then for weeks we lived from hotel to hotel, and from house to house, never knowing where to go from one night to the next. Generally we were working in our Bureau up until midnight, and then we would go out and find a cheap hotel. After weeks of this I gave out and collapsed, due to rheumatism of the heart. Then I came out of the hospital after a month. We were followed night and day by British spies, and by the help of friends tried to get hold of them and have them arrested for illegal police activities. My husband received warnings time and again to be careful. Then about two weeks ago a terrible thing happened to him: we drank chocolate in an Islamic restaurant with some friends, and within a short time he lay unconscious on the floor; diarrhea and vomiting started as soon as he came to. The physician we consulted said he had been given arsenic, and a large dose which fortunately caused vomiting. For days he was very ill, but recovered. But before this was complete, two English agents came with [skeleton] keys and tried to break into the room where we live with a little old lady. Failing, they went away and came later. The little old lady went outside to meet them and asked them what they wanted; they said they wanted to rent a room and wanted to go inside and see her rooms. She refused, saying she had no rooms to rent, and had never had in her life. She did not understand English, and said the men were foreigners and spoke a foreign language which she could not understand. But both had on high military boots and coats.

Then our wanderings started again and continue to this day. We work very hard during the day, trying to build something which will remain in Germany, and at night we go where we can. . . . We are no longer bothered by the German police, who know all about us, but the British spies make our lives a hell.

Smedley noted that the handgun given to her for protection by their mutual friend Josephine Bennett at the time she left New York for Germany was a great comfort to her.

To add to Smedley's mood of despondency, the news about the Indian independence movement in the United States was not encouraging.

Without her, the Friends of Freedom for India had gone rapidly down-hill, and it collapsed in 1922.[4] According to Baldwin and Das, infighting among the Indians and Ghose's incompetence had succeeded in alienat-ing the organization's key American backers, such as Robert Morss Lovett and Margaret Sanger. To Das, the loss of Smedley as a bridge be-tween the two cultures was irreparable.

On June 1, 1922, Smedley wrote to Florence that she was near ner-vous collapse and completely exhausted; she said she had recently spent two weeks in a sanitorium in Mecklenberg. The same letter also carried the seeds of a new humiliation: it was the first in a long series of requests for money to pay mounting medical expenses. To assuage her guilt, Smedley was sending Florence Indian saris which she hoped could be sold to repay the debt. She asked Florence not to tell anyone that her friend Taraknath Das was sending her money.

By the fall of 1922 she was feeling well enough to take a paying job "polishing" English at home for a commercial magazine, but her spirits continued to sink. On November 22 she wrote to Florence: "Germany is terribly depressing. . . . I don't know when I have heard a person laugh a really joyous laugh. The only time they laugh is when they have beer before them, and then their laugh is heavy and deadly. I am weary of Germany, just as one wearies of suffering, dullness, and ugliness over a long period of time. Perhaps my weariness is due to prolonged illness or to—God Forbid—advancing age! I long for a rest in a fresh happy atmosphere."

Behind her mood lay the disintegration of her "marriage." As she ex-plained to Florence on June 4, 1923, she and Chatto were miserable to-gether and miserable apart:

> I've married an artist, revolutionary in a dozen different ways, a man of truly "fine frenzy", nervous as a cat, always moving, never at rest, indefatigable energy a hundred fold more than I ever had, a *thin* man with *much* hair, a tongue like a razor and a brain like hell on fire. What a couple. I'm consumed into ashes. And he's always raking up the ashes and setting them on fire again. Suspicious as hell of every man near me—and of all men or *women* from America. My nervous collapse quieted him much. I told him once when I was on the verge of unconsciousness: "Leave me in peace; leave me alone personally; if I can't have complete freedom I shall die before your eyes." But he is ever now and then blazing up again. And he is always smouldering. I feel like a person living on the brink of a volcano crater. Yet it is awful to love a person who is a torture to you. And a fascinating person who loves you and won't hear of anything but your loving him and living right by his side through all eternity! We make a merry hell for each other, I assure you. He is rapidly growing grey, under my influence, I fear. And that tortures me.

Chatto, whether consciously or not, was making Smedley pay in guilt for undermining him politically by what he considered her previous "sexual exploits." He was now openly ashamed of her. Their differences in class background heightened the tension. He was embarrassed to introduce Smedley, not only to his family but to upper-class friends of his family as well. A year or two later she gave a new friend, the Danish writer Karin Michaelis, this vivid account:

> Once some well-known Indian men and women came to Berlin, and my husband was to go and meet them. This same night some American friends invited me to the theatre. My husband was angry because I was going out with these Americans—although he had the appointment with the Indians. In defiance, I went to the theatre. But I could not enjoy myself, I felt so miserable that I had not come to an agreement with my husband. Then I got up and left the theatre in the middle of the first act and decided to go to my husband and tell him I could not enjoy myself because of the difference of opinion between us. In happiness I rushed to that hotel where he was to meet the Indians. I went in through the doors and saw him in the midst of the Indians. I ran up to him, happy and smiling. But he was very much embarrassed and led me away and said: "You see, why have you come *here?* Do you not know that it makes my position impossible? I cannot introduce *you* to these people—they know my family. How then can I introduce *you* to them?" And I, stunned and shocked, asked, "Your family, but why should you not introduce me to people who know your family?" And he said, "Oh, it is impossible. You must go away." And he took me to the door, and I went out on the street. I looked back and saw that all the Indians were staring after me. They thought I was some woman from the street, some prostitute or something. . . .
>
> Well, for hours I walked the streets of Berlin. Finally, I went home and lay in silence through the long night. I heard my husband come home and stand by my bed to see if I was asleep. Then, when he heard no sound he went to bed.
>
> An American girlfriend was living with us at the time. I was unable to get up from bed the next day, and after my husband was gone she asked me why. I broke down and told her. In anger, she went to my husband and accused him. He came in the room, locked the door and began to ask me why I betrayed him to outsiders as I had done to this girlfriend. I told him I was so unhappy, so miserable, that I must tell my sorrow to someone. He accused me, he beat his own head, he accused me of all my past "sins." In the end, to get peace, and because I was so sick that I feared another nervous attack, I said, "I am sorry to have mentioned the subject. Of course I should not have come to the hotel last night. You were right; you could not possibly have introduced me to those Indians. They were such beautiful women, in silk Indian costumes, and I was badly dressed; and I am of the working class. And you have a wife in England. I am sorry that I did not see clearly."
>
> And then he said, "Yes, now I hope you see your mistake and act differently in the future. Now the matter is settled."
>
> And so there was peace! But at what a price![5]

Later Chatto also compromised and seemed to come to terms with his conflicting feelings on these issues. Eventually family members, including his sister and nephew, stayed with the couple and addressed Agnes as "Auntie."

Compounding such tensions were cultural differences. In the Eastern tradition, no traveler should be turned away. And since Chatto was seen as the intellectual patriarch of all the Indians in Europe, a steady stream of Indians, mostly male, visited their household expecting to find temporary food and lodging.* Hindu and Muslim religious festivals were often celebrated there, "until the very walls of our home seemed to be permeated with the odor of curry." And of course the burden of cooking and cleaning fell on Smedley.

Chatto's attitude toward money ensured that their personal comfort came last. He saw money merely as a means of working for the independence of his country. He never owned more than one suit of clothing, and Smedley was constantly darning, patching, and pressing it. Nor did he care what he ate. Twenty years later, in *Battle Hymn of China*, Smedley could see this indifference as a positive trait: "When he had money, he gave it to anyone in need, so that we were forever in debt. His attitude toward it had been formed by the great joint families of India and in particular by that caste of Brahmin teachers and scholars who gave their knowledge freely. Years later I found the same attitude among those intellectuals of China who also came from families in which the clan cared for the individual" (p. 14). But by 1923 Smedley was beginning to consider her place in Chatto's world as intolerable. She described the situation in a letter to Michaelis:

> For three years . . . I have lived in silence, and I never said a word against him. I helped him. I borrowed money and supported both of us. And even then I washed our clothing, ironed them, scrubbed the floor, cooked and washed dishes. I did everything, from mending his clothes and washing them, to borrowing money and loading myself with debt for many years to come. In the meantime, he gave his services *free* to the Indians here, and I had to pay even for the postage. He searched for rooms for every business-man or student who came along, he helped them shop, he also did national

---

*Now and then a student "straight off the boat" would strike a maternal chord in Smedley, and she would try to help him not make a fool of himself. In *Battle Hymn of China* (New York, 1943), she mentions a student who bought a straw hat with a bunch of grapes hanging down the side: "It looked like a turban, and only with difficulty could we induce him to cease wearing it." Chatto for his part "would argue with [all visitors]— attacking Hindu caste prejudices and Muslim superstitions, eating beef in front of Hindus and pork in front of Muslims and showing contempt for those who looked primarily to England for culture and learning" (pp. 14–15).

work. He brought them home at mealtime, two or three extra ones day by day, and I had to sacrifice my food day after day because he wanted to enter- tain his guests. There were days when I did not have enough to eat because Indian hospitality demands that a man must be fed. But I had to cook for these men who were not idealists, who had never raised a hand to help free India. My life was given to India, but I had to cook for businessmen. And I would sit and listen to them talk about [how] "all European women are pros- titutes." Then from morning until late at night I answered doorbells and tele- phone bells [from] men who demanded that my husband pay them money— money which he had not taken, but which other Indians had taken and he agreed to pay it back because he said "the honor of India is at stake." But *I* had to pay that money. "The honor of India" be damned! It came out of my body, and never did I have one second of rest and peace trying to do my housework and at the same time trying to make extra money writing. And hearing nothing but requests for money. And all day long my husband tele- phoned for the Indians, and these Indians came to our house to telephone [so] they [would] not have to pay. And month after month I had to meet tele- phone bills which ran up into the hundreds of marks, and often the telephone was cut off. That is the economic side of the question, only.[6]

Smedley was also repulsed by feudal Indian customs, including the women who were their victims. As she wrote to Florence Lennon on August 25, 1924:

We are living with a Mohammedan man and his wife. It is her first year out of purdah. These innocent purdah ladies! She knows more of sex than the freest woman of America. And such miserable, intriguing habits! She listens at key- holes to what the men are saying in the other room, and seems to think I understand it. She, the innocent, has gonorrhea, carried to her by her dear husband from the brothel—the husband who believes women must live in purdah in order that they may be protected from the cruel world. And she thinks that gonorrhea is an ailment something like a cold on the lungs. We found out the trouble only after they moved in, and they moved in only be- cause she is the sister of a very dear young man who is very close to our hearts. The old gent who gave her the disease is very religious and prays five times a day in good Muslim style. And he raves against the immorality of the West! The rest of the time he eats his opium and sits contemplating.

This all is a great experience for me. I would never have learned of it had I not lived through it. They leave, thank God, in five days.

As Smedley's emotional fury mounted, she became more introverted. In her letters to America in early 1923 she stopped discussing politics— a clear sign that something was seriously wrong in the life of this politi- cal woman. The shock of discovering the prejudices of "revolutionary" men was intensified because the most paralyzing daggers were thrust at her by her own "revolutionary" husband, Chatto. In anarchist fashion,

she blamed an institution—in this case, the institution of marriage,
which she saw as corrupted by the notion of "ownership."

The only friends she was seeing in the spring of 1923 were Alexander
Berkman, Emma Goldman, and their German anarchist-syndicalist
friends. As her physical collapses became more frequent and her dependence on sleeping powders grew, these friends became deeply concerned. At their urging, Smedley sought the help of a psychiatrist early
in 1923. On May 8, she explained the situation to Florence:

> You ask me why I don't "drop in at Vienna and have a consultation with
> Freud." Why not advise me to drop into heaven and have tea with God? It is
> far from the possible, I assure you. Freud charges money; it also takes money
> to go to Vienna; and it requires a passport which I don't happen to have. . . .
>
> I am better now. About two weeks ago I had a fearful attack which laid me
> out for a week in a state of semi-consciousness. Since then I have started
> working again and seem to be submerging myself in work because I am get-
> ting better each day. But always around eleven o'clock in the morning and
> three or four in the afternoon I feel my throat begin to tighten and my head
> to swim. Yesterday, for the first day, I did not feel this. But today it is back
> again. As I wrote you, I have been going to a psychoanalyst [name unknown],
> a student of Freud's and a man of some note here in Germany. But he refused
> to touch my case save in certain spots regarding my personal life. I slept for
> the first time in months after going to him for a time. But he says he can't
> cure me, and there is no need of his deceiving me. He says he can only act as a
> prop now and then when I need him. So when I am very bad, I rush to him
> and we talk about things in general. He hypnotised me to take away a part of
> my misery, but the hypnosis has now worked itself away again. . . . My
> psychoanalyst has tried to induce me to write a novel based upon some of my
> own experiences. But the idea was crushed out of me by an incident after I
> had written three chapters. . . . He made a serious psychological blunder
> once which has driven me away from him for a month now, and I can't bring
> myself to return unless I am seriously ill. . . .
>
> Please write me. I am sorry to write a letter all about myself. But there is
> no one here in whom I have full confidence that tomorrow they will not take
> my misery and make a joke of it for every street corner, or at best, for draw-
> ing room gossip.

Smedley's withdrawal was so uncharacteristic that it surprised even
Florence, who implied that perhaps she was overreacting to her personal situation. What Smedley had not made explicit to Florence was
the fact that her analyst had tried to seduce her. Instead, on June 4,
Smedley wrote:

> Your letter dated May 20 came this morning. I have read it with interest. It is
> the most "grown up" letter you have ever written. Of course nothing you say
> in it offends me, as you seemed to think it would. I bristled at a sentence or

two . . . [but] only because my Ego is very active, owing to long suffering, and because what you say is true. I still bristle, however, at your remarks on my obsession that my freedom is being forever limited. Perhaps I am over-sensitive on that point. But surely you admit that the one thing people love to do is to boss it over another, to influence another, to assert their authority. And the male of the species, after a few billion years of bossing, finds it a part of him. . . . I often think freedom is more valuable than happiness, except that the two are perhaps but synonyms. Believe me, I am not using my imagi-nation in my present situation. The thing bore down upon me month by month, and no one was more surprised than I; and I fought a battle worth fighting. But I lost. And I'm sick. My nervous collapses come back at least twice a month, leaving me prostrate in bed for a week at a time. I'm taking high sun rays treatment as well as high-frequency electric treatment.

I gave up my psychoanalyst who was treating me. I don't care to say why, exactly. But he became too personal.

Now, with her distrust of men nearly total, Smedley launched a crusade to protect her friends against the institution of marriage. Breaking up marriages became a cause for the rest of her life. At the same time her suspicion of men led her to seek help almost exclusively from women.

During the summer of 1923, Smedley was saved temporarily by the generosity of an Indian nationalist she had first met in New York, Lila Singh, a woman of about fifty, wealthy by birth and marriage, and a vet-eran fighter for Indian independence and for women's rights and educa-tion.[7] Passing through Berlin on her way to England in 1923, Singh was appalled by Smedley's condition and offered to give her enough money to spend two summer months away from Chatto in the Austrian Alps.

At about the same time Smedley wrote to Florence that Karin Michaelis had invited her for a visit to her home on an isolated island in Denmark:

I look forward to the island. It is isolated and we shall live alone, rowing, writing, and doing what we will. Karin herself is a much older woman than I. She is 53. Have you not heard of her? She is a well-known novelist, author of *The Dangerous Age* and many other books. For some unknown reason we two struck up a strange, interesting friendship while she was here. She is not old, for all her age. I have an idea that she wants me to come [so she can] get a lot of "copy" out of me about my life for a novel! Really! . . . One of her closest friends and advisers is Georg Brandes, and I shall meet the great man. Karin is a wise woman and a seemingly frivolous one. She talks rot, but she seems to dive down deep into all women. She looked me over and decided I should be one of her next victims in a book. And then she fastened on me like a leech. I was very tired and ill and couldn't be interesting. But she is wiser than she sounds, I assure you, and she knows what ails women. . . . I have helped her break up her own married life right here in Berlin. She has now

left the man. He is younger than she by far. He exploited her for her name
and connections, and he used all her money. He was a rat. I don't care to use
names.

Finally deciding that she was not ready to be used as source material for someone else's book, Smedley wrote to Michaelis on July 14,
politely declining the invitation by asking for a raincheck. Instead she
accepted Lila Singh's offer. She spent most of July in a shepherd's hut on
a mountainside near the Bavarian village of Gerstruben. Although she
found the dances, folk songs, and festivals there entertaining, neither
these diversions nor the supposedly therapeutic Alpine sun put an end
to her sleeplessness and terror at night. In early August she moved to
Berchtesgarten, a small resort town near the site of Hitler's mountain
retreat. She wrote to Florence on August 11:

> Here in Bavaria, I am in the stronghold of reaction. At night I am often
> awakened by the military commands and the march of men (Monarchists)
> who are training at night in the forests and in the mountains. It is a gruesome
> feeling—this secret training of men to kill other men. And these men being
> trained are peasants and working-men—not the class we usually think of. In
> Saxony the same thing occurs; there at night the men who are under training
> are also working-men, but the leaders are Communists. And they are prepar-
> ing to kill their kind also. Sometimes I see no difference between the two.
> What is this business everywhere—men preparing to murder their own kind
> for the sake of an idea? Not their own idea either, but that of men who use
> them as tools to set themselves in power. We only wait for the day when the
> two groups will start massacring each other. Both groups are bitterly op-
> posed to passive resistance as a method; it isn't bloody or sadistic enough.
>   There is no need to send the money unless the sari is sold. I have decided
> definitely, anyway, not to go to Vienna because it is about ten times as expen-
> sive as Germany, and I haven't the money. I hope to be well enough by Sep-
> tember or October to enter Berlin University in October and drown my
> troubles in work. I shall use the money from my sari for that instead of a
> psychoanalyst. Of course, if it is absolutely necessary, I must return to Berlin
> for a month or two. But I can't have everything. In Berlin there live two of the
> best living analysts, aside from Ranke and Freud (Dr. Abraham and Dr.
> Eitingon), and I shall try to get on the lists of one of them if absolutely neces-
> sary. I have a job in Berlin for the winter at four pounds (about twenty dol-
> lars) a month, and with a little writing for the Indian press I shall perhaps
> bring it up to 5 pounds. I shall just be able to live on this, and I plan to take
> an hour or two a day at the University. I tried to find work in Switzerland and
> go there, but the people whom I approached told me that foreigners could
> not draw salaries in Switzerland because of unemployment. So I have given
> up Switzerland.
>   In Berlin I am [going to get] a passport under my own name, and I am
> going to live alone. A friend is finding a room for me about an hour from the

city. Chatto is in agreement with my plans. Faced with my total destruction or with a total separation, he said he would give up all claims on my attention, etc., and would give me perfect freedom in all things; he is not to make one single demand or personal request. Upon this condition I [shall] return to Berlin, go my own way, and no longer have his perpetual jealousy and suspicion to face. You must not think [that those things were] imagination on my part. I have faced not only death, but worse than that, insanity. And I am not completely well by any means. The least little thing sets me on edge for days even now, and weeks pass [when] I do not sleep without strong sleeping powders.

Her desperate letters to another old friend in New York, Ellen Kennan, brought more than words of comfort. In Munich Smedley joined Ellen Kennan, who had come to Germany to lend Agnes her moral support and visit her other old friend, Emma Goldman. The two women attended the Wagner Festspiele in Munich and then proceeded together to Berlin.[8]

Upon returning to the capital in September, Smedley immediately ran into obstacles in her attempt to gain admission to the University of Berlin. She frantically wrote for transcripts from New York University and her schools in California and also contacted her lawyer, Gilbert Roe. The job she thought she had lined up turned out to be volunteer work, offering only a vague promise of future income. By this time Kennan had returned to New York. As Smedley's prospects evaporated, friends in America urged her to return. In response, she told them that Chatto was holding her by threatening to quit his work for Indian independence and come to America with her, swearing that he could not live without her. Fully aware that she would be miserable if she lived with him again, Smedley gave in to his pleas and in October moved back in with him. She told Florence that she had agreed to stay with Chatto only for another six months, and that if she failed to gain entrance to the university by spring, she was determined to return to the United States.

By this time Smedley's guilt about accepting money from friends was weighing her down. She wrote to Florence on October 8:

Please do this for me—do not send any money at all unless [the sari] has been sold. I shall refuse it and return it at once. I have decided never to accept another cent of money which I have not earned. I can't always feel like a worm as I do now because of the money I have received which does not belong to me. I am improved in health. But I am not enthusiastic about my life anymore. I shall never be again, I think. The only hope I have is to bury myself in work and go through life with a dead heart. . . .

I am wasting my life and I know it, and yet there is no other way open to me. I am 31 years of age and still an ignorant, uncultured, undeveloped animal.

The disintegrating political situation of Weimar Germany brought more economic chaos. Smedley's desperation over finding enough money to survive, and her growing anxiety about death, were by no means idiosyncratic. Many artists and writers, such as Käthe Kollwitz, George Grosz, and Ernst Barlach, had similar feelings and captured in their art the misery of the working people of Germany as inflation continued to devour the weak. In an article published in the *Nation* on November 28, Smedley wrote:

> The week has witnessed looting of many shops in various parts of the city, unrest in most cities throughout the country, and actual street fighting in many. Looting and rioting are regarded as so much grist to the mills of the Communists and the reactionaries alike. The Communists take advantage of it and preach their dogma; the monarchists do the same. They smile cynically when they read of the frightful increase in the cost of living and say, "It has not yet gone far enough. It must be worse still before the masses realize the mistake they have made in establishing a republic! We shall wait a bit longer." But most of the townspeople are so weary, so destroyed by uncertainty and long years of nervous strain, that they do not care what happens. They are tired of it all.

By November, Smedley noted, inflation had soared until one dollar was worth 2.5 trillion marks, and the cost of a loaf of bread had risen from 900 million to 1,200 billion marks.

Smedley's earlier fears, voiced from Berchtesgarten, over the increasingly polarized political situation also intensified, and in a letter to Lennon on September 16, 1923, she predicted civil war, to be followed by a Fascist victory. Her predictions began to be realized in October, with the brutal suppression of Communist uprisings in the provinces of Saxony and Thuringia and in the city of Hamburg.

As the economic and political order in Germany crumbled around her, Smedley's letters to Florence became more preoccupied with death. Tucked inside a letter that arrived in October was a handwritten note that read: "I have collapsed once again." On November 12, she described visiting the deathbed of Surendranath Karr, the Indian nationalist who had spread more vicious gossip about her than any other person in Berlin with the exception of Gupta himself. Confronted with death, she said, one could "forget political or temperamental differences."[9] Six days later she wrote to Florence: "I can never pass through the winter in Germany. If I remain here, I die."

CHAPTER VI

Psychoanalysis, 1924–1925

By late 1923, Smedley's "revolutionary marriage" was disintegrating, even though in many ways Chatto was a better match for her than Ernest Brundin. She shared Chatto's revolutionary goals; they agreed to make political work, and not childrearing, their cementing concern. Both had been married and had come together only after separately establishing their credentials within the independence movement. Emotionally, both were intense and moralistic, with a burning need to exert themselves in the larger body politic. But Chatto's jealous rages over Smedley's "premarital affairs" had finally shattered her self-esteem. In letters to Karin Michaelis and Florence Lennon, she tried to generalize about her predicament:

> I assure you, Florence, that when you marry your desired man, you will suffer tortures of which you do not today dream, at the hands of your husband, because you have dared use your vagina before you met him. Before you marry him, he will talk of freedom, of liberty, and [your equal right] to have lived and loved. But wait until the sense of property enters his head after marriage! . . .
>
> Before I met my husband I had had relations with other men. I had been married once. All this I told my husband when we were married [so] that there might be no misunderstanding. He also had lived with *many* women and was not only once married but is married to this day—his wife is an English woman and lives in England. . . . [But] after one month, my husband began to accuse me of being a woman of weak character because I had had sex relations with other men. And he said that he "got the leavings" from other men. Now when a man strikes at a woman like that, in view of the fact

that he is also "the leavings from other women" it is not only unethical, it is
contrary to all the laws of decency and fair play. But I was sick and I felt
guilty. He also locked me up from the Indians, and refused to let me go into
the Indian work, [saying that] the Indians would learn of my sex life and ruin
him because of it. For three years he refused to let me write. . . . He was hostile and bitter because I wanted to write and said it was only a desire to
"show off." And if I wrote I was to write only the things he told me to write,
in order that he might see whether or not they were correct. So I did not
write at all. Each month I became sicker and sicker until I began to have serious nervous attacks, something like epileptic fits, in which I would lose
control of my body and mind, fall to the floor and tremble for five or ten
minutes. I lost all ability to sleep and for ten months became a drug fiend,
taking stronger and stronger sleeping powders. Then I would try to rebel, or
when I would talk back to my husband about these things, he attacked me
physically. Three times he choked me and bit me, and after these attacks I fell
to the floor in these terrible fits.

   I will never forgive him. . . . When any other human being strikes at the
spiritual and intellectual life of a person, he may as well drive a knife into his
heart and be finished with it.[1]

Hampered by her poor command of German, Smedley's political community in Germany was mainly a small circle of anarchist-syndicalist
friends like Emma Goldman and Alexander Berkman. Goldman's admiration for Smedley's courage in seeking her out in Moscow had
been their initial link. Her lifelong friend and former lover Alexander
Berkman found Smedley all the more interesting when he learned that
part of her childhood had been spent near Ludlow, before the massacre
of 1914. Goldman had passed through Denver just after the strike and
was upset when labor leaders rejected her offers of support. Berkman
did much to publicize the massacre and is alleged to have been the chief
strategist in an aborted attempt to place a bomb on the Rockefeller estate, in protest. By 1923, Smedley and Chatto were regularly attending
study group meetings with Goldman, Berkman, and some of the leading
anarchist thinkers in Europe, including the German Rudolf Rocker and
the Italian Armando Borghi, a former associate of Mussolini's.[2] Although working with and intellectually exploring anarchist-syndicalist
ideology, to Lennon in New York Smedley portrayed herself as holding
back from total commitment:

Miss Miller [a friend in New York] is romantic. She thinks that if there is a
Monarchist Reaction here I would suffer. Not at all. I know some of the most
prominent Monarchists and some of them are very interesting and cultured
people. I don't agree with their political opinions, but I render unto Caesar
what is Caesar's. If I were in trouble from the Monarchists, I'd go to such

people and ask them what they mean. Similarly with the Revolutionaries. Of course, I work with the Syndicalists and Anarchists, [so that] if the Communists came [into power], I'd perhaps get my head chopped off, for of all people most hated by the Communists, the Anarchists and Syndicalists stand in the first rank, even ahead of Hitler and his gang.

You need not worry yourself thinking if there is a revolution that I'll run out on a barricade and dare them to shoot me. Thanks. I've decided not to die for a time yet. And if I do, it won't be in Germany. [February 16, 1924]

Not surprisingly, given this company, Smedley expressed her feelings about her personal problems by continuing her assault on marriage as an institution. Arguing with Florence Lennon on the nature of man-woman relationships, she had written on November 12, 1923:

You say . . . that although girls should not be feebleminded, they should not attempt to take the place of men in nature. I answer this: I do not know just what woman's "place in nature" happens to be, except sexually—that "place" is quite clearly marked out. But as to socially, I do not know but that nature has been mauled over the head by men, and woman has been forced to occupy positions for which she is not fitted by nature, but which she is forced to fill only because it pleases the vanity of men. I think the development of the human species in the future is going to see woman occupying a place other than she occupies today. Your line of argument is dangerous: the old-time gentlemen used such arguments when they said women should not enter churches, when women could not sit in anti-slavery congresses because of their sex, when they were not able to vote because of their sex, when they were forced out of the medical, legal, and every other profession because of their sex. To the old reactionaries—may their souls roast forever—women were trying to "take the place of men in nature."

I have no objection to a man being a man, however masculine that may be. I hate female men. But I see no reason why a woman should not grow and develop in all those outlets which are suited to her nature, it matters not at all what they may be. No one yet knows what a man's province is, and how far that province, as conceived of today, is artificial. There are many men—such as those often to be found among the Indians—who are refined until they have qualities often attributed to the female sex. Yet they are men, and strong ones. I am not willing to accept our present social standards of woman's place or man's place, because I do not think that present society is rational or normal, either as regards men or women or the classes. I bow to nature, but I don't bow to a social system which has its foundation in the desires of a dominant class for power. That system perverts the very source of life, starting with the home and the schools. Thousands of women are crushed and [made] inarticulate by that system and never develop as their natures would force them to develop were they in a decent environment.

I do not know whether you have me in mind when you say that a "trained nurse or a revolutionary may abnegate his or her personal happiness and reproductiveness for what seems to him a larger cause, but for that reason he need not limit himself with the niggardly attitude of sour grapes." I believe that I am a type of many revolutionaries. And to us, our work is our personal happiness. Personally I have no objection to women having as many babies as they want. What I do hate is for men, particularly, to think that a woman who does not have a bunch of children hanging around her skirt is damned forever more. Furthermore, happiness does not lie [only] in reproductiveness. . . . As for sex, I shall certainly help myself to it when I feel that I need it. But as for children, there are too many women today who merely breed without purpose. To my manner of thinking, to give birth to a child is a terrible thing unless you think you know the meaning of life and why you are bringing new life into existence. . . .

You say: "My point is this: each of us is strongest when functioning along the lines he was *originally intended for*." That sounds to me as if you have accepted the idea of God, and that this gentleman "originally intends" us to be or do something. To me, life is a development only, and there is no intention about it. Because I am born a woman does not mean I can only do certain things and nothing else. Physically only do I admit that.

Nor do I deny what you say about the influence of love. But I can't place love too far in the foreground of life today because I see [for] myself that love is usually divorced from reason, and that it can be perverted and warped. To me now, as always before, love is nothing but sex in action. . . . And to my point of view, intelligence is of equal importance in the universe; to me it is far more important . . . because it is such a child in the scheme of the universe. Emotion is as old as life, but the intellect is so young that it must be cherished. And it is precious enough to cherish.

Writing in this vein may have brought Smedley some temporary relief, but her friends were alarmed by her personal situation and urged her to seek help again, this time from a woman psychoanalyst. Smedley agreed. Backed into a corner by Chatto, who derided psychoanalysis as priestcraft and superstition, she felt a desperate need for a breakthrough. As she told Florence on December 8, about a month after beginning work with a new analyst: "I prefer death to these spells and to sleeplessness. . . . Upon my analysis my life depends; there is not a shadow of doubt in my mind now."

Smedley's new analyst was a middle-aged woman, Frau Dr. Elizabeth Naef, an associate of the Berlin Psychoanalytical Institute.* At this time, the Institute was building an international reputation as the world's

---

* Little is known of Naef except that she was Jewish and a Socialist; her father, named Rosenbaum, was an official in the Lithuanian legation in Berlin in the twenties; and she was married and had children. After she died in 1933, Ernest Jones eulogized her as follows: "Berlin has suffered the loss of Frau Dr. Naef, a woman whose striking personality gave her an influence much greater than strangers might suppose from her writings. I first met her in Zurich in 1907 and always esteemed her as a valued colleague" (Ernest Jones, "Report," *International Journal of Psychoanalysis* 15 [1934]: 516).

most important psychoanalytic training center. Loosely affiliated with the University of Berlin, it departed from Freud's Vienna group in promoting research into the social causes of emotional disturbance and requiring all its practitioners to be medical doctors. Its early members included Karen Horney, Helene Deutsch, Melanie Klein, and Wilhelm Reich.[3]

When Smedley began analysis with Naef in late 1923, the issue of the development of the feminine identity was being hotly debated among members of the Institute. Horney, among others, was challenging Freud's theories of the "castration complex" and "penis envy" and was also questioning the ideal of monogamous marriage. Dr. Naef, however, was apparently a more orthodox Freudian than Karen Horney. After three weeks of analysis, on November 27 Smedley wrote to Florence: "I am too young in the analysis business to tell you what is wrong with me. But you may be interested to know that I have a deep castration complex which colors all my relationships. I gained the earliest impression that I was made into a girl by my penis having been cut off! Someday I'll be able to relate many interesting things to you. You may, however, get some light on my contempt for women as a sex and at the same time my bitter feminism. Likewise my lifelong man-ishness." Two weeks earlier she had written: "My doctor is wonderful. Aside from the real help I get from analysis, I find it frightfully interesting as a study. When I find the origin of things which hurt me, I'm so interested that I forget to be hurt. Really, it is quite an uncanny business." Recovering her sense of humor, she also offered Florence a "comic-supplement" of "Babu-isms," the efforts of "half-baked Indians trying to write English poetry." One example was: "On the trodden sands of time / I saw the footprints of a vanished hand."

As her self-assertiveness returned, Smedley wrote the first article she had published in almost two years: in "Starving Germany," for the November 28 issue of the *Nation,* she reported on the desperate situation caused by inflation and rising unemployment. She had resolved to earn her living by writing, but when this article brought her a check for only $17.50 from the *Nation,* she had to reconsider, for her analysis alone cost $62 a month. Florence had sent $20 in two letters in November and had promised to send $30 more, but she also reported that she had been unable to sell the rather gaudy sari and broken string of pearls that Smedley had sent her. Smedley advertised for typing work, and when the American Embassy answered to invite her for an interview, she went—at great risk, because she had no passport to show. After extended questioning, an embassy official told her that no typing job was available. But in her determination to become self-reliant, she refused to confide in her "husband." As she explained to Florence on November 12: "I have never told Chatto about the arrival of the money [you sent] or about the money I pay my analyst. He is so bitter because I am being analyzed that there is little communication between us."

On December 1, Smedley decided to quit analysis until she could pay for it herself. But after only five days without Dr. Naef, her throat convulsions returned and she sank into a suicidal depression. In response to Florence's urging that she return to the United States, she said that she intended to return, but only after analysis was completed. On December 8, she wrote again, pleading for money: "Please try to understand. You have done more than your share for me. I feel it an imposition even to write this to you. I have no right. Yet I have no one else." As Smedley later admitted, she was turning once again to "sleeping powders" or drugs to help her face life without analysis and combat new convulsions. Florence Lennon and Josephine Bennett quickly responded by sending her enough money to pay her doctor's bill.

As she told Florence on December 20, she was trying to fight her way toward some sense of purpose: "During the days I try to do things—work, sing, beat the piano—to bring myself back to a realization of reality; I try to bring back the illusion (you say I'm cheated if I don't have it) of life. So I try to bury myself in trivial things." But by January 3 she had to report a serious two-day attack: "I have been *sick*. I had hallucinations that Chatto was locking my door and was going to murder me. Yet I was awake and not dreaming and I found myself screaming in the middle of the night." During this crisis, with Smedley threatening to leave immediately for America, their landlady telephoned Dr. Naef, who began treating Smedley again on January 3 and agreed to carry her bill until she "could afford to pay." Chatto, terrified by this episode, finally acquiesced in her continuing analysis.

Smedley welcomed Dr. Naef's support in her battle to rebuild a positive image of herself as a writer. By contrast, she resented the "realistic" suggestion of her former sister-in-law, Thorberg Haberman, that she seek financial help from Chatto's upper-class relatives so that she could return to New York and open a Hindu restaurant. On January 19, after noting that she had recently sold articles to *Deutsche Allgemeine Zeitung*, one of Berlin's largest newspapers, Smedley wrote to Florence: "As for starting a Hindu restaurant (!), I'd about as soon start a Thompson's lunch room! If I return, I go as a reporter or writer on the *New York World*, on which I am practically assured a good position. That prospect draws me continually. . . . I love Thor, and I'd do anything for her—but start a restaurant. I can't cook, and I hate it; I can't buy; I can't add two and two together, so as a bookkeeper I am out of the question. I have but one work: writing. I'd rather starve and write than make a good living in a restaurant." She went on to imply that she was successfully working through her writer's block:

> I realize that I speak better than I write. Why, I don't know. I hope analysis will free my mind from my idea (of very early origin) that anything in books represents the god-like, and that [anything] in myself represents the vile. I need time, is all. When I have a good day I feel equal to anything. . . . As my doctor says, I am more or less dominating and masculine in mind and character. [She] says I have forced my way through three generations of culture in 31 years, and in the process I have hidden, repressed, and suppressed every tendency which seemed to belong to a . . . lower characteristic of human nature. Even with her I fight for days and days before I will admit a fact which has always seemed base to me. Even she seems mechanical in her interpretations at times. I admit the love of my father—it was an early recognition and I didn't oppose it at all—and I admit a dislike of my mother. All such things I admit freely and without conflict. They are simple things compared to spiritual cravings.
>
> Nor do I agree with you that my castration complex [means simply] that "I have wanted a penis and have made Chatto suffer because he had it and I did not." The psyche is not so simple, as you must know, Florence. It has not been a "want of penis," it has been the impression that I have been left a half-person, and I have tried to make up [for that] in other ways.

In the same letter, she said that Dr. Naef's willingness to fend off Chatto was proving crucial to her recovery. For example, when Emma Goldman obtained an invitation for her to lecture on Gandhi's ideas in February before the English Department at the University of Berlin, Chatto opposed the idea, but Dr. Naef ran interference for her: "My doctor called Chatto the past week and talked with him for an hour or two. She has asked him to restrain himself from opposing me in every wish which does not come from himself. For instance, he called me an idiot for wanting to speak at the University—not because it was the University, but because my subject was India. He can't endure *anything* which doesn't come from himself. He crushes me. She has told him 'hands off' if he wishes me to recover at all." The result was salutary. She wrote Florence on February 16:

> Nothing more was said until yesterday before my lecture, when [Chatto] asked me if I had any objection if he came to hear me. I permitted it and even he, who is a hostile critic of such things, said I did well. . . .

My doctor was a wonderful person about it all. Had it not been for her urging me to accept the invitation [and] her help in analyzing my emotions about an audience, I could never have pulled through. It was a very strange thing for me to stand on a high platform and see a thousand [educated] people looking to me to tell them something they didn't know—and to be able to look each one of them in the eye without the shrinking I have always felt.

I worked night and day both on my lecture and on myself. It meant a great deal to me, since it was my emergence from my long years of illness, it was the first time I had ever appeared as a lecturer before a University audience, and the subject I had was such a broad one.

February was also a good month financially. Although still dependent on her parents for money, Florence promised Smedley $25 a month for analysis as long as she needed it. Smedley herself felt self-confident enough to take a job with an Indian commercial magazine, and with Germany's currency now stabilizing, she gained a taste of financial security. More important in her mind, she continued to sell articles on India to all kinds of newspapers and journals—Irish, French, Indian, German, and American.

By early March, however, the strains of analysis and the tensions of living with Chatto were becoming intolerable. And when their landlady completely incapacitated herself with a drug overdose, Smedley's patience snapped. She left Chatto and moved into a maid's quarters in a friend's house—a small room with one bed and one chair. Chatto followed her there and quickly collapsed, from exhaustion and an illness for which the doctor prescribed morphine injections. For the next two weeks, Smedley became a day-and-night nurse to the man from whom she had been running away. Chatto begged Smedley to remain with him and promised his full support, and at the end of the month they found new quarters together.

In the spring of 1924, Smedley worked with Dr. Naef to discover how her attitudes toward women and sex had been formed. In two remarkable letters to Florence Lennon, she described the insight she had gained from this effort. On April 1 she wrote:

When I was a girl, the West was still young, and the law of force, of physical force, was dominant. Women were desired, of course, but the rough-and-ready woman made her place, and often the women of the West, the mothers of large families, etc., were big, strong, dominant women. A woman who was not that was scorned, because the West had no use for "ladies." And the woman who could win the respect of man was often the woman who could knock him down with her bare fists and sit on him until he yelled for help. At least this was so in my class, which was the working class. Of course my mother, being frail, quiet, and gentle, died at the age of 38, of no particular disease, but from great weariness, loneliness of spirit, and unendurable suffering and hunger. She wasn't big enough to hammer my father when he didn't bring home the wages, and so we starved, and she starved the most of all so that we children might have a little food. And my father, a man of tremendous imagination—a Peer Gynt—lived in a world of dreams; the minute he had a little money, he went on a huge carouse in which reality played no part, in which he dreamed of himself as a great hero achieving the impossible, etc.

Now, being a girl, I was ashamed of my body and my lack of strength. So I tried to be a man. I shot, rode, jumped, and took part in all the fights of the boys. I didn't like it, [but] it was the proper thing to do. So I forced myself into it, I scorned all weak womanly things. Like all my family and class, I considered it a sign of weakness to show affection; to have been caught kissing my mother would have been a disgrace, [and] to have shown affection for my father would have been a disaster. So I remember having kissed my mother only when she went on a visit to another town to see a relative; and I kissed my father but twice—once when he was drunk, because I read in a book that once a girl kissed her drunken father and reformed him and he never drank again!

Another thing which forced me into a masterful attitude toward life was my ugliness. My hair was thin and all the other girls had long hair and took great pains with it. Because hair, of course, is a sex allurement. My grandmother—a huge, black-eyed woman who whipped her grown sons if they didn't obey her—used to laugh at my thin hair and compare me with her daughter who had lovely hair. Her laughter wounded me from the time I was a child. So as a child, and as a girl, and later as a young woman, I was never attractive to the boys. I looked like a scarecrow in dainty dresses, and laces [only] accentuated my yellow complexion and my awkwardness. So, of course, I copied my father in living in a world of imagination in which I *was* attractive. And, of course, I tried to compensate for my physical unattractiveness by developing my brains, imitating my father. . . . Of course, I was useful to my father when he had accounts to make up, and this brought me into contact with more and more men who worked with or for my father. And I was treated by them almost as a boy, and they had respect for me because I was "smart"—that is, I knew a lot. And I thus got huge influence over my father, and my mother used to deal with my father through me; if she wanted anything done, she asked me to have my father do it. Of course, father didn't always do it, because what she wanted done wasn't romantic enough; she only wanted bedsheets, a new bed, a new table, etc., while he dwelt in more romantic heights. And so instead of buying the things she needed, he got drunk and imagined he had a palace filled with the riches of the earth. And I admired my father in my heart, because I believed his stories, and I had contempt for my mother! But outwardly I acted as if I loved my mother and didn't care much for my father.

With such conflicts most people have to [deal], of course. But you can perhaps not know the long years of uncertainty, of indefinite struggle, which marked my life until I was twenty years of age. I hungered after something, but *what,* I didn't know. It forced me to oppose all things, to fight for many things. Nothing gave me happiness, nothing gave me peace. . . .

One more thing before I close: My attitude toward sex was primitive. [Before marriage] I had often been tortured by a vague dissatisfaction, physically, but when men had approached me in a sexual manner, as many had done in my wanderings, my terror of the sex act, my ignorance regarding it, forced me into an attitude of horror of everything concerned with sex relations. And even after I was married, I had relations with my husband only after we had been married eight months. I considered the sex act a horrible, degrading act, particularly degrading for the woman. My attitude toward this question was responsible for the destruction of my first marriage. I was so ashamed of myself because I was called "Mrs." that I could hardly look people in the face, and this secret shame forced me into a sick attitude toward my husband, [so] that he could never broach the subject to me. When I was divorced—divorce is very easy in the West—I felt clean once more; I felt like a bird with wings, I felt very very friendly to my husband, and felt that I could take him by the hand and run and dance with him from pure joy and friendship. For the first time I regarded him as my friend and my relationship to him as a clean one.

You must also realize that in America, children are taught that the sex act, or anything connected with sex, is a shameful, disgraceful thing, and every time the subject is broached a wave of horror or silence spreads over an audience. It is a shameful subject! The word "sex" itself is enough to throw "proper" people into a fit of stony silence, and the person who mentions it is an outcast for the rest of the evening. Now imagine what it means for a child, when her whole attitude toward life is formed in this period, to have the foundation laid in this manner. Then imagine a young woman with this attitude, suddenly married. Two minutes before, she is supposed to think that the sex act is a degrading, debasing, shameful act; then she is married with a few words; and society tells her that now she may have sex relations every hour of the day if she wishes. Of course, an attitude formulated during the early years of her life cannot be changed in two minutes by the words of an official or a priest. There is a terrible conflict over this question; it is enough to disrupt the life of a nation. It develops hypocrisy at the *best.* I believe it finds outlets in a thousand other ways, terrible outlets. If the woman is sensitive, she becomes psychologically if not physically ill. An honest woman brought up in such a manner has no choice before her but to remain an ascetic all her life—or if she departs from the ways of asceticism, to be broken in health. I often wonder if this national attitude of prudery in America does not find outlet in the lynchings of Negroes, the racial hatred, etc. I don't know.

In her other letter to Florence, dated two days earlier, Smedley wondered how she could ever come to terms with the kinds of deprivation and suffering she had known as a child:

Let me tell you, I long for my own kind very often. Next year if you do not come here I am returning for a visit to America. And I hope to have money enough to go to New Mexico to see my father before he dies. I think one has the right to look upon one's creator once before he dies. The only thing which holds me back is the emotional strain upon me. I shall not only see my own father, but I shall see a poverty which I cannot improve. The memories of my childhood will perhaps be understandable by the time I return, but they will be dark ones, nevertheless. I often wonder what course to take. I have left a world of misery, a world of poverty, of prostitution, of ignorance, of dirt. Shall I go back and look upon it once more without being able to help? And then once more go away, with the wounds reopened, with the pain sharper than ever? I cannot forget, and yet I cannot rationalize such things, which were the earth in which I grew.

Continuing in this vein, she compared her own efforts with those of women friends in Germany—social reformers, writers, and artists, many of them rich or famous:

Karin Michaelis [the Danish novelist] has written [to ask] me to meet her tomorrow, with Emma Goldman, and to go with her to see a kitchen for poor artists opened by an Austrian woman physician friend of hers. . . . And I am invited by the Austrian physician to come to her home in Austria for the summer. And I repeatedly wonder, "Shall I go on in this life meeting and knowing people who are doing things in the world of thought, looking upon kitchens which they [set up] for poor artists, and ignore the vast sea [of people who] live always in poverty and hunger, the sea from which I came? . . .

My nice new house [with Chatto] is a mockery for it seems empty of something, and I think that something is achievement. I feel that I should live in a house which corresponds to my mind and my achievements. And it would be then one little bedroom, with no pictures on the wall and with only one bed, one chair, one place for my clothing. And my clothing just two things—a change while the other things are being washed. Then I should feel in harmony with life. Now I do not.

On March 17, Smedley wrote to Florence that her fragile state of mind had led Dr. Naef to suggest that the two of them take a three-week summer vacation together, so that the analysis could continue without interruption.

In April, Dr. Naef left Berlin to attend the International Psychoanalytic Congress in Austria. The day before she left, Smedley had another attack. She told Florence in April: "[The attack] prostrated me completely for four hours. Since then I've been ill and she's been away. I don't know what to do, Florence. I need analysis for my very life. . . . I have come to look old and ugly, and have no desire to improve my appearance in any way. I have interest in *no* thing and I become actually physically and mentally ill at the least occurrence. . . . Always I remember your phrase that a person who hasn't the *illusion* that life is worthwhile is being cheated. I wait and hope that analysis will give me that illusion back."

Florence had spoken of coming to visit Smedley in the summer, but now she said she would not be able to come until February of the next year. (Her parents disapproved of her relationship with Smedley and insisted that she graduate from college before traveling to Europe.)

By May, Smedley again felt overwhelmed by the burdens of everyday life and petty debt. In search of a loan, she turned first to Karin Michaelis. Michaelis declined, saying that her young husband was spending all her extra money, but suggested a famous Austrian woman physician who might be able to help. Smedley contacted this woman, but found no help: she refused to grant a loan, told Smedley that analysis was worthless, and advised her to go back to the United States. In response to this setback, Smedley began to reveal the extent of her emotional problems to friends in New York other than Florence Lennon and Josephine Bennett. She wrote first, on May 9, to Margaret Sanger: "You also have lived through such a life as mine. And I believe you have known the meaning of petty debt. I have at last written you because I know your life in the past has drawn you into contact with women of means who were able to help you when you passed through deep water. . . . I know that such people know your work to have been of greater social significance than mine in the immediate present, yet I approach you." Sanger responded by promising to pay Smedley's analyst $50 a month for a year, while at the same time urging her to return to the United States.*

This renewed contact drew Smedley back into birth control work. In June she sent Sanger a detailed set of instructions on how best to introduce birth control information in India, along with a list of Indian doctors who might be willing to help. She enclosed a letter of introduction to Chatto's sister, Sarojini Naidu, the most prominent woman politician in preindependence India. But from bitter personal experience, she also offered this advice:

> It is better not to stress the woman's freedom viewpoint until you have a foothold. India is more reactionary than you think. But from the national and racial betterment viewpoint, and from child hygiene viewpoints, you can make headway. Even the elevation of the working class plays no great part in India now.
>
> You should mention also the [birth control] centers in Japan and China,

---

* During the fall of 1924, Smedley received another loan of $1,000 for six months through Robert Morss Lovett, who appealed to the Garland Fund in New York on her behalf. See Smedley letters to Sanger for 1924.

and the reception given [to them] by the Japanese government. Bear in mind that India tries to emulate Japan—the one independent spot in Asia. We can't very well stress "Western" viewpoints regarding social subjects, but we can go hard on what Asia is already doing.

In India everything depends on the personality of the person who presents this subject.

Despite frequent complaints that her analysis was "moving at a snail's pace" and that her writing output was low, Smedley's letters over the spring and summer of 1924 suggest a period of real growth and development on many fronts.

In May she spoke of reading Rebecca West's *The Judge* and Somerset Maugham's *Of Human Bondage* and *One Little Boy,* sent to her by Florence, and Evelyn Scott's *Escapade,* given to her by Emma Goldman. Inspired by these works, she told Lennon on May 23: "Someday when I am out of purgatory, financially and mentally, I'm going to write something creative. Now I can write only things that sell at once, from day to day. My doctor is constantly astonished at my energy and the way in which, in one or two days, I come from the depths of melancholy to a level on which I write for hours."

In June, after a brief reunion with Lajpat Rai, who was on his way back to India after petitioning the British Parliament for an increase in pace in setting up Indian self-rule, Smedley wrote her most successful article of the summer, "Akali Movement," published in the *Nation* in July. It described another massacre by British soldiers in the Punjab, in which the victims were members of the Akali, a Sikh reform sect that had been protesting British attempts to seize its lands. In an August letter, Sanger praised the article and remarked on the improvement in Smedley's writing style.

Driven by the desire for more education, Smedley still planned to enter the university, and by June she had maneuvered indirectly toward that goal, strengthening her position by developing a personal connection with a professor of English at the University of Berlin. On the seventeenth she wrote to Lennon:

A damned German Prof from Berlin University is on my trail. He thinks I'm a Miss and I am! He is arranging for [me to give] a course of English lessons in Berlin University. So he, as a true German, invites me to lunch with him *every Tuesday at 1:30!* We talk literature and I try to prevent myself from saying, "As my husband was saying yesterday . . . ." The Prof is a bore, such a bore I can't even hate him. Today is Tuesday and I telephoned him [to say] I was spending a week in Potsdam! My life has become such a burden with a suitor who is a bore—such a bore as I have never seen in my life. And I know some day at 2:45 he'll take out his handkerchief, spread it on the floor, kneel on it in the proper attitude and ask me to *accept his hand!* Oh I know I'll yawn and tell him I'll let him know next week at 2:45. He's the sort of man who writes a Doctor's thesis on why a period was in a certain place in a Greek manuscript and then after he has his degree [he'll find] the period to be a fly-spec. He's a philologist who traces the evolution of "a" into "o." It all is a reflection upon me. I'm 32 and drab and unbeautiful. The only sign of life left in me is my swearing and cursing.

But by August 25, she told Lennon, quite emphatically, that because Chatto also had problems with his attitudes toward sex, she had struck a bargain with him—they could remain together only if he started analysis:

Chatto enters the analysis on the first of September and is being taken free of charge by the most important analyst in Germany [Max Eitingon, founder of the Berlin Psychoanalytic Institute]—all because he is such a wreck and is a Hindu, whom they wish to study. It will be very hard for him, for he is 43 and his habits are bands of iron. Yet I could never live with him unless he were analyzed. He is almost ruined. And he ruins me daily because of his pressure upon me. It is a great relief to know he is going into analysis.

Am I married, you ask. Yes, to my sorrow, and I'll be for another six months at least; I'll wait for Chatto to lose his baby dependence on me through the analysis before I do anything else. If you mean sexual marriage, I may say I'm seldom married! I'm sick of being bound. I want a vacation. Do you remember Ibsen's *Lady from the Sea?* Well, that's me, with the exception that I'm partly the Lady and partly Peer Gynt. And the Lady's psychology is mine. I want to go because someone tries to hold me.

In a dramatic reversal of her mood earlier that summer, Smedley no longer described herself as old and ugly and unattractive to men:

You say you repel men and are beginning to despair of the possibilities of a love-life. Ayah, my dearest, I wish I could go halves with you in my own sex nature—any pair of pants going, from the garbage man up, stops and tries his chances with me, or wishes he could. I feel his wishes although he doesn't say anything. The so-called "soul" has a language of its own! But like you, I'm polygamous! And polygamous women aren't popular as wives. I don't live polygamously, but I can't help my emotions. It's pretty hard to have said all through my life that I don't give a damn for sex and then to learn that I'm polygamous. My only desire, however, is to take my polygamy out in writing instead of in bed (pardon the vulgarity).

In this letter Smedley, who had once called herself Mrs. Agnes Smedley-Brundin, criticized a mutual friend for adding her husband's name to her own.

If Smedley had hidden from Chatto some of her friendships and meetings with men, such as those with the German professor, there was one relationship that she did reveal to him, and for which she "made him pay." After learning that Florence had fallen in love over the summer, Smedley wrote on October 28:

> Yet I must betray myself to you; and you and my doctor are the only souls on the earth to whom I can speak. In my misery with my husband because of his jealousy even of my private thoughts (and of my doctor, and of you), I suppose it was but natural that my suppressed feelings should search the landscape for a victim and find one. Said victim is a young man eight years younger than myself who has the pain not only of worshipping me but of being a very close friend of my husband's, bound to him by ties of friendship and idealism. Think of loving your friend's wife—saying so to him and the wife! And think of the wife saying: "I love you also, tenderly as I would a child in my arms, and yet savagely as a wild person protecting its young. My love doesn't require a sex relationship, yet it is a deep and tender love."
>
> Now think of the husband in the case: dark, passionate, and intense in every act of his life, moved by an overmastering love for his wife. Think of the pain of the man and his attempts to control himself; of his inability to do so, and of his weeks and months of useless talks with his wife. And of more tragic things: the young man leaving the country, calmly and clearly, holding the wife in his arms and kissing her as he leaves, and taking the attitude "This is an affair only between us two." And then writing letters in the same strain, just as if the husband does not exist in [that] relationship. . . .
>
> I'm an indecent woman! Do you remember Candida and her love for a younger man; or Galsworthy's "The Dark Flower"—the first part? Strauss's opera [Rosenkavalier] is playing here. It deals with the same subject—the love of an older woman for a younger man. Like all women in such a case, I have been eaten by shame, guilt, remorse, untold misery, and it took me months to face the truth. But the most difficult of all parts has been that of my husband's. I suppose I'll "sublimate" my love for the young man. In my analysis I have traced my feeling for him to the feeling I had for my dearest brother, who was much younger than myself and to whom I was practically a mother. The feeling is almost identical.
>
> So you see, I'm not a respectable married woman. The walls of marriage will never hold my love, my desires. May God pity all men who love me, especially my husband, who expects marriage to bind my love hand and foot! A vagabond in life, so in emotion, I remain!
>
> Florence, dear, men will love you through all eternity if you beat them! Do you remember Chekov's story of the little Russian man who had two wives: the first one—gentle, tender, loving, self-sacrificing—he practically beat to death. She loved him; he had no use for her. After she died he married a woman who beat him daily—hammering hell out of him. She was accidentally killed, I believe, but for the rest of his life that man mourned for her, kept her grave covered with flowers and often sat by her grave in tears—and the other wife's grave nearby was absolutely forgotten! I have always inspired the most remarkable love in men—big and little, thin and thick; and it has

been because I have scorned them or turned on them a face filled with dislike or active anger! Note my present husband! It is sad, for he is a creative soul, and should not be subjected to me. He will change, I believe, for he is to start analysis with Dr. Eitingon, perhaps the most noted analyst in Germany. It is the only hope for him. But it may lead to our final separation.

Over the summer, as friends urged her to return to America, Smedley had continued to struggle with her contradictory feelings about Chatto. With no passport and the certainty of British opposition, Chatto could not possibly go with her to America, and neither of them would be allowed in India. She was still reluctant to give up what she considered to be Chatto's genuine love and concern for her. On April 19 she had written to Michaelis: "Life is a very short experience at best and to lose love, or to deliberately give up a great love, is very difficult. There are many other men I could live with, but my knowledge of men tells me that I would suffer a worse fate at the hands of most of them than I suffer now. And, let me tell you, Karin, dear friend, I do not intend to live without men!"

Chatto began analysis in November of 1924, about the time Smedley began teaching an English-language conversation and debating course at the University of Berlin. On December 10, Smedley wrote a letter to Margaret Sanger, then on a speaking tour of England, in which she introduced her young Indian lover, an Oxford student by the name of Bakar Ali Mirza, to Sanger as "my son." By January of 1925, Smedley and Chatto had agreed to a six-month separation. Smedley moved in with an old American friend, Mrs. A. Marshall Bullitt Grabisch, diplomat William C. Bullitt's sister, who was collaborating with another American, Mary Kellerman, in setting up a European literary agency to sell English translations of European literary works in the United States.*

In a letter written on January 16, 1925, Smedley seemed to support Lennon's recently announced marriage plans, but she offered this caveat: "I'm not a friend, you know, of the 'marriage' relationship on a permanent basis." A month or two later she asked Florence to find her a literary agent in the United States, complaining that "almost all I write these days is returned to me. . . . I'm taking more and more to teaching to

---

* William C. Bullitt was a member of the American Peace Treaty Commission under President Wilson and head of the American delegation that produced the Bullitt Report, which recommended recognition of the new government in Russia. William Bullitt himself would soon marry an old acquaintance of Smedley's from New York, Louise Bryant. Bryant's first husband, John Reed, had died in 1920 in Moscow, where they were covering the Russian Revolution. In Smedley to Michaelis, June 27, 1925, Smedley introduced Mrs. Grabisch as William Bullitt's sister.

make a living." Perhaps by this time Smedley had saturated the market for articles on India.

Smedley began to put more energy and research time into academic writing. Her long article "India in World Politics" was published in Germany's most prestigious political journal, *Zeitschrift für Geopolitik*, in June of 1925.

In the spring, although her personal predicament was rather more abstract, since young Bakar Ali Mirza had been out of the country for months, Smedley had a series of exchanges with Emma Goldman and Karin Michaelis about the heartaches suffered by a woman who falls in love with a younger man. To complicate matters, Smedley could not tolerate Karin Michaelis's young husband. She believed that he was a homosexual who had married Michaelis only to acquire a "financial base." She did not "speak plainly" to Michaelis about her suspicion, but her hostility toward the husband grew to such a point that in July she again declined Karin's invitation to visit them in Denmark—a hard refusal to make, because she was desperate to get away from Berlin and Chatto.

For his part, Chatto pleaded daily with Smedley to stay "married" to him. He argued that he was too old to start over again, and that it would be irresponsible of her to desert him now after ruining him both politically and emotionally. But as Smedley had told Karin on February 2, "I will die for his ideas and his country; but I won't be his wife."

By the summer of 1925, Smedley felt that her analysis had come to a dead end; she wrote Florence that she "couldn't talk" to Dr. Naef anymore. On July 20 she stopped analysis. After asking Sanger for help in finding a job in the United States, she fled Berlin and Chatto for Czechoslovakia, in the company of a student-actress friend. Just before leaving (probably in July), she wrote to Emma Goldman:

> Chatto will be better eventually. He is now in Saxony. He is in [Berlin] a few days during the week only and the rest of the time is collecting advertisements for his magazine in order to make money. He is under treatment only twice a week, and that is too little. He is looking very tired and old. My heart is filled with pity. I could erase that look and give him back much strength, if I would return and live with him, or even tell him that I intend to do so. But I cannot. Often I think that he is of far more value than I am; everybody knows that—all of you anarchists and revolutionaries, all of the Indians, everybody who knows us both. But I cannot force myself back. . . . I know that if I return to him, I shall kill myself within a month. And I often wonder if I shall not do it eventually anyway, even if I do not return. . . .
>
> During the summer I shall be in Denmark and Czechoslovakia and I hope

that in this manner the chains will be broken, for he will know that I am in Europe, and yet he will be separate from me and will be forced to find new friends and associates . . . and I hope other women.[4]

Chatto's reaction to her flight was pathetic. He asked her young Indian lover, Bakar, to go to Czechoslovakia and plead with her to return to him. Bakar did as he was asked, but to no avail. In order to put off further confrontations with Chatto, Smedley begged Karin Michaelis for another invitation and the money to join her in Denmark in late August. From the small island of Thurö in Denmark, Smedley wrote to Sanger on September 5:

> Here I am in Denmark, living a very primitive existence on a little island with my friend Karin Michaelis, the Danish woman writer of whom you perhaps know. I came two weeks ago and I am still hoping that I shall feel better soon, for I was much run down in health and very nervous. But it is so cold here—and there is always a high wind from the sea—that it takes a long time to get accustomed to it. . . . Karin wants me to stay here until December 1 and write my first book during that time. I think I will stay here if I can get my visa prolonged, for I don't want to be in the same city with Chatto for a few months more. . . . Yet I know that it is impossible for me to write a book inside three months. I can at best outline it and make the first draft. Karin offers to help in the plan. It will be based upon my life and I plan to make it a document that will be direct and true—and which will lose me most of my friends because they will be ashamed to be a friend of mine after that. I won't lose you and Karin and a few other such, but most I shall lose. I am brought to writing the book in the baldest manner possible because my health is never a thing I can depend on, and my mind is so destroyed that I never know what I am capable of. I am so utterly unhappy all the time that I don't care much for life and I think if I write a book I may either feel better afterwards, or it will be finished anyway and I will have done what I could in this damned experience called life. It will be about all I have to give.

But on November 12, Smedley announced to Florence:

> Here . . . guess . . . what. I have written a book based upon my life. I have done the first draft.
>
> The name of my book is *The Outcast* or *An Outcast*. I don't know yet.
>
> You are in my book—do you know that? And your name is Florence there. But nothing else.
>
> Karin says my book is excellent. We shall see. Note the enclosed chapter and let me know what you think. And try for the love of mercy to sell the damned thing, for I shall live in a garret and cook over a spiritus lamp until I sell a few articles and until I finish typing my book and post it to the publisher.
>
> I am almost certain of the success of my book. . . . Karin says it will go marvellously. Alexander Berkman is here as a guest and he says it will be ac-

cepted at once by a publisher. Then maybe I'll be rich! Oh God, for a place to hang my head [*sic*] at last.

Thus Smedley's first book, eventually called *Daughter of Earth,* was born on a windswept Danish island, with the Danish novelist Karin Michaelis and the exiled Russian-born anarchist Alexander Berkman acting as midwives. Her original title, *An Outcast,* is revealing. Over the past four years, her letters had combined expressions of isolation and distrust, and deep feelings of worthlessness and intellectual inferiority, with powerful bursts of willfulness and defiance. Her unsophisticated language often gave her writing—like her speech—a melodramatic or comic-opera quality. And because she often appeared to distrust and manipulate her friends, Lennon and Goldman, Michaelis and Sanger, Chatto and Bakar, who offered her love and support, they sometimes found it hard to appreciate the depths of her loneliness. As Emma Goldman had written to Alexander Berkman on May 28:

> I know the agony of loneliness and yearning. I therefore agree fully with you that both men and women need some person who really cares. The woman needs it more and finds it impossible to meet anyone when she has reached a certain age. That is her tragedy.
>
> However, I do not see how this applies to the condition of Agnes. In the first place, she has a number of men who care violently about her—Chatto, Mirza (Bakar), and others. She has outgrown Chatto, but she seems to be very much in love with the other. I don't know what it is; she certainly is a nervous wreck. And I myself am too miserable most of the time to be of any comfort to others. Still, I will have to write her soon.[5]

CHAPTER VII

Smedley as Eliza Doolittle, 1925–1927

Smedley returned to Berlin in December of 1925, full of unrealistic expectations: she would quickly polish the first draft of *Daughter of Earth,* find German and American publishers for it, and begin to experience financial independence at last. But almost immediately she found herself preoccupied with the practical problems of earning a living. To support herself, she resumed teaching English, not only at the University of Berlin, but also privately. And one of her private students, Tilla Durieux, quickly assumed a major role in her life.

Ottilie Godeffroy, the daughter of a Viennese chemistry professor, began her theater career as "Tilla Durieux" in 1901. Two years later, as the discovery of the Berlin director Max Reinhardt, she rose to stardom with her portrayal of the heroine in Oscar Wilde's *Salome.* She became famous for her roles as Hebbel's Judith and Ibsen's Hedda Gabler and is credited with introducing George Bernard Shaw's plays to Germany. In 1913 she played Eliza Doolittle in the first Berlin presentation of Shaw's *Pygmalion.* By the time she met Smedley, she was one of Europe's leading actresses and an influential patron of the arts. (Pierre-Auguste Renoir's 1914 portrait of Tilla Durieux in her Eliza costume now hangs in the Metropolitan Museum of Art in New York.)[1] Furthermore, she had been married to Paul Cassirer, one of the leading promoters of innovation in the Berlin art world and a member of a family of famous intellectuals.*

---

*The Cassirers, a Jewish family originally from Breslau, made their fortunes in the mid-nineteenth century in the timber trade, engineering, and the manufacture of copper

Paul had always been in poor health. By the early 1920s, medication could no longer prevent frequent episodes of severe pain, and in the late fall of 1925 he was told that he had only a few months to live. When Tilla, unable to bear his prolonged illness, divorced him, he committed suicide.[2] In guilt and sorrow, Tilla withdrew from her friends until one of them (probably the artist Käthe Kollwitz, Smedley's friend and a member of the Berlin Secessionist group) encouraged her to get her mind off mourning by taking English lessons from a complete stranger. The stranger was Agnes Smedley.

In her memoirs, Durieux described her first encounter with Agnes:

> One day a young woman came. She wore a simple dress, had wild blondish hair and a pair of enormous blue-grey eyes. She was very hostile. She gave the name of an acquaintance and said sullenly that she could give a few lessons. My knowledge of English was not very good, and I have no talent for languages. But as I talked with her, I was increasingly struck by her hostile attitude. Her very simple dress showed me that she needed to give lessons for the money and came for no other reason. So I was in no way intimidated by her. We set the time and conditions. Just the effort to try and win over this stubborn, unfriendly person had a good effect on me. She was Agnes Smedley, who later became one of the most important journalists in China.[3]

Within weeks a patron-protégé relationship developed, and before long Durieux had cast Smedley as Eliza Doolittle opposite her Professor Higgins in a real-life drama.

It was Tilla Durieux who persuaded an editor at the *Frankfurter Zeitung* to read Smedley's book manuscript. By early spring of 1926 Smedley had sent six chapters but was having trouble finishing the last section of the book, which dealt with her involvement with the Indian nationalists. Knowing Smedley needed uninterrupted time to write, Durieux offered her the chance to stay with her for two months in Salzburg and Munich. Durieux also promised to give her a personalized course in literature, theater, music, architecture, and the arts. Because Durieux had never discussed her relationship with Cassirer, Smedley was fascinated by Durieux's offer but wary about her motives. With

---

and steel cables. Before World War I, Paul and his cousin Bruno had become important figures in the art world as gallery owners, with Paul exerting influence as an esthetic theorist as well. Another cousin, Ernst, became a noted philosopher and historian. As Jews in the Weimar Germany of the 1920s, the highly visible Cassirers had often drawn criticism in the past for their daring and innovative exhibitions of painters like Manet, Monet, and Renoir. And the group of modern artists known as the Berlin Secessionist Movement, sponsored chiefly by Paul Cassirer, was accused by National Socialists of being part of an international Jewish-Communist plot to undermine the values of the Fatherland. See Peter Paret, *The Berlin Secession: Modernism and its Enemies in Imperial Germany* (Cambridge, Mass., 1980).

mixed feelings, she finally decided to accept the offer for July and August of 1926.

For Smedley, who had spent the last five years living in shabby rooming houses in the company of impoverished students, penny-pinching landladies, and furtive revolutionary nationalists, it was a shock and a challenge to live in the most fashionable hotels in Europe, surrounded by cultural leaders and persons of vast wealth. She wrote to Florence from Austria:

> Here in this hotel I have seen things that have awakened many, many thoughts in me. There is an orchestra that plays the best there is in music, and in the evenings we sit there and read or smoke or meet interesting people—and we always talk. There are children who come with their parents and sit there. Lovely, clean, well-dressed, and well-fed children. . . . They will grow up the best and most cultured, and they will scorn the working class and say that the working class could have what it wanted if it only tried. Then I remember all the children we pass on the street; the only music they hear is the cheap trash they hear in the kino—for which they pay ten pfennigs. Cleanliness to them is a bath once a month or once a year. Conversation to them, and intelligence, is what Susie said to Mary about the new dress . . . Mary's mother bought for the baby. I see more and more that we human beings are products of our environment, to a very large extent. I do not speak of the occasional genius or selfish person who does otherwise. They do not count in the scheme of things unless they destroy the ugly things. Then I look about in the lobby and see slick, well-fed, rich men smoking their cigars and offering drinks and paying with a gesture that shows that money is nothing to them. And I think of them grasping and collecting the good things of life and holding them for themselves, and using their brains to justify their actions. I know they have big bank accounts somewhere—more money than they need for life. Yet they keep the money and continue to add to it, and I see that each [Deutschmark] means the sacrifice of a worker's baby somewhere. Then I hear them talk about "anarchy" and the "danger of Bolshevism and Communism." As I sit and listen I doubt their humanity at all—I really doubt if they have the attributes of human beings. . . . And I long for the day to come when the working class will be sufficiently conscious to shake the earth to pieces and drown these people in a flood of their own blood.
>
> I am glad I have come here. It has not corrupted me as I thought. It has only brought me face to face with the most terrible injustice that has ever existed—the inhumanity of man to man: His callousness before the dog-like existence of the masses. Madame Durieux I excuse. . . . She does not hide her face from the truth of the present social system—nor from the eternal truth that is beyond all social systems—the equality of all men before eternity and their equal rights in this life to all that is good. . . .
>
> Pardon if I judge you. I do not class you among the rich people of the world. I do not ask you to give up the little money you have to live on. You would not help society by doing it. But as I see it, your life, your very exis-

tence, is not worth anything at all if you live passively in the midst of injustice, and at the same time think only of protecting yourself and yours. You
are not better than others—and I am no better than others. If you live, or
bring others into existence, others who are protected from knowing what the
vast masses suffer, then think of protecting only them and yourself, you are a
selfish, utterly selfish person. . . .

   If I am always tortured by misery about me, you must know that is because I was born in misery and my roots are in misery. I shall be analysed
enough one day to not be hurt so much, but then I shall be all the better
revolutionary and I shall use my brain like a weapon. . . .

   You consider me neurotic that I feel misery so deeply. Then I wish to remain neurotic. If I thought my analysis would take me away from the class
struggle, then I would never be analyzed. If I thought love would blind my
eyes to it, would make me think that me and mine were the only things worth
while, or the chief things, then I would stop the analysis. The class struggle, I
say, and mean the international struggle with which India is so intimately
bound. It just happens that I have taken the Indian end to work with.

Durieux had challenged herself to change Smedley's defiant attitude,
but she was finding her to be a more reluctant Eliza Doolittle than
her ficticious Shaw counterpart. Instead of becoming more tolerant,
Smedley was alienated even further in Salzburg, so that for the first time
in a private letter Smedley used the term *class struggle* and made it clear
that she thought everyone had to choose sides. But her admiration for
Smedley's intelligence, thirst for knowledge, and commitment to helping
the poor convinced Durieux to continue to support Smedley's attempts
at self-improvement. In another letter to Florence Smedley wrote of a
new Durieux proposal:

   Madame Durieux has offered to give me an income until I take my doctor's
   degree from Berlin University. I have not made up my mind definitely yet.
   I want to do it . . . and I want the German method of research. . . . Never
   before have I been able to study for a month without working [to pay] my
   way through. This would give me the opportunity. The only thing that holds
   me back is the mental feeling of dependence. I dream of it and think of it with
   depression, and that may be worse for me than anything else. I must decide. . . . I do not like the idea so much as if I were working on my own
   money; but later I may make enough money from my book to drop her income and live from my own work.

A Bakar visit in late July provided Smedley with a week's reprieve from
life at the hotel. The two of them went off together to a small Gasthaus
in Linz on the banks of the Danube. Their meeting resolved nothing,
but they agreed that they would not see one another until the coming
December, after they both had another six months of analysis. Smedley

wrote to Florence that she still dominated Bakar too much, but she re-asserted her commitment to work for Indian independence.

By the time she left Salzburg, Smedley had sent off a completed manu-script to Durieux's editor friend at the *Frankfurter Zeitung*. Smedley's lawyer in New York, Gilbert Roe, was also sent a copy, with the request that he help her find a publisher.

On the way back to Berlin, Durieux and Smedley visited Munich, where Smedley took the opportunity to go into the Bavarian hills to see Professor Karl Haushofer, the founder of the Institut für Geopolitik.* He had been responsible for publishing, in June of 1925, a paper by Smedley in the prestigious academic journal *Zeitschrift für Geopolitik*. The article, on India's place in world politics, included the prefatory statement that the nation that ruled India would be the master of Eu-rope. During Smedley's visit Haushofer agreed to sponsor her entrance into the University of Berlin for one year, after which it was expected that she would come to his Institut to finish her degree under him per-sonally. Haushofer clearly saw her as a valuable tool for keeping in touch with the Indian nationalists.

After returning to Berlin, Smedley was disappointed to learn that the *Frankfurter Zeitung* wanted major revisions on her manuscript. She found herself in an awkward personal situation as she waited for Durieux to work out the details of a financial stipend. Durieux herself was extremely busy preparing for the opening of Frank Wedekind's play *Franciska*. Of even greater significance was the launching of another major theater project. In the fall of 1926 Durieux persuaded her future husband, Ludwig Katzenellenbogen, to put up 400,000 marks as a guarantee on a complete first season for a new theater group to be headed by the left-wing director Erwin Piscator. Durieux had been deeply impressed by Piscator's *Robbers* and was excited by the possibil-ities of a new experimental theater with intellectual and political bite.**

---

* Haushofer had been a German general in World War I and a military observer in Japan before that. It seems likely that Smedley had met Haushofer in Berlin a year earlier, before the publication of her research paper; see *Battle Hymn*, p. 20. Unbeknown to Smedley, Haushofer was concealing at his institute in 1926 the General Staff of German Imperialism. It was he and his General Staff who were furnishing Hitler at the time with such demagogic ideas as *Blut und Broden*.

** It was in 1926 that politics "invaded" the German theater. Bertholt Brecht, Erich Engel, Leopold Jessner, and Piscator were all attempting topical modernizations of the classics. Sergey Eisenstein's film *The Battleship Potemkin* had been released, after much debate, to great critical acclaim. Maxim Gorky was due in Berlin for the November 10 opening of his *Lower Depths* with Piscator as director. That summer Piscator, Engel, Ernst Toller, Wilhelm Herzog, and Otto Katz had discussed the possibility of founding an

Considering Durieux's growing commitment to leftist political theater, it seemed that Eliza was having as much influence on Higgins as vice versa, and perhaps more.

Without funds, waiting for Durieux's promised stipend, Smedley resumed private English teaching, borrowed money to pay her rent, and wrote feature articles on the summer's cultural scene in Salzburg. Consuming most of her energy, however, was a series of articles crusading against a traveling human freak show brought to Europe from India that was being exhibited at the Berlin Zoo. Finally October came, classes started at the university, and Smedley received her stipend. Now that her play had opened, Durieux once again had time for Agnes: she decided to introduce her to Berlin society at an opening-night theater party. But Smedley's debut in high society was not as successful as Eliza Doolittle's well-rehearsed performance at the ball. The extent to which Smedley refused to play a role is suggested in a letter she wrote to Florence on November 5, 1926:

> Frau Durieux has had her premiere in *Franciska*, Wedekind's play. It was good. Afterward [at Durieux's] home, I talked with an English gentleman whom I did not know, and this was the conversation:
>
> ME: Are you an American?
>
> HE: No, I am English. Are you?
>
> ME: No. I'm American. How did you like the play?
>
> HE: I don't like it. It grates on my English nature. A girl appearing naked on the stage was too much for me.
>
> ME: Oh, that! Well, that didn't bother me. It was so natural.
>
> HE: I don't like all these things in Germany.
>
> ME: Well, I think Wedekind wasn't exactly a normal man.
>
> HE: No, he suffered that . . . that . . . that . . . difficulty of Carlyle.
>
> ME: Oh. You mean he was impotent?
>
> HE: Well, yes, if you wish to call it that in so many words. But then that is the reason he gives such emphasis to all such things as this . . . well, as that problem or so-called problem we saw tonight.

---

epic theater to develop their innovative ideas, both technical and political. By the following year, all but Engel were on Piscator's payroll. Engel would team up with Brecht and Casper Neher to produce *Man ist Man* and *The Threepenny Opera* in 1928. But it was the funds provided by the intervention of Durieux and her wealthy fianceé that turned Piscator's dreams into a reality. Katzenellenbogen's only condition was that the name of the group should not include the adjective "proletarian-revolutionary." He also expected that Durieux would be offered a part in the production. See Erwin Piscator, *The Political Theatre: A History, 1914–1929* (trans. Hugh Rorrison, New York, 1978), especially pp. 175–76; also John Willet, *The Theatre of Erwin Piscator* (London, 1978), p. 67.

ME: You mean the sex problem?

HE: Well, yes if you wish to call it that in so many words.

ME: You think sex is no problem?

HE: No, it's not. Its just a lot of freaks who say it is.

ME: And do you think that marriage is no problem?

HE: No, it's not either. Things have always been like this and they will always be like this. There has never been any progress and there never will be any and we may as well make up our minds to it and stop complaining. Such things as we see these days on the stage aren't natural at all.

ME: You remind me of the monkey who must have watched the Neanderthal man stand upright and walk. The monkey undoubtedly thought it wasn't natural to walk upright. That no progress had ever been made and never would be made.

HE: Well, not much progress *has* been made.

ME: Not much—with some people.

A silence settled over us. To break it, I said:

ME: What's your profession here?

HE: Guess.

ME: A newspaper correspondent—perhaps the *Times* or *Morning Post*.

HE: No—I'm in the diplomatic service.

ME: Oh. Are you in the Consulate here?

HE: No, I'm in the Embassy.

ME: Oh, is that so—in what capacity?

HE: I'm the Ambassador.

ME: (A silence from me and then I laughed.)

He sat looking at me and wondering what I was laughing about. He couldn't see the joke. But *I* saw the joke. A girl came and took him away and I asked Frau Durieux who he was. "He is the British Ambassador," she said. Well, well, said I to myself in a corner, this is too jolly. So I went back and tried to pry the girl away from him—she was a young actress who was kissing him in the corner. So, I asked him how long he had been ambassador, and he said six years and was going home. I told him I knew some British subjects here— Australians and Indians and things like that. I waited for a reply but none came. Then I asked him where he had been before, and he said he was ambassador in Peking. So I asked him what he thought of the Pan-Asiatic movement. He said he didn't know anything about it. So I told him it was a league of Asiatic peoples for self-defense. He looked at me and said nothing. And the girl took him away again to a back room—perhaps to kiss him in peace.

Now if you think I'm relating a drama that I have manufactured, you are wrong. I swear before God in whom I do not believe, that what I have told you is the truth and nothing but the truth.

It is clear from interviews that Smedley's upper-class Indian friends, who had been mixing socially with Europe's cultural and political elites, were distressed by Smedley's behavior. One of them described Smedley at this time as a pathetic, scrawny creature wearing expensive hand-me-down clothes from Durieux that made her look "ridiculous"; the relationship between the two women, he said, was "curious," possibly lesbian.[4] Given the fact that Smedley was now crusading against marriage and denouncing men, it is not surprising that many Indians thought this a possibility. But earlier, in the spring of 1926, Smedley had confronted the issue in psychoanalysis and rejected it as a possibility for her. To Dr. Naef she had expressed her underlying anger at Florence's recent marriage. Hints in Smedley's letters as well as references to an early draft of an autobiographical short story suggest that Dr. Naef had asked her if she had latent homosexual feelings toward Florence. As a Freudian, Dr. Naef is likely to have talked with her about homosexuality as an alternative that could emerge in women like Smedley who have been repulsed by intercourse and see it as degrading for women. Smedley was so angered by the suggestion that she briefly considered giving up Dr. Naef, a woman, for a male analyst. Although she distrusted marriage and men, Smedley countered that her reaction toward Florence's pending visit with her new husband had more to do with anger at feeling indebted to someone who seemed to enjoy emphasizing Smedley's weaknesses and eccentricities. Even before Florence arrived, Smedley had started trying to distance herself. In a 1926 letter to Florence she wrote: "There may be a chance that you and I will have to start our friendship over; for I am almost a new person now and you may not find it agreeable. My picturesqueness that you often mention is gone, I think."

To Florence's suggestion that Smedley meet them in Austria and then travel together, Smedley responded that she was accepting Durieux's invitation instead so that she might work on her book. When the Berlin reunion with Florence finally occurred, in late spring of 1926, Smedley seldom saw the couple alone and did not see them off at the train station when they left the city. Although in the process of distancing herself, she attempted to divest herself of obligations to Florence by serving up connections to famous and interesting people as an exchange for debts owed. Smedley introduced Florence as a poet and an old friend to such people as Käthe Kollwitz and Alexander Berkman, and she took Florence along with her to Kollwitz's home to celebrate the artist's birthday.[5]

But as she began cutting her ties with Florence, Smedley reached out once again to another old New York friend, Margaret Sanger. In April of

1926, after months of silence, she wrote Sanger of her trouble in finishing the book, of going back into analysis with Dr. Naef, and of her continuing concern with women's questions. She also offered to help with introductions to Indian women at the scheduled fall conference in India on birth control, and she extended an invitation to Sanger from German women physicians to come to Berlin on her way to India.

Since her involvement with the Friends of Freedom for India in New York in the late teens, Smedley had served as a cultural bridge between the Indian nationalist movement and progressive American women in the United States. As these groups developed a history of mutual support, Indian students and leaders like Das were often asked by progressive Western women to write about birth control as it pertained to India. This, needless to say, put them in a bind. Their natural constituents abroad were liberals who sympathized with their fight for Indian independence and did not view them as racially inferior. The Indians were trying to present an image of a sophisticated people fighting to regain the right to govern themselves and retain a different culture based on non-Western religions and traditions. In the fight against racial and cultural prejudice, they were reluctant to admit to any problems that would not be cured by the removal of the British. Fearing the effectiveness of British propaganda in using such admissions of backwardness against them as proof of Indian "unfitness" for self-rule, Indian men dodged the problem of birth control in India by writing abstractly about the geopolitical concerns of the issue, much to Smedley's chagrin. Bitter and disillusioned by the sexist attitudes of many Indian nationalist leaders, Smedley complained to Sanger about their position on birth control in a letter in the spring of 1925:

> Dr. Das has just sent me a copy of his paper for your conference. Dr. Das is a very dear friend of mine, but I simply can't agree with his viewpoint [on birth control] in this paper, and I'm surprised that you have accepted it. . . . I've an article appearing in *Die Frau* [Germany's leading women's magazine], and I know [that because of it] many Indians will brand me as a betrayer of their cause. I agree that poverty is great in India, and [that] 50 to 80 percent of it is caused by exploitation by England. But the population is too thick even if India could support four times as many. The rabbit habits of human beings seem so utterly useless. Men always seem to think human beings should breed like lice as long as they can feed themselves. For what purpose? . . . What's the big idea? I [can] understand [those who] work on a Christian hypothesis of filling heaven with souls; but many don't even believe that asininity, and I don't understand them. India produces droves of weak slaves which are pulling the nation to the earth. I'm sick of this viewpoint of Mr.

B. K. Roy and Dr. Das. We're far stronger in meeting our opponents if we agree to all India's evils and merely prove that we are the ones who recognize them and are willing to change them; we don't need the British government or Christian missionaries to do it. It irritates me to see people talk in terms of percentages and competitive populations; I don't find women talking that way.

To Smedley, who held muckraking journalism as an ideal, the practice of hiding weaknesses, even if they were your own, was inconceivable if progress was your goal. Problems couldn't be solved if they weren't identified.

By the fall of 1926, many Indians in Europe who were not familiar with how effective Smedley had been in advancing their cause in the United States were openly embarrassed by their self-appointed champion. Most believed that she had stunted Chatto's political career and made his personal life miserable, even though unintentionally. Needless to say, they were also worried about how she would portray Indian nationalists in her forthcoming book.[6] By this time, rumors of the content of Smedley's book were circulating among the English-speaking community in Berlin. One shocked manuscript reader, Smedley's friend Grabisch, was a likely source of these rumors. Smedley noted Grabisch's negative reaction in an August 1926 letter to Florence:

> She nearly smashed me up before I left Berlin. She came over and read the last part of my book and then she told me she considered it highly unethical of me to expose to the public my most sacred feelings, etc. . . . She said I had written a sensational book on my most "sacred experiences" for the sake of money—had exposed Chatto and my own life for the sake of money. Then she proposed that it be published under another name and I refused. . . . The last two days in Berlin were hell for me and I was on the verge of withdrawing my book from the publishers.
>
> Of course, the last part is not only Chatto. I put in a lot of Bakar—at least the things I feel about Bakar. But I could not tell her that. So I wrote Bakar and asked him if he thought I was selling him out for money.
>
> My book has now gone off and it is finished. I worked like hell to get the last part done, and corrected it and worked on it, and since I came here [Salzburg] have done nothing else. Now it can go or not—I am finished with it and am tired of it and am sick of it and hope never to see its dirty face again.

Other Indian nationalist leaders, like her New York teacher Lajpat Rai, took a more positive approach to Smedley, seeing her as a passionate partisan who ought to be kept under control. Rai had sought her out in July, 1926, after attending an international labor conference in Switzerland. No doubt both curious and anxious about her forthcoming book, he flattered her with an invitation to submit articles to his weekly Lahore newspaper, *The People*.

For her part, Smedley felt that she had more than paid her dues and deserved to be treated as an equal member of the Indian nationalist family, fully entitled to criticize particular members and aspects of the movement. Until 1925 she had followed the unwritten rule of keeping the movement's public face intact by not revealing weaknesses to outsiders. In that year she started publishing articles in Europe critical of the lack of a birth control program in India, and then in 1926 in articles she sent to India she began to preach in a condescending manner. Predictably, both were resented.*

When classes began at the University of Berlin during the fall of 1926, Smedley was in high spirits. Exhilaration turned to apprehension as she realized the intensity of graduate work and the inadequacy of her background. She chose "Opium, a Historical and Economic Study" as a thesis topic for an economic geography class. In a class on "The British Empire," she focused on China. The demand for increased sophistication in German vocabulary alone posed a formidable barrier.

As the pressures increased, Smedley's health deteriorated. Ugly colds and coughs often kept her from attending classes. But Frau Durieux's backing never wavered. In a November 12, 1926, letter Smedley wrote to Florence: "When I have to go anyplace, Frau Durieux sends her car these days and I feel like a princess." Durieux continued to include Smedley at theater and dinner parties, including those for the celebrated Maxim Gorky when he visited Berlin. Smedley was also continuing analysis, as well as attending lectures with such titles as "Psychoanalysis and Marxism" at the Psychoanalytical Institute.

By late November, Smedley voiced serious doubts about being able to

---

*Her tone was particularly condescending in a January, 1926, article in the *Modern Review* (Calcutta) in which she ridiculed Indian students and their knowledge of "theatre": "But of all things [of] which India can learn from Europe stands the theatre as a place of culture and learning. In this respect, nothing can be learned from England, which is notorious throughout the cultured world for its cheap, trashy, inartistic theatres. There Indian students learn little they cannot see in India; it is actually painful to see Indian students come from England to the Continent and ask for the theatres; the places they want to see are not the National Theatre where the great thought of the world is to be met face to face, but the cheap reviews, the varieties, the vaudevilles, the cabarets. They know nothing else—that is "the theatre" for them. But that is not "the theatre" on the Continent, where men and women devote a lifetime to the serious study of acting and drama, and where the serious men and women artists are the associates and equals of scholars and thinkers in every other branch of life. There India has a world to learn—and a world to gain."

keep up with her classmates. In mid-December, Bakar arrived for a Christmas visit. He found Smedley in bed with influenza and soon left. Writing Florence on January 31, 1927, that she had been in bed for over five weeks with "the rottenest influenza you can imagine," Smedley was still cheery enough to congratulate Florence on the coming of her first child. But what seemed to rouse her the most was the news of a forthcoming visit to Berlin of an old American friend, Roger Baldwin. After the founding of Friends of Freedom for India in 1919, Baldwin and Smedley had become good friends and quite possibly occasional lovers.[7]

Baldwin was coming to Berlin to see Chatto as well. His trip was the result of a year of careful planning by a handful of people, spearheaded by Chatto, for the convening in Brussels in February of 1927 of a new organization to be called the League Against Imperialism. As an international organization designed to take unified stands in support of nationalist movements in Asia, Africa, and South America, the League Against Imperialism was formed to counter the League of Nations' status-quo position on colonialism. The intent was to focus world attention on acts of imperialism such as the use of Indian troops to protect British interests in treaty-port China. The idea for the League and the planning for the Brussels meeting originated with Chatto in Berlin. Initial financing was provided by the Comintern, which thereafter deliberately refrained from exercising direct control over the organization, so as to avoid tainting it as Moscow-dominated. Chatto himself, however, had just joined the German Communist Party. He worked closely with such labor organizers as L. Gibarty of Hungary, Edo Fimmen of Holland, and Comintern figure Willi Münzenburg of Germany. In its initial years, the League received the active support and endorsement of such non-Communist international figures as Bertrand Russell, Albert Einstein, Henri Barbusse, Romain Roland, Mme. Sun Yat-sen (Song Qingling), and Jawaharlal Nehru—all of whom attended the inaugural meeting in Brussels.*

* The arrival the year before of Jawaharlal Nehru had been a major event for the Indian nationalist community in Berlin and was later important to Smedley. Nehru was general secretary of the Indian National Congress and since 1921 had been Mohandas K. Gandhi's right-hand man. He spent the summer of 1926 in Switzerland with his wife, who was recovering from an illness. In the fall, Nehru came often to Berlin to investigate and encourage the European-based community of nationalists in exile. His visits bestowed recognition and a sense of legitimacy on the propaganda of Chatto, Smedley, and their colleagues. Nehru paid special attention to Virendranath Chattopadhyaya as the acknowledged leader of the community, and he met Agnes Smedley on a number of occasions. Although Smedley said little about Nehru at the time, their relationship would grow in significance to her, with the two of them remaining in contact until Smedley's death in

The Brussels meeting was a success, resulting in a manifesto that focused on two main issues: the rising struggle of colonies for national independence, and the prediction that a war against the Soviet Union was imminent and would be waged by imperialist countries within the year. Labor leaders noted the shift of industry and mining in the West to colonies and emphasized that workers around the world would have to act in concert if they were ever to gain control of their economic lives. The concluding session adopted a constitution and elected an executive board that included Nehru, Baldwin, Mme. Sun, and others. Chatto became the League's executive secretary.

Reactions from the British and French to the Brussels conference were prompt. Both protested to the Belgium government about providing facilities for it. The French arrested board member Leopold Senghor, the black delegate from the "French African Colonies," thus making it impossible to set up the League's office in Paris as planned. The British labeled the group as a front for the Comintern, and U.S. intelligence accepted that conclusion without comment.[8]

Both Chatto and Bakar attended the meeting. Smedley, not wanting to be with them both at the same time and place, did not. But she followed the League's activities closely and was certainly encouraged by the thrust of the meeting.

Smedley continued to attend classes during the spring of 1927, but with growing frustration. She published more magazine articles, usually on theater or on women professionals and pioneers. Roger Baldwin was her personal refuge that spring as she shared her knowledge of the city, its organizations and people, with him. After four months of silence Smedley wrote to Florence on May 6, 1927, to inquire whether or not her baby had come and to confide her loneliness:

> Roger Baldwin was here and I was often with him as he investigated organizations here. It was like meeting a brother I loved, and he awoke in my heart the bitter need of having friends like him whom I instinctively understand and who understand me. When he left I lay awake all night trying to reconsider my life so surrounded by public work and thought but so lonely person-

---

1950. Chatto convinced Nehru of the utility of taking a unified public stand around the world against imperialism through the League Against Imperialism. Chatto introduced Nehru to Mme. Sun and other Chinese Nationalist Party (Guomindang) officials. By December, 1927, it was announced in Delhi that Nehru was to stay on in Europe to represent India at the Brussels meeting. See A. C. N. Nambiar, interview, 1971, ms. at Nehru Memorial Museum and Library, New Delhi, as well as All-India Congress Committee Files, supplement no. 127, on the League, in the same location; also Jawaharlal Nehru, *Toward Freedom* (New York, 1942), pp. 121–27.

ally. You might think that I fell in love with him—but I didn't. He showed me—well, I don't know if these were individual emotions or racial or national understanding. He showed me, without knowing it, the gulf between me and the Indians. I wrote him so. He says he thinks that it is our particular relationship. Perhaps he is right. . . . With most Americans I feel a deeper gulf still. But even with Americans whom I regard as enemies of the human race, I instinctively know just where I can hit them the hardest. But with the Indians . . . I don't know where to touch them the most deeply. An Arabic or a Sanskrit phrase calls up no memories in me. . . . I haven't seen Chatto for two months and would rather not see him at all. So many miserable things come to light about him that I've tried to draw back for a time. They weren't miserable in themselves—I felt miserable is all. Regarding Bakar—the summer will decide what we do. Just now we do not even write to each other—by agreement.

By June, Smedley had come to a decision. Acknowledging that an academic degree was beyond her, she gave up her "scholarship," so that her financial obligations to Frau Durieux, at least, ceased to mount. Although failing to become an academic, Smedley had found Durieux's contacts invaluable in placing articles and in finding a German publisher, the *Frankfurter Zeitung,* for her book *Eine Frau Allein* (*A Woman Alone,* the German title for *Daughter of Earth*). If Smedley was playing Eliza Doolittle, it was in a *Pygmalion* written by Brecht, not Shaw. As an Eliza Doolittle of the left, she embraced the message coming out of the Brussels conference and pervasive within the foreign student communities of Berlin: the revolution was coming—and within the year![9]

CHAPTER VIII

Speaking Her Mind, 1927–1928

During 1927 Smedley became convinced that within a year or so Britain would go to war against the Soviet Union in order to stop Bolshevik influence from spreading across the British Empire in Asia.[1] On June 29 she reported to Florence: "I am writing . . . for the Indian press, counteracting British propaganda against Russia, for . . . if another war breaks—and it is bound to within a year at the latest—[we hope that] India will strike for its freedom and that all Asia will at last be free."

In Berlin, Smedley could see that German political life was heading for a crisis: fascism was on the march, but so was the German Communist Party. She was more sympathetic to the Communists, of course, but she differed sharply with them in several ways. Perhaps most of all she was angered by their simplistic glorification of the working class as full of selfless idealism. Her own experience in the American West had convinced her that this attitude was fatuous and self-serving and that the problems of poor people would not immediately disappear after a successful political revolution. In an August article in the *New Masses,* she admitted that she had joined the Indian independence movement "not only because it was a movement for freedom but also because it was a movement just about as distant from American life and thought as any movement can be."

She was convinced that Marxism had to deal with the psychological problems of the working class in order to erase the scars of educational and economic poverty.* Under the influence of Tilla Durieux and her

---

* Smedley's own analyst, Dr. Naef, was associated with the Berlin Institute, which pioneered the study of the psychological problems of working-class men, returning soldiers in particular.

left-wing friends, she argued in the *Modern Review* for January, 1927, that a true people's theater offered one way to attack this problem:

> We know that in the soul of every individual, as of the masses, both social and anti-social instincts slumber, and that anti-social instincts, [when] denied creative outlet or application, break out in open or subtle anti-social actions—in cruelty, crime, and even in war. The possible value of the theatre as an institution for using up and sublimating this energy cannot be underestimated. It gives the opportunity to act out every kind of emotion, not in an evil but in an artistic and creative manner. When mankind has the opportunity to live creatively everything within it, war, with its dramatic appeal and its opportunity for lawlessness of every kind, will have no hold on the masses.[2]

Smedley also differed from the Communists in believing that the rise of workers to power would not in itself solve problems of sexual identity for women. In short, Smedley was elated over the coming revolution but ambivalent about Communist leadership. As she had told Florence on June 29: "I have joined an 'Arbeitsgemeinschaft' for the study of Marxism and Imperialism. . . . Our leader is a well-known Marxian economist. Within my own opinions I remain nonpolitical insofar as the Communist Party is concerned, and could never join it. I am more and more interested in economic action alone. But I must know other things also."

In May of 1927, in a *Modern Review* article on Helena Lange, who founded the first girls' *gymnasium* in Germany and created the women's magazine *Die Frau*, Smedley criticized anarchist and Communist philosophies for refusing to address the "women's problem" within the revolutionary working class. Much to the anger of party members, she argued that the "secret shame" of working-class women—the way they were treated as property or "sex slaves" by working-class men—had to be exposed and dealt with. Clearly, her concern was rooted in personal experience, not ideology. At about this time she had written to Margaret Sanger:

> You have touched a problem that is more real than most people know—that of the rapidity of man in sex union. Few women will be frank enough to say that they are generally left in a most awful nervous tension, to lie awake in bitterness all night long, while a man slumbers peacefully. . . . The cause of this in men you did not fully treat. . . . One cause is that many men get their sex start in life with prostitutes, [who want] to get through the business as soon as possible. I've heard that they often say to a man: "Well, for Christ's sake, aren't you through yet!" In such a relationship a man need think only of himself—never of the woman. In brothels for soldiers—as on the Rhine after the war—each soldier was allotted 15 minutes with a prostitute. . . . In this way decent women get husbands whose sex training has been gained from

prostitutes. This training is as deadly as syphilis. It is the revenge of the prostitute against the "respectable" women who consider themselves better. [dated only January 13]

Smedley's work with Dr. Naef had increased her appreciation of the complexities that go into the molding of a sexual identity. Having gained a new understanding of the relationship between the drives for power and for sexual gratification, her sympathy for Chatto and her understanding of men in general grew. She acknowledged the deep hostilities and resentments behind her own striving for equal power, and even decided that men had the more difficult task, because sharing was harder than taking. But she was also convinced that individual men, like colonial powers, would not give up their positions of dominance except under the threat of force. If even Chatto, who at least intellectually accepted the notion of equality between the sexes, could not give up his drive for dominance, what chance was there for the wives of working-class men? Always impatient with the idea of slow progress through political reform, Smedley favored radical—and personal—action. In a letter to Sanger on December 27, 1927, she suggested that working-class women use sexuality as a political weapon: "I myself would advocate the use of birth-control methods, a complete birth strike, and a change in the form of society by revolution."

Emboldened by psychoanalysis, Smedley attempted to address American audiences on the subject of sexual identity. But the candor with which she discussed sexual problems, as well as the real and potential perversions in her own emotional life, were seen by most U.S. editors as too scandalous for publication. In her June 29 letter to Florence she wrote:

I have an article to appear soon in the *New Masses* ["One is Not Made of Wood," August 1927]. It is anonymous and was submitted to *The Nation* for its series on "These Modern Women." They were afraid to publish it and sent it to the *American Mercury*. But [the editor of the *Mercury*, H. L.] Mencken—according to a letter from the *New Masses*—also got cold feet and said the post office was watching him too closely. So it went to the *New Masses* and they said if I would give it to them they would fight on the issue. But even they wanted to cut out the word "homosexuality" and change a whole paragraph. I have let them. In the meantime I have a letter from *The Nation* telling me that they could not have published the article without toning it down [because] "our readership, advanced as it is, also has its definite limitations." Then [Oswald Garrison] Villard [editor of *The Nation*] is good enough to go on and say: "May I say to you that I think that yours is one of the most extraordinary human documents I have ever read, for its frankness,

its self-revelations, and the moving character of the story." Now if he really
thought that, why did he not run it . . . ? And why didn't Mencken? Well,
read the article yourself when it appears and see if you think Villard has
merely flattered me. But I wish you would not tell [others that I am the one]
who wrote it, outright just like that. The Indians will always use it against me
anyway. What I think is that America is frightfully backward in such things.

As Smedley became more stridently forthright, the strain in her relations with Indian colleagues increased and led to a public debate with
Lajpat Rai. Smedley's overriding priority was to convince modern Indian nationalists like Rai that the time had come for them to choose
sides. As she saw it, the choice was either the capitalist West and con-
tinuation of India's colonial status; or it was Communist Russia, and
ideally, the abandonment by nationalist leaders of their upper-class
status in return for independence and social justice.

Soon after the League Against Imperialism was formed, Smedley began implementing one of its main objectives: getting news about China
into the Indian press. The Chinese Nationalist Party (Guomindang) had
established an information bureau in Berlin. From this source, she
wrote articles on the activities of Indian nationalist organizations in
Canton (Guangzhou), Hankou, and Shanghai; of Indian officers court-
martialed in Shanghai; of Harbant Singh, an Indian revolutionary who
shot and killed the head of the Indian police in Shanghai; of seventy Indian policemen who went over to the revolutionary Canton government; and of a "whole brigade" of Indian troops sent back from China
for being untrustworthy. Obviously, these articles were meant to suggest
that the Chinese and the Indians, as fellow victims of British imperialism, should unite in an attempt to rid themselves of the British. (This
message was not lost on British intelligence agents in the Home Rule
Office, who began to keep closer tabs on who in India were receiving
and publishing Smedley's articles.)[3]

Reading these articles written for Indian audiences gives one the feeling of having stumbled into the middle of a family feud—which, of
course, was exactly the case. Smedley was India's divorced daughter-in-
law, albeit one who was still a strong advocate for many of the views of
her former husband. She was taking sides in a clash within the Indian
nationalist movement between domestic leaders like Gandhi and Rai
and overseas leaders in exile like Chattopadhyaya. The leaders in India
felt that those in exile were out of touch with realities inside India and
too heavily influenced by foreign values and perceptions. The leaders in
exile felt that their counterparts in the homeland were too parochial and

did not see the larger international forces at work. In "The Indian Revolutionary Movement Abroad," published in *The People* on August 11 and 18, 1927, Smedley tried to demonstrate the superiority of the "internationalist" view, but she undercut the effectiveness of her argument by using insulting and condescending language. For example: "The Indian leaders [in India] are nearly all poisoned by their English education or their dependence upon an English interpretation of world events. The Indian exiles, living as they do in many lands, can see the world situation through Indian eyes, and not just through British eyes. But most of the Indian leaders are afraid of them—it isn't safe and it isn't respectable to see the world except through the crooked spectacles of England." She added that the 1917 Russian Revolution and the worldwide Socialist movement had caused Indians "whose brains are still mobile" to revise their outlook.

In a five-part series entitled "England's War Plans Against Asia," Smedley argued that Britain saw Russia as a threat to her domination of India and China, whose raw materials were essential for her factories. As evidence that war was about to break out between Britain and the Soviet Union, she offered the following: the British raid on the Russian Trade Delegation in London, and the subsequent suspension of diplomatic relations between the two powers; increased anti-Russian propaganda in the British press; British support of former Russian Czarist officers in Europe, the existence of the headquarters of a Czarist government in exile in England, and British support of Czarist armies in China; and Britain's building of air bases, military camps, and a military railroad through the Khyber Pass to the Afghan frontier. Smedley urged India, Russia, and China to stand together against the British or any other imperialist power that might threaten one of them. As for those who believed that the Comintern might be a front for Russian imperialism, she wrote: "Such people are absolutely ignorant of the fundamental and underlying principles of Socialism, or in a more restricted sense still, Communism. . . . [They] are unable to get out of their own skins and conceive of an economic system whose life is built upon principles that make imperialism absolutely impossible. To excuse their own cynical ignorance, they try to read into the Socialist system all the rottenness of the capitalist system."[4]

In India, Smedley's rhetoric hit like gasoline on a fire. In an angry response, her old mentor Lajpat Rai, the publisher of *The People*, pointed out on October 13 that Smedley had nothing new to tell Indians. They had known for two hundred years, he said, that Britain used

India as a base for all her wars in the East, both defensive and offensive, and that Britain was not ruling India out of philanthropic motives. As for the Russians, Rai said he was not convinced that they were disinterested friends, as Smedley claimed. He questioned what would happen when Russia gained the same power in the world as the British Empire. Addressing Smedley's condemnation of communalism in India, Rai said Indians knew quite well that it was a poison to true nationalism. But, he asked, wasn't communism itself a kind of communalism, the organized war of one class against another? Clearly, she had stung him: "Miss Smedley is mistaken if she thinks we are all babies and do not understand even elementary politics. Sitting in Berlin and writing from her place of vantage, she can call us traitors, cowards, and fools. But we know we are nothing of the kind. Only we realize what our power is and what our resources are and what we can do and what we cannot do. . . . Miss Smedley has not told us what we should do. Should we organize a rising against the British and get our heads and bones and bodies powdered into smithereens? Will India be a bit freer or happier if some of us are out of the way?"

On November 17 Chatto's sister-in-law, Kamaladevi Chattopadhyaya, published a letter in *The People* that was even more hostile toward Smedley (confirming Smedley in her belief that Chatto's family despised her because of her working-class background). Rejecting the suggestion that Soviet Russia was the answer to India's problems, Kamaladevi called Agnes a Communist and attacked her personally: "[Indians abroad] fail to see that these Communist friends are usually those who either have no opportunity of becoming capitalists, and thus convert a disadvantage into a virtue, or bourgeoisie who play the superficial role of the Communists as a sort of recreation or amusement."

It is clear that Kamaladevi was upset by the influence she perceived Smedley as having on the life of her brother-in-law and on other young Indians abroad. In 1927 Chatto had joined the German Communist Party and was followed a year later by a brilliant young physicist and protégé of Einstein's, Gangadiri Adhikari, who was convinced that Smedley and Chatto were right to see international communism as the only hope for India. At about this time Chatto's sister, Suhasini Chattopadhyaya, also became a Communist. Still, the Communist Party of India remained quite small and had little influence on Indian domestic politics—another reason why Kamaladevi saw joining the Communist movement as a waste of effort.[5] But the crux of Kamaladevi's disagreement with Smedley was philosophical: "The theory that equal opportunities both physical and mental are going to solve the problem of misery is a most fallacious one, at least as it is interpreted by the Communists. If everyone learns to read and write and every stomach is fed, the world is not going to become a paradise. Happiness can begin when we learn to hold life sacred. Then alone can we say the movement brings comfort and relief to a grief-stricken world." Smedley did not believe paradise would arrive with the advent of communism. But having grown up in poverty, she viewed Gandhian notions of "love" and the "sacredness of life" as fine sentiments that could not be indulged until the fight for basic necessities had been won.

Each was reacting to the other emotionally, for each had been hit at the most vulnerable spot: Smedley was challenged on her ability to comprehend political realities; Rai and Kamaladevi were accused of being provincial and unwilling to sacrifice their privileged status and position. But this three-way collision only reconfirmed the previous goals of each. Rai wanted India to be given Dominion status so that it could proceed with gradual reform, which would allow him to protect his Hindu constituency in the Punjab from what he considered to be a hostile Muslim community surrounding it. Kamaladevi wanted to bring about independence and reform without loss of life and without sacrificing ethical ideals. Smedley wanted the liberation of India and all colonial peoples to come about as quickly as possible at whatever cost, because for her, seeing others locked into poverty and ignorance was intolerable. Rai, it appears, was able to understand Smedley's emotional commitment to her cause. Smedley cared deeply about Rai's opinion of her, but she felt she had the right "to go beyond" her teacher. And at this time, she could only view Kamaladevi's talk about the sacredness of life as a hypocritical dodge of the real issues.

Smedley was defended by several people, including M. Acharya and Jaya Surya Naidu, the son of Chatto's eldest sister. In the December 15 issue of *The People,* Rai tried to terminate the debate with an apology:

> I could have and should have pitched my comments in a milder key. I have known Miss Smedley for the last ten years and I have never doubted her sincerity. She is not a person who can be bought for money. She is a born revolutionary and has all the mentality, tendencies, and habits of one. Her life spent in constant struggle for living and honour has if anything, added to these tendencies. Personally, her motives are absolutely pure and clean. She is a woman capable of great sacrifices for her friends and her cause, and I can say from personal knowledge that gold has no temptations for her. . . .
>
> We have no love for our chains and Miss Smedley knows it. We are working according to our lights. Miss Smedley ought to know that I, for one, have

no other occupation in life. All the same I am very sorry if I have hurt her. I should have known that coming from me the remarks could not but hurt her. Here the incident must close.

On January 29, 1928, Smedley had the last word; in an unusually lengthy essay in the *Forward* (Calcutta), she defended the strident tone of her earlier articles as an attempt to rouse Indian leaders into action. By this time the personal vindictiveness of the debate had dissipated, largely because Smedley had joined the critical attack on Katherine Mayo's recently published *Mother India,* which was then being highly publicized in the United States. By giving the impression that only the Christians and the English were addressing India's social, political, and economic problems, Mayo seemed to be making a case for continued British rule, and thereby offended Indian leaders of every political persuasion. (For example, she deplored the evils of the caste system without mentioning that Gandhi, the acknowledged leader of the untouchables, not only continually denounced it but also practiced what he preached. And she failed to say that enlightened families like the Nehrus and Chattopadhyayas had worked not only to elevate the status of the women in their families but also to break down such social practices as child marriage, purdah, and permanent widowhood.) Nehru and Gandhi attacked the book. Lajpat Rai wrote editorials against it in *The People* and even produced a point-by-point refutation of its charges and distortions. Given the level of concern, Smedley's noisy campaign against the book was much appreciated. Rai was particularly grateful to have an American woman activist take on Mayo. It was one month after the appearance of Smedley's first review of *Mother India* for the *New Masses* that Rai published his "apology" to Smedley.[6]

In December of 1927, during the heat of battle with her Indian comrades, Smedley received a visit from her old friend Margaret Sanger, who arrived with her husband, J. Noah H. Slee. Besides making the necessary personal arrangements for them, Smedley set up two speaking engagements for Sanger. The first and larger one was sponsored by the Association of German Medical Women, a group of physicians who were campaigning against a proposed law that would make abortion a crime. Sanger's second lecture was delivered to a joint meeting of the Hindustani Association of Central Europe and the Chinese Student Association. During their ten days together, Smedley also introduced Sanger and her husband to several famous German friends: Dr. Helena Lange, founder of the first girls' *gymnasium* in Germany; Adele Schreiber, a former member of the Reichstag who had written an introduction for a

German translation of Sanger's latest book; Käthe Kollwitz, who agreed to illustrate Sanger's next book; and Dr. Helene Stocker, director of the League for the Protection of Mothers.[7]

Bakar spent a quiet Christmas with Smedley at her apartment. She was flat on her back with a hot water bottle on her stomach, for an as-yet-undiagnosed complaint. One source says that Bakar proposed marriage and that Smedley refused, knowing it would ruin his career. At any rate, early in 1928, having completed his doctoral degree, Bakar returned to India. The two never saw each other again.[8]

Before returning to America, Sanger asked Smedley to work for the prompt establishment of a birth control clinic in Germany. In mid-January, Smedley was joined in this project by Josephine Bennett, an old friend from Indian and birth control work in New York and a close associate of Sanger's. In considering how to organize a clinic, Smedley decided to form a working advisory committee made up strictly of medical professionals who had the commitment and the political backing to withstand the inevitable public outcry. Although birth control was not illegal in Germany, the Catholics and the National Socialists (the Nazi party) were trying to have it outlawed, and it was receiving only token support from the Communists and the Social Democrats. On the advice of Käthe Kollwitz's son, Dr. Hans Kollwitz, she turned to Dr. Richard Schmienke, a Communist Party member and the commissioner of health for the Berlin working-class district of Neukölln, who had already tried to establish a birth control clinic in Saxony. Because the majority of elected representatives in this district were Communists and Socialists, they expected minimal opposition. Schmienke had read Sanger's articles and wanted to model the first Berlin clinic after Sanger's clinic in New York. But in February of 1928, the best he could offer was three free rooms in a clinic set up to treat venereal diseases. Smedley, unwilling to risk letting the public associate birth control with venereal disease, rejected the offer; but she did win Schmienke's commitment to search further for space and to organize women doctors in his district to help with the work.[9]

There is no doubt that during this period Smedley was working closely with the German Communist Party. The Communists and Socialists with whom she was associating were an impressive group of artists, doctors, and professionals. On February 21 she spoke in German on the labor movement in India to the Congress of Proletarian Women, a large Communist-front organization (it claimed 30,000 members in Germany). When she finished her speech, the audience rose to its feet and spontaneously began to sing the "International." It was heady stuff. Fascism may have been on the march in Germany, but to Smedley in Berlin, so were the Communists. In her experience, it was the Communist and Socialist professionals who were giving the most generously of their time and talents to help the poor and the workers of Germany.[10]

Since December, and throughout Sanger's visit, Smedley had been struggling with her health. Sometime in January her analyst, Dr. Naef, had diagnosed the problem as appendicitis and recommended an operation. But Smedley, short of money and fearful of being anesthetized, balked at the suggestion. Instead, she started on a special diet and began taking the drug atropia to control possible spasms.* By late February Smedley admitted that her pain had become unbearable, and she appealed to Sanger to ask her husband for the money to have an operation. On March 2, with Jo Bennett at her side, Smedley submitted to an operation to remove her appendix and repair her uterus. Even after a rectal anaesthesia was administered, she fought against the taking of ether until Bennett finally calmed her. After the surgery she had a four-day bout with postoperative fever and complained of pain around her heart, which was treated with "electric baths" and heat pads. Käthe Kollwitz visited Smedley in the hospital, and they tried to work on a translation of a Sanger manuscript, but Smedley was too weak to make much progress. Instead, Kollwitz made several sketches of Smedley in her hospital bed. On March 16, Smedley was finally released from the hospital, and two days later Jo Bennett wrote to Sanger: "She has certainly had a hard fight all her life against poverty, ill health, and I believe, almost insanity. But she is better now than I have ever seen her."

Indeed, by April Smedley seemed full of energy. She was teaching two courses again at the university, walking three evenings a week to the homes of private students, and working to finish revising her book. When Jo Bennett contracted a severe case of influenza, Smedley nursed her at home and then visited her regularly in the hospital until she was well. By the end of May, Jo Bennett had completely recovered and moved to Paris to work on birth control there. Smedley was to join her in Paris for the month of August.

Other minor problems cropped up to delay the opening of the Berlin

---

* Smedley was also having some sort of gynecological problem and for a while debated the merits of having a hysterectomy when they took out the appendix. She consulted several women doctor friends and decided against it after hearing that women who had such operations often "become fat and . . . look like female eunuchs" (Smedley to Sanger, February 14, 1928).

clinic, which had been scheduled for June 1. Much discussion led to a
decision that the clinic should not be named for Margaret Sanger, because that would encourage monarchists, Catholics, and National Socialists to attack it as a foreign-funded institution. And, as Smedley explained to Sanger on July 7, the fact that the clinic had Communists on
its advisory board could make Sanger even more vulnerable in the
United States. (Smedley knew that Sanger had already been criticized in
New York for seeking an invitation to visit birth control clinics in Russia.) On July 7, after crucial last-minute help from Dr. Kurt Bendix, a
prominent Social Democrat, the Beratungstelle für Geburtenregelung
(Birth Control Clinic) opened its doors.

At some point during the winter of 1927–28, Smedley made the political and personal decision to go to China as a journalist. The night
before the opening of the birth control clinic, she had given a lecture at
the University of Berlin entitled "The Revolt in Asia." She had believed
for some time that a showdown between Asian nationalists and European imperialists, particularly the British, would soon occur. China,
Smedley thought, would be center stage, and she intended to be there.
More important, Smedley made the decision because of a perceived mission for which she thought she was uniquely qualified.[11]

The formation of the League Against Imperialism had stimulated the
Indian National Congress into taking steps toward establishing direct
formal ties with the Guomindang government in Nanjing. All attempts
by the National Congress, from the exchange of Congress and Guomindang Party representatives to sending the Chinese an ambulance and
medical team, were vetoed by the British. Since the formation of the
League Against Imperialism, Smedley had focused her attention on getting more news about China into the Indian press. But the British cen-
sored many stories from China, such as those about strikes against
British-owned factories that were at all supportive of the workers. This
censorship was proof enough for Smedley that the British considered
such stories incendiary and were afraid that the sparks of nationalism
and anticolonialism might spread from China to India. Therefore she
decided to defy the British by personally becoming a catalyst linking the
two nationalist movements. Her plan was to go to China to write news
stories for the Indian press and to help put the Indians in the treaty
ports in touch with the Chinese nationalists in Nanjing. Smedley had
been cultivating contacts within the Chinese nationalist community in
Berlin. As an activist in the Indian cause, she already knew how to

evade British mail censorship and publish in the Indian press. Now she had to get herself to China.

Her first problem was the lack of a passport. It took her lawyer in New York, Gilbert Roe, six months to collect sworn affidavits from her father and from the doctor who had attended her birth, and divorce papers from Ernest Brundin. These, along with her seaman's pass and sworn statements from Josephine Bennett and Roe himself, finally proved sufficient, and Roe sent her her passport in the first week of July.[12] Her second problem was financial: she intended to work in China as a journalistic stringer for the *Frankfurter Zeitung* and various American and Indian publications, but she needed money to pay for her passage and her living expenses when she arrived. The answer to this problem was provided by a new American friend, David Friday, who had been president of Michigan Agricultural College (now Michigan State University) from 1921 to 1923, and who now generously offered to loan her enough money to get through a year in China and, he hoped, establish a birth control clinic there.[13] Another piece of good news reached her in late June: Gilbert Roe had negotiated a contract with Coward-McCann for publication of *Daughter of Earth*, but some further revisions would be required.

With her preparations for China well underway, Smedley spent August in Paris with Jo Bennett, who was doing birth control work there. Another purpose of the trip was to meet with her American editor and make the final changes on her manuscript. In early September, she took the train from Paris to Frankfurt, where she worked intensely for six weeks with Julian Gumperz, who translated her book into German.* On October 16, 1928, she wrote to Karin Michaelis: "You will find the book much changed. The murder theme has been taken out entirely. . . . I wonder what you will think of it as it is now." Gumperz, she said, had

---

* Julian Gumperz was an independently wealthy German-American citizen who had studied political economy at the University of Halle, where he became a student of Marxism. When World War I broke out, Gumperz moved to Berlin and published an antiwar magazine called *The Oppositionist* (*Der Gegner*). This experience led him to the idea of founding a publishing house that could bring out inexpensive, good books "for the masses"—the first paperback books. The Malik Verlag's handsome paperbound editions of leftist and progressive works (those of Upton Sinclair, for example) startled the German publishing world. Politically, Gumperz was usually aligned with the German Communist Party, but he never actually joined. In 1928 he had just returned from a year in the United States, where he developed a strong interest in rural American politics and economics, about which he was writing a doctoral thesis. Smedley's autobiographical manuscript about growing up in rural America seemed a perfect fit with Gumperz's interests and politics. Smedley's respect and affection for the man rose rapidly (see letters to Sanger, Au-

translated her book into German and would arrange for its publication in other European countries; reminding Michaelis of her offer to review the book, she added that Gumperz would send her one of the first copies of both the English and German editions.[14]

Smedley left Frankfurt for Berlin on October 27 after giving Julian Gumperz power of attorney to act for her in all matters in Europe. Arrangements had been completed with the *Frankfurter Zeitung* certifying her as a correspondent in China. With all decisions on her book now behind her, and her passport and visas in hand for the trip to China, Smedley's thoughts turned to the few loose ends left in Berlin.

Smedley's exuberance was damped in Berlin when she received a letter from Josephine Bennett informing her that she had been visited and questioned by the police after Smedley's August visit. She became apprehensive about her personal safety en route to China, fearing harassment from British agents along the way. Smedley was convinced that Scotland Yard was still keeping track of her. She reminded Sanger in an October 30 letter that Sanger herself had been questioned by British authorities in detail in both Hong Kong and Penang about her connections with Smedley and the Indian nationalists. Smedley asked for Sanger's help in case she disappeared or was arrested. Melodramatically, she gave specific instructions to Sanger to contact her lawyer and friend Gilbert Roe if necessary, and even explained how he should be paid. She requested that should anything happen to her while in China, Sanger should notify Roe that everything, including her book royalties, be turned over to Mr. Gumperz to do with as he thought best.

With her thoughts now turned toward China, Smedley spent most of the next six weeks crossing the Soviet Union. During a stopover in Moscow she met Mme. Sun Yat-sen. Although impressed by the general improvement of conditions since 1921, Smedley was concerned about the large number of orphans still wandering the streets. She visited orphanages and wrote an article about the problem for the *Nation*. Smedley spent a week touring Moscow and then boarded a train for China toward the end of November, 1928.[15]

While Smedley was on the train to the Sino-Soviet border, events were

---

gust 21, 1928, and to Karin Michaelis, dated simply "Frankfurt, Friday"). Besides the translation effort, Smedley and Gumperz collaborated on an article about current literary trends in Germany for an English-reading audience (*Modern Review* [February 1929]; repeated in *Survey,* February 1, 1929). On Gumperz see Hede Massing, *This Deception* (New York, 1951), pp. 43–65; and 1976 interview.

occurring in India that increased the interest of British intelligence in her whereabouts. On November 17, 1920, Smedley's mentor, Lajpat Rai, the Lion of the Punjab, died in Lahore of injuries sustained in a nonviolent protest march two weeks earlier. Rai's death was attributed to wounds received at the hands of a British police officer, J. P. Saunders. In the Punjab, young men thirsted for revenge and called for the assassination of the police officer. In late November, as Smedley made her way across Russia, Saunders was gunned down on the steps of Lahore's police headquarters by a young radical Sikh revolutionary from California.[16]

CHAPTER IX

The Shanghai Years, 1929–1933

When Agnes Smedley crossed the Soviet-Manchurian border into China in late December of 1928, British intelligence officers sprang into action. They informed the U.S. consul in Harbin that she was an undesirable who had forfeited her U.S. citizenship by marrying a British subject, Virendranath Chattopadhyaya. Convinced that her purpose in coming to China was to incite Sikh soldiers and police to rebellion in the treaty ports, they asked the U.S. consul to declare her passport invalid so that they could deport her. When questioned at the U.S. consulate, Smedley mentioned her family connection to the American Revolution and pointed out that she had never been legally married to Chatto, who was, she said, in any case still married to an Irish nun.[1]

Wintering in Manchuria (now China's northeastern provinces of Harbin, Liaoning, and Heilongjiang) is a harsh experience under the best of circumstances. In 1928 the region was ruled by a combination of warlords and foreign powers. Foremost among those powers were the Japanese, who had been turning Manchuria into a semi-colony since 1915. A few months before Smedley's arrival, radical elements in the Japanese military had assassinated warlord Zhang Zuolin, hoping either to provoke a war or to find a more pliable instrument in the person of Zhang's Japanese-educated son, Zhang Xueliang. The result was even greater confusion, a breakdown in law and order, and heightened international tension, especially after the son proved to be even more nationalistic and anti-Japanese than the father. Banditry was rife in Manchuria. For decades, pillage by marauding bandits or unattached "soldiers" had been an annual occurrence. The people were exhausted and picked clean. The poverty of the peasants was more profound than any Smedley had ever seen, and conditions in the principal cities of Harbin and Mukden (Shenyang) were desperate. Emotionally overwhelmed by what she saw and shaken by harassment from authorities, she collapsed and spent over a week in bed.

One of the first subjects Smedley wanted to explore for the *Frankfurter Zeitung* was the position of women in China. The result was one of her first works of reportage from Manchuria, "Five Women of Mukden." Although Smedley had yet to realize it, the subject was even more highly charged in China than in India or Western Europe. In China by 1929, a generation of reformers had made the plight of women a symbol of the backwardness of the old society, and thus of the need for drastic social change; the issue had become fundamental, dividing right from left. In her early stories for the *Zeitung*, Smedley most often illustrated the tradition of oppression of women by reference to the brutal practice of footbinding, the reduction of the adult female foot to an elegant "golden lily," three inches from heel to toe. With some regional and class variation, footbinding had been inflicted upon Chinese women since the tenth century. Economically and socially, women lived in bondage, although here again, the form varied from class to class and region to region. Often, as Smedley wrote in one article, lower-class women were bought or sold as *meicai*, household slaves. How marriage institutionalized the subordination of women to men was another theme of Smedley's stories. To begin with, all marriages were arranged by parents, and a bride usually left her home (the wealthier ones, with a dowry) to live and work in the home of a stranger, her husband. Only within the institution of marriage, as a breeder of males, could a woman rise in status. Otherwise, as the old proverb went, "a woman married is like a pony bought—to be ridden or whipped at the master's pleasure." Infanticide of baby girls was common among the lower classes. Traditionally, the only escapes for women were suicide, prostitution, or a Buddhist nunnery.

The seeds of revolutionary change in China, for women and men alike, were planted as early as the mid-nineteenth century, with the Opium War (1839–42) and the Taiping Rebellion (1851–64). The Taiping Rebellion was brutally suppressed by 1864, but the Opium War was only the first in a series of confrontations with imperialist powers, first Western nations and later Japan. The result was the piecemeal loss of Chinese sovereignty and a growing cultural defensiveness about many issues, including Western criticism of the lack of education for women and the practice of footbinding as barbaric.

By the late 1890s, prominent male reformers within the Qing dynasty bureaucracy, notably Kang Youwei and Liang Qichao, had attacked footbinding and supported formal education for women, and by the turn of the century the first women revolutionaries appeared in Sun Yat-sen's movement against the dynasty. Most of them, members of the privileged classes, were graduates of new women's colleges in China and abroad, particularly in Japan. Like their Western feminist models, these early radical women in China used the press to advocate women's right to own property, to have free choice in marriage, to pursue education, and to vote. Unlike their Western counterparts, however, they justified their claims with a nationalist appeal: to become a strong nation in the twentieth century, China needed strong, independent wives and mothers.[2]

The cultural link between nationalism and feminism was strengthened by the May Fourth Movement of 1919, a series of student demonstrations and merchant boycotts in major cities against the Treaty of Versailles, by which Western powers recognized Japanese special rights that challenged Chinese sovereignty in Shandong and Manchuria. The May Fourth Movement had radicalized the generation of Chinese women that Smedley would soon meet in Shanghai, Yan'an, and elsewhere. (One of them was Deng Yingchao, a Tianjin student activist and later the wife of Zhou Enlai.) Through the 1920s Ibsen's plays, especially *A Doll's House,* were translated and widely performed. Footbinding was beginning to die out, and women's organizations were being established in most cities and in some rural communities.

At the same time, urban politics, influenced by the May Fourth Movement, took a more progressive and nationalistic direction. In 1923 and 1924 Sun Yat-sen reorganized his followers along Soviet Bolshevik lines into the Guomindang. He also formed an alliance with the then tiny Chinese Communist Party (established in 1921). Efforts were made to organize and politicize urban workers and peasants, particularly the former. In large treaty-port cities like Shanghai and Guangzhou, a trade union movement emerged in which women were important. In 1923, some 20,000 women silk workers in Shanghai struck successfully for a ten-hour day and a wage of five cents a day. Often the women who led such strikes—Xiang Jingyu, Deng Yingchao, and Ding Ling, for example—were Communists and anarchists from upper-class backgrounds. Smedley had already heard about the role played by women in several major confrontations with Western imperialism such as the one on May 30, 1925, when British police in Shanghai opened fire on a large crowd of strikers and student demonstrators. Once in China, she met the participants and wrote about them for the *Zeitung*.[3]

Sun Yat-sen's death in 1925 produced a permanent ideological split within the leadership of the Guomindang. Initially the left wing of the Guomindang, which sent delegates to the League Against Imperialism meetings in Brussels in 1928 and was supported by Mme. Sun Yat-sen, seemed to be in control. But in retrospect, it seems clear that its power peaked with the completion of the Northern Expedition of 1925–27, a military campaign against warlords that unified south and central China under the Guomindang.

The liberation of Shanghai by a workers' uprising in March of 1927 brought a surge of hope to the left—which was promptly blasted away in the White Terror (or Reaction, as Smedley called it) unleashed by the commander of the Northern Expeditionary forces, Chiang Kai-shek. In April of 1927, without warning, Chiang ordered all Communists rounded up and executed. The left Guomindang, centered at Wuhan, was also driven from Nationalist Party leadership, but the Communists were Chiang's main target. Thousands died, including much of the leadership of the party, and the rest went underground. In desperation, surviving Communists attempted uprisings in several cities, but all of them failed, bringing even greater losses to their ranks. Women with closely cropped hair and unbound feet, symbols of the new Chinese woman, were hunted down as targets for persecution. One of those to fall was Xiang Jingyu, the highest-ranking woman in the Communist Party. In Guangzhou on a single occasion, between two hundred and three hundred women were executed simply for having closely cropped hair (like Smedley's). Over one thousand women leaders were killed in the White Terror. The cost to the revolution and to the women's movement was enormous and forced major changes in the directions both would take.[4]

By the time of Smedley's arrival, in late 1928, open political activity on the left had died down in most major cities. In a few, however (notably Shanghai), Song Qingling, Sun Yat-sen's young widow, became a rallying point for resistance to Chiang Kai-shek's reborn conservative Guomindang. Chiang's marriage to Qingling's sister, Song Meiling, in late 1927 added the dramatic dimension of a family feud to the left-right split within the Guomindang. This split forced the center of gravity of the Chinese revolution to shift slowly back to the countryside, where in the early 1930s, in the remote mountainous regions of the southeastern province of Jiangxi, an alliance was eventually forged between peasants and battle-hardened urban intellectuals, many of whom had been educated in Moscow and the West.

For Smedley, the political context in which the Chinese peasant was living during the early 1930s was defined by war. There was a civil war going on between Chiang Kai-shek and the Communists in the Jiangxi area; and there was an imperialist war in Manchuria, where Japan's Kwantung Army was seizing more and more territory by force of arms. In fact, it was the threat of Japanese imperialism that surprised Smedley most during her first few weeks in China. She had always seen Britain as the main imperialist threat and Japan as anti-imperialist and even a positive model for countries like China and India. Her views changed quickly, and she sent several articles to the *Frankfurter Zeitung* about the seriousness of Japanese aggression in Manchuria. In disbelief, her German editors refused to publish these articles until the Japanese invasion and occupation of Mukden in 1931 convinced them.[5]

In Mukden, Smedley probed social as well as political realities. In retrospect, it was her ability to empathize with individual Chinese— rich or poor, old or young—that set her apart from other foreign journalists. This can be seen in some of her first works of reportage from Manchuria, the best of which, "Five Women of Mukden," appeared in the *New Republic*. The high point of the vignettes is a scene in which an old footbound beggar woman slips and falls on the frozen street. When people gather to laugh at her lying sprawled on the road, the old woman suddenly turns and bellows at the crowd, cursing its members, individually and collectively; it was "as if a sudden blast of Siberian weather" had struck. In a final cameo portrait, Smedley added a note of hope to her theme of defiance: idealistic students, male and female, ostentatiously break the established social code by offering their seats on a crowded bus to a tired old man. For more than a decade, Smedley had been writing secondhand about the plight of the poor and downtrodden in India. In autobiographical reportage, she was finding her métier. Her autobiographical novel, *Daughter of Earth,* was just coming out in the United States and Germany. Now, in China, she would use direct contact and personal narrative to bring to life her advocacy of a new cause: the revolutionary hopes of the Chinese poor.

In late winter Smedley began to move south, first to Japanese-occupied Dalian-Lushan (Port Arthur) and then on to Beijing, where she met with the Y.M.C.A. reformer James Yen and a young missionary couple at Yenching University (now Beijing University). In her letters to Margaret Sanger in 1929, Smedley reported on their discussion of birth control and the possibility of establishing clinics in China like the one Smedley had left in Berlin.[6] She then crossed the Yellow River and headed for Nanjing, the capital of Nationalist China on the Yangzi River. Here she wrote a long article on the fanfare with which Sun Yat-sen was reburied in a huge mausoleum on the outskirts of the city. She noted the many political ironies and tensions in the situation, not the least of which was the conflicting speeches given by the Song sisters, Mme. Sun Yat-sen and Mme. Chiang Kai-shek.[7]

In Nanjing, just as in Mukden and Beijing, Smedley sought out members of the small community of German diplomats and journalists, who welcomed her warmly. Several of them, like the *Frankfurter Zeitung*'s famous Beijing-Tianjin correspondent, Herbert Mueller, were politically left of center, which British intelligence took as further evidence of a German-Russian-Comintern plot to make trouble for the British in China so as to undermine Britain's colonial position in India and elsewhere. The British were in earnest about this. On March 29, 1929, in Meerut, a small town in India about 100 miles east of Delhi, they opened a trial: thirty-one suspected Indian Communists and fifty-one absent co-defendants—including Smedley—were charged with "conspiracy to deprive the [British] King [and] Emperor of sovereignty." Among those standing trial were Sikh activists, who were charged with publishing in Urdu articles sent from Berlin by Smedley (whom they had never met), including the articles in which she predicted war between Britain and Soviet Russia. In fact, it was the assassination of the British officer who had wounded Lajpat Rai at a protest march in Lahore the previous October, as well as other terrorist acts by Communist revolutionaries in the wake of Rai's death in November, that had provoked the British into launching a major attack on the tiny Indian Communist Party and staging the show trial at Meerut. Learning of Rai's death only when she reached Tianjin, Smedley wrote a note of tribute to Rai, expressing her shock and remorse, which was published in India in April of 1929. The show trial dragged on for three years without a conclusion, but it did succeed in keeping the defendants incarcerated until 1933, and in provoking considerable expressions of sympathy for Indian Communists by Nehru, Gandhi, and others in the mainstream of the Indian nationalist movement. At any rate, just as British intelligence suspected she would, Smedley made contact with Sikh police and other Indian nationalist activists in Nanjing. She also gave lectures on Indian nationalism in both Beijing and Nanjing. But within a few weeks, feeling uneasy and confined in Chiang Kai-shek's Nanjing, she boarded a train for Shanghai.[8]

As China's most populous city (3.4 million) and largest treaty port, Shanghai was in its prime in 1929 and would remain so until 1937. Economically, it had been the most important city in China since the turn of the century. Now, precisely because Chinese politics had reached their nadir and the country was helpless against the machinations of foreign powers, Shanghai thrived as a political and cultural center. Over half of the city was made up of concession areas that were owned and governed by various foreign powers under the overall leadership of the British. It was a unique arrangement and a unique moment in Chinese history. Shanghai, the point of maximum Western penetration of Chinese civilization, had also become a haven for Chinese intellectuals and political dissenters fleeing Guomindang jurisdiction. By 1929 almost every writer and artist of importance, who in normal times might have been in Nanjing, had gravitated to Shanghai. It was home to immensely wealthy and privileged families like the Songs who were allied to powerful (and wealthy) underworld leaders like Du Yuesheng; it harbored the greatest concentration of Guomindang power in the country, and also the underground headquarters of the Chinese Communist Party. This was the heady atmosphere that kept Smedley in the city for the next seven years and provided the background for her first China book of social commentary, *Chinese Destinies* (1933).[9]

When she arrived in Shanghai in early May of 1929, Smedley went immediately to the French concession area, in hopes of diminishing the effectiveness of British surveillance tactics. Her first step was to look up Gertrude Binder, a young student that Scott Nearing had told her about in Berlin. Binder was working for the most important U.S.-owned newspaper in Shanghai, the *China Weekly Review,* and was a stringer for a few Midwestern newspapers in America. Smedley proposed that they live together on the second floor of a rooming house on 85 Avenue Dubail, Binder's present residence. Problems soon arose, because Smedley was not alone: she had brought with her a young Chinese writer she had picked up in Mukden, who had been serving her in the dual capacity of translator and lover. This arrangement was soon abandoned.* But the

---

* In Mukden, Beijing, and Nanjing, Smedley had left her friend—he was ten years younger than she—in their hotel room while she went out to see other foreigners. One day on Avenue Dubail, when everyone was out, the young man found a bottle of crème de menthe and managed to drink all of it. The White Russian landlady returned to find him

young Manchurian's departure did not bring calm to Avenue Dubail. Smedley, still sexually defiant after her experiences in Berlin, told Binder that she intended to "take sex like a man." For several weeks she seemed to bring home "anything in pants that she found around town." Binder remembered that one night a young Marine suddenly bolted from the house, frightened by Smedley's aggressive advances. As in New York in 1919–20, however, Smedley soon became satiated and disgusted with herself, and by midsummer her liaisons became longer and more meaningful.[10]

Shanghai's Sikh community was the first focus of serious attention by Smedley. She found this community under heavy surveillance and severely faction-ridden. Nevertheless, during the summer of 1929 she was able to goad the American editor of the *China Weekly Review*, J. B. Powell, into having a lively debate in print with counterparts in the British press over the treatment of Indian (mostly Sikh) nationalists who were being arrested and murdered in the British concession area. Incensed, the British doubled their watch on Smedley's movements and tried once again to persuade the U.S. and Chinese authorities to hand her over for deportation. But Smedley's involvement with the Sikhs ended abruptly in the fall of 1929, when she returned home one day to find the severed head of a Sikh comrade in her wastebasket. It was the result of murderous in-fighting between Sikh factions—exactly the kind of revenge cycle that Lajpat Rai had warned against. For Smedley it was too much, and she had little more to do with the Sikhs of Shanghai.[11]

Most of the Americans with whom Smedley had friendly contact in Shanghai were reporters at the *China Weekly Review*. The editor of the *Review*, J. B. Powell, was a crusty old China hand and former lecturer at the University of Missouri School of Journalism. Although he supported the Guomindang and Chiang Kai-shek, he was anti-British and anti-Japanese enough to find common ground with Smedley and to ask her to write book reviews for the paper. Working under Powell was a young reporter, fresh from Missouri, named Edgar Snow. Smedley befriended Snow, who was ten years her junior, and wrote him a warm letter of introduction to Nehru, which Snow took with him on a trip through In-

---

writhing on the floor, foaming a green liquid at the mouth. Terrified that he might be succumbing to something like rabies, she called a doctor. The doctor rushed over, got one whiff of the patient, and laughed heartily. The landlady was embarrassed and angry, and Gertrude Binder, herself only twenty years old, was amazed. Smedley, who paid the doctor, was not amused and decided on the spot that it was time for her companion to leave (Interview with Gertrude Binder).

dia in 1930. Smedley's American contacts outside the *Review* seemed limited to one or two journalists such as Randall Gould, the editor of the daily *Shanghai Mercury*. She stayed away from U.S. diplomats at the consulate because of their cozy relationship with the British secret service and police.[12]

Of greater importance to Smedley was Shanghai's small community of German leftists, whose political views were closer to her own. They all patronized the Zeitgeist Bookstore near Soochow Creek in the International Settlement, and the manager of the Zeitgeist, Irene Wiedemeyer, became Smedley's good friend and confidante. Through Irene, Smedley located Gerhart and Elli Eisler. (Gerhart had been married previously to Julian Gumperz's present wife, Hede, and Elli was Hede's younger sister.) She also found two old Berlin acquaintances, Arthur and Elsie Ewerts. Gerhart Eisler and Arthur Ewerts were Comintern representatives in Shanghai. (In 1936 Arthur was arrested by Nazi agents in Brazil and brutally tortured into a state of permanent insanity; Elsie died in a Nazi camp at about the same time.) The Eislers and the Ewerts, like Julian Gumperz, were sophisticated Berlin intellectuals. They welcomed Smedley warmly, and she saw her association with them as a natural extension of her Berlin community of friends.[13]

Historians have concluded that at the time of Smedley's arrival in Shanghai, the Comintern was in disarray. Moscow was too preoccupied with internal factional fighting over Stalin's growing influence to give its Shanghai representatives any serious attention or coherent direction; in any case, its main concern was strengthening Soviet Russia for its struggle against the Western imperialists led by the British. For most of 1929, Earl Browder, an important figure in the U.S. Communist Party, was in Shanghai setting up a small organization that Arthur Ewerts subsequently ran without much direction from Moscow.[14] As we have seen, Smedley had known Browder in New York and had described him in Moscow in 1921 as "effeminate and a fraud as head of a workers' movement."[15] It is doubtful that she would have seen much of him in Shanghai. In short, those who knew Smedley best accepted her self-assessment: she was a freelance revolutionary operating on a global scale. She shared the anti-imperialist goals of the Comintern and consciously cultivated friendships with leftists like the Eislers and Ewerts, whom she undoubtedly knew were Comintern representatives, but a Comintern or Communist Party member she was not.*

---

* For the rest of her life, Smedley had to face allegations—originating in Shanghai with British intelligence in the early 1930s—that she was a Comintern agent when she arrived in Shanghai; as evidence, it was claimed that while on her way to China, she had attended

Smedley's first Chinese contacts were with Western-educated intellectuals, a highly refined group of poets, scholars, and writers with whom she attended elegant dinner parties and took moonlit rickshaw rides. Of these friends, the one best known in the West was Hu Shi, a university professor and disciple of John Dewey, who served during World War II as the Guomindang ambassador to Washington. More liberal politically was Yang Quan, a noted anthropologist with the Academia Sinica.[16] The figure to whom Smedley was most attracted was Xu Zhimo, China's leading romantic poet (who would die tragically in a plane crash in 1931). To a romantic imagination, Xu was the perfect union of East and West. He was Oxford-educated and a favorite of the British critics I. A. Richards and H. G. Wells; he was a disciple of the great Indian poet Rabinandrath Tagore, whom he had hosted in Shanghai shortly before meeting Smedley; and his wife had just taken a lover, making their marriage the talk of literary Shanghai. Tall, thin, and looking poetically sensitive in his Chinese scholar's gown, he could be equally eloquent in English and Chinese. By midsummer of 1929, he and Smedley were having an affair, the high point of which was a two-week boat trip down the Yangzi to the Xu family country estate.[17]

But Smedley was not bedazzled for long. In *Battle Hymn of China*, she contrasted her "patrician" Chinese friends with the rickshaw men who pulled them around the city: "[My desire to become a patrician myself] became mixed up with thoughts about my rickshaw coolie silently running like a tired horse before me, his heaving breath interrupted by a rotten cough. Suddenly his broad shoulders began to remind me of my father's. I was a dog, the whole lot of us were dogs!" (p. 57).[18]

Smedley's grip on herself and on Chinese realities grew firmer during the fall of 1929. In this process, two men played a crucial role. The first was Chen Hansheng, the head of Shanghai's new Institute for Social Science Research and the father of modern Chinese social science. Brought

---

the Sixth Congress of the Comintern in Moscow. But that was clearly impossible; in August of 1928, while the Comintern was meeting, Smedley was in Paris, visiting Josephine Bennett and working on the final revisions of *Daughter of Earth* with her American editor. The remaining evidence of a Comintern connection is circumstantial, based on the fact that in the 1930s Smedley was friendly with a number of Shanghai Comintern figures, beginning with Ewerts and Eisler. But according to everything known about the workings of the Comintern, Smedley could not have been a member unless she had also been a member of a national Communist Party or at least acceptable for membership. And no evidence of such a relation to the American, German, or Indian Communist Party has ever been found. Even British intelligence would often categorize her as an anarchist-syndicalist and not a Communist (Shanghai [British] police assessments in F.B.I. 100–68282–1B32 [Exhibits]).

up traditionally in a scholar family, by 1924 Chen had university de-
grees from Pomona, Harvard, and Berlin. Thereafter, he pioneered in
rural socioeconomic survey work; he taught at Beijing, Johns Hopkins,
Tokyo, Delhi, and elsewhere; he edited journals and wrote over a dozen
books in several languages; and all the while, he said, he was "making
revolution"—as a member first of the Comintern (1928–35) and then
of the Chinese Communist Party.*

During the fall of 1929, Chen invited Smedley to join him for two
weeks of survey work in the wealthy lake region of Wuxi west of Shanghai. Landlordism in this area was a more powerful institution than in
Manchuria, where everyone, the few landlords included, was comparatively poor. By studying the landlord-tenant relationship firsthand,
Smedley began to understand the fatalistic acceptance of great poverty
existing next to great wealth. She also witnessed, for the first time, suspected Communists being beheaded in the street by local authorities.
She could no longer be charged, as she had been in the past by Indian
associates, with naïveté about social and economic realities in Asia.[19]

The other person from whom Smedley learned much in 1929 was
Rewi Alley, a thirty-year-old New Zealander who was inspecting labor
conditions for the municipal government in all foreign-controlled factories in Shanghai. With Alley, she tasted the Dickensian world of Shanghai industrial life. As Alley wrote in 1952: "She asked to be shown some
factories, and we had just been around some of the shocking sweatshops
which were all too common in the 'model settlement' of Shanghai. I can
still see her great eyes looking at me intently over the table as I told her
some of the suffering, some of the tragedy, some of the denial of life I
moved amongst in industrial Shanghai."[20] In some strong pieces on
child labor and the abuse of women (for the *Frankfurter Zeitung* and
later for *China Forum*), Smedley drew on this experience and on data
from Chen Hansheng's pioneering studies of Shanghai's contract labor
system.[21]

With the help of Chen Hansheng and Rewi Alley, Smedley was seeing
that in China the injustices were so great, and the choices so clear, that

---

* Chen is one of the last of a remarkable generation of Chinese intellectuals who, like
former Premier Zhou Enlai, were equally at home in China or abroad, and whose commitment to a socialist revolution was international in premise. In numerous interviews over a
ten-year period, he told stories in which Smedley appears as anarchistic, promiscuous,
and hot-tempered; but he emphasized her integrity and wit, her intuitive sense of the essential, and her capacity for self-sacrifice in the cause of the oppressed. He said that she
had never been a member of the Comintern or a Communist Party, and that what he admired most of all about her was her principled internationalism. A loyal friend, he kept in
contact with Smedley for the rest of her life.

there was no ambiguity left in the situation. Here a personal commitment to the oppressed could be made meaningful, and here, if she could endure many hardships, she might have a real impact. As this awareness grew, she lost her passionate interest in the Indian independence movement and in the prospects of war between the Soviet Union and Britain. Toward the end of 1929 she parted with her American roommate, Gertrude Binder, and began to live alone. Her friendships with Chinese became less frivolous, her love life more subdued.

By 1930 Agnes Smedley was well settled in Shanghai and in touch with the underground revolutionary movement. She was writing a great deal and had completed some of her best pieces of feature writing, such as "Hsu Meiling" and "Silk Workers."[22] Her spirits were high. In the United States and Germany, *Daughter of Earth* was attracting attention and receiving praise in the sort of journals that mattered to her, such as *New Masses* and *The New Republic*. On April 2, 1930, she wrote to her old friend Karin Michaelis about finding a new identity:

> I live now only for an idea. This surprises me more than anything else. More and more I become political [and] intellectual, with emotions being crowded completely or nearly completely out of my life—I mean any emotions of personal love. I work about 18 hours a day out here, and there is no rest even when you do no work, for the poverty of Asia . . . presses in upon you on every side. . . . Here is a handful of rich Chinese and foreigners living in the midst of indescribable poverty which pushes its way right under their windows—and here are the big battleships of many lands riding at anchor in the river, and here are armed soldiers and marines from many foreign lands "guarding" the handful of foreigners who live in wealth. Here, in the midst of riches, poverty, a vast network of espionage, of murder, kidnapping, executions of idealists, crimes of every sort, sometimes I almost seek rest in philosophy. . . . Always I think that I shall write one more book before I die—just one book in which I shall, many years from now, try to show what the capitalist system, with its imperialist development, has done to the human being—how it has turned him into a wolf. Only inhuman creatures who have become wolves could for a moment try to perpetuate the system that has reduced Asia to its position today. And yet the armed forces and the battleships are here for this purpose.

On June 23 she wrote to Michaelis about love:

> China has done me much good. It has made me a sane woman; sane and clearheaded and hard in mind. All my bondage to Chatto has gone from me, once and forever. I recall my life with him as a frightful mess and a ghastly thing for both him and me. No man will ever get his hooks in me again. I shall have men friends and I shall now and then live with a man whom I admire intellectually and who appeals to me physically; and the basis of our union must be a broad and generous friendship. But I am now a sane

woman. There is always a little tendency in me to long for the old kind of love
that is senseless and dependent and cruel. But I try to analyze that out of my
mind and heart. . . . I hope to socialize all my emotions in that respect. But
all this does not mean I am or ever will be a hardboiled woman. I can tell that
by the response of the Chinese to me: I have countless friends whose devotion to me knows no limit. . . . The thing is that I love the Chinese and all
Asiatics, and they feel that.

As Smedley became immersed in China, correspondence and contact
with most of her old friends in Germany and the United States faded
away. For example, in her first letters from China to Margaret Sanger,
she discussed the possibility of establishing birth control clinics in Beijing
and Shanghai on Sanger's behalf, and Sanger sent seed money for a
short-lived pilot project that Smedley helped organize in Beijing. By
1931, however, Smedley had come to believe that a birth control movement could never make progress in China until the country experienced
a social and economic revolution, and she said so publicly in an article
for *The Nation*. Thereafter correspondence between the two women
dropped off.[23]

Smedley's break with another old friend, Emma Goldman, was more
dramatic and emotional. The issue was Goldman's persistent and sweeping denunciations of Moscow and all Communist movements. In her
last note to Goldman—the woman who had once been her model, and
from whom she had learned so much about politics and love—Smedley
argued that in China the Communists were worth supporting because
they were "the only ones who offer any hope for the peasants." She said
she did not want to see Goldman again, because "I do not want to think
of you with bitterness."[24]

When Smedley wrote to Karin Michaelis in June of 1930, she was
seriously involved with a new man. He was Richard Sorge, alias Johnson, who was ostensibly a German living in Shanghai as a correspondent for the German press. But his real mission, which eventually made
him one of the most intriguing figures of World War II, was rather different. His reputation today rests on his record as a master spy for the Soviet Union operating in Tokyo from 1937 to 1941. Between 1939 and
1941, in particular, Sorge and a Japanese collaborator, Ozaki Hotsumi,
transmitted to Moscow high-level communications between the German and Japanese governments. Moreover, many scholars now believe
that they had a significant influence on German and Japanese foreign
policies because of their trusted positions as Asian experts. Both men
were arrested by the Japanese in 1941 and executed in 1944. It was later

alleged that Smedley was connected to the spy ring because she had introduced Ozaki to Sorge in 1931.[25]

When Sorge arrived in Shanghai, he immediately sought out Smedley. Sharing literary and intellectual interests, he and his wife had been friendly in the late 1920s with the Eislers and with Julian Gumperz. (But Smedley had *not* met Sorge in Germany or the Soviet Union, as some have claimed.) Except for Smedley and one or two others, Sorge avoided contact with the Shanghai radical community. As "Johnson" he was gathering military intelligence and cultivating German officers like Colonel Hermann von Kriebel, who was advising Chiang Kai-shek's armies, by exchanging information. According to Chen Hansheng, Sorge and Smedley became romantically involved soon after they met in 1930, and they spent the late spring and summer together in south China around Guangzhou.[26]

Sorge was a big, Nordic, ruggedly handsome man three years younger than Smedley. Born in Russia of a German father and a Russian mother, he had lived in Germany after the age of eleven; he had become a Communist after serving in the German army in World War I, when he was wounded three times. (Interestingly, his grandfather Friedrich Sorge was a prominent Socialist who knew Marx and Engels and, later, Samuel Gompers.) Like Smedley, Sorge had a taste for the flamboyant, a good sense of humor, and a fondness for drink. Their relationship was apparently based on mutual respect and attraction, with no strings attached. As Smedley wrote to Florence Lennon on May 28, 1930: "I'm married, child, so to speak—just sort of married, you know; but he's a he-man also, and its 50–50 all along the line, with he helping me and I him and we working together or bust, and so on; [it's] a big, broad, all-sided friendship and comradeship. I do not know how long it will last; that does not depend on us. I fear not long. But these days will be the best in my life. Never have I known such good days, never have I known such a healthy life, mentally, physically, psychically."[27]

Smedley was impressed by Sorge's sophistication and eagerness to learn about China. She knew about his life in Germany and his war experiences, and she assumed that, like Eisler, he was really a Comintern agent.* She introduced him to some of her Chinese friends, notably Pro-

---

* In reality Sorge's mission was to provide intelligence to the Soviet Red Army; his orders were to avoid association with foreign Comintern members or members of the Chinese Communist Party. See Chalmers Johnson, *An Instance of Treason: Ozaki Hotsumi and the Sorge Spy Ring* (Stanford, 1964), pp. 68, 74–75. Recently Walter Prange (*Target Tokyo* [New York, 1984], p. 22) and others have said that Sorge sponsored Smedley for

fessor Chen Hansheng. The three of them soon began meeting on a regular basis and exchanging information. Sorge became increasingly concerned about Japanese troop movements in Manchuria and their political implications for the Soviet Union, and he accompanied Chen on a trip into northwest China during the spring of 1932.

It was through Smedley that Sorge found most of the Asian contacts who gave him significant information over the next two years. The most important of these, of course, was the Japanese journalist Ozaki Hotsumi. When Smedley introduced the two men in 1931, she knew Ozaki well, as he was already translating *Daughter of Earth* into Japanese. In recent years the Smedley-Ozaki-Sorge friendship in Shanghai has become part of the legend surrounding the accomplishments and romance of the later spy ring. Their relationship was even dramatized by a leading Japanese playwright, who mistakenly portrayed Ozaki as Smedley's principal lover.[28]

For two months during the winter of 1930–31, Smedley's personal crusade to stop Western imperialism led her to investigate the political situation in the Philippines. The United States had promised eventual independence with the adoption of the Jones Act in 1916. As of 1931, that promise was still to be realized. Smedley knew that public opinion in the United States was still divided on the issue. On this working holiday, Smedley researched a series of articles critical of the U.S. colonial presence in the Philippines. Using contacts suggested by her old friend Scott Nearing, she wrote about Filipinos from all walks of life, including interviews with members of the then embryonic Philippine Communist Party.[29]

After returning to Shanghai in February of 1931, Smedley was absorbed by a crisis that shook Shanghai's community of German leftists. In June, Paul and Gertrude Ruegg, known as Mr. and Mrs. Hilaire Noulens, were arrested. Allegedly, they were Comintern agents organizing a branch of the League Against Imperialism in Shanghai. (The Noulens were Swiss, but did not have valid passports.) It was an unusual move for French and British police, who, after making the arrest in the foreign concession area, turned the Noulens over to Chinese authorities as Communists. Smedley knew the Noulens because of the anti-British propaganda work they had done together with Indian nationalists and labor unions in Shanghai. Their arrest soon produced tension in Smedley's

---

Comintern membership—a claim that came not from Sorge himself but from his Japanese interrogators when they were questioned by MacArthur's staff after World War II.

relationship with Richard Sorge. The issue was what to do about the Noulens' young son. Smedley made a point of openly helping the boy and asked friends and acquaintances to take him in. One of the persons she approached was Ruth Kuczynski, a young German Communist Party member she had met about six months earlier. When Sorge persuaded Kuczynski to refuse to take the child, on the grounds that public association with the Noulens would identify her as a Communist, Smedley was outraged. She wrote Kuczynski an angry letter accusing her of not being a true revolutionary. And she began to give up her romantic attachment to Sorge, whose affairs with other women had already made her jealous.[30]

As usual, Smedley was defiantly open about her position: she joined Chen Hansheng and Mme. Sun Yat-sen on the Noulens Defense Committee, which worked to bring international publicity to the case, to apply pressure for the couple's release. The Noulens were tried by court-martial in late 1931; both were sentenced to life imprisonment. In 1933, the Soviet Union, which had broken off relations with the Nationalist government after Chiang's purge of Communists in 1927, reestablished diplomatic relations. It may well have been because of an increasingly close relationship between Chiang and Moscow that the Noulens were released from prison and deported in September 1937.[31]

Well over a year before she became involved in the Noulens' defense, Smedley had begun associating with members of an underground literary movement—writers who rejected the romanticism of literati figures like patrician Xu Zhimo (known as "the Chinese Shelley"). For Smedley, the key figure in this process was Mao Dun, probably China's leading novelist at the time. As she and Mao Dun worked on translations of literary works in 1930, she began to see that a revolution was taking place in Chinese arts, drama, and literature. Socialist-oriented experimentation was everywhere—and so was Guomindang censorship and repression. The struggles Smedley described in a series of pioneering articles on the arts were intense, dangerous, and creative.[32]

Smedley's excitement and desire to help were irrepressible. In 1980 Mao Dun recalled:

> Knowing her was as if I had seen a comet shooting loftily and leisurely across the sky and then suddenly it disappeared. Agnes Smedley was an unforgettable person, whether you liked her or not, and we Chinese liked her very much. She was the most thorough-going internationalist I have ever met. There also was absolutely no smack of feudalism in her. And to us Chinese, this is so rare a quality that it made her just that more attractive. She radiated

a kind of nobility that is unforgettable—a mixture of incisiveness (at times akin to abrasiveness), alienation from worldliness (at times akin to novelty-seeking), and hatred for evil (at times akin to a lack of forbearance), as well as devotion to others (at times akin to self-denial).[33]

It was through Mao Dun that Smedley met the man who since the May Fourth Movement of 1919 had been at the center of the movement for change in the arts: the author and critic Lu Xun.

As an essayist, poet, and short-story writer, by 1929 Lu Xun had won recognition as China's finest living writer. During the 1920s he had wandered from north to south and finally settled in Shanghai, where he married and began to raise a family. He lived in the International Settlement area, down a side lane in a European-style row house. Today his home is a museum, furnished just as it was in the early 1930s. With the late afternoon sun filtering through the curtains of the second-floor study, one can easily imagine Lu Xun and Smedley sitting in the rattan chairs by the front window, discussing literature and politics. From this study, Lu Xun presided over the Shanghai literary scene—encouraging the young, lashing out at Guomindang repression, and urging unity within the literary left. Lu Xun was steadfastly internationalist in outlook; he had studied in Japan and had translated major German and Russian works (his favorite author was Maxim Gorky).

Smedley first met Lu Xun at his home in December of 1929. Finding that they could communicate in German, the two quickly became friends. Lu Xun had been reading *Daughter of Earth* in German, and he eventually found a translator and publisher for a Chinese edition. The editor of a literary journal, he got Smedley into print, for the first time in Chinese, by publishing an article of hers on conditions in rural China.[34] For her part, Smedley introduced Lu Xun to the graphic work of her Berlin friend Käthe Kollwitz, and she soon became an intermediary for correspondence between the two of them. It is possible that she also introduced Lu Xun to the work of the German Socialist cartoonist George Grosz.[35]

During the spring and summer of 1930, Smedley and Lu Xun worked with the organizers of a new League of Left Wing Writers. The League was an umbrella organization for young writers who accepted a common set of explicitly revolutionary political principles and agreed to work in cities like Shanghai as "cultural guerrillas," counterparts to the guerrilla fighters in the countryside. Smedley concentrated on publicizing the work of the League in Europe, India, Soviet Russia, and North America.

Within a year, her association with Lu Xun had enabled Smedley to meet most of the prominent new writers in Shanghai, and in 1930 she wrote several of the first articles in a Western language on the new social realist movement in Chinese art and literature. Predictably, her concern was more political than esthetic. She applauded the discipline and political commitment of these young Chinese intellectuals. Compared to their Indian counterparts, she wrote, they were less troubled by factionalism and had a record of action and sacrifice. The majority were not what she and Lu Xun called "salon Socialists," a class more common in Europe, North America, and India.[36]

Smedley's idealistic devotion to her Chinese mentor Lu Xun was reminiscent of her earlier admiration of the veteran Indian nationalist Lajpat Rai. On September 7, 1930, Smedley and the League of Left Wing Writers put on a fiftieth-birthday party for Lu Xun at a Dutch-Indonesian restaurant in the French concession area. Her account of that evening (in *Battle Hymn of China,* pp. 77–83) brings to life the tense political atmosphere and the powerful personal and cultural aspirations Smedley shared with her friends in Shanghai:

On the afternoon of the birthday celebration I stood with my two friends at the garden gate of a small Dutch restaurant in the French concession. From our position we had a clear view of the long street by which the guests would come. [They were on the lookout for police and Guomindang informers.] Lu Xun, accompanied by his wife and small son, arrived early. . . . He was short and frail, and wore a cream-colored silk gown and soft Chinese shoes. He was bareheaded and his close-cropped hair stood up like a brush. In structure his face was like that of an average Chinese, yet it remains in my memory as the most eloquent face I have ever seen. A kind of living intelligence and awareness streamed from it. His manner, speech, and his every gesture radiated the indefinable of a perfectly integrated personality. I suddenly felt as awkward and ungracious as a clod. . . .

As the guests went by, my two friends explained that they included writers, artists, professors, students, actors, reporters, research scholars, and even two patricians. This last pair came not because they shared Lu Xun's convictions, but to honor his integrity, courage, and scholarship.

It was a motley and exciting gathering—pioneers in an intellectual revolution. One group, poorly dressed and apparently half-starved, was pointed out as representing a new [theater group] trying to edge in social dramas between Wilde's *Salome* and *Lady Windermere's Fan.* A more prosperous-looking group proved to be Fudan University students led by Professor Hong Shen. They had produced some of Ibsen's plays and one or two written by their professor, who was also a director of one of the first Chinese motion picture companies. A third dramatic group was made up of young leftist actors, writers, and translators who had produced plays by Romain Rolland, Upton Sinclair, Gorky, and Remarque. Much later they produced *Carmen,* were raided by police after the third performance, arrested, and closed down. Detectives in the audience had not liked the last scene, in which Don José stabbed Carmen to death: as Carmen hurled her ring at her cast-off lover, she uttered words that reminded them of the split between the Communists and the Guomindang.

From my place at the gate I now saw a number of people approaching. One tall, thin young man walked rapidly and kept glancing behind him; he was clearly a student, and as he passed, my friends whispered that he was editor of the *Shanghai Bao,* an underground Communist paper which conducted a kind of journalistic guerrilla warfare in the city. Shortly after came one whose foreign suit was wrinkled and whose hair was wild and disheveled. He had just come from months in prison. He had been suspected of representing the Chinese Red Aid; the charge had been true, but money had proved stronger. His family had spent a fortune bribing his captors [to release him].

When darkness began to fall, half of the guests left. Others took our place as sentries and we went inside the restaurant with the other guests.

After the dinner, speeches began and one of my friends translated for me. The Dutch restaurant owner understood no Chinese, so he did not worry us, but the Chinese waiters stood listening intently. When the man with the wild hair made a report on prison conditions, we watched every move of the servants. After him came the editor of the *Shanghai Bao,* giving the first factual report I had so far heard on the rise of the Red Army and on the "harvest uprisings" of peasants who had fought the landlords and then poured into the Red Army like rivulets into an ever-broadening river.

A short, heavy-set young woman with bobbed hair began to tell of the need for developing proletarian literature. She ended her address by appealing to Lu Xun to become the protector and "master" of new League of Left Writers and League of Left Artists, the initial groups which later became the Chinese Cultural Federation.

Throughout, Lu Xun listened carefully, promptly turning his attention to new speakers, his forefinger all the while tracing the edge of his teacup. When all had finished, he rose and began to talk quietly, telling a story of the half-century of intellectual turmoil which had been his life—the story of China uprooted. . . .

He was now asked, he said, to lead a movement of proletarian literature, and some of his young friends were urging him to become a proletarian writer. It would be childish to pretend that he was a proletarian writer. His roots were in the village, in peasant and scholarly life. Nor did he believe that Chinese intellectual youth, with no experience of the life, hopes, and sufferings of workers and peasants, could—as yet—produce proletarian literature. Creative writing must spring from experience, not theory.

Despite this, he would continue to place the best of Western literature and art before Chinese youth. He was willing to help guide youth, or, as they requested, to be their master. But protect them? Who could do that under a regime which called even the mildest social literature criminal? As "master," he urged educated youth to share the life of the workers and peasants, and draw their material from life, but [to] study Western social literature and art for form. . . .

[Lu Xun] often spoke to me of his plans for a historical novel based on his life, but the social reaction in which his country wallowed seemed to leave no time for this. So deep was his hatred of "the slaughter of the innocents" and the violation of men's rights that after a while he was using his pen only as a weapon—a veritable dagger it was—of political criticism.

Of all Chinese writers, he seemed the most intricately linked with Chinese history, literature, and culture. It was almost impossible to translate into English some of his "political criticism" because, unable to attack reaction openly, his writings were a mosaic of allusions to personalities, events, and ideas of the darkest periods of China's past. Every educated Chinese knew that he was comparing present tyranny with that of the past. Through these political criticisms ran rich streams of both Chinese and Western culture, couched in a style as fine as an etching.* He introduced literary magazine after literary magazine to the public, only to see each suppressed. These introductions, compact and chaste, were flown like proud banners. To him freedom of thought and expression was the essence of human achievement. So distinctive was his style that pseudonyms failed to shield him, and censors began to mutilate his articles until they often appeared senseless. Writers, editors, and artists associated with him began to disappear without trace; only his age and eminence protected him from arrest.

On the night of February 7, 1931, five leading members of the League of Left Wing Writers, including the editor of the *Shanghai Bao,* were summarily executed by Guomindang authorities. Alarmed, Smedley smuggled the writer Ding Ling, the wife of one of the executed men, out of Shanghai. Lu Xun's answer was an article entitled "Present Conditions of Literature and Art in Darkest China," which he asked Smedley to translate and have published abroad. Smedley consulted with Mao Dun and others and decided to wait, because she genuinely feared that publishing it would lead to Lu Xun's arrest and execution. Instead, she and Mao Dun persuaded Lu Xun to write an appeal for help from the League which would be less of a direct challenge to the Guomindang. The two of them then translated the letter and arranged for it to be hand-carried to New York, Berlin, Moscow, and elsewhere. In the United States, this appeal appeared in the June, 1931, issue of *New Masses,* and

---

* Smedley liked to call Lu Xun the Voltaire of the Chinese revolution, and certainly his writing had an erudition and polish that made it quite different from her own, which was bluntly emotional and verged on the melodramatic.

it had the desired effect. Hundreds of letters and telegrams of protest poured into Guomindang headquarters from writers and artists around the world.[37]

Smedley had met Mme. Sun Yat-sen in Moscow in November of 1928, when she was on her way to China. In 1929 the two women met again in Shanghai, and within a year Smedley was helping Mme. Sun with correspondence and writing her speeches, especially in regard to the League Against Imperialism. (Mme. Sun was an executive officer of the League, and Smedley was personally acquainted with some of its leading figures, such as Nehru and Roger Baldwin.) By September of 1929, Smedley felt free to write on the flyleaf of a copy of *Daughter of Earth*, "To Mme. Sun Yat-sen, whom I respect and love without reserve as a revolutionary who keeps the faith."

Mme. Sun, although related to many of the Guomindang leaders, steadfastly refused to join the Guomindang and chose instead to oppose the Nanjing government and support a series of left-of-center causes. As with Lu Xun and Smedley, it was impossible for the Guomindang to arrest or assassinate her because of her international reputation, and of course she was nationally respected as Sun Yat-sen's widow. But she was under constant surveillance by Guomindang police, and she was made to watch as those around her disappeared into prison or fell to the assassin's bullet. By 1931 Smedley was working so closely with Mme. Sun on various projects that many considered her to be an official speechwriter and aide. The two women collaborated publicly, for example, at the time of the Noulens affair, forming an international defense committee with Chen Hansheng and others to publicize the case and pressure the Guomindang for the couple's release.[38]

In September of 1931, Japan's Kwantung Army, acting on the pretext that the Chinese had sabotaged the South Manchurian Railroad, drove the Chinese army of warlord Zhang Xueliang out of Manchuria. In the Manchurian Incident, as it quickly became known, the Japanese army had boldly formulated foreign policy on its own, without the consent of civilian officials in Tokyo, and this shocked even Smedley's Japanese journalist friend Ozaki Hotsumi. Throughout the autumn of 1931, Smedley, Ozaki, and Sorge continued to trade information from various sources on the latest Japanese moves and Chinese reactions. It was probably concern with the new political situation at home that prompted Ozaki to return to Japan in January of 1932. He left just in time.[39]

On January 30, 1932, hoping to frighten the Chinese into accepting their takeover of Manchuria, the Japanese launched a naval landing against the Chinese quarter of Shanghai. They were met by the Chinese Nineteenth Route Army, reinforced by divisions of students and regular soldiers from Nanjing. Finding the resistance stronger than they had expected, the Japanese resorted to a massive aerial bombardment of the old city—the first large-scale bombing of a civilian population in history. A week of bloody house-to-house combat followed, until the Chinese withdrew to a defensive perimeter around Shanghai. A truce was signed on May 5, ending what is now called the Shanghai Incident of February, 1932. Essentially a Japanese victory, the truce created a large demilitarized zone in and around Shanghai in which Chinese troops were not allowed. It also provoked a real upsurge in Chinese nationalism. From this point on, popular impatience and anger with the impotence of the Nanjing government grew steadily. It eventually led to the Xi'an kidnapping of Chiang Kai-shek in 1936, as well as the formation of a united front with the Communists, and declaration of war on Japan in 1937.

To Smedley, the Shanghai Incident—or war, as she called it—meant two things. First, it reinforced her conviction that Japan was the chief imperialist menace in the Far East, the enemy against whom all should unite. In her view, the Japanese threat had become far more important than the British or the civil war between the Guomindang and the Chinese Communists. This put her at odds with the mainstream Comintern view and the Chinese Communist Party line, which gave top priority to protecting the Soviet Union and engaging in class struggles within China against Chiang Kai-shek. Second, the Shanghai Incident gave Smedley her first opportunity to work as a war correspondent, and she made the most of it. Hitching rides back and forth between the battle lines, she wrote extensively on Japanese and Chinese tactics, the human suffering caused by the bombing, and the heroics of the Nineteenth Route Army and its civilian supporters.[40] At one point the Japanese bombed the area where Lu Xun lived. Smedley managed to sneak through the Japanese barricades and rushed in panic to his home, which was badly damaged. As she wrote in *Battle Hymn of China*: "I hammered on the doors and shouted in English and German, but no one answered. Marooned in their homes, many Chinese refused to respond to anyone, and some of them died of hunger rather than open their doors. . . . Only when the [Shanghai] war was over did I learn that Lu Xun and his family had been rescued and hidden by Japanese friends" (p. 107).

Just before the Japanese struck Shanghai, Smedley was dismissed by the *Frankfurter Zeitung;* there had been decisive changes in the political climate in Germany, and Guomindang-leaning intellectuals such as Hu Shi had made complaints about her to the German Embassy. Thus her reports on the Shanghai Incident appeared in a number of Indian and American journals, but not in German publications.[41]

During 1932 Smedley was also putting together a book of reworked old and new pieces, *Chinese Destinies* (1933), and starting a new work on the Jiangxi Soviet, *China's Red Army Marches* (1934). Also in that year she and Chen Hansheng became heavily involved in a short-lived new group, the China League for Civil Rights, which was dedicated to curbing the harassment and persecution of intellectuals.[42]

As Smedley's political activities expanded, her friendly contacts with fellow American journalists narrowed to a few leftists, such as Harold Isaacs and Frank Glass. Isaacs was a wealthy young New Yorker who had come to China at the age of twenty, right after graduating from Columbia University. In search of adventure, he first worked for the Chinese-owned, Guomindang-controlled English-language press in Shanghai. Eventually he fell under the influence of Smedley and Frank Glass, an older South African journalist who was a fervent Trotskyist with a committed Chinese following. After a trip into the interior with Glass, he experienced something like a conversion; he returned a committed leftist, with increasing Trotskyist tendencies. Early in 1932, with encouragement from Glass, Smedley, and Mme. Sun, Isaacs founded the *China Forum,* an English-language weekly that expressed views close to those of the Chinese Communists. Smedley, Chen Hansheng, Frank Glass, George Kennedy, and others contributed heavily to it with anonymous articles, including the first translations of several short stories by Lu Xun and other members of the League of Left Wing Writers. The *China Forum's* most noticed production, however, was *Five Years of Kuomintang Reaction* (May 1932), a detailed book-length indictment of Guomindang rule that Smedley and Isaacs co-edited. It immediately attracted censorship and created consternation in Shanghai's official foreign circles.[43]

On occasional trips to Beijing, Smedley kept in touch with Edgar Snow, who in mid-1932 had moved north to teach at Yenching University. She also visited a young American historian, John K. Fairbank, and his artist wife Wilma, who had appeared in Shanghai in 1932 with a letter of introduction from the widow of Fairbank's uncle and Smedley's lawyer, Gilbert Roe. In December, 1932, Smedley stayed for a month with the young couple in Beijing while on an organizing mission for the

League for Civil Rights, and afterward she used them as a maildrop for Beijing members of the League.[44]

Not surprisingly, Smedley's problems with the Guomindang-controlled English and Chinese press led to vicious personal attacks on her morals as well as her politics—a tactic to which she was hardened by now. The nadir was reached in a 1933 Guomindang dispatch which claimed that on a visit to the Jiangxi Soviet base, she had brought cases of whiskey with her and had stood nude before a mass rally, singing the Internationale.[45]

In fact, although she certainly wanted to, Smedley never managed to visit the Jiangxi Soviet, where between 1929 and 1934 Mao Zedong and Zhu De were establishing a base and attempting to recoup the declining fortunes of the Chinese Communist Party. But beginning in 1932 she did shelter many refugees from Jiangxi, hiding their documents, obtaining medical treatment for them, and questioning them thoroughly. Her most prominent visitors were two Red Army commanders, Zhou Jianping, who was killed in battle in 1938, and Chen Geng, who would become China's senior military adviser to Vietnam in the 1950s. From the materials she collected in this fashion, Smedley began to write the first articles in a Western language about life in the liberated Jiangxi area. Moreover, it was partly through Smedley that Otto Braun made contact with the Jiangxi Soviet and arranged to go there as Moscow's permanent military representative and adviser. Finally, intelligence about her Jiangxi connection stimulated even tighter surveillance by Guomindang and British police, and Smedley began making frequent changes of address within the French concession. At one point Glass and Isaacs took turns sleeping on Smedley's front porch to protect her from the Guomindang thugs she thought were lurking in the shadows across the street, waiting for a chance to break in.[46]

In January of 1933, Richard Sorge left Shanghai for Moscow and Germany. The scene of his subsequent career and rendezvous with Ozaki Hotsumi would be Japan. Smedley, who apparently saw much less of Sorge in 1932, would never see him again.[47] In February, Smedley and Mme. Sun played host to George Bernard Shaw, then on a whirlwind tour of the Far East. When introduced to Lu Xun, Shaw quipped: "They call you the Gorky of China, but you are more handsome than Gorky." "Oh," replied Lu Xun with a smile, "As I grow older I will become still more handsome." In a now-famous photograph of Shaw with Lu Xun and other luminaries in Mme. Sun's garden, Smedley appears tense and depressed.[48]

Indeed, by the early spring of 1933 Smedley was exhausted and anxious. Many of her friends had departed, and Professor Chen Hansheng was about to leave for Japan. It was now evident that she could not soon visit the Jiangxi Soviet areas. She was also depressed about having to fire her male secretary and translator, Feng Da, whom she suspected (correctly, as it turned out) of having ties to the Guomindang; Feng's recent marriage to her friend the left-wing writer and activist Ding Ling worried her greatly.[49] Smedley's principal concern, however, was with finishing her book on the Jiangxi Soviet. At this time, she was one of the few Westerners conversant with developments there who also sensed both the long-term significance of the Chinese Communists' success in organizing peasants and the growing seriousness of Guomindang military campaigns against it. Her mission, as she saw it, was to get the full story out as soon as possible, but the distractions and pressures of her life in Shanghai were making this difficult. Thus when a publisher in Moscow offered her an advance for the book, she accepted quickly and left in May of 1933 to finish writing it in the Soviet Union.

CHAPTER X

Moscow, New York, and Shanghai, 1933–1936

Smedley spent ten months in the Soviet Union, from June, 1933, until April, 1934. Soon after she arrived in Moscow, doctors advised her to go to a sanitorium for heart patients in the Caucasus Mountains at Kislovodsk. She paid for the summer's stay there by using the advance from her Moscow publisher and by selling over a thousand of the photographs she had taken in China. Although she found the rest she needed in Kislovodsk, her attention was diverted from the Jiangxi book when she learned in June of 1933 that her friend Ding Ling, the left-wing writer and Lu Xun's protégé, had been arrested. Smedley's suspicions of her secretary and Ding Ling's husband, Feng Da, proved correct, as it was his defection to the Guomindang that had led to Ding Ling's arrest. Hurriedly Smedley put together a collection of translated short stories, by Ding Ling and others, to publicize the persecution of writers in China.[1] This task completed, she began to make real progress with her book on the Jiangxi Soviet. She returned to Moscow in September, still hoping to finish the book quickly and leave for China in November, via Europe and New York.[2]

Smedley lived in the capital in a second-class residential hotel, cooking meals on a small stove and keeping house for herself. One night the Chinese poet Emile Xiao, a boyhood friend of Mao Zedong and an early Chinese Communist Party member, visited Smedley to invite her to his home for dinner. Later, at his request, Smedley gave a talk to Moscow's International Congress of Writers on literary developments in China. Xiao remembered Smedley as a sad and lonely woman who was restless and anxious to get on with her work. He recalled her simple life-style and the courtesy she showed the old and infirm on the streets of the city. She was definitely not being treated as part of the Comintern family or the *Moscow Daily News* crowd, whose life revolved around the old Hotel Lux. Emile Xiao's impressions jibe with the few letters that survive and with the recollections of another Chinese friend in Moscow, Jack Chen.[3]

Although she published nothing about the Soviet Union, Smedley's letters suggest that she was impressed by the improvement in living standards and cultural life since her first visit in 1921. But except when she was visiting Chinese friends or going to the ballet and opera with Archie Phinney, a Nez Percé Indian from Idaho who was working in Moscow, Smedley felt isolated and restless. This was especially true when her work bogged down and she found herself haggling with her Russian editors over her book. (For example, despite her protests they deleted a chapter in which she described the shooting of landlords by Communists.) She also complained about the *Moscow Daily News* circle, with whose leader (and editor of the *News*), Michael Borodin, she had clashed in 1921.[4]

In January of 1934, feeling increasingly uncomfortable in Moscow, Smedley moved to Leningrad to complete her book. There she had a reunion with Virendranath Chattopadhyaya, who had arrived the year before from Berlin, after the Nazi Party had risen to power. By 1934 Chatto was settled into Leningrad's Institute of Ethnography and had a Russian bride who was expecting their first child. The reunion was friendly and platonic, and finally closed a painful chapter in Smedley's life.[5] In Leningrad Smedley was able to put the finishing touches to her book. In March she returned to Moscow, where she received word from Madame Sun that she wanted Smedley to help her with a new project: finding funds and personnel in New York for a new English-language journal that might serve as a consistent voice for the underground communist movement. Smedley heard from Mme. Sun that the *China Forum* had collapsed after a sharp swing in a Trotskyist direction by the *Forum*'s editor, Harold Isaacs. After seeing her editors, by early April Smedley was off for New York via Europe. She stopped in Paris for a few days to visit an old friend from the Greenwich Village birth-control movement, Josephine Bennett Brooks, and then she sailed for New York.

Smedley was met at the wharf by her former roommate Florence Lennon, whom she had last seen in Berlin in 1925. Now divorced, Florence had brought along a new male companion, and almost immediately an argument began. After the boyfriend denounced the Soviet and Chinese Communist parties in Trotskyist terms, Smedley asked Florence to renounce him. Florence refused, and the two women never saw each other again.[6]

Smedley was returning to the United States in the middle of the Depression after twelve years abroad. She arrived in New York in a comparatively self-confident mood and sure of her political position. So far as she was concerned, economic conditions in the United States proved that imperialism and capitalism were on the wane. In New York Smedley hoped to raise funds for Mme. Sun's new journal and line up reporting jobs for herself. Smedley's New York stay was hectic. She visited the offices of the *New Masses,* Thorberg Brundin, Margaret Sanger, the widow of Gilbert Roe, and her publishers—in addition to addressing groups about China. In the Depression, funds and jobs were scarce. She failed to line up a full-time job as a foreign correspondent for a major paper or wire service. Her biggest success was the negotiation of a new Coward-McCann abridged edition of *Daughter of Earth,* with an introduction by Malcolm Cowley. *Daughter of Earth* had received critical acclaim but not sold well, and Cowley believed that a shorter, better edited edition could have mass appeal.[7]

Like many intellectuals of the period, Malcolm Cowley had been radicalized by the Depression. Having witnessed the organizing of miners in Appalachia, Cowley had reported that the lives of ordinary people were given new dignity and meaning when they joined together to fight for better conditions. But Cowley was reexamining his revolutionary enthusiasm when he first met Smedley in New York in May of 1934. His New York City milieu was the well-intentioned intellectual left community, similar to Smedley's Greenwich Village in 1918–20. To Cowley, Smedley in 1934 was the personification of a dedicated working-class revolutionary with qualities of fanaticism that he found both attractive and repulsive. He first encountered Smedley when she was the guest of honor at a political dinner:

> Agnes Smedley is fanatical. . . . Her hair grows thinly above an immense forehead. When she talks about people who betrayed the Chinese rebels, her mouth becomes a thin scar and her eyes bulge and glint with hatred. If this coal miner's daughter ever had urbanity, she would have lost it forever in Shanghai when her comrades were dragged off one by one for execution. . . . This evening I'm drawing back. . . . I don't wait to hear Agnes Smedley give her speech, which will be more convincing than the others, as if each phrase of it were dyed in the blood of her Chinese friends.[8]

Not long after this meeting, Cowley wrote an enthusiastic review of Smedley's *China's Red Army Marches* for the *New Republic.* He wrote in part:

There are a good many tricks of narration that [Smedley] could easily learn if she had leisure for study; and there are other tricks that she seems to have learned from writing Sunday feature stories and ought to abandon. But she has an extraordinary subject here, and she has something else besides—an attitude of reverence for her subject, a faith that calls to mind the medieval chroniclers and bards. Mind you, she is dealing with historical facts. They are obviously simplified, worked smooth by retelling, yet they are facts none the less, such as can be checked by official records. Reading this book, with its heroes and villains (and no shades of characters between them, only the brave Reds and cowardly Whites), one can't help thinking of Roland against the Paynim, of Richard Lionheart against the Saracens, of the saints and martyrs that crowd the Golden Legend.[9]

By June Smedley was in California, where reunion with her family proved painful. Myrtle Smedley, who owed her college education to Agnes, was now the principal of a primary school in the San Diego area. Their younger brother, Sam, was also in San Diego and recently married, but having difficulty holding down a job. Their hard-drinking, unemployed father, Charles, had moved in temporarily with his children. Agnes had not seen any of them since 1916, when the president of San Diego Normal School advised her to leave the area so as not to ruin Myrtle's chances of finding work. By 1934, Myrtle was the family's only stable breadwinner, and when she imagined what might happen if the community discovered that her sister was a "red sympathizer," she became so overwrought that the nerves in half her face became temporarily paralyzed just before Agnes's arrival. Smedley preached socialism to the family anyway. She constantly urged Sam to put the cause of the workers' revolution above his own immediate interests and join the U.S. Communist Party, then at the height of its strength. Sam's new wife, Elizabeth, didn't seem to mind, but Sam told Agnes in no uncertain terms to "knock it off." Smedley's first husband, Ernest Brundin, and his wife Elinor also came to see Agnes, a visit that was very painful for Elinor.[10]

Smedley left California for China in early October of 1934. When her ship stopped for one day in Yokohama, she visited the only person she knew in Japan at the time—the Japanese translator of *Daughter of Earth*, Ozaki Hotsumi, whom she would never see again.[11] As was duly noted by a British agent, V. A. Pitts, Smedley arrived in Shanghai on October 22, 1934. Shortly thereafter, perhaps hoping to receive some official protection from the U.S. consulate, she presented the following letter of introduction from Secretary of State Cordell Hull: "At the instance of the Honorable Robert F. Wagner, Senator of the United States from the State of New York, I take pleasure in introducing to you Miss Agnes Smedley of New York City, who is about to proceed abroad. I cordially bespeak for Miss Smedley such courtesies and assistance as you may be able to render, consistent with your official duties." [12]

The letter of introduction did not help. For Smedley the next two years in Shanghai would be more difficult and less productive than the 1929–33 period. She wrote much less and relied chiefly on income from earlier work—several articles she had sold to American journals in 1934 and the royalties from three books, including the 1935 Coward-McCann abridged version of *Daughter of Earth*. The few articles she did publish reveal a pervasive sense of isolation and near-paranoia about political persecution. Her swings in mood, from long periods of depression and poor health to brief bursts of happiness and physical energy, became more pronounced. It is not surprising, perhaps, that eight years later, in the autobiographical passages in *Battle Hymn of China,* she said nothing at all about this period of her life.

Part of Smedley's problem was rooted in her frustration over the deteriorating political situation. From their new colony of Manchuria, the Japanese were creeping slowly toward Beijing. The Guomindang government in Nanjing was taking little direct action to stop them, concentrating its efforts on exterminating Chinese Communists. In the spring of 1934 the Guomindang began its fifth encirclement campaign against the Communist guerrilla bases in Jiangxi; and by October, relying heavily on German advice, technical help, and blockhouse strategy, Chiang Kai-shek had the Communists pinned down and in serious trouble. In cities like Shanghai, the Guomindang was thus in a more confident mood. Nanjing launched a Confucian-oriented revivalist campaign, the New Life Movement, to combat the growing appeal of Marxist thinking among the educated urban populace. In Shanghai especially, this propaganda effort was accompanied by increased repression and censorship by the Guomindang police.

In 1934 the Communists were deeply divided over strategy. After the party headquarters moved from Shanghai to Jiangxi in 1932, a serious split in the leadership developed. The founders of the Jiangxi Soviet, Mao Zedong and Zhu De, argued that mobile guerrilla warfare was necessary to counter the Guomindang encirclement campaigns. But the twenty-eight "Bolsheviks" in the party leadership, who followed Moscow's more traditional position, insisted on the need to fight fixed battles from a secure base. The larger "Bolshevik" faction in the leadership won out, and by the summer of 1934 they had put Mao under virtual house arrest. The area held by the Jiangxi Soviet was diminished as the Guomindang pincers tightened, and when the situation became desperate in late October, 100,000 men broke through Guomindang lines and headed west, leaving behind a rear guard made up mostly of Mao's old comrades, including his brother, Mao Zemin. Within a matter of days the rear guard was overrun and most were killed or captured by the Guomindang. This was the beginning of the epic Long March, which over a year later brought 20,000 ragged survivors to Baoan in the northwest, where they reestablished a Soviet and a party headquarters under the leadership of a new party chairman, Mao Zedong.

During this period the leftists with whom Smedley associated in Shanghai became divided. For example, within the League of Left Wing Writers, by late 1935 one group was in contact via intermediaries with Mao in the northwest; but another group, probably the larger one, was receiving directives from Mao's antagonist, Wang Ming, the Chinese Communist Party's man in Moscow in 1935. In early 1936, most Shanghai Communists were still following Moscow's lead: they consistently downplayed the issue of Japanese imperialism in China in favor of promoting class struggle within China and protecting the Soviet Union internationally. But in the spring of 1935, at about the time the Seventh Congress of the Comintern was meeting in Moscow, the Chinese Communist Party had changed its line and called for a united front with *all* parties and classes against the Japanese. Within the League, then, Smedley's friends were arguing bitterly over how best to carry out Moscow's new united front policy in cultural work, and how far committed leftist writers should go in dropping their posture as revolutionary cultural guerrillas.

Although Lu Xun and others in the League had already spoken out about the seriousness of the Japanese threat, they now opposed the new line. Lu Xun believed that the new thrust under the slogan of National Defense Literature, as advocated by several writers close to Moscow, notably Zhou Yang and Xia Yan, was too compromising: it involved too great a capitulation to the authority of the Guomindang, and it could only undermine the principles and goals of a social revolution. He proposed an alternative slogan, Mass Literature for the National Revolutionary War, and refused to join a new group of writers being organized by Zhou Yang to replace the League of Left Wing Writers. Lu Xun was supported by prominent figures such as Feng Xuefeng, who had recently arrived from the new northwestern guerrilla headquarters of the Chinese Communist Party and claimed to speak for Mao and other leaders on this issue. Characteristically, Smedley's friend Mao Dun tried to mediate between the two sides and was attacked by both. By the spring of 1936 the personal tensions that had been simmering for some time exploded into heated denunciations, the echoes of which are still heard today in Beijing. In the end, the majority of Party activists rallied around the Moscow-leaning writer Zhou Yang, and the League of Left Wing Writers was dissolved.* The unity among politically concerned intellectuals that had been carefully built up around the League since 1930 was permanently damaged by the war of words that raged through the summer of 1936.[13]

Further depressing Smedley was a fight with Frank Glass and Harold Isaacs shortly after her return to Shanghai. Although she had once worked closely with Isaacs and Glass on the *China Forum* (which ceased publication in early 1934) Smedley was now upset by their Trotskyist associations and views: she saw their open opposition to the Chinese Communist Party as playing directly into the hands of the Guomindang. Her dispute with them became public in the pages of the *China Weekly Review* during the summer of 1935, to the delight of the Guomindang and the treaty-port press. Smedley was denounced as a Stalinist, and she in turn accused her old friends of sabotaging the cause of the revolution and jeopardizing the lives of key figures such as Mme. Sun Yat-sen. This episode also temporarily cut off Smedley's cordial relationship with J. B. Powell, the American editor of the *China Weekly Review*, who took the opportunity to ridicule both sides in print.[14]

Throughout this second sojourn in Shanghai, Smedley's personal life

---

* Throughout this period of ideological conflict, Smedley seemed to side consistently with Lu Xun. She met Feng Xuefeng on several occasions and took special interest in his account of the Long March. She was particularly upset about the dissolution of the League of Left Wing Writers, with which she had worked since its formation in 1930. During the spring of 1936, before his death, she continued to work closely with Lu Xun when he came under direct attack. One important project was the joint editing and financing of an edition in Chinese of selected Käthe Kollwitz prints (see Bibliography). With Lu Xun's encouragement, she also developed friendships with his younger protégés—for example, a couple from Manchuria, Xiao Jun and Xiao Hong, and the Hunanese Zhou Libo, with whom she would work closely a few years later.

As early as 1935 Smedley had been concerned about Lu Xun's failing health, urging him repeatedly to go to a sanitorium in the Soviet Union and bringing to his home in 1936 the most noted specialist on tuberculosis in Shanghai, an American doctor named Tenney. As a last resort, one day in 1936 she secretly took Lu Xun and Mme. Sun to the Russian consulate, hoping that an official invitation in Mme. Sun's presence might persuade the writer to leave Shanghai for a rest cure. Lu Xun steadfastly refused, saying: "Everyone cannot run away! Someone must stand and fight." Interviews: Mao Dun; Zhou Libo; and Qian Junrui. *Lu Xun riji*, diary entries for 1936. Exhibit at Lu Xun Museum, Beijing, in March, 1978; *Battle Hymn*, pp. 83, 133. See also Mao Dun, ed., *Lu Xun huiyi lu* (Beijing, 1978).

was lonely. She had returned to Shanghai emotionally and physically exhausted and had to spend her first two months there recuperating in and
out of the hospital. She had few close friends left in the city. Ozaki Hotsumi, Sorge, and Chen Hansheng were gone. Edgar Snow was in Beijing.
Ding Ling had been arrested and was presumed dead. The League for
Civil Rights had been dissolved after the assassination of its general secretary, Smedley's friend Yang Quan. The old friends who remained were
Lu Xun, Mme. Sun, and Rewi Alley. Alley and Smedley were neighbors
in the Bearn apartment complex on Rue Joffre. The Bearn straddled a
whole city block which was hexagonal in shape. The complex had more
than twenty entrances and exits and was thus ideal for harboring fugitives and evading surveillance by French, British, and Chinese police.
For one under heavy surveillance, as Smedley was, the advantages of so
many entrances and exits were obvious. Together she and Alley hid fugitives from the Guomindang Blueshirts and found ways to get them out
of Shanghai. One such fugitive was Professor Chen Hansheng, who un-
expectedly turned up on Smedley's doorstep in May of 1935. Chen, who
had been in danger when he fled Shanghai for Tokyo in 1933, had returned on a secret mission, only to find that his Shanghai contact had
just been arrested. He hid first in Smedley's apartment and then in
Alley's; his wife, Susie Gu, was brought from Tokyo to Shanghai and
housed with a German couple. After several weeks Smedley booked passage for them on a Russian freighter bound for Vladivostok. In the actual escape, the emphasis was on costuming. On the day of departure,
Chen Hansheng appeared at dockside dressed as a wealthy Chinese,
sporting a pith helmet and a bouquet of gladioli, who was seeing off
foreign friends (Alley and Smedley). The German couple and Susie Gu
put on a similar charade. Minutes before the ship cast off, Smedley
ushered the Chinese couple into the captain's toilet, where they remained behind a locked door until the ship was well outside port and
down the Huangpu River.[15]

On another occasion, Smedley and Alley protected Liu Ding, an important Communist Party operative and survivor of a small soviet in Fujian province which the Guomindang had crushed in 1933–34. Late in
1935, Liu was brought to Rewi Alley for hiding, and for a few weeks it
became necessary for him to live in Smedley's flat. Smedley recorded in
detail his stories about the Fujian soviet and was especially intrigued by
the ingenuity the Fujian peasant guerrillas had shown in making their
own firearms. Early in 1936 Liu was asked to undertake a delicate mission: to be the party's liaison with the Manchurian warlord Zhang

Xueliang, who was then in control of Xi'an in the northwest. As he boarded a plane for Xi'an, Smedley handed him a large canister of surgical anesthetic; both were ignorant of the danger involved in transporting this highly explosive substance. When Liu casually handed the canister to delighted Red Army medics at their new base camp a few miles outside of Xi'an, he was dressed down for taking such risks.[16]

Although Smedley's circle of friends was smaller than before, she exercised an important political influence on several Western newcomers. One of these was George Hatem, a young American doctor who had come to Shanghai in search of adventure and personal fortune. Smedley shook him with her penetrating analysis of the misery of Shanghai and her stories of the Red Army in the northwest. At her insistence that he discover the truth for himself, Hatem joined Edgar Snow in the spring of 1936 on a journey to the Red Army's new base camp outside Xi'an. Finding an enormous need in the Red Army for his skills, he stayed on; he fell in love with a young Chinese comrade, joined the Chinese Communist Party, and did not return to Shanghai until the 1940s.[17] Smedley also played a significant part in the life of the Snows, Edgar and his first wife, Nym Wales (Helen Foster), whom she had known in Shanghai. In December of 1935 she stayed with them in Beijing, where the three of them became highly involved in the December Ninth Movement, a series of student strikes and demonstrations in Beijing against Japanese imperialism and the Nanjing government's failure to respond to it.* After spending most of the month with the strikers, she brought messages from them to Mme. Sun Yat-sen in Shanghai. She then helped organize the National Salvation Association, headed by Mme. Sun, which demanded a united front of the Guomindang and the Communists in a war of national defense against the Japanese. Smedley was the Snows' link to this organization as well as their link to Lu Xun. And, of course, it was Smedley who urged Snow to go to the northwest with Hatem in 1936 to meet the Communists as they came out of their Long March.[18]

Smedley seems to have been much less involved with Shanghai's German community of leftists after she returned in 1934. The Eislers, Ewerts, and Sorge had left China; Irene Wiedemeyer's bookstore had been closed; and of course Smedley was no longer writing for the Ger-

---

* Smedley also took the opportunity to take a day long fact-finding trip with United Press Beijing bureau chief F. McCracken Fisher, Frank Smothers of the *Chicago Daily News,* and Edgar Snow into the country east of Beijing where the Japanese were setting up their puppet East Hebei "Autonomous" regime under Yin Rugeng. In 1987 "Mac" Fisher recalled: "On the long ride home Agnes taught us 'The Streets of Laredo,' even making that lugubrious ballad seem rollicking!"

man press. Her German friends during this period were newcomers
such as Trudy Rosenberg and her husband, Hans Shippe. Regularly on
Sundays they dined on fried chicken and argued such theoretical points
of Marxism as the definition of feudalism or Oriental despotism. In
anger, Smedley would insist that Trudy should divorce her bullheaded
husband. She also advocated the dissolution of marriage as an institution and insisted that having children restricted a woman's involvement
in politics.[19]

As her Shanghai world began to unravel in the spring of 1936,
Smedley's most serious problem was the breakdown in her relations
with Mme. Sun, who had been a key figure in her life since 1929. The
trouble had begun the previous year, when Mme. Sun had given Smedley
the task of finding someone to edit and publish a new journal in Shanghai to replace the *China Forum*. The two women were agreed on the
need for a publication that would openly criticize the Guomindang and
report on political developments from an anti–Chiang Kai-shek, pro-
Chinese Communist perspective. By necessity such a journal would have
to be in English, edited by foreigners whom the Guomindang could not
touch, and published in the concession areas where the Nanjing government had no jurisdiction. Seed money to organize this enterprise was
given to Smedley three times by Mme. Sun, probably during the latter
half of 1935.

In several letters to New York, throughout 1935, Smedley asked Earl
Browder, secretary-general of the U.S. Communist Party, to send someone to Shanghai who could edit and publish the new journal. Finally, in
1936, after desperate appeals from Smedley, Browder sent his own secretary, Grace Granich, and her husband Manny. In the meantime Smedley
had gradually spent much of the seed money on what she considered to
be emergencies, such as financing the escape of fugitives and publishing
the book on Käthe Kollwitz's etchings. Mme. Sun was quietly furious
about the delay and the "wasted" funds. She was also angry that Smedley
sometimes described herself publicly as Mme. Sun's "associate" or "secretary." Mme. Sun, a very private person who wished to avoid being
identified with her followers, resented this deeply. Finally, when the Granichs arrived in Shanghai, Smedley apparently believed that she would
share editorial authority with them; but the Granichs refused to accept
this arrangement and received Mme. Sun's backing. Thus although
Smedley wrote articles for the initial issues of *Voice of China* (under the
pseudonym Rusty Knailes), she resented the new journal's success and
quarreled increasingly with the Granichs, especially Grace, who became

as outspoken and shrill in her criticisms as Smedley herself. Mme. Sun soon cut off relations with Smedley entirely, and eventually issued a public statement that Smedley had never been her secretary.[20]

This estrangement was probably inevitable. Although Smedley and Mme. Sun were both women of action who agreed politically and communicated perfectly in English, Mme. Sun was genteel, emotionally restrained, and taciturn, whereas Smedley was coarse, tempestuous, and outspoken. Even in the best of times, they probably were never intimate; the clash in style and personality was too great. In this light, it is not hard to see how Smedley's actions in the *Voice of China* matter could bring an end to her working relationship with Mme. Sun. The break continued to pain Smedley deeply as late as the 1940s.

By midsummer Smedley decided she had to leave Shanghai. She was suffocating politically, alienating herself from her remaining friends, and falling into poor health again. Characteristically, her next move was based on an earlier friendship. Liu Ding, the Red Army veteran whom she had sheltered a few months before, was now in Xi'an, the biggest city in northwest China, working closely with the Manchurian warlord Zhang Xueliang. When Liu wrote inviting her to come to Xi'an, she accepted immediately. In Xi'an, she could rest, write, and enjoy a more progressive political atmosphere. And there was another attraction: the new base of the Red Army was only thirty-five miles away.[21]

CHAPTER XI

Smedley as "White Empress": The Xi'an Incident, 1936–1937

In 1936 Xi'an was a poor, dusty city in a forgotten corner of China. During the Tang dynasty (686–906 A.D.), as the eastern terminus of the Silk Road across Central Asia, it was the biggest, richest, and most cosmopolitan capital in the world. In the tenth century it was sacked and demolished and thereafter grew very slowly over the centuries to the condition in which Smedley found it in the autumn of 1936: a sprawling, dingy, windswept trade center, protected by thick medieval walls from the rugged, impoverished countryside of Shaanxi province. Its foreign community consisted only of a handful of missionaries and an itinerant merchant or two.

Smedley's contact, Liu Ding, had been in Xi'an since early 1936 as a top aide to "the young marshal" Zhang Xueliang, a refugee Manchurian warlord-general.* Liu's assignment from the party was to serve as a secret liaison between Zhang, then only thirty-two years old, and the Red Army to the north. In May of 1936 he had arranged a secret meeting between Zhang Xueliang and Zhou Enlai in an old Catholic church at the county seat of Yan'an, then under control of Marshal Zhang's troops. The purpose of this meeting explains why Liu asked Smedley to come to Xi'an in September. Zhou Enlai and the Communist

---

* After earning a degree in engineering in Germany, Liu Ding returned to China in 1933 and joined the Chinese Communist Party; he first worked in a munitions production at a Red Army guerrilla base in Fujian province. After the Fujian and Jiangxi Red Army base camps were broken up by Chiang Kai-shek in 1934–35, he took refuge in the Shanghai apartments of Smedley and Rewi Alley (Liu Ding interview).

Party leaders hoped to induce Marshal Zhang and other warlords in the region to force Chiang Kai-shek to join the Communists in a united front against the Japanese. If progress could be made toward this end—and success seemed near—they wanted an international correspondent of progressive sympathies on hand to report the results.[1]

The reasons the Communists thought Marshal Zhang Xueliang in particular might be susceptible to their wooing were complex. Marshal Zhang had inherited his position and his army from his father, Zhang Zuolin, the notorious bandit turned warlord whom the Japanese had assassinated in 1928 as an early step in their takeover of Manchuria. By 1932 the Japanese had completed their occupation and driven the young warlord and his army out of Manchuria. Aching for revenge and the chance to win back his territory, the young marshal was given command in the south at Wuhan, and throughout 1934 he supported Chiang Kai-shek as the only leader who could muster the military strength to take on the Japanese. By 1935 Zhang Xueliang's patience with Chiang was wearing thin, and Chiang was beginning to see Zhang's army as a potential threat to his own regime—a loose cannon on the deck of central China. Chiang's solution was to send Zhang and his men northwest to Xi'an with the task of suppressing the Communists in the area.

In 1935, Xi'an was already under the control of a Shaanxi warlord, Yang Hucheng, a man of the old school whose army had a reputation for rapaciousness. Yang was not interested in fighting either the Japanese or the Communists, but he was fiercely independent and resented Chiang Kai-shek's authority. Wisely, the young marshal Zhang Xueliang kept his troops clear of Yang Hucheng's men. As the two warlords consulted personally and worked out separate spheres of military responsibility, however, they found that they could more than coexist; they were actually agreeing on a number of issues. Soon their two staffs were working together on intimate terms—in part because both staff groups were heavily infiltrated by Communists.

In the summer of 1936 the two warlords believed that the Communists, whose strength had been sapped by the Long March, posed no threat to them, even in Shaanxi province, as Chiang Kai-shek alleged. They saw a much greater threat in the Japanese, who by summer had reached the suburbs of Beijing and were now heading west, toward Shaanxi. The generals' point of view matched that of public opinion in major cities like Beijing and Shanghai, as articulated by Mme. Sun's National Salvation Association, which was dedicated to pressuring Chiang

Kai-shek into fighting the Japanese. Somehow the Japanese had to be stopped.

When she arrived in mid-September, Smedley was not disappointed by the political climate in Xi'an. Since August, politically active students and intellectuals from Beijing and Shanghai had been migrating to Xi'an, where repression of the student-intellectual community was minimal. Anti-Japanese street demonstrations were openly condoned by local authorities. Moreover, although direct contact with the Red Army to the north was still forbidden and access closed to foreigners, it was now possible surreptitiously to go there in disguise and under escort. Dissident students from Beijing and Shanghai such as the future foreign minister Huang Hua passed through Xi'an on their way to the Red Army base camp.

Liu Ding greeted Smedley warmly upon arrival, but she stayed in the city proper for only a few days. Liu wanted her close at hand but not in the public eye, where she might prematurely raise suspicions and draw fire from Nanjing. For her part, Smedley was content to lie low and wait for an invitation and escort to visit the Red Army. At this point the warlords Yang and Zhang did not interest her much, and she had already seen a lot of the anti-Japanese student movement in Shanghai. Thus, when Liu Ding arranged for her to stay in Lintong, about twenty miles to the east, she did not object.[2]

Lintong is one of China's most ancient resort towns. Built around fine sulphur hot springs, it was once the elegant playground of Tang dynasty emperors and their consorts, and its mix of temples, baths, and covered walkways, all in a classical Ming-Qing architectural style, invited nostalgia for the romantic past. Smedley lived quietly in Lintong until late November, regaining her health and working on a new book about the Long March. As a girl she had loved to ride horses, and now she began to take regular excursions on horseback. (One of her favorite destinations was the nearby tomb of Qin Shihuangdi, China's first emperor and the builder of the Great Wall.) Every week Liu Ding would send out an aide with bread, mail, and news of the outside world. Chinese friends also paid occasional visits, and one day in late October a young woman from Shanghai brought her word of Lu Xun's death. At about the same time, she learned of the death of her father in California, which provoked a brief but sharply painful spasm of guilt and reflection about her family.[3]

Smedley interrupted her Lintong retreat only once, for a trip to Xi'an in late October to see Edgar Snow, who had just returned from four months with the Communists at their base camp near Baoan. It had been a trip that Smedley had encouraged and helped to arrange when she was in Beijing in December, 1935. The Communists had wanted the first journalist visitor to be someone without any association with the international left. Smedley understood politically, but at a personal level Snow's journalistic opportunity left her burning with envy. Containing her jealousy well, she greeted Snow warmly.

The high point of this visit was a dramatic reunion one evening with Ding Ling, the writer friend she had presumed to be dead after her arrest in Shanghai in 1933. Ding Ling now said that the international attention Smedley drew to her arrest was responsible for saving her life. The reunion was held at the compound of a German dentist, Dr. Herbert Wunsch, where Ding Ling was hiding from Guomindang police disguised as a servant. Dr. Wunsch, whom Smedley had persuaded to come to Xi'an from Shanghai, worked on Zhang Xueliang's teeth, but his real job was to serve as a conduit for medical supplies to the Red Army. Forty years later, Ding Ling recalled the laughter and tears of that October reunion at Dr. Wunsch's, and how hard she had worked to prepare a chicken for the occasion. It was a joyful, rousing evening dominated by talk of the doings of the Red Army and a preview by Snow of the material he had collected for *Red Star over China* (1938). A few weeks later Ding Ling slipped out of Xi'an to join the Red Army near Baoan.[4]

In late November Smedley was told abruptly that she would have to leave immediately for Xi'an. Chiang Kai-shek was about to arrive in Lintong. He intended to consult with his warlord generals, Zhang Xueliang and Yang Hucheng, and to insist that they put more energy into suppressing Communist "bandits." On December 7, Chiang made Lintong his headquarters for private meetings with the Xi'an generals. Chiang's staff and most of his officers remained in Xi'an, where they were billeted at the very guest house Smedley had moved into a week earlier.

Although Chiang Kai-shek thought war with Japan was inevitable, he had various reasons for wanting to postpone it. First, he was negotiating with the Japanese, trying to buy time to develop and modernize his army. Second, he had just embarked on an ambitious three-year industrialization plan which he hoped would provide the kind of industrial base he would need to hold out against the Japanese. In these efforts he was counting heavily on German assistance, and he hoped that the Germans would act as a restraining influence on Japan, their new ally in an anti-Comintern pact. Third, he was confident that his new security apparatus, modeled on the systems developed in Fascist Germany and Italy, gave him more control of China's major population centers than ever before. In these circumstances, Chiang believed he had time to deal with the Communist "bandits" in the northwest. He tackled this unfinished business late in 1936 by making two visits to Xi'an: the first for a day or two in October, to order a suppression campaign; and the second in December, to oversee the execution of his orders in person.[5]

The atmosphere in Xi'an in early December was electric. Although she was making frequent visits to the local missionary hospital because of back trouble, Smedley spent as much time as she could in the streets. As generals Zhang and Yang held strained talks with Chiang Kai-shek at Lintong, student marchers swept through the city demanding that all Chinese unite against Japan. The first demonstration was to protest the November 27 arrest in Shanghai of "the seven gentlemen," leading liberal journalists and non-communist intellectuals who had called publicly for a united front of the Guomindang and the Communists. Having worked in Shanghai with these "gentlemen" on behalf of Mme. Sun Yatsen, Smedley shared the student outrage over their arrest. The climax came on December 9, when students marched to commemorate the demonstrations and shootings of a year earlier in Beijing, which had led to the formation of the National Salvation Association under Mme. Sun. Xi'an police, emboldened by the presence of Chiang Kai-shek and his private guards, opened fire on the marchers, killing nine and arresting dozens. The young marshal, Zhang Xueliang, was furious and demanded the release of the demonstrators. Supremely confident in his authority, Chiang gave generals Zhang and Yang a two-day ultimatum: cease disobeying orders and launch a military campaign against the Communists or be relieved of command. The reply took all sides by surprise, including the Communists.

Before daybreak on the morning of December 12, Zhang Xueliang dispatched a small number of troops to arrest Chiang Kai-shek at Lintong and bring him back to Xi'an. Simultaneously, Yang Hucheng's troops were sent to detain Chiang Kai-shek's staff officers at the guest house in Xi'an, where Smedley was also staying. In Lintong, hearing a few gunshots outside his quarters, Chiang scrambled up a nearby cliff in his nightshirt. He was found near the top of the cliff in a shallow cave, his feet too bloodied to climb further. The officer who was leading the expedition apologized to the general, carried him down the cliff on his back, and hustled him back to Xi'an by car. Chiang was in shock and at first refused to speak.[6]

Whereas the young marshal's men had captured Chiang Kai-shek at Lintong without violence, and given him treatment that was almost courtly, Yang Hucheng's troops assaulted the Xi'an guest house and arrested Chiang's staff before dawn in a more traditional fashion. Here is Smedley's account in *Battle Hymn* (pp. 141–42):

> Rifle butts crashed against my door. Unwilling to help in my own murder, I backed into a corner just as three rifle shots splintered the wood and the glass panel crashed and scattered. I heard shouts of "Japanese" and thought in terror: "God, they're going to kill me under the pretense that I'm a Japanese."
>
> A soldier's head appeared through the door panel and stared wildly about. I recalled enough Chinese to say: "I'm not Japanese. I'm an American."
>
> Someone pushed him and he tumbled into the room. A crowd of gray-clad soldiers, rifles ready, poured after him and then milled around confusedly. Some dashed into the bathroom, others jerked open the door of the clothes closet, and then all but two streamed out and began beating on the manager's door, which was next to mine.
>
> The two soldiers left in my room began moving around. One suddenly thrust his rifle barrel into my stomach and pushed me back against the wall, while the other dumped everything out of my dressing table. He filled his pockets with everything that struck his fancy—my eyeglasses, rolls of film, flashlight, and batteries. He gathered up my woolen sweater and woolen underwear with particular exclamations of satisfaction.
>
> The soldier pinning me to the wall reached out and flipped over the pillow on my bed. There lay my purse, with all my money. With cries of joy the two soldiers pounced on it and divided up the money. One took my fountain pen and one my pencil, then each clipped his trophy into his breast pocket. Finally each dragged a woolen blanket from the bed and disappeared down the hall.

A few hours later, when the shooting and looting had subsided, Dr. Wunsch, the German dentist who had hosted Smedley's reunion with Ding Ling and Edgar Snow the previous October, arrived at the gates of the guest house. He was refused entry. Insisting that he had an eight o'clock appointment that had to be met, he brushed the guards aside and pushed through the gates. He was gunned down on the spot. Smedley contacted Wang Bingnan, the underground Communist and one of Yang Hucheng's top aides, who rushed over to handle the situation. Forty-two years later Wang, who had studied in Germany, described how he buried his friend on a small hill in the suburbs of the city with great sadness and embarrassment.[7]

On the morning of December 12, in shock over the loss of all her worldly goods and the death of her friend Wunsch, Smedley at first thought the raid on the guest house had been part of an action by

Chiang Kai-shek's Blueshirt police against the warlord troops in the city, but by midday Liu Ding had told her what had actually happened.[8] By afternoon Smedley was on the streets with a military pass to do first-aid work. In a remarkable letter written May 19, 1937, from Yan'an to Shanghai newspaperman Randall Gould, she described the scene:

> For the first week of the Sian [Xi'an] events I was a first aid worker in the streets of Sian. I had plenty to do, and the foreign hospital gave me bandages, lint, gave me some instruction in first aid whenever I was up against a problem, and took me through the wards to show and demonstrate the care of wounded. The hotel manager gave me cognac in small bottles, and I bought alcohol, iodine, and other first aid medicines. I once took care of thirty Yang Hucheng soldiers in the streets [where] an accident [had] killed eighteen on the spot, and wounded the rest. I found myself battering down the doors of merchants to get water. The merchants are as a rule rotters when something uncomfortable happens on their door steps. Then, when the four hundred political prisoners were released (all of them Red Army men, women and children), I became the only medical attendant. One hundred of the three hundred men were wounded—some with untended old wounds that would soon kill them, some with wounds that festered along, some with leg ulcers, and many with the big, hard, bare feet of peasants—feet swollen and bloody from marching and fighting in the winter's snow. I washed the feet of these men, disinfected their wounds, bandaged them—and returned to the missionary hospital to ask for instructions about certain wounds. . . .
>
> So I had to be the doctor to these wounded men until we could remove them to the hospital. There were fifty-four women and forty little boys with the Red Army prisoners, and I went daily to take care of them also. Nearly all were poor peasants, and some had been slaves. I felt always that I was walking down one of the most tragic and terrible corridors in human history when I worked with them. The sight of poor peasants or slaves who had known nothing but brute labor all their lives, lying there with no covering, no bed, on stone floors, with untended and unhealed wounds, with big, hard, bloody feet—no, I shall never forget that, and shall carry that with me to my grave. I have written for years of the Red Army, yet my first living contact with it was with these peasants. They did not understand me. I was the first foreigner they had seen, most certainly; I wore wool dresses, a fur coat and hat, warm stockings, and leather shoes. I could not talk with them. Those men watched me with hostile eyes at first, many standing back and scowling at me. I do not know what they thought when I washed their feet and tended their wounds. Perhaps they thought me an insane *yang kweitze* [*guizi*, foreign devil].
>
> Later, many of those prisoners were sent to Yan'an. Now and then in the theatre some little boy whom I do not remember comes and cuddles up near me, and holds my hand. I know he is one of those "prisoners of war." One day I was passing through the streets when a crowd of women surrounded me and began caressing my hands, face, and shoulders. You see, it is not always easy if you have a foreign background, because many of these women

had trachoma. But they embraced me, caressed me, and some cried. They were those poor peasant women, prisoners of war, whom I had tended in Sian—women who had fought with guns in the Red Army, or who had followed their sons or husbands in the army because the poor have no protection but the Red Army.

Five days after the kidnapping, Zhang Xueliang dispatched Liu Ding in a plane to pick up Zhou Enlai and two other members of the Communist Party's Central Committee; he was to bring them to Xi'an to join in negotiations with Chiang Kai-shek. Smedley talked at least briefly with Zhou and his colleagues soon after they arrived in Xi'an. We know little about what was said, but within days Smedley began making forty-minute broadcasts in English every evening from Zhang Xueliang's headquarters. She would summarize major developments of the day in Xi'an and interview key players in the drama, such as Marshal Zhang and General Yang. When her programs were picked up in Shanghai, as intended, they caused considerable stir. Except for the official Guomindang communiqués emanating from Nanjing, which were hostile to Zhang and Yang as well as to the Communists, Smedley's reports were the only daily news coming out of Xi'an. Not incidentally, the person in charge of the radio broadcasts was Wang Bingnan, the man who had buried the German dentist, Wunsch, on the day of the Xi'an Incident. Then thirty years old, Wang had recently returned from Germany, via Moscow, with his German wife, Anna. In Moscow he had joined the Chinese Communist Party and received orders to try to join the Xi'an staff of General Yang Hucheng, with whom he enjoyed close family ties. He soon became one of Yang's most trusted aides.[9]

The Xi'an broadcasts made Smedley an international figure and stamped her permanently as an apologist for the Chinese Communists. Within China's foreign community she was already legendary—as heroine or pariah, depending on the political point of view. Now she became an international celebrity, and an infamous one in most circles. By early January of 1937, American newspapers were giving her front-page coverage under sensational headlines: "Huge Army at Her Back," "U.S. Girl a Red Peril," and "American Woman Aids Chinese Rising."[10] The appeal to popular ignorance and stereotypes was not confined to headlines. In a flight of irresponsible fantasy, a long Associated Press background story described her as "the one-time American farm girl who may become a virtual 'white empress' over yellow-skinned millions." Even Upton Sinclair, who had admired Smedley's early Socialist impulses, wrote an overblown popular portrait of her for *Liberty* magazine, under the title "America's Amazing Woman Rebel in China." Ironically, the American Communist paper, the *Daily Worker,* taking its cue from Moscow, attacked Smedley on its front page for her public criticism of Chiang Kai-shek and her obvious jubilation over his kidnapping, thus putting Smedley and the American Communist Party at loggerheads once again.[11]

The Xi'an Incident caught both the Russian and the Chinese Communist parties by surprise. The Chinese Communists had hoped only that Marshal Zhang and General Yang would refuse to launch an extermination campaign against them, thereby creating a split in loyalty within Chiang Kai-shek's military forces. They had never dreamed that the warlords might kidnap Chiang. When the news reached them at their base camp, they were shocked and began emotionally charged discussions about what to do next. At first many argued for revenge: execute Chiang and then form a united front. Then came Moscow's reaction, by telegraph: condemn the kidnapping as a Japanese plot and demand Chiang Kai-shek's release unconditionally. This message perplexed and embarrassed the Chinese Communists and shocked Zhang Xueliang. But Mao and Zhou won out against the comrades who wanted Chiang executed, and managed to forge a compromise. Chiang would be released, but on three conditions: he would call off his campaign to exterminate the Communists, he would join the Communists in a united front against the Japanese, and he would formally declare war on Japan. Mao and Zhou were willing to go this far, but no further, because they believed at this time Chiang was the only figure behind whom the Chinese people could unite.

This was the position that Zhou Enlai and two other party leaders brought to the negotiations between Chiang Kai-shek and his warlord captors. After ten days of discussion, in which Mme. Chiang and her brother, Song Ziwen (T. V. Soong), participated, a bargain was made. Its provisions are still a mystery, but its immediate result is suggestive. Chiang was released and flown back to Nanjing on Christmas Day. By the end of February, 1937, Chiang had announced that he would cease hostilities against the Communists. Not until July, after the Japanese attacked Lugouqiao (Marco Polo Bridge outside Beijing), did both sides publicly commit themselves to a "united front" against Japan, Chiang formally declaring war.[12]

Until January, 1937, Smedley knew little about the furor her broadcasts had stirred up. Then, besides learning of denunciations from Nanjing, she heard that U.S. consular officials in Nanjing were trying to get her passport revoked. The State Department had received complaints from the Chinese ambassador in Washington. The consulate was also influenced by reports from Christian missionaries in Xi'an, who charged that Smedley was a leading conspirator in the Xi'an kidnapping, a political agitator who was about to lead the once-contented peasants of Shaanxi province in a massive Communist uprising.[13] These missionary tales were the main source of the fantastic charges leveled against Smedley in the Western press. At this point the U.S. government solidly supported Chiang Kai-shek's reluctance and hoped to delay a full-scale war between China and Japan, and official Washington thus expressed outrage at Chiang's kidnapping and named the Communists as its instigators. Over the next few months, however, Smedley successfully rallied friends like Margaret Sanger, Upton Sinclair, and Roger Baldwin to speak out in Washington in her defense. She also set the record straight by publishing a long factual account of the Xi'an Incident in *The Nation* on February 13.[14]

Smedley's credibility outside Xi'an was improved by the arrival, and subsequent participation in the broadcasts, of James Bertram, a young New Zealander. Bertram had arrived in Beijing in early 1936 on a Rhodes traveling fellowship to study the Chinese language and see China after graduation from Oxford. He made the acquaintance of Edgar Snow and John Fairbank and began writing for the British press about the encroachments of the Japanese, the anti-Japanese student movement, and the conclusion of the Communists' Long March to the northwest. In England he had been sympathetic to left-of-center causes such as that of the Republicans in the Spanish Civil War. Not surprisingly, in Beijing he began to abandon scholarly pursuits in order to concentrate on the current political situation. He befriended a number of Chinese journalists and students from Manchuria, at the time occupied by the Japanese and the home province of the young marshal in Xi'an, Zhang Xueliang. Then in December, electrified by the news from Xi'an, Bertram resolved to break the news blockade and somehow get to Xi'an. He made it, with a Manchurian friend, in eleven days, by train, rickshaw, donkey, and military truck. He arrived on December 27—two days after Chiang Kai-shek's release and return to Nanjing.[15]

Bertram joined Smedley as the only other foreign resident of the Xi'an guest house, which now billeted Marshal Zhang Xueliang's staff officers. Their first meeting was not a success:

A woman of something over forty came striding down the corridor, my card in her hand. She was short, strongly built, with a brown weather-beaten face and short hair, and with extraordinarily wide-set, candid eyes.

"Mr. Bertram?" The voice was harsh and sounded hostile. She wore a red woolen jersey, brown skirt, and heavy baroques.

"Yes," I said. "You won't know me, but I've met some people you know in Shanghai." I gave the names.

"Indeed," said Agnes. "And what are you doing here?"

It was the question I had wanted to ask her. But I explained that I had come out of a natural curiosity to find out what was happening in Xi'an, and to do some writing about it. I had a connection, I added, with some English newspapers.

"What papers?" Agnes was relentless. I mentioned the *Daily Herald* and—in a weak moment—the *Times*.

"The London *Times* is no friend of China." Her mouth shut like a trap. "How did you get here? For all I know you may be a British spy."

This was unpromising. "I came in with a Dongbei [Manchurian] man," I said. "Would you like to meet him? We're going out to Lintong with Sun Mingjiu."

This name, which had been unknown [to the public] three weeks ago, made a more favorable impression. Agnes Smedley was not unwilling, it seemed, to meet the man who had captured Chiang Kai-shek. But she was still a little suspicious about me. "Do you know anyone else in Sian?" she asked.

I drew a bow at a venture and mentioned the young editor of Zhang Xueliang's daily. Fortunately, she had met him.

"Yes, I know him. Is he a friend of yours?"

"We used to live in the same rooms in Beijing. He'll tell you I'm not a spy."

"Good," said Agnes decisively. "I'll ask him." [16]

Smedley's suspicion of an Oxford-educated Englishman is not surprising. But within a few days Bertram proved himself. He found Smedley tough and uncompromising, yet "one of the most human and lovable people I have ever met." He joined her in the streets, helping to minister to the medical needs of Red Army women and children. By New Year's Day, 1937, they were making daily radio broadcasts together from the primitive transmitter in Xi'an. As Bertram wrote:

We divided the news of the day between us, and sometimes gave short descriptions of various activities going on in Xi'an and in the countryside around. We tried very hard to be objective, and always satisfied ourselves that the facts we announced were accurate. But Agnes had a fine slashing style that was not very well-suited to diplomatic statement, and an incurable fondness for the word "masses." In fact, the way she pronounced this word, with a broad "a" and a vigorous enunciation of the sibilants, would—I felt sure—identify her voice to anyone who had ever spoken to her for two minutes. By contrast, I tried to make my voice sound as unemotional as possible, modelling my delivery on the soothing accents of the B.B.C. . . . We would come back from the radio station each night, and make coffee in Agnes's room. All kinds of people drifted in during these evenings—journalists, students, officials, soldiers—and we would talk over the general situation, or speculate on the probable plans of the Japanese. Agnes, who had renounced most home comforts, retained an American taste for good coffee; she made it over an alcohol lamp with a skill that excited my envy.

Bertram was astonished by Smedley's knowledge of the Red Army:

> One night a tall, slim young man in a plain khaki uniform came in with a friend. I noticed at once his beautiful carriage and the healthy glow of his brown cheeks. He was a Red Army commander and had been for nine years with Peng Dehuai, fighting in Hunan and Jiangxi, and then on the long trek to the North. Peng Dehuai was Agnes Smedley's favorite Red leader; she knew every campaign he had fought. They settled down to discuss details of strategy five years old. The newcomer flushed with pleasure when he found that this foreigner knew the name of obscure villages in the South, once given a brief fame as the scene of fierce engagements. Their conversation sketched the ten years' history of the Chinese Red Army. It was as vivid as a novel by Stendhal.[17]

In retrospect, it is hard to overestimate the importance of the Xi'an Incident as a turning point for the Chinese Communists. At a time of great military weakness, with one stroke of luck the Communists recouped the fortunes of their movement.*

In early January, 1937, a messenger slipped into Xi'an from the new Communist headquarters of Yan'an and handed Smedley an official invitation to visit. This was the opportunity for which Smedley had been waiting for years. There was a modest farewell dinner party attended by Bertram, Wang Bingnan, and his German wife, Anna. "The resources of the Sian [Xi'an] Guest House were getting rather low after almost a month's economic blockade. Agnes wore a Red Cross armband; 'officially' she was going on a trip to the front to do first-aid work. . . . That was the last I saw of Agnes Smedley in Sian. She left the Guest House early the next morning, a businesslike figure in heavy riding breeches and the familiar red sweater. Always she wore it like a banner."[18]

---

* Only the outcome had been unpredictable. Despite the fact that the Communists were clearly surprised by the kidnapping of Chiang, it is difficult not to see in the Incident the catalytic effects of masterful behind-the-scenes maneuvering by such party operatives as Liu Ding and Wang Bingnan.

CHAPTER XII

Yan'an, 1937

After the Xi'an Incident, the Red Army moved into the mountain citadel of Yan'an, an ancient county seat and traditionally the most important marketing and administrative center in impoverished, mountainous northern Shaanxi province. Lying about one hundred miles south of the Great Wall, it had long been the gateway through which trader or invader would pass to Xi'an. It was through Yan'an, for example, that Genghis Khan and his Mongol cavalry swept into China proper in the thirteenth century. Edgar Snow described Yan'an in 1936 as "cradled in a bowl of high, rock-ribbed hills, its stout walls crawling up to the very tops. Attached to them now, like wasps' nests, were newly made fortifications."[1] A river served as a moat running around the city's ancient and modern battlements. But despite its importance and antiquity the city was tiny: it had a main street lined with one-story shops and a population of fewer than a thousand. At one end of the street was a large abandoned Catholic church and at the other a magnificent gate dating from the Song dynasty (954–1268 A.D.). Perched high on a mountain overlooking the citadel was an eighth-century Buddhist pagoda.

Before he was kidnapped, Chiang Kai-shek had set up a military blockade around Xi'an to contain the Communists. His aim was to cut the Communists off from the province's major source of supplies and to control access to the area. Foreign journalists were explicitly prohibited from entering the Red Army strongholds. Now anxious to proceed to Yan'an, on January 12, 1937, Smedley took advantage of the confusion in the wake of the Xi'an Incident to sneak past the blockade, in the back of a truck provided by her Red Army escort.

Smedley spent three weeks getting to Yan'an, traveling slowly by truck through central Shaanxi, where the Red Army was integrating shells of villages into a new soviet area. The surrounding countryside reminded Smedley of the blasted landscape she had known in her youth in the American Southwest: "The countryside was desolate, without population. Now and then we came to a tiny village with a few houses and a few ragged peasants. . . . [Further to the south we] came out on high plateaus. They reminded me of the broad mesas of southwestern America . . . [except that] the sides of the plateaus were terraced and, in many places, cultivated. But there were times when we traveled for a whole day and saw not one cultivated terrace. The rains had washed many of them away and grass had grown over them. They had not been used for years."[2] The lack of cultivation Smedley observed was the result of the Great Northwest Famine: between 1928 and 1933, about three million people—almost half the population of Shaanxi province—died of starvation. Alternating periods of flood and drought had ruined agriculture. Missionaries had organized an International Relief Commission, but it had faced formidable obstacles. It tried to send grain, but the province had no railroad or river system for transporting it; even the roads were inadequate for the purpose. And throughout the famine, absentee landlords and competing warlords protected their most reliable cash crop by keeping the best land in opium poppy production, and also siphoned off much of the famine relief for themselves.[3]

Besides wanting to examine rural conditions for herself, Smedley was eager to visit Red Army units. She found her first chance at Tongli, a half-deserted county seat that was now serving as headquarters of the First Red Army Corps, after she had spent three days traveling forty miles across rough terrain. The commander of the First Corps was Zuo Chuan, one of the soldiers she had sheltered in Shanghai; shortly after arriving she was greeted by Ding Ling, who, as her official host, had been sent from Yan'an to escort her the rest of the way. Just to the east and west of Tongli were units commanded by two Red Army heroes she had never met: the dashing, jovial He Long, and the ugly, austere Peng Dehuai. She stayed in the Tongli area for two weeks, spending many hours interviewing He and Peng. She described her first impressions in *Battle Hymn of China*:

"Shades of the Taiping rebels!" I exclaimed to myself, for He Long looked not like a Chinese, but like some old print of a mustachioed folk-tale Mongol or Central Asiatic. He was a man in his middle forties, but he walked with the lithe grace of a panther. As he drew near I saw that his dress seemed so strange and vari-colored because it was made up of the remnants of many uniforms. His jacket was of faded gray and his trousers black, the latter fitting so tightly that he appeared to be made up for some medieval drama. Above his blue cloth Chinese shoes white socks showed, and from his ankle to the knee was a splash of green puttees wrapped tightly in a long, leaf-like pattern. Something seemed missing from his uniform—oh yes, a blazing sash and a curved scimitar! . . .

Ding Ling and I rode to a large village near [a] snow-covered mountain [Bei Wutian Shan], where Peng Dehuai had his headquarters. He was of medium height, built like a stocky peasant, and perhaps in his middle thirties. He was ugly, but as he smiled in welcome his face was pleasant. His eyes were level and penetrating, his voice gruff. . . . When we arrived he was ill. The Long March had left him with gastric ulcers and in addition he had been kicked by a horse shortly before our arrival. But no one dared refer to his illness in his presence. Since [the others present] were anxious, they pushed me forward and I, innocent and unabashed, talked to him about his health. I also suffered from gastric ulcers and carried powders, milk, and soda crackers. I shared these with him, and because I was a guest he had to listen to my advice.

(pp. 156–160)[4]

For the rest of the way to Yan'an, Smedley was accompanied by Ding Ling, the only prominent female Chinese Communist she knew whose views about women and marriage approached her own. Both women were outspoken, reckless, flamboyant, and accustomed to living freely "like men." Both admired the Russian revolutionary Alexandra Kollontai. Despite the fact that they had trouble communicating—Smedley had only broken Chinese—mutual respect developed between them.[5]

Smedley and Ding Ling arrived in Yan'an at night and were taken immediately to see Zhu De and Chairman Mao in their respective mountain caves overlooking the town. Smedley's first impression was that Zhu De was gregarious and down-to-earth; Mao, aloof and "spiritually isolated." The next day, asked to address a formal welcome meeting before most of the population of Yan'an, she spoke for almost an hour. She talked about her early days on a dirt farm in Missouri and gave a dramatic account of her imprisonment in 1918 because of her anti-imperialist activities. She said that the American people understood the feelings of the Chinese in their struggle against the Japanese aggressors. "You do not stand alone, nor is your struggle an obscure one," she concluded. "You are part of a world wide anti-fascist movement." It was a stirring speech, filled with personal emotion. Even as they heard it through a Chinese translator, the crowd was mesmerized by the words of this foreign woman with the broad Roman forehead and penetrating blue eyes. When she ended, they stood and applauded loudly.[6]

Smedley did not come as a complete stranger, of course; she was well known as one of the few foreign friends of the Chinese Communist movement. On hand to welcome her personally were Chen Geng, Liu Ding, Ding Ling, Zhou Enlai, and other comrades she had either sheltered in Shanghai or worked with in Xi'an; George Hatem, the American doctor she had talked into going to the northwest a year earlier; and Wang Bingnan and Anna Wang, the couple who had befriended her in Xi'an. Thus the atmosphere surrounding her arrival was one of joyous public reunion with old friends, beyond the reach of Chiang Kai-shek's hated Blueshirts.[7] Also, Smedley felt oddly at home in the geographical and social setting of Yan'an. Despite its distinctly Chinese landmarks, it reminded her of the one-horse frontier towns she had known in the American West at the turn of the century. With amusement, she compared the newly arrived Red Army soldiers to greenhorn cowboys fresh off the range: "This was a large town for the Red Army boys—so large that the merchants swindled them right and left."[8]

After staying for several days in a rat-infested downtown building, Smedley was moved to a roomy cave carved into the mountain walls that enclosed the citadel. Here, not far from Mao's and Zhu De's quarters, she spent her first weeks interviewing Mao, Peng Dehuai, Zhu De, Zhou Enlai, and others; the sound of her portable typewriter could be heard late into the night as she hammered out the results.[9] In the course of this work she developed a close working relationship with her young interpreter, Wu Guangwei, or Lily Wu, as Smedley and other foreigners called her. Lily was an attractive divorcée, a college student turned revolutionary and an actress in Ding Ling's drama troupe. (It is likely that Smedley had first met her in Xi'an.) She soon moved into the cave next to Smedley's and the two became close friends.[10] In a military encampment, Smedley, Ding Ling, and Lily Wu were a unique group: three strong-minded, divorced women who were critical of traditional marriage and wanted to see women given more power in a socialist society.

By April, Smedley had settled down to work on longer-term projects, the most significant of which was a biography of the Red Army's legendary peasant commander-in-chief, Zhu De, meeting him regularly for long sessions in the evening. A combination of Chinese, German, and English was used, and for help at sticky points they turned to Lily Wu, Hatem, and Huang Hua. The result, though not published until six years after Smedley's death, was *The Great Road* (1956). In China, where it is still regarded as a classic, millions of copies of a new translation have been sold in recent years.[11]

Characteristically, Smedley did not restrict herself to interviewing and writing but threw herself into several other projects at once. Her international appeals to bring supplies and doctors to Yan'an were responsible in part for enticing Norman Bethune, the celebrated Canadian surgeon, Communist, and Spanish Civil War hero, to come to northwestern China. She became an energetic librarian and took charge of expanding the foreign-language section of Yan'an's new Lu Xun cave library to serve the burgeoning student population; the *New Masses* of New York was the most popular, due to its combination of graphics and politics. She worked hard to attract foreign correspondents to Yan'an, urging them to break through the Guomindang blockade at Xi'an. By May and June she was beginning to succeed, with the arrival of Victor Sheen, Earl Leaf, and Helen F. Snow, among others. She even mounted a birth-control campaign but had to give up quickly when neighboring villagers, thinking the blue-eyed foreigner was offering them a potion of miraculous powers, drank the lemon-based douche she had imported from Shanghai. Much more successful was Smedley's anti-rat crusade, accompanied by much propaganda about the importance of sanitation. At first many scoffed at her Western "obsession" with rats, but they fell silent when Mao Zedong threw the full weight of his authority behind her campaign. Before long, rat traps imported from Shanghai and Beijing were having an impact on Yan'an's ancient rat population.[12]

Smedley was pursuing all these activities during a six-month lull in fighting before the Sino-Japanese War of 1937–45—probably the most relaxed period in the thirty-year history of the Communist Party's climb to power. Mao and his comrades were in a mood to experiment, even with Western social and cultural forms. New social, economic, and political measures were being introduced as part of the Communist Party's new united-front line: cooperation among *all* elements of the population who were willing to fight the Japanese. In the villages, new united-front political coalitions were formed, and elections were held for the first time. Land-reform measures directed against landlords were curtailed. Women's and youth organizations that cut across class lines were organized, and literacy campaigns were undertaken.[13]

Exhilarated by all these activities—feeling, perhaps, that here in Yan'an she was seeing the future of the revolution—Smedley took a step she may have been considering for years: in March or April of 1937, she applied for membership in the Chinese Communist Party. Her application was denied. When she received the rejection she burst into tears and, to the amazement of those on hand, became nearly hysterical.

Party propaganda chief Lu Dingyi tried to soften the refusal by explaining that she would be of greater use as a journalist outside the party.[14] But although she continued to devote her life to the cause of the Chinese peasant, this rejection in Yan'an was a devastating blow from which Smedley would never fully recover. In retrospect, it is clear that there were a number of reasons for the rejection, such as her unbridled individualism and Chinese doubts, especially after her fight with Mme. Sun Yat-sen, about her ability to accept party discipline. All of these factors related to a controversy that had been brewing ever since Smedley arrived in Yan'an and that culminated during the summer—after her rejection by the party.

In February, Mao, Zhu De, Zhou Enlai, and others had encouraged Smedley in her efforts to introduce a new pastime: social dancing, Western style. Smedley was convinced that the grim survivors of the Long March needed to learn to relax and play. She also thought dancing might help break down the rigid social code imposed by the wives of leading cadres. Somehow she found an old phonograph and some Western records, and by March she and Lily Wu were conducting evening dance classes in the old Catholic church. The Red Army husbands came without their wives, but they were joined by a sprinkling of young women and men who had recently arrived from campuses in Beijing and Shanghai to serve the united front and the revolution. Edgar Snow wrote:

> Since she had been raised in the American West among cowboys, [Smedley] liked folk songs such as "On Top of Old Smokey," "Red River Valley," and "She'll Be Comin' Round the Mountain When She Comes." [With records of songs like these] she taught square dancing. . . . At first there were very few women who would dance, and frequently only the men danced. Agnes said that when the dancing was over she felt as if her feet had been trampled on by a whole army division. At this time she was 44 and her hair had already begun to turn gray; but she had the energy of a child, and knowing the pleasure of play, she made the dance parties with these "country bumpkins" a more joyful and pleasant experience than a first-class New York dance.[15]

Smedley was playing with dynamite but didn't seem to know it. Doubtless her own staunchly Western feminist views about marriage and freedom between the sexes blinded her. But the dancing parties were creating an explosive social atmosphere in the caves of Yan'an. Increasingly Smedley and her beautiful companion and interpreter, Lily Wu, came under sharp criticism from the women comrades of Yan'an. The situation came to a head in a most extraordinary fashion in June of

1937. Here is the story as Smedley told it to Edgar Snow, who retold it (in Japanese) after her death:

When the women of Yan'an first noticed an atmosphere of defiance among the men of the town, they suspected Agnes as the primary cause. For instance, they thought it strange that a foreign woman should spend so much time talking with their husbands in her cave. . . . It was said that General Zhu De's wife—a combat veteran in her own right—did not like the fact that her husband was being interviewed alone for long periods of time by Agnes, and she told him so. When Zhu De laughingly told Agnes this, her blue-gray eyes widened in surprise. And she said to Zhu De, "Isn't it bourgeois to think that there is only one thing men and women talk about when they are together?"

It was Mao's wife, He Zizhen, who appreciated Smedley the least. In return, Agnes made it plain that she thought Zizhen led a colorless, cloistered existence and did not have the necessary qualifications to be a revolutionary leader's wife. She made this clear by ignoring Zizhen. As a result, although there had been no specific quarrel between the two women, there was much mutual animosity.

Agnes had the habit of reprimanding young communist officials for being afraid of their wives. She told them half-jokingly that if they could not free themselves from women's oppression, they probably could not liberate China. . . . Agnes's introduction of square dancing to Yan'an was the last straw. It galvanized the wives into open opposition.

What we should not forget here is that the Red Army had just arrived in northern Shaanxi province after their famous Long March. The hardships had been great and many had been sacrificed along the way. Only a small number of women survived. Most were the wives or future wives of important party figures or Red Army commanders.

Even with the establishment of the communist base area around Yan'an, the number of women cadres was extremely small. Neighboring peasant women, behind the times politically and not beautiful physically, did not exist as rivals for the communist women. The women cadres controlled their husbands easily by applying the time-honored technique of not sleeping with their spouses. As a result, they gradually ignored personal appearance. They thought it bourgeois to braid one's hair prettily, and so they let their hair grow long and unkempt, casually cutting it short with a knife when it became bothersome. A few of these women had bound feet, so they especially were opposed to dancing and considered it immoral and "suggestive."

In one letter, Agnes wrote delightedly, "Mao said that because the women can't dance, they are all opposed to dancing." And again, "I have not yet corrupted Mao with dancing but I'll probably succeed soon. He wants to learn dancing and singing in case he has the chance to go abroad. Thus it was imperative he learn the latest fox trot. I think that if he has this chance to travel he'll have to leave his wife behind. His poetry has definitely progressed over these past few weeks." Since I knew nothing about Lily Wu at this time, I did not understand Agnes's reference to Mao's poetry.

Lily Wu was the star of the "social dances" that were taking place in the evenings. She also was a leading player in the "contemporary theater" troupe of Yan'an. Her specialty was leading roles in Western plays. From the beginning, Lily seemed a brilliant fairy-tale princess in contrast to the dull women of Yan'an. To the men of Yan'an, who had lived a long time among only peasants, Lily was more than a pretty face. She was comparable to Yang Guifei, the most beautiful woman in Chinese history.

Lily interpreted for most of Smedley's conversations with major leaders. Agnes and Lily were a good combination and became close friends. Often when high officials visited Lily without their wives, Agnes acted as Lily's chaperone.

The Red Army was enjoying a few months' interlude of peace between wars. And it was spring, with young rice plants coloring the red earth with green, and apple blossoms coming into full bloom. Mao, finally freed from battles which had lasted years, read many books and wrote essays on politics and philosophy. What is not well known is that Mao was also writing a large number of poems to instruct and guide Lily Wu. Right after sunset, before he went to work, Mao frequently went with one guard to Agnes's cave, and they talked together while drinking tea or rice wine. He showed a great deal of interest in foreign countries. He and Agnes were the same age, and he questioned her in detail concerning her life, including her love life. Mao had read some Western poems in translation, and he asked Agnes whether she had ever experienced romantic love of the type poets such as Byron, Keats, and Shelley praised.

Agnes discussed her marriage to V. Chattopadhyaya and described how, as lovers and compatriots, they had struggled together for Indian freedom. She stated that Chatto was the one true love of her life. Then Mao wanted to know exactly what "love" meant to Agnes, how she and Chatto had expressed it in their daily lives, and how the two of them could have argued and finally separated if their marriage linked the spiritual with the physical.

Agnes later said to me, "I was surprised at his childish curiosity." And again, "He said that he wondered whether the type of love that he had read about in Western novels could really exist and he wondered what on earth it was. Among the people he had met, I was the first one who seemed to have experienced this sort of love. He seemed to feel that somehow he had missed out on something." Lily appeared to be reviving within him youthful fancies about delicate and refined sentiment. She always acted as mediator in conversations between Mao and Agnes, and we may assume that certain questions Mao asked Smedley were directed at Lily. She was fresh and sensitive as well as elegant. Thus, when Agnes discussed romantic love with Mao, she thought the conversation was aimed at Lily Wu. During their discussions, Mao wrote poems. Naturally Lily was able to appreciate them better than Agnes. Lily would respond poetically herself, using the same rhythm as Mao had in his poetry, and this pleased him. They discussed at length man-woman relationships in the new post-revolutionary liberated society where men and women would be equals. These thoughts were woven into their poetry, which was classical in form.

Late one evening after Agnes had already gone to bed there was the sound of cloth shoes outside her cave and she heard the sound of Mao's soft southern accent. The chairman was in Lily's cave next door and the light was still on. Smedley had heard him knock, then the door opening and closing. She tried to go back to sleep and just when she finally was drifting off, she heard the sound of footsteps rushing excitedly up the hill. Then the door of Lily's cave was pushed open and a woman's shrill voice broke the silence: "You idiot! How dare you fool me and sneak into the home of this little bourgeois dance hall strumpet."

Smedley leapt out of bed, threw on her coat, and ran next door. There was Mao's wife standing beside the seated Mao beating him with a long-handled flashlight. He was sitting on a stool by the table, still wearing his cotton hat and military coat. He did not try to stop his wife. His guard was standing at attention at the door looking perplexed. Mao's wife, crying in anger, kept hitting him and shouting until she was out of breath. Mao finally stood up. He looked tired and his voice was quietly severe: "Be quiet, Zizhen. There's nothing shameful in the relationship between comrade Wu and myself. We were just talking. You are ruining yourself as a communist and are doing something to be ashamed of. Hurry home before other party members learn of this."

Suddenly Mao's wife turned on Lily, who was standing with her back against the wall like a terrified kitten before a tiger. She railed at Lily, saying, "Dance-hall bitch! You'd probably take up with any man. You've even fooled the Chairman." Then she drew close to Lily and while brandishing the flashlight she held in one hand, she scratched Lily's face with the other hand and pulled her hair. Blood flowing from her head, Lily ran to Agnes and hid behind her. Mao's wife now directed her anger against Agnes.

"Imperialist!" she shouted. "You're the cause of all this. Get back to your own cave." Then she struck the "foreign devil" with her flashlight. Not one to turn the other cheek, Smedley flattened Mrs. Mao with a single punch. From the floor, Mao's wife, more humiliated than hurt, shrieked: "What kind of husband are you? Are you any kind of man? Are you really a communist? You remain silent while I'm being struck by this imperialist right before your eyes."

Mao rebuked his wife, saying "Didn't you strike her even though she had done nothing to you? She has a right to protect herself. You're the one who has shamed us. You're acting like a rich woman in a bad American movie." Furious but restraining himself, Mao commanded his guard to help his wife up and take her home. But she made a fuss and refused to cooperate, so Mao had to call two more guards, and they finally led Mao's hysterical wife from the room. As they proceeded down the hill, Mao followed in silence, with many surprised faces watching the procession from their caves.

The next morning the whole town was talking of nothing else. It got to the point where Mao had to regard the problem as important, so he assembled the Central Executive Committee, explained his actions, and left the final decision to them. The committee decided to treat the case as a "secret matter" and they issued a command that forbade speaking more about it.

But no one could keep Mao's wife quiet. She got the other women together and asked for their support in banishing Smedley, Lily, and Mao's guard—she believed that he also had a part in this "intrigue"—from Yan'an. And she tried to put a stop to the dancing.

Soon there was animated discussion in the streets of Yan'an about the pros and cons of romantic love versus marriage. The young people began to ask: "If Mao can't control his wife, what sort of order can he impose on other people?" Finally, Mao went to Smedley's cave and said: "We swore that we wouldn't say a word about that embarrassing event. But my wife has broken her promise, and now this town is filled with suspicion and slander. It is an unbearable situation. I am convinced now that it is necessary to act publicly and counterattack the slander. This time I shall break completely with Zizhen. I think everyone will know the truth when I announce my reasons for the separation. Thus you are freed from your vow of silence. You may speak out [and defend yourself] if you wish."

For a second time Mao discussed this question with the party's Central Executive Committee. He asked for their consent to a divorce in order to clear up the matter once and for all. As they pondered his request, there was heated debate throughout Yan'an. Wives urged their husbands to intervene and save Mao's wife, but many men considered the situation from the opposite point of view. It was possible then [under Party regulations] to obtain a divorce by simply inserting an account of the situation in the official records and signing it. But Mao knew that if he wanted to maintain his authority, the officials would have to study previous cases for moral principles and fundamental guidelines that could serve as precedents for this act. Only then would the politburo be able to come to a systematic conclusion.

At just this point in time [July 7, 1937], the Lugouqiao [Marco Polo Bridge] Incident occurred and war was formally declared [by China], putting Yan'an suddenly on a war footing. The Committee therefore made a quick and simple decision. Mao's divorce was formally granted. Mao's wife was reprimanded for acting inappropriately for a Communist and revolutionary. "Political education" was necessary. He Zizhen promptly left Yan'an, going first to a remote village and later to the Soviet Union for continued "political education." Wu Guangwei [Lily Wu] was also banished from Yan'an. She was sent to the front lines with [Ding Ling's] theatrical group. Crying softly, Lily Wu burned Mao's poetry before leaving Yan'an. She and Mao probably never met again.

Agnes Smedley was not formally banished. Yet about a month after Lily Wu, Smedley also left, and some women leaders of Yan'an took credit for her departure. The dancing, however, continued. Smedley considered this a significant victory—a step toward removing the vestiges of feudal thinking from Chinese society. Square dancing became popular beyond Yan'an. After adapting a number of steps and rhythms from traditional peasant dances (*Yang ko*), "popular dancing," as it was called, eventually spread from the villages to the cities of northern China.

As I try to look back on it all today [1954], the image that springs to mind is that of the wide roads of Yan'an and rats in packs searching for a place to hide. And in the background, I can hear, faintly, an old phonograph playing strains of "She'll Be Comin' Round the Mountain When She Comes." [16]

In a shorter version of this story told by Nym Wales (Snow's first wife), it was said that He Zizhen threatened to kill Smedley.[17] Certainly the conflict was a deep one, pitting Yan'an's veteran women revolutionaries against Smedley and the few Chinese women who had just arrived from the cities and knew little about life in the countryside. Although both sides agreed that in the new society women should be economically independent, each had a radically different assessment of marriage as a social institution. Smedley had long believed that marriage was an oppressive institution for all women. The women veterans, however, considered monogamous marriage a great victory for Chinese women— a cultural advance to be protected and strengthened. They were not ready to tolerate the introduction of a "free-love" system; this had been tried earlier in the Jiangxi soviet and had victimized many women.[18] Needless to say, the ease with which Mao was being granted a divorce also upset them. In retrospect, it seems clear that Smedley's position in this controversy and the resentment aroused by her "liberated" Western behavior gave party leaders ample reason to deliberately ease her out of Yan'an.

The rejection of her application for membership in the Chinese Communist Party in the spring and then the Lily Wu affair in July were heavy blows to Smedley's spirit.[19] During her last two months in Yan'an, she tried to compensate by keeping as busy as possible. Defiantly, she continued the dance classes. But she also turned to gardening and acting as a foster parent. In letters that have survived, she tried to hide her disappointment by painting her life in idyllic terms. On July 21 she wrote to Randall Gould:

> In the midst of wars and rumors of wars, I've an American flower garden here. A friend outside sent me seeds; all kinds, including vines, nasturtiums; also some vegetables—eggplants, beans, squash, cucumber. I've shovelled and hoed for months until now my flowers are just starting to blossom— beautiful things that draw admirers. When they go to seed, I'll distribute [them] to many peasants so we will have a few new kinds of flowers up here.
>
> I walk on the hills and through the valleys early mornings and pick wild flowers—larkspurs, a big orange-red lily, iris, and a few other kinds. Up here they are gorgeous. Then I ride like the wind through valleys and over hills on my beloved "Yunnan"—a pony captured by He Long in Yunnan and given me by Zhu De.
>
> I work also—writing the life of Zhu De, and I keep chickens and ducks for food and do my own cooking. I'm a nurse also to one of my bodyguards.

He's been sick for three months, first with pneumonia and then weak lungs. He's a Sichuan peasant boy about twenty who lies in bed week after week, reading aloud in a sing-song voice. And now that he is better, [he is] singing dozens of peasant and Red Army songs. I'm also "attached to" a *xiaogui* [little devil] about eleven. He is the smartest thing in this part of the world. He lives in my house/cave, does small chores, and goes to school. I want [to bring] another *xiaogui* here also, because he has T.B. and needs a mother's care. He is one of the child prisoners of war formerly in Xi'an prison but released during the Xi'an event. He's a Sichuan peasant child about eleven also.

My present *xiaogui* is a character. Until I made him build a chicken house, he kept the chickens and ducks under his bed at night. Over his bed is a swallow's nest with four young just learning to fly. The peasants who share our compound have pups and kittens and my *xiaogui* had established a protectorate over them. Each day he carries our two ducks down to the river and the three of them go swimming together. He collects tin cans, nails, string, boxes, and pictures galore from magazines I throw away. And just like little American boys he has made himself a telephone with tin cans to which long strings are attached. He is a *xiaogui* in reality, and will fight any lad twice his size who tries to impose on him. My sick guard sort of fathers him and helps him study each day. I like his belligerency.

In other words, I've a calmer, more marvelous life than I have ever dreamed of. Never in Shanghai or America could I live so freely or so happily.

In late August Smedley fell off her horse and injured her back, thus delaying her departure. Her mood as she prepared to leave was bittersweet. She had often been genuinely happy in Yan'an. She knew that Zhu De and Zhou Enlai, among others, still had much affection for her; Zhu De had even given her his horse, Yunnan, in a gesture of friendship. But she had grown bitter toward Mao Zedong, perhaps seeing him as the cause of her rejection. In her future characterizations of Chairman Mao, whom she never saw again, she would be cutting, as in this example from the 1940s:

> I saw Mao Zedong on many occasions in Yan'an, either in the cave where he worked or elsewhere. I found him at first physically repulsive. It was difficult to meet his eye and he would answer my questions in a roundabout, impersonal way. There were times when he would not answer them at all and [thus] give me the impression that he had not heard them. He seemed somehow unsure of himself, even though his popularity and authority were not to be questioned. I attended several public meetings at which he spoke. They took place in the open air and the audience was enormous. His elocution was not good. He spoke as if his mouth were full of hot congee and his voice did not carry well. He was certainly aware of this and expressed himself in short, clipped, simple sentences, but slowly and with many pauses, during which those listeners in the front rows relayed his words to those further back who had not been able to catch them. A general murmur of approval then went

through the crowd and Mao waited for this to die down before proceeding. He would begin his speeches very quietly, keeping his hands still. Then, gradually, he would start gesticulating and his elocution then grew worse. It didn't matter much because that was precisely when those close to him began to clap their hands and of course the clapping was taken up by everyone present. It was rather impressive because it gave one the feeling that no matter what Mao said, he was the spokesman of his every audience.[20]

Smedley finally left for Xi'an in September of 1937, bruised but unbroken, already planning a way to rejoin Zhu De and Zhou Enlai in the field with the new Eighth Route Army. She was determined to fight on for the Chinese revolution. But her mission would remain only a self-appointed one.

China, 1929–1941

Smedley in Shanghai in
1930. (Courtesy of Gertrude
Binder.)

Lu Xun at his birthday party,
Shanghai, 1930. Photo by
Agnes Smedley. (Lu Xun
Museum, Shanghai.)

Richard Sorge in 1938. (Courtesy of Osaki Hotsuki.)

Left to right: Agnes Smedley, George Bernard Shaw, Mme.
Sun Yat-sen, Cai Yuanbei, Harold Isaacs, Lin Yutang, and Lu
Xun. In Mme. Sun Yatsen's garden, Shanghai, 1933. (Lu Xun
Museum, Shanghai.)

Osaki Hotsumi and daughter Yoko in Shanghai,
1932. (Courtesy of Osaki Hotsuki.)

Agnes Smedley in Yan'an with friends
Lily Wu (Wu Guangwei) and Anna
Wang, Spring, 1937. (Courtesy of Earl
Leaf.)

Zhu De and Smedley in Yan'an, 1937. (Courtesy of Ayako Ishigaki.)

Smedley with her "little devil" friend in
1937. Photo appeared in *China Fights
Back* (New York, 1938), following
p. 42.

On grounds at U.S. embassy, Hankou, 1938. Left to right: Frank Dorn, Zhou Enlai, Agnes Smedley, Evans Carlson, and consular official Robert Jarvis. (Smedley papers, Arizona State University.)

"Last Ditchers" dinner party in Hankou, August, 1938. Left to right: Agnes Smedley, Frank Dorn, F. McCracken Fisher, Jack Belden, A. T. Steele, Evans Carlson, Freda Utley, Zhang Hanfu, John P. Davies. (Courtesy of John P. Davies.)

Outside Bishop Logan Roots' residence, Han-
kou, 1938. Left to right: Bishop Roots, Anna
Louise Strong, Peng Dehuai, Francis Roots, and
Agnes Smedley. (Ralf Sues, *Shark's Fins and
Millet* [New York, 1944].)

Agnes Smedley and Frank Dorn, Hankou,
1938. (Courtesy of John P. Davies.)

Smedley being welcomed by a New Fourth
Army unit in Anhui battle zone, September,
1939. (Smedley papers, Arizona State
University.)

Hong Kong, 1940. Left to right: Agnes
Smedley, Emily Hahn, Hilda Selwyn-Clarke
and daughter Mary, and Margaret Watson
Sloss. (Smedley papers, Arizona State
University.)

Smedley in Guomindang uniform, worn by Communist and Guomindang troops in central China
during the United Front period, 1937–45.
(Smedley papers, Arizona State University.)

CHAPTER XIII

The Eighth Route Army and the Magic of Hankou, 1937–1938

For Smedley the ten-day march from Yan'an to Xi'an went badly. The back injury she had sustained in August flared up; she collapsed and at times had to be carried on a stretcher. Heavy rains had washed away whole sides of hills, making passage through the loess country unusually slow and dangerous. The conditions of famine she saw along the way depressed her. She was also unhappy with Mr. Zou, the translator assigned to accompany her now that Lily Wu was gone. Zou was a former schoolteacher from Beijing, and his contemptuous attitude toward the peasants and their health problems galled her. He was an urban intellectual of the sort she had found insufferable ever since her days on the Socialist *Call* in New York City.[1]

Another source of irritation was the presence of Nym Wales, who was also traveling to Xi'an. Wales had just spent three months gathering materials for her first book, the classic collection of Yan'an vignettes entitled *Red Dust*. Although they had been acquainted since 1934, the two women had never been friendly, and in Yan'an they steered clear of one another. Smedley was more than ten years older and considered Wales politically naive, intellectually superficial, and vain about her looks. Wales considered Smedley a psychotic prima donna of the left, and a shrill one at that. During the Lily Wu affair in Yan'an, Wales had tacitly opposed Smedley by siding with such Chinese women veterans as Kang Keqing and Deng Yingchao. But on the road to Xi'an the two women kept up an appearance of friendship, for the sake of their Chinese comrades. Forty years later, Wales still had little sympathy for

Smedley and expressed doubt about the seriousness of Smedley's back injury.[2]

Smedley arrived in Xi'an on a stretcher in mid-September of 1937, feeling irritable and useless, and very worried about her back, which she wanted x-rayed at the local missionary hospital. Refusing to go to the Xi'an guest house with Nym Wales and partake of its Western comforts, she spent the first week or so flat on her back at the Eighth Route Army headquarters, an old-style compound just outside the city walls, which she had known as the home and office of her friend the German dentist Wunsch, who had been killed on the first day of the Xi'an Incident.[3]

Although personally miserable, Smedley found the general atmosphere in Xi'an much improved since January, and this buoyed her spirits and eventually improved her health. Since the implementation of the united front, political tensions had slackened and Communists could move freely about the city. In an article entitled "The Chinese Red Army Goes to Town," Smedley described the astonishment of seasoned Red Army veterans discovering the wonders of big-city life—moving pictures, electric light bulbs, the flush toilets of the Xi'an guest house. At the Eighth Route Army headquarters she found high spirits and much optimism, even about confronting the Japanese. When, on September 26, news came of a Red Army victory at Pingxing pass in northern Shanxi, Smedley was swept up in the general euphoria:

> A meeting was held. I got out of bed and went. Everybody in the building was present, from all the men in charge to the cooks and cooks' assistants. There were many released political prisoners from Nanjing and Xuzhou, students from Beijing and Tianjin going to Yan'an, political workers from Yan'an en route to various places in China, Red Army men, guards, "little devils," and two foreigners [Smedley and the New Zealander James Bertram].
>
> This meeting was a wildly enthusiastic one. We were told of the victory in the north and men interrupted the speaker to shout slogans. Zhou Enlai's wife [Deng Yingchao] led the celebration. The New Zealander contributed an aboriginal Maori dance of his country. I tortured the audience with two songs—but then, many of these men had made the Long March or been in prison for years, so they could stand almost anything. A student back from Japan tortured me when he sang what he called a Japanese love song. A Red Army man told an incident of the Long March—how the Red Army [had] crossed the treacherous Datu River in Xizang [while] enemy troops raked their ranks from across the river. As he ended, Deng Yingchao rose and sang two stanzas from a beautiful Long March song.

By early October, Smedley's back was on the mend and she was growing restive. When she received an invitation to join the Eighth Route

Army in the field, she accepted immediately, but on one firm condition: Mr. Zou should not be her interpreter. This created a problem, since Zou was the only person available who had the requisite command of English. After a few days a solution was found by Zhou Yang, a party operative Smedley had known in Shanghai; he recommended that Smedley accept his young assistant, Zhou Libo. Zhou Libo's English was halting at best, but Smedley liked him at once and agreed to work with him.[4] In about a week, with Zhou Libo at her side, Smedley caught up with the Eighth Route Army at Taiyuan, the political and commercial center of western Shanxi. There she was welcomed and briefed by Zhou Enlai and then sent on to Zhu De's headquarters in the hills to the north. For the next three months Smedley remained there, interviewing and traveling by day, typing the results by night. In 1978 Zhou Libo and Zhu De's widow, Kang Keqing, remembered how Smedley worked at a furious pace. Besides writing individual articles, she was shaping her copious notes into a diary-style narrative that would be published the next year in New York and London as *China Fights Back*.

Smedley's courage and sense of detail still comes through in the clean, driving prose of *China Fights Back*. As always, she was passionately honest about her identification with her subjects and she unabashedly mixed reportage with autobiography:

> Tonight as these hungry men sang, and then as they marched away to their beds of straw or cornstocks spread on mud floors, their singing had more meaning to me than ever before. Their voices were like a strong orchestra in the night. I, who have food this day, realized that I can never know fully the meaning, the essence of the Chinese struggle for liberation, which lies embedded in the hearts of these workers and peasants. I am still an onlooker and my position is privileged. I will always have food though these men are hungry. I will have clothing and a warm bed though they freeze. They will fight and many of them will die on frozen battlefields. I will be the onlooker. I watch them blend with the darkness of the street; they still sing. And I hunger for the spark of vision that would enable me to see into their minds and hearts and picture their convictions about the great struggle for which they give more than their lives.
>
> (p. 123)

Smedley took an almost maternal interest in Zhou Libo's intellectual and physical well-being. Zhou recalled that he affectionately called Smedley *lao taitai,* "the old lady," to friends. Smedley saw him as too young and too intellectual for the Eighth Route Army—a fish out of water.* In *China Fights Back* she worried about his future and that of Xu Quan, another struggling young writer-soldier:

> The real story of China can be told only by the Chinese workers and peasants themselves. Today that is impossible. I do not believe that my companions [Zhou and Xu], Chinese though they are, can write the real story of the struggle of the Chinese people. They are true Chinese intellectuals, as removed from the life of the masses as I am. And one of them, Xu Quan, is first of all interested in "style." If you ask him about a book, he will tell you first of all of its style. Later on you can pry out of him something of the content. Libo is more interested in content, it is true. But the life he lives is so hard now that he is often too weary to make use of his experiences. Later on he will become hardened to this life, I think.
>
> (p. 148)

Smedley saw Zhu De, the commander of the Eighth Route Army, almost daily, and an extraordinary rapport developed between them. This gave rise to the rumor, both inside and outside China, that they must have had an affair.[5] But beyond Smedley's hero-worship, there is no evidence to support it. Weighing against it is the fact that Zhu De's young wife, Kang Keqing, was always in the vicinity and in later years actively promoted Smedley's image in the People's Republic of China. For Smedley, Zhu De was another father figure, a successor to Lajpat Rai and Lu Xun. Because Zhu himself had grown up in rural poverty, Smedley's identification with him was often painfully personal. Later, in *The Great Road*, she wrote:

> Sometimes, when General Zhu himself talked [about his parents], I would be unable to go on and he would regard me with curious and questioning eyes. "Sometimes," I would explain, "you seem to be describing my own mother. We did not work for a feudal landlord, but my mother washed clothing for rich people and worked in their kitchens during holidays. She would sometimes sneak out food for us children, give us each a bite, and tell us of the fine food in the home of her employer. Her hands, too, were almost black from work, and she wore her hair in a knot at the nape of her neck. Her hair was black and disheveled."
>
> "And your father?" he asked in wonderment.

* In March of 1978 the authors interviewed Zhou Libo, a large–framed, sickly, and bespectacled figure with a thick Hunan accent. Having just survived ten years in prison on trumped-up charges of political crimes during the Cultural Revolution, he was being fully rehabilitated and honored in the Chinese press as one of China's most important living novelists (*Renmin ribao*, March 23, 1978). Now he was being shown off to foreign visitors. We did not know that he was dying of cancer and would not live out the year. We wondered, however, what Smedley, who had absolute confidence in his personal and political integrity, would have thought about his recent treatment as a member of the Chinese Communist Party.

"In my early childhood he was a poor farmer who plowed the fields in his bare feet, but wore leather shoes most of the time. He ran away periodically because he hated our lives, and left my mother alone. He was not so disciplined as the men of your family. Then he became an unskilled day laborer, and we never had enough to eat."

"The poor of the world are one big family," he said in his hoarse voice, and we sat for a long time in silence.

(p. 18)

Shortly after her arrival, Smedley began working with Zhu De on a project of importance to the future of Chinese relations with India. Seeking medical aid for the Chinese, they established the first formal contact between the Chinese Communists in Yan'an and the Indian nationalist movement led by Gandhi and Nehru. Smedley knew Nehru personally and had corresponded with him since coming to China in 1929. She now persuaded Zhu De that Nehru was sincere in his international outlook and had genuine sympathy with China's struggle against imperialism.

Smedley wrote to Nehru on November 23, 1937, and Zhu De followed with a letter on November 26. Both noted the serious problems the Eighth Route Army was having in feeding and caring for its troops, particularly the new volunteer units, and they made a broad appeal for help. Nehru responded quickly. He publicized the letters, began raising funds, and revived an earlier Indian National Congress idea for a medical mission to China. By the summer of 1938 a relatively well-equipped medical mission of five Indian doctors was organized and ready. Smedley met them when they arrived in Hankou in October, 1938, and was instrumental in the mission's final decision to go to Yan'an and join the Eighth Route Army.[6] Their host in Yan'an was of course Zhu De. One of the doctors, Dwarkna Kotnis, decided to remain in China throughout the war and married a Chinese woman a year before dying in the service of the Eighth Route Army. In short, the medical mission was a great success, and it remains today a major symbol of friendship between the Indian and Chinese peoples.[7]

In mid-December of 1937, into Zhu De's headquarters walked a man who would become one of Smedley's closest friends. He was Evans Carlson, forty-one years old, a Marine captain and the fervently devout son of a Congregational minister in Connecticut. He had come to investigate the Eighth Route Army and study its guerrilla tactics. Carlson had the tall, rawboned, Nordic look of Smedley's first husband, Ernest Brundin, and more recently, her lover Richard Sorge. As it turned out, he was also a friend of Edgar Snow's, and, like Smedley, was disarmingly straightforward, open-minded, and daring. According to Smedley, Carlson's principles "were deeply rooted in early American Jeffersonian democracy; that must have been why he felt at home in the political and ethical atmosphere of the Eighth Route Army." [8]

When they first met, however, Smedley refused even to speak to Carlson, because he was an American official: "I considered him a military spy sent by the American Embassy and the Marine Corps. . . . I regarded him not only as a spy against that army, but a traitor to the principles on which the American Republic had been founded. Because of [his] background in Nicaragua and with the Marine Corps generally, I had little faith that he would understand the Eighth Route Army. He did not know my deep-seated hostility to all that he represented. We had only coffee in common, it seemed." [9]

For his part, Carlson was startled by Smedley's appearance. He wrote in his diary that she looked "woefully grim in her military uniform . . . [and] her face had the signs on it of suffering. . . . But absolute honesty in thought, speech, and action was written all over her." Soon the two were spending much time together, walking and talking, exploring each other's lives and ideas. "She was grand, attractive, alive, animated, wise, courageous, a wonderful companion, impetuous, wants things done right away." He also saw in her a Christian vocation of self-sacrifice: "She had forsaken the comforts of what we regard as civilization for a primitive life among an alien people. Her one desire was to remain with these people who were making such a valiant effort to realize the ideals for which she had consistently fought." [10]

The rejection in Yan'an had already forced Smedley to begin reconsidering her views on America. Now, as she came to know Carlson, there were signs that she was beginning to move toward a less dogmatic and more tolerant political position; she began reaching out once again toward well-meaning liberals, even officially connected ones. Clearly, Carlson touched the native American roots of her radicalism: "[He] reminded me of the words of the Battle Hymn of the Republic: 'As He died to make men holy, let us die to make men free.'" [11]

Christmas Eve, 1937, was their last night together before Carlson departed for the field. In his diary entry for that evening, Carlson describes a touching scene in his room. Agnes brought some coffee, and Carlson supplied a half-pound of peanuts. When the pot was hissing on the charcoal stove, Agnes suggested they celebrate "in our own style." Carlson asked if she knew any Christmas carols, and Agnes said she couldn't remember any, but she knew a few Negro spirituals. "You sing the spirituals," he said, "and I'll play some carols on my harmonica." Agnes sang "Let my people go." Carlson played "Silent Night," and then, characteristically, the Marine Corps song, "From the Halls of Montezuma." Then Agnes asked for a favorite of hers. At her request, the two stood up by the stove while Carlson played and she sang out loudly, "My Country 'Tis of Thee." [12]

On the twenty-sixth, Carlson was to go to the front lines. Smedley had asked permission to accompany him. When Zhu De told her he could not let her go because she was a woman, she was furious. Kang Keqing, Zhu De's wife, remembered that Smedley pouted for a day and, much to everyone's amazement, even tried tears. But Zhu De and others stood firm, insisting that Smedley should leave the increasing dangers of the field and go to Hankou, where she would be much more effective as a writer and an organizer of medical supplies. Smedley, of course, had no real choice in the matter. Carlson left with Zhou Libo, and Smedley began preparing for departure as cheerfully as she could. [13]

Hankou, part of the tri-city industrial complex known as Wuhan, straddles the Yangzi River midway down its long course from the Himalayas to the sea. After the Japanese capture and rape of Nanjing in December, 1937, it became China's new capital. Helped in part by a major victory at Taierzhuang in April, 1938, the Chinese were able to hold onto the city until mid-October. In January, 1938, when Smedley arrived, the international community had joined Nationalist and Communist politicians in descending on the city. Spirits were high. For the first time in a decade, there seemed to be some unity of purpose in China. Hankou seemed to represent a fresh start. In retrospect, the next ten months were the most romantic of China's wartime experience.

With Franco's victory over the Loyalists in Spain, the international press began to see Hankou as the most prominent new arena in the worldwide struggle against Fascism. The city quickly became almost a tourist stop for journalists, diplomats, and political radicals. It attracted veterans of the Spanish Civil War—notably the Canadian doctor and Communist Norman Bethune. Film-makers Joris Ivens and Frank Capra turned up, as did such leaders of the U.S. Communist movement as Earl Browder and Mike Gold, with whom Smedley had been sparring in recent years. Anna Louise Strong had just arrived from Moscow. The writers W. H. Auden and Christopher Isherwood passed through. The German, Italian, and Russian military officers advising Chiang Kai-shek added yet another international dimension. The Russians were particularly important, because Russian planes and pilots provided the only air defense against the intensifying Japanese bombing raids. Smedley thrived in this exciting atmosphere, and because of her myriad Chinese contacts, she enjoyed something like celebrity status. Everyone, it seemed, wanted to meet her or use her as a go-between.[14]

After arriving in Hankou on January 9, 1938, Smedley's first stop was the U.S. embassy, where she delivered a letter from Carlson and briefed the ambassador and assorted military attachés on the activities of the Eighth Route Army in northwestern Shanxi. The first of many visits she made to the U.S. embassy, this was the beginning of her regular contact with such figures as John Davies, Frank Dorn, Joseph Stilwell, and Claire Chennault, all of whom later became important in the shaping of America's China policy.

Clearly, this new relationship with official America was an about-face for Smedley. For years she had had difficulties with U.S. consular officials in Berlin, Shanghai, and Guangzhou. It was the rejection in Yan'an, the changed political situation in Hankou, and the anti-Japanese war that made the difference. Hankou offered a fluid and open environment in which Smedley and her new diplomatic friends could interact. Smedley found that she shared with Evans Carlson's cohorts a hostility toward Japan and an impatience with official U.S. reluctance to confront Japanese expansionism. Moreover, for the first time the embassy was interested in making contact with the Chinese Communists, and Smedley seemed an ideal go-between. Thus in Hankou we see Smedley returning to the coalition-oriented, political organizer role she had played during 1919 and 1920, when she had effectively lobbied and raised funds among New York and Washington elites and unions around the country for the Friends of Freedom for India. Perhaps the most striking evidence of her new approach to political work was her friendship with the British ambassador, Sir Archibald Clark Kerr. Suspicion of the British, who had harassed her for many years because of her anti-imperialism and her commitment to Indian nationalism, was an old habit. But Clark Kerr, the leading liberal of the Western diplomatic corps, won her over with his interest in the Eighth Route Army and medical aid. Within months he became a friend and one of the strongest supporters of her causes.*

---

* Sir Archibald Clark Kerr (1882–1951) proved to be one of the most important and controversial British diplomats of the World War II and postwar periods. As ambassador to China (1937–42), Moscow (1942–45), and Washington, D.C. (1946–48), he demonstrated remarkable empathy for the problems of the countries to which he was posted. In

Smedley's second stop in Hankou, after the U.S. embassy, was the humble headquarters of the embryonic Chinese Red Cross, where she delivered requests for medical supplies from the Eighth Route Army. Smedley had been working since 1934 to get medical supplies to the Red Army. Now, in the director of the Chinese Red Cross, Dr. Robert K. S. Lin (Lin Kesheng) she found a leader, a man whose personality, experience, and energy seemed to promise hope at last for the Chinese soldier. Lin was indeed a man of parts. Born in Singapore, he had been a professor of physiology from 1924 to 1937 at China's most important medical school, the Rockefeller-funded Peking Union Medical College. He was a Christian who spoke beautiful English with a pronounced Scottish accent, having received his secondary and university education in Scotland. He was attracted to Fabian socialism and admired the Russian physiologist Ivan Pavlov. With his knickers and cane, he looked very much the Anglo-Chinese gentleman, a familiar cultural type. But as a Chinese, he was deeply nationalistic. By 1938 he was one of China's best-known medical figures. He also had considerable organizing experience behind him, including the field directorship of the Medical Relief Commission during the north China famine of 1933. In late 1937 he came to Hankou to organize a new Chinese Red Cross Medical Relief Corps out of the remnants of the civilian Chinese Red Cross which had survived the rape of Nanjing. Considering the difficulties he faced, Lin was astonishingly successful in Hankou and afterward. (By 1943 he had set up a medical supply system for the army, with more than one hundred units and two hundred ambulances in the field. And in Hankou he started a medical-service training school, which later moved to Guiyang and maintained five branch schools in the field, that is estimated to have given training to more than thirteen thousand people.) [15]

When Lin and Smedley began working together in 1938, the only organized Western medical care in China was provided by missionary doctors and hospitals. The rest of Western medical practice in China was

the case of China this meant supporting medical aid, economic reconstruction, and resistance to the Japanese. He also adopted a consistently liberal or tolerant view of Moscow and the Chinese Communists, positions which some historians in recent years have considered naive. Thus Clark Kerr's enthusiasm in 1938 for Smedley's causes came naturally—laying a base for a relationship which continued through Clark Kerr's Washington, D.C., days and their joint condemnation of the Cold War. Clark Kerr is in need of a good biographer; for basic facts see the *Times* (London), July 6, 1951, and, on his role in Anglo-American World War II China policy, the frequent references in Christopher Thorne, *Allies of a Kind: The United States, Britain, and the War against Japan, 1941–45* (Oxford, 1978).

entirely private and could be found only in large cities. The soldiers in China's armies—those who served Chiang Kai-shek, as well as the warlords—were expected to fend for themselves on a minuscule medical supplement added in cash to their salaries (and often expropriated by their officers). By 1938 several Chinese Red Cross committees had been organized by missionaries to care for the civilian refugee population. These committees received almost all the medical relief funds raised abroad, but the missionaries assiduously followed the practice promised by the myriad international fund-raisers: no medical care would be provided to wounded combatants, whether Chinese or Japanese. Thus by 1938, the second year of total war in China, the problem of medical care for the Chinese wounded had reached crisis proportions.

For the next ten months, Smedley devoted most of her energies to raising funds for the Chinese Red Cross and publicizing the misery and heroics of the Chinese wounded. Her articles appeared first in the *Manchester Guardian* and the *China Weekly Review,* and later in *China Today,* the *Nation,* the *Modern Review, Asia,* and even *Vogue.* In her fund-raising efforts, she ferreted contributions out of every conceivable source in Hankou: the American and British embassies, Standard Oil, and high Guomindang government officials were all fair game. Her biggest success came at a dinner party when she publicly shamed Finance Minister T. V. Soong (Song Ziwen) into contributing 10,000 Chinese dollars to the cause. Her journalist friends remember being dragooned on several occasions into visiting hospitals, to sing songs to the wounded and to leave substantial contributions. For Dr. Lin, Smedley wrote to the United States and Hong Kong appealing for help. As it turned out, the lion's share of aid in money and medical supplies was effectively solicited from overseas Chinese, especially those in Hong Kong. By midspring, Lin and Smedley had the support of the British Hong Kong medical establishment in the person of Hilda Selwyn-Clarke, the wife of Hong Kong's medical director and a very able fund-raiser, who was by then a fervent convert to the cause of the Chinese Red Cross.[16]

Smedley grew intensely loyal to Dr. Lin, and he to her, but both paid a political price for the relationship. For Smedley the problem was Dr. Lin's association with Mme. Chiang, which at times brought him into fund-raising competition abroad with Mme. Sun and her China Defense League, which was often at odds with the Chiang government. This fact reopened Smedley's old conflicts with Mme. Sun and tended to isolate her from such friends as Edgar Snow, Rewi Alley, Elsie Cholmeley, and Israel Epstein, who were working closely with Mme. Sun on various projects. For Dr. Lin, the problem was Smedley's close ties to the Communists, which regularly got him into trouble with the Guomindang leadership. (Once in 1940, when he was detained in Chongqing and threatened because of Smedley, he was saved only by the intervention of Mme. Chiang Kai-shek.) In sum, Smedley's alliance with Dr. Lin was another sign of the more independent political course she was now charting. Increasingly, she was moving away from political positions, alliances, or publications that were exclusively associated with the organized left in the United States, Europe, and treaty-port China.

When Smedley arrived in Hankou, she stayed first at the home of an Episcopal cleric, Logan Roots, who was known at the time as "the pink Bishop" because of his contacts with the Chinese Communists. The atmosphere at the Roots compound was extraordinary. Zhou Enlai paid regular visits there, as did other Communists such as the Moscow-oriented Wang Ming. At lunch came a steady stream of Guomindang officials, missionaries, diplomats, and journalists of various political persuasions. Other missionaries called the Roots' luncheon table the "Moscow-Heaven Axis." Sharing the spotlight with Smedley at these lunches was Anna Louise Strong, whom Smedley had presumably met in Moscow in 1933. Between them, they put on quite a show, Smedley describing the exploits of the Eighth Route Army and Strong analyzing the international situation from Madrid to Hankou. Strong was more ideological and still oriented toward Moscow; Smedley was passionately down-to-earth in her concern for the wounded and the details of the war itself. Strong later liked to tell friends a story that illustrates well how the two women differed. She once invited Smedley to join her for a dinner with H. H. Kung (Gong Xiangxi), her one-time classmate at Oberlin College and nominal head of state as president of the Executive Yuan. According to the biography co-authored by Strong's nephew:

> In the midst of an elegant banquet and innocuous conversation, [Smedley] suddenly interrupted Dr. Kung and asked for a large donation for the peasant guerrillas who were fighting the Japanese in Shanxi, Kung's home province. Anna Louise froze with embarrassment, knowing as Agnes certainly also did, that Kung was a bitter enemy of the Communists. As Anna Louise expected, Kung exploded angrily that he disapproved of people collecting extra money for the Communist Eighth Route Army, which, he said, should be content with its regular wages and not ask for special gifts. All three of them knew the injustice of Kung's response; the Eighth Route Army was twice as large as the number of troops for which Chiang Kai-shek was paying. Agnes did not attempt that argument. "Oh, Dr. Kung," she protested, "I am not asking for anything for the Eighth Route Army. Of course they are satisfied

with their wages. I am asking you for the peasant guerrillas of Shanxi, who
are protecting your property, Dr. Kung, against the Japanese." Agnes left the
party with a large check for her peasant guerrillas, and Anna Louise retired
to their quarters with a new sense of the difference between her and her
housemate. Her good middle-class upbringing, she concluded, would never
have allowed her to dare such a request. "But Agnes never recognized im-
possibilities." [17]

Despite their differences in style and background, Strong and Smedley
seemed to respect each other and did not clash directly. Strong wrote an
introduction for *China Fights Back*, which Smedley was just finishing,
and she may well have been responsible for its speedy acceptance and
publication.

Neither Strong nor Smedley stayed with the Roots for more than a
few weeks. Strong soon left for the United States and the Soviet Union.
Smedley, after borrowing money from a Chinese engineer friend from
Shanghai on the strength of her promised advance for *China Fights
Back*, rented a small apartment in town. From there she began to write
for the *Manchester Guardian*, an assignment that by summer turned into
a position as special correspondent—her first in years, and a sign that the
quality of her war reporting was gaining international recognition.

She also began to socialize a bit, though warily. Captain Frank Dorn,
General Stilwell's debonair aide, later recalled his first "date" with her:

> Getting in touch with Zhou Enlai was a tougher nut to crack since I felt it
> essential that I meet him under auspices acceptable to him. So [the journalist
> Walter] Bosshard arranged for me to meet Agnes Smedley at a luncheon in
> the Y.M.C.A. dining room. She was now a correspondent for the *Manchester
> Guardian*—when she took time off from her aggressive assaults on the for-
> eign community for money and hospital supplies to alleviate the neglect with
> which the Chinese treated their sick and wounded soldiers. She was without
> much conventional charm or femininity; her face was squarish, as was her
> figure. Her blonde hair, streaked in shades of sun-scorched yellow, was cut in
> an indifferent bob; she wore clothes for the sole purpose of covering her
> body, with no thought for fashion. . . . She had little use for most military
> officers, except of course her beloved Chinese Reds. In her eyes the military
> were all politically naive, an opinion she promptly stated in an abrupt and
> somewhat harsh voice. But after this initial phase of putting me in my place,
> she settled down and we got along pleasantly enough. During coffee I invited
> her to have wiener schnitzel the next evening at the Austrian-Chinese restau-
> rant. Though her eyes widened momentarily with surprise, she accepted.
> That evening, after the third gimlet, Agnes set her glass down with a thump
> and said flatly:
>
> "What's this all about, Captain Dorn? I know damned well I'm not the
> type that *your* type asks out on a date."

"I want you to introduce me to Zhou Enlai and to ask him to be frank with me."

"Well, at least you're honest about it. That's to your credit . . . aside from all these drinks. I like honesty. Even though I think I'm being taken in, I'll see what I can do. I've got an appointment with Zhou tomorrow morning."

We finally shook hands across the table, and I began a long friendship with this intense, unhappy woman. A radical with a great heart, she refused to submit to any form of discipline and distrusted all political leaders.[18]

One of Smedley's closest friends and confidants in Hankou was Freda Utley. A British Communist and graduate of Oxford, Utley had gone to the Soviet Union in the 1920s and married a Communist official. After he disappeared in a purge in the mid-1930s, she made her way with her small son to Tokyo, where she began working as a journalist. She arrived in Hankou in 1938 fiercely anti-Russian but not hostile to the Chinese Communists. Compared to Strong and Smedley, she knew little about the Chinese situation. But she had written lucidly about the Japanese as fascists, and she saw the Chinese struggle as a prelude to World War II. In Hankou she and Smedley soon became a twosome. In 1970, after having turned rabidly anti-Communist, she wrote:

> [Agnes] was one of the few people of whom one can truly say that her character had given beauty to her face, which was both boyish and feminine, rugged and yet attractive. [She was] one of the few spiritually great people I have ever met, [with] that burning sympathy for the misery and wrongs of mankind which some of the saints and some of the revolutionaries have possessed. For her the wounded soldiers of China, the starving peasants and the overworked coolies, were brothers in a real sense. She was acutely, vividly aware of their misery and could not rest for trying to alleviate it. Unlike those doctrinaire revolutionaries who love the masses in the abstract but are cold to the sufferings of individuals, Agnes Smedley spent much of her time, energy, and scant earnings in helping a multitude of individuals. My first sight of her had been on the Bund of Hankou, where she was putting into rickshaws and transporting to the hospital, at her own expense, some of those wretched wounded soldiers, the sight of whom was so common in Hankou, but whom others never thought of helping. Such was her influence over "simple" men as well as over intellectuals that she soon had a group of rickshaw coolies who would perform this service for the wounded without payment.[19]

Smedley was attracted to Utley for several reasons besides her admiration for Utley's first book, *Japan's Feet of Clay* (London, 1937). The two shared a background in radical politics, and both had husbands arrested in Stalin's purges. (Smedley had just received word of Chatto's arrest. It is unclear how much she knew as yet about Stalin's purges.) Utley was younger, more attractive, and leading a very complicated love life in a deliberate rejection of marriage. It is possible that Smedley saw in her a faint reflection of her own life ten years earlier. At any rate, by summer the two women were the center of a high-powered, tight-knit social circle of diplomats and journalists (nearly all of them male) which included Evans Carlson, who was back with news from the front.

The international press corps in Hankou had quickly developed a unique sense of camaraderie. As Frank Dorn has written, the increasingly frequent Japanese air raids heightened belief that the city's days were numbered: its fall and pillage were inevitable. But working conditions were favorable: for one thing, there was less censorship being applied than in any Chinese capital before or since. Moreover, there was political consensus about the job that needed to be done, that is, to report the heroic struggle of a united Chinese people against the brutal and Fascist Japanese invaders. One expression of this convivial spirit, and a common interest in seeing who could stay in Hankou the longest, was the Hankou Last Ditchers Club. Beginning in the summer of 1938, its members staged regular farewell dinners for "deserters," with the rhetorical and comical flavor of press club "roasts." One such dinner in September was staged as a "trial" of the guests of honor, Evans Carlson and Freda Utley, who were about to leave for Shanghai. Smedley attended many of these dinners, and when she herself left Hankou in October she wrote a long note, addressed simply to the Hankou "gang," in which she lovingly sketched each of them as characters in a play she might someday write.[20]

Smedley's Chinese associates in Hankou shared some of the hope and exhilaration felt in the foreign community. Politically, the united front was at its most cordial stage, and Chiang Kai-shek's secret police were much less active than they had been (and would be later). In most ways, it was the freest atmosphere Chinese intellectuals had seen in years. Zhou Enlai and Guo Moruo, both Communists, held high government posts. Hankou buzzed with intellectual activities—new magazines, plays, and art exhibits. Lao She, the head of the writers' association, was there, as were other important writers Smedley had known in Shanghai, notably Mao Dun. The poet and scholar Guo Moruo, who seemed to preside over the cultural scene, later devoted a volume of poems to the "spirit of Hankou." Smedley was interviewed often by Chinese reporters and made friends with some of the young journalists who in the 1980s hold top management positions in the press of the People's Republic of China. She also wrote articles expressly for Chinese publications; Lu Xun, Japanese prisoners, and the Chinese wounded were favorite subjects.[21]

Smedley's most significant contact was with the medical men and women of Hankou, the most important of whom was Dr. Lin. She made regular trips to Changsha, a day's drive to the south, to deliver medical supplies and ambulances, as well as to monitor conditions there for Dr. Lin. About fifteen years later, in the Chinese press a Y.M.C.A. worker named Liu Liangmo described Smedley's appearance at a large Chinese fund-raising event in Changsha in 1938, at which he served as her translator.* According to his report, she spoke quietly first of the Eighth Route Army's victories over the Japanese. Then, her voice rising gradually to a passionate intensity which seemed to transform her physically, she described the desperate needs of the Chinese wounded, ending with a dramatic appeal for funds. She sat down abruptly, exhausted, and there was a long silence. Then the crowd stirred and began donating money, in large amounts. Liu was amazed; it was the most successful fund-raising event of the year in Changsha.[22]

Hankou fell on October 17, 1938. A few days earlier, Smedley had slipped out of the city, first to Changsha and then onward to join the newly formed Communist-led guerrilla units of the New Fourth Army. There were many successes ahead for her, in terms of writing and medical relief efforts, but she left in a mood of melancholy and regret. In June of 1939 she wrote to Freda Utley:

> The last days of Hankou still remain in my mind as rare, unusual days from the psychological and human viewpoint. I still think of Shaw's *Heartbreak House* when I recall them. As you remarked at the time, no person on earth is more charming than the American journalist abroad, particularly the cultured, serious-minded one. But I wonder what it would be like were I to meet those same men on the streets of Chicago. Gone the magic! The only ones who have maintained some contact with me are Evans [Carlson] and Frank [Dorn]. Evans wrote me a short note from Shanghai and sent it here by [Jack] Belden, who came here for a week. Then Evans remembered to send me a copy of one of his articles in *Amerasia*. And, as Frank Dorn returned to

* Westernized and a highly committed social worker, Liu Liangmo was a Christian in the mold of James Yen and Robert K. Lin. Shortly after he met Smedley in Changsha he would become instrumental in introducing mass singing to China on behalf of the war effort. Choosing to return to China (from the United States) after 1949, he was a leading figure in Y.M.C.A. and other social-welfare work in Shanghai through the 1950s. His outspokenness and Christian Y.M.C.A. background made him vulnerable during the Cultural Revolution. In a 1978 interview he denounced Chairman Mao in no uncertain terms and charged the authors with the task of telling the world that Mao had ruined the lives of four generations of his family.

America, he wrote me a long, human letter from the ship. But then a ship is much like Hankou—an island on which one is thrown back upon oneself. I suppose he has forgotten me by this time. Once [Tillman] Durdin asked someone in Chongqing where I am—so he remembers I am somewhere in the land of the living.

I sort of pine for the magic of Hankou. It was the bright spot in one decade of my life. There I met foreign men, some of them rotters, but most of them with the charm that belongs to many men of the Western world. They themselves do not know how very different they are from the Chinese. Though I have never liked to be treated as bourgeois women are treated, still the foreign men from England, America, and perhaps France, have a deep and unconscious attitude of respect for women; a little feeling of protection for women; of helping a woman; and a kind of gentleness toward her. Often [their] kindness blended a bit with tenderness or a breath of romance. It is difficult to explain, because it is there as an atmosphere. In the Chinese man this is totally lacking in all respects. There is not even friendship and comradeship between man and woman in China. The foreign word "romance" has been taken into the Chinese language and means promiscuous sexual relations. And "love" means sexual intercourse in its usual use in China. For a Chinese man to even touch a woman's arm or hand means something sexual and arouses shock.

So, for ten years I lived in this desert [China], and because of this, I found a magical place. Since then I have thought much of this. Shall I return to the Western world, or shall I remain here? I fear I must remain in China. Hankou was a rare exception, and I believe all of us felt the same about it. I wish to retain it as a precious memory. I think often of the play in which many persons of different classes are on a foundering ship in mid-ocean. Class distinctions fall away as they face death together, drawn closer by humanity. But when the storm passes and the ship is saved, the old cold and cruel class distinctions return. I believe that to be Hankou.[23]

CHAPTER XIV

At the Front, 1939–1941

A few days before Hankou fell to the Japanese in October, 1938, Smedley headed south in a medical van. At Changsha, between bombing raids she conferred with Dr. Lin and pondered her next move. There seemed to be three alternatives. First, she could move further inland to the remote mountainous retreat of Chongqing, along with Chiang Kai-shek's government and most of the Hankou "gang" of international correspondents. By withdrawing to Chongqing and giving up vigorous resistance to the Japanese, Chiang hoped to survive without major losses until the Americans and others could be drawn into the war. Or, second, she could return to the United States via Hong Kong. Third, she could join the Communist-led guerrilla units in central China, the most dangerous war zone of all, as a war correspondent and medical worker.

The first two options were not hard to reject. Chongqing was far from the battlefield, and with the censorship and police harassment Smedley could expect from Chiang's regime, the atmosphere was likely to be as stifling for her as it had been in Shanghai in 1936. The United States had even less to offer her in the way of professional opportunities. The popular mood there was still isolationist, there was little interest in Asia, and the American left was increasingly split over Stalin's purges. Personally, she felt little emotional pull to return. Her father was dead, she was not on good terms with others in her family, and over the years she had drifted apart or broken off friendships with women like Florence Lennon and Margaret Sanger. For better or worse, China had become her personal and professional home. Choosing the third option,

211

then, came naturally. Four months with the Eighth Route Army in 1937 had given Smedley a taste of war reporting, and she loved it. The recognition being given to *China Fights Back* (1938), as well as the encouragement she was getting from editors at the *Manchester Guardian*, were a tonic for her self-confidence. Perhaps most important, she filled an essential role as a spokesperson for medical needs of the wounded in central China. The units would soon be served by her friend Dr. Lin and his associates, who were setting up a medical delivery system for the Communist-led New Fourth Army in the hills to the east of Changsha.

Despite the fact that the Lily Wu affair had rendered her persona non grata with the Eighth Route Army in Yan'an, many Communist leaders, particularly Zhou Enlai and Zhu De, appreciated Smedley's value as a sympathetic writer and go-between in dealings with the West. At Hankou she had proven herself on a variety of fronts, and Zhou Enlai had developed a genuine personal respect for her. Thus Zhou did not hesitate to recommend Smedley to the commanders of the New Fourth Army, Ye Ting and Xiang Ying, and they in turn gave her blanket permission to travel in the war zone.

From November of 1938 to April of 1940, Smedley wandered the hills north and south of the Yangzi River as it flows east from Wuhan—a vast region that encompassed Hunan and Hubei provinces to the south and Anhui and Henan provinces to the north. Most of her time was spent visiting resistance units under both Communist and Guomindang leadership. Hers turned out to be the longest sustained tour of a Chinese war zone by any foreign correspondent, man or woman, including Edgar Snow and Jack Belden. It was an exhilarating experience and probably the high point of her career as a journalist. But the conditions were rugged and dangerous, and Smedley paid a price in steadily deteriorating health.

In *Battle Hymn of China* (1943), one of the best works of war reporting to have come out of World War II, Smedley chronicled her eighteen-month experience in great detail. War and revolution were her subjects, and she painted them in broad dramatic strokes through a series of colorful vignettes about battles, Japanese atrocities, and heroics on the Chinese side. Determined to arouse American sympathy for the struggle of the whole Chinese people against the Japanese invaders, she deliberately emphasized unity of purpose between the Communists and the Guomindang. Her attacks on the Guomindang, for example, were muted, and she praised pro−Chiang Kai-shek warlords like Li Zongren and his Guangxi troops almost as much as the Communist-led New Fourth Army.

From the historian's point of view, one of *Battle Hymn*'s great strengths is its description of the social transformation that took place in the Chinese countryside as the result of the war. Through Smedley's eyes we see how peasant women were being organized to take an active role in military and social life, how basic literacy grew through mass education campaigns, and how democratic practices were introduced into village politics as an integral part of mobilizing against the Japanese. It was largely because of these changes that Chiang Kai-shek was unable to regain control of the Chinese countryside after the war.

What Smedley does not reveal in *Battle Hymn* is the complexities of her own personal and political life in the central war zone. The tone of the book is upbeat and exuberant, but from a letter she wrote to Freda Utley in June of 1939, we know that she often felt isolated and alone after the camaraderie she had enjoyed in Hankou. And despite the rosy picture of national unity she painted in *Battle Hymn*, she knew that the Communists and the Guomindang remained bitter rivals, and even that the Communist leadership of the New Fourth Army was seriously split.

The New Fourth Army had taken shape in 1938 from guerrilla units operating in the hills of the lower Yangzi River valley, which runs east from Anqing to the outskirts of Shanghai. The army was recruited and led by Communist veterans of the Long March, and by the fall of 1938 it had over 12,000 uniformed men. Split into four detachments, the main body operated south of the Yangzi. Only one detachment of about 2,000 men operated to the north. The headquarters was in southern Anhui at Yunling, about fifty miles south of the river port of Wuhu. Because Chiang Kai-shek insisted that the commander of the New Fourth Army could not be a Communist, a compromise was made: the leader would be Ye Ting, a former Communist who was now on good terms with Chiang. But because Ye was kept busy commuting back and forth between Yunling, Nanchang, and Chongqing, the real power lay with his strong-minded Communist vice-commander and political commissar, Xiang Ying. Xiang had been a major figure in the Red Army and the Communist Party since the Jiangxi soviet of the early 1930s. Politically he was allied to the more doctrinaire, Moscow-trained, "Bolshevik" faction led by Wang Ming and Bo Gu, which rigidly supported the united-front line. Owing to his earnest pursuit of the united front, Xiang Ying's relations with Guomindang counterparts in the Fifth War Zone were often better than those of his commander, Ye Ting.[1]

Throughout 1938 and 1939 the New Fourth Army managed to become enough of a nuisance to attract Japanese air attacks and mop-up campaigns—which was precisely what Chiang Kai-shek had hoped would happen. A major reason for the New Fourth Army's resilience was its medical corps. Smedley worked closely with this corps from the very beginning, and her role in its success is now offici. ly acknowledged in Beijing.[2]

In November, 1938, Smedley moved from Changsha to the New Fourth Army headquarters at Yunling, ostensibly to prepare an extended report for Dr. Lin and the Red Cross. But her real mission, as she saw it, was to publicize the New Fourth Army Medical Corps in Shanghai and Hong Kong. During the winter of 1938–39 she wrote a series of articles for the *China Weekly Review* of Shanghai (reprinted later in the *Manchester Guardian*) which reported at length on the condition of the New Fourth Army and its medical needs. Privately, she appealed to such British friends as Sir Archibald Clark Kerr, the ambassador, and Hilda Selwyn-Clarke, wife of the director of Hong Kong's health services, as well as to the American branch of the International Red Cross. By spring, significant aid was coming in from British and Red Cross sources, and in the eyes of her Chinese colleagues, Smedley was a heroine.[3]

The director of the New Fourth Army Medical Corps in Yunling— who was later to become one of the leading figures of Chinese medicine—was Dr. Shen Jizhen, a German-trained native of Hunan province and a teacher at Beijing Medical College until Dr. Robert K. Lin personally appointed him to the New Fourth Army job. During the winter of 1938–39 Dr. Shen escorted Smedley on an extensive tour of more than twenty medical teams attached to the three detachments of the New Fourth Army south of the Yangzi. Forty years later, in an interview in Beijing, Dr. Shen recalled how hard Smedley had worked and especially praised her personal ministrations to the wounded. Most of Dr. Shen's doctors and nurses were from big cities like Shanghai and Hong Kong and felt uneasy in the countryside, as well as being terribly frightened by the Japanese bombing raids. Smedley seemed much less concerned about both, and often risked her life to help the wounded during bombing attacks.[4]

A contemporary account by a young writer for a local guerrilla publication captured the excitement surrounding Smedley's arrival at New Fourth Army headquarters in November, 1938. The author, an aspiring novelist and playwright named Wu Jiang, considered Smedley a celebrity before she arrived. Three weeks earlier, at a memorial meeting honoring Lu Xun, the father of modern Chinese literature, he had heard Smedley referred to as a close friend and comrade-in-arms of the great man. Now here she was, the great American writer herself, rafting into Yunling with a group of guerrillas and students. Seeing themselves as part of an international struggle, the whole community gathered in an old ancestral temple to meet her. The welcoming speeches were warm, not only from medical corps director Shen but also from Xiang Ying, the hard-nosed Red Army veteran who was in charge. Smedley's words of response were well translated by a young American-trained doctor, Fang Lianbai. It was her standard melodramatic performance: she described her poor rural roots, her jail experience in New York, and her revolutionary marriage to Chatto, and concluded by praising the Chinese struggle as a crucial part of the international fight against fascism and imperialism. As usual, she brought the crowd to its feet. At the end of the evening, she led a rousing rendition of the "Internationale" in Chinese.[5]

Smedley spent her first days in Yunling inspecting medical facilities and writing reports. At night she met by candlelight with students for discussions of world politics and literature. She seemed indefatigable. In an interview in 1978, Wu Jiang remembered that she took time to talk with him personally and at length about how to write plays and how to collect material in the midst of a war.[6]

After a few weeks at Yunling, Smedley and Dr. Shen began to tour medical units in outlying areas. In a valley not far from headquarters, she was allowed to visit the New Fourth Army's secret arsenal and munitions center—an expression of unusual trust, since the arsenal's existence technically violated the united-front agreement with the Guomindang.* Quickly recovering from the shock of having a foreign visitor, the arsenal's managers proudly showed Smedley around the factory and explained its improvised equipment. With characteristic forthrightness, Smedley asked to try out the product. She was handed a pistol and bullets and led to the outskirts of the compound, where a target was put up against a tree. Like a true daughter of the Wild West, she loaded the

---

* Under the terms of the agreement between Yan'an and Chongqing, the New Fourth Army was to get its arms only from Chongqing and was not to produce munitions on its own. Chiang Kai-shek, always wary of any increase in Communist power, sent only enough arms for the army's size in mid-1938 and thereafter supplied few replacements. To accommodate the army's swelling ranks of guerrilla units, the leadership decided they had to develop a makeshift arsenal of their own. See sources cited in note 1.

pistol expertly, whirled toward the target, and fired. All three shots were on the mark. She handed the gun back to her astonished hosts, and at the end of the tour she told them: "I've traveled in America and Europe, and visited many countries and factories, but I must confess I have never seen anything like your arsenal. It's unique."[7]

In the spring of 1939, when Smedley returned to Yunling from one of her excursions, she was surprised to find Hans Shippe in camp. Shippe was a German writer and maverick Communist whom Smedley had known in Shanghai in 1935. Writing under the pen name Asiaticus, he had criticized Edgar Snow's *Red Star over China* as soon as it appeared. Essentially he argued that Snow, whom he called a Trotskyite, had exaggerated the independence of the Chinese Communists from Moscow and had not understood the need for the Communists to subordinate their identity to the united front with the Guomindang. A similar position on *Red Star* was being taken by Communist Party reviewers in Europe and America—in the New York *Daily Worker,* for example.[8]

When Shippe visited Yan'an in 1938, he had arranged for a Chinese version of his critique of Edgar Snow to be circulated before his arrival. In his first audience with Mao, he repeated his attack on Snow. The response was silence, and other senior figures refused to see him. A few weeks later, he asked to see Chairman Mao again. This time Mao did all the talking: he delivered a stern rebuke and told Shippe to hold his tongue about Snow if he had any hope of being restored as a member of the German Communist Party. Shippe later told Smedley: "Mao had been too severe with me. He was really too cruel."[9]

When Shippe visited the New Fourth Army headquarters for two weeks in the spring of 1939, he and Smedley saw each other daily and argued vociferously, not only about Snow but about other matters as well. Their opposing positions are worth noting because they mirrored disputes taking place within the Communist leadership of the New Fourth Army generally. Smedley sided with Ye Ting and Chen Yi, whose views resembled those of Zhu De and Mao in Yan'an: she wanted the Communists to maintain considerable independence of military command from Chiang Kai-shek's Guomindang and hence enough military power to avoid another betrayal by Chiang. Shippe's views were closer to those of Xiang Ying of the New Fourth Army and Wang Ming and Bo Gu in Yan'an: he wanted the Communists to accept political and military subservience to the Guomindang and more guidance from Moscow. After all, he argued, Stalin was providing major assistance to

Chiang Kai-shek, and so long as this aid continued, Chiang would not dare attack the Communists. The daily arguments between Smedley and Shippe were so noisy and bitter that their Chinese hosts arranged for Smedley to leave on a field trip earlier than planned, and Shippe left for Shanghai shortly thereafter.[10]

While Smedley was defending Edgar Snow in her arguments with Shippe, she took a position on another issue that on the surface seemed to contradict her stand on the need for independence from the Guomindang. In letters to Edgar Snow, she was demanding that he choose sides between her and Mme. Sun Yat-sen on the issue of medical aid. Both women were raising money in Shanghai, Hong Kong, and the United States for China's medical needs, but they felt locked in competition. A central issue was the role of Dr. Robert K. Lin, whom Mme. Sun disliked chiefly because of his close ties to her sister and arch-rival, Mme. Chiang. In Mme. Sun's view, accepting the united front to the point of working mainly through Dr. Lin on medical aid meant handing over supplies and money to the hopelessly corrupt Nationalist government of Chiang Kai-shek. In her opinion, little if any medical aid would then reach Communist-led troops. But Smedley was fiercely loyal to Dr. Lin, and, as she had so many times in the past, she put her trust in the proven character and abilities of an individual. He had demonstrated his willingness to provide medical care to all Chinese soldiers, not just those passing the ideological litmus tests of the Guomindang or the Communists, and Smedley firmly believed that he was best able to deliver the needed health-care system. Unfortunately, because of her past fights with Mme. Sun, Smedley's old friends could not always separate her demands from what they felt was a personal vendetta between the two women. In this context Smedley now demanded that friends like Snow, Rewi Alley, and James Bertram choose sides. At first the Snows tried to remain neutral, but by mid-1939 their relationship with Smedley had broken off. On the other hand, Hilda Selwyn-Clarke in Hong Kong chose to side with Smedley, and became a close friend and staunch supporter in her fund-raising.[11]

Because of this dispute, Smedley found herself getting along better with leading British figures in China such as Sir Archibald Clark Kerr and Hilda Selwyn-Clarke, than with American friends, like the Snows—an ironic turn of events, considering her long-standing hostility toward the British over their colonial policies. This estrangement from several old friends and colleagues intensified the loneliness Smedley felt during

her work with the New Fourth Army, but it also heightened her emotional commitment to the mission of the Chinese Red Cross, Dr. Lin,
and the New Fourth Army Medical Corps.

By the fall of 1939, under the leadership of Chen Yi, major units of
the New Fourth Army had begun moving north across the Yangzi River
into northern Anhui province. Smedley, who accompanied one of the
units, recalled her crossing in *Battle Hymn:*

> On September 3, before crossing the Yangzi, we took our last rest in a de-
> serted temple high in the mountains. Before going to sleep we ran up the
> highest peak and looked down on the gleaming river, ten miles away. We saw
> the black bulk of what seemed to be a cruiser nosing its way up river. To the
> west we could see a pall of smoke over the Japanese-occupied river port [of]
> Tikang. Feng Dafei [the commander] pointed to two towns lying on the plain
> below us, about five miles from the shore of the Yangzi. "Those are the enemy
> garrison points," he said. "Tonight we will pass directly between them."
>
> Nearing the mighty Yangzi, we came out on top of the high earthen dikes
> that hold back the river during the floods. Dark lagoons slumbered on either
> hand—breeding places of the malarial mosquito. Then a traitor appeared:
> the red half-moon rose like a balloon over the mountains behind us and cast
> its ruddy glow across the white dikes and the dark lagoons. I could see a part
> of the long column in front of me. We cursed under our breath and began to
> hurry and even run. Our carriers dropped into a slow, rhythmical dog trot,
> breathing heavily. . . .
>
> [Upon reaching a junk at the water's edge] many of our people were ex-
> hausted and two women nurses had been sick for hours with a malarial at-
> tack. Ignoring the danger, they all fell flat on the deck, closed their eyes, and
> slept like the dead. The great oar at the stern of our junk began to creak and
> we saw that we were pushing off. Soon we came out on the broad bosom of
> the Yangzi, blanketed in a silvery haze. A rolling and mighty river, it stretched
> before us like an ocean. At this point it was five miles wide as the crow flies,
> but actually seventy *li* (about twenty-three miles) from our place of embarka-
> tion to the village where we were to land. . . .
>
> We anxiously peered at the dark shore and disappearing buildings behind
> us. The half-moon was now high above, casting a long silvery path over the
> waters. Flaky clouds floated across its face. The wind blew strong and fresh,
> and we cried out in joy as it bellied out the great ragged sails and sent us
> leaping forward. Our eyes scanned the mist, watchful for enemy gunboats;
> and we strained our ears for any sound of firing. . . .
>
> The trees on the north shore became clearer and, beyond them, buildings.
> Down the river shore we saw the dim figures of sentries, rifles on their backs.
> As our junks touched land we leaped over the sides and ran excitedly towards
> a crowd of people. The whole village was up, waiting for us. A man in a
> white jacket and trousers came forward, introducing himself as the *qu* official.
>
> We walked into the village and came to rest on a broad flat threshing floor
> which gleamed white in the faint moonlight. A group gathered, put their

heads together, and began singing the Guerrilla Marching Song. Ten minutes later the second junk landed, and our commander, Feng Dafei, congratulated us on our military discipline. We had done much better than he had expected.   (pp. 304–13)

Smedley spent October of 1939 at Lihuang, on the Hubei border.* At the time of her visit, the small city of Lihuang was in the hands of relatively progressive troops led by a group of Guangxi warlord generals. For a fleeting moment, before its fall to the Japanese in February of the next year, it was the center of united-front resistance in central China. Writing for the *Manchester Guardian* about conditions there, Smedley said she was impressed by how well the united front seemed to be working, noting especially that a concerted effort to establish a new school system was underway. She saw hope in the position of the local newspaper, whose liberal editor, Zhang Beiquan, was advocating democracy in local government. For Dr. Lin and the Chinese Red Cross, she wrote a long report about the hospital in Lihuang, calling it the best she had seen yet in wartime China. In *Battle Hymn of China* she went on for several chapters in this vein, explaining to an American audience how conditions in Lihuang set a hopeful precedent for the anti-Japanese war effort in the future.[12]

Because Smedley was the first (and last) foreign reporter to visit Lihuang during the war, her presence was treated as a major event. She was invited to speak at several large rallies. On these occasions she illustrated international support for the anti-Japanese struggle by citing the contributions of Indian nationalists—particularly the medical mission from India that was already in full operation in northwestern China. (Smedley was in touch with Nehru, who had just arrived in Chongqing on a goodwill visit, and was trying to bring him to Lihuang on his way to other guerrilla bases to the north.)[13]

In Chinese accounts of Smedley's stay in Lihuang, she appears as something of a Pied Piper, always followed by a band of young, patriotic intellectuals who were refugees from Shanghai and elsewhere. Through her energetic, American-educated interpreter, Dr. Fang Lianbai, Smedley

---

* The region, long notorious for its bandits, had been the power base of Cao Cao, the third-century A.D. villain of the popular Ming novel *Tale of Three Kingdoms* (*San guo yanyi*). The ancient and present name of its main city was Jinjiachai; it had recently been renamed for a fallen Guomindang general, Wei Lihuang, and made the capital of unoccupied Anhui province. On the region in general and its place in modern Chinese history, see Elizabeth Perry, *Rebels and Revolutionaries in North China, 1845–1945* (Stanford, 1981).

engaged these young people in long conversations, which in some cases became dialogues that continued throughout her stay.[14] One of these young persons was Meng Bo, then twenty-four years old and a choral director and musician-composer, who talked with her about music and its relationship to politics, with interesting results.*

Smedley's interest in local culture was real enough and her emotional identification with the Chinese very strong, but she could not divorce these interests from the immediate political situation. In *Battle Hymn*, for example, she reported the following event. One evening, more than a thousand people gathered to see some short plays performed by a local Guomindang troupe. One of them, which concerned a battle six months earlier at Anqing, where Guangxi troops had surprised and smashed a Japanese garrison, gave a sympathetic portrayal of a Japanese officer who had been born and educated in China, and this upset many in the audience. Smedley wrote:

> When the performances were finished, I was asked to speak. Instead, I rose and suggested that the audience discuss the plays. My suggestion was op-posed by an official who declared that the audience was too undeveloped to discuss them. The actors, still in their make-up, supported my idea and asked me to lead the discussion. Two of the playwrights offered to reply to criticism.
>
> I spoke of the excellent acting, but objected to the idea of showing a Japa-nese staff officer as a friend of China. If he was a friend of China, why did he remain in the Japanese Army? The playwright replied that his Japanese char-acter was drawn from life; that there really had been such a man in Anqing during the May 4 fighting.
>
> The dam had broken. A dozen men, some soldiers, some students in the various training camps, asked for the floor. They strode up the aisles, leaped to the stage, and told what they thought of the plays. And they talked intelli-gently. One soldier declared that one play was too filled with lofty talk which the common people could not understand. Still another pointed out that one of the plays showed a gang of Japanese and Chinese puppets [collaborators] having a feast and gabbing about the threat of guerrillas, but that the guerril-las never attacked, and only the wife of the puppet leader had killed herself out of fear. No play, he declared violently, should ever show that treason

* One day over tea Smedley asked Meng Bo, "Do you know any choruses from Beetho-ven's 9th?" Surprised and defensive, Meng Bo said his group had been performing some Bach cantatas with band accompaniment. "Why don't you give Beethoven a try?" she sug-gested. She sang the chorus from the finale for him several times and then went over the words. Finally Meng Bo sang it back, and they tried singing it together. When he had it at last, Smedley let out a big cheer and rushed over to hug him. As a result, the final chorale of Beethoven's Ninth Symphony was published, in translation, in a local music magazine (interview with Meng Bo). In the 1960s, during the Cultural Revolution, Meng Bo was severely criticized at the Shanghai Conservatory of Music for his advocacy of Beethoven.

pays: the guerrillas should have killed every low-down dog at the banquet table!

Ah, replied the playwright, was that reality? If the enemy was always lying dead on the stage, what was the use of continuing the war? Arouse the people by showing the facts!   (pp. 355–56)

In November of 1939 Smedley again joined guerrilla units in the field. First she headed north into southern Henan province, where she encountered ancient peasant mutual-protection associations with secret-society names like Red Spears.[15] These groups were cooperating with local Communist-led guerrilla units in harassing the Japanese behind the lines. Toward the end of December, as the situation there became more dangerous, Smedley moved southwest into the barren, windswept Dahong mountain range along the Anhui-Hubei border, where she stayed for three months with a special commando unit affiliated with the New Fourth Army. This unit was commanded by Li Xiannian, a carpenter turned Robin Hood, Communist guerrilla leader, and charismatic folk hero. (In 1949 he would become the first Communist governor of Anhui province, and in 1984 he was named president of the People's Republic of China, the titular head of state.)

Smedley devoted three chapters in *Battle Hymn* to her experiences with Li Xiannian's troops. She paid special attention to the ways women were being organized in the New Fourth Army areas. With her old Brownie camera, she took a remarkable set of pictures documenting women's meetings, literacy classes, and women as soldiers.[16]

Smedley was keenly interested in Chen Shaomin, the only woman commander in the area. "Big Foot" or "Big Sister" Chen, as she was known at the time, had joined the party in the late twenties as a teenager, and by 1939 she had earned wide respect in northern China as an underground party operative. By the time Smedley met her, she seemed a kindred spirit—tough as leather, very businesslike, and still single. Smedley was impressed by the respect Chen seemed to command from male troops, taking it as a sign of growing emancipation on the part of the Chinese male peasant. To Smedley, Big Sister Chen superseded the traditional Chinese heroine—the woman warrior disguised as a man who becomes a battlefield commander, an Eastern Joan of Arc—because Chen went undisguised.[17]

By March of 1940 Smedley's health had deteriorated, and as Japanese pincer movements tightened around the guerrillas, Li Xiannian advised Smedley to leave the war zone and head for Chongqing. There, he said, she could regain the strength to carry on with her most important mission—telling the world about the struggle in central China. Smedley was familiar with this argument and knew she would have to leave, but the prospect hurt her in a personal, even maternal, way. She had become so attached to her "little devil," a boy named Shen Guohua, that she wanted to take him away from the front and send him to school. As the time for her departure drew near, she begged for permission to adopt him. Thus she wrote in *Battle Hymn:*

> When [Li Xiannian] asked me why I wished to adopt Guohua, I tried to give my reasons a scientific basis. The child had a scientific turn of mind, I argued, and I mentioned his observations of lice, of wind and snow, the way he learned to read and write so quickly, and how he could tell the directions from the stars at night. Good, Li said, I could adopt the boy if I wished and if the boy himself consented. A burly fellow leaning against the door frame remarked that he could do all the things I said Guohua could do. And he felt certain that he knew much more about lice. Would I like to adopt him too! The conversation became a little rowdy.   (pp. 474–75)

In the end, the boy himself refused to leave with Smedley, saying that she could adopt him "after the final victory." Sadly, Smedley left on foot for the long trek southwest to Yichang on the Yangzi River, where she caught a boat going upstream to Chongqing.

Chongqing rose high on a rocky promontory overlooking the confluence of the Yangzi and Jialing rivers. Until the arrival of Chiang Kai-shek's government in December of 1938, it was a remote medieval city of impressive natural beauty, locked away in the mountains of the southwestern province of Sichuan. The city's largely bamboo and mud structures seemed to be stacked up like sandcastles on the riverbank. Economically, it had been a bustling regional trading center with few industries, known locally for its rats and its scarcity of fresh water. Between 1938 and 1940 its population doubled, swelled by a cosmopolitan refugee population; shabby makeshift housing covered the foothills south of the city. And although the city was mountainous, its latitude was approximately that of Cairo, Egypt, so its winter chills produced thick fogs that obliterated the sun for days, providing ideal protection from Japanese bombing raids. In warm weather, however, the fog dissipated and the city became clearly visible from the air. Caves carved into nearby mountains thus became second homes for the city's Chinese and foreign population. During the summers of 1939 and 1940, the visibility was good and the bombing was the most intense of the war; the city proper became a smoldering ruin, and bodies were seen daily floating down the Yangzi.

Politically and socially, Chongqing had been dominated since the 1920s by a group of notoriously ruthless warlords who were only loosely allied to Chiang Kai-shek. Furthermore, General Dai Li, Chiang's minister of public security, was exacting bribes and terrorizing the Chinese population. His men made special targets of Smedley's friends from Shanghai, such as the liberal noncommunist newspaper editor Zou Taofen; while Smedley was in Chongqing, Zou fled for his life to Hong Kong.[18]

Despite these depressing conditions, Chongqing, like Hankou, had one advantage for Smedley: it put her in touch again with the international journalistic and diplomatic community. At the U.S. embassy she got along well with the senior military attaché, the Chinese-speaking David Barrett. And she renewed her friendship with the British ambassador, Sir Archibald Clark Kerr, who made another contribution of money for medical relief and found her a place to stay at the Jardine-Matheson headquarters, on a high bluff overlooking the river and city. Within the foreign community in general Smedley was a notorious, mysterious figure and therefore often invited to give talks. Her first was to the International Women's Club of Chongqing, where she appeared "in blue slacks in keeping with her mannish haircut" and spoke in sober terms about conditions in the central war zone. Between talks and stays in the hospital for severe chest pain, Smedley visited friends at the International Press Hostel, a rickety old bamboo structure in a banana grove on the edge of the city. She avoided the Chinese Ministry of Information next door; its director, Hollington Tong, had been trying for several years to censor Smedley's writings or have her deported from China. At the press hostel, Smedley made new friends among the younger generation of China reporters, notably Hugh Deane and T. H. (Theodore) White, who had just arrived fresh from Chinese studies at Harvard. Deane in particular has recalled how much he benefited from Smedley's long discussions with him about the situation in China.[19]

Although generally depressed by conditions in Chongqing, Smedley was encouraged by two developments she found there. The first was a network of hospitals and medical schools, established throughout unoccupied China by the Nationalist government's new Ministry of Health, under the direction of her friend Dr. Lin. She saw this—correctly, as it turned out—as a basis for socialized medicine, or at least a national health system.* She was also excited by the privately funded Industrial

* The roots of the contemporary Chinese health care system combine a foundation laid by Dr. Lin and his associates with elements of guerrilla medicine developed in Yan'an.

Cooperative Movement led by Rewi Alley, Mme. Sun Yat-sen, Chen Hansheng, and others. With capital raised from hundreds of overseas investors, small industrial cooperatives were being formed in the hinterland. Again, this seemed to augur well for a socialist shape to the postwar economy.

In mid-June of 1940, Dr. Lin arrived in Chongqing on one of his periodic visits from his mountain medical training center at Guiyang, in neighboring Guizhou province.* Shocked by the state of Smedley's health, he insisted that she return to Guiyang with him, to rest and be examined for a possible gall bladder operation. Smedley, probably tired of Chongqing by now, eventually consented. By the end of the month the two of them were heading south for Guiyang in an ancient Red Cross truck (donated by overseas Chinese from Indonesia), rattling over a twisting, unpaved road strewn with abandoned vehicles. Smedley arrived in Guiyang bedraggled but in good spirits, and moved into the guest cottage next to Dr. Lin's compound.[20] There she rested, enjoyed Lin's library, and continued to work on writing her experiences with the New Fourth Army. The serenity of this interlude was broken only twice by Japanese bombing raids. As she wrote in *Battle Hymn*, the first was directed at the city of Guiyang, but the second hit the clearly marked medical compound at Duoyunguan:

> On July 28 enemy naval planes made a special detour to bomb the Red Cross headquarters and the medical center. After that raid—when doctors had to operate on wounded men injured a second time and convalescent soldiers had to help prepare temporary shelters for the night—Dr. Lin began plans to decentralize and scatter the wards, a layout which would make medical work still more difficult. That evening Dr. Lin brought in a huge bomb fragment and, looking at it speculatively, said, "I've half a mind to make special medals of it and confer them on American firms that sell war material to Japan."
>
> (pp. 508–9)

---

* Dr. Lin had come to Guiyang from Changsha in 1938 and within two years had built the mountain suburb of Duoyunguan into the new headquarters of the Chinese Red Cross. As the director of both, with the rank of lieutenant general, he gathered around him a remarkable staff: faculty and students from China's top medical facility, the Rockefeller-funded Peking Medical College, were joined by fifteen European medical doctors and technicians, whose release from French concentration camps in Spain (where they were captured during the Spanish Civil War) Dr. Lin had secured on the condition that they work in China. At Guiyang, Dr. Lin was helped in this recruitment by the Yugoslavian doctor, Berislav Borcic, whom Smedley had known in Shanghai. By 1940 the physical facilities, built with British and Indonesian Chinese money, were impressive: classrooms, dormitories, and laboratories; a major hospital for the severely wounded; a motor pool of three or four hundred ambulances from Indonesia; five large storage warehouses for medical supplies and equipment; and three cooperative drug-producing factories in which outpatients worked. For sources see note 20.

As she regained strength, Smedley spoke at mass meetings and made a few radio broadcasts. On one memorable occasion, she even danced the night away at a party given in honor of a new group of wounded soldiers from Britain who had been fighting the Japanese in Burma. But her gall bladder was still giving her trouble, and in August she and Dr. Lin agreed that she should ride east two hundred rough miles by truck to Guilin and from there fly to Hong Kong, where she could get the kind of sophisticated operation she needed. Her plan at the time was to recover in Hong Kong and then return to Duoyunguan, to continue her writing and her work with Dr. Lin.

Smedley arrived in Hong Kong at 3:00 A.M. on August twenty-sixth, after a night flight over Japanese lines, as the only passenger in an un-marked mail plane.[21] As she left the plane she was met by British immigration officials, politely taken into custody, and told that she must appear at a hearing the next day. Here, in the Crown colony of Hong Kong, she had set foot for the first time on British soil, and without a visa. British intelligence agents had been tracking her since 1918, when her arrest in New York had revealed her association with the Indian nationalist movement, and during the 1930s colonial service agents in Shanghai had built up a substantial file on her. Since there was a large Indian community in Hong Kong, they were concerned to discover whether she was still bent on promoting dissent or even rebellion there. At the hearing the next morning, a British judge in robes and wig recited Smedley's past offenses against the British Empire, especially her support of Indian independence, and accused her of being a woman of questionable moral character. Smedley responded in kind, denouncing British imperialism and defending her right to sexual freedom.* In the end a bargain was struck: Smedley could remain in Hong Kong for medical treatment as long as she refrained from making speeches or engaging in political activities. Most probably, it was her connections to Sir Archibald Clark Kerr and Hilda Selwyn-Clarke that prevented the authorities from deporting her within days.

Hong Kong's population in the fall of 1940 was about one million, one-fifth its size in 1980. Much of the island and most of the New Ter-

---

* There are many stories about how Smedley handled the British authorities in Hong Kong. According to Ram Chattopadhyaya, Virendranath's nephew, who saw her in Boston in the late 1940s, she answered the judge as follows: Yes, she had slept with many men. But if one of them had been English, she simply couldn't remember, because "he made so little impact on me." After a moment of embarrassed silence, the judge's voice rang out, "Case dismissed" (interview). See also Emily Hahn, *China to Me* (New York, 1944), p. 222.

ritories (on the mainland peninsula) were still rural. But the sudden influx of war refugees had overtaxed the colony. There were severe shortages of housing and decent health services. Malaria and cholera had
reached near-epidemic proportions. What made the situation seem desperate for all, rich and poor, foreigners and Chinese alike, was the
knowledge that a Japanese attack was inevitable. The colony had been
surrounded since the fall of Guangzhou in 1938, and the Japanese were
simply waiting for the right moment to strike. The atmosphere resembled that of Hankou two years earlier: tension and a sense of impend-
ing disaster combined with giddy feelings of unity and camaraderie.

The influx of Chinese war refugees had turned Hong Kong into an
important arena of Chinese politics. Mme. Sun Yat-sen, for example,
was living there, providing a focal point for noncommunist opposition
to the Guomindang government in Chongqing. Hong Kong was the
headquarters for the Industrial Cooperative Movement being led by
Rewi Alley, Chen Hansheng, Mme. Sun, and others. Moreover, with the
closure of the Burma Road and the application of tight Japanese con-
trols on Shanghai, most international medical aid for China was being
funneled through Hong Kong. Finally, Hong Kong was a center of international intrigue and espionage. During the winter of 1940–41 it was
widely rumored that secret meetings were being held there between
Japanese agents and representatives of Chiang Kai-shek. Chiang, it was
feared, was about to make a deal and accept a peace settlement—an apprehension temporarily fueled by Mme. Chiang's arrival in Hong Kong
at the beginning of 1941.

In cultural terms, Hong Kong had become a haven for a number of
major Chinese writers and artists, such as Mao Dun, Xiao Hong, and
Xia Yan, all of whom Smedley had known in Shanghai. Supporting these
writers were the newspapers and publishing ventures being launched by
Smedley's friend Zou Taofen, a recent political exile from Chongqing
who was probably the most distinguished Chinese journalist of his
generation.[22]

With Hilda Selwyn-Clarke acting as her guarantor, Smedley was released from hotel arrest by immigration officials in early September of
1940. Hilda was a substantial figure in the colony. Her husband was the
medical director of the colony's health services, and she herself was
probably the colony's most effective social activist. Fervently committed
to the anti-Japanese struggle in China since 1938, she had been deeply
involved in organizing medical aid. She was the type Smedley liked—a
handsome, hard-drinking, independent woman who enjoyed life while
she fought for social causes.

As soon as Smedley was released, Hilda marched her straight off to Queen Mary's Hospital to have her gall bladder examined. Within a few days Smedley underwent surgery. Her doctor was Paul Wilkinson, a red-bearded, sultry professor of internal medicine at the University of Hong Kong Medical School. Smedley and Wilkinson quickly became friends and an affair developed. On the surface at least, they were an unlikely pair. Wilkinson was a moody recluse who took great pride in his classical education and his ability to recite Latin and Greek verse. Although he had Socialist leanings, he took little interest in British, Hong Kong, or Chinese politics. Many of his British friends at the university, however—for example, Norman France, a history professor—were Communists, and in social situations, Smedley delighted in needling them about the rigidity of their positions, especially their present tendency to dismiss the Sino-Japanese and European conflicts as simply wars between capitalists.

While still confined to bed in Queen Mary's Hospital, Smedley wrote a scathing indictment of British health, education, and welfare policies in Hong Kong. Supported by statistics provided by Hilda Selwyn-Clarke, her study appeared in two installments in the *South China Morning Post* and was signed simply "American Observer." Within days it drew a series of outraged responses, to which Smedley responded in kind. Although her identity as the "American Observer" was never publicly revealed, Smedley was indirectly announcing her arrival and clearly testing the strength of the British prohibition on political activity.[23]

Shortly after Smedley was released from the hospital, Hilda Selwyn-Clarke introduced her to the Anglican bishop of Hong Kong, the Reverend Ronald O. Hall, a liberal community activist like Hilda (or like Bishop Roots in Hankou). He invited Smedley to convalesce for a few months at his country place in Shatin (then a rural market town on the railway line, today completely engulfed by Hong Kong's urban sprawl and the Chinese University of Hong Kong). Smedley accepted and spent much of the rest of 1940 in Shatin, resting and writing. On forays into town, she saw Wilkinson, Hilda, and old Chinese friends such as Chen Hansheng. She also spoke publicly a few times before student groups. She tried to bring the war to life by talking about battlefield conditions, the heroics of the New Fourth Army, and the desperate medical needs of those fighting the Japanese. But in general, she seemed to be heeding official British strictures and maintaining a low profile.[24]

Other reasons for Smedley's subdued, reclusive mood were her arguments with the senior Chinese Communist Party representative in Hong Kong, Liao Zhengzhi, and her continued difficulties with Mme. Sun Yat-sen. Smedley was repulsed by Liao personally, as she wrote to Malcolm Cowley on July 24, 1941: "The Communist representative sitting in Hong Kong since the war began . . . [grows] fatter and fatter the longer he [sits] on his rear in the rear." She was upset that he was paying more attention to the American Communist Party line on relations between Washington, the Guomindang, and the Chinese Communists than checking with Zhou Enlai about realities in Chongqing. As for Mme. Sun, although Hilda made an attempt to reconcile the two women, the break between them remained deep and bitter. They disagreed over tactics for raising medical aid funds abroad, and Mme. Sun continued to be upset about Smedley's support of Dr. Lin and Chiang Kai-shek's medical establishment in Chongqing. Moreover, she told friends that Smedley was too emotional and unreliable to work with. The feud continued to put their mutual friends—among them, Rewi Alley, Israel Epstein, Elsie Cholmeley, Chen Hansheng, and James Bertram—in a difficult position, and this in turn tended to isolate Smedley further. Alley and Chen, in whom she confided at the time, said she struck them as a melancholy figure, tortured by the break with Mme. Sun and still deeply hurt by what she considered her rejection by the Chinese Communist movement, to which she had given so much of her energy since the early 1930s.[25]

In early January of 1941, events in China changed Smedley's plans about returning to the interior. In southern Anhui province, fighting broke out between the New Fourth Army and Guomindang forces. The New Fourth Army units defending the Yunling headquarters south of the Yangzi were destroyed, the commander, Ye Ting, was arrested, and Xiang Ying was killed. This was the first major combat between Communist and Nationalist units since the united front had been declared in 1937.[26] With the New Fourth Army Incident, as this engagement was dubbed, relations between the two sides broke down. For the rest of World War II, there would be no more military collaboration between the Chinese Communists and the Guomindang.*

---

* The New Fourth Army Incident had a tragic personal sequel for Smedley. A few months later, she learned that Dr. Fang Lianbai, her favorite interpreter at Yunling and Lihuang in 1939, had been killed, along with Hans Shippe, in a Japanese ambush. After Shippe had returned to Shanghai in 1939, he and his wife, Trude, had played a major role in smuggling out medical supplies to New Fourth Army units. In early 1941, just after the Incident, Shippe decided to visit surviving units in northern Anhui. Just before he was killed, he filed a long analytical article on the fighting strength of surviving units of the New Fourth Army. His intent was to counteract Guomindang propaganda to the effect that the New Fourth Army had been destroyed. Asiaticus (Hans Shippe), "New Fourth Army Area Revisited," *Amerasia* 5, no. 3 (September 1941): 287–94; also Wang Huo, "Hansi Xibo," *Geming wenwu*, no. 4 (July–August 1979): 38–41.

News of the New Fourth Army Incident left Smedley feeling shocked and helpless. Here she was, the foreign journalist who knew the New Fourth Army best, stuck in Hong Kong at the hour of the army's greatest trial. Because the Guomindang had imposed a news blackout and was issuing only its own version of events in Anhui, Zhou Enlai in Chongqing was desperate to get his view of the Incident to the outside world. He managed to send it out with Anna Louise Strong, who happened to be in Chongqing at the time, and after some misadventures she was eventually able to get it placed in the *New York Times*. On her way to New York, Strong passed through Hong Kong, apparently without seeing Smedley—another painful reminder for Agnes of her rejection by the Chinese Communist Party.[27]

The cumulative effect of the Incident, along with the news that political difficulties in Chongqing because of his relationship with her had forced Dr. Lin out of Guiyang, convinced Smedley that for the time being she could no longer be of much use in China. She decided it might be best to return to the United States, regain her health, write a book, and work to influence public opinion there in favor of China's war effort. Evans Carlson passed through Hong Kong shortly after the Incident, and Smedley spoke with him about her plans. When she said lack of money was a problem, Carlson offered to wire her the fare for a return passage when she was ready to leave.[28]

By the spring of 1941, Smedley was spending most of her time back in Hong Kong proper. In April, for example, she promoted a pamphlet on China's wounded that she had written as a fund-raiser for the Chinese Red Cross and its orthopedic center in Guiyang. In its distribution she was greatly helped by David MacDougall, a young Scotsman who was head of the Hong Kong Information Service and by then a good drinking buddy. She met frequently with such Chinese women friends as Rosie Tan and Dr. Eva Hotung (of the famous Anglo-Chinese Hong Kong family), often at tea time in the lobby of the Gloucester Hotel. The press noted Smedley's presence at art exhibits and cultural events in the company of Dr. Wilkinson. And toward the end of the month, Ernest Hemingway arrived from Chongqing and Smedley met him at a reception. She described him as "breezy, self-confident, and virile," and he solicited a story from her for his forthcoming edited volume, *Men at War*.[29]

In late spring Smedley stayed for about three weeks with Emily Hahn. More recently known as a writer on the natural sciences for the *New Yorker*, "Mickey" Hahn had fled the comfortable Chicago suburb of Winnetka in the mid-1930s to seek adventure as a writer in war-torn China. A short, heavy-set, handsome young woman with jet-black hair, she sashayed down Chinese city streets in minks, smoking a black cigar. Her trademark was a pet gibbon riding on her shoulder—intended, she said, to ward off unwanted men. At the time Smedley stayed with her, Hahn was winding up a long affair with a Chinese poet, Sinmay, and was expecting a child out of wedlock fathered by Charles R. Boxer, a British intelligence officer. She was also writing a popular biography of the Song sisters, Mme. Chiang, Mme. Sun, and Mme. Gong. China, for Hahn, meant Chongqing, Hankou, Shanghai, and Hong Kong. Her political sympathies lay with the Guomindang, but she was not deeply concerned with politics and knew next to nothing about conditions in the Chinese countryside. But Smedley appreciated her as a fellow writer and as a lively conversationalist with a fondness for the well-placed four-letter word. And because she gaily rejected conventional social norms, Smedley sympathized with her and seemed to delight in acting as a confidante and supporter. Hahn, in turn, took a sympathetic interest in Smedley's affair with Paul Wilkinson.

In an interview thirty-five years later, Hahn recalled Smedley lounging in silk pajamas, her severe, weatherbeaten Roman head in stark contrast to her supple and seemingly young body. Smedley, she insisted, was highly sensual, still liked a good time, and could flirt with the best of them when she wanted to. But an equally strong attraction was her energy, the electricity about her, the strength of her intellectual and emotional concerns:

> The world to Agnes is full of dragons which she is forever battling. A world of easygoing people just doesn't exist in her conception of things. She didn't worry about it, though. There would come a time, she knew, when I would need a champion, and then she could do her job. Agnes carried with her, always, an atmosphere of tenseness. [The weather] could be as calm and gentle out of doors as anything, and yet when she came in you thought of blowing winds and flying sleet and snow, and clouds whizzing past the mountaintops. One evening I was sitting peacefully at my desk, and I'll swear it was as sweet a spring evening as you'll find anywhere along the Pacific. Then suddenly the door burst open and Agnes stamped in, frowning. She shook snowflakes off her sturdy shoulders. I could almost hear the stamp of the horse outside and smell the sweaty saddle leather, and the frosty pine needles that they had bruised in their headlong flight. . . . "I've brought a chicken for you," growled Agnes.[30]

It was probably Emily Hahn who introduced Smedley to Mme. Chiang Kai-shek in 1941. Smedley had been in correspondence with Mme. Chiang since October of 1940 and was writing a chapter on the Chinese Red Cross for a book entitled *China Shall Rise Again,* a collection being edited under Mme. Chiang's name. Smedley approached

Mme. Chiang in the spirit of the old united front, knowing well that the meeting would irritate Mme. Sun, Mme. Chiang's sister and rival. She wrote in *Battle Hymn:* "I met [Mme. Chiang] and found her cultivated, tremendously clever, possessed of charm and exquisite taste. She was groomed as only wealthy Chinese women can be groomed, with an elegant simplicity which, I suspect, must require a pile of money to sustain. Next to her I felt a little like one of Thurber's melancholy hounds. She was articulate, integrated, confident. As the years had made her other sister, Madame Sun Yat-sen, older and sadder, so had they increased Mme. Chiang's assurance and power" (p. 523).

Despite her meeting with Mme. Chiang, Smedley's sympathies remained constant. Fully aware that Guomindang repression in unoccupied China was tightening in 1940–41, she was concerned about the fate of Chinese intellectuals in flight from General Dai Li's White Terror in Chongqing. She was particularly worried about the writer Xiao Hong, a young woman she had known in Shanghai as a protégé of Lu Xun's. Xiao Hong, on the run from her native Manchuria since the early 1930s, had already managed to write three first-rate novels and several short stories—clear evidence that she was an important talent of her generation.

Smedley's concern about Xiao Hong was more than political. She knew of Xiao's masochistic weakness for selfish and insensitive men. By 1940, when she fled to Hong Kong, she had been abandoned by her first husband, the novelist Xiao Jun, with whom Smedley had known her in Shanghai. By early 1941 she was living in a hovel in Kowloon with two genuine scoundrels. When Smedley found her in March of that year, she was seriously ill with tuberculosis. At first Smedley brought her for a few weeks to Bishop Hall's cottage in Shatin. But in April, after consulting other writers, including Mao Dun and his wife, she got Xiao admitted to Queen Mary's Hospital and appealed to friends for the money needed to pay for her convalescence through the summer. But Xiao Hong never recovered. She died at the age of twenty-eight in December of 1941, a few days after Hong Kong fell to the Japanese. She was hastily buried near Repulse Bay by her two lovers, who immediately fell to quarreling over who had the best claim to royalties from her works.[31] In *Battle Hymn,* Smedley contrasted Xiao Hong with Mme. Chiang. Mme. Chiang represented the old elite. Xiao Hong represented the new woman of China, changed by the war and social upheaval around her: she had lived in poverty and had devoted her short life to writing about social justice for women and the rights of the poor.

Early in May of 1941, Smedley decided she could stay on no longer.

With a loan from Evans Carlson, she booked passage on a Norwegian freighter bound for California. In *Battle Hymn* she wrote of her voyage:

> Among the twelve passengers on board were three Pentecostal missionary ladies, one of whom was my cabin-mate. She did not even know who Hitler was. These ladies had originally come from the American South, where they had had Negro servants; and in China they had had Chinese servants. Thus when they once discoursed on heaven, they described it as a place where truly pious Christians would sit on the right hand of God through all eternity, while the less pious would be their servants.
>
> Another passenger was a young Belgian priest who had become a Chinese citizen. He and I agreed about most things in China, so we spent four weeks on the Pacific arguing about religion and the future of society.   (p. 526)

The woman who was returning in 1941 was not the same Agnes Smedley who had crossed the Pacific in the fall of 1934. She had been reshaped by two events: her quarrel with Mme. Sun Yat-sen, and the rejection by the Communist Party of China. These events had made her feel more melancholy and isolated than ever. In America she would have to find new friends or renew very old acquaintances, and she knew that she would not find them on the organized left. Politically, Smedley was convinced that now, in 1941, the key to the future in the Far East lay in Washington, D.C., and with American public opinion. She was returning to be at center stage and in a position to contribute to the debate.

CHAPTER XV

California Revisited, 1941–1942

A timeworn Agnes Smedley, now forty-nine years old, arrived penniless in Los Angeles in late May of 1941, wondering how she would be received by people she had not seen for seven years. In seeking a place to stay she had written to her ex-husband Ernest Brundin and his wife Elinor in the Los Angeles suburb of Montabello. She had maintained sporadic contact with them while in China, most recently to solicit funds for the Chinese Red Cross, and they agreed to put her up. For Elinor Brundin, Smedley's two-week stay was uncomfortable but revealing. While making arrangements for her next move, Smedley tried to be a good house guest. She helped with the daily chores and entertained the Brundins and their children with stories of her experiences with the Chinese guerrillas. But she also threw a tantrum that amazed and enlightened Elinor.*

Smedley must have felt great stress about returning to America. Except for a brief visit in 1934, she had been out of the country for twenty-one years. Now, in 1941, she had reason to fear that her left-wing friends from those years—especially the Communist ideologues she had known in New York—would reject her. Her strident ideology of the

---

* When the Brundins' family doctor prescribed a vitamin shot for Agnes's fatigue and back pain, Smedley agreed until she saw the needle. Then she panicked, 'first groaning, then doubling up in fright and shouting. Elinor was dumbfounded. Could this be the same woman she had seen in photographs from China, personally tending the wounded? Embarrassed and ashamed, Elinor fully understood Ernest's reaction thirty years earlier, when Smedley had acted the same way on a streetcar (Interview with Elinor Brundin).

early 1930s had been crucially modified. For this reason, no doubt, she sought help from Julian Gumperz, the man who had translated *Daughter of Earth* for her in Germany. Gumperz (who had retained his original United States citizenship) had become a successful financier in New York. Though now politically inactive and disillusioned with the Communist Party in the United States and abroad, he remained a generous friend to his acquaintances formerly on the political left. He had always admired Smedley for her honesty, idealism, and courage. And so when Smedley wrote to him in May of 1941 that she wanted to write a book that would tell the American people, in flesh-and-blood terms, what the Chinese people were doing to resist the invasion by a fascist Japan, he understood. He became Smedley's chief "angel," the man who contributed much of the money Smedley needed to continue working on her book about China.[1]

To raise additional funds, Smedley lined up speaking engagements in southern California. Her credentials as a journalist with established newspapers such as the pre-Nazi *Frankfurter Zeitung* and her unique experiences as a woman war correspondent for the *Manchester Guardian* made her a marketable speaker and good press copy. Fortunately for her, the international situation in 1941 tended to overshadow her past political stands and gave her a chance to redefine her personal beliefs.

During the summer of 1941, public attention was being focused on the crisis brewing in the Far East. Events earlier in the year had forced President Roosevelt to reexamine his China policy, which had been to give evenhanded support to both the Guomindang government and the Communists, as the most effective strategy for tying down the Japanese.

Before 1940, Chiang Kai-shek's desire to move against the Communists in Yan-an had been held in check by the fact that his government, and not Mao Zedong's movement, was receiving almost all the military aid being sent from the Soviet Union. Stalin had shared Roosevelt's belief that keeping Tokyo's forces bogged down in China was the best way to deter Japanese expansion: and he had more faith in the ability of the Nationalists to accomplish this than he had in the peasant-based Communists, over whom he was not confident of control. Precisely because of Stalin's support, Chiang had been hesitant to move against Yan'an.

But with the increasing German threat to Russia in 1940, Stalin was forced to reduce Soviet aid to Chiang. The Americans quickly stepped into the vacuum. Although Roosevelt and his advisers wanted to prevent civil war and opposed the idea of encouraging Chiang to move against Yan'an, they felt obliged to offer Chiang aid in response to the recent

military alliance between Germany and Japan. The need for this deci-
sion was reinforced in November of 1940, when Tokyo recognized Wang
Jingwei's regime as the "true government of China." Within days of
Tokyo's recognition of Wang's puppet regime, Roosevelt pushed through
Congress a one-hundred-million-dollar loan to China. And it was just
weeks after the loan was negotiated that Chiang's generals attacked and
destroyed units of the Communist-led New Fourth Army south of the
Yangzi River.

Realizing that civil-war in China would free troops for a major Japanese push into Southeast Asia, Washington was anxious to see the
united front patched up. In an attempt to force reform, pressure was applied on Chiang to democratize his regime, wipe out corruption, and
quit fighting the Communists. With the cooperation of Time-Life publisher Henry Luce, Chiang was popularized in the American press and
encouraged to promote a sort of New Deal in China. Roosevelt wanted
to blunt the political appeal of the extreme left within China, so that
when the war was over America would have China, the greatest power in
Asia, as a friendly ally. To further strengthen Chiang's hand, the administration urged its friends abroad to treat the Nationalist regime as a
"Great Power."[2]

On the other hand, though few in Roosevelt's administration thought
the Chinese Communists' peasant army was worthy of support, selling a
patched-up united front to the American public required polishing the
image of the Communists. The problem was that probably no more
than twenty non-Communists in America had much familiarity with
the Chinese Communists. These few included military men—Evans
Carlson, Joseph Stilwell, Frank Dorn—and journalists such as Edgar
Snow. One of the very few persons now in the United States who had
real up-to-date contact was Agnes Smedley. Therefore her initial appearances in southern California were opportune and welcome to a variety
of political circles. In her talks, she effectively projected an image of a
working alliance between the Chinese Communists and Nationalists as
they waged war against a common Japanese enemy.[3]

Smedley's first major engagement was a dinner speech at the faculty
club of Pomona College. She was extremely nervous. Ernest Brundin
and Elinor drove her there, to provide moral support. During the drive,
according to Elinor, Smedley doubled up on the back seat and began to
moan and "carry on," claiming she was too ill to give the talk. The
Brundins were amazed: despite years of speaking experience in Germany and China, she seemed genuinely terrified of facing an American

academic audience. When they arrived, Smedley sent the Brundins into town to find sandwiches and asked them to wait outside while she spoke.

Once inside the faculty club, Smedley gave an impassioned speech. She urged the United States to stop supplying the Japanese with war materials. She described the situation she had just left in Hong Kong and warned that someday soon the United States would be forced to confront the Japanese head-on. When she finished with an emotional plea for more American support for the heroic Chinese, who were already fighting the good fight, the response was enthusiastic.

When Smedley emerged from the faculty club, quite late, and climbed into the car with the waiting Brundins, she was transformed, recited limericks, told off-color jokes, and sang cowboy ballads and Chinese army songs. Then, sometime after midnight, the car ran out of gas on a lonely stretch of road. Smedley was immediately indignant. She called Ernest stupid for having let them run out of gas and demanded that he find a way to call a taxi right away, so the triumph of the evening would not be ruined. But Ernest stoically left the car and walked down the road with Elinor to find gas. It was the second time in one evening that Elinor had witnessed a tantrum by Agnes. She marveled at Smedley's heightened sense of emotion and her ability to squeeze every ounce of drama out of a situation. She also understood, at last, why Smedley's temperament had always made anything more than a friendship with Ernest impossible.[4]

A few days after the Pomona speech, Smedley left the Brundins to visit her sister Myrtle and her brother Sam in Chula Vista, near San Diego. Her arrival was greeted by a story in the *San Diego Union* on June 11 which announced the presence in the city of one of six foreigners who was on Japan's "most wanted" political enemies list. The story helped to stimulate interest in a series of talks Smedley proceeded to give around town.[5]

On June 22, Germany invaded Russia and President Roosevelt was quick to send aid to the Soviet Union. In July, after signing a mutual assistance pact in Moscow barring each nation from making a separate peace with Germany, British and Russian forces jointly occupied Iran to stop German expansion. Thus, overnight Soviet Russia became an ally of the West. In public, therefore, Smedley felt that for the sake of the Chinese cause and the war effort she had to refrain from strong criticism of Soviet policies, which had contributed to the ambush of her beloved New Fourth Army, and, earlier, to the disappearance of Chattopadhyaya in Leningrad during Stalin's purges.

On July 24, Japan began its occupation of French Indo-China. Two days later, President Roosevelt froze all Japanese assets in the United States, which brought Japanese-American trade to a halt and cut off Japan's major source of petroleum. He also nationalized the armed forces of the Philippines and placed them under the command of General Mac-Arthur. Americans of all political persuasions were beginning to accept the idea that a strong and united China was the key to protecting American interests in Asia generally. After this time, when questioned about fighting between Chinese Nationalists and Communists, Smedley answered by saying she was sure that the Japanese invasion had given them both reason enough to be united for quite a while.

At talks Smedley was frequently harassed by American Communist Party members who considered her too generous in her treatment of President Roosevelt and the Guomindang. In a July 24 letter to Malcolm Cowley she responded angrily:

> I was dumbfounded at the Communist Press before the U.S.S.R. was attacked. In a series of small audiences where I spoke just after I landed, Communists challenged my knowledge by stating that Roosevelt had ordered the Chinese government to wipe out the Communist armies, otherwise they could not get the American loan! That was a lie. . . . Time and again in my small lectures Communists came up to me, pointed a finger at me, and called Roosevelt a dozen kinds of names. . . . Of course, I have not been sitting in New York in Party headquarters, dispensing wisdom. I have only been at the Chinese fronts and in the enemy rear, and in Chongqing. . . .
>
> The truth is that the Chinese Communist Party represents the most democratic force in China, that they fight for their country and people, that they have considered any peace talks [with Japan] as national treason. But they are not the only progressive force, and their armies are not the only fighting armies of China. I used to think that they were. I support them for their social policy—bringing China out of feudalism to elementary democracy. [This] viewpoint infuriates the American Communist Party for they have the theory that once you refuse to follow their Party line, you go right over into the ranks of the moneylenders. But I am what I always was—a real American democrat of the original brand of democracy, yet demanding that it be extended to economic democracy. I will watch and study the American Communist Party program, sympathize with any progressive thinking they undertake, any line which seems to me the right one. My mind may not be the right kind of mind, but it is all I have to go by, and I have not yet been convinced that it can be handed over to the Party to play with as they wish.

But Smedley still found that she had friends on the unorganized political left in California. In the San Diego area, though she visited her sister and brother in Chula Vista, Smedley lodged with Harry Steinmetz, an activist and professor at San Diego State College, with whom she had enjoyed a political relationship for several years. Steinmetz had first met Agnes during the summer of 1934 when he heard her speak at the Labor Temple on the situation in Shanghai and Guangzhou. Afterward he introduced himself and invited her home for further discussion, and there she met Steinmetz's father (Harry H. Steinmetz), a doctor of medicine and a ham radio operator. Smedley quickly developed a special relationship with the two men, and when she returned to China she began to send news stories and other messages from Shanghai to America via the Steinmetzes, through a circuitous route. First she would give what she wanted transmitted to an American doctor in Shanghai, a thyroid specialist by the name of Miller. He in turn would give it to a banker friend, who sent it either by messenger or air mail to Manila; from there it was transmitted to San Diego by ham radio. Harry Steinmetz recalled in 1976 that most of the messages were about Guomindang Blueshirt activities and police crackdowns in Shanghai. In 1938 and 1939 Smedley successfully solicited medical aid for the New Fourth Army from the San Diego area, using this system.*

Harry Steinmetz was an independent leftist who preferred to stay outside the Party, sometimes joining movements and activities supported by the American Communist Party and sometimes opposing the Party line. He recalled Smedley's hostility to the idea of submitting to party discipline and her unkind words for the U.S. party's leadership. He was also convinced that Smedley was in love with Evans Carlson and had strong hopes for a future relationship with him. He recalled being present at one of their meetings in San Diego, and he knew that they wrote to each other frequently.

Carlson had been a close friend of Smedley's since 1937 when he arrived as a Marine Intelligence Officer at Zhu De's Eighth Route Army headquarters with a letter of introduction from Edgar Snow. Carlson, a devoutly religious man, had shocked his superiors with reports not only that the Communists were fighting a war of liberation but that their conduct toward the people was "truly Christian." Warned by the navy that if he said another word in this vein he would be court-martialed, Carlson resigned in 1938. He wrote a book about his experiences, *Twin*

---

* Harry Steinmetz noted her increased self-confidence and a generally more relaxed, less frantic approach to politics in the 1940s. In 1934 she had been strident in her belief that Depression conditions made it imperative for all workers to join the American Communist Party. In 1941 there was no such talk, and she had little to say about the Soviet Union. Her focus was the need to aid China, and in particular the Chinese Communists, whom she carefully compared to Tito's partisans in Yugoslavia.

Stars over China (1939), and lectured across America with Walter Judd
and others urging U.S. opposition to Japanese expansion in the Pacific.
On the eve of Pearl Harbor, most likely through his connection to President Roosevelt (he had been F.D.R.'s bodyguard), Carlson reenlisted
in the Marines to form an experimental batallion of volunteers to be
trained in the techniques of guerrilla warfare on the model of Zhu De's
guerrilla units in north China. One of "Carlson's Raiders" was Roosevelt's son Jimmy. The military were reluctant to allow Carlson to implement his unorthodox method of using political indoctrination in the
ideals of democracy as a key component of military strategy, but in
1941, he had the political backing of the president for his experiment.
Smedley would later incorporate many of Carlson's ideas into her talks
for U.S. military personnel, since many of his criticisms were similar to
her own. As he wrote to Smedley in 1943:

> There were two factors which modern military leaders do not seem to under-
> stand or prefer to ignore. One, comfort and personal convenience are not
> consonant with the conduct of military-naval operations against an alert and
> tenacious enemy; two, men are inspired to fight with all that is within them
> only by leadership based on merit, a profound knowledge of the reasons they
> fight, and the conviction that the things for which they fight are worth fight-
> ing for. We will win because of our economic strength, but the sacrifice in
> men and treasure will be out of proportion to our effort and far beyond what
> it would be if we as a nation had learned that there is no smooth road to
> freedom.[6]

On August 14, President Roosevelt and British Prime Minister
Churchill issued the Atlantic Charter, a joint statement of principles for-
mulating the broad postwar aims of the two countries. The third point
supported the right of peoples to choose their own form of government.
On September 24 it was announced that fifteen anti-Axis nations, including the Soviet Union, had endorsed the Atlantic Charter.

Roosevelt seemed convinced at the time that this war would unleash
nationalism in Asia and bring an end to colonialism. The right to colonize, of course, was at the heart of the dispute with the Japanese, who
argued that they were a new world power who, because of racism, were
being denied their legitimate right to colonize. Japan claimed the right
to take over French Indochina in order to liberate the people there from
the white men's rule. In Roosevelt's vision of a postwar world, economic
competition and cooperation would replace colonialism. He obviously
viewed the Atlantic Charter as a tool to undercut racist Japanese propaganda and encourage nationalist forces to stop Japanese expansion, an

aim not shared by Churchill. Smedley was impressed by Roosevelt's anticolonial rhetoric and had been convinced by such prominent Englishmen as the ambassador to China, Clark Kerr, that many of his countrymen had accepted the end of colonialism as inevitable.

Given her past antagonism toward most Englishmen, it is ironic that introductions from Anglican clergymen in Hong Kong to Anglican clergy in Los Angeles were among the most helpful in obtaining speaking engagements for Smedley in the United States. In September, Bishop Ronald Hall himself arrived from Hong Kong, and he and Smedley toured together as a twin billing in the Los Angeles area.

Smedley and Hall became part of the broad coalition of political, church, business, academic, and media people who formed the Los Angeles Committee to Support China. In addition to clergymen, the group included Alfred Hitchcock, Senator Robert W. Kenny, editor Carey Williams, and Sir Cedric Hardwick. With handbills and advertisements proclaiming "China Fights on for Democracy," the Committee booked Bishop Hall and Smedley into the Philharmonic Auditorium on September 29. Advertisements promised that the audience would hear firsthand accounts of how China was fighting back in a "struggle to the death" against the "Japanese devils." By September, Smedley was arguing that the United States should declare war on all the Axis powers, including Japan.[7] Throughout October and November of 1941, Smedley continued to lecture under the auspices of the Committee. At the same time she began to organize her notes and articles and outline the book she was planning.

Steinmetz, who had already found temporary housing for Smedley on Selma Street in Hollywood, now introduced her to Gladys Caldwell, a public librarian in Los Angeles, who had the ideal place for Smedley: a summer cottage in Ojai, California, in the mountains just east of Santa Barbara. Recognizing that Smedley needed peace and isolation in order to write her book, Caldwell offered her the cottage. By November, Smedley had received a small advance from Alfred Knopf. This, she thought, along with the contribution from Gumperz, would free her from the need to take on more speaking engagements. She now desperately wanted to finish her book.[8]

But at this point Smedley, like everyone else, was overtaken by events in the Pacific. On November 29, the Japanese premier asserted that British and American influence must be eliminated from Asia. Then on December 7, the Japanese stunned the nation with their attack on Pearl Harbor. Smedley was in San Diego at the time to give a talk. In sketchy diary entries she noted that the city was blacked out and she had helped patrol the streets; and that there were rumors that fifty Japanese planes had been seen flying over San Francisco. On December 8, Smedley spoke before a Town Hall meeting in Los Angeles and outlined the situation in China. On December 10, she spoke for two hours to the local Foreign Trade Association, chiding the businessmen for having "armed and equipped" Japan. She noted that the Japanese were beginning their attack on Hong Kong and landing in the Philippines. In her last available diary entry, December 16, she indicated that Warner Brothers had approached her about a film and that she was going to be on the radio on December 29 to speak on behalf of the Fight for Freedom Committee.[9]

In her speeches Smedley continued to hit hard. She pointed out why the Japanese were so quickly chalking up victories in Southeast Asia and why in some places they were being welcomed as liberators: "The canker at the heart of our civilization is being exposed. This canker is the assumption that white people are superior and are destined to rule the colored races. The Japanese are smashing that conviction—drowning it in our own blood, while appealing to subjected Asiatic people to grasp this historic opportunity to drive out the white man."[10]

She pointed out that the Burmese, for example, were actively helping the Japanese in order to rid themselves of white men's rule. She also cited the infamous case of a popular Bengali nationalist and former mayor of Calcutta, Subas Chandra Bose. As an advocate of a free India since before World War I, Bose had been imprisoned several times by the British and had finally turned to Japan for help. Smedley, who had known Bose, pointed out that he had a large following in Bengal, which borders Burma, thus making it vulnerable—perhaps the next domino to fall after the Japanese conquest of Burma. Smedley was careful to explain, however, that most Indian nationalists, Gandhi and Nehru in particular, saw nothing to be gained by exchanging British chains for Japanese ones.

Smedley concluded most of her speeches by arguing that the only effective response to Japanese propaganda appeals to race hatred was to give full support and aid to China as an equal. Britain, she contended, had brought about its own defeat in Hong Kong by its racist attitudes. By way of illustrating this, she said British officers had told her that England had refused to reach an agreement with the Chinese for a joint defense of Hong Kong for two reasons. First, Britain did not want China to have a claim after the war for the return of territory. Second, they noted that in facing China, the Japanese so far had only been fighting "a third-rate power," and that when they faced a first-rate power in Britain

they "would learn what real fighting is." The British had been confident
that they could hold Hong Kong for two or three months until their
naval fleet arrived with reinforcements. In fact, Hong Kong fell after
seventeen days. The lesson in this, Smedley concluded, was that the
United States should accept the Chinese as equal allies. She strongly implied that neither the Nationalists nor the Communists would accept a
position as an American puppet.[11]

Emotionally, Smedley was riding high. The Pacific war had put her in
the spotlight, and she felt confident she could write an important book,
one that could make a real impact on U.S. policy. She was in no mood,
therefore, to hear a voice from her wretched Missouri childhood.

Press reports about Smedley's talks had reached Osgood, Missouri,
and were noticed by her closest childhood friend, Mamie Weston. On a
visit to California, Mamie tracked Smedley down by telephone. But the
voice on the other end of the line said No, she didn't remember any
Mamie or any exchange of watch chains in 1903 with pledges of ever-
lasting friendship. Mamie was crushed. Smedley went on to say that she
was sorry, but it was so long ago, and she had lived through so much
since then, that she simply couldn't recall. And she did not want to see
Mamie.[12] Smedley was still bitter about her childhood. With *Daughter
of Earth* she thought she had buried it for good. Now full of purpose
and patriotic fervor, she did not intend to let the past consume her
again. Smedley was anxious to move forward, and for once the policy
concerns of her government coincided with her own.

In early February of 1942, Smedley excitedly moved to Ojai to get on
with her writing. It was not long before she had developed a new support system, the John Taylor family. In an interview with the Taylor family in 1975, Aino Taylor, John's wife, said her friendship with Agnes was
the most intense of her life, before or since. When Smedley first came to
Ojai, Aino was a housewife in her twenties, and her husband John was
a schoolteacher then making $1,750 a year. Also in the household were
a five-year-old daughter, Ingrid, and Aino's mother, Elviira. Elviira was
a professional masseuse, and it was this fact that first led Smedley to the
Taylors' door seeking relief from her back pain. For the Taylors, Smedley's
love of life, hearty laughter, vitality, and intense curiosity seemed to per-
meate the valley. Aino's vivid memories included talks over many cups
of coffee, classical music, tears over newly written chapters in Agnes's
manuscript, and raucous laughter over earthy passages in the *Canter-
bury Tales*, which Smedley read and reread with delight. Aino and

Agnes took long outings on borrowed bikes to a vineyard, where they bought and savored warm grapes. On Easter morning in 1942, they gathered around a small, orange-sized cantaloupe growing on a vine under an oak tree. Smedley remarked on the vitality and courage with which it had grown to maturity despite the hard, acidic soil. This, she said, was a miracle "as great as a resurrection and far more real." She was still an enthusiastic gardener.

The Taylors remember Smedley as a twentieth-century Cassandra who proclaimed that no one—whether American, Christian, Buddhist, Hindu, or Communist—had the whole truth. What she believed in was education and, of course, getting politically involved. Smedley took Aino Taylor under her wing and continually preached that she must never allow herself to become a dull housewife with her head in a diaper pail. She was emphatic in her opinion of housewives who were indifferent to what was going on in the world, and she emphasized that it was the duty of each person to keep up with what was happening in government in order to fight for their rights. At Smedley's insistence, Aino read the *Congressional Record*, which Smedley herself devoured daily. Consistently cynical about men and the rich, she insisted that only pressure would wring concessions in the form of rights for the poor and women.

Aino refused to accept Agnes's view that marriage was "the root of all evil," and Smedley could not believe that Aino did not somehow feel oppressed by her husband. But the two women agreed to disagree. John Taylor and Smedley also became good friends. John cut firewood for her, and the two had intense discussions about literature and politics. Smedley made it clear to both Taylors that it was not John she disliked, but simply the institution of marriage.

Smedley received some interesting visitors at Ojai. One was Theodore White, who was on his way to China via India and dropped in to ask Smedley for introductions to prominent Indians. More memorable from the Taylors' point of view was Smedley's reunion with Thorberg, Ernest, and Elinor Brundin, which included picnics under the nearby eucalyptus trees. Smedley had last seen Thorberg in 1934 in New York. By this time Thorberg had divorced Robert Haberman, married an Eastern European intellectual, Basil Ellison, and moved to a farm near New Paltz, New York. She had taken a train to California in the summer of 1942 in order to see her brother Ernest in Los Angeles and with him drive to Ojai to visit her former sister-in-law, Agnes. According to a

1975 interviews with Thorberg, Elinor, and the Taylors, the visit went well on the whole.* Smedley at last felt unreservedly friendly toward Thorberg. Having written four books on China, plus her autobiographical novel, she had demonstrated that she was capable of doing more than starting an Indian restaurant in New York (as Thorberg had suggested to Smedley in 1924). She even fantasized with the Brundins about someday forming a cooperative farm and growing old together.

In the congenial atmosphere of Ojai, the rough draft of *Battle Hymn of China* rolled steadily off Smedley's typewriter. In early October of 1942 she left Ojai with the nearly completed manuscript in her suitcase and moved back to Hollywood to tie up a few loose ends before traveling to New York, where she intended to put the finishing touches on the manuscript with the help of her editor at Knopf. She was already feeling personally fulfilled, but before she left Hollywood she was excited by an event that seemed to suggest that profound changes for the better were taking place in America.

A director from Warner Brothers, interested in the film possibilities of her *Battle Hymn* manuscript, invited Smedley to a dinner sponsored by the C.I.O. The occasion was the christening of a new naval merchant ship, the *Booker T. Washington*. The ship's captain was Black, as was the chief engineer, and seamen from eighteen allied nations made up the rest of the integrated crew. At the dinner, representatives of the Ladies' Garment Workers Union gave all the members of the crew fur-lined jackets, and Jewish songwriters from Hollywood sang humorous songs. Smedley was especially delighted by a song about the Atlantic Charter. As she wrote to Aino Taylor in early October: "The Atlantic Charter song set the audience whooping until we could hardly hear the words and they had to sing it again. It told of one Franklin Roosevelt who said to Churchill, 'give me your fountain pen,' and they sat down on some stools and drew up the Atlantic Charter—with its points one, two, three and four. Everything [was] there, but it was so folk songsey that it was just short of genius. . . . The whole tone of the evening was unrestrained; they were all working men working together." Clearly Smedley was impressed by the progress unions had made since 1934, especially their seemingly sincere effort to break down racial barriers—an effort that seemed to be taking place even in Hollywood.

---

* Aino, however, recalled feeling as if she were in the presence of two queens competing for a place on center stage. Agnes was the "doer" and Thorberg the "intellectual," a term Aino defined in our interview as one who talked about ideas without noticing what obviously needed doing to implement them.

Smedley left for New York in mid-October full of optimism about America's future and her own prospects—financial stability at last, and perhaps even a film to be made from *Battle Hymn*. As she hastily wrote in a departing note to Aino Taylor (dated "October something or other—Monday"): "I finished my book yesterday and sent it off today. I leave Wednesday evening for New York going via Salt Lake, Omaha, Chicago, and trying to meet all my old lovers at every place the train stops. I expect mobs and mobs, and intend to tell them to organize a union and join the C.I.O."

Bittersweet Homecoming: New York, 1942–1943

Smedley left California in a buoyant mood, optimistic about her prospects and excited by what she had seen of wartime America. The contrast between conditions in 1934 and 1942 was striking. The war had brought women into the work force and produced nearly full employment for men. For ordinary people such as her relatives in San Diego, the standard of living was appreciably higher. Social changes that in 1934 she had seen as obtainable only by revolutionary means—racial integration, economic independence for women, and political enfranchisement of unions, for example—seemed to be taking place peacefully in 1942. In short, under Roosevelt the United States seemed to be realizing the domestic and foreign policy goals for which she and her friends had marched and campaigned since her days with the *Call* in 1919. In this new political context, Smedley thought she could be an effective advocate of American support for a united Chinese war effort against the Japanese.

As in 1928, when Smedley left Europe to take up the fight against colonialism in China, her mission as a propagandist in America was a self-appointed one. She saw herself as representing "progressive" elements in China, and by this she certainly meant the Communist leadership in Yan'an, especially such coalition-minded leaders as Zhou Enlai. But she made her own independent analysis of the Chinese situation; she was not, like Anna Louise Strong, a designated spokesperson.[1] In *Battle Hymn of China,* the "progressives" she championed included Dr. Robert K. Lin, Guangxi warlord generals, and independent urban intellectuals, as well as the Communists. She hoped that civil war might be avoided in postwar China and thought that this was possible if the right kind of American influence were exercised on Chiang Kai-shek. Thus Smedley's top priority in 1942 was to get to New York, the media center of the nation, and establish herself as a writer and authority on China.

Smedley's train to New York was packed with soldiers, and Smedley talked late into the night with as many of them as she could. En route to Chicago, she wrote to Aino Taylor:

> My respect for the men of my country mounts daily. The soldiers are edu-
> cated men on the whole and seem intelligent. They lack international infor-
> mation, but they are a fine lot of men and I'm proud. I like so many things
> about my countrymen—their informality. Everybody talks with everybody
> else, every one makes jokes about each other. A very respectable woman with
> me, one of the lousy rich Mellons, became my chum. She was about my own
> age and fine looking and before long she dropped all her high-nosed attitude
> and joined in with the soldiers. She and I just prowled about talking with
> them, arguing and debating about this and that, and we were soon joined by
> a serious, handsome WAAC woman about 30 years of age returning to her
> camp in Des Moines. A Negro girl joined us—the wife of a Negro soldier—
> so we were four. One night we started singing folk songs in a group and soon
> we had the whole lounge car, and groups of soldiers who came in, singing at
> the top of their voices. We sang our way right through the history of America.
>
> When we awoke one early morning passing through Wyoming we found
> snow lying in deep drifts and Cheyenne was completely covered. Farmers, as
> big as the side of a barn, got on the train in Nebraska. They were fully 6 ft. 6 in.
> tall and broad shouldered as oxes and wore checkered shirts. They looked
> worn out from labor. The soldiers looked like gentlemen of leisure in
> comparison.

Smedley's one stopover was in Chicago. She had promised Emily Hahn in Hong Kong that she would personally deliver a photograph of Emily's out-of-wedlock baby to Emily's mother in Winnetka. Especially now that Hong Kong had fallen to the Japanese and Emily Hahn's where-abouts was unknown, Smedley felt duty-bound to fulfill her promise.[2] Two of Emily Hahn's sisters met Smedley at the station in Chicago and the three toured the city until evening, ending up at the Hahns' north-ern suburban home. Smedley was impressed by the family's efforts for the war. Some served on the State Civilian Defense Commission, some wrote articles for *Harper's* and *The Atlantic*. One of Emily's nephews was in the air corps, and the women were involved with the Red Cross and cooperative sewing bees. Smedley was warmly welcomed, despite the disturbing news of Emily.[3]

Smedley was also impressed by the *Chicago Sun Times,* founded and

financed by Marshall Field, pronouncing it the best newspaper she had
ever seen: "Responsible, depressingly accurate; thorough; non-sensa-
tional; progressive; opposing all reaction, all Fascism in the country. Today's issue had a thorough report about Guadalcanal; and it runs the
diary of their correspondent with the Marines in the Solomons. . . . But
leaving Chicago for New York, my pullman is filled with businessmen
who read the vicious *Chicago Tribune*. Tomorrow at 9:30 we reach
New York. This is a different world and it seems like a dream."[4]

Smedley now believed that acceptance of a united front in China by
middle-class America was the key to U.S. government policy. Like Margaret Sanger in her evolving tactics for promoting birth control, Smedley
was willing to downplay ideology and concentrate on working toward
an immediate goal. As for her own political position, she was still searching, and still repulsed by authoritarianism whether on the left or the
right. Much more flexible politically than during her last visit to New
York, in 1934, she hoped that the established media would accept her.
But the memory of her dogmatic political statements from the 1930s,
and her reputation as a foul-mouthed and "loose" woman, made that an
impossibility. In a November letter to Taylor, she gave this account of her
first appearance at the Overseas Press Club, in late October, soon after
her arrival in New York:

> There were three or four guests of honor and we had to stand up and take a
> bow. . . . As I stood up, cries from the Far East [contingent] went up in vari-
> ous corners. . . .
>
> Now what do I think of that Club? Well, the speeches were interesting, but
> . . . [if] kings and queens are more high-nosed, they achieve a lot. I believe
> commanders on the battlefield must feel most insignificant with men of my
> profession. Well-dressed, slick, hard-boiled, each one writing a book a month;
> and each one with a look on his face that says: "I'm so famous. . . ." As for
> myself, I sort of felt that my pants were falling down and I seemed to drag
> around the room in insignificance. It's amazing how an atmosphere can wipe
> one out. After the luncheon one of the "Far Eastern" correspondents came
> up, bent down knowingly and asked me: "Give me the low down—were you
> and Sir Archibald Clark Kerr lovers?"
>
> He looked accusingly at me, and so help me Hannah, I felt that he had
> caught me stealing a penny from the church plate. This also shows the power
> of attack. It took me a few minutes to rally and say the rumor was untrue, but
> so fierce was the attack that I began to wrack my brain to determine if I had
> or had not had a love affair with the British Ambassador. Perhaps I had for-
> gotten, I thought. But I'm really quite certain that I never did have. . . .
>
> After the meeting, I kissed the Far Eastern crowd and they kissed me, and
> the wives of some of the men I kissed remarked in astonishment: "Good-

ness me: I always expected to find you very ugly; but you're not so very." So I learned that their husbands, whom I had kissed, had all told them that I was ugly.

Smedley had a total of four hundred dollars with her when she arrived in New York. She had already taken an advance against royalties on *Battle Hymn of China,* and—not surprisingly—her editor at Knopf wanted more cuts and rewriting, which meant more delays before she could draw any money from that source. In this pinch, Smedley did not try to find housing in Greenwich Village, rationalizing that she "did not want to get mixed up in all those small political cliques which make the Village their hang-out." [5] She found a forty-dollar-a-month studio apartment uptown in a "second or third rate" building somewhere between Central Park and Riverside Drive; the communal kitchen where she kept her food—primarily milk and cottage cheese—was down the hall, as was the shower. Her financial woes were increased by trouble with her teeth; she wrote to Taylor that she was hoping to sell an article soon in order to pay for new bridgework.

Among those who opened their doors to Smedley were her publishers, Alfred and Blanche Knopf. During her first months in New York, Blanche often invited Smedley to the Knopf home for cocktail parties where the rich and powerful mixed with famous artists and writers. It was at one of these parties that Smedley met Henry Luce. She wrote to Taylor on November 20:

> Into this party strode Henry Luce, magnate, owner and publisher of *Life, Time,* and *Fortune.* Mrs. Knopf introduced him and he bowed here and there, but when she brought him to the couch where I sat in state, he shook hands and plunked himself by my side and there we sat marooned on the couch for an hour, talking. Then he got up, bowed, and left, after saying he wanted to see me again. Mrs. Knopf took me aside, and in a low impressive voice, told me that "Harry came only to see you." For "Harry" is very romantic about China, and once his wife had been squelched in China by the British Ambassador when she tried to get all the dirt on me. Well, Luce is the only attractive man I've met so far, and I'd think this had he never even looked at me during the party. He's amazingly attractive; which is rather distressing when you consider that I so thoroughly disagree with all his ideas— if these ideas, which I hear on all sides, are true. He told me about his experiences in China and I sometimes had to laugh at him for being taken in. He's not used to having anyone laugh at him, for he's a millionaire. People just don't scoff at millionaires, you know.
>   So I'm getting a bad reputation for associating with the rich and powerful. However, everyone rich enough to do so calls Mrs. Knopf "Blanche" and

they call Henry Luce "Harry." If my book is a howling financial success and I
can make enough noise by writing, I may one day be able to call them
"Blanche" and "Harry."

It was not surprising that Henry Luce and others in the New York
publishing world would probe to see if Smedley could fit her political
message into their world view. In 1942 New York was a center for ex-
Communist intellectuals from around the world. One of Luce's principal intellectual advisers at Time-Life was Willi Schlamm, the former
editor of the Communist daily newspaper in Vienna. Another of Luce's
editors was the ex-Communist Whittaker Chambers, who became an
informant for the F.B.I. in 1942 and was known to encourage other ex-
Communists to bare their souls to him.[6] Luce quickly discovered that
Smedley shared his own attraction to intensely committed people: she
had been a friend of ex-Communists Julian Gumperz and Freda Utley;
she had her differences with members of the American Communist
Party; she had been upset by the Stalinist purges and had been privately
critical of Russian policies toward China. She had also been outspoken
in her admiration of the progress made in the United States under Roosevelt's New Deal.

Henry Luce clearly thought of himself as a national policymaker, and
the war in which America found itself was, in his view, a war for men's
minds, an ideological contest. He had been born in China, the son of
missionaries, and the establishment of a Christian China was part of his
obsession. This fact, coupled with a century of U.S. missionary commitment in China and Chiang Kai-shek's conversion to Christianity, led
both Luce and American Christian churches to assume a self-interested
loyalty to the Guomindang. This in turn produced such extravagant
praise for Chiang that he became a legendary hero almost overnight,
and any criticism of him became inadmissible.[7]

Luce and many ex-communists believed that the public was inca-
pable of absorbing a complex picture of conflicting realities and therefore
needed an elite to point out the right policy or the right man to support.
When it came to raising funds for missions or choosing an ally in China,
the public was not to be confused with any information about the potential weakness of Chiang or his government. This type of thinking led
the *Missionary Review of the World* to proclaim after Chiang's conversion: "China now has the most enlightened, patriotic, and able ruler in
her history."[8]

Freda Utley tried to bring Smedley into her circle of professional ex-

Communists when Smedley approached her to renew the friendship they had had in Hankou in 1938. But after seeing Utley in New York, Smedley had her doubts. In two letters to Taylor she wrote:

> Last week I was at the home of the English woman writer, Freda Utley, who once married a Russian who was put to death by the Soviets. Never in my life have I seen a woman in whose heart and mind every hope on earth has been slain as has hers. She used to be a leading British Communist; now [she is] a black-minded cynic. She believes in nothing at all. . . . [According to her] the Russians fight out of fear; the Americans and British and Chinese are merely bringing Fascism to life.
>
> (December 2)

> Two nights ago I was at a Greenwich Village evening party [at Freda Utley's home]. One distinguished-looking elderly man [there] had once been a high functionary of the American Communist Party but [had] resigned because of the purges in the Soviet Union. He kept saying to me: "Agnes (I had never seen the fellow before in my life), you and I will never live through such glorious days as in the past, will we?" The man seemed to think we were buddies who had grown old and disillusioned, and was dreadfully disappointed because I refused to take my place by his disillusioned side. Freda, who is cynical and disillusioned, kept saying of me: "Oh, she feels just the same as we do, but will not admit it." They had it all down pat.
>
> (December 4)

Alfred Kazin, who worked for *Time* during this period, noted that one was always meeting ex-Communists in New York whose contempt of the masses amounted to an intellectual style. Freda Utley certainly fit this description. This was the same kind of intellectual arrogance toward "the masses" that had caused Smedley to be hostile and defensive toward New York Communists twenty-four years earlier.[9] In 1942 she found that not only ex-Communists but active Communists had not changed much in this regard. She told Taylor: "A few evenings ago I went to a woman's apartment and found a group of Communists gathered. With withering scorn they condemned everyone else to perdition—as 'half-baked liberals, corny illiterates, Fascists'—and they said Hemingway must be crushed. . . . They say everybody is running to them now to get knowledge and wisdom and they are dispensing it to the worthy. I decided that I am not worthy to associate with the American Communists; and I shall not seek their company nor tolerate it in the future" (December 24).

At a time when Smedley herself was searching for an ideological home, others in the publishing world besides Luce were trying to figure out just what her political position actually was. The editors of *Reader's Digest*, for example, explored the question for months. On November 20 Smedley wrote Taylor:

> I went by train about an hour or two up the Hudson to a place called Chappaqua, near which [*Reader's Digest*] has its hang-out. There Mr. Wallace, owner of the *R.D.*, and one Palmer, the new editor, met me by car and took me to lunch for three hours in a little house furnished, as they said, like the "parlor" of a Justice of the Peace where shotgun marriages are performed. That man Palmer is known as a pro-Fascist connected [to] some of the Bundists now in jail. He is a big hulking man who sometimes smiled, but more often reminded me of British soldiers in Libya who do not advance until they have poked sticks in the sand to detect land mines. So Palmer approached me with stick in hand, sticking it cautiously about lest he strike a mine that might blow him up. He is very anti-Negro, very much one for Aryan race purity. His anti-color prejudice extends to the Chinese and all Asiatics, and he asked me to just please tell him if I thought the Atlantic Charter should be applied to China, and if that meant Chinese could enter this country, and if it meant we would have to go in and build up China after the war and feed all those 400,000,000 people. He used the words "yellow peril." The man does not seem to realize that Chinese have always worked for a living, and I told him that if it had not been for our sale of war materials to Japan, they would need no help at all from us. Well, since a few hundred dollars per article was sticking out [toward] me, I tried to turn the subject to reality and talk of things I knew. I assured him that I was no authority on loans and investments, and that my voice is not quite decisive in our State Department. Wallace asked me to write one article to start with, on Japanese treatment of the Chinese.

By this time, Smedley was living on money borrowed from a loan company. On January 13 she told Taylor that after several rewritings, *Reader's Digest* was still not satisfied:

> They [said they] did not know when, where, or if they could publish the article at all. It [might be] too shocking to American readers. The editors of that magazine said to me: "Tell us about Japanese rape. We like to hear about rape." So I wrote about that, among other things, in my article. However, I did not make rape attractive, as so many people like to think about it. I showed how Japanese soldiers, fifteen or so in a bunch, rape a woman until she goes insane or dies, then often kill her in disgust afterwards. And I told how Chinese women, left pregnant by Japanese, kill the babies at birth.

Smedley's dream of financial stability and acceptance as a writer slipped away as article after article was returned for toning down and revision. In February, she reluctantly borrowed the money to have three teeth removed and a bridge put in. Though sliding further into debt, she steadfastly refused to be edited: she would not avoid criticizing Chiang Kai-shek, or try to make the war in China seem more palatable for middle-class readers. She stuck by her convictions: only if the public had the harsh facts could it understand what was at stake in China.[10]

During the fall of 1942, Preston Schoyer's novel *The Foreigners* came out. Smedley proclaimed it to be a "very good thing on China but in which I appear . . . as tough and bitter as they make them." Toughness and stridency were indeed the dominant traits that Smedley communicated in public. But this image of toughness, though frightening to publishers, was attractive to military men and government officials, both British and American, who were involved in the war effort. They were continually coming up to visit her in New York or inviting her to Washington. Most of them had been in China or were about to be sent there.[11] Typical was Joseph Barnes, a department head for the Office of War Information. He and Smedley met regularly on a personal basis, working closely together and trading information: "He [Barnes] gave a dinner party for me, with five other people and his wife. It was an evening spent in political discussion and debate and I learned all the latest from China. He also gave me a big bundle of documents."[12] Clearly, important people on the East Coast were deciding that Smedley had pertinent military information and could be effective in conveying the need to support whoever in China was fighting the Japanese. For these reasons it was suggested to the new Canadian ambassador to Chongqing, General Victor Odlum, that he see Smedley. On March 17 or 18, she wrote to Taylor:

> Last night I went to dinner with General Victor Odlum, the new Canadian Minister to China. We then went to his apartment and stayed there until midnight, walking the floor, waving our arms at each other, and talking about war, Fascism, liberalism, Communism, etc. He's a very naive simple-minded man who will be lost in China in the hands of kid-gloved politicians. Yet he has the mind of a common man still—he sees behind much deception and intrigue and I liked him immensely. We had a fine time together and I sometimes laughed myself sick at him or with him. For instance, he told me that Americans all say that Canadians are so very colorless and so dreadfully proper. The Prime Minister, Mackenzie King, for instance, is straight-laced, colorless, and always recalls a man from a diplomatic post if he belches by accident. General Odlum wrote him yesterday and told him for God's sake to become a little colorful for the sake of the Four Freedoms; but, he says, Mackenzie King may fire him for making the suggestion. Then, the General and I were discussing the Nazi-Soviet battlefront, and he was trying to demonstrate military tactics by using a wrestling match as an example. To do this, he got up, stood before me, and threw himself in the position of a wrestler grappling with an opponent. . . . While he talked I screamed with

laughter at the prospect of wrestling with a General. I told him that it's a fine idea; that I've never yet seen a Senator cry, an elephant fly, nor have I yet wrestled with a General. Lord Chesterfield, I told him, once remarked that the pursuit of knowledge is like wrestling with a beautiful woman. Had we two not been alone, had there been a third person present, I would actually have wrestled with General Odlum. But since we were alone and he is a Canadian, I feared he might think me too colorful. So I merely proposed that he write Mackenzie King and tell him that he has been wrestling with a woman in pursuit of knowledge, and having a colorful time.

Smedley also contacted organizations sending medical aid to China. She found an acquaintance from Hong Kong, Dr. J. Heng Liu, working as head of the American Bureau of the Chongqing government's Department of Medical Supplies, and she was asked to give a report to the directors of the United China Relief, a Rockefeller-backed organization headed by Henry Luce.[13]

Pearl Buck and her publisher husband, Richard Walsh, also offered to open doors for Smedley. The two women had more in common than they realized: they did not know that at different times each had had an affair with Xu Zhimo, the romantic poet from Shanghai who had died in a plane crash in 1931. Buck asked Smedley if she would accept a few speaking engagements if Buck arranged them for her—an offer Smedley readily accepted. Smedley was impressed by Buck's energy and courage and was particularly excited by a speech in which Buck criticized the racism inherent in parts of the missionary movement in China. Buck and Walsh reintroduced Smedley to an old Shanghai acquaintance and intellectual adversary, Lin Yutang. Smedley was impressed by the way the war had changed Lin. He seemed more confident, more sophisticated, and fiercely patriotic; she was happily surprised to find that he bitterly opposed the limitation of the Atlantic Charter to white nations.[14]

Smedley had introductions of her own to offer. One of her Scotch-English friends from Hong Kong was David MacDougall, who had been wounded and captured by the Japanese and had then escaped. By January of 1943 the British government had sent him to Washington to manage propaganda in favor of Britain's colonial policy. He came up to New York several times to visit Smedley and invited her down to Washington to visit him. Smedley introduced him to Pearl Buck in New York in February, and the three argued about British policy in India. On February 7, Agnes wrote to Aino:

> But when [MacDougall] told me that he thought Jawaharlal Nehru should be imprisoned, he and I nearly engaged in physical combat. I told him that he is

disgracing himself; that he is a young man, a liberal, and that he belongs to the new world, not to the old. I told him frankly that I for one refused to surrender him to the old world; that he must help us defeat colonialism; that he must help us free Nehru and other Congress [Party] leaders in India and stop shipping Indian Quislings around this country to do propaganda for British rule in India. Pearl Buck and Dick Walsh and the C.I.O. leader [unknown] all supported my view. We told David that we want Lord Halifax shipped out of this country and Sir Archibald Clark Kerr brought here; . . . David thought Pearl Buck "a danger" before he met her. But after he met her, he saw as I did that she was a lovely, simple, direct woman, utterly without guile or subterfuge. She is the best that America has produced—intelligent, idealistic, honest, uncomplicated in mind and attitude; and very, very frank. . . .

When I saw her in their town apartment, I saw how very beautiful she can be. Last night I received a note from Pearl Buck—one such as must endear her to the hearts of others as it does to mine. She wrote, amongst many other things, "I feel that I know you now—and I *like* you so much." She told me that both she and Mr. Walsh will be at my lecture on "The Fighting Chinese" on the 24th of March.

Because of the war, a spirit of bipartisanship prevailed in foreign policy. Former political opponents now agreed that since Japan was proving a much more formidable enemy than expected, an international effort was needed to preserve a united front in China. And with Germany poised to invade Britain, Russia was desperately needed as an ally against Nazi Germany, no matter what conservatives or liberals thought of Stalin's purges of the 1930s. The mood of the time was reflected at a November 7, 1942, meeting at Madison Square Garden commemorating the anniversary of the Russian Revolution.* With no end to German ex-

---

*Smedley did not attend this meeting, but she did attend similar smaller affairs at which she renewed an acquaintance with the Soviet ambassador to Washington, Maxim Litvinov, and his British wife, Ivy, whom Smedley had met in Moscow in 1934. Maxim Litvinov (1876–1951), a Polish Jew, was one of the founding members of the Russian Social Democratic Labor Party who had joined Lenin in breaking off in 1903 and forming the Bolshevik Party. After the Soviet Union was established in 1917, Litvinov was deputy people's commissar of foreign affairs from 1921 to 1930, when he became commissar. It was Litvinov who had negotiated U.S. recognition of the Soviet Union in 1933. Thereafter he was the principal spokesman for the policy of collective security by which the Soviet Union sought cooperation with Great Britain and France against Nazi Germany. In 1933–34, the Litvinovs made a point of getting to know and help Westerners who turned up in Moscow. They seemed less mechanical in the application of theory than many other Russian officials. Anna Louise Strong, for example, considered them quite successful in bridging cultural differences. Not surprisingly, Maxim Litvinov had been dismissed from office in May, 1939, on the eve of the Hitler-Stalin Pact. After the German attack and the Soviet-U.S. alliance, he was reinstated and was named ambassador to Washington in 1941. It was in this wartime context that Smedley saw the Litvinovs in New York and once in Washington. In mid-1943, Litvinov was recalled as U.S.-Soviet relations hardened again. No fur-

pansion in sight, it was not only Communists and fellow travelers who made up the audience of 25,000. Speakers included Vice-President Henry Wallace; the former U.S. ambassador to Russia, Joseph E. Davis; and a general representing Chief of Staff General George Marshall. And loudspeakers transmitted to the crowd a radio message of support for our Russian allies from General Dwight D. Eisenhower in Africa.[15]

Smedley was well aware that the world political situation in 1942 was different from what it had been in 1920. Although she resisted at every stage, her political naïveté had gradually been stripped away over the years. Her recognition of the realities behind political rhetoric had steadily widened, as if in concentric circles. Yet at the core she remained the same person, and thus in 1942 she turned to the old group of independent, idealistic, liberal and leftist friends she had made before 1920— people she knew could understand her political odyssey. Foremost among these were women with whom she had worked in Greenwich Village and in Germany in the birth control movement: Thorberg Brundin, Josephine Bennett, Mary Knoblauch, and Ellen Kennan. Smedley's personal and social life in 1942 revolved around these women.* With the possible exception of a poet who was teaching English at New York University, Smedley apparently had no sexual relationships with men. She was now in her early fifties, and her sexual needs appear to have diminished. To Taylor, she referred to sex with disdain, always distinguishing it from friendship and love. From current plays and movies about the war, she complained, one might conclude that "capitalism has given the American people nothing to live and die for except sex," and she criticized publishers and moviemakers for teaching youth that "love solves all problems, while in reality love should merely enrich lives."[16] In contrast to Yan'an, where she had fought against excessive puritanism, now in the U.S. she found herself reacting to what she thought was another extreme—an obsession with sex.

---

ther direct contact between Smedley and Soviet officials is documented after the Litvinovs returned to Moscow (Strong and Keyssar, *Right in Her Soul: The Life of Anna L. Strong* [New York, 1983], pp. 205, 233–34; Henry Roberts, "Maxim Litvinov," in Gordon Craig and Felix Gilbert, eds., *The Diplomats* [Princeton, 1953], pp. 344–77; for Smedley's contact, see Smedley to Taylor, June 1, 1943).

* Smedley's closest friend was Josephine Bennett, whom she had last seen in Paris in 1934 on her way back to the United States from Russia. Mary Knoblauch, once on the editorial board of the *Birth Control Review*, now widowed and in her seventies, was living comfortably and independently in New York on an inheritance from her side of the family; she enjoyed entertaining writers and academics at her Wyoming Apartments flat. Also widowed and in her seventies, Emma Goldman's old friend Ellen Kennan was still teaching Latin in New York and living in the Village. After renewing their friendship, Smedley and Kennan frequented the theater together (Smedley to Taylor, December 12, 1942).

Running into old friends and being teased about her past love life made Smedley uneasy and even embarrassed. In another letter to Taylor she wrote:

> Speaking of men, a fellow came to town and telephoned me and told me romantically to meet him "in the same room in the Public Library where we used to meet." I remembered the fellow but could not remember having met him in any room anywhere. I agreed to lunch with him and asked him to meet me by the lions in front of the library. We met and the years had not been unkind to him. But when he kept touching my shoulder I remembered, unfortunately, that I *had* met him in a room now and then. This repelled me so much that I nearly insulted him and I hated the ground he walked on. He kept telling me sadly that I had changed so terribly much. Yes, I said, three times over, for one changes entirely every seven years. . . . I really think the man's a moron. He talks like a broken phonograph record, and once or twice I said to him: "You were saying that same thing a quarter century ago." He replied: "There isn't anything else to do but repeat." Afterwards this rat went to a man I know and told him that he and I had once been lovers. The man gave me a strange smile when the fellow's name was mentioned, then asked me if the statement were true. I told him it perhaps was; that I had been such a sap that anything would have been possible; but that I found him the most dreadful bore I have ever met. The friend stopped smiling at that.
>
>   What a rotten life I must have led while a girl. If only I could meet one man whom I could be proud of, and say: "I slept with him!" But I have to creep off in some corner by myself and contemplate such things in shame. Shaw was right to say that sex is the most transitory and unreliable of human passions. Only if linked with the deepest friendship and affection can it be tolerated.
>
> (January 27)

In January of 1943, at a formal banquet in support of Indian independence, her sense of déjà vu was overwhelming. Even the toastmaster, Roger Baldwin, was an old lover. Smedley sat at the head table, but it was Pearl Buck, not Smedley, who was chosen as the main speaker. She understood why. It was the same old sexual-political problem that had plagued her throughout her marriage to Chatto. She told Taylor:

> I sat at the speaker's table with about thirteen others that night. . . . So I met all the leading Indians in the city, and there was not a man of them but that knew that I had lived with an Indian for years. So they sort of took possession of me as one of themselves! Funny, isn't it? All Asia believes not only in wives, but in concubines, or sub-wives, of which I was one. Roger Baldwin was toastmaster at the dinner, and he came [formally] dressed and was as handsome as the day. We stood in the big reception hall and went through a regular rite which we have repeated in Germany, Moscow, China, and various other cities in the U.S.A. He saw me, uttered a glad cry, held out his arms and embraced and kissed me, then continued to hold on and chatter dear noth-

ings. We finally separated and he introduced me to his watchful wife. I told
her that Roger and I act like this on every continent but immediately separate
and forget each other until we meet again; then we repeat the process and say
"good-bye," just like that.

(January 27)

The next night Smedley was expected at a fund-raising banquet for the
birth control movement, but after the nostalgic trauma of the Indian affair she decided not to attend. Still, though deeply embarrassed by the
abundant reminders of her youthful "energy," she could respond play-
fully when confronted with the evidence. She wrote, again to Taylor: "In
Washington I met an old friend, a Swiss journalist, who was jolly as
ever. . . . He asked me to live in his flat when I return, but I laughed at
him and told him that I'm a re-conditioned old maid" (February 27).

Although she continued to delight in bawdy stories and language,
Smedley now thought of sex as potentially corrupting. In praising a
1943 play about Thomas Jefferson, she commented to Taylor: "Even the
liberal drama critics say the play was without 'color and intimacy' by
which they mean scenes of sex passion which have corrupted America.
They cannot conceive of intellectual passion as colorful, intimate, and
magnificent. To me, the play was more magnificently colorful and inspir-
ing than anything I've seen on stage" (January 30).

Smedley was trying to get back in touch with her country, and she
found books, movies, and plays a convenient way to feel its pulse. By
October, Lewis Gannett, a critic at the *New York Herald Tribune* and a
longtime admirer of Smedley's, had become an acquaintance. When he
suggested that a play based on her experiences in China would be timely,
Smedley, who always loved the theater, was enthusiastic about the idea
and decided it would be her next project.[17]

But Smedley drew most of her conclusions about the political climate
in the United States in the winter of 1942–43 from personal contacts
and friendships. In this respect, two persons were particularly important for her assessment of the possible acceptance of U.S. support for a
united-front government in China: Republican Congressman Dr. Walter
Judd, a former medical missionary to China; and J. B. Powell, the editor
of Shanghai's *China Weekly Review* in the 1930s. Convinced of their
personal integrity, Smedley trusted that their "Old China Hand" camaraderie and common anticolonial and antiracist positions would allow
them to work together effectively to publicize the situation in China.
Both men were respected political conservatives, and Smedley's desire to
work with them reflected a new realism on her part. For Smedley, the

only hope for China's rural poor lay with U.S. support for a united-front government, and she saw the involvement of "old hands" like Judd and Powell as the key to winning bipartisan acceptance in the United States.

In early November the Swedish ship *Gripsholm* had reached the United States carrying correspondents who had been prisoners of the Japanese. Among them was J. B. Powell. Powell had been brutally tortured by the Japanese; all that remained of his feet were stumps. Smedley was a frequent visitor at his bedside in New York and spent New Year's Day of 1943 at the hospital with him. She could not get it out of her mind that she too was on the Japanese political-enemies list and would have met the same fate had she remained in Hong Kong. Powell had been given a contract by Macmillan for a book. In addition, Chiang Kai-shek and the National Press Club in Washington had sent Powell $10,000 and $8,000, respectively. Powell was genuinely moved. He weighed only 109 pounds and was still too weak to face a writing project, but his inability to get anything done was depressing him. Smedley's visits were a tonic for his morale, since her presence always seemed to stimulate a political argument they could both enjoy.* When the debate was about to go too far, Smedley would ask, "Well, what can I get you?"—her signal that it was time for her to leave.[18]

Smedley finished her final draft of *Battle Hymn of China* on January 4, 1943, and delivered it to her editor at Knopf, who told her she could expect a May publication date. Her arguments with Powell on the possibilities for a united-front government in China had depressed her and she now anticipated that her book would be "blown out of the water" by Powell's book because hers "would be considered too controversial."[19] She continued to search for some common ground between them. Later that spring she thought she had found it. On March 25, Smedley sent a taxi, nurse, and wheelchair to pick up Powell, his wife, and his son at the hospital and take them to a Broadway theater to meet Smedley, Thorberg Brundin, and Mr. and Mrs. Lewis Gannett. Powell had not seen a play in the United States since 1921, and Smedley thought he might like this one, *The Patriots* by Sidney Kingsley. The play's hero was Thomas Jefferson, and it focused on the writing of the Declaration of Independence, the Bill of Rights, and the struggle between Hamilton

---

* On that New Year's Day, Mrs. Powell couldn't resist asking "if her husband's friendship with me [Smedley] had been platonic. I tried to remember, but I could not exactly recall; and he was too polite to insist that it had been" (letter to Taylor, January 3, 1943); Smedley's "lack of memory" was for effect—she never had had an affair with J. B. Powell. The International Concession area of Shanghai had been occupied by the Japanese immediately after Pearl Harbor in 1941; Powell was among the first Americans arrested.

and Jefferson. The performance concluded with the audience standing to sing the "Star-Spangled Banner." Powell himself insisted on standing, with the aid of crutches. Hearing Smedley sing along with wholehearted gusto, he couldn't resist the teasing remark, "I didn't think you knew that song." * * Smedley had arranged for the theater to donate the seats for the Powell family as well as to set up a private party backstage with sandwiches and wine as a tribute to his bravery.[20]

Throughout the spring of 1943 Smedley praised to friends the stance on China being taken by Republican Congressman Walter Judd and urged them to read his speeches in the *Congressional Record*. The two now were in contact with one another. As she wrote to Taylor on April 24, Judd had helped arrange for her to speak at the National Press Club in Washington on April 20, where "the audience was small but intelligent and interesting and there was considerable discussion afterwards, with Representative Judd and other officials taking part." Reporting on her other recent activities, she continued: "I had a four-hour conference with the Surgeon General's office on the Chinese Army medical system, and since returning home have made an extensive report and sent it off this morning. Then I spent a morning in conference with the Cultural Division of the State Department. Had two cocktail parties and three dinners and argued my way through one crowd after another. General Magruder, of the Office of Strategic Services, gave a cocktail party for me. I learned that Generals do not read books; that they live luxuriously; that they are good cocktail party hosts and charming personally, but totally out of focus and out of step with the times."[21]

Since early winter, Smedley's many discussions with Powell, Judd, and various generals had caused her distress about the opinions being expressed in the business and military communities. She had written to Taylor on January 27:

> Mr. Powell told me other serious things he has heard. Many big business and Army men think there should be peace with Japan . . . [because], they say, China may go Communist, and together with the Soviet Union "menace" the world. They consider Japan a bulwark against Communism and they also say that Japan was America's best customer before the war began. There is one thing they all forget: that it is Japan who would decide all things; and American businessmen would have to go crawling up to Japanese boots, asking for the right to sell a few piddling things; that is, if Japan is victorious. In any

---

* * Smedley had, in fact, been genuinely moved by *The Patriots*. She had already seen it once, in January, and in Washington in February had gone to the Library of Congress to see the writings of Jefferson for herself (Smedley to Taylor, February 27, 1943).

case, the world is in a hell of a state, and America is the least prepared of all nations to think in terms of a new and socialist world.

Smedley had also been worried for months about Chiang Kai-shek's increasingly effective China lobby. She had written to Taylor on February 7: "It was interesting and more than depressing to talk with [a friend in the Office of War Information] about internal conditions in China today. Madame Chiang Kai-shek remains in a hospital in New York here, and she brought a whole regiment of men with her, it seems, and all of them are busily engaged in trying to drive out of official and newspaper positions every American in this country who speaks favorably of the democratic forces inside China. They work through Henry Luce, millionaire and powerful owner of *Life, Time,* and *Fortune,* and head of China Relief."

By early 1943, informed observers had concluded that the Guomindang could not escape a major domestic challenge after the war. Few were sure of the outcome. George Atcheson, a U.S. diplomat who had twenty years of experience in China, reported in May of 1943 that the situation was deteriorating rapidly. Pearl Buck wrote to Eleanor Roosevelt: "It is a peculiar and interesting situation. It cannot of course last. I fear an outbreak from the people immediately after the war, or at least as soon as the people can recuperate sufficiently to make it." [22]

On March 22, 1943, *Time* published an eyewitness account, by Theodore White, of the terrible Henan famine of 1942–43. According to White, however, they had not published the whole outraged account he had submitted. He had reported on the "stupidity and inefficiency of the relief effort, the continued collection of taxes from starving peasants by local officials, [and] the bland equanimity of Chongqing because officially all taxes had been remitted." He had mentioned corruption and profiteering and had said he was convinced that the loyalty of the peasants of Henan had been "hollowed to nothingness by the extortions of their government," which was of course Chiang Kai-shek's Guomindang regime. None of these charges appeared in the *Time* story. They had been cut out by Whittaker Chambers, who had taken over as editor of the foreign news section. [23] In 1952, in his book *Witness,* Chambers acknowledged that during this period he was "writing or rewriting a fourth to a third" of the magazine's foreign news section and that he was doing so to make an ideological point: "I reversed the magazine's news policy toward Russia, making it clear on the basis of the weekly news that Russia was not a friend, but an enemy who was actively using

W.W. II to prepare W.W. III. With the same weekly insistence, I pointed
out that China was the key to world politics and that to lose China to
Communism was to risk losing W.W. III."[24] Chambers, of course, had
never been to China.

On March 25, Smedley wrote to Taylor that she had signed up with a
lecture agency in order to earn some much-needed cash:

> Lecture agencies have a system of calling organizations to send represen-
> tatives . . . to hear short speeches by lecturers. I felt like a horse being pa-
> raded out for possible buyers to look over. Perhaps in time I'll get used to
> this. There were 100–150 representatives of clubs and other organizations
> present, each writing busily while the speakers did their stunts. I took an
> episode of the China war, which they seemed to like. . . . I've told the head of
> the agency that I want schools and universities, serious clubs, and Army
> training camps, but there is almost no money in it. They pay a flat $10 a day
> only, whereas clubs pay from $100–400 a lecture. But I'd like to speak be-
> fore Army camps now and then.

By this time, the only articles Smedley was able to place were book
reviews in the *Progressive*. For its May 10 issue she wrote a short but
hard-hitting piece entitled "The Mind of China's Ruling Class," in which
she reviewed Chiang Kai-shek's *All We Are and All We Have* and Mme.
Chiang's *We Chinese Women*. Smedley warned that attempting to use
another government strictly for America's own purposes might backfire
and implied that it was naive to think that the other party wouldn't play
the same game: "In a way, it is up to us to become truly democratic and
to realize the freedoms for which we say we are fighting. If we wage this
war as merely an alliance of political forces, some of them fascist or
semi-fascist, and if we continue to support British imperialist policies in
India, we cannot expect China to do more than protect itself against us,
utilizing this war as we do for our own selfish aims."

This piece developed a theme from Smedley's first review for the *Progressive*, on March 29, of Jack Belden's *Retreat with Stilwell*. Belden had
ended his book with Stilwell's confession that "the Japs ran us out of
Burma. We were licked." What Belden witnessed and reported, Smedley
restated in even blunter terms: the outcome in Burma was the inevitable
result of the white man's imperialist sins. The Burmese so hated the
white man, Belden reported, that when the Japanese came, Burmese civilians had themselves tattooed with an ancient symbol of revolt and then
went gunning for any white man they could find. Smedley also noted that
"someone" was trying to prevent Belden's book from being distributed to
American soldiers because it was critical of Chiang's troops.

By the early spring of 1943 Smedley realized that it was probably financial suicide to step up her criticism of Chiang Kai-shek. She tried not to be discouraged. As she wrote to Taylor on March 17, she took heart from another American who had fought against racial discrimination:

> I went to see Helen Hayes in *Harriet* the other night. It's a play of Harriet Beecher Stowe's life, of the way she wrote *Uncle Tom's Cabin* and the uproar it caused before and during the Civil War. The play was disconnected, not well constructed, but there was a lot of humor throughout. I decided that I love many Americans, for the whole Beecher family is shown—a dozen brothers and sisters at least—all fighting over one problem or another at the top of their voices. Some were anti-slave, some pro-slave, and one of the sisters was one of the first suffragists. . . . I loved it. No milk and water, but conviction. And finally we see the anti-slave Beechers with guns in their hands, fighting the Kentuckians who crossed the Ohio River and tried to capture escaped slaves. The Beechers took up their guns and fired. They melted up lead and made bullets in their own kitchen. Lord, I love anyone who would do that. Harriet, then lukewarm and seeking escape from reality, tried to prevent them and screamed at her father, a famous preacher, to stop them from fighting. The old gray-haired man shouted: "If they do, I'll disown the lot of 'em."
>
> Well, I've sent my article for the [*Saturday Evening*] *Post* to my agent, but both he and I know it will scare the *Post* to death; and it is going to be rejected, of that we are both certain. So place no hopes on seeing that article in the *Post*. I've broken my heart and head trying to emasculate it, and failed. But after seeing Jefferson and Harriet Beecher Stowe plays, I've decided to fight as they fought, and take defeat as it comes; and it is coming.

Riding High: Yaddo and the Lecture Circuit, 1943–1944

By March of 1943 Smedley had decided that she could no longer afford to live in New York City while awaiting the publication of *Battle Hymn*. Her dream of lucrative feature-writing for publications like the *Reader's Digest* had fallen through. She had used up Knopf's advance on the book, and she could not face accepting more help from old friends like Julian Gumperz, Jo Bennett, and Mary Knoblauch. Her only income was from speaking engagements and publication of a few advance excerpts from *Battle Hymn,* which she placed in *Vogue* and the *New Republic.* In short, Smedley was destitute again. As a temporary solution, she accepted an offer from her former sister-in-law, Thorberg Brundin Ellison: free housing in exchange for work on Thorberg's farm near New Paltz in upstate New York.

Smedley had always taken pride in her rural roots. In China and in California, she had gardened whenever she could. And so in New Paltz, with customary zeal, she threw herself into farm work. She wrote to Aino Taylor on March 7: "I'm doing farm work with a vengeance. Can find little time for anything else. Thor grades and packs thousands of eggs a week—It's something like knitting when you once learn how." But soon it became too much. On June 1 she told Taylor: "About two weeks ago, Thor suddenly decided—as she often does—that she had had enough of farm work and that she would go for a toot in New York City. She's like that—totally irresponsible, periodically. I was on the farm and she knew I would take over. She got out of it by saying that her mother needed her. So off she went without apologies, and of course I took over and could not lift my head above the waves." So after Thor returned, Smedley took a trip of her own to New York, ostensibly to make a shortwave broadcast on Armed Forces radio: "The Army telephoned me to come down to broadcast. . . . Anyway, when the crucial hour came, a soldier and a sailor took me up to the microphone and we three were on the air, one after the other. I had taught the Army band the Chinese soldiers' marching song before the broadcast—and my speech ended with that song played by the Army band." After the broadcast, she lingered in the city through the last week of May, staying with Mary Knoblauch, seeing two plays, and taking in an open-air exhibit of contemporary abstract art in the Village which left her perplexed: "I don't belong in the art world. I am merely a farm laborer, I learn."

Smedley returned from her visit desperate to leave New Paltz and find a place where she could work full-time on her new project, a play focusing on the political choices of a Chinese officer in the Sino-Japanese war. From an old acquaintance and supporter, the critic Malcolm Cowley, she learned about Yaddo, the prestigious foundation-supported retreat for creative artists located near Saratoga Springs, New York, where selected writers, artists, and composers were invited to live and work free for several months at a time, usually in the summer. Cowley was on the board of directors and urged Smedley to apply. On the basis of his recommendation, which was seconded by Blanche Knopf, Smedley was accepted. In high spirits, she took up residence at Yaddo in early July. A month later she wrote to Taylor:

> I've a place here until the third week in August and hope to remain until the end of September. It's unspeakably beautiful here. . . . There is a big lake on this estate, with beautiful shadows caused by overhanging forests; and there's a huge fountain before the mansion in the shadow of a gigantic Norwegian spruce tree. . . . The architecture is a strange mixture, but the main part of the building is the same as a royal palace in Rumania. . . . We each have a room in the mansion, and some have studios in the mansion attached to their bedrooms. There are a number of wooden shacks amongst the pines, in isolated spots, and some of us have these. I have one. An old barn has also been transformed into a studio, now occupied by the Negro girl poet, Margaret Walker.*
>
> (August 6, 1943)

* In a 1986 telephone interview, Margaret Walker, best known for *Jubilee* (Boston, 1966), remembered Smedley trying hard to make her feel comfortable and appreciated at Yaddo. She was the first Black woman guest and was feeling shunned by the white Southern women writers among the small group in residence that summer.

The Yaddo Foundation had been established in 1926 by the Norwegian-American Trask family and further endowed by Mrs. Trask's second husband, the philanthropist George Foster Peabody. The managing director of the foundation was Elizabeth Ames, whose sister, Marjorie Peabody Waite, was Peabody's adopted daughter. Mrs. Ames ran the retreat with a firm matronly hand. The working guests were assured of absolute privacy from daylight until 4:00 P.M., after which came cocktails, dinner, and conversation.[1]

Because of the war, Yaddo was hosting only a small group in the summer of 1943. Smedley's fellow residents were Carson McCullers, Langston Hughes, Alfred Kantorowitz, Kappo Phelan, Rebecca Pitts, Paul Zucher, Hans Sahl, Isabella Howland, Margaret Walker, Harold Shapiro, Jean Stafford, and Smedley's old friend the Danish novelist Karin Michaelis, now a refugee from the Nazi occupation of her country.

In a letter to Taylor dated July 26, Smedley described her new companions and new activities at great length. A few excerpts will suggest her high spirits and the flavor of life at Yaddo:

Langston Hughes, the Negro poet and playwright, is here also. I have known him for many years, having met him once in Russia and once in China. One of his "processional" dramas was produced in Madison Square Garden this past winter with a cast of 250 people. [It] was a pageant of the Negro race, with white much mixed up in it of course; it was a combination of singing, acting, and dancing. With all his talent, Hughes is the most American creature I've ever met. He's bedrock practical, yet you feel in him that horizonless being that absorbs and considers all things. I feel hidebound compared with him. Only certain things penetrate my hard soul. I have standards and principles and prejudices and weaknesses. Hughes looks on and listens and absorbs everything—that makes him an artist. I suppose I'm interested in Rebecca Pitts more than the others because I like her. She is struggling with the problems of life which she was unable to solve by herself, and I suppose that's why she began to study philosophy—she wanted to try and find a solution to many things that seem to elude explanation.

I'm drinking too much up here! These people drink a lot. Sometimes they give parties, with wine. Last night, before dinner, I took my turn and gave a cocktail party. We had dry Martinis. And were we drunk! I [haven't] been so thoroughly tight for ages. I think my vulgar nature came out. The party was really a bawdy one. Since it came at 5:30, and since we had only a light lunch in the middle of the day, even a little was enough to set people on their ears. . . . In the midst of the party, the news came over the air of the abdication of Mussolini, and that caused everyone to take another cocktail or two. I simply refused to get excited about Mussolini or about the new Premier who has taken his place. The three German refugees here became very erudite and excited, but I failed to see much in the replacement of one rascal by another. The only value in the whole thing is that Italy may collapse soon and can be used as a base against [the Nazis in] Germany, France and the Balkans.

I have begun work on a play about China, and find myself wading up to my neck in my own ignorance. I've read four books on the techniques of play-writing. It's a regular precision technique and I have never had any precision in my being. I'm a sloppy writer on the whole, at least in the first stages of a ms. . . . If my play is a failure, I shall at least have learned the problems of play-writing, and will henceforth see plays with an entirely different outlook.

Smedley and the writer Carson McCullers became friends at Yaddo. Then in her twenties, the young McCullers was fascinated by the stories Smedley and Karin Michaelis told. McCullers's biographer has written: "An old-line revolutionist, [Smedley] was totally undisciplined and doubtless would not have made a fit member of the American Communist Party, about which she was completely negative. Carson was fascinated by . . . Smedley's tales of her life in China and listened thoughtfully to her ideologies." [2]

In the summer of 1943, Director Ames was struggling with more than wartime shortages. She was also trying to care for her sister, who had suffered a stroke the previous November that left her paralyzed and often mentally confused—a condition her doctors said would steadily grow worse. Characteristically, Smedley volunteered to relieve Mrs. Ames now and then from her nursing duties. The help she provided created a bond between the two women that would soon prove invaluable to Smedley.

On July 15, 1943, Thorberg Brundin Ellison received a telephone call from the F.B.I. asking for Agnes Smedley. Thor informed them that Smedley was now residing at Yaddo, but that she would ask Smedley to call their New York office. When Smedley called, an interview was arranged for August 30. The F.B.I. wanted her help in their investigation of Carroll Lunt, an American whom Smedley had debated several times in Los Angeles in 1941. At that time, Lunt was urging U.S. businessmen to continue trading with Japan, and the F.B.I. was now looking into possible connections between Lunt and Japanese espionage in the United States.

Thus Smedley's first direct contact with the F.B.I. had nothing to do with her own activities. The bureau's official report on the August 30 interview quoted Smedley as saying that Lunt had advocated Japanese control of China. Smedley probably also repeated her earlier public charge that he had been paid by the Japanese government. [3]

During the summer, Smedley heard from her California friends the Taylors. She had been urging them for some time to move away from isolated Ojai and broaden their experiences; in particular, she had been prodding Aino to write a book, or get a job, or do anything but be "just a housewife." Aino now wrote to say that for the summer they had moved to the Los Angeles area, where John had taken a job in a bank and she was working in a war production plant. When Aino wrote that her fellow women workers were not interested in joining the union, Smedley answered angrily:

> It seemes strange to me that the women workers should hate the unions. Had it not been for the unions, they would be working for a dog's wage. If they have a decent life, it's because so many trade union men fought and suffered for so many decades to make it possible. Those women ought to see the German workers, or the Chinese, who are not permitted to have independent unions of any kind. And in China there are generally no unions at all. The hours of labor were always around sixteen a day. For a time, in 1925–27, when the revolution gave the workers the right to have unions, they got the ten-hour day and a few strong unions got the eight-hour day. After the unions were destroyed by the reaction . . . the old conditions were imposed [again] and the workers given just enough money to keep life in them and enable them to continue living and working for their bosses. Women workers ought to get a few brains into their damned heads. I'm afraid they plan to work only until the war ends. So they don't care what happens to workers after that. They won't have to stand the gaff; and they're narrow-minded from their home lives. They ought to learn something about the history of labor, for a change.

(August 6)

Battle Hymn of China finally appeared in bookstores around New York City at the beginning of September.* On the official publication day Smedley was interviewed twice on local radio, and Mary Knoblauch threw a small party in her honor. The first reviews, in the *Times*, the *Tribune*, and *Newsweek*, were strongly positive.[4] Smedley was elated. Praise for the book soon appeared in newspapers across the nation and was reiterated by the end of the month in major literary and political journals like the *New Yorker*, the *Saturday Review of Literature*, the *Christian Register*, the *Nation*, and the *New Republic*.[5] Smedley was surprised to receive generally positive reviews from across the political

---

* *Battle Hymn* remains in print today (1986) as a classic work of World War II reportage and an important source on the Sino-Japanese war before 1941. Because of its autobiographical character, the book has been cited repeatedly in previous chapters. For the authors' summary and evaluation of its contents in historical perspective, see above, especially Chapter 14.

spectrum, from Freda Utley and the *New York Post* on the right to the Communist Frederick Field in the *New Masses* on the left. Field, however, criticized Smedley for raising questions about the status of women in the Soviet Union and the Soviet-German nonaggression pact of 1939: "Another complaint about the book is that Miss Smedley is prone to making political howlers. Granted she does this when writing of something foreign to her, like the position of women in the Soviet Union (she is upset because women do not make speeches at Red Square celebrations) or like the policy of the U.S. Communist Party before June, 1941 (it is incomprehensible and reprehensible to her)."[6]

Smedley's discussion of women in *Battle Hymn of China* provoked a heated debate in an unlikely place: the *Shanghai Evening Post and Mercury,* an English-language daily which was publishing temporarily and infrequently from New York because of the Japanese occupation of Shanghai. The debate began with a review of *Battle Hymn* by Grace Cook, an old Shanghai friend of Smedley's from the early 1930s. When she first met Smedley, Cook was struggling to combine work as a journalist with motherhood after the birth of her daughter, Cynthia, in 1928.* In her October review in the *Post and Mercury,* Cook wrote that Smedley's "biting scorn" for "mere wives" had hurt her deeply—though she conceded that while Smedley seemed to despise married women as a class, she also could be "gentle" with individual wives. Cook then went on to challenge the value of any "social consciousness" that rejects the traditional claims of motherhood:

> I am not belittling Agnes' work. I am, maybe, suggesting that she should not belittle mine. But what I am really thinking of is my daughter. She and I have known a lot of wandering correspondents in our time, all the way from frank hedonists out for excitement to sincere crusaders like Agnes, and none of them fit in very well with raising families. One of the halfway-betweens said to me in 1937, exhilarated by the Shanghai war, "I can stand anything but monotony."
>
> This, to a fifteen-year-old [and] her ex-newspaper [writer] mother, sounds marvelous, but we both know it won't fit with formulas, vitamins, school hours, measles. Maybe some of those clubwomen you despise, Agnes (after all, they did come to hear you) are trying harder than you know to fit a social consciousness into their children's schedules.
>
> What shall I tell Cynthia, Agnes? We need leaders like you, but where is

---

*Grace Cook was married to Frank Glass, the old friend and later Trotskyist rival whom Smedley blamed for leading Harold Isaacs astray and bringing on the demise of *China Forum.* Cook and Glass had left Shanghai for the United States before the Japanese occupation of 1941 (Interview with Cook and Glass).

your working pattern for us ordinary women? You resent your own neglected
childhood; you have great tenderness for children. Shall the state rear them?
But even that involves [the sort of] sex relationship to which you "have never
been able to reconcile" yourself. What shall we put in place of marriage to
populate the world? Or shan't we? And if not, why bother to save the world
at all?

It's ten years since you took pictures of Cynthia in our garden, Agnes.
She's fifteen now, she thinks you're wonderful, and she needs to know.[7]

Despite her personal tone, Cook was raising a crucial issue and one
that remains as important to feminists today as it was in 1943. Smedley
knew this, and she responded seriously in the October 29 issue of the
Post. She argued that a distinction should be made between marriage, a
man-made institution with varying laws, and motherhood, a universal
natural phenomenon:

Children—all children—should be considered as the general wards of
society. We have government institutions to protect wild life and farm animals. . . . It's my belief that children are as valuable as hogs or cattle, to say
the least. It's also questionable if many parents are worthy of having children,
or of bringing them up after they have them. The minds of many, many
people are distorted in childhood by ignorant and selfish parents. . . .

Grace thinks that a social consciousness which makes no provision for
society to survive is questionable. Right. But the existence of human beings
without social consciousness is also questionable—as witness this present
war, and contemplate future ones in which men and women without social
consciousness massacre each new generation. . . .

Yes, in China, I did indeed view most foreign wives with a jaundiced eye. I
had plenty of reason. . . . The Shanghai factories were filled with wives and
mothers and with their children laboring twelve to fourteen hours a day,
without the well-to-do raising a voice of protest. When Chinese mothers and
wives and their children went out of factories to strike, the police would
shoot them down or beat them. No protest came from the well-to-do, white
or colored. Where was sacred motherhood?

Where was the voice of American mothers and wives while their husbands
sold scrap iron and gasoline to Japan to slaughter the Chinese? I've little use
for selfish motherhood, and I'll continue to insist to my dying day that wives
and mothers should assume the full responsibilities of citizenship and cease
to be "simple souls" who leave the affairs of the world to those moved solely
by predatory greed. . . .

Since returning from China, I've met countless women—and girls and
boys, too—who grew up during the Depression. They are afraid of the future, afraid of life. In our country, the richest on earth, many of our soldiers
are getting the first regular meals, decent clothing, medical and dental care
they've ever had. Why did we have to leave our children to find refuge in war
and death?

You might argue, Grace, that this has nothing to do with wives and mothers. It has, because it has to do with social consciousness and children and the care of children. . . .

It's not enough to merely take care of our own. Not even our own race. Our social consciousness should embrace the world, and we should create a society that cares for all human beings. We would find like minds to ourselves in every land, for we privileged Anglo-Saxons are not the chosen people of God.

You say with sarcasm, Grace, that wives could not leave their children and run off to the Eighth Route Army, as I did. . . . There were many married women in the armies. In the war zones I saw countless wives and mothers who, while they did their duties as mothers, were also striking off the shackles that had impeded their sex. . . .

The time [may] come, for the new generation, when motherhood will be regarded as a profession worthy of protection—but a profession that is merely part of citizenship as a whole.

By September 8, Smedley had left the whirl of activity in New York and retreated to Yaddo for a short rest before embarking at the end of the month on her first lecture tour—which she told Taylor she "dreaded"—to try to earn her livelihood.[8] Politically, however, she had already begun to take advantage of the success of *Battle Hymn*. In a long letter to the editor of the *New York Herald Tribune*, dated September 6, she attacked British colonialism and the appointment of Lord Philip Mountbatten as supreme allied commander for Southeast Asia. She argued that anti-British feeling was so strong in Southeast Asia that Mountbatten, whom she called a playboy, could never be effective. Citing the fall of Burma as evidence of the success with which the Japanese had used antiwhite feelings against the Allies, she insisted—no doubt with a keen sense of irony—that Chiang Kai-shek would have been a far wiser appointment.

The dreaded speaking tour began in October with a reassuringly successful talk at nearby Skidmore College. The college newspaper, the *Skidmore News*, reported: "From experience we can tell you that she's more vibrant than a [movie] thriller and more intoxicating than a Worden beer."[9] After this she spoke at several small colleges in upstate New York and around New England, and she completed the tour at the end of the month with well-publicized talks in Boston and New York City, where she made radio appearances as well.[10]

Newspaper accounts described Smedley as "hard-hitting," and "pulling no punches." Her descriptions of war were more graphic than most audiences, especially women's groups, were used to hearing. She emphasized the heroic sacrifices the Chinese were making in fighting the Japanese against such great odds. She also challenged her audiences to examine America's China policy for racism. The Chinese, she said, were fighting to be free of *all* foreign domination, not just domination by Japan. Chinese of all political persuasions felt that by fighting together with the Allies against fascism, they had earned the right to be treated as equals. Thus they hoped that after the war, all foreign powers would give up their special privileges in China and restore true sovereignty to the nation.

Smedley spent November in Yaddo, but by early December she was back on the lecture circuit. This time she was on the road for a series of three tours over the next six months. After an initial appearance in New York City, she headed south to Georgia and then west by bus and train on a zigzag course to Anniston, Knoxville, and Jacksonville. From Mississippi she continued to New Orleans and various small towns in Louisiana. Then she headed across Texas to Houston, finally ending the first tour at Southwestern University in Georgetown, Texas, on December 17.[11]

After Christmas in Yaddo, a second tour began, covering a much smaller area, Philadelphia to Boston, during January of 1944. Then it was back to Yaddo before a swing at the end of February north into Canada, which was followed immediately by a long trip south to Louisiana at the end of March. From New Orleans Smedley went to Chicago, and she did not arrive back at Mary Knoblauch's apartment in Manhattan until mid-May, having come via Cleveland, Ohio, and a number of small colleges in western New York. After a few more appearances in Boston and New York, in mid-June she finally resettled at Yaddo. She wrote to Taylor: "Well, I finished with my goddamned lecture tour and I never want to lecture again. My agent is up in arms because I told her I'll lecture only during March of next year—not any other time; that I want to write. She told me how she's fought and suffered and bled for my sake! But I did the fighting and the suffering and the bleeding and found that what I have to say is simply an amusement for most audiences. So I want to finish my play and start on another book—the biography of General Chu Teh, whom you like best of all" (June 11).[12]

Though physically exhausted and near collapse, Smedley was also exhilarated. She drew confidence in the years ahead from the knowledge that she had proved popular and effective as a speaker before a variety of mainstream American audiences—the Council on Foreign Relations, church groups, women's clubs, college students, and military training groups, to name a few. Even when challenged by hostile questions, she appeared to enjoy herself much of the time. As she told the Taylors: "I'm a good lecturer, darlings. Better speaker than writer by far, I think. But it does wear me out. . . . I always work and worry a lot before each lecture, trying to do my best. I know that I'll have opponents in every audience. But I like opposition, for it whets the mind and keeps you on your toes, intellectually speaking" (February 4).

Indeed, wherever she went there were those in the audience who were suspicious of her motives and background. In Chicago, for example, after a speech at the Palmer House to the Council on Foreign Relations, she was asked directly whether she had helped "set up a Communist empire in North China" at the time of the Xi'an Incident, as was suggested by reports in U.S. newspapers in 1937. In response, she explained the circumstances of the Xi'an Incident and said she had done no more than report, in several radio broadcasts, the views of Chiang's opponents and the motives of the kidnappers.[13]

Smedley tailored her message to her audience. In the North, she could emphasize the dangers of a racist American foreign policy in which business interests outweighed moral concerns; she could also say that she considered a showdown between the Guomindang and the Chinese Communists inevitable, and that she considered the Communists the more democratic party. But in the south, she avoided condemnations of racism and praise of the Chinese Communists, stressing instead the importance of continued support for the Chinese: "Our destiny, our fate is bound up with the fate of China—China is our chief land base of operations in Asia, and if China should collapse it would be a disaster for America." She often concluded with a strong appeal for contributions to medical relief in China, challenging her audiences to show a determination equal to that of the Chinese people in the fight against the Japanese.[14]

Although publicly she modified her speech and behavior in the South, privately what Smedley saw there outraged her. For example, on December 7, 1943, she wrote to Taylor:

The treatment of Negroes in the south has humiliated and shamed me so deeply that my blood runs cold in my veins. Traveling by bus, with the rain pouring, the driver ordered a dozen Negroes to step back and let two handsome white women aboard first. They came on, then the driver saw they had Negro blood in their veins—perhaps their hair showed it. The driver slapped his leg and bawled with laughter and said to the white passengers: "Now ain't that a joke! I thought they was white and they are Niggers." The faces of the two women and of all the colored passengers were frozen. Mine froze too. Some of the white passengers broke into a laugh at the *joke*. . . . I saw a northern white soldier ask a colored soldier to sit down by him and the latter did so; then the bus driver stopped the bus and said: "Stand up, Nigger!" The colored soldier stood up. The white soldier said: "Aw hell!" and stood up also. But had that white soldier not been in uniform, I don't know what would have happened.

Now when I heard this, I should have stood up and killed the driver. But I sat there petrified, sat there like a traitor to the human race. I kept thinking of what Jesus would have done, and knew that he would perhaps have allowed Himself to be killed. I didn't. I didn't do a thing for many reasons: because I was warned a dozen times by white people that if I did anything it would be the colored people who suffered for it. The whole south whispers if the least thing breaks out. In one town in Georgia a fight started in the colored section of the town. So great is the tension that the minute it started, the railway engine on the train began to toot, the air-raid sirens went off as if there was an air raid, police cars and motorcycles roared through the street, and I heard the firing of guns. A street fight starts such a night alarm. . . .

I spoke at a colored college in that town, and a white woman put me up. Of the college she said: "They are nice Negroes—make no trouble at all; well-behaved." The assumption being that Negroes generally "make trouble" and are not "well-behaved."

Smedley did not remain silent for long. As soon as she returned from her first Southern tour she began a one-woman campaign to send books to a woman in Louisiana who wanted to set up a library for the "colored people." She contacted librarian friends in New York and Los Angeles and started sending appeals to the press. But they were more than appeals; they were direct attacks on Southern racism, and they were published in a number of Black newspapers around the country. One of the most inflammatory appeared in the *Los Angeles Tribune* under the headline "White Author Indignant over Southern Prejudice" and ended with the words "We can't treat men like dogs and expect them to act like men." [15]

Interestingly, it was Smedley's public attacks on Southern racism, not her statements about China, that apparently prompted the first F.B.I. investigation of her activities. At the end of August, 1944, Representative John S. Gibson of Georgia had his complaints against her recent activities entered in the *Congressional Record;* and on the basis of references to her in the 1938 report of the House Un-American Activities Committee (or Dies Committee, after its chairman, Martin Dies), he connected Smedley to international communism and suggested an F.B.I. investigation. He said, in part: "[Earlier] I brought to the attention of the House a very ugly attack made on the South by an Agnes Smedley. . . . She is the author of many books which portray the glory of the Communist Party and its great cause. . . . She was the author of *China's Red Army*

Marches in which she described in glowing language how the Reds with people other than whites had overcome whites in revolution. She pictures the great benefits received from the Communist revolutions."[16] The F.B.I. took up Gibson's suggestion immediately. In September of 1944 the secretary to Yaddo's director, Elizabeth Ames, was enlisted to keep track of Smedley's movements and provide copies of any lecture notes or correspondence she might type for Smedley. The investigation was run from the Albany office and seemed at first to have had rather low priority at F.B.I. headquarters in Washington; apparently the bureau was concerned chiefly with being prepared to answer any congressional inquiries about Smedley.[17]

Yaddo during the summer of 1944 was much quieter than when Smedley arrived the year before. The mansion was closed and few guests were in residence. Besides Smedley, there were only Carson McCullers, Helen Eustis, and Gerald Erlich, who was accompanied by his wife Sophie and their baby daughter. Like Elizabeth Ames and her sister, and the caretaker and the cook, they lived in small out-buildings and ate together in a converted garage.[18] Living nearby, however, was a former Yaddo resident in whom Smedley took special interest: Katherine Anne Porter.* The two became friends in part because of a mutual friendship with Thorberg Brundin Haberman Ellison. They also discovered that their early careers had been shaped by an overlapping Greenwich Village "period."

In 1919 Porter, a native Texan, moved from the West to Greenwich Village, where she associated with some of the same women who had supported and nurtured Smedley. She was an aspiring journalist with political views similar to Smedley's, and the Sacco-Vanzetti anarchist case absorbed her energies off and on over the next seven years. Outside of news stories, Porter's first literary works were children's stories that were strongly feminist in tone. And for many of the same reasons that Smedley had been drawn into the Indian nationalist movement, Porter was attracted to the Mexican revolutionaries and artists living in New York in 1919. Porter went to Mexico City in 1920 to take a job on the *Magazine of Mexico,* and during the 1920s she shuttled back and forth between Greenwich Village and Mexico.

It was in Mexico that Porter met Thorberg Brundin, there as a reporter for the newspaper *El Heraldo.* Thorberg's first husband, Rob-

---

* Porter (1890–1980) had fallen in love with the upstate New York countryside during her stay at Yaddo in 1940 and had bought a nearby farmhouse (Joan Givner, *Katherine Anne Porter: A Life* [New York, 1982]).

ert Haberman, was working as a pharmacist and a teacher, but he was also smuggling guns to peons on behalf of the socialist congressman from the state of Yucatán, Felipe Puerto Carillo. Thorberg owned the Greenwich Village building in which Porter had an apartment until 1929. In 1977 Porter said that when she had known Smedley at Yaddo, they had agreed "on most issues" largely because of these early parallels in their lives.[19]

At Yaddo, Smedley also had Chinese visitors whom she asked for advice about the play she had been working on. Her main consultant, introduced to her by Pearl Buck, was Wang Yong, a young actress whose background reminded Smedley of that of theatrical friends like Lily Wu in Yan'an or members of the New Fourth Army's guerrilla theater. In trying to make her characters and scenes believable, Smedley had found she needed more cultural insight. How was love expressed between two married Chinese intellectuals? Under what circumstances might a young Chinese army officer be attracted to a foreign woman? If he followed such an attraction, that would he hope for, and what would he fear, as the relationship developed? Smedley asked Wang Yong to discuss these questions with her male companion and future husband, Xie Hegeng. Wang Yong responded earnestly in several detailed letters. While thinking about the play, Smedley decided to postpone further actual writing until her collaborator, playwright Leonard Ehrlich, was discharged from the U.S. Army Signal Corps.[20]

In June, Smedley described her activities in two letters to Aino Taylor. She had started work on her biography of Zhu De and found herself struggling: "I'm working on my new book, and, as usual, wish I'd never been born. In the first place, I don't even know what kind of book I'm going to write. I know the material I'll use, and I'm writing, but don't know what form to put it in yet. So far what I've written gives me a pain. Writers always get a pain in the neck at what they write—a writer who is satisfied with what he writes is someone to beware of" (June 12). She was concerned, as always, about gardening and crop raising: "Wet spring—farmers not even able to get in potatoes—rot in ground—good for grass, but you can't eat grass" (June 13). She asked Aino to send Elizabeth Ames one crate of California lemons a month during the hot weather, because they were hard to find in Saratoga Springs. She was also doing a lot of reading. She said she still loved Chaucer, and she recommended Ignazio Silone's *Bread and Wine:* "Silone takes the soul of man through all the stages of the purgatory of the present age and his product is infinitely richer than Dante's *Divine Comedy.* I suppose many scholars would protest. Let them. I simply don't like Dante, though he gives a picture of the ideas and superstitions and reflects in his work the political oppression of the early Renaissance. But Silone does this and much more" (June 12).

The only time Smedley left Yaddo during the summer was at the end of July, when she went to New York to participate in a roundtable debate, with three university professors and two apologists for the Guomindang government, on the present situation in China. She told Taylor that on her way back she stopped off to visit Thorberg Brundin Ellison at New Paltz and "pulled weeds for a week," assuring herself a bout with back pain.[21]

In August Smedley told Taylor about another new friend, Caroline Slade, a novelist and social worker whose husband was the current president of the Yaddo Corporation: "Mrs. Caroline Slade, who has written a number of novels based on the lives of girls (Mrs. Slade was a social worker for twenty years) has told me about her many girl cases. It is a depressing story. Many, many poor girls who work as servants in middle-class homes are either seduced or raped by the head of the family and set on the road to 'delinquency.' Often these girls come [not only from] alcoholic families but simply [from] families ruined and made degenerate during the Depression. Caroline Slade and I argue all the time about the origin of delinquency, its cure, etc." (August 15). Through the summer and into the fall, Smedley enlisted Slade and Porter to work with her on various fund-raising projects for the China Aid Council of United China Relief. Also in August, she gave Taylor her reaction to *Pacific Story,* an NBC radio play from Hollywood that used a script based on *Battle Hymn of China:* "Isn't it wonderful that Americans had to stick in a 'Mr. Scott'—a man instead of a woman marching with the guerrillas. The fact is that no American man had the guts to march and live with the guerrillas. Anyway, I thought the broadcast exceptionally good" (August 9).

All in all, the summer of 1944 was an unusually productive and happy one for Agnes Smedley. She was riding high from the success of *Battle Hymn of China* and her speaking tour. And at Yaddo, she had found security and an important friend in Elizabeth Ames. As she wrote to Taylor on July 21: "Yaddo is a perfect place for working and writing, and I'm so damned poor that it is life for me. Apart from that, I have a dear friend here [Elizabeth Ames], the woman who manages the place, and this is a precious acquisition that gives me peace and quiet and which should enable me to write."

Friends Become Enemies: The Debate over China Policy, 1944–1945

The calm of Smedley's life at Yaddo ended in October of 1944, when President Roosevelt recalled General "Vinegar Joe" Stilwell, the U.S. commander of the China/Burma/India theater (C.B.I.), and Smedley's friend since her Hankou days in 1938. This extraordinary action would quickly draw Smedley into a storm over America's China policy.

In the summer of 1944 the war in the Pacific was far from over. In Burma the Japanese were advancing north from Rangoon, and in China they were in the midst of a major offensive, making significant gains inland from the southeastern China coast. In part, this new offensive was intended to stop the vigorous air war which had been conducted since 1942 by General Claire Chennault's "Flying Tigers," operating from bases in southern China. By September of 1944 the Japanese were threatening Chennault's main base at Guilin, and this forced theater commander Stilwell to order the evacuation and destruction of the base. The success of the Japanese thrust also drove a political wedge between Stilwell and the Chinese head of state, Chiang Kai-shek. Chiang remained confident that he need only wait for the Americans to beat the Japanese; Stilwell blamed Chiang for his battlefield losses in Burma. Like *Time*'s T. H. White and many other observers, Stilwell saw Chiang's Chongqing government as foundering in a sea of poor leadership, corruption, inflation, and secret police executions. Moreover, Chiang had refused Stilwell's urgent request that he transfer 200,000 of his crack troops to the southwest front, away from the northwest where they were blockading the Communists. Chiang had answered that Stilwell could save Guilin by bringing British and American troops up from Burma.[1]

By the end of the summer, Stilwell's impatience with Chiang Kai-shek's "mishandling" of the war effort had reached a boiling point. In his communications with Roosevelt, Stilwell insisted that he should be given direct command of all Chinese troops, Guomindang and Communist alike. He also urged that the United States consider backing someone other than Chiang Kai-shek—or "Peanut," as he called him privately—as head of state. Stilwell thought he could strengthen the war effort in northern China if he could treat the Communist and Nationalist armies as equals. He had been encouraged briefly when Chiang reluctantly consented to permit the "Dixie" mission of official U.S. military observers to the Communist capital of Yan'an.* But then Chiang Kai-shek stiffened and by September, when Guilin had to be abandoned, Stilwell and Chiang were locked in a power struggle. On September 28, Chiang made a desperate move. He cabled Roosevelt an ultimatum: Stilwell must be recalled or he would resign as generalissimo and president of China (head of state).

The Japanese offensive of the summer of 1944 also broke up a bipartisan foreign-policy consensus in Washington. As the debate over China policy and U.S. support of Chiang Kai-shek grew hotter, it divided opinion among "old China hands" now working in the press and military, many of whom were Smedley's friends. Matters came to a head in late October of 1944, when Roosevelt finally decided to remove Stilwell as his C.B.I. theater commander and send Chiang a new ambassador, Patrick Hurley, who was ideologically more sympathetic to the Guomindang government.

In retrospect, F.D.R.'s motives seem clear enough. This was a presidential election year, and he did not want to give Republicans—especially powerful opinion-makers like Henry Luce—an opportunity to attack him for vacillating in his support of Chiang's government. He was also concerned about the possibility of a postwar power vacuum in China if Chiang's government should fall and China be consumed by civil war. He still hoped that a strong and united China would provide postwar stability in the Far East, and he wanted China to play the role of a great power in the Security Council of the new United Nations, which was to be established in San Francisco the next year. Thus against the

---

*The Dixie military observer mission remained in Yan'an from July to November, 1944. It was led by the military attaché to the embassy in Chongqing, Col. David Barrett, and was named Dixie because of the Guomindang and American view of the Communists as rebels and the song title "Is It True What They Say about Dixie?" For an overview, see E. J. Kahn, Jr., *The China Hands: America's Foreign Service Officers and What Befell Them* (New York, 1975), pp. 103–34, or Barrett's memoir, *Dixie Mission: The United States Army Observer Group in Yenan, 1944* (Berkeley and Los Angeles, 1970).

advice of most China experts, both inside and outside the White House, Roosevelt felt that he had no choice but to sack Stilwell and send new representatives to Chongqing who could get along better with Chiang Kai-shek. At the same time, he urged his new ambassador, Patrick Hurley, to do what he could to prevent the outbreak of civil war in China and asked him to actively promote the idea of a coalition government in which the Communists would have a secondary role.[2]

The press reaction to Stilwell's sacking, though overshadowed by the election as a news story, was strong and noticeably divided. The conservative *Chicago Tribune* and Scripps-Howard papers such as the *New York Daily Mirror* praised Roosevelt's decision; the *New York Times,* the *New Republic,* and *PM* decried it. The most interesting response came in *Time* magazine. The first part of its lead story of November 13 quoted from a dispatch filed by its Chongqing bureau chief, T. H. White, and was pro-Stilwell and critical of Chiang Kai-shek. But in the middle of the piece, the tone abruptly changed: Chiang was praised and the decision to sack Stilwell was applauded. This was the work of *Time*'s foreign news editor, Whittaker Chambers. *Time*'s publisher, Henry Luce, was of course a fervent supporter of Chiang Kai-shek. Thus when his Chongqing bureau chief loudly protested the contradictory editorial additions, Luce supported Chambers and eventually forced White's resignation.[3]

These events took place in a new Cold War atmosphere in New York and Washington. With the war nearly over in Europe, the Soviet Union began to be seen as the new enemy and the Chinese Communists as its puppets; thus Chiang Kai-shek had to be supported as part of the effort to stop the spread of Communism in Europe and Asia. This was the reasoning of Whittaker Chambers and some of Smedley's old China friends, notably J. B. Powell and Walter Judd. Smedley had come home from China determined to be politically independent and open-minded. But having lived under Chiang Kai-shek and then under the Chinese Communist Party, she was convinced that the poor of China would be better off under the Chinese Communists than under Chiang. She refused to give up her belief that a Communist Party forged by an indigenous nationalist movement would act independently of Moscow. From her experience in the Indian and Chinese movements, she knew the strength of nationalism. She also refused to accept the view that communism and democracy were mutually exclusive.

Before General Stilwell's recall, Smedley had already been upset and feeling personally wounded by the anti-Communist stands of her Hankou friend Freda Utley and her Hong Kong friend Emily Hahn. Hahn had attacked Smedley in the spring of 1944 in her book *China to Me*. Since Hahn was a good friend of T. V. Soong's and was the biographer of Madame Chiang Kai-shek, her political position could hardly have surprised Smedley. What did surprise her was the fact that Hahn made her a personal target. Claiming that the average American was "full of hooey" because "he thinks the Chinese guerrillas are the only soldiers doing any fighting in China," Hahn argued that Agnes Smedley, Edgar Snow, and Evans Carlson were the "perpetrators" of this misconception. "I am not trying to run you down, Agnes Smedley, Ed Snow, and General [*sic*] Carlson, and the rest of you; I'm only trying to undo some of the harm you have unwittingly done to your friends." Smedley concurred privately with Carlson's response that Hahn's book was "an abortion."[4]

The rift with Freda Utley hurt more, and again it involved Carlson. In *China at War* (1939), Utley had been the first on-the-scene observer to claim in print that the Chinese Communists were basically agrarian reformers. More recently, however, she had been making sharp anti-Communist statements—statements so sharp, in fact, that Carlson and Smedley wondered if she had become a paid publicist for the Guomindang.[5]

Since his formation of an elite Marine battalion trained in the guerrilla tactics he had observed in northern China, Carlson had continued to make waves in the military. At Guadalcanal from August, 1942, to February of 1943, Carlson's Raiders had won the first victory against the Japanese in the South Pacific, losing only sixteen men while destroying Japanese installations and killing over eight hundred Japanese. Nevertheless, Carlson's superiors told him frankly that they were afraid of his unorthodox ideas and tactics, and in May of 1943 he was kicked "upstairs" to be executive officer of the Raider regiment and stripped of direct command of his battalion. He continued his fight to change practices within the military by supporting such projects as the writing of pamphlets "on the contribution of the Negro to our military efforts."[6] By 1944 he had stirred up enough controversy with his statements about China to be condemned by Luce and Hearst publications. He was one of the chief architects of American strategy in the battles of Tarawa and Saipan, where his arm was badly shattered as he attempted to remove a wounded soldier from the line of fire. (Because of his wound, he would be forced to retire from the Marines in 1945. He returned to the United States with the idea of running for the U.S. Senate from California.)[7]

While Smedley and Carlson were being criticized from the right by supporters of Chiang Kai-shek, Smedley also received criticism from old friends on the left, such as Anna Louise Strong.[8] Most such criticisms were still being made in private. Not until September of 1944, when the debate over Stilwell began to heat up in Washington, did Smedley drop her united-front position and respond publicly by sharpening her attacks on Chiang's government. On September 18 she wrote to Taylor:

Since writing you I went down to Woodstock to lecture. It was interesting. Woodstock is an artists' colony; about 180 writers, painters, sculptors, musicians, and theater people live in the stretching mountains. They have small wooden cottages somewhat like mine at Ojai, and they go there in the spring and stay until the cold drives them out. But one needs a car to get about because they live in isolated places in the hills and valleys. I was the guest of Dr. Harold Rugg . . . a professor at Teachers College of Columbia University and a very interesting man. I had a young Chinese Army officer (Guomindang), an old friend from China with me, and we were both given a tremendous reception. Dr. Rugg arranged a private social party on Saturday evening (my lecture was on Sunday evening). He invited 15 but 45 came. They all brought their suppers in boxes and we sat on his lovely plateau-like lawn overlooking valleys and mountains and had a picnic supper. When it grew dark we went inside and a number of musicians played. . . . After this, my Chinese friend and I sat in the circle of friends and answered questions . . . about conditions in China. I was afraid for this Chinese friend, for he has the unfortunate habit of speaking the bitter truth [about the reactionary Chinese government]. Once I stopped and asked the audience to remember that if they repeated a word he said, he could be arrested and sent back to China. I was particularly afraid because Mrs. Shotwell and her daughter were present. Prof. Shotwell is a historian—he is a Prof. at Columbia; and he's an advisor to our State Department and is in close contact with Chinese officials. So I directed my appeal to Mrs. Shotwell. Her husband, fortunately, was in Washington that weekend. Everyone promised—but I am a little worried still. . . .

Prof. Shotwell had tried to prevent me from saying anything against the Chinese government dictatorship because, he said, our government recognized it. He and a rich woman had originally arranged for me to speak in the town hall [at Woodstock]. When I refused to allow Shotwell or our State Department to abridge freedom of speech and press, they were furious. I refused [Prof. Shotwell's invitation] to go to Woodstock. Then some writers [Dr. Rugg] asked me to come to a meeting which they would call and in which I could say anything. So I went. To the amazement of the Shotwells and the rich woman, I had [a Chinese] Army officer in uniform with me—and he was far more critical of the Chinese govt. than I was. They were simply flabbergasted. After the meeting, Mrs. Shotwell tried to assure me and the officer that they believed absolutely in free speech, press, assembly, etc. I listened in silence and let her squirm. Even the rich woman came to my meeting and afterward came up and sadly shook hands with me. I congratulated her on her bravery in coming and she squirmed and asked if I wanted her to help take down the exhibits—for we had put up a [photo] exhibition. I told her that she need not help—as the Chinese Army officer would take them down; he was in charge of them.

If there was any group of individuals thoroughly familiar with Smedley's political views, it was the publishers and editors of the *New Republic* and the *Nation*. Smedley had established working relationships with both magazines at the time of her involvement in Friends of Freedom for India. With the aim of representing independent liberal views, which included strong anticolonialist positions, both magazines had published Smedley's stories during her early days in Germany. Over the years the editors had become acquainted with her independent anarchist-socialist leanings and had often seen her stand up to the American Communist Party, refusing to become anyone's tool. They had watched as she criticized the "feudal" personal attitude toward women taken by the Indian nationalists, even though she knew they would see it as a betrayal. Thus when Smedley returned to the United States in 1941 hostile to Soviet policy in Asia and critical of factionalism within the Chinese Communist Party, but still firm in her belief that the CCP offered a greater hope for democracy in China than Chiang's Guomindang government, they took her arguments seriously. And because of her understanding of the military situation in China—shared publicly by Carlson and Snow, and privately by Stilwell and other U.S. diplomats—her editors accepted the view that a long hard war remained to be fought by U.S. troops in China and that it was therefore in America's interest to support the Chinese ally who would be of greatest aid to our troops. The Communist-led guerrillas seemed, in the judgment of many American observers, to be the more effective fighters against the Japanese. And since Chiang had not yet implemented democracy in China but was only holding it out as a promise for the future, many suspected that he was cleverly manipulating the Americans for his own purposes. The rash of books and articles arguing the case for exclusive support of Chiang only served to confirm their suspicions.

Earlier, in a November 13, 1943, review for the *Nation*, Smedley had taken on Mme. Chiang Kai-shek, the figure who, by her speaking tours and cover-story publicity in Time-Life publications, best personified U.S. friendship with the Guomindang government. The author under review had called Mme. Chiang "the mother of every wounded soldier in China." He went on to claim that Mme. Chiang had never been "captivated by the luxury and superficial brilliance of modern New York," but dressed "like a simple and modest Chinese wife." As a leader of the

New Life Movement, she was said to live frugally and to "abjure those
new-fangled frivolities which are quite out of keeping with their digni-
fied Chinese traditions." Smedley did not let such claims go unchal-
lenged: "Mr. Tsui [the author] perhaps gets his Soong sisters mixed up.
That description might apply to Madame Sun Yat-sen, but never to
Madame Chiang. The paragraph was perhaps written before Madame
Chiang's visit to this country with a retinue of relatives and retainers.
Jade and diamonds, mink and sables, silks and satins, do not constitute
frugal and plain living and are totally out of harmony with the bitter
lives of the soldiers and common people of China."

Madame Chiang struck back through Emily Hahn, who made a personal attack on Smedley in *China to Me.* As a biographer of Madame
Chiang, Hahn's opinions mirrored those of high Guomindang officials in
Washington. Madame Chiang's anger was confirmed privately to Smedley by Pearl Buck, who quoted her as saying that Smedley would never
be allowed back into China.[9]

In 1944, as the Luce publications intensified their "hard sell" of the
Chiang government, the *Nation* and the *New Republic,* both independent journals, turned to Smedley as a person well qualified to refute distortions that Guomindang spokespersons might try to put forward as
truth. By the fall of 1944, Smedley was more convinced than ever that
what she called "reactionary forces" were lining up behind Chiang in a
full-fledged propaganda war. Their goal, she thought, was to ensure that
the United States gave full support to Chiang's government and cut off
all support for the Communists. Further proof was the recruitment into
Chiang's propaganda "camp" of the conservative businessman Arthur
Kohlberg.[10] On December 16, Smedley wrote in the *Nation:* "Many
Americans are today campaigning for that dictatorship and [held] up
everywhere as 'friends' of China though they know little about that
country. An American businessman [Kohlberg] made a three-month trip
to China last year, was made a general in the Chinese army, and is now a
sort of high advisor to the official Guomindang propaganda headquarters in New York."

On October 22, the liberal New York newspaper *PM* published a
background article on China by Smedley under the headline "Crises in
China: Defeat and Disunity." Smedley laid out the disintegrating mili-
tary situation in China and urged that the Guomindang blockade of the
Communists be lifted and their troops released to fight the Japanese.
She also accused the Guomindang of sending propagandists to the
United States to persuade Republicans, clergymen, and "reactionary"

newspaper publishers to label any criticism of the Guomindang as interference in China's internal affairs or as "Red-inspired." Smedley named
Dr. Walter Judd and Clare Boothe Luce as examples of those who had
"swallowed their line." *

Two days later J. Edgar Hoover, the director of the F.B.I., sent the
following memo to his Albany office:

> It is respectfully requested that Agnes Smedley, of Yaddo, Saratoga Springs,
> New York, be placed on the regular Censorship Watch List, and submissions
> of all communications and telephone conversations to, from, or regarding
> her be forwarded to the Bureau.
>
> *Purpose:* Agnes Smedley is recognized as one of the principal propagan-
> dists for the Soviets writing in the English language. Agnes Smedley is con-
> sidered an authority on Communist activity in the Far East, and as the
> operations of the United States Army and Navy come closer to the Asiatic
> Mainland and the Japanese home islands, Communist activity in those areas
> will be of increasing importance to the Bureau.[11]

With this memo, the F.B.I.'s investigation of Smedley intensified and the
surveillance of her through the Yaddo secretary was stepped up. From
reading her mail, an early discovery was correspondence with German
Communists in exile in Mexico City.

Soon after her arrival in New York, Smedley had been asked by the
German-American community to write articles and make broadcasts
urging Germans (in Germany) to rise up and overthrow the Nazis, which
she did. It was probably through this community that she made contact
with the refugees in Mexico City. Among them was the celebrated Czech
journalist and political commentator Egon Erwin Kisch, whom she had
known in Shanghai. With others in Mexico City, Kisch had started a
newspaper, *Fries Deutschland,* to serve the German expatriate community around the world. Smedley began subscribing to the paper, and it
was this subscription that triggered closer examination of her mail by
the F.B.I. It was noted in her F.B.I. file that a "highly confidential source"
(said to be at the Knopf publishing house) claimed that he had forwarded to Smedley a letter from Mexico City that ended with "best
regards of [names blanked out by F.B.I.] all of whom are outstanding
German Communists now refugees in Mexico." From this and other
"evidence," F.B.I. headquarters in Washington concluded that "Mrs.
[*sic*] Smedley had been for several years a notorious Communist expert

---

* This piece, written on short notice, represented a regression in Smedley's writing
style. Unlike her last book or her recent lectures, articles, and book reviews, it was a heavy,
muckraking article filled with clichés and name-calling.

on the Far East." Thereafter all mail for Smedley from Mexico was to be examined by the Office of Censorship before delivery.[12]

J. Edgar Hoover was in close contact with the anti-Communist right in Congress. By raising the status of the Smedley investigation he was responding to allegations like those of Congressman Gibson that Smedley was a Soviet agent. The point of his investigation was to find evidence of Smedley's ties to the Soviet Union (possibly through American or German Communists) as an agent, a spy, or both.

Smedley's F.B.I. file from late 1944 onward shows a heavy reliance on newspaper accounts to trace her speaking appearances, which were considered proof of her Communist sympathies. Agents apparently assumed that any coverage of Smedley by what they considered to be a Communist publication proved that the U.S. Communist Party, and therefore Moscow, had approved of what she had said. From all available evidence, no F.B.I. agent read any of her books at least until 1947; the bureau simply selected book reviews for summaries of their content. In choosing interviewees, the F.B.I. appears to have restricted their list in Smedley's case to "reliable witnesses"—by which they meant persons who were known to be anti-Communist. Evidence from persons of "unknown reliability" was of course suspect. In spite of the fact that Smedley's friends held diverse political, ideological, and religious positions, any continuing contact with Smedley automatically put them in the "unreliable" category. Finally, in the material released in 1984, neither the F.B.I. nor military intelligence reported on Smedley's talks to military groups or high military officers, even those who knew her well like Carlson and Stilwell. In short, from its outset the F.B.I. investigation was strikingly superficial and blatantly biased.

Thus, by late 1944, both the left and the right on the China issue began to anticipate conspiracies, and both began to oversimplify the motivations of those holding the opposite point of view. Those supporting recognition of the Chinese Communists became the "puppets" or "stooges" of Moscow, and those supporting the Guomindang became the "running dogs" of big business, both Chinese and American.

Stilwell's removal from command was not publicly announced until after he had arrived in the United States. He was asked to give no public statements, an order he obeyed. Most likely Stilwell had anticipated this, for he had been careful to give his version of events to *New York Times* correspondent Brooks Atkinson and to T. H. White of Time-Life before he left China. In a piece for the October 30 edition of *PM*, headlined "Stilwell Scapegoat for Chiang's Defeat," Smedley argued that

Chiang was trying to deflect growing internal criticism of losses to the Japanese by blaming them on American policy in China. Noting that she knew Stilwell personally as a blunt military man, Smedley surmised that he had probably spoken too directly with Chiang about the military situation, as well as about corruption and other problems within the Guomindang government. She called his removal a victory not for Chiang but for the Japanese.[13]

Smedley published another piece in *PM* on November 21 denouncing the cabinet shift within the Guomindang as meaningless, a "new hand with an old deck" that would do nothing to bring democratic reforms to China. Her final piece for *PM*, published on December 10, was entitled "Open Letter to Henry Luce Challenging Time-Life Articles on the China Situation." During the first week in December, *Life* magazine had asked Smedley for her collection of photographs to illustrate an upcoming article. She had written a letter to Luce explaining that she would not turn over the photos to him until she was told in what context they were going to be used. After citing examples of what she claimed to be distorted editing, such as the published version of T. H. White's story on the sacking of Stilwell, Smedley said she feared her pictures might be used in a similar manner to support the Guomindang's cause. She accused Time-Life of following a "Guomindang line" by using materials provided by a Guomindang supporter and member of the staff, Mrs. Y. Y. Sung, after having them tidied up by an "American editor." Although she did not name this editor, it is clear from the examples given that she meant Whittaker Chambers. She also spelled out her growing sense of conspiracy:

> [Guomindang agents] began to feed a regular "Guomindang line" of propaganda to American reactionaries who have been willing to "front" for them. This activity has been accompanied by secret efforts to have Americans in many institutions of the country discharged because they have criticized Guomindang reaction. The regime which *Time, Life,* and *Fortune* have chosen to champion is crumbling. Not until the Japanese were actually knocking on its front door has this regime been willing to yield a step to the Chinese democratic forces—which include the Communists. It scorned even the democrats within its own ranks. It sent its agents to the United States to lie to and deceive the American public, and you opened your publications to them.
>
> That America is in part responsible for the whole Chinese debacle goes without saying. Americans who for years wrote the truth about China were defamed as Reds, idealists, visionaries, and what not. I am one of those so-called "partisans" because I would not sit on the fence and pretend that Fate could protect us.

It [the Guomindang] would have fallen, had our moneyed interests not supported it in power.

Now the cry goes up that the Chinese Communists will dominate all China and fight the war, while American influence will wane. Let us thank God that some Chinese force remains intact to fight on in cooperation with us. American democrats will thank God that this new China, rising in the ashes of the old, will not sell their country to American and British industrialists and financiers.

Within the ranks of the Chinese Nationalist armies are hundreds of thousands of honest and democratic patriots. It is they who must pay for the sins of the [Guomindang] regime, and those who escape death in this debacle will find ways of uniting with other men like themselves, including the Communist armies, to continue the war and to build a democratic government.

That government will not be "totalitarian Communism," as your *Time* article stated, for that is not and never has been the program or purpose of the Chinese Communists. If we try to destroy [a Communist] government in order that China may become a puppet state, as Greece and Italy are British puppets, we may cause decades of suffering and bloodshed, but we will merely end by becoming the most hated of imperialists.

On November 5, Evans Carlson wrote Smedley and praised her articles in *PM:* "It is good to have the spotlight turned on the true state of affairs inside China. Stilwell has done a magnificent job. I know of no other man who could have accomplished what he has in the face of all the obstacles out there. And while doing it he supported the highest ideals of American democracy and decency. What has happened to Walter Judd? That was a lousy statement he made about Stilwell's recall." This letter also contained news that was probably painful for Smedley. Carlson had remarried. This was the first letter in which he spoke of his new, young wife, calling her a "grand companion." Perhaps to soften the blow, he added: "I am eager for you two to know each other. She is a great admirer of yours, Agnes." It was signed, "With love, as always, Evans."

As public concern about U.S. China policy grew, Smedley appeared on "The People's Platform" over CBS radio on November 18 in a debate with John Gunther, J. B. Powell, and Vincent Sheean. She also spoke at several veterans' hospitals, and in December she sent Aino Taylor a picture of herself at Halloran Army Hospital on Staten Island.[14]

On December 7, Smedley joined an organization she thought would be receptive to her message: the National Citizens' Political Action Committee, an off-shoot of the C.I.O. Political Action Committee.* She

---

* Although a forerunner in name of the P.A.C. in American politics since the 1970s, the National Citizens' P.A.C. was concerned with public education on political issues, *not* funneling funds to a particular candidate. In its heyday in the mid-1940s, however, the

had seen unions as a force for political education ever since 1920, when she had won union support in her efforts to stop the deportation of Indian nationals. And in China, she had witnessed the power of student movements to stir the conscience of a nation. Now, in December of 1944, she urged the students at Skidmore College to join the National Citizens' Political Action Committee to fight what she called "a new brand of imperialism." On December 7, after her appearance there, the *Skidmore News* printed some of her comments:

> Our great newspapers and magazines, such as the Luce publications, began to propagate a new brand of imperialism, saying this is the "American Century," that America will determine the future fate of the world. The question—a life and death question—for us is: are we going to become a politically enlightened people who understand every issue of our country and of the world? [Or are] we going to go on, as in the past, leaving politics in the hands of the professional politicians, who, in most cases, are representatives of the great industrial barons of our country? Are we going to be, as before the war, mortally afraid of every new idea that might disturb the groove in which our minds run? Are we going to approach the mighty people's resistance movements in Europe and Asia as if they were a menace to our pocketbooks, even when most of our pocketbooks are flat? Are we going to be afraid to listen or sit in the presence of a progressive American lest we catch Communism? We possess the political democratic machinery with which to become a torch in the world's darkness. But will we prepare ourselves to use it?—Halt, think! You *are* your brother's keeper!

Smedley also used her Skidmore appearance to lead a petition drive protesting the British killing of Greek Resistance fighters. It gathered three hundred signatures, and the F.B.I. noted that it was sent to the president, the State Department, and several major newspapers.[15]

If Smedley and many of her old friends from China disagreed over China policy, they still seemed united on India. In November, Smedley, Lin Yutang, and Pearl Buck's husband Richard Walsh had published articles in *Voice of India* in support of Indian independence. The issue was dedicated to Jawaharlal Nehru on his fifty-fifth birthday and urged the British to release him from jail.* In her article Smedley compared Nehru to Thomas Jefferson and used quotes from Katherine Anne Porter and Elizabeth Ames to demonstrate the anti-British feeling that the treat-

---

National Citizens' P.A.C. was used by Henry Wallace to attract liberal-minded intellectuals to his causes. See William O'Neill, *A Better World, the Great Schism: Stalinism and the American Intellectuals* (New York, 1982), pp. 143–45, and Joseph Gaer, *The First Round: The Story of the C.I.O., Political Action Committee* (New York, 1944).

    * Without an immediate commitment from the British to Indian independence, Nehru, Gandhi, and other nationalist leaders refused to cooperate in the British war effort and were therefore jailed from August, 1942, to May, 1945.

ment of Nehru had aroused in America. She also pointed out that Nehru's book *Toward Freedom* had been translated into Chinese and published serially in the New Fourth Army's monthly magazine. The Chinese, too, she noted, were watching to see if India would be granted independence.

Smedley's visibility after the publication of *Battle Hymn of China* led a curious young student from India, then studying at M.I.T., to seek her out during the fall of 1944. He was Ram Chattopadhyaya, the nephew of Virendranath Chattopadhyaya and the son of Kamaladevi. In a 1977 interview Ram said he and Smedley met a number of times. In New York, they went to the theater or concerts; in Boston, he would join her for dinner at a Chinese restaurant. They talked much about Ram's uncle, Chatto. Smedley told him that the period during which she lived with his uncle had been the most formative of her life. Chatto, she said, had been her teacher. Ram also said that Edgar Snow had explained to Smedley the circumstances of his uncle's death after Snow returned from a trip to the Soviet Union in 1944 or 1945. Chatto had disappeared in 1938, during the time of Stalin's purges. In 1941, his Russian wife was informed only of his death. According to Ram, Snow told Smedley he had heard that Chatto had died in a labor camp. Ram helped to arrange a meeting for Smedley with Nehru's sister, the future ambassador, Madame Pandit. He said Smedley had been extremely emotional on this occasion and had nearly cried as she said how honored she was to meet the sister of such a great man as Nehru. Ram himself lost touch with Smedley sometime after 1946. He added that what he remembered most clearly was her fiercely anti-British attitude.

The beginning of 1945 saw Congress voting by a narrow margin (207 to 186) to give permanent status to the House Committee on Un-American Activities. That committee had recently recommended the dismissal of approximately 3,800 government employees, a list that was narrowed down to 36 by F.B.I. investigation. This was the atmosphere in which Smedley continued to speak. An F.B.I. agent noted that at a Rotary Club in Saratoga Springs on January 4, she defended Stilwell and attacked the Guomindang. She told the group that Stilwell had been dismissed because he had sought to supervise the distribution and use of lend-lease money given to the Guomindang. Smedley said that this money, meant for use in the fight against the Japanese, was being used instead to fight the Communists or was being eaten up by large-scale corruption.[16] During a ten-day lecture swing in late January, Smedley continued her attack on the Guomindang government. She urged the

United States to support the establishment of a coalition government that included the Communists and what she called progressive democrats, primarily Chinese intellectuals of the type represented by Dr. Sun Fo. The *New York Times* covered her talk at Vassar College.[17]

The event that best illustrates the growing split among the "old China hands" in early 1945 was a radio debate in which Smedley joined Walter Judd, Lin Yutang, and Harrison Forman of the *New York Herald Tribune* on NBC's "America's Town Meeting." Less than two years earlier, Smedley had privately praised Judd for delivering "the best and most learned speech [on China] to be made in Congress so far."[18] Now she found herself in direct conflict with both Judd and Lin Yutang. She wrote to Taylor on February 27:

> You were right, I nearly had a fight [on the air] with Lin Yutang. Before the program began I asked him why he didn't come right out and tell the public that he represents the Military Affairs Commission of the Chinese govt., and that he got a big fat check in American dollars from a Chinese govt. bank for his trip, etc. Lin turned pale yellow and screamed at me with all hands and legs flying in the air: "I'll sue you! I'll sue you! I'll sue you!" he screamed. He has not done so yet. . . .
>
> Well, I was on the verge of laughing a belly laugh when I finished Judd's famous letter [in which he mentions Guomindang] generals with venereal disease. . . . I wish you could have seen Judd's face after I read the letter. That is not even one-tenth of the letter. A magazine took it from me afterwards and it will be published. Judd will never write another letter until the day he dies, I think.* Afterwards, as I was leaving the Hall, Judd stopped me on the street to shake hands and say goodbye. Shaking hands, I said: "What a liar you are, Walter Judd—for a missionary, you did well at that." Then the fight began. He and I stood there debating everything all over again. Crowds coming from the hall stopped and closed in and before long the street was packed. Then the crowd began to take part, and I went to the reception next door. The crowd had Judd well in hand when I looked back. Lin left by some back door and refused even to come to the reception. But the bitch Emily Hahn came, and of course we [did] not speak.
>
> Town Hall says they have never had a more exciting meeting. The 2,000 people in the hall were packed [in]. Every seat was taken, then the platform [was] jammed with extra chairs, and [there were] crowds in the wings. They

---

* The infamous letter to which Smedley referred is from Dr. Walter Judd to another missionary, Logan Roots, in Hankou. The letter is dated Fenzhou, Shanxi province, January 14, 1938. As a medical missionary Judd commented at length on the conditions and politics of Guomindang troops as the Japanese were defeating them in Shanxi province. In the letter Judd favorably compared the Communist-led Eighth Route Army with the conduct of Guomindang troops and those of local warlord Yan Xishan. The full text is to be found in Smedley papers, Box I, item 55; Roots presumably passed the letter on to Smedley, who was staying in his home at the time of its receipt.

had to close the doors at 8 P.M. to keep out more crowds. I had friends in the audience who got so excited that one woman simply could not follow the arguments at times. Another could not come to the reception afterwards because she got a violent headache and had to go home to bed. You who only hear, cannot see the audience. Hundreds of Chinese were there, including the Ambassador and his gangster wife. . . . But not one Chinese democrat dared stand up and even ask a question. There were some there, including two secret members of the Chinese Democratic League in Chungking [Chongqing]. A friend of mine sat near two Chinese. Everytime I spoke they slid forward anxiously, and if I drubbed Judd or Lin, they slid back easily and smiled. It was like that all over the theater. The crowd straining forward and backward and around and about. When I read Judd's letter about venereal disease a yelp started to go up, but Denny, the master of ceremonies, ran from one side of the stage to the other, waving his arms to the crowds not to laugh. The audience was busting.

The F.B.I. sent two agents to cover the radio debate. They noted that Smedley accused the Chinese secret police of activities in the United States, but that one of their "reliable" informants had told them Smedley had "no foundation for the above allegations." [19] Apparently, from the files released, it did not interest the F.B.I. that the U.S. army still valued Smedley's information on military matters in China. As she wrote Taylor on February 27, she continued to make periodic trips to the army's special training school at Harvard, where she gave seminars to the graduate student officers. Talks such as these were not included in her file.

In addition to the public pressures on her, Smedley had been coping with the personal grief of Elizabeth Ames, whose sister had finally died in December. She also had to manage her own ambiguous feelings over the slow death from cancer of her sister, Myrtle Finney. In two letters to Taylor, she wrote:

> I don't know how I can drag my roots out of Yaddo. The woman who runs it is deeply attached to me. I've sort of taken the place of her sister, who was paralyzed and unable to speak for two years and who died last winter. So I'm bound in some obscure way because Elizabeth needs someone near her. She's a strange, reserved woman, disliked by most people. She insists that I make Yaddo my home. I do—but I've a hankering for Ojai.
>
> (March 27)

> Life has been depressing for me at times. My sister died about two weeks ago—of cancer. She kept calling for me, but you know what it costs to go and come from California. My disagreement with her made the situation all the more depressing and I became sick. I tried to telephone her but she was unconscious. While she was still conscious I wrote to her almost daily. She did not know she had cancer or that she was dying, so I wrote accordingly,

planning to have her come east next winter to see the play which I hope will be ready for the stage by that time. She had agreed to come. Then she died.

I'm working on my new book [on Zhu De] but the going is slow and painful. I keep trying to write a biography but it always turns out a novel. Then I start all over again.

Carlson is in the Pacific, but his Saipan wound has maimed him for life and he writes me that he will be forced to leave the service for good and return home. Why can't Ojai have him speak? [His] address [is] Escondido, Calif.

(June 1)

During the spring of 1945, Smedley once again set out on an extensive lecture tour to earn money. When it was over, she wrote Taylor: "I'm worn out, but I've earned a lump of money to do me for a year of writing" (June 1).

The F.B.I., continuing its investigation of Smedley, discovered from its newspaper morgue that she had been arrested on espionage charges in 1918. But apparently its agents never saw or requested the Justice Department's back files on the case, for they never noted any of its details. A check also was run on Wang Yong, the Chinese actress helping with background information for Smedley's play. F.B.I. agents who attended Smedley's lectures often described the composition of her audiences. For example, in their report on her speech at the Community Church in Boston on March 10, 1945, an attendance was noted of 450 people, 30 of whom were Chinese and "about 20 per cent" of whom were Negro. In attendance also was a professor [unnamed] from Cornell who had lived in Japan before the war. According to their files, he had contacted the F.B.I. after the speech because of his concern about the activities of Guomindang secret police agents among Chinese students in the United States. Describing them as Chinese "Gestapo," he relayed the information that two such agents were known to be at Harvard watching Chinese students there. He suggested that they interview Smedley on the subject and said that from talking to her and attending one of her lectures he was sure she was not a Communist. He described her as intelligent and said she stuck to factual material in her presentation. He also advised the F.B.I. to ask General Stilwell about Smedley, saying that he would vouch for her. There is no evidence in the F.B.I. files that Stilwell was ever interviewed by any intelligence agency on the subject of Smedley.[20]

The F.B.I. did, however, pay attention when Nationalist China lobbyist Alfred Kohlberg made a hostile reference to Smedley in a letter to the editor of the *New York Herald Tribune*. The agent reported:

"Kohlberg stated that inadequate and distorted as Miss Smedley's version of Guomindang-Communist differences is, her letter is of real value. It indicates the line of thought of certain groups with regard to the postwar dismemberment of China."[21] Kohlberg's letter is evidence that he had now made Smedley a target in a propaganda battle, with the F.B.I. watching.

On May 10, 1945, the F.B.I. first asked Whittaker Chambers, the senior Time-Life editor and former Communist, what he knew about Agnes Smedley. The file reads:

> Chambers recalled that sometime during 1936, he learned that Agnes Smedley, well-known writer and author of *Battle Hymn of China* [1943] and other works, was in New York and he told J. Peters (former treasurer of the Hungarian Communist newspaper) he would like to meet her. [Smedley was in China in 1936.] Peters said to meet Smedley in an Automat somewhere in the east '70s. . . . Smedley had said upon meeting him, "I thought I was going to meet Edwards [an alias of Gerhart Eisler]. . . .
>
> Chambers was asked whether he had any evidence of Communist affiliation of Smedley and he pointed out that he did not have any actual evidence but that everyone knows she is a Communist. He stated, "there is absolutely no question about it."
>
> [Chambers] recalled that Peters had close contact with her and that she always "hung around" the ninth floor of the [U.S. Communist Party's] headquarters.

According to the file, Chambers concluded by telling a story he thought he had heard from Earl Browder: that "Smedley's Chinese husband," a Communist, had been arrested and then killed by the Guomindang in Nanjing.[22] The Chambers interview about Smedley came six months after she had used strong language to criticize publicly the editing of China stories in *Time* magazine. At about the same time, on June 6, the journalist Mark Gayn was arrested by the F.B.I. as one of six principal suspects in the Amerasia espionage case. The F.B.I. had found Smedley's name in Gayn's address book and noted also that he had given Smedley's book a positive review.[23]

In the summer of 1945, Yaddo was still operating on a wartime footing; food supplies, especially meat, were still difficult to get, and the number of guests in residence was only slightly larger than it had been the previous two summers.* Smedley had first met one of them, the

---

* Besides Carson McCullers, the group at Yaddo included the writers Haru (Ayako) Ishigaki, Eleanor Clark, Howard Doughty, Jr., Kappo Phelan, Ruth Domino, Leonard Ehrlich, and Agnes Smedley; the composers Klance Blazek and Alexei Haieff; and the painters Hobson Pittman, Ester Rolick, and Eitaro Ishigaki (Virginia Spencer Carr, *The Lonely Hunter: A Biography of Carson McCullers* [New York, 1975], pp. 257–58).

painter Eitaro Ishigaki, through the sculptor Gertrude Boyle in Greenwich Village in 1918. Ayako, Eitaro's wife, had come to the United States in the 1920s as the daughter of a Japanese diplomat. In 1928 she met Eitaro in Greenwich Village and refused to return to Japan with her family. The two were married and in the 1930s became a part of a small group of antimilitarist Japanese exiles who after 1941 worked in various capacities for the U.S. government. To allay any possible fears and misunderstanding by the citizens of Saratoga Springs, the press release given by Yaddo to the local newspaper made the Ishigakis' loyalty perfectly clear: "Mr. and Mrs. Ishigaki are loyal Japanese now in the employ of our government. He is in the War Department and she is in the Office of War Information." [24] The Ishigakis' loyal friendship with Smedley over the next few years would eventually lead to their deportation.

Smedley received two important Chinese visitors during the summer of 1945. Dong Biwu's weekend visit in August with his interpreter put Smedley back in direct contact with the leadership of the Chinese Communist Party for the first time since she had seen Zhou Enlai in Chongqing in 1940. [25]

Dong Biwu (1886–1975) was one of the greybeards of the Chinese Communist revolutionary leadership. Along with Mao Zedong and eight others, he was a founder of the Chinese Communist Party in 1921. He had early been an associate of Sun Yat-sen, and during the period of Communist-Guomindang alliance (1924–27) he had become a leading Guomindang activist. (For example, he had played a key role as political officer in the successful Northern Expedition led by Chiang Kai-shek in 1926.) After Chiang's sudden bloody purge of Communists in 1927, Dong escaped to Japan disguised as a sailor. Forced by Japanese security police to flee again, he made his way to Moscow. Four years later he returned to China to join the leadership of the Communist Party at the Jiangxi Soviet in Ruijin. Dong first met Smedley as part of the negotiating team that flew into Xi'an with Zhou Enlai at the time of Chiang Kai-shek's kidnapping in December of 1936. He was also in Yan'an when Smedley was there in 1937, and the two had seen each other most recently in Chongqing, when Smedley had passed through in 1940.

On March 26, 1945, Chiang Kai-shek's Nationalist government had announced that it would send a ten-man delegation, including one Communist, to the inaugural meeting of the United Nations in June and July in San Francisco. The Communists wanted to send Zhou Enlai, but the leader of the delegation, Foreign Minister T. V. Soong, insisted on Dong, whom he had known in Wuhan in 1926–27. At the San

Francisco conference, Dong and his two aides remained inconspicuous,
and afterward they toured the United States for about four months. At
several press conferences, Dong called for a unified, democratic government and the avoidance of civil war in China, while at the same time
decrying the corruption of the Nationalist government. Oddly enough,
official Washington took little interest in Dong's visit—which is regret-
table, since it turned out to be the last visit to the United States by a
senior member of the Chinese Communist Party until the late 1970s.[26]

Smedley was exuberant in her welcome. She spent many hours walking in the woods of Yaddo with Dong, talking at length about Chinese
politics, and Dong gave her some of the materials for her Zhu De biography that she had requested in letters to China. It was a very informative visit for Smedley, but so quiet that it was barely remembered
by other Yaddo residents years later, when the F.B.I. gave it serious
attention.

Dong Biwu arrived in Yaddo on August 7, just one day after the first
atomic bomb was dropped on Hiroshima, and he doubtless discussed its
implications during his visit. Smedley thought possession of the bomb
would change the balance of power in Asia and worldwide, in part by
making the fate of anticolonialist movements more dependent than ever
on U.S. policy. For the Communists in China, she believed, it meant that
the Soviet Union could no longer be effective as a neutralizing force if
the United States chose to back the Nationalists in a civil war. She was
convinced that if the civil war were allowed to run its course without
Soviet or U.S. interference, the Chinese Communists would prevail. But
she feared that the United States, as sole possessor of the bomb, would
find the temptation to meddle in China too great.[27]

The September, 1945, Chicago Round Table conference on the future direction of U.S. policy toward China proved even more explosive
than Smedley's debate the previous February with Walter Judd and Lin
Yutang. It convinced her that public advocacy of a middle position had
finally become impossible and that it was time to "choose sides." Discussion papers written for the Round Table by Max Eastman, J. B.
Powell, Tillman Durdin, Dr. Walter Judd, Edgar Snow, and Smedley had
been distributed prior to the meeting. Writing before Dong Biwu's visit,
Smedley had argued that when the war was over, Chiang Kai-shek
would not be able to use "war necessity" as an excuse for delaying the
implementation of a democratic constitution and elections. She predicted that when the lend-lease money dried up, Chiang would no
longer be able to buy the cooperation of the coalition of military forces

that was propping up his government. Durdin's piece focused on the recent Sino-Soviet Treaty negotiated by T. V. Soong and Stalin, in which the two sides agreed that the Chinese Communists were to receive no material assistance from the Soviet Union. Snow's piece "Must China Go Red?" was written earlier, before the dropping of the atomic bomb or the Sino-Soviet treaty. It argued that leaders in both Britain and the United States ought to recognize legitimate Soviet security interests vis-à-vis China, because they had "frankly staked their future in history on making a success of keeping the peace by sharing world power with the Soviet Union."

Before Hiroshima and Nagasaki, many in the United States had been willing to concede the necessity of sharing world power with Russia. Now, however, some influential voices began to call for the United States to challenge the Soviet Union more aggressively for moral rather than political reasons. One of those voices belonged to Smedley's old friend J. B. Powell, who co-authored a paper with Max Eastman attacking the Chinese Communist Party. Claiming that the Guomindang "commands the loyalty of an immense majority of the Chinese everywhere," Powell and Eastman argued that all Communist actions in China had been "executed under orders from the Kremlin."

Dr. Walter Judd was much more subtle in his anti-Communist conclusions. Like Smedley, he was committed to the use of American influence to prevent European powers from reasserting colonial authority in Asia. He conceded that the real strength of the Chinese Communist Party was based on the democratic practices followed within the party itself, but he questioned whether either the CCP or the Guomindang, as a ruling party, would ever treat its opposition democratically. He then asserted that it had been the Communists who had refused to put their troops under American command, and that Chiang had always been loyal to the United States. He also claimed Chiang had told him that he had not wiped out the Communists because he was a Christian, not a barbarian. The thrust of Judd's final argument was basically religious and paternalistic in tone: the United States owed Chiang loyalty because he was a Christian convert who had stood by the United States in spite of hardship at home and criticism from abroad, even from America. He argued:

> But if after [the Chinese people] have held the line so valiantly they are let down and our commitments are not fulfilled, then there is no place they can go next time except to the Communists and a world class war, or to Japan and the world race war. If we fail this time, we will have two-thirds of the

people in the world who are colored against the one-third who are white. We can win all the battles, but we will still lose the war because they can out-work and undereat the white man, they will out-suffer him, they will outwait him, and they will outbreed him.

Are the Chinese, the most numerous and incomparably the strongest of the colored peoples, to stay on the side of the democracies, or are they to be driven in despair to the other side? The answer to that is still in our own hands. We must understand what we are up against, grit our teeth and stay at it until we get not just the defeat of Japan, but a victory which really frees China and assures all Asia of ultimate freedom as its people work and struggle and grow to full nationhood and independence.[28]

In a letter to Taylor written on September 7, shortly after the debate, Smedley described her own sense of betrayal:

Well, the U. of Chicago Round Table went off, but the real fight between Powell and me went on the evening and morning before the broadcast. Powell seems to be financed now by some powerful Fascist organization, and I sus-pect the National Manufacturers Assn. He's been lecturing before chambers of commerce and businessmen's clubs against Russia, and against every force that opposes the Guomindang dictatorship in China. They seem to have egged him on in grand style, so that he has now come out as a savage reac-tionary agitating for war against Russia unless Russia bows and goes [down] on her knees to American finance capital.

In the six-hour discussion with three U. of Chicago men the evening be-fore, in which Powell and I locked horns, Powell accused me of having been present and participating in the murder of two American missionaries who, he said, were murdered by the New Fourth Army "to celebrate a Russian national holiday." You know, I was so appalled that I could not even think, let alone speak. Prof. MacNair took Powell on and silenced him with facts, and I finally asked Powell if knowing me for years as he had, he really believed such an atrocious story. He said he "believed I knew more about the matter than I would admit." Then I replied: "Before your god and in the name of your god, you lie." And he fell silent.

That ghastly meeting went on from 6:30 to 12:30 P.M. Finally MacNair said to Powell (MacNair paced the floor), "You belong to two different worlds." And one of the other men echoed him.

No one knows why Powell has swung over to the reaction. He used to be a liberal—opposed to the Chinese Communists, indeed, yet always willing to protect free speech and press and never to allow his magazine to be used for vilification. He once fired a man for publishing a vicious article against me. Now he makes vicious charges himself.

My friends tell me that I did an excellent job on the radio. I hardly re-member what I said, for I did not sleep the night before because of Powell's change and his atrocious charges. Anyway, we are no longer friends. We are enemies.

The F.B.I. agent who monitored the Round Table Discussion over the radio drew the unfounded conclusion that Smedley "upheld Russia's intentions in the Far East."[29]

In the *New Republic* for November 26, 1945, Smedley reviewed Powell's book, *My Twenty-Five Years in China*. In a head-on attack, she accused him of having become a spokesman for American business interests in China. Although she praised him for having taken an early stand against Japanese imperialism and for behaving honorably and courageously during his imprisonment, she suggested that he had experienced China "through the eyes of a foreigner living in a treaty port. . . . History had passed him by." Smedley accused him of twisting facts to appeal to "American chauvinism," citing as one example his statement that no Chinese who had attended an American university in the United States or China had ever become a Communist. And she identified several other distortions by Powell that especially bothered her: that Communists within the Nationalist army were solely responsible for attacks on foreigners in 1927 in Nanjing; that Chiang Kai-shek had nothing to do with the massacre of 5,000 Chinese workers and students in Shanghai in 1927; that Mao Zedong and Zhu De were both "trained in Moscow under Trotsky and Radek"; and, finally, that during the Xi'an Incident, Mao, Zhu De, Zhou Enlai, and other Communists had gone to Xi'an "to confer with her." Although he had not named her, Powell had referred to Smedley in his book as the "American woman leftist . . . utilized by the Reds" who was part of an international plot to kidnap Chiang Kai-shek.

Powell, Judd, and Smedley had more in common than they would have liked to admit, but they felt forced to choose sides. Each took a "leap of faith" in support of the faction he or she thought could best lead the people of China. And as they became locked into defending their respective faiths, they lost sight of their common fight against poverty, racism, colonialism, and injustice and began to see each other as adversaries. Once friends, they became bitter enemies on the field of Cold War politics.

CHAPTER XIX

The Cold War Begins, 1945–1948

For Smedley, the period from 1945 to 1948 was relatively calm and productive. Most of her time was spent in upstate New York at Yaddo, where she stayed on at the personal invitation of its director, Elizabeth Ames, and managed to finish writing the first draft of her biography of Marshal Zhu De.[1] Her concentration seemed curiously aided by the growing Cold War atmosphere, civil war in China, and increasing attacks on her for her open support of the Chinese Communists. By 1946 she had become too controversial to be booked on the popular lecture circuit as she had been during 1944 and the spring of 1945. She continued to accept frequent public speaking engagements, but with the exception of one quick trip to Chicago, her appearances were confined to the Boston, New York, Albany-Schenectady axis and were often made before sympathetic left-of-center audiences. Her radio broadcasts also became fewer in number.

In the years 1946 through 1948 the F.B.I.'s interest in Smedley grew, but the intensity of its investigation fluctuated in response to outside political pressures from the right. In January of 1946, the bureau reported that it was investigating Smedley's old friend Mary Knoblauch in New York City. A field agent noted in frustration that Smedley had no phone at Yaddo and that he had been "advised that the subject had very few visitors." About the same time, however, army intelligence sent the bureau's Albany office a report on a Smedley lecture at the Old South Meeting House in Boston. In the course of the lecture Smedley had denied that she was a Communist, and this provoked an investigation into her background by the F.B.I.'s Boston bureau office. In their report, the Boston agents wrote that Smedley had been called a Communist in Elizabeth Dilling's book, *Red Network*. They noted that *Battle Hymn of China* had been offered by the Book Find Club, which, "according to information available locally," was "a Communist Book of the Month Club." They also pointed out that *Battle Hymn* had been favorably reviewed by Mark Gayn, who had been arrested the previous June as one of the six principals in the Amerasia espionage case.* The report ended with a melodramatic warning that "the subject was reported to at all times carry a sidearm of heavy calibre." [2]

On May 31, 1946, the F.B.I.'s New York bureau had "ascertained that the book entitled *Daughter of Earth* by Agnes Medley [*sic*], 1931 edition [*sic*] was out of publication—no copy available." From this point on, the name Medley was listed in the F.B.I. files as one of Smedley's "aliases." [3] On June 2, Albany agents tried round-the-clock physical surveillance for the first time, following Smedley from Yaddo to New York City. From the time she left until midnight on June 7, agents tailed Smedley and three Skidmore students with whom she had come to New York to attend a performance of *Oklahoma!* After tracking all four women for five days, the agents reported no suspicious behavior or contacts with possible espionage figures. Smedley had spent most of her time with Mary Knoblauch, whom the reporting agent described as "seventy years of age and childless, brilliant mind, quite hard of hearing, and slowly dying from a 'cause' with which the informant was not familiar." After this experience, the Albany bureau decided that future coverage of Smedley's activities could be handled through "spot checks." [4]

But in mid-July of 1946, F.B.I. headquarters in Washington put Smedley on its special Security Watch List. This was a list of suspected Soviet agents or spies, who were candidates for "custodial detention" if "their presence at liberty in this country in time of war or national emergency would be dangerous to the public peace and safety of the U.S. government." Smedley's Security Watch Index card was captioned simply "Smedley, Agnes: Native Born Communist." Noted below were various aliases, including Brundin, her married name, and biographical data

---

* On the Amerasia case see Chapter 18, note 23. The F.B.I. report neglected to say that Gayn was never indicted and charges against him were dropped by August, 1945.

that faithfully preserved the numerous typographical and factual errors that had crept into her file since 1944.[5]

This sudden upgrading of Smedley's case was not the result of any new information. It reflected the rising Cold War tensions in Washington: in the spring and summer of 1946, J. Edgar Hoover launched a concerted propaganda campaign against an alleged internal Communist conspiracy, and in the process Smedley and many other leftists in the public eye were elevated to Security Watch Index status.[6]

From the beginning, the aim of the Smedley investigation had been simple: find concrete evidence of her membership in the American Communist Party and her connections to the Soviet Union. The assumption behind this effort was likewise dazzling in its simplicity: if Smedley could be sympathetic to the Chinese Communists, she must be either a member of a Communist Party or a Soviet agent, or both.

In fact, of course, Smedley's independence from the American Communist Party was a matter of record. In 1937 the *Daily Worker* announced twice that she was not a party member. She was friendly with certain individual Communists, like Anna Louise Strong, but she had always kept her distance from the American Party itself. She was on particularly bad terms with the party leaders—most notably, Earl Browder, but also Grace and Manny Granich, with whom she had fought in Shanghai. In *Battle Hymn* she had gone out of her way to criticize the American Communist party. And in private and in public, she had repeatedly denied being a party member.

At this point the F.B.I. had no concrete evidence that Smedley was a Soviet agent—indeed, none existed. Despite this, the F.B.I. was convinced of her guilt, because she had not publicly and categorically denounced the Soviet Union. In fact, her attitude toward the Soviet Union in 1946 was complex. Smedley's independence from Moscow was a matter of record. Stalinism repulsed her, especially after she learned of the disappearance in 1938 and death in 1940 of Chattopadhyaya. When Anna Louise Strong, still a party member, visited Smedley at Yaddo on her way to Moscow in 1946, Elizabeth Ames's secretary reported to the F.B.I. that the two women had "bitter arguments relating to Communism, Stalinism, and Marxism."[7] On the other hand, the Cold War atmosphere, the atomic bomb, and her angry debates with Powell, Judd, and others had driven Smedley to the despairing conclusion that another World War was inevitable. Thus in April of 1945, when the Soviet Red Army became the first of the Allied armies to reach Berlin, she wrote Karin Michaelis:

It is a satisfaction to know that the Red Army took Berlin. It was of the utmost importance . . . that the Russians give the warning to all Fascists throughout the world of what will happen to anyone who tries to emulate Hitler. May they take warning—though I do not think they will. This is not the last war. So long as the capitalist system exists, it will try to smash any cooperative country that dares lift its head. We have so many American Fascists who would much rather have joined with the Nazis against the U.S.S.R. They will bide their time—and they will engineer another world war. You and I will not be on this earth by that time, but I am convinced that that will be the last world war and that a socialist system of society will thereafter rule the earth. I do not think that ruling classes learn anything from history.

This next world war, Smedley believed, would be fought for control of newly liberated colonial countries, whose only protector among the great powers was the Soviet Union. Because of its role as protector, then, the Soviet Union should not be attacked. And in the 1940s Smedley had come to feel that the United States had replaced Great Britain as the major enemy to legitimate national aspirations around the globe, particularly in China.

Smedley's lifelong involvement with radical Indian and Chinese nationalists led her to an early appreciation of what today is recognized as national communism, or the phenomenon of Communist parties rising to power on the crest of nationalist forces. By the 1940s Smedley saw it as natural and appropriate that the nationalist, anti-imperialist aspirations of a people should play the leading role in creating a socialist state and defining its foreign policy. Soviet Russian models no longer interested her, as they had briefly in the early 1930s. This is evident from her concern about Yugoslavia, as well as China and India.[8] But although she didn't want to attack Moscow, the potential protector of new socialist nations, she was afraid Moscow might not fulfill that role; she was concerned above all with the fate of the poor and oppressed in China, and the 1945 treaty with Chiang didn't look promising to her. Thus she was guarded in her reaction to the Sino-Soviet Treaty between Stalin and Chiang Kai-shek's Guomindang government signed in August of 1945. In public, the Communists in Yan'an had felt obliged to endorse the agreement; and in order to avoid further isolation from the Great Powers, they had begun negotiating directly for a political settlement and a coalition government with Chiang Kai-shek in Chongqing. But privately, the Chinese Communist leadership was surprised and angered. Smedley must have sensed this from discussion with Dong Biwu when he visited Yaddo, as well as with other Chinese friends on the left.

In an article for a compendium of diverse views on China published by the United Nations in the winter of 1945–46, she stated that the Chinese Communists would continue their efforts without Soviet support:

> On August 14, 1945, a Sino-Soviet treaty of alliance was signed in Moscow in an effort to prevent another world war. Conservative sections of the American press proclaimed that the treaty had "knocked the props out from under the Chinese Communists." One might ask, what props? For years Moscow had recognized and dealt with only the Guomindang Nationalist government. The only "props" on which Chinese Communists could depend were the Chinese people, whose interests they represented. Since the needs of the people had not changed, the Communist and guerrilla armies did not evaporate when the Sino-Soviet treaty was signed.*

Smedley's radio confrontation with Powell and Judd in August had foreshadowed a larger public debate over China policy that unfolded during the fall of 1945. Hearings on China in both the House and the Senate were climaxed by the appearance before the Senate Foreign Relations Committee of Ambassador Patrick Hurley, who charged that the foreign service officers under him were anti-Chiang and obstructive. Taken as a whole, these hearings and the public airing of views on China policy that went with them represented the first national debate on the subject. The results were inconclusive; support for Chiang Kai-shek remained ambiguous, neither increased nor reduced. In a sense, the Truman administration cut off the debate by dispatching World War II hero General George Marshall to China in December, 1945, on a special peacemaking mission which was to last until January, 1947. It was the failure of the Marshall mission to create a coalition government and prevent civil war, coupled with Chiang Kai-shek's losses on the battlefield in 1947 and 1948, that turned China policy into a major domestic political issue and produced the venomous debates in 1949 over "who lost China."[9]

In this controversy, many American scholars and journalists with expert knowledge of China sided neither with the Guomindang nor with

---

* Smedley's thirty-three-page article, entitled "Social Revolution," appeared in *China* (Berkeley and Los Angeles, 1946), edited by H. F. MacNair of the University of Chicago. (Until the mid-1950s, this book was widely used in college survey courses on Chinese history, culture, and thought.) Throughout her piece, Smedley stressed the importance of national communism and argued that the Communists were seen at the grassroots as a more democratic alternative to Chiang Kai-shek's government. Although she questioned the impartiality of America's China policy after Stilwell's dismissal, Smedley concluded her article by expressing hope that the Marshall peace mediation mission, then in its initial stages, would succeed.

the Communists. Their sympathies lay with a group of Chinese intellectuals, many of whom they knew personally, who had organized a new party, the Democratic League. China experts like John K. Fairbank of Harvard or the journalist T. H. White hoped that somehow these liberal democrats might emerge to lead a coalition government in Nanjing. Indeed, it was Chiang's systematic persecution of them between 1944 and 1946 that made Fairbank and White lose faith in the Guomindang government. Their cause célèbre came in 1946, when Professor Wen Yiduo, a nationally famous poet and literature professor, was gunned down in the streets of Kunming, and Yang Chao, a prominent journalist who worked closely with Western newsmen, was arrested and executed. Smedley helped to organize the protest petitions that promptly appeared in the *New York Times*. To her, the situation in China in 1946 reminded her of Shanghai in 1933, when the civil rights leader Yang Jie was murdered and Lu Xun launched his bitter attacks on the Guomindang government. The time had come, she thought, for liberals like Fairbank and White to choose between the Communists and the Guomindang. In her view, the Democratic League had no hope of success: its independent intellectuals, many of whom were her friends as well, simply had no military or mass support.[10]

Throughout the period between 1945 and 1948, with its maze of negotiations and intensifying civil war, Smedley depicted the Communists as the popular choice of the Chinese people. She publicly denounced the presence of U.S. Marines and naval forces in northern China coastal ports and their active defense of Chiang Kai-shek's interests against the Communist-led guerrillas in the surrounding countryside. On January 15, 1947, shortly after the failure of the Marshall mission, she wrote her friend Anna Wang in China about a confrontation she had had in Boston with Harvard professor Arthur Schlesinger, Jr., over the activities of the U.S. Marines.

In Boston I had a fierce and ugly fight with Arthur Schlesinger, an Associate Professor at Harvard and author of the new book *The Age of Jackson*, who told me with fierce anger:

"You whitewash everything the Chinese Communists do—such as the attack on the American Marines at Anping. They lied about that incident, yet you whitewash them."

My viewpoint is this: the American Marines had no right to be at Anping or at any other place in China. . . . If we had peaceful motives in China, we had no right to be transporting ammunition. If foreign troops were on the soil of the United States, I also would ambush them and kill as many as possible.

Schlesinger said: "The Communists denied attacking. They lied. There is such a thing as *truth*."

I replied: "You are taking a small truth and putting it above the major truth, which was that the Marines had no right to be there; that Chinese soil belongs to the Chinese people; and that we were there supporting a Fascist regime. The guerrillas had as much right to ambush that convoy as the French underground had to ambush German Nazis in France."

He said: "The Communists lied."

I said: "Marshall has lied, by commission and by omission. When he blames the Communists for the anti-American feeling in China, he lies. Anti-American feeling is nation-wide, affecting all classes of the Chinese people. There would be none if we did not arm and finance the enemies of the Chinese people."

Both [Schlesinger] and others in my audiences have spoken of the "totalitarian" goal of the Chinese Communists, but I have declared that they have not been afraid to arm the people, or to place democratic power in their hands. Then I have said time without number that our government is not opposed to totalitarianism, because we recognize, arm, and support it in China when we recognize and support the Guomindang and Chiang Kai-shek.

In my lectures I am stating also that a few weak liberals cannot establish a democratic government in China, and that Chiang has not the slightest intention of permitting a democratic government to be formed. He makes a few statements directed at ill-informed Americans, playing for American loans.

So far, I have been surprised to find that the public does not swallow Marshall's report without question. They are, above all, afraid of military men in such a key position[s]. . . . One man said if Roosevelt were alive, he might have such a man as Secretary of State without danger, because Roosevelt was stronger than such a man. But President Truman is so weak and so mediocre that Marshall will be master of the government—which means that our War Department will direct our foreign policy. Furthermore, even our Congress is much more reactionary than General Marshall, and its leaders have already announced their intention of insisting on a Chinese government without the Chinese Communists. Marshall will soon be called before the most powerful government body, the Senate Foreign Policy Committee, to testify. So I expect Marshall to bend before the reaction. That reaction is furthermore backed by great newspaper monopolies like Henry Luce's publications [and the] Scripps-Howard and Hearst combines.

As an old-fashioned advocate journalist, Smedley saw the American media as a sophisticated instrument of propaganda. In her view, the battle for control of the press and radio was being won in the mid-1940s by the political right. She continued in her letter to Anna Wang:

Henry Wallace [F.D.R.'s Vice President, 1941–45] and such men are fighting the reaction, but we are weak, financially, and our public organs cannot even attempt to compete with the great newspaper monopolies.

So far as I can see, nothing can offset the reactionary policy of our government toward China except the mass movement of the Chinese people. I hope the Communists and the democrats will entertain no illusions about this country or our policy. Our progressives will continue to fight as best we can, but we cannot really make any impression on [U.S.] policy toward China. The student movement threw a scare into our reactionary circles, and it is unfortunate that it has died down. I wish the [Chinese] Communists had someone with them who is conversant with American conditions and reactionary propaganda. For instance, Marshall accuses the Communists of [obstructing road and railway routes between Guomindang and Communist areas]. The Communists should put out releases charging that [these routes] are merely used to transport Guomindang armies for civil war [purposes] and that the actions of the Communists differ in no way from that of the French underground resistance against the Nazis and the government of Petain in France during the war.

Above all it is important to have such men as General Yang Jie [Guomindang general] make public statements [against U.S. involvement]. Otherwise Marshall will give the impression to the U.S.A. that only the Communists are anti-American.

We are in for a hard and bitter era in this country. Some people may take comfort in the coming depression, but that depression is the great danger, for when it comes, American men will enter the Army, Navy, and Air Force to earn a living. The capitalist class always solves its problems by war; and the danger is that with the coming depression we will have the dreaded Third World War. Even now many, many men have remained in the armed services or have rejoined, because they are afraid of unemployment in the future. My own nephew has done that. So the problem sits right on my own doorstep. My nephew lives on the West Coast, and a few letters from me can never offset the daily, hour-by-hour propaganda pounded into his head by the Army. He is typically American—politically ignorant. He does not even read my books, let alone others.

Teddy White's new book [*Thunder out of China*] has had a great influence on the country, but while a million people may read it, 12 million read such a weekly magazine as the *Saturday Evening Post*, while others have circulations of 3 to 15 million. Everyone today with even liberal ideas is being called a "fellow traveler" of the Communists, if not an outright "Red." Our people swallow the most amazingly superficial propaganda. I sometimes think that Madame Sun Yat-sen might have a very good influence on this country if she came for a lecture tour. But she would have to become tough to endure the slanderous campaign against her by the reactionary Chinese and Americans. Yet this country is the center of power, and what it does will be decisive. Only the mass power of the Chinese people is capable of disrupting its machinations. I sometimes grow sick with the very thought of the suffering the Chinese people must endure to offset the reaction of my own country. I want to come back to China, and as soon as my new book is finished, I shall come by some means.

Later, in a lecture in Chicago entitled "The Struggle for Democracy in China," Smedley tackled the charge that the Chinese Communists were "totalitarian." She described the occasion to Anna Wang on February 5:

The audience was tremendously enthusiastic. I was amazed with their response. There was only one hostile question—from a very finely dressed man student, who reminded me that Marshall says the Chinese Communists may advocate democracy today but they have a totalitarian Marxist goal. That is the one reactionary cry in this country today, and it is very important. . . . Speaking to the young man who asked the question, I asked:
"Have you ever studied Marxism?"
"No," he said.
"Neither have I, very much," I replied. "I am an American in that, I fear; and it is a weakness. For the majority of people [in the world] today are inspired by Marxist principles. I have read here and there, from the works of Marx and those that came after him. But not thoroughly. From what I have read, however, I have learned that human societies take on the coloring of their background—from the history and culture of specific countries. Chinese Communists are Chinese, rooted in the soil of their country. They have used Marxism as a method of understanding their history and culture. They indeed aim at a socialist system of society, but this does not mean that they will follow Soviet Russia, or America, or any other country. All they think and do is, and will be, influenced by their own history, culture, and needs. If they are forced, by a combination of Chinese and American reactionaries, to create a totalitarian system that denies civil rights to people, that will not be their fault. They may be forced to fight for their lives and the lives of their people, against all opposition. But from what I know of them, they would prefer it otherwise. They have believed in the power of persuasion. They have believed that they could convince even landlords to advance with them toward more progressive forms of government. During the war I saw them in action. I was often more "leftist" than they, for I could not believe that feudal landlords would surrender their stranglehold on the peasants without violence.
When we Americans say we fear totalitarianism, I question them because, if we feared totalitarianism, we would not support the totalitarian regime of Chiang Kai-shek. Yet we [have] supported that regime for the past twenty years, and we [have done] the same with Hitler, Mussolini, and Franco. We found nothing wrong with them, though they violated every aspect of democracy, denied civil rights to the people, and ruled by totalitarian violence. It is dishonest for our government to speak of totalitarianism of the Chinese Communists in some distant future while supporting Guomindang totalitarianism today."

Applause shook the building.

Yet, as I spoke, a woman sat in the front row and took down every word I said in shorthand. Later she asked me to lunch with her, and said she was from the Military Intelligence Service (54th Army Command). I had another engagement and did not lunch with her, which was too bad indeed. I should have gone.

How long it will be before I land in some concentration camp, I do not know. Our Congress is just like the beginnings of Nazi-ism.

I was also booked for a 15-minute broadcast in Chicago. The sponsor which puts on the program is a big department store. I sent in my script, as is required, and they . . . cancelled the broadcast because they said it was "controversial" and critical of General Marshall's statement. Two weeks before they had had Dr. Walter Judd on the same program, and he had advocated an all-out American support of the Chiang Kai-shek regime.

In the spring of 1947, as Cold War tensions increased in Europe, particularly in Greece, Smedley saw rightist conspiracies everywhere. A mirror image to her reaction was occurring on the right in American politics. In 1946 Smedley's former friend J. B. Powell had joined forces with polemicist Alfred Kohlberg to form the American China Policy Association, with Powell as its first president. Behind it coalesced the increasingly influential "China Lobby" of journalists and politicians, led by Henry and Claire Boothe Luce, who advocated increased U.S. aid for Chiang Kai-shek and opposition to the Chinese Communists. In March of 1947 the National Industrial Conference Board, a business group associated with the China Lobby, issued the following statement, which was duly recorded by the F.B.I.: "The pro-Chinese Communist propaganda in this country has been so pervasive that it has made it almost impossible for the American people to get an objective picture of the situation. The books, articles, and speeches of such persons as Agnes Smedley and others, forever smearing the legal government of China as 'Fascist' and misrepresenting the Communist quislings as mere agrarian reformers, all have supported and strengthened the official policy of appeasement." [11]

In the meantime, the F.B.I. had continued to focus its investigation of Smedley on her alleged connection to the Soviet Union. A late 1946 classified study of "Underground Soviet Espionage Organizations (NKVD) in Agencies of the U.S." said: "Agnes Smedley, for many years, has been an important fanatical Soviet propagandist and has made frequent trips to the Soviet Union and contiguous territory." [12] The trouble was that surveillance and mail censorship had still not produced any evidence of a direct Soviet connection or Communist Party membership. For the spring of 1947, the major entry in Smedley's file was a report that she was one of the signers of a letter sent to House Speaker Joseph Martin by the Civil Rights Congress protesting as a violation of the Bill of Rights the proposed Rankin Bill, which would fine and imprison school-teachers if they "conveyed the impression of sympathy with Communist ideology." Along with Smedley's were one hundred other names, including those of Archibald Cox, Elmer Benson (a former governor of Minnesota), Margaret Sanger, and Arthur Miller. In May of 1947 the Albany office of the F.B.I. announced that after watching Smedley for over three years they had found nothing illegal about her activities, and thus notified headquarters: "The Subject's name is being deleted from the Key Figure List of the Albany Division. In view of SAC Letter #44 dated April 17, 1947, it is not believed this subject warrants active investigation. It is requested that the Subject's name be removed from the Bureau's Key Figure List. This case is being closed in the Albany Office." [13]

During this period a network of Chinese friends living in New York gave Smedley their perspectives on conditions in China and on U.S. policy. Three of these friends were women: the actress Wang Yong, who helped Smedley with the play she was trying to write at Yaddo; Huang Shaoxiang, a student of American history who helped Smedley with translations; and the journalist Yang Gang. Not incidentally, all three were women of great accomplishment, and two of them later became victims of the Cultural Revolution.*

Yang Gang (1905–57) was the most experienced politically. In the mid-1930s she had participated in the student movement at Yenching

---

* Huang Shaoxiang was interviewed by the authors in Beijing. In the 1950s she wrote what became the standard work on American history in China, *Meiguo tongshi qian pian* (Beijing, rev. ed. 1979). As a faculty member of Beijing University, she was criticized severely during the Cultural Revolution for her American past. By the late 1970s she was working in a new Chinese Academy of Social Sciences in Beijing as the dean of China's America historians.

Wang Yong was arrested by U.S. immigration authorities in the early 1950s and finally deported, in part because of her association with Agnes Smedley. She then worked in Chinese theater during the 1950s and became increasingly critical of the overly stylized, ideologically restricted productions. She herself was first criticized in the anti-rightist campaign of 1957—ironically, for her relationships in America with figures like Pearl Buck. The attacks became vicious during the Cultural Revolution of the mid-1960s and Wang Yong died in prison. A memoir written in the 1950s about her life in America, *Liangzhong Meiguo ren,* was published posthumously in Beijing in 1980 and introduced apologetically by the great dramatist Xia Yan (Interviews with Wang Yong's husband, Xie Hegeng, and a friend, Frank Xu, as well as Xia Yan).

Yang Gang rose in the 1950s to be vice-editor of the *People's Daily* and one of the most important journalists in China. She too was often impatient and outspoken about the traditionalism and slow pace of Chinese journalism. Her suicide in 1957 was apparently for personal reasons and not, as has often been alleged in the West, because she was under political attack as a rightist (for which there is no evidence). Sources on Yang Gang are cited in note 14.

University in Beijing and had joined the Chinese Communist Party shortly thereafter. She moved to Shanghai in 1937 to become literary editor of the influential *Da Gong Bao*. After the Japanese occupation, she followed the paper first to Hong Kong and then, in 1941, to Guilin. She had left her daughter behind in Hong Kong and lost track of her after the Japanese took the city. She came to the United States via India in 1945 on a Radcliffe fellowship to study literature and to write a series of columns for the liberal non-Communist press in China about life in the United States. These columns included descriptions of racial prejudice in the South and on the streets of New York as well as positive portraits of individual Americans like Agnes Smedley. To Smedley, Yang Gang was like many of the heroines she had known and written about in China. The two women apparently saw each other often in New York and Boston until Yang Gang's departure in 1948. The writings of the two women about conditions in the United States and China in the 1940s are strikingly similar in point of view.[14]

One of the two most important senior figures in Smedley's circle of Chinese friends was Professor Chen Hansheng. Smedley had first met him in Shanghai in 1929, and it was he who introduced her to conditions in the Chinese countryside by taking her with him on an economic field survey outside the city of Wuxi in central China. In 1932, Smedley had hidden Chen and his wife, Susie Gu, from Guomindang police and smuggled them out of Shanghai in disguise, which, according to Chen, had saved their lives. When they arrived in New York in late 1945, Smedley had not seen them since 1941, in Hong Kong. Professor Chen remained in the United States until 1950, teaching and writing at Johns Hopkins, the University of Pennsylvania, and the University of Washington. He was also the designated representative of the Chinese Communist Party in the United States at the time. Although Chen traveled a great deal, he and Smedley kept in regular contact, and he and his wife visited Smedley at Yaddo on at least one occasion.[15]

Smedley's other important Chinese friend at this time was the writer Lao She, who had established his reputation in China in the 1930s with works like *Rickshaw Boy*, based on neighborhood life in the old capital of Beijing where he had grown up. Although he became bitterly opposed to the Guomindang during World War II, when he was head of the Chinese Writers Association, he was not a Communist. He came to the United States in 1946 at the invitation of the State Department, a translation of *Rickshaw Boy* having been a bestseller and Book of the Month Club selection in 1945. He remained in the United States for three years, in part to avoid assassination or imprisonment at the hands of the Guomindang police, who in 1946 had murdered his close friend and fellow writer Wen Yiduo. It was in the United States that Lao She completed what many today consider his masterpiece, *Four Generations under One Roof,* the story of a Beijing neighborhood during the eight years of Japanese occupation. Lao She returned to Beijing in the fall of 1949, angry about U.S. support for Chiang Kai-shek and doubtless also disturbed by the attacks being made on his friend Agnes Smedley at the time of his departure.[16]

Smedley and Lao She had met in China, probably first in 1938, in Hankou. Soon after he arrived in the United States in early 1946, they met again in New York and Smedley arranged with Mrs. Ames for him to come to Yaddo. Lao She lived in the Saratoga Springs area as Smedley's guest for about six weeks in August and September of 1946. For Smedley, his visit was invaluable to her work and a great boost to her spirits. They talked at length about patterns in modern Chinese history, the historical setting into which she was laboring to place Zhu De in her biography. Doubtless they also discussed the political situation in China; and it is quite conceivable that Smedley was a major source of Lao She's increasing disillusionment with U.S. policy toward China. By the time he left in 1949, his disgust extended to almost everything American, including films, ice cream, and Coca Cola. He allegedly committed suicide during the Cultural Revolution.*

During Lao She's visit to Yaddo, Smedley had been invited to speak to veterans' groups in Albany and Schenectady, New York. She took Lao She with her, and together they spoke on September 16 and October 15, 1946. The F.B.I. agent who was present noted that Smedley read letters from General Stilwell that were critical of the Guomindang government. In one letter, in reference to Chiang Kai-shek, Stilwell allegedly wrote that he did "not want to fight [along] with a skunk." Smedley's version was more colorful:

> Lao She went to town against American policy in China. To the question of a man who seemed to be a businessman in the audience—about Chinese attitudes toward American bankers and businessmen—Lao She said something

* In the 1950s Lao She was best known as a playwright and a prominent figure in the writers' union. During the Cultural Revolution, however, he came under heavy attack from Red Guards and was physically beaten. After such a beating in 1966 his death by drowning occurred: either his tormentors killed him or he committed suicide (the latter seems to be the view of most, but is not accepted by his widow, Hu Xieqing) (Interview with Hu Xieqing; see also Jonathan Spence, *Gate of Heavenly Peace: The Chinese and Their Revolution, 1895–1980* [New York, 1981], pp. 389–94).

like this: "We don't like you and we don't want you there. You support Chinese reactionaries and they support you. You have only one interest—to exploit the Chinese people."

A young G.I. who had been in Kunming stood up and complained against the Chinese. The minute Japan surrendered, he said, their attitude towards Americans changed. He was traveling in a jeep in the country, he said, and he immediately saw their attitude—they asked him when Americans were going to get out of China. The young fellow thought that pretty mean of the Chinese.

Lao She answered that one by telling the young fellow that every egg in the province of Yunnan had to be delivered to the Americans during the war; [and that] farm animals were also taken and slaughtered.

The young fellow said: "We paid for them."

"But the people had no eggs, no chickens, no meat at all," Lao She said. "You can't eat American bank notes."

"Oh," exclaimed the young fellow, "you mean you're thinking of it from the view of the peasant?"

"Certainly," said Lao She. "Even if you paid for it, our people had to do without food."

One fellow [recently returned] from China was wonderful. He said something like this: "They wanted us to get out just as we'd want foreign soldiers to get out of this country. Our fellows acted pretty bad—black marketeering, women, and a contempt for all Chinese. Now in India and in China both, I watched Indian and Chinese coolies loading or unloading our airplanes. . . . They were underfed and thin—they can't do as much work as an American. Or take General Chennault. I was in his air force. It was said that he owned an interest in every restaurant and wine shop in Kunming, and in every industry in the province. That was why he had such a conflict with Stilwell."

Another fellow from Chennault's air force said the same thing.[17]

In July of 1946, after much prodding by Dong Biwu and Anna Wang, Marshal Zhu De, the commander-in-chief of the Red Army and the subject of Smedley's biography in progress, sent her by courier more biographical materials about himself in Chinese, adding that he had faith in the American people's ability to move their government in the direction of supporting "peace and democracy" in China. When she finally received this letter in December of 1946, Smedley replied with a warning. She said she had heard rumors of a secret agreement between Chiang Kai-shek and Washington by which Qingdao would remain a permanent naval base for the U.S. Seventh Fleet. She said she believed that U.S. relations with China were "determined entirely by our War and Naval Departments" and that "the State Department does not even know what the policy is." She continued: "America is becoming a vast militaristic imperialism, but there is a serious storm brewing inside this country.

Within a year the storm may break. There are powerful reactionaries in this country [besides] Luce, Vandenberg, and others . . . and the most dangerous are the agents of the great banks and corporations who are in the Navy and War Departments with the highest ranks." As for the effectiveness of the organizations trying to counter Luce and the influence of the Navy and War departments, Smedley was gloomy. She told Zhu De: "The Committee [for a Democratic Far Eastern Policy] works under great financial hardship. We all support it and I am giving all my lecture fees to it. I wish I could say that we made a wide impression. [But we only] make a little impression on important people here and there." [18]

The Committee for a Democratic Far Eastern Policy had been formed in late 1945, at the time of the first public debate in Washington over postwar China policy. Its purpose was to lobby actively in Washington against the Guomindang, organize public rallies in support of "democratic" China, and, eventually, publish a monthly magazine, *Far East Spotlight*. For the old China hands among its founders, such as Edgar Snow, it represented an open break with Henry Luce and his umbrella organization, United China Relief, through which most private aid for China had been funneled during the war. The first chairperson of the Committee for a Democratic Far Eastern Policy was Smedley's good friend Evans Carlson.

From the beginning, Smedley supported the new committee and appeared regularly at its functions. She was on friendly terms with such leading committee activists as Elsie Cholmeley and Israel Epstein, but she stopped short of lending her name to the committee's letterhead or becoming involved in the organizational work. Her reasons were mostly personal. She was unwilling to work with certain activists such as Nym Wales and Ida Pruitt, with whom she had had poor relations since the 1930s, and later she became troubled by the increasing influence of the U.S. Communist Party on the organization. Moreover, she remained fiercely loyal to Dr. Robert K. Lin, who after the war became the Nationalist government's medical director, and to Mildred Price, who, as head of the China Aid Council of the United China Relief, was in charge of medical aid to China and continued to direct money and supplies to Dr. Lin. Some committee leaders, however, thought Price and Lin had "sold out" to the Nationalists. Smedley's solution was to position herself midway between Price's China Aid Council and the new committee by being friendly with both. She felt closest to the committee when it was led by Evans Carlson and was publicizing the anti-Guomindang position of General Joseph Stilwell. [19]

By 1946, General Stilwell was stationed in California and deeply depressed by the silence imposed upon him. He had deliberately not been brought to Washington to testify at China policy hearings in the fall of 1945 because of the controversy he might stir up. His rival, Claire Chennault, had Joseph Alsop to champion his case in print. But so far, Stilwell had no one to tell his side of the story of his conflict with Chiang Kai-shek. He had begun to confide in T. H. White and Brooks Atkinson in Chongqing at the time of his dismissal in 1944, but because he was still on active duty, he had to obey orders to limit his comments.

In late February of 1946, T. H. White gave a party in his New York apartment for General and Mrs. Stilwell, and Smedley was among the invited guests. She wrote on February 19 to her friend Aino Taylor in California:

> I returned tonight from a 24-hour trip to New York to see General Stilwell and Mrs. Stilwell. Teddy White gave a party of China people for them in his home. Present also were Eric Sevareid; Betty Graham (who is leaving soon for India as a freelance writer); Jack Belden, whose new French wife will have a baby any day now; Richard Watts, Jr.; Maxwell Stewart; Elsie Fairfax Cholmeley and Eppie; Major Schoyer; Annalee Jacoby; Harold and Viola Isaacs; and groups of others. Sevareid's new book will be out soon, Teddy White's book will be ready by June, Elsie's book will be ready about the same time, or appear at that time; all on China. . . .
>
> General Stilwell is . . . a very sad and lonely man. I wish Madame Sun could be induced to write him [so] he might know that the Chinese still honor him. Yesterday he spoke at the party and said he had no faith whatever in the Guomindang carrying out its side of the new military agreement; and he thinks that as soon as Marshall leaves the Guomindang will start killing again. C.K.S. [Chiang Kai-shek], he said, now faces an *idea,* and has not the slightest knowledge of the meaning of that idea; he thinks in military terms, and is not so very good in such matters either.

Smedley was one of those in whom the general confided, not only in letters but during a visit to Yaddo, when he was in the area to see his aunt. According to Smedley, they had long talks. He told her that he intended to resign in November of 1946 and write a book focusing on the Chinese situation.[20] But November would not be soon enough. Joseph Stilwell died suddenly from a heart attack in California on October 12, 1946.

For Smedley, the news was a terrible blow. She wrote to Taylor on October 22: "You perhaps read of the death of General Stilwell. . . . Now the facts of China will not be told from his viewpoint ever. He was a real democrat and his loss is irreparable." Quickly realizing the importance of the letters Stilwell had written to her, Smedley sent copies off to Israel Epstein, for use by the Committee for a Democratic Far Eastern Policy, and to Jack Belden, Upshire Evans, a Colonel Robins, and Elmer Benson of the National Citizens' Political Action Committee. She also urged that they get in touch with the former executive secretary of the American Veterans' Committee for access to Stilwell letters in their files. She added, however, that before publishing any letters they should first receive permission from Stilwell's widow, as she herself was, for the letters in her possession.[21]

Soon there was a consensus among Stilwell's China friends that some sort of book should be written presenting his point of view to the American public. Who should write it was the question. On December 18, 1946, Smedley wrote to Israel Epstein: "As for someone to do the Stilwell book, I am at sea. Frank Taylor asked Jack Belden to do it when he returns six months hence, and Jack gave some kind of tentative agreement. Only someone like Jack, very close to Stilwell, could write the book; and Mrs. Stilwell would never release papers to anyone who had not been close to him. Jack was the closest of all correspondents to him and he spent many days with Mrs. Stilwell after the General's death. Even at this, Mrs. Stilwell wrote me that she herself intends to write the book. I think she'll drop that after a few chapters. I am, of course, out of the running."

Smedley considered herself out of the running for a number of reasons. She realized that because of the attacks on her by Powell, Judd, Lin Yutang, and others, she was becoming notorious enough to injure Stilwell's credibility if she were to do the book. She had just been stung by her inability to place an article on Stilwell in either the *New Republic* or the *Nation*. Indeed, the *New Republic* had stopped publishing any of her articles and book reviews after 1945, and the *Nation* had followed suit after 1946. Moreover, she still considered her most important task the completion of her Zhu De biography. In the end, the Stilwell project fell to T. H. White, whose edition of the general's papers was published in 1948.[22]

In May of 1947, only eight months after Stilwell's death, Smedley suffered another grievous loss: Evans Carlson died suddenly, at the age of fifty-one. (He suffered a heart attack during a conversation with former Vice President Henry Wallace and Michael Straight, both of the *New Republic*, about the U.S. policy of support for Chiang Kai-shek.) Smedley attended the military funeral at Arlington National Cemetery, and on January 25, 1948, at the Roosevelt Hotel in New York, she delivered the main eulogy for Carlson at a memorial meeting of the Committee for a Democratic Far Eastern Policy. It was a speech full of righteous anger, sprinkled with quotations from Carlson's last letters to her.

Indeed, Smedley said, over the last two years—and especially after Stilwell's death in late 1946—she had watched Carlson grow more cynical and discouraged. He had called Winston Churchill's "Iron Curtain" speech at Fulton, Missouri, "the most arrogant insult to the American people from an Englishman since the time of George III," an attempt to arouse support for "bankrupt policies of colonialism, special privileges, human exploitation, and military balance-of-power alliances." He had become convinced, from bitter personal experience, that the name-calling and Red-baiting now common in U.S. politics were "designed to obscure the vigorously conducted campaign for economic domination of Eastern Asia by American industrial interests, which jeopardizes the political independence of Asiatic peoples." In concluding her eulogy, Smedley emphasized Carlson's commitment to building a new social order and a new foreign policy on the basis of Roosevelt's Four Freedoms: freedom of speech and worship, and freedom from want and fear.[23]

Smedley's F.B.I. file contained two reports on the Carlson memorial meeting. One stated that she chaired the proceedings; the other said it was chaired by Congressman Hugh DeLacey, who turned it over to Smedley to give the main eulogy. A brief summary of her remarks emphasized her point that Edgar Snow had helped to change Carlson from a reactionary to a "fighter for the people" at Beijing during the mid-1930s.[24]

By early 1948 the F.B.I.'s investigation of Smedley had intensified again. The agency was probing her activities in Germany in the 1920s by conducting interviews in New York with two old German acquaintances of Smedley's who were known to be "reliable" anti-Communists. But these two persons—internal evidence strongly suggests that they were Julian Gumperz and Karl Wittfogel—offered no proof of the long-sought Soviet connection. They emphasized Smedley's work with the Indian nationalists in Germany and said they were positive that she had not been a Comintern agent or a Communist Party member. One of them described her as an anarchist-syndicalist, and both added that party members at the time had thought her unreliable and emotionally unstable.[25]

The F.B.I. was taking a renewed interest because in October of 1947 it had received a summary report from General MacArthur's G-2 (the Far East command, Military Intelligence Section) which claimed that

Richard Sorge

Smedley had been connected to a Soviet spy ring in Tokyo before the war. This ring allegedly originated in Shanghai in the early 1930s and centered on Richard Sorge, who along with certain other members had been arrested in 1941 and executed by the Japanese. The sources of the allegations were Sorge's interrogation and Japanese police reports uncovered by MacArthur's intelligence chief, General Charles Willoughby, in Tokyo. The charges as summarized were undocumented but were provocative enough to cause J. Edgar Hoover to order increased surveillance and deeper investigation into Smedley's activities in the 1920s and 1930s. In a memorandum to district offices, Hoover said: "The Subject was active in Russian intelligence work in China from approximately 1930 to at least 1934. You are requested to be on the alert for any such present activities on part of the Subject." [26]

By December of 1947, guilt by association with Agnes Smedley had become a common feature of right-wing attacks on liberal organizations. For example, Smedley was named as a Communist Party member in an editorial in *Counter-Attack*, one of J. Edgar Hoover's favorite political journals. This editorial was part of a larger attack on Progressive Citizens of America, a civil liberties group that had defended Hollywood writers, directors, and producers who had recently been named as Communists or Communist sympathizers by the House Un-American Activities Committee. Smedley was a member of Progressive Citizens of America and one of sixty-five persons who had signed a public petition in defense of the Hollywood figures. [27]

On January 1 and 2, 1948, the *Chicago Tribune* carried a two-part news story, datelined Tokyo, which had been leaked to the reporter Walter Simmons by General MacArthur's intelligence chief, General Charles Willoughby. The story began: "Details of the most successful Communist espionage ring ever exposed, whose operation probably helped precipitate World War II, have been pieced together by the *Tribune* from once top-secret Japanese documents." Certainly the way the story was "pieced together" gave it a sensational slant that neatly coincided with the prevalent conservative view that the American media had been infiltrated by persons sympathetic to Moscow. One of the two reporters named in the story was the Swiss journalist Gunther Stein; the other was Agnes Smedley.

The *Tribune* story described Smedley as a former Colorado schoolteacher who had "aided radical movements in Asia for years" and "become a principal apologist" for the Chinese Communists. The writer, Walter Simmons, stopped short of saying that Smedley had actually been a member of the spy ring, but he quoted Sorge as "crediting" her with introducing him to his key accomplice, Ozaki Hotsumi. He emphasized that the spy ring had "picked the brains of their newsmen" and had used "left leaners" of all nationalities to gather facts "concerning the military and economic potentials of non-Russian countries" to be sent to Stalin.[28]

Yaddo had been a haven for Smedley during the war years. The small number of guests had included writer-refugees from war-torn Europe. All had been concerned with the progress of the war, including the Asian front, and Smedley's expertise was valued. But all that slowly changed after the war ended. By 1947, Smedley was feeling increasingly isolated at Yaddo as the new artists- and writers-in-residence were no longer preoccupied with the war. As pressure on her increased, Smedley's self-confidence in her writing ability began to waver. On November 12, 1947, she wrote to Malcolm Cowley:

> Since writing comes so hard to me, I always think I am not a writer. I have a feeling of guilt about my writing—as if I am an imposter who pretends to be a writer but is something else. There are two me's inside me: one that seems compelled to diddle with a typewriter and paper and without which my life would not be worth another day of living; the other me sits back and watches in disgust, sometimes with contempt, sometimes with despair. Guests at Yaddo have actively contributed to this latter state of mind—most of them do not consider me a writer in the fine, noble style. They turn to Joyce, Kafka, Sartre, etc, spending endless evenings splitting hairs about writing and writers, tossing lesser mortals into the burning pit. Kafka and Sartre bore me to tears, Joyce merely amuses me, in spots. You see, I lack the proper approach to writing. Instead of a perfectly balanced sentence with or without commas or periods, I see armies of barefoot peasants in China and other parts of the world reaching for the stars of humanity but being shot to death for their endeavors.

Earlier that summer she had written to Karin Michaelis of her frustration at not being able to finish the Zhu De biography, but she had ended with a more positive assessment of herself: "Do you remember my first book, written in your home? Without you that could never have been. I have written only five books in my life, which is a small harvest. But I have turned out thousands of political articles which have never been collected. I have no idea how much I have written in my life, but on the whole I'm rather contented. I have not been the writer I had hoped to become, but I have done fairly well with such poor equipment as I was fitted with in the beginning" (July 21, 1947).

Frustration with her writing, the deaths of Stilwell and Carlson, and

the increasingly vicious political attacks on her left Smedley feeling depressed, isolated, and vulnerable. But it was an event at Yaddo in the
spring of 1948 that turned her private mood of bitterness into one of
desperation. In late February of 1948 a public radio debate was held at
Skidmore College, Saratoga Springs, between a White Russian refugee,
Countess Tolstoy, and the Communist Party organizer of the northeastern subdistrict of New York State, Harold Klein. After the debate
Smedley held a reception and cocktail party for Klein in her room at
North Farms on the Yaddo estate. Some students from Skidmore attended. (F.B.I. informants later said Smedley "had tried to convert
[them] to the Communist cause.") When they heard about this event,
several townspeople from Saratoga Springs complained to Yaddo's Board
of Directors. In response to irate parents, Skidmore college officials
added their voice to the protest. They had already complained a few
months earlier after Smedley had disrupted a lecture at Skidmore by
rudely interrupting and attacking the speaker. Elizabeth Ames had expressed embarrassment then, but she now felt forced to confront Smedley, and a bitter quarrel ensued. With steely righteousness, Smedley insisted that she had a right to her own political views and did not have to
explain them or apologize for her guests to anyone. Mrs. Ames, seeing
no sign that the controversy would blow over, decided that in order to
protect the integrity of the Yaddo corporation, she had to ask Smedley
either to promise to be more discreet or to leave. Smedley's reaction was
shock followed by hysteria. On March 9, 1948, she moved abruptly out
of Yaddo, leaving most of her packed belongings behind until she could
find a place to live.[29]

United States, 1941–1950

Agnes Smedley with Dong Biwu, Chinese
Communist delegate to United Nations, August, 1945. (Courtesy of Ayako Ishigaki.)

Yaddo, summer of 1943.
From left to right: Hans
Sahl, Agnes Smedley,
Karin Michaelis, Lang-
ston Hughes, Carson
McCullers, and Alfred
Kantorowicz. (From the
collection of George S.
Bolster.)

On Yaddo grounds, 1946, with visitors. From
left to right: Yang Gang, unidentified man,
Agnes Smedley, and Chen Hansheng. (Courtesy of Chen Hansheng.)

Agnes Smedley speaking at memorial
service for Evans Carlson in New York,
January 25, 1948. (Courtesy of Hugh
Deane.)

A SURGE

.D HERE SINCE
TOTAL 1,500.

ector Advises Put-
hildren Showing
.ash Cold
.nptoms.

the old-fashioned red
severe kind—the real
appearing in epidemic
.re and in several other
nation this winter.
ted since January 1 to
ity health department
rs. Bessie W. Smith,
.e communicable dis-
aid today.

:TEADY RISE.

started in December,
City cases reported,
three cases in De-
It continued last
.1 cases, compared
January last year.
days of this month
.es were reported.
.idence is the high-
.5, when 1,741 cases
· the entire year.
-three cases were
y.
.hood disease, oc-
ike a young adult
.wn to all babies
hs old.
receding the rash
.esemble those of
. L. Dwyer, city
explained today.
nny nose, watery
and coughs from
before the rash
the last phase,
.ncubation period
· weeks.

CAUTION.

.r to bed when
.s appear," Dr.
call your doc-
.ments.
on that the
.on't force him
'arm and as

appears first
the hairline
.eal measles,

AMERICAN WOMAN INVOLVED IN SPY DIS-
CLOSURE—Agnes Smedley, an American writer, described as a native of a Missouri farm, shown in a camera
study made today before she conferred with her attorney
in New York. The United States army had released a report
on the amazing Russian spy ring which operated in the
Far East before the Pearl Harbor attack. The report
links Miss Smedley to the ring as its Shanghai operative
and states she is "a spy and agent of the Soviet government"—(Wirephoto).

MURDERED IN A TRAILER

VICTIM NEAR WELLINGTON A
RETIRED CHENEY FARMER.

Saturday Business Hours to
Prevail on Lincoln's Birthday.

Most places of business will op-
ate as usual on Saturday, Lincoln's birthday.

RED SPIES AT TOP

Army Reveals Startling Operations in Tokyo Before Attack
on Pearl Harbor.

TIP ON THRUST AT RUSSIA

Knowledge That Japs Would Not
Attack Siberia Set Up De-
fense Against Nazis.

STILL MAY BE MENACE

MacArthur Says Remnants of
Ring Could Be Active in
World Capitals.

(ADDITIONAL STORIES AND ILLUS-
TRATIONS RELATING TO THE SOVIET
SPY RING IN THE FAR EAST ON
PAGE 5.)

BY DAYTON MOORE.

Washington, Feb. 10.
(UP)—A Communist spy
ring, perhaps the mos·
successful of all time
kept Russia informed o
Japanese and Germa
war plans for nine year
before Pearl Harbor, th
army reported today.

The ring operated out
Tokyo. Its twenty memb
were headed by a Gern
Communist, Richard So
who posed as a Nazi journ:
and hoodwinked high Ger
as well as Japanese off

Tip to Nazi Attack

Sorge tipped off the]
that the Germans w·
Russia in June, '
Ozaki also rep·
nese would
against

Agnes Smedley in New York City on February 10, 1949, the day the army publicly accused her of being a Soviet spy.
(Kansas City *Star*.)

Agnes Smedley in her vegetable garden
at Sneeden's Landing, summer, 1949.
(Courtesy of Ayako Ishigaki.)

Rewi Alley, close friend from her
Shanghai days, at Agnes Smedley's grave
at Babaoshan, the Cemetery for Revolutionaries on the outskirts of Beijing,
March, 1978. (Photo by authors.)

CHAPTER XX

The Last Act, 1948–1950

By the time Agnes Smedley was leaving Yaddo under a cloud, the civil war in China had taken a dramatic turn. The Communist counter-offensive launched in late 1947 had proved more successful than any-one anticipated. Chiang Kai-shek's armies, badly overextended and poorly led, were quickly driven from Manchuria, and large numbers of Guomindang troops and their equipment were captured. The old guer-rilla capital of Yan'an in the northwest was recaptured. By April of 1948 the Communist armies were in control of the countryside north of the Yellow River, and major cities like Beijing and Tianjin were at their mercy. And it was reported that they were preparing a major campaign in Shandong, China's most populous coastal province, which straddles the mouth of the Yellow River.

This news from China cheered Smedley and relieved some of her anxiety about the break with Elizabeth Ames and the problem of find-ing food and shelter. In her speeches she spoke out more strongly than ever against the hopelessness and immorality of continued U.S. aid to Chiang Kai-shek. At the same time, however, her political enemies be-gan to attack her more vigorously and to lobby for more U.S. aid to Chiang Kai-shek. Thus Alfred Kohlberg, after a visit to Tokyo in which he stayed at General Willoughby's home, devoted an entire editorial in his magazine *Plain Talk* to Willoughby's still secret report that included the charges that Smedley was a Soviet spy, "at large" since 1930, who had engaged in "traitorous" conduct.[1]

Under pressure from Kohlberg and others, such as the editors of

Counter-Attack, to support their allegations, the F.B.I. was anxious to make a breakthrough in the Smedley case. Privately, Hoover was concerned about the lack of concrete evidence. In April of 1948, after receiving from the army copies of Willoughby's detailed sixty-four-page report about the Sorge spy ring and Agnes Smedley's role, he seemed unconvinced and commented in a memo to a bureau chief: "It is readily apparent that the author of the report was involved with motives to the detriment of facts regarding the operations of the Sorge group."[2] Moreover, Hoover saw little evidence as yet of a connection between the Sorge group in the Far East and Soviet espionage in the United States. In anticipation of future requests for more information about Smedley, the F.B.I. felt under pressure to find the necessary evidence. Hoover chastised his Albany bureau for having been half-hearted about the Smedley case and ordered them to continue their investigation of Smedley even though she had moved from their jurisdiction. The New York bureau was now given major responsibility for the case and was urged to step up the investigation of Smedley so as to produce every shred of evidence about her alleged Soviet spy connection.[3]

When Smedley fled Yaddo in March of 1948, she went first to Thorberg Brundin's farm at New Paltz and then, about two weeks later, to New York City, where she moved in with Mildred Price, a friend and China medical relief worker. As if to demonstrate that she could not be intimidated politically, she spoke publicly and wrote letters in adamant opposition to the proposed Mundt-Nixon bill in Congress, which would require the registration of alleged Communist-front organizations. Her China speeches became more strident. For example, at a "Get out of China" rally on April 4, 1948, in New York's garment district, she denounced U.S. imperialism in China and bluntly criticized General Marshall and President Truman. Sharing the podium with her were the singer Paul Robeson and the former warlord Feng Yuxiang, an old political opponent of Chiang Kai-shek's who had come to the United States to sell himself to Washington as a viable alternative to Chiang.* By sup-

---

* Paul Robeson (1898–1976), a Phi Beta Kappa at Rutgers, the first Black All-American football player, and a graduate of Columbia University Law School, was considered to be one of the most accomplished Black artists of his generation. Although he never joined the Communist Party, Robeson was well known as a fellow traveler. Like others who had suffered discrimination in the United States, Robeson found the alternative ideology as preached by the Soviet Union, championing the poor and minorities, to be attractive. Just as Smedley's defense of the Chinese Communist Party stiffened when she came under attack, Robeson's views on Russia were only reinforced by the personal attacks on him after the start of the Cold War. See Paul Robeson, *Here I Stand* (New York, 1958).

porting Feng, Smedley and the Committee for a Democratic Far Eastern Policy hoped to encourage the formation of some kind of new coalition government with the Communists that could end the civil war. But Feng was rebuffed in Washington and afterward stormed off to seek aid from Moscow. (He died in a ship fire while crossing the Black Sea.)[4]

By June Smedley had worked out a new living arrangement. Since her arrival in New York in 1942, she had kept in touch with her old friend Josephine Bennett and Bennett's husband, Ricard Brooks.* The Brookses, who knew Agnes well, foibles and all, now invited her to live with them at Sneeden's Landing, a village nestled in the woods near Palisades on the western bank of the Hudson River, about an hour by train from Manhattan. By mid-June Smedley had settled in at Sneeden's Landing and, with the F.B.I. watching, was giving speeches in nearby towns opposing the Nixon-Mundt bill and supporting Henry Wallace's 1948 presidential campaign on the Progressive Party ticket.[5] On September 13, in a letter to Aino Taylor, she described her new life on the banks of the Hudson and her return to large-scale gardening:

> I moved to the half-built country home of the Brooks family—old friends of mine—where I have a very small room and a private bath. The couple have also moved in and by winter the house will be in good condition. For weeks I abandoned my book—mental shock over conflict at Yaddo and, after coming here, the hammering of carpenters and the noise of workmen generally. So I put in a big garden—big enough for the three of us and for about a dozen families who are friends. I put in tomatoes (about 3 doz. plants) two dozen eggplants, 1 dozen peppers, broccoli, carrots, lettuce, turnips, beans every 2 weeks, New Zealand spinach, mustard spinach, 2 kinds of squash (6 huge hills of them). . . .
>
> To give you an idea of the garden; yesterday a large camp of veterans near here . . . held a big picnic to auction off things to raise money for the Wallace [for president] campaign. I sent boxes of fresh vegetables direct from the garden—they sold for $35. I supply some of the veterans with green vegetables regularly, supply two families near us, and send boxes to New York to a friend whenever I have a chance. My garden has been a sensation in this region, most of the others having partly failed. I had corn in the summer—until a raccoon got in and ate dozens of ears each night. . . .

* Jo Bennett, an heiress to a railroad fortune, had been Margaret Sanger's secretary when she met Smedley in 1919. She found in Smedley a common devotion to women's rights, the birth control movement, and Margaret Sanger, and the two became close friends. She had nursed Smedley back to health in Berlin after an appendicitis operation in 1927, and Smedley had visited her in Paris before leaving for China in 1928. In the early 1930s, she married Ricard Brooks, an independently wealthy mural and portrait painter, and Smedley had visited the couple in Paris in 1934. In 1948, Jo Bennett Brooks was still active in birth control work (*New York Times,* obituary of Ricard Brooks, June 23, 1954; interview with David and Mary Loth).

We have a house about 300 ft. from the Hudson—we sit on the verandah and look at the river below. There are great forests along the Hudson down to the city, you know, so it's very beautiful. This community is a kind of artists' community—largely people who commute to New York: theater people, musicians, composers, writers, a few professors and other professional people who live here but work in New York. But I see little of them. . . . My health has never been better—it is excellent since I left Yaddo. My ulcer has disappeared.

The autumn of 1948 was a relatively quiet and productive one for Smedley. She revised a draft of her Zhu De biography, and at the end of the year she sent it off to Knopf and then to Edgar Snow for a reading.[6] By this time, however, she had lost favor with the literary establishment of New York. Her booking agent for speaking engagements had dropped her. She rarely appeared on college campuses. Editors, and not only those at the *New Republic* and the *Nation,* were keeping their distance. Smedley was finding that she could now place articles only in the limited-circulation journals of the Socialist left, such as *Far East Spotlight* (published by the Committee for a Democratic Far Eastern Policy), *China Digest* (Hong Kong), and the *National Guardian* (New York). China lobbyists such as Judd and Powell would no longer debate her on the radio; her last radio broadcast had been in May of 1948, sponsored by the Committee for a Democratic Far Eastern Policy.[7]

When Smedley spoke on China publicly outside New York City, she was often heckled. In June of 1948, for example, there was much furor about her scheduled appearance before a veterans' group near Palisades. Armed with the accusations in Kohlberg's *Plain Talk* that Smedley was a traitor, a handful of local residents protested for a week before her talk. Smedley spoke anyway, without disruption, but the atmosphere was tense and reportedly she dropped the usual question-answer session. The press was hostile. The *New York Mirror* described her as "indifferent" to the local community around Palisades and ridiculed her "as a stocky woman whose varied hair dyes have become a topic of interest around Palisades."[8]

Anti-Communist sentiments had been fanned in August of 1948 by rumors leaked to the press about the testimony of Elizabeth Bentley, the "Red Spy Queen," to a New York grand jury (though no indictments were handed down). By December the wave of espionage stories and accusations of Communist infiltration within the U.S. government itself had reached a crest in the deadlocked confrontation between Whittaker Chambers and Alger Hiss. Although Chambers had been an F.B.I. informer since 1942, it was not until after December 2, 1948, when the House Un-American Activities Committee visited his farm to be shown the famous "pumpkin papers" that he changed his accusation against Hiss to include the charge of espionage on behalf of the Soviet Union. In the same month the committee also questioned Chambers about the Far East and Agnes Smedley, and it was at this time that he changed his story. In his 1945 F.B.I. interview, he had reported having a casual meeting with Smedley at *his* request, in an Automat in New York *in 1936;* he had added, "everyone knows that she is a Communist." Now, in December of 1948, he said the meeting had occurred *in 1935,* was not casual, and was not at his request: John Loomis Sherman, a member of the American Communist Party who was about to go to the Far East on a special mission and needed to see Smedley on official business, had asked Chambers to make contact with her.*

On December 31, the nationally syndicated columnist Drew Pearson wrote that Smedley was a key Soviet spy who had worked in Japan as a member of a Soviet spy ring from about 1934 to 1941.[9] Also about this time, leading China lobbyists like Kohlberg, Utley, and Judd, realizing that Chiang Kai-shek's position was virtually hopeless, began to adopt a new slogan: who lost China? Their answer, of course, was not Chiang Kai-shek. The war, they said, had been lost in the United States, in no small part because sympathizers and outright Communists like Agnes Smedley had succeeded in softening public opinion and weakening support—especially in the State Department—for the massive aid package that Chiang needed to remain in power.[10]

The year 1949 started quietly enough for Smedley. On January 21, she spoke in Palisades before the local Wallace for President Club with Liu Liangmo, the Christian Y.M.C.A. worker with whom she had worked so closely on medical aid in Changsha in 1938. It was a happy occasion, and she and Liu were very warm about the prospects for China's future. But January, it turned out, was the lull before the storm. On January 31, *Time* magazine falsely named Smedley as a contributor

---

* F.B.I. summaries of Chambers interviews are in 100–68282–139 and 103, p. 14; 61–6580–127, p. 241. Chambers was wrong, of course, in both versions: Smedley was in Shanghai in 1935 and 1936. It was at about this time that Chambers also told the F.B.I. that a letter from Smedley had been hand-carried to the New York office of the *New Masses* in 1932 by a young foreign service officer, O. Edmund Clubb. In 1951 Clubb was grilled at length about this incident by the House Committee and ultimately was forced to retire from the foreign service: O. E. Clubb, *The Witness and I* (New York, 1974). Chambers later changed his story about Smedley yet again (see note 37); for his final version, see Whittaker Chambers, *Witness* (New York, 1952), p. 399.

to the *Daily Worker,* the official organ of the American Communist Party.[11] On February 1, the army and the C.I.A. requested copies of all F.B.I. reports on Smedley. On February 8, a U.P.I. reporter informed the F.B.I. that the army was about to release a 33,000-word report on a Soviet spy ring in which Agnes Smedley was one of the key figures.[12] On February 10, at a press conference in Washington, Colonel George Eyster released the report. Eyster's report, based on Willoughby's report from General MacArthur's headquarters in Tokyo, described a wartime spy ring working for the Soviets in Japan; by supplying vital intelligence, it said, this ring helped the Russian armies turn back and defeat the Germans (absurd, since Sorge was arrested in 1941). The leaders of the ring were identified as Dr. Richard Sorge, a Russian posing as a Nazi press attaché in Tokyo, and a Japanese newspaperman and China expert, Ozaki Hotsumi, who was a friend of Prince Konoye's. Both were arrested by the Japanese in 1941, along with a number of others, and were executed in 1944. But the origins of the spy ring were traced back to Shanghai in 1929.

The gravest accusations against a living person were lodged against Agnes Smedley. She had indeed introduced Ozaki to Sorge in Shanghai in 1930, when all three were there as newspaper correspondents. Although there was no evidence of her involvement after 1934, the report flatly declared that Smedley was "still at large" as "a spy and agent of the Soviet government." Moreover, she was described as "one of the early perpetrators, if not the originator, of the hoax that the Chinese Communists were not Communists at all, but only local agrarian revolutionaries innocent of any Soviet connections." This view, the report alleged, had been so effectively popularized by Smedley that "today high American government officials find it difficult to believe any other interpretation of China's Communists."[13]

With her attorney, O. John Rogge, at her side, Smedley held a press conference in New York on the same day. (Rogge, a former assistant attorney general under President Roosevelt, was probably the best-known civil liberties lawyer in the country at this time.) She vehemently denied the allegations, saying that she had never been either a Soviet spy or an agent for any country. She also accused General MacArthur of sinister political motivations and said that his attack on her was linked to the fall of Chiang Kai-shek's regime in China.[14] That evening, on a Mutual Broadcasting System radio program, Smedley threw down a challenge: "General MacArthur proposed no action against me. He knows I am not guilty of the charges brought against me. He makes his charges while hiding behind the protection of a law which says that he, as a top Army official, cannot be sued for falsehood. I therefore call him a coward and a cad. I now say to him: waive your immunity, and I will sue you for libel." [15]

By the next day, February 11, the army spokesmen in Washington were having second thoughts. They made a flurry of requests to the F.B.I. for more information. Eyster was reluctant to release the full report to newsmen, saying that it "contained opinions as well as facts." [16] By February 16, he was telling the *New York Times* that the "report contained several opinions that are now embarrassing the Army here" and that he "believed that Miss Smedley should not have been mentioned by name until the appropriate authorities had investigated her." As much as possible, army officials in Washington were trying to place responsibility for the whole affair on MacArthur's headquarters in Tokyo. [17] Finally, on February 18, the army apologized publicly and retracted its charges against Smedley. The *Times* reported:

> The Army acknowledged publicly tonight that it had made a "faux pas" in releasing a "philosophical" report of Communist spying in Japan and China, and said it had no proof to back charges that Miss Smedley, U.S. author, had been a member of the alleged spy ring. [Colonel Eyster] stated firmly that it was not the Army's policy to issue statements making accusations against persons such as Miss Smedley "when the proof is not in our hands." He emphasized he was not saying there was no proof concerning Miss Smedley, but merely that "it was not in our hands at the time the report was issued." Colonel Eyster said it was not the policy of the U.S. government to "tar and feather people without proof." [18]

The reaction at Tokyo headquarters was indignation. The report had been written and sent to Washington in 1947 by MacArthur's chief of intelligence, General Charles A. Willoughby. Why was it being released now? But it was Smedley's threatened libel suit and the army's retraction a week later that really outraged Willoughby. On February 21, he held a press conference in Tokyo to announce that he would drop his military immunity so that Smedley could sue him. Smedley never took up his challenge, chiefly because of the expense involved and because she had already won an apology and retraction from the army. In any case, the secretary of the army, Kenneth C. Royall, refused to let Willoughby waive his immunity and tried to dismiss the whole affair on "Meet the Press" on February 25 as an "inadvertence." [19]

Undaunted, General Willoughby took the next year off to gather evidence in support of his charges. His efforts produced a special report to the House Un-American Activities Committee and a highly inflammatory book, *Shanghai Conspiracy* (1951). Neither one succeeded in proving that Smedley was a Communist Party member or agent or that her connection with Sorge and Ozaki extended beyond 1932. Nevertheless, Willoughby and his report were a cause célèbre with the China Lobby and have remained one to the present day with conservative groups like the John Birch Society.[20]

Like J. Edgar Hoover, army headquarters in Washington had been under increasing pressure from such China lobbyists as Alfred Kohlberg to release Willoughby's report. These lobbyists were distressed that army leaks to friendly reporters such as Walter Simmons, Drew Pearson, Joseph Alsop, and others had not received much attention. And Kohlberg, who was a close friend of Willoughby's, was particularly impatient with the army for sitting on the report. Disastrously, as it turned out, Colonel Meade buckled under the pressure and released the report without the approval of his boss, Secretary of the Army Kenneth Royall. On the same day the report was made public (February 10), Kohlberg held a press conference. He applauded the army's action and challenged "the Army and the F.B.I. to follow the lead of General MacArthur and make a full disclosure of the results of their investigations of Soviet spy rings." He added: "The two writers mentioned in the MacArthur report are now living in this city and . . . there should be some further account of their activities in this country."[21]

Not surprisingly, given Tokyo's reaction and Secretary Royall's embarrassment over the affair, the chief of intelligence for the army, Colonel Meade, and apparently also the information officer, Colonel Eyster, were removed, as the men responsible for releasing the report. Their transfers quieted a call on February 19 by two congressmen for an investigation into the army's motives and its handling of the entire affair.[22]

Press reaction to the release of the February 10 report and the army's subsequent retraction varied enormously. In lead articles for the March and April issues of *Plain Talk,* Kohlberg spoke for the right and the China Lobby: "The whitewashing of Agnes Smedley must not be permitted to victimize a great and esteemed soldier and to stain the honor of the U.S. Army." Henry Luce's *Time* and *Life,* the *New York Mirror,* the *Chicago Tribune,* and Scripps-Howard papers like the *World Telegram* all expressed the opinion that it was about time Communists like Agnes Smedley were exposed. On the left, the *Daily Worker* charged that the attack on Smedley was a response to the fall of Chiang Kai-shek and implied that MacArthur had ulterior political motives. In the middle were liberal editors and columnists like Marquis Childs and Harold Ickes writing for the *Nation,* the *New York Times,* the *Washington Star,* and the *New York Post.* They were shocked by the absence of concrete evidence to back up the charges and feared that despite the army's retraction, more witch-hunts lay ahead.[23]

The publicity given to the spy charges had serious repercussions in some unlikely places. Within a little more than a week after the February 18 retraction of the report, F.B.I. agents visited Yaddo and interviewed two of the four residents at the time, Edward Maisel and Elizabeth Hardwick, as well as the executive director, Elizabeth Ames. The main focus of the questioning was Agnes Smedley. Until Smedley had left Yaddo a year earlier, the F.B.I. had kept track of her for four years through Ames's secretary, who regularly "dropped off information at a certain place in Saratoga for forwarding to the F.B.I."[24] An open visit at this time, a year after Smedley's departure, could be seen as an ominous expression of concern about Smedley's long residence. And if the intention of the visit was also to intimidate, it certainly succeeded.

Startled by the F.B.I.'s sudden interest in an alleged Communist past at Yaddo, the four guests in residence—Hardwick, Maisel, Flannery O'Connor, and Robert Lowell—began to entertain suspicions about Elizabeth Ames. Of the four, only Maisel had ever met Smedley. Nevertheless, within days of the F.B.I. visit, the four of them, led by the poet Robert Lowell, got in touch with local board members and expressed their concern about the "sinister" atmosphere at Yaddo. They noted that the "F.B.I. seemed to have no confidence in either the words or motives of the executive director of Yaddo, Mrs. Ames . . . but thought she had protected Mrs. Smedley [*sic*] to the point of misrepresentation."[25] On February 26, 1949, a formal meeting of the board was convened at Yaddo to discuss the matter. The long-winded case against Mrs. Ames as delivered by Robert Lowell is summarized here by his biographer, Ian Hamilton:

> The transcript of the meeting makes fairly ugly reading. Lowell's introductory statement demands that Mrs. Ames be "fired" and that this action be "absolute, final and prompt." The "exact" charges were that "It is our impression that Mrs. Ames is somehow deeply and mysteriously involved in Mrs. Smedley's political activities," and that Mrs. Ames' personality is such that "she is totally unfitted for the position of executive director." Lowell goes on from this to employ "a very relevant figure of speech." Yaddo, he says, is a "body" and Mrs. Ames "a diseased organ, chronically poisoning the whole system, sometimes more, sometimes less, sometimes almost imperceptibly, sometimes, as now, fatally. . . ." Lowell then cross-examines the

other guests, extracting from each of them a series of supposedly damaging "impressions." Hardwick for example, testifies: "I personally feel that at times there is a discrepancy between Mrs. Ames' surface behavior and her true feelings, not toward me, but toward most matters. I only know the surface . . . I cannot read her heart." There is mention of other Communist writers who have been entertained at Yaddo, of a "proletarian novelist" called Leonard Ehrlich, who was a long time friend of Mrs. Ames and a frequent visitor at Yaddo, of Agnes Smedley's proselytizing among the students at nearby Skidmore College, of mysterious Japanese and East German visitors, of suspicious jokes about "Molotov cocktail parties," of Mrs. Ames' unpatriotic caution in her dealings with the F.B.I. and so on. All in all the "evidence" is a patchwork of devoured hearsay and rather desperate speculation: not one of the witnesses challenged Mrs. Ames' "surface" friendliness and efficiency.[26]

At the end of the meeting, Elizabeth Ames defended herself. She explained that she "felt indebted to [Smedley] after Marjorie [Ames's sister] died, as she had helped so much with the nursing and everything." This, she said, was why she had permitted Smedley to stay on so long. She did not apologize for Smedley's presence at Yaddo or back away from her earlier characterization (to Lowell) of Smedley as "an old-fashioned Jeffersonian Democrat." She was shocked and hurt by these attacks from guests with whom just ten days ago she had been on such amicable terms.[27]

Malcolm Cowley was present as a Yaddo board member, and he defended Smedley and Mrs. Ames. Nobody, he said, denied that Smedley was at times sympathetic to Communist causes, but he belittled the idea that she was either a Communist or a former espionage agent. The account in Smedley's F.B.I. file quoted Cowley as telling board members: "As early as 1940, [when] she had just left China . . . Smedley wrote me an eight-page letter from Los Angeles about her troubles, which were considerable. The [American] Communists were all turning on her. They were seeing to it that she did not get speaking engagements. She was hard up. After that, she came East and was working as a farmhand and wrote again that she had heard about Yaddo and I told her to write to Mrs. Ames."[28]

The meeting ended with an agreement to discuss the matter again and make a final decision at the board's next meeting in New York City at the end of March. The resulting scene at Yaddo is best described by Cowley in a letter to a friend:

> In the end nothing was done, nothing could be done, but everything was deferred to this new meeting in New York (in about two weeks or less) at which

some sort of decision must be taken. The guests departed, vowing to blacken the name of Yaddo in all literary circles and call a mass meeting of protest. The directors departed. I stayed one day because I had to do a big review and would be too tired to finish it if I waited till I got back to Connecticut, but then I left too, feeling as if I had been at a meeting of the Russian Writers' Union during a big purge. Elizabeth [Ames] went to a nursing home. Her secretary resigned. Yaddo was left like a stricken battlefield.[29]

Over the next three weeks, Lowell wrote circular letters to Yaddo alumni urging the dismissal of Mrs. Ames. A counter-petition in her defense was prepared by Malcolm Cowley, Alfred Kazin, John Cheever, and others. It was signed by a resounding fifty-one alumni, including many of Smedley's old Yaddo friends such as Katherine Anne Porter and Carson McCullers.[30] McCullers left Georgia immediately and came to New York to help defend Mrs. Ames. By the time the board met on March 26, its decision was a foregone conclusion: Mrs. Ames was reconfirmed as executive director. Robert Lowell, who probably never understood Mrs. Ames's role in the founding of Yaddo, took the overwhelming vote for her as a personal defeat.*

Thus for a month in March of 1949, Agnes Smedley became the talk of the town in New York literary circles. Unfortunately, much of this talk simply strengthened the impression that she was a dangerous radical, and quite possibly a Communist and a spy. As a result, she emerged from the affair an even greater pariah in the eyes of the New York literary establishment than she had been at the time of her expulsion from Yaddo a year earlier.

The army's release of the Tokyo spy report also jolted the F.B.I., which was suddenly put under pressure to provide more evidence of Smedley's Communist connections. Alfred Kohlberg, for example, called for the F.B.I. to make public what it knew about Smedley, and there was talk of a grand jury investigation into the Smedley case, in which the F.B.I. would have to play a major role.[31]

In the summary reports it had been sending to such other government agencies as the C.I.A. and Army Intelligence, the F.B.I. had

---

*Ian Hamilton, *Robert Lowell: A Biography* (New York, 1982), p. 152. Ironically, in February Lowell had been leading a campaign in defense of Ezra Pound; arguing that art stood above politics, he defended Pound's right to receive the Bollingen Prize for Poetry. Pound, of course, was a highly controversial choice because of his overt support of fascism during the war. The left opposition to Lowell argued that the prize should be withheld from Pound on moral and political grounds—precisely the grounds of Lowell's attack on Elizabeth Ames's qualifications to run an artists' colony. See Hamilton, chapter 10.

consistently indicated that Smedley was a Communist "according to reliable sources."[32] The problem was that it had only one "reliable" ex-Communist source who claimed to be sure that Smedley was a party member: that was Whittaker Chambers, and he had no evidence at all. Its interviews with such ex-Communists as Wittfogel and Gumperz, as well as Smedley's speeches and writings, tended to prove only that Smedley had been a Communist sympathizer or an "anarchist-syndicalist" in the 1920s—not a Comintern agent or Communist Party member. Moreover, the Sorge spy charges were as yet unsubstantiated. Hoover complained about the inattention the case had received and ordered an interagency review of the Smedley files.[33] In particular, he again criticized the Albany office for having "mishandled" the case.

In its response, the Albany office took a firm stand. It admitted an "inexcusable delay" in submitting reports, but added: "there was apparently nothing in the way of any pertinent activity by the subject in the Albany division to report." In answer to Director Hoover's question about why no action had been taken after the initial Sorge report was received in late 1947, the Albany bureau explained:

> It is to be noted that this [1947] summary discloses no pertinent data on subject's activities in the Far East beyond 1934. In fact, the last sentence of this summary states that Sorge informed one of his agents, Ozaki, that it was dangerous to have any further contact with subject. . . . Upon receipt of this summary the Albany office determined that subject still remained at the estate [Yaddo] and was doing nothing inconsistent with her occupation as a writer. She seldom left her residence and according to the informant [Mrs. Ames's secretary], she made no trips of any consequence. . . . Furthermore [up to 1949] investigation by the Albany and New York offices had failed to disclose current espionage activity on her part.[34]

The New York office, though more obliging in its answer to Hoover, was also troubled by the lack of evidence: "At no time has it been possible to definitely ascertain that Smedley has acted or is acting as an agent for the Soviets. The investigation revealed that she has maintained pro-Communist sympathies and associates with persons and organizations of like character. It is believed that a continuance of this investigation will undoubtedly compile additional information of the type already obtained."[35] To produce a breakthrough, New York recommended interviewing Smedley herself, by means of a grand jury subpoena if necessary. The interview should explore at length her "associations in Europe, particularly in Russia, the personalities with whom she was in contact in the Orient while working with the Chinese Communist armies, and the extent of her relations with Dr. Sorge." But after agreeing that Smedley's influence and associations in the United States deserved a major investigation, the New York office said that "great caution should be exercised to prevent any embarrassment to the Bureau in covering leads."[36] After the embarrassing publicity the army had just received, this warning was not lost on J. Edgar Hoover, who promptly rejected the idea of interviewing Smedley directly by means of a grand jury subpoena.

In March, after the F.B.I. learned—much to their chagrin, from a newspaper article two months after the fact—that Whittaker Chambers, in testimony given to House Un-American Activities Committee members in December, had implicated Smedley in possible espionage, they reinterviewed him. Chambers contradicted his 1945 F.B.I. account, as we have seen, but the F.B.I. report of the interview made no note of the discrepancy. As for Smedley being a Communist, it is unclear what Chambers had told the House Committee in December, but by March his language was more cautious than it had been in 1945: "I had no information that [Smedley] was a CP member, but gained the impression that she was at least a CP sympathizer."[37] As the year progressed, the F.B.I. interviewed several people who had known Smedley in China in the 1930s, including Tillman Durdin, Freda Utley, Harold Isaacs, and Frank Dorn. Smedley's first husband, Ernest Brundin, and his sister, Thorberg, were investigated, and Smedley's tax returns were examined. Smedley's mail and her movements around Sneeden's Landing were watched more closely.[38]

Of the journalists Smedley had known in China, most now avoided her. There were a few exceptions and Smedley welcomed a letter of support from one in March of 1949. T. H. White, writing from Italy, said:

> And even if I wrote you a long letter I couldn't begin to tell you how angry I feel at the s.o.b.'s who so casually smear a person of your record. Willoughby, whom I used to know, is an effeminate, evil old bastard. The last time I saw him (Manila, 1945) he was bawling the hell out of a Negro soldier in the middle of the street, saying: "You Nigger son-of-a-bitch what do you mean getting in my way!" He was saying it in that guttural foreign accent of his which always reminds me of the fact that his father was a Prussian general in Kaiser Wilhelm's army. For that jerk to set himself up as a steward of your loyalty is grotesque. . . . All of us all over the world who love you are standing by. . . . Somehow you and I and a number of others seem to have lived through a period when the spirit and the will counted; and are now caught up in the hands of mechanical men who measure faith by the yard and loyalty by lead counters."[39]

With F.B.I. surveillance both tightening and surfacing, Smedley was feeling like a hunted woman, much as she had in Shanghai when she was under the eyes of the French, British, and Chinese secret police. As before, her public reaction was one of defiance. In a short article for *Far East Spotlight* entitled "Tokyo Martyrs," she praised the contributions of Ozaki and Sorge as anti-Fascists. She also continued to send clothes and money to Ozaki's daughter in Tokyo.

In an inspired move, Smedley recruited the support of Harold Ickes, who had been Roosevelt's noisy and controversial secretary of the interior for over a decade. Although now in his mid-seventies, Ickes was still rambunctiously active as a syndicated columnist and sponsor of liberal causes in his daily column in the *New York Post*. He and Smedley had been in correspondence since late 1947 about the situation in China. In February and March, Smedley deliberately fed him derogatory material about Willoughby, hoping he would use it as ammunition in an attack on the China lobby, General MacArthur, and the Truman administration. Ickes embraced Smedley's cause with a vengeance. In two columns in mid-March, he called General Willoughby a racist and near-Fascist (among other things), with the desired effect: he put the China lobby and Willoughby temporarily on the defensive and kept them spluttering for years afterward.[40]

At O. John Rogge's suggestion, and perhaps to tweak the nose of the New York literary establishment, Smedley put in a symbolic appearance at a three-day Cultural and Scientific Conference for World Peace at the Waldorf Hotel at the end of March. The conference, organized by intellectuals who had backed Henry Wallace's Progressive Party campaign in 1948, was an effort to keep the Wallace movement alive and also to combat the growing Cold War mentality in the nation. The plan was to invite major Russian and Eastern European intellectuals to discuss contemporary culture with their American counterparts. Rogge, one of the conference's key organizers, wanted Smedley to appear at the meetings as a symbol of political repression in the United States.

The State Department denied visas to most of the Eastern Europeans who had been invited, but such major Soviet figures as the writer A. A. Fadayev and the composer Dmitry Shostakovich came. There were over a hundred participants on the American side, ranging politically from right to left, from Robert Lowell to Norman Mailer to Clifford Odets. Outside, demonstrators marched to protest the allegedly pro-Soviet point of view of the organizers and audience; inside, some writers, including Dwight MacDonald, Sidney Hook, and Robert Lowell, raised hostile questions whenever possible. The debates were heated and the polemical fallout in literary and political journals lasted for years.[41]

In general, in the continuing controversy the organizers lost more than they gained. In at least one case, there were tragic consequences. The literary critic F. O. Matthiessen, partly in response to the personal attacks against his politics, committed suicide the next year. Nor did Agnes Smedley emerge unscathed. Although she said little at the conference (China was not discussed), her photo appeared in the *New York Times*, and when she did speak she spoke in defense of the Soviet Union, asking rhetorically: "If 25 million Russians had not died in the war, would we be sitting here today?"[42] Thus in many of the articles written about the conference (and in historical works written years later), Smedley was tarred with the same brush as Matthiessen: she was called a staunchly unrepentant, Stalinist fellow traveler.[43]

Smedley recognized that she was irrevocably labeled in the public eye as a pro-Soviet fellow traveler and suspected Communist spy. The sad truth was that in 1949 Smedley's strongest tie to an Eastern bloc country was not to Russia, but to Yugoslavia. Since the middle of 1948, Yugoslavia under Marshal Tito had broken defiantly with the Warsaw Pact and Moscow's leadership. Smedley's sympathies with the Communist-led Yugoslav guerrilla movement dated back to her friendship and admiration for Dr. Borcic in Hankou in 1938. In public addresses in the 1940s she often drew parallels between the Yugoslav and Chinese Communist movements (a comparison that finally won scholarly acceptance in the 1960s). In 1949 Smedley was a regular visitor at the Yugoslav information bureau in New York and became especially close to one of its directors, Marjia Vilfan. Vilfan later wrote that there was no question in her mind that Smedley sympathized with the Yugoslavs in their fight against Soviet hegemony.[44]

Smedley still spoke at rallies, like the one in New York in June that was sponsored by the Committee for a Democratic Far Eastern Policy. The theme was "Hail New China—Ally for Peace," and appearing with her were the folksinger Pete Seeger, Henry Wallace, and Liu Liangmo, her old Y.M.C.A. friend from Changsha.[45] But in general, she was afraid that such appearances would do her sponsors more harm than good.*

---

* In October of 1949 Smedley wrote to Zhu De: "I was still known to the public as a suspected spy. I therefore refused to speak to many radical organizations, and appeared only before those that had some ability to protect themselves. I refused to speak to Communist audiences because the Communists have enough problems without being charged with entertaining a suspected spy."

By appearing at this particular rally, Smedley was trying to demonstrate neutrality about a major split that had developed within the committee. The issue was Anna Louise Strong. After her sudden expulsion from the Soviet Union and her return to New York in January of 1949, Strong had angered the American Communist Party by criticizing the Soviet Union in a series of articles for the *New York Herald Tribune*. As a result, committee leaders—Elsie Cholmeley, Maud Russell, and others—refused even to speak to Strong, and in reaction a number of Smedley's friends, notably Edgar Snow, resigned from the committee and boycotted its activities. Smedley, like Snow, was sympathetic to Strong. The two women had stayed in touch throughout the spring of 1949 and shared the same lawyer, O. John Rogge. On the other hand, Smedley remained on good terms with individual committee members and made a point of continuing to appear at their functions.[46]

Despite her public posture of defiance, Smedley was deeply depressed. As during earlier crises, her physical health reflected her state of mind. In mid-February of 1949, she wrote to a friend that she could not sleep at night without drugs, that she was having heart trouble, and that she felt exhausted all the time, as if she had suddenly grown ten years older. As on earlier occasions, she said the political atmosphere around her was a suffocating one of retrenchment and witch-hunts. She apologized for being so tired and depressed at the time of the Red Army's great triumph in China, and once again thought about escaping: "My friend, why didn't I go to China and become a Chinese citizen months ago? I could have worked in peace there. But this country is no place for anyone who loves liberty. A general can simply say 'A.S. is a spy and an agent of the Soviet govt.' because she defends China."[47]

But this crisis was different from earlier ones. In the past, Smedley had always been able to rely on a network of friends for material and spiritual help. In 1949, the remaining members of her network—the Brookses, Edgar Snow, Mildred Price, and Jack Belden—were almost daily becoming more vulnerable to political harassment because of their association with her. In the past, she had always had a sense of personal mission, a feeling that she was needed by others to do important work. After the Waldorf conference she felt useless and counterproductive. Her Communist friends were about to come to power in Beijing; Chiang Kai-shek was gone. What could she contribute now to the making of a new China? Perhaps she would only get in the way. Finally, her independence was being threatened by her inability to lecture or publish. And the prospect of becoming totally dependent upon friends, whether in the United States or in China, was unacceptable to her.

Ayako Ishigaki and her husband Eitaro, in New York City, were part of Smedley's network of supporters during the spring and summer of 1949. Eitaro had known Smedley since her Greenwich Village days after World War I and had renewed their friendship at Yaddo. Ayako later remembered that by June of 1949, Smedley's troubles were multiplying. At Sneeden's Landing, her hosts the Brookses were being harassed by local residents and boycotted by their relatives. A faction within the local American Legion spread the rumor that Smedley was signaling Russian ships going up and down the Hudson. F.B.I. surveillance also tightened. For weeks, two agents parked in front of the Brookses' home. To avoid being seen coming or going, Smedley sometimes hid in the trunk of their car. Not wanting to cause her friends more trouble of this sort, Smedley decided to leave and find a place to live in Manhattan.[48]

Before leaving for New York, however, Smedley found a moment of mirth in Sneeden's Landing, at the wedding of Edgar Snow to Lois Wheeler, a young actress. (Snow had been separated from his first wife, Nym Wales, since 1944 and had recently—over her protests—obtained a divorce. In the late 1970s, Wales still partially blamed Smedley, her old adversary, for the divorce.) Smedley took great delight in helping with the wedding plans. In fact, according to Lois, Smedley organized the entire affair, hiring the musicians and arranging the outside reception on the Brookses' patio. She infuriated the neighbors by filling the foyer with flowers "borrowed" from their gardens. For Smedley, it was great fun and an emotional release. But more basically, it was an expression of her friendship for Snow, who by this time was the most supportive and influential of her remaining friends from her China days.[49]

In July, Smedley moved in temporarily with Mildred Price in Manhattan. After a few weeks of futile apartment hunting, she took a room in a small residential hotel, the Carteret. It gave her privacy but cost more than she could afford, and to save money she often shared the costs of meals with Ayako and Eitaro.[50] At about this time she received another blow: her editors at Knopf wanted substantial revisions of her Zhu De manuscript. They were critical of her long quotes from Zhu De himself and her intensely sympathetic view of the Chinese Communist movement; and they asked her to write about the relationship between the Chinese Communists and Moscow, a subject she had not touched. Smedley became angry and began to suspect that Knopf's objections were the result of the worsening Cold War atmosphere and MacArthur's charges against her. She asked Edgar Snow for his opinion, but he said he agreed with many of Knopf's comments; the manuscript did need major revisions and shortening. In the end, Smedley decided to break with Knopf, revise her manuscript, and rely on Snow to help her edit it and find a new publisher.[51]

By August, Smedley's savings had run out. She had recently paid over $1,500 in legal fees, and had sent $500 to her brother in San Diego. Breaking with Knopf made her financial future seem even more precarious. The only solution she could see was to leave the country as soon as possible. She planned to live first in Europe, where it was cheaper, and finish her book and from there to arrange passage to China.[52]

Smedley had begun to apply for a passport in July, but she was rejected several times, with no reason being given. Friends such as Roger Baldwin tried to help, but to no avail. Finally Rogge, her attorney, was told by the passport division that she was not being given a passport because she was a Communist and the War Department had accused her of being a spy. In October, as a last resort, Smedley enlisted the help of Harold Ickes in applying pressure on the passport division head, Ruth Shipley. At last Shipley relented and Smedley was issued a passport that (according to letters from Smedley to Ickes) would expire in October of 1950 and be good only in England, Italy, and France. Although she was unaware of the reasons, these restrictions were tailored to meet the needs of the House Un-American Activities Committee. Its members planned to question Smedley in 1950 and perhaps bring her before a grand jury.[53]

In October of 1949, while Smedley was still waiting for her passport, Jawaharlal Nehru visited the United States for the first time, as prime minister of an independent India. It was an emotional and highly publicized trip, important not only symbolically but substantively, because Nehru was also seeking aid. Many people wanted to see Nehru, among them Agnes Smedley. The two had corresponded erratically since first meeting in Berlin in 1928, and in the 1940s Smedley had been comparing Nehru publicly with Jefferson as one of the great statesmen and democrats of our time. Twice after his arrival she tried to reach him by mail through the Indian embassy but received no answer. Then at a press conference in Washington, a friend of Smedley's asked Nehru why he had not answered her letters. Seemingly stunned, Nehru sent word to Smedley that she should call him that evening. Smedley called and could not get through to Nehru. She talked to a man she concluded must be an

F.B.I. agent posing as Nehru's secretary, since she knew that his real secretary was a woman. Eventually, by another means, she did succeed in having an hour privately with Nehru at his suite in the Waldorf in New York. He asked her about the new government in China, its leadership, its land reform policies, and so on. Smedley urged him to go to Beijing and see for himself. Nehru reassured her that his government would be recognizing the new Chinese government soon. Smedley also spoke about racial prejudice in the United States and her own situation. Nehru was politely sympathetic, but after their meeting Smedley confided to a Chinese friend that his condescension and "bourgeois behavior" had offended and disappointed her. Nehru did not renew a previous invitation to come to India.[54]

The interview with Nehru probably opened up old wounds for Smedley. Although she believed that she was being kept from Nehru by the F.B.I., it seems more likely that the Indian officials around Nehru were trying to keep him from seeing her. Some of them would have remembered her shrill public debates with Lajpat Rai and Kamaladevi Chattopadhyaya in 1927. And by 1949 she was too controversial for Indian leaders to embrace publicly. If Smedley guessed at any of this, it would have increased her sense of isolation.

Late in September, before she met Nehru, Smedley had received $2,000 in cash from an emissary of the new government in Beijing. The emissary was her oldest and closest Chinese friend, Professor Chen Hansheng, who with his wife, Susie Gu, had been in the United States since late 1945. The money was for the express purpose of returning to China.[55] During the week leading up to October 1, the day of the official establishment of the People's Republic of China, Smedley seemed happy and relaxed. She wrote a short article for the *National Guardian* in praise of the Communist triumph, and she brought a cake and candles to the Ishigakis' apartment for a celebration. When her passport finally came through at the end of October, she acted quickly. She left most of her papers and possessions with her friend Toni Willison, who lived in upstate New York near Yaddo, for later shipment to China. She urged Ayako not to see her off at dockside because of the omnipresence of the F.B.I. Ayako remembered her during those last days as a haggard, exhausted figure wearing an empty smile as she said goodbye.[56]

And indeed, Smedley was worried. Politically, she wondered if China needed her now, and she feared she might be useless. And as she had told Freda Utley in 1939, in her remarkable letter about the magic of Hankou, in China she had always felt herself an outsider, never understanding intuitively the rhythms, nuances, and moods of the society around her. Thus it was a sad figure whom Josephine Bennett Brooks, Chen Hansheng and his wife, and the Snows saw off at a New York pier on November 15, 1949. Smedley boarded an American liner bound for Le Havre, France; from there she would cross the channel and enter England, where friends awaited her.

Ship life buoyed her spirits. To begin with, no one on board seemed to know who she was. She was traveling tourist class and was especially active at cocktail hour, old-fashioned in hand. She mixed with the crew as much as with her fellow passengers. To her delight, a controversy developed over labor politics. The Red-baiting head of the National Maritime Union was on board, traveling first-class to London for a meeting. He and the crew got word in mid-passage that a riot and coup against him in New York had just been carried out by the left wing of his union. A meeting of union members was held, with all the crew participating and Smedley cheering on the sidelines. At issue were the racial and political biases of the union. Later Smedley met with a number of the Black crew members in her cabin, where they talked about Red-baiting in the union and her acquaintance with Paul Robeson. All in all, it was an exhilarating trip. When it was over, she used her connections with the crew to make off with satchels of surplus food for her friends in London.[57]

Upon disembarking at Le Havre, Smedley's high spirits were reinforced by her success with British customs officials, whom she cajoled into letting her bring in the extra food and provisions as gifts. England in 1949, of course, was still suffering major food shortages and rationing caused by the war.

Smedley was greeted in London by Hilda Selwyn-Clarke and Margaret Watson Sloss, old friends from Hong Kong. Hilda and her husband had sat out the war in a Japanese concentration camp, from which they emerged malnourished and white-haired. Hilda's husband was still in the colonial service as acting governor of the Seychelles Islands off the coast of Africa. Hilda and her teenaged daughter, Mary, remained in a large flat in Wimbledon, where a room and private bath awaited Smedley.[58]

The plan was that Smedley would stay with Hilda, complete the revisions on her book, and arrange to go to China as soon as diplomatic relations between London and Beijing were reestablished. Hilda was working a full eight-hour day as a Labour Party activist. Her daughter, Mary, was away at boarding school. Thus Smedley would be left alone to work on her book.

The first three days at Wimbledon were spent catching up and swapping stories. Smedley was initially impressed by the Labour government's achievements: the National Health Service, pensions for ordinary workers, and social welfare programs. She worried, however, about what she called "contaminations" from the United States. There were signs of growing Red-baiting by some British Labour leaders, and she saw this as symptomatic of trouble ahead. In foreign affairs she was concerned about vestiges of British imperialism in Asia and Africa. With Hilda Selwyn-Clarke especially, she argued about the British determination to retain Hong Kong.[59]

In general, during December and the holiday season with Hilda and her daughter Mary, Smedley was in good spirits, working on her book, baking apple pies, and feeling relatively hopeful about her personal future. At least that was the tone of the warm, chatty, circular letters she addressed at the time to "Dear family": Mildred Price, the Snows, Jo Brooks, and the Ishigakis. She also sent genial thank-you letters to Aino Taylor in California, who had been sending her packages of food, clothes, typing paper, and coffee. In these first letters from England, her pessimism and sarcasm seemed confined to discussions of the situation in America, which she characterized as one of growing fascism at home and imperialism abroad.

Through January and February of 1950, Smedley lived a secluded life at Wimbledon. She seldom went out and did almost no public speaking. Her social life was confined to joining Hilda and her Hong Kong friends at the Wimbledon flat, attending an occasional meeting of the Britain-China Friendship Association, or visiting with new friends she had made after speaking at a Chinese Student Union meeting. One of these new friends was Hu Ji'an, a Chinese Communist Party member who was working for a degree in international law. In 1978 Hu recalled that Smedley invited him and his friends to her flat for Chinese meals and wide-ranging discussions. He remembered being shocked at her describing the government of the Soviet Union as harshly autocratic and saying that she had no intention of returning to China through Moscow. She was also sharply critical of the British intention to retain Hong Kong.[60]

She had been keeping in direct touch with China by writing regularly to Anna Wang, sending parcels of books, film, and records to her through Zhou Enlai's trusted associate Gong Peng in Hong Kong. In London she made good use of the Chinese students as couriers. In April, for example, when Hu Ji'an came to say goodbye, she loaded him down with books and records for Gong Peng, Dr. George Hatem, and friends in Beijing.[61]

In early March of 1950, in a burst of energy Smedley wrote her last two articles. In both, she castigated the accelerated bombing of cities on the mainland China coast, being carried out by U.S. planes based at Chiang Kai-shek's refuge in Taiwan. Increasing tension in Korea and the bombing of the China coast, she argued, were being orchestrated by the United States—as represented in Tokyo by General MacArthur—in order to draw the Soviet Union into a major confrontation. This clash, she argued, would probably start in Korea or Indochina, and once it had started the "rattlesnake" Chiang Kai-shek would strike from Taiwan. Urging all "progressives" to rally around China, as they had once rallied to the Republicans in the Spanish Civil War of the mid-1930s, she wrote:

> A dreadful war plot is being hatched in the Far East, and it includes not only Formosa and Japan, but Indo-China. Yet the secret forces behind this plot are not yet known to the people of the world, certainly not to the peoples of Japan, America, Britain, and the peoples of some of the countries of Europe. To expose and protest, and finally to appeal to the people of America in particular, is the role of every peaceable man of the Western world. But it must be done soon, otherwise the plot will reach its fulfillment in a new world war, beginning in the Far East.[62]

Polemics of this sort now disturbed Hilda Selwyn-Clarke every morning at breakfast, as Smedley read the American news in the morning's *Herald Tribune*. And they seemed to be growing more vituperative, lasting longer, and consuming more of Smedley's energy—especially after she read that Senator McCarthy had made Owen Lattimore his number-one target in his crusade against the State Department.* Nonetheless, Smedley still saw her main task as finishing the biography of Zhu De, and she would usually spend the rest of the day working quietly on revisions. She was also reading: Margaret Mead's *Male and Female;* novels by a new British friend, James Aldridge; Morton Thompson's *The Cry and the Covenant;* and translations of Chinese poetry by Arthur Waley.

In a letter to Edgar Snow, her sympathy for the downtrodden seemed heightened by her own comfortable but socially isolated circumstances:

* In Senate subcommittee hearings in February, McCarthy accused Lattimore of being the Soviet Union's top secret agent in the United States. Lattimore was a professor at Johns Hopkins University and in 1941–42 had been an adviser to Chiang Kai-shek's government as well as to Washington. In testimony he was combative and apparently bested McCarthy in the hearings and in the press (see his *Ordeal by Slander* [New York, 1950]). A year later, however, probably because of the Korean War, it was a different story: the McCarran subcommittee was able to discredit Lattimore in the public eye and have him indicted for perjury (December 16, 1952). Although he was never convicted, his career and reputation were in tatters and he left the country.

"Day before yesterday I saw the Italian movie 'Bicycle Thief.' I went alone and stood in a queue for two solid hours to buy a ticket. It was worth it. That little child sits enthroned in my heart. God of gods, but the human animal is savage! On every hand, everywhere, the human being can look on the most appalling injustice, the most blatant poverty due to the ownership of the earth by a few, without rising in their wrath. I can never understand that, and it fills me with despair."[63] Within the confines of her Wimbledon flat, Smedley's identification with the poor was played out in a relationship with Hilda Selwyn-Clarke's charwoman. In a March 17 letter to Elvira, the mother of her California friend Aino Taylor, she wrote:

> I wish you could see this woman as she is generally, and see what her reaction was to the suit [a gift from Aino Taylor]. She is the mother of three children and her husband, a truck driver, has been in the hospital for weeks with a fractured spine. She is perhaps 42 but looks ten or more years older. She wears threadbare cotton dresses up to her scrawny knees, with an old apron over [the dress]. When she came this week I made coffee and she and I sat down together and drank it, with toast and butter. She was very uncomfortable sitting down with a "lady," until I told her I wasn't a lady but that my mother had been a charwoman and a washerwoman.
>
> I asked her about her child, her family, etc. Her mother, she said, had washed clothing and "charred" for a living. "We often lived on nothing but bread and drippings . . . for often we could not afford anything else. When I grew old enough I also began to char, and I still do. . . . Now why are you so good to me? This costume and the other things cost very, very much money. I could never save enough money to buy the costume and blouse. The children need so many things."
>
> I asked about eggs, which are soon to go off the rations. Well, she said, eggs are piled up because workers cannot afford to buy more than one egg for each child per week. It seems hard to understand, yet it is so. I had heard of that before but could hardly believe it.

In mid-March, Smedley's health took a dramatic turn for the worse. The stomach ulcer that had plagued her throughout her adult life began hemorrhaging painfully. Hilda finally persuaded her to see a local physician. He said she might need an operation, but for the time being he prescribed a strict diet of mild, soft foods and no smoking. According to Hilda, Smedley's mood was one of deep depression. Her outbursts at the breakfast table over the *Herald Tribune* became longer, almost hysterical, and a dangerous waste of energy. The arguments over Hong Kong were becoming sharply personal, and a distance was growing between the two women.[64]

By April, Smedley knew she was seriously ill but feared that an operation would delay her departure for China or even leave her an invalid. She was also feeling terribly alone, dependent, and unhappy in Hilda's flat. When Hilda's daughter Mary returned for Easter vacation, Agnes started nasty arguments about the additional noise in the house. On April 10, she sent a short and alarming note to Mildred Price in New York: "I've not written because I've been sick for three weeks and am still sick. I had an internal hemorrhage—this duodenal ulcer. The doctor urges me to have an operation, but I hesitate because one-fifth of my stomach would have to be cut away. I'm depressed about everything. Can't work, can't walk about, live on milk, and am sick of life."

On April 16, 1950, matters came to a head. Hilda returned from delivering her daughter back to boarding school to find Smedley gone. When Smedley returned that evening, they had a long and difficult talk. Smedley said that she was desperately unhappy and wanted to find a room by herself—that she needed to live like a monk. In the end, Hilda talked her into going to visit their mutual friend from Hong Kong, Margaret Sloss, in Oxford for a rest, after which she could return to live with Hilda under quieter and more restful conditions.[65]

Smedley took the train to Oxford the next day. She arrived sick, went straight to bed, and was soon taken to the University Hospital, where experts x-rayed and examined her. Their diagnosis was that two-thirds of her stomach would have to be removed—a major operation, but normally not life-threatening. By the end of April, as she was resting and waiting in the hospital for the operation, she wrote Hilda a series of notes, most of them medical and grim in tone. One of them ended: "I live in one hope—that I can go to China. But I doubt now that a Chinese embassy will ever arrive here. Nor do I see why it should. My time is running out" (April 29). In a letter to Jo Bennett Brooks on May 2, she tried joking about the prospects of death: "Margaret Sloss will notify you if I should go to join my ancestors—God forbid, for I've no interest in them. I'll hope to join the Chinese who [have died] for the revolution instead. How very interesting that would be! No research on my book— just talk with them! And what stories they could tell me! What a great loss I can't go to meet them—and do a few books on our talks!"[66] On the same day she wrote to Harold Ickes: "I expect to pass thru the operation, yet I have little interest. American Fascism, and what in reality is my exile, has caused this serious situation. I see no hope in sight for myself or for the U.S.A. I will be here for three weeks, then must recuperate someplace. I have longed for China but my passport confines me to England, France, and Italy. It expires in October. I prefer death to returning to the U.S.A. So I enter the operation in a very dark frame of mind. In case I do not recover, I bid you an affectionate farewell and send you my enduring thanks for all you have done to help in the past years."

As a precaution, Smedley also wrote a few letters of a more formal nature, spelling out what should be done with her royalties and her possessions in case of her death. The most important of these, dated April 28, she left with Margaret Sloss:[67]

> My Dear Margaret,
>   I don't expect to die under the operation before me, but in case I do, I'd like to inform you of a few things and ask you to do me a favor or two.
>   My last will is with my lawyer John Rogge. . . . I own no property. All I possess is with me: $1,900 in Government Bonds (in my purse) and a book of Thomas Cook's Travel Checks, also in my purse. I wish you to take the Cook's Travel Checks, and meet all expenses concerned with me, down to the very last. . . . I do not recall the exact terms of my will, but I think I left $1,000 of my Government Bonds to my little niece, Mary Smedley. All income from my books, everywhere, all go to General Zhu De, Commander-in-Chief of the People's Liberation Army of China, to do with as he wishes. . . . Which means the building of a strong and free China.
>   By the terms of the will, also, I have asked specifically that my body be cremated and my ashes sent to General Zhu De to be buried in China. Could you see to that? If the new embassy comes, they could be delivered to it to ship. I wish the simplest possible funeral, and the cheapest that can be had in these islands. I do not believe in wasting money on such things.
>   I am not a Christian and therefore wish no kind of religious rites over my body—absolutely none. I have had but one loyalty, one faith, and that was to the liberation of the poor and oppressed, and within that framework, to the Chinese revolution as it has now materialized. If the Chinese embassy arrives, I would be thankful if but one song were sung over my body: the Chinese national anthem, "Chee Lai" [Rise up]. As my heart and spirit have found no rest in any land on earth except China, I wish my ashes to live with the Chinese Revolutionary dead.
>   I thank you, Margaret, and I thank Hilda, for your friendship. We may differ in many ways, but you have nevertheless remained my friend.

Smedley's surgery was performed on the afternoon of May 5. By evening it was over, she was coming out of anesthesia, and Hilda wired friends in New York that she was all right. But the next day, May 6, 1950, Agnes Smedley died, with Margaret Sloss at her side. According to the death certificate, the cause of death was pneumonia, acute circulatory failure, and the effects of the partial gastrectomy the day before.

Within a month, the war that Smedley had predicted broke out in Korea, delaying the reestablishment of a Chinese diplomatic mission in

London. Eventually her ashes were taken to China by a British "people's delegation," and on May 6, 1951, after a long memorial meeting in Beijing, they were placed in the Cemetery for Revolutionaries in the western suburb of Babaoshan. The Chinese characters inscribed on her gravestone are in Zhu De's hand: "In memory of Agnes Smedley, American Revolutionary Writer and Friend of the Chinese People."

Conclusion

On May 7, 1950, Agnes Smedley made headlines for the last time in the U.S. press, when a spate of stories sought to explain her death in England under seemingly mysterious circumstances. Congressman Harold Velde, a former F.B.I. agent and zealous member of the House Un-American Activities Committee, accused "the Communists" of murdering her. Smedley, he argued, was about to return to the United States under subpoena and publicly reveal to his committee her activities as an espionage agent on behalf of the international Communist movement. Spokesmen for the new Chinese government in Beijing made the reverse accusation: Washington was responsible for Agnes Smedley's tragic death. Friends blamed the Cold War atmosphere, and some raised the possibility of suicide.[1]

Smedley's career as a journalist and champion of the downtrodden in China, India, and elsewhere was recalled at memorial meetings in New York City. Moving eulogies were given by Edgar Snow, Harold Ickes, General Stilwell's widow, and others. The obituaries in *Time* and *Newsweek* concentrated on General Willoughby's charge, made public in 1949, that Smedley was still "at large" as a Soviet spy. It was because of this charge that no member of Smedley's immediate family attended a memorial service or sent a message.

Shortly before her death, Smedley had predicted a war in Korea or Vietnam that would bring on a military confrontation between the United States and the Soviet Union over Asia. When war broke out in Korea a month after her death, it provoked a wave of anti-Communist hysteria and a witch-hunt led by the junior senator from Wisconsin, Joseph McCarthy. Smedley was mentioned frequently as the woman who conspired to weaken U.S. policy and bring the Communists to power in China. Alfred Kohlberg charged:

> Miss Smedley played an important part, by her writings and speeches, in bringing about the downfall of our friends in China, and the triumph of our enemies. General Douglas MacArthur revealed that she had acted as a Soviet espionage agent in connection with the Sorge spy ring.
>
> As a friend and adviser of General Stilwell, Agnes Smedley influenced that general's attitude. In his recent testimony General Marshall stated that he had been influenced in turn by General Stilwell. Americans who are confused about the situation in the Far East need not feel apologetic. The revealed confusion of General Marshall and General Stilwell, which stems in part from Agnes Smedley, who was not confused, furnishes a complete excuse for the confusion both in the press and in the public mind.[2]

Despite such allegations as Kohlberg's, the F.B.I. closed its investigation of Smedley on June 27, 1952. After acknowledging that there was no evidence of party membership, the report concluded: "No facts have been developed which would indicate that subject was engaged in espionage activity on behalf of a foreign government nor have any further facts been developed as to her alleged espionage activity in the Far East as alleged by the Dept. of Army in the Sorge Case."[3]

One of the last entries in Smedley's F.B.I. file—dated October 11, 1954—was a military intelligence report of an interview with an American soldier who had been taken prisoner by the Chinese during the Korean War; the soldier, it said, had been made to read portions of *Daughter of Earth* in an attempt to "educate" him about the evils of the capitalist system. This conveyed perfectly the extreme right's image of Smedley: she was the disloyal American whose willingness to show the weaknesses of the American system made her a tool the Communists could use in undermining the United States.[4]

The charge that Smedley was a simple tool of the Communists—or, as Freda Utley claimed, a naive fellow traveler—obscures the true nature of Smedley's political life and moral commitment, in all its disturbing complexity. Beginning with her days on the Socialist *Call* in 1919, Smedley understood political advocacy as the heart and soul of journalism. As a working journalist, she considered it a part of her job to interpret events from her own political point of view, regardless of ideological positions taken by those in power. Thus in the 1920s she spoke out against Comintern opposition to the creation of a united front in India led by the bourgeoisie; in the 1940s she supported the China Aid Council, which supplied medical aid to the Guomindang. Most significantly, in the mid-1930s, the Chinese Communist guerrillas she loved had rejected her application for party membership, precisely because of her individualism. Moreover, if she was ever used politically, she was well aware of it and accepted the possibility of being labeled an apologist. In December of 1936, when she made daily broadcasts from Xi'an to counter Guomindang propaganda about the kidnapping of Chiang Kai-shek, she knew what to expect.

By the time Smedley came under attack by General MacArthur's staff, she knew quite well that she could save herself personally if she would publicly denounce the Soviet Union and the American Communist Party. But as much as she hated some of the policies of the Soviet Union and despised the arrogance of many American Communists, she could not bring herself to do this. To Smedley, the Cold War rhetoric of the late 1940s seemed a reworking of the old British anti-Bolshevik propaganda of the late 1920s, a smokescreen designed to mask the building of a new American empire. Smedley was not convinced in 1950 that colonialism had been dealt a mortal blow, and she was bitterly disappointed with the United States for abandoning the anticolonial principles of the American Revolution. In addition, having witnessed Attorney General Palmer's anti-Bolshevik raids of the late 1910s and early 1920s, Smedley knew that politically innocent people would suffer as targets of indiscriminate ideological attacks by the right.

Throughout her life, Smedley's motivations for pragmatically aligning herself with the Communists were complex and varied from issue to issue. Also, she frequently defied both official Soviet and Chinese Communist positions, as when she voiced her support of Tito in 1948 and 1949. Although she considered violence a last resort, to be applied only after democratic processes had broken down, she accepted the Communist premise that only the threat of violence would cause a redistribution of power, an end to imperialism, and the redressing of social wrongs.

Loyalty was the most troublesome ethical issue that Smedley faced throughout her life. Interestingly enough, from the very beginning of her career the groups for which she chose to fight were reluctant to embrace her as one of their own. Even after her death, the embrace has been hesitant. To all, she lacked the key qualification for membership, the willingness to express uncritical public loyalty to an image or cause. Time and again she was denounced as a heretic because she was unwilling to accept the classification of anyone as an enemy if she herself judged that person to have good motives and ethical principles. When she defended such people as Dr. Robert K. Lin, Bishop Roots, and Anna Louise Strong and when she refused to renounce her American, Indian, and Chinese friends, she paid a political price. Smedley's insistence on the paramount right to decide for herself made her a thorn in the side of all groups and organizations. Although she publicly championed the Chinese Communist cause, Smedley openly criticized individuals she did not like, including Mao Zedong and Mme. Sun Yat-sen. Although she advocated birth control and Indian nationalism, she refused to idealize either women or Indians as a group.

Psychoanalysis in the 1920s helped Smedley turn her rage into creative anger, but it could not completely heal the wounds inflicted on her by the poverty of her youth and the discrimination she experienced as a woman. In her personal relationships, Smedley consistently took risks by insisting that any friend or lover must accept her exactly as she was. Throughout her life, sponsors or patrons tried to co-opt Smedley as an Eliza Doolittle figure, the lower-class girl who could be molded and made respectable. But Smedley remained fiercely independent, and in each case it was unclear at the end who had influenced whom the most, patron or protégé. After analysis, she decided never to let a personal relationship compromise her professionally or politically. Her feminism focused on causes such as birth control, which offered increased freedom and power to women.

Smedley's extreme militancy made her pursuit of feminist emancipation most difficult and contradictory for her. Her attempt to resolve her own sexual conflict by renouncing the interdependence of men and women came at the cost of some loneliness, but it was this position—combined with her blatant refusal to abandon sexual pleasure in her thirties and forties—that made her an embarrassing maverick, not only to the public at large but to most of the women with whom she worked.

Smedley was once described as living in a world "full of dragons which she is forever battling."[5] Impetuous, often tactless, and always restless, her behavior bordered on the melodramatic. When depressed or feeling insecure, she often collapsed physically. But just as often, and seemingly overnight, she would bounce back to meet a major physical or political challenge with a burst of energy. Then she was happiest: singing cowboy songs, reciting bawdy limericks, organizing dancing parties, and madly gardening.

From the first years of her involvement with the Indian nationalist movement, Smedley idealized the martyr to principle. In 1949, although hunted and isolated, and even deserted by most of her liberal friends, she felt a certain sense of satisfaction in seeing what others had called her expressions of paranoia vindicated by the attacks from the right.[6] These attacks became part of a self-fulfilling prophecy, reinforcing her belief that the struggle for liberation from poverty and ignorance was a war in the literal sense, one in which she herself had become a martyr to principle.

Smedley's faith in the Chinese Revolution as led by the Communists sprang from the democratic spirit she had seen in the guerrilla armies with which she lived in the 1930s. That this democratic promise has yet to be fulfilled in the 1980s would have deeply disappointed her, and one wonders how she would have reacted to events in China during the 1950s and 1960s. Like Smedley herself, many of her close Chinese friends—the independent intellectuals Lao She and Liu Liangmo, for example, and the dedicated Communists Chen Hansheng, Zhou Libo, and Ding Ling—were eventually accused of disloyalty and punished when they criticized government policies or decried the lack of democracy within the Communist Party. It was a hopeful sign in 1978 when the Communist Party of China publicly acknowledged that the policy of treating these intellectuals as enemies had been a tragic mistake.

To the end, Agnes Smedley was a self-appointed warrior, a freedom fighter for the poor and powerless. She was also a fanatic gardener, a mother-figure for homeless "little devils," and a woman who organized rickshaw pullers in Hankou to transport wounded soldiers. While she threw herself into practical work, such as medical relief in China, she assaulted the consciences of the rich and privileged, whom she bullied, cajoled, entertained, and insulted with lower-class bawdiness, defiance, and passion.

Smedley's militant and creative use of personal rage evoke the same disturbing emotions as do the images of the poor we find in the etchings by her friend Käthe Kollwitz. Like Kollwitz and Emma Goldman, she did not romanticize the poor or the working class, and she never glorified their way of life. Indeed, most of her close friends were from the middle and upper classes. And it may have been precisely this, her success in sending a radical message across class boundaries, that most frightened such China lobbyists as Kohlberg and Judd. The events of the last years of her life led Smedley to believe that American capitalist interests were opposed to the interests of the poor—in China and India, but implicitly in America as well.

Throughout her life, in her writings and her public statements, Smedley's self-appointed task was to communicate the desperate, endless nightmare of poverty and ignorance. Her goal was the overthrow of these two dragons. Her life was a battle, without truce or compromise, to that end.

Notes

1. BITTER ROOTS, 1892–1912

1. Although Smedley was still considered an embarrassment to most kinfolk living in the area in 1976, two widows were more than willing to talk about her. At the foot of a hill, one road over from Main Street, lived Mamie Weston Mc-Cullough, the one remaining friend from Agnes Smedley's childhood. At the top of the hill, in a larger house filled with porcelain figurines and patriotic pictures painted by the owner, lived the other widow, Ruth Ralls Fisher, former Republican Party county chairwoman, town historian, and remote Smedley relation.

2. Goodspeed Publishing Co., *History of Adair, Sullivan, Putnam and Schuyler Counties, Missouri* (Chicago, 1888), pp. 80, 192; Ruth Ralls Fisher, *This Small Town—Osgood* (Milan, Missouri, 1975), pp. 28–31.

3. The Smedley family Bible, in the possession (1976) of Elizabeth Smedley, Chula Vista, California, records Charles (b. October, 1863; died September, 1936) and other children: Nellie (b. September 12, 1889; d. September 13, 1909), Myrtle (b. March 11, 1894; d. May 22, 1945), John (b. August 25, 1896; d. April 12, 1917), and Sam (b. October 3, 1899; d. August 11, 1952).

4. In school Agnes was especially good at spelldowns. Agnes and Mamie had a pact: neither would ever spell down the other. Mamie remembers Agnes as a "smart girl, smarter than her older sister Nellie, but not so spunky as Myrtle" (her younger sister).

5. Data from exhibits and materials at Colorado Historical Society, Trinidad (Baca House, Bloom House, and Pioneer Museum); photographs at Altman Studio (Trinidad); *Trinidad City Directory* (Trinidad, 1904–1910), vols. for 1904 to 1910, at Trinidad Public Library.

6. U.S. Commission on Industrial Relations, *Final Report* (Washington, D.C., 1916), vols. 7, 8; quote is from George P. West's preliminary report on the Colorado mines to the commission, dated 1914 and cited in Allan Nevins, *John*

D. Rockefeller (New York, 1940), p. 667; see also Graham Adams, Jr., *The Age of Industrial Violence, 1910–1915* (New York, 1966).

7. Quotations are from *Daughter of Earth* (New York, 1929), but the facts of the Smedley family history were verified as follows:

(1) Postcards written during this period and saved by Charles Smedley, then passed to Agnes's sister Myrtle who, in turn, passed them to Sam. As of 1976, the originals were with Sam's widow, Elizabeth, with copies in the Arizona State University archives.

(2) Elizabeth Smedley's statement (1976) that the family was very upset by *Daughter of Earth*—but none of them denied that the family history in it was true.

(3) Photographs owned by Elizabeth Smedley, with copies at Arizona State University.

(4) Interviews with Thorberg Brundin and Elinor Brundin (Ernest's widow).

(5) *Trinidad City Directories,* Smedley entries.

(6) Personal visits to Trinidad and sites of Tercio and Delagua in 1986.

8. Short history in manuscript of Delagua by Barbara Hallas Lei, dated 1984, at Trinidad Public Library; *Trinidad City Directory,* vol. for 1910 on Delagua; *Chronicle News* (Trinidad), April 17, 1907, p. 5. For the Ludlow massacre of 1914, see Philip Foner, *History of the Labor Movement in the United States* (New York, 1980), vol. 5, pp. 196–213.

9. Materials at Colorado Historical Society, Trinidad, and Public Library; representative memoir: Banon B. Beshwar, *Out of the Depths* (Denver, 1942).

10. Photo in Smedley collection, Arizona State University. For Tercio, see another memoir: Jose M. Romero, *El Valle de los Rancheros* (no date, no publisher), chapter 12, and *Trinidad City Directory,* vols. for 1904–07. Tercio belonged to the Colorado Fuel and Iron Co.

11. Mamie said about their 1908 reunion, "Agnes didn't talk of hard times." She was a "saucy" sixteen-year-old and proud of being a schoolteacher. Mamie never saw Agnes again. She married a railroad man at nineteen and has lived ever since in the Osgood-Campground area, except for a "brief period of fourteen years" when she lived in a small town to the north. But over the years she saved Smedley's childhood photos and newspaper clippings that appeared on her friend in Missouri newspapers. She did not believe that Agnes was ever a Communist or a spy, "just a smart girl making her way. . . . One who wasn't much for loving, but she'd do anything for you." Although she lives in the more middle-class town of Osgood, Mamie's loyalty to Campground as her roots and home to the poor people of the community was still strong in 1976. Mamie had decided that she wanted to be buried in the Campground cemetery, not in Osgood's "new" one. "I'll feel more like I'm with my own."

12. Postcards dated 1908–10 in Smedley collection used to trace movements. On Raton, see New Mexico State University Engineering Experiment Station *Bulletin,* no. 8 (1959): 8–9; also oral histories in manuscript, New Mexico State University, courtesy of Joan Jensen. For example, on the schools: "Raton was a small mining community sharply divided between miners and business people. . . . Father worked as a schoolteacher while mother, a qualified home economic teacher, stayed home and took care of the family. Italians, Spanish speakers, and Slavs attended Longfellow school where father taught. Living in such a deprived area made father aware of the poverty his students lived with

. . . like boys walking barefoot in the snow, or boys and girls not going to school because they didn't have suitable clothing to wear." (Patricia Murphey to M. C. Martinez, December 20, 1976.) See also memorabilia, Raton Museum, Raton, New Mexico.

13. Letters from Vera M. Keeney, April 3, 1973, and Eva Hance, December 17, 1972, and April 6, 1973; "Recalls 'Red Empress' as Student at Tempe," *Phoenix Gazette,* January 11, 1937; school photographs preserved in the University Archives, Arizona State University.

14. Smedley articles cited fully in Bibliography. Her first signed story was an imagined interview with an old-timer about the history of cowboy days in Tascosa, Texas, which did not mention her illness and threatened rape. "The Magazine Agent" was again autobiographical. She acknowledged the hostility she had experienced from other women but left out negative sexual overtones and romanticized her interactions with men. The tone is defensive, explaining that she took such a job in the first place because of bad health. For a memoir of a Smedley contemporary at Tempe Normal School see Jim Kimball, "Woman's Memories of Early Arizona Brings History to Life," *Minneapolis Tribune,* April 27, 1975.

2. THE DILEMMA OF MARRIAGE, 1912–1916

1. *Tempe Normal Student,* April 26, 1912.

2. Smedley, *Daughter of Earth,* p. 186.

3. See Thorberg Brundin, "Light Reactions of Terrestrial Amphipods," *Journal of Animal Behavior* 3, no. 5 (September–October 1913): 334–52. The original thesis is in the library of the University of California, Berkeley.

4. Ernest Brundin's widow, Elinor, told of finding a letter from Agnes among his papers after his death. In this letter, written in 1913, a few months after her abortion, Agnes poured out her intense anger. Hurt that her husband had saved this letter for so many years, Elinor tore it up on the spot.

5. Smedley references in Normal School records are not clear. She attended classes in 1913 and 1914, but apparently never graduated from the two-year program. Smedley references in *Normal News* (San Diego), January 7, 28, March 19, May 13, June 11, 18, 1914, and passim through June 21, 1915.

6. *Normal News,* scattered miscellaneous references in spring issues of 1915.

7. *Normal News,* April 29 and June 21, 1915. The liveliest account of the San Diego affair is still Emma Goldman's *Living My Life* (New York, 1931), pp. 557–58. For recent evaluations see Alice Wexler, *Emma Goldman: An Intimate Life* (New York, 1984), pp. 179–82, and Candace Falk, *Love, Anarchy, and Emma Goldman* (New York, 1984), pp. 159–89.

8. Goldman, *Living My Life,* p. 558, and George Edwards, "Free Speech in San Diego," *Mother Earth* 10 (July 1915): 182–85. Open Forum founders included George Edwards, a musician at the Conservatory of Music, and Dr. A. Lyle de Jarnette, a Baptist minister who resigned from his church to found the Forum.

9. *Normal News,* October 28, November 18, 1915; January 20, February 17, 1916.

10. Upton Sinclair, "The Red Dragon," unpublished ms. from Upton Sinclair papers; *Normal News*, January 17, 1916.

11. James Weinstein, *The Decline of Socialism in America* (New York, 1967), p. 53.

12. *Normal News*, October 19, 1916, and *Fresno Morning Republican*, September 15, 1916.

13. *Normal News*, 1916: October, November, December issues.

14. Interviews with Harry Steinmetz and Elizabeth Smedley.

15. *Normal News*, January 11, 1917; letter to Florence Lennon, October 24, 1924; interviews with Elinor Brundin and Thorberg Brundin.

3. FINDING A CAUSE, 1917–1918

1. June Sochen, "Henrietta Rodman and the Feminist Alliance: 1914–1917," *Journal of Popular Culture* 4, no. 1 (Summer 1970): 57–65.

2. See Joan Jensen, *Price of Vigilance* (New York, 1968); and specifically about intelligence surveillance of Indians and Smedley, see her forthcoming *Passage from India: Asian Indians in North America* (New Haven, 1988).

3. For Rai's early impressions of America see *United States of America: A Hindu's Impression* (Calcutta, 1916). The best single work on Rai's life is still V. C. Joshi, ed., *Lajpat Rai, Autobiographical Writings* (New Delhi, 1965). In New York Rai wrote and published two books: *England's Debt to India* (New York, 1917) and *The Political Future of India* (New York, 1919).

The literature on the anticolonial movement in turn-of-the-century American politics is vast. For the Anti-Imperialist League in particular see E. Berkeley Thompkins, *Anti-Imperialism in the United States: The Great Debate, 1890–1920* (Philadelphia, 1970). For the connection to the Indian nationalist cause, see Alan Raucher, "American Anti-Imperialists and the Pro-India Movement, 1900–1932," *Pacific Historical Review* 43, no. 1 (February 1974): 96–100.

4. Of the many studies of the Ghadar movement, four are noteworthy: A. C. Bose, *Indian Revolutionaries Abroad* (Patna, 1971); G. S. Deol, *The Role of the Ghadar-Party in the National Movement* (New Delhi, 1969); S. S. Josh, *Hindustan Ghadar Party* (New Delhi, 1977); and L. P. Mathur, *Indian Revolutionary Movement in the United States of America* (Delhi, 1970); and for early activities of the party in California see Emily Brown, *Har Dyal: Hindu Revolutionary and Nationalist* (Tucson, 1974).

5. As early as 1915, the British had begun to forward informal complaints about the Ghadar Party to the U.S. State Department, but it was not until February of 1916 that the British ambassador, Cecil Spring-Rice, lodged a formal protest and an agent was dispatched to do undercover work in New York in the Indian community. By 1917, reports were being funneled to London and selected information was then forwarded to the British embassy in Washington. Bundles of papers on the activities of the "East" Indians were then sent regularly to the State Department. Included in these were memoranda linking San Francisco and Berlin Indians to a 1915 confiscated shipment of guns aboard a ship, the *Annie Larsen*. The U.S. Justice Department continued its own investigation,

but Attorney-General Thomas W. Gregory wrote Secretary of State Robert Lansing in February, 1917, that there was nothing illegal about the *Annie Larsen* shipment unless it was part of a military expedition. Testimony concerning Indian passengers on the other ship involved, the *Maverick*, was hearsay and thus of no value in proving violation of law. Moreover, the British had not offered to bring their witness to the United States to testify. The Justice Department, insisted Gregory, had been "particularly scrupulous" in maintaining its obligation to enforce the neutrality laws. With Gregory's arguments in hand, Lansing composed a memorandum defending the United States and insisting that neither of the two ships had violated the neutrality laws of the United States. (Joan Jensen, "The 'Hindu Conspiracy': A Reassessment," *Pacific Historical Review* 48, no. 1 [February 1979]: 65–83; Don Dignan, "The Hindu Conspiracy in Anglo-American Relations during World War I," *Pacific Historical Review* 40, no. 1 [February 1971]: 73–74.)

6. *New York Times,* March 11, 12, 13, 1917, and M. N. Roy, *Memoirs* (Bombay, 1964), p. 37; see also Jensen, *Passage from India.*

7. Isaac Deutscher, *The Prophet Armed: Trotsky, 1879–1921* (New York, 1954), pp. 241–47; Ram Chandra, *An Appeal of India to the President of the United States* (San Francisco, 1917) quotes Trotsky; see also Chandra Chakravarty, *New India* (Calcutta, 1950), pp. 34–38; *New York Times,* March 7, 9, 1917; *Washington Post,* March 11, 1917.

8. Jensen, "Hindu Conspiracy," p. 81. The *Larsen* case is discussed in note 5, above.

9. National Archives, Justice Department, RG 60, file 193424, section 1; Bose, *Indian Revolutionaries Abroad,* p. 257; Mathur, *Indian Revolutionary Movement,* p. 126.

10. Taraknath Das (1884–1958) was a dedicated nationalist who would become a close associate and longtime friend of Smedley. In his teens Das joined the nationalist movement in Bengal, which was the hotbed of nationalist ferment in India at the turn of the century. In 1905, at the age of twenty-one, Das was forced to flee the country disguised as a Sadhu monk. He stopped first in Japan, where he stayed a year before moving to the United States. In San Francisco Das worked as a freelance journalist and established *Free Hindustan,* the first overtly nationalist Indian publication to appear in the United States. He also worked with Har Dyal in founding the Ghadar Party, although Das never formally became a member. By 1910 he was a major publicist of the Indian cause in the United States—known, for example, for his exchange of letters with Tolstoy on Indian independence, serialized in the popular journal *Twentieth Century* in 1909–10. In 1914 he became a U.S. citizen and began work toward a Ph.D. in international relations at Georgetown University in Washington, D.C. In 1915, while doing research at the University of Berlin, he became deeply involved in the developing Indo-German plot to smuggle arms and men into India for major uprisings. See the lengthy entry in *The Dictionary of National Biography* (Calcutta, 1971–74), vol. 1, pp. 363–64.

11. One of their first joint ventures was the publication of a small book or pamphlet written by Das in Japan, which had been confiscated by U.S. immigra-

tion authorities upon Das's arrival in San Francisco. The title of the book seemed innocent enough—*Isolation of Japan in World Politics*—but the contents, according to the U.S. Justice Department, were "disruptive and traitorous." Certain chapters were strongly anti-British and pro-German. Japan was portrayed as a pivotal power in Asia, alienated from Britain and possibly willing to join the fight to dismantle the British empire in Asia. On November 22, 1917, Das wrote to Smedley from San Francisco asking for help in arranging for publication of his book in New York. This Smedley proceeded to do, with money sent her by Das. By the following March, over two thousand copies were printed, bound, and ready for distribution. (National Archives, Justice Department, RG 60, file 193424, memoranda on cases against Ghose and Smedley.)

12. Ibid.

13. Called Juan Diaz in *Daughter of Earth*. Convincing evidence that the man was Herambalal Gupta includes the following: (1) National Archives, Army Intelligence, RG 165, file 10541722/42, report dated September 26, 1918, indicating that Gupta forfeited bail and left for Mexico in February, 1918. (2) Interview with Florence T. Lennon. (3) The alias Gupta used in the United States and Mexico was Juan Lopez. (4) Gupta resurfaced in Berlin in 1921 and gossiped about the incident (see Chapter 5). The best summary of his career is the numerous references in Bose, *Indian Revolutionaries Abroad*.

14. National Archives, Justice Department, RG 60, file 193424, and Military Intelligence, RG 165, file 10541722; *New York Times,* March 19, 1918.

15. Interview with Elinor Brundin; *New York Times,* April 2, 1918; *Call,* April 5, 1918.

16. Margaret Sanger, *An Autobiography* (Boston, 1938), pp. 252–53; *Call,* April 5, 1918; Gilbert Roe papers, Box H7.

17. *New York Times,* June 12, 1918. The second indictment refined and expanded upon the same charges and became the focus of prosecution efforts; but both indictments remained on the books.

18. Sanger, *Autobiography,* p. 351.

19. *Call,* March 22, 1918.

20. Jensen, "Hindu Conspiracy," pp. 82–83.

21. Robert K. Murray, *The Red Scare: A Study in National Hysteria, 1919–1920* (Minneapolis, 1955), p. 14; see also Chapter 4.

22. Smedley, "Cell Mate, No. 3."

23. Smedley, "Cell Mate, No. 4."

24. Peggy Lamson, *Roger Baldwin: Founder of the American Civil Liberties Union* (Boston, 1976), pp. 144–45. The Baldwin papers at Firestone Library, Princeton University, have much material on Baldwin's subsequent association with Ghose, Smedley, and the Friends of Freedom for India movement.

25. Joshi, ed., *Lajpat Rai,* pp. 212–20; N. S. Hardiker, *Lala Lajpat Rai in America* (New Delhi, n.d.); *Young India,* March 19, November 20, 1919; Bose, *Indian Revolutionaries Abroad,* pp. 189–91; also Raucher, "American Anti-Imperialists," pp. 83–110.

26. National Archives, Justice Department, RG 60, file 193424, plus Gilbert Roe papers, provide abundant documentation; for interpretation see Raucher, "American Anti-Imperialists," and Jensen, *Passage from India.*

4. ADVOCATE JOURNALIST, 1919–1920

1. *Birth Control Review* 2 (January–December 1918), 11 issues, and 3 (January–December 1919), 12 issues; Sanger, *Autobiography*, p. 252; Sanger correspondence for 1919 in Sanger papers.

2. Smedley's first signed article for the *Call*, "Sidelights on Women in India," appeared on March 16, 1919. She emphasized the role that Indian women were playing in the struggle for independence and argued that although Indian women had many problems indigenous to their culture, they could not possibly gain equality with men until India was free.

3. Murray, *Red Scare*, pp. 58–66.

4. *Call*, February 13, June 16, 23, July 16, 1919; for a biography emphasizing Minor's later career as a Communist, see Joseph North, *Robert Minor, Artist and Crusader (1884–1952)* (New York, 1956).

5. *New York Times*, January 29, 1919; February 10; February 12; February 13; *Call*, February 13, 1919. See also U.S. Congress, House, Committee of Immigration and Naturalization, *Deportation of Interned Alien Enemies and Convicted Alien Enemies* (Washington, D.C., 1919), p. 9. The definitive general work is Jensen, *Passage from India*.

6. Beard to Louis Post, February 27, 1919, in National Archives, Justice Department, RG 85, file 53854–133. See also Ellen Note, *Charles A. Beard* (Carbondale, 1983), p. 84.

7. William Wilson to Charles Beard, March 3, 1919, in National Archives, Justice Department, RG 85, file 53854–133.

8. Friends of Freedom for India collection, correspondence for 1919–20.

9. Friends of Freedom for India, eds. (pamphlet), *India's Freedom in American Courts* (New York, 1919); Robert M. Lovett, *All Our Years: The Autobiography of Robert Morss Lovett* (New York, 1948), pp. 158–59; Sanger, *Autobiography*, p. 351; Raucher, "American Anti-Imperialists."

10. *Call*, April 12, 1919; Lovett, *All Our Years*, p. 158.

11. *Call*, May 3, 7, 10, June 13, 1919; see also Murray, *Red Scare*.

12. The classic general work is Theodore Draper, *The Roots of American Communism* (New York, 1957).

13. F.F.I. collection, correspondence 1919–20; National Archives, Justice Department, RG 85, has a huge file of letters from many organizations.

14. *Call*, April 14, 15, 1919; N. S. Hardiker papers, Nehru Library, New Delhi, correspondence with Lajpat Rai, March 1, April 17, 1919. See also Bose, *Indian Revolutionaries Abroad*, p. 189, and D. P. Singh, *American Attitudes toward the Indian Nationalist Movement* (New Delhi, 1969), p. 303.

15. F.F.I. collection, correspondence, 1919: Smedley to San Francisco office F.F.I., July 1, August 24; Smedley to Morrison, August 26; Gompers to F.F.I., July 2; Smedley to labor unions, undated; Morrison to Smedley, August 25. More labor correspondence with immigration in National Archives, Justice Department, RG 85, file 53854–133.

16. F.F.I. collection, correspondence, 1919: Smedley to San Francisco office F.F.I., September 4; and *Call*, August 29, 1919. With further documentation, Gilbert Roe papers, Box H8.

17. F.F.I. collection, correspondence, Smedley to San Francisco office F.F.I., undated. Frank Walsh was a nationally prominent civil rights attorney and important liberal figure in the Democratic Party. In 1915 he chaired the influential U.S. Commission on Industrial Relations. The next year he managed President Wilson's campaign for New York State, continuing into the 1920s as the party's liberal whip for New York.

18. The New York indictments were not dismissed until 1923. See National Archives, Justice Department, RG 60, file 193424, Roe correspondence for September and October, 1919, and file 9–19–0, section 1, February 28, 1923; also briefs and correspondence in Roe papers, Boxes H7, H8. For military intelligence reports see National Archives, Army Intelligence, RG 165, file 10541–722.

19. *Call*, October 30, 1919; F.F.I. collection, correspondence, 1919: Smedley to San Francisco office F.F.I., October 31.

20. F.F.I. collection, correspondence, 1919: Smedley to San Francisco office F.F.I., November 11, 17.

21. *Call*, September 7, November 29, December 7, 1919; *Young India* 3, no. 1 (January 1920), is devoted to Rai farewells.

22. *Call*, December 4, 5, 1919.

23. Raucher, "American Anti-Imperialists," pp. 96–100, and F.F.I. collection, correspondence, 1919, items dated October 31, November 17, and December 18.

24. F.F.I. collection, correspondence, 1919: Coblentz to Gammons, December 15.

25. F.F.I. collection, correspondence, 1919: International Brotherhood of Electrical Workers, Stockton, to San Francisco office F.F.I., October 2.

26. *Call*, November 12, 1919.

27. F.F.I. collection, correspondence, 1919, contains the letters quoted here and below.

28. *Call*, October 29, December 15, 19, 1919.

29. The best general account of the "Red scare" is still Murray, *Red Scare;* for Smedley articles see Bibliography.

30. *Call*, February 29, 1919 (special issue), pp. 1, 12.

31. F.F.I. collection, correspondence, 1920: Smedley to San Francisco office F.F.I., August 5, 17, and undated (Autumn); *Call*, August 16, 1920.

32. F.F.I. collection, correspondence, 1920: Das to San Francisco office F.F.I., December 18.

5. SEXUAL POLITICS AND BREAKDOWN, 1921–1923

1. For location of Smedley-Lennon correspondence see Lennon papers in Bibliography.

2. Chatto had already traveled to Moscow in November of 1920 to win agreement for such a meeting. Final details and financing were worked out in Berlin by the Comintern's representative, Michael Borodin, early in March of 1921. Smedley, of course, had come to Berlin from New York explicitly to represent the Indian movement in the United States at the Moscow summit.

3. Arun C. Guha, *First Spark of Revolution* (n.p., 1971), pp. 499–514;

Muzaffar Ahmad, *Communist Party of India and Its Formation Abroad* (Calcutta, 1961), p. 112; M. N. Roy, *Memoirs,* pp. 477–85; G. Adhikari, ed., *Documents of the History of the Communist Party of India* (New Delhi, 1971), vol. 1, pp. 81–82, 85–89, 250–61, is the best analysis to date of this complex meeting in Moscow. To a growing number of contemporary Indian historians, the Berlin committee's advocacy of an alliance with bourgeois nationalists like Nehru and Gandhi now seems correct and closer to Lenin's position at the time than Roy's more left-wing line emphasizing proletarian solidarity. See Sobhanlal Datta Gupta, *Comintern and the Colonial Question: The Decolonisation Controversy* (Calcutta, 1976), and Adhikari, ed., *Documents,* pp. 250–61.

4. On the collapse of the Friends of Freedom for India, see the Roger Baldwin papers, as well as F.F.I. collection correspondence.

5. Smedley to Karin Michaelis, Michaelis papers, dated only "February 21," but probably 1924.

6. Smedley to Michaelis, dated only "February 21."

7. On Lila Singh, see the *Dictionary of National Biography,* vol. 4, pp. 209–12.

8. Smedley to Lennon, September 16, 1923.

9. As a writer and speaker with his own following, Surendranath Karr had been a troublesome figure within the movement. In New York he had bitterly opposed Das and Smedley in the Friends of Freedom for India and in Berlin he led personal attacks on Smedley and Chatto. Thus her visits to Karr's deathbed surprised her comrades. Embarrassed, Smedley explained her actions in terms of basic humanity: "Before he died he asked that I see him once. I went twice and did all I could—which was little. During his illness I kept him supplied with eggs, butter, broth, bread, meat, and all he needed. Before death one can only think of life. . . . Please tell Tarak [Das] of Karr's death. I shall write to Tarak soon. I do not write, mostly in shame for my weakness. But in a human relationship like this, the road is not sharp and clear—there does not seem to be but one or two ways of action" (Smedley to Lennon, November 12, 1923). For Karr's obstructive role in New York, see Gilbert Roe papers, Box H8.

6. PSYCHOANALYSIS, 1924–1925

1. Smedley to Michaelis, December 8, 1923; Smedley to Lennon, February 21, 1925.

2. A. C. N. Nambiar letter to authors, December 31, 1977; Margaret Vallance, "Rudolf Rocker: A Biographical Sketch," *Journal of Contemporary History* 8, no. 3 (July 1973): 75–95. On Goldman and Berkman and their interest in the Ludlow, Colorado, 1914 massacre, see Wexler, *Emma Goldman,* pp. 219–20.

3. By 1934 the Institute was forced to close its doors in the face of growing hostility and anti-Semitism from the right. The international flavor, the large number of Jewish staff, and the Institute's work among the employed poor made it a target. Most of its prominent members left Germany, and a significant number of them came to the United States. See Peter Gay, *Weimar Culture* (New

York, 1968) and *Freud, Jews and Other Germans* (New York, 1978); Psycho-analytical Institute, ed., *Zehn Jahre Berliner Psychoanalytisches* (Berlin, 1930); *International Journal of Psychoanalysis* (volumes 1–15 for 1920 to 1934); Paul Roazen, *Freud and His Followers* (New York, 1975); Vincent Brome, *Freud and His Early Circle* (New York, 1968); *Selected Papers of Karl Abraham,* 2 vols. (New York, 1927); Jack Rubins, *Karen Horney* (New York, 1978).

4. From Emma Goldman papers, Amsterdam, as quoted in Richard Drinnon and Anna Drinnon, eds., *Nowhere at Home: Letters from Exile of Emma Gold-man and Alexander Berkman* (New York, 1975), pp. 135–37.

5. Quoted in Drinnon and Drinnon, eds., *Nowhere at Home,* p. 128.

7. SMEDLEY AS ELIZA DOOLITTLE, 1925–1927

1. Barbara Erlich White, *Renoir: His Life, Art, and Letters* (New York, 1984), pp. 265, 271; and *New York Times,* February 22, 1971 for Durieux obituary. For Renoir portrait, see illustrations.

2. Personal letter, Peter Paret to authors, June 7, 1982.

3. Tilla Durieux, *Eine Tür steht offen Errinerungen* (Berlin, 1965), pp. 246–47. How much Smedley knew about Cassirer's suicide is not clear. In *Battle Hymn of China* (New York, 1943), pp. 19–20, she described Durieux as "strange." In 1931 Durieux fled to Yugoslavia, and during the war she worked for Tito's underground resistance. In 1951, at the age of seventy-one, Durieux returned to West Berlin and renewed her career on stage. At eighty-five, she played the starring role of Madame Karma in André Roussin's *The Clairvoyant.* Her last role was as an old peasant woman in the motion picture *The Last Bridge.* After her death in 1971, the Cassirer family honored her request for burial next to Paul.

4. Interviews: A. C. N. Nambiar; Kamaladevi Chattopadhyaya.

5. Interview with Florence T. Lennon.

6. Interviews: A. C. N. Nambiar; Kamaladevi Chattopadhyaya.

7. Oral history interview in Roger Baldwin papers; see also Lamson, *Roger Baldwin,* pp. 144–45.

8. G. Adhikari, "India and League against Imperialism," *Mainstream* (Delhi), annual for 1976, pp. 37–38, 151–54; Bakar Ali Mirza, "Congress against Imperialism," *Modern Review* 41, no. 5 (May 1927): 554–64; S. Gopal, ed., *Selected Works of Jawaharlal Nehru* (New Delhi, 1973), vols. 2–4 has numerous letters on the League.

9. Smedley to Lennon, June 29, 1927.

8. SPEAKING HER MIND, 1927–1928

1. This was the year Britain's conservative government broke relations with Russia after the police raid on the Soviet trade delegation (ARCOS) in London turned up evidence of spying.

2. One reason for Smedley's strong friendship with Käthe Kollwitz, who was a Socialist and not a Communist, was that although Kollwitz was committed to class struggle and revolution, her work was a painfully honest portrayal of both

the strengths and the weaknesses of the working class. See Smedley's portrait in "Käthe Kollwitz: Germany's Artist of the Masses," *Industrial Pioneers* 2 (September 1925): 4–9.

3. See Smedley's "China and the Indian Press"; "The Chinese Peasant Movement in 1926"; "Factory Life in China"; and "The Chinese Woman Today: An Interview with Madame Sun Yat-sen," as cited in Bibliography. As for the British reaction, Smedley pointed to the sudden flood of articles in Europe and India by Bertram Simpson, the British propaganda director for the notorious Chinese warlord Zhang Zuolin, an anti-Communist who recruited White Russian generals after their failed effort to capture Siberia: "Who Is Putnam Weale?" *People,* August 18, 1927, pp. 136–37. Evidence of the growing concern of British intelligence about what Smedley was sending to India was found in archives in New Delhi, India: the P. C. Joshi Collection and the Meerut Conspiracy Case Exhibits (see Bibliography).

4. The five-part article ran in Lajpat Rai's *People* on August 25, September 1, 8, 22, and October 13, 1927; the quoted material is from September 22. These articles also were published in India by Sohan Singh Josh as a pamphlet titled *India and the Next War* (Amritsar, 1928). Smedley mistakenly claimed that Zhang Zuolin was a British puppet. She also blamed the White Russians for raids carried out in Shanghai and Hankou against Russian official residences and for the murders of leading Chinese Communists. At first Chiang Kai-shek's White Terror of 1927 was attributed in the Western leftist press to "foreign" (meaning British and White Russian) influence.

5. G. Adhikari, ed., *Documents,* vol. 1, pp. 82–83; as well as Adhikari interview recollections about Smedley's influence. Kamaladevi became a major politician: see J. Brijbhushan, *Kamaladevi Chattopadhyaya* (New Delhi, 1976). For background, see John P. Haithcox, *Communism and Nationalism in India* (Princeton, N.J., 1971), and Sankar Ghose, *Socialism and Communism in India* (Bombay, 1971).

6. Manoranjan Jha, *Katheran Mayo and India* (New Delhi, 1971), and Lajpat Rai, *Unhappy India* (Calcutta, 1928). Smedley's reviews appeared in *Modern Review* (September 1927): 296–99, and *New Masses* (November 1927): 26–27. Mayo had earlier written a book defending U.S. retention of the Philippines as a colony.

7. "Margaret Sanger Comes to Berlin," *Birth Control Review* 7, no. 2 (February 1928): 50–54, 66.

8. Karin Michaelis's introduction to the Danish translation, *Kun en Kvinde,* of *Daughter of Earth* (Copenhagen, 1933). In India Bakar married a doctor and became a prominent Hyderabad politician and parliamentarian, serving in the 1950s and 1960s on a number of United Nations commissions. He died in the early 1970s.

9. Smedley wrote two articles for *Birth Control Review* on the Berlin clinics: June 1928, March 1929. See also James F. Cooper, "Birth Control Movement in Germany" (October 1929): 288–89, as well as Sanger's own brief account in her *Autobiography,* pp. 388–90. Details are abundant in Smedley-Sanger correspondence, February to October, 1928. A recent study is R. P. Newman, "Working Class Birth Control in Wilhelmine Germany," *Comparative Studies in Society and History* 20, no. 3 (July 1978): 273.

10. The experience produced an article, "Germany's Red Front," *Nation* 127 (August 1, 1928): 116–17; see also Smedley to Sanger, February 21, 1928.

11. Smedley to Sanger, May 18 and July 7, 1928.

12. Smedley to Sanger, May 18, June 22, July 7, August 21, October 26, 30, 1928; and to Ernest Brundin, March 22, June 27, 1928; the Gilbert Roe papers are strangely mute, although an earlier inventory left with the Wisconsin State Historical Society suggests the former existence of a manuscript, "Struggle of Earth," and perhaps correspondence.

13. David Friday (1876–1945) was probably Smedley's most respectable American lover. At the time he was a banker, a professor of political economy at the New School for Social Research in New York and a lecturer with the Brookings Institution in Washington, D.C. Friday frequently testified before legislative bodies and would become the president (1938–39) and chairman of the board (1940–41), and a director since its inception of the National Bureau of Economic Research (*The National Cyclopaedia* [New York, 1948], vol. 34, p. 137). Smedley evidently thought a great deal of Friday (see letters to Sanger, July 7, August 21, October 26, 30, 1928). The supreme irony is the fact that since the 1940s the charge has been made that the Comintern sent Smedley to China; in fact the trip was sponsored by David Friday, financier and economist.

Just before Friday entered her life, Smedley spent a few days with Scott Nearing, the famous American socialist whom she had known earlier in New York. She arranged for Nearing to lecture at the Charlottenburg town hall. His audience was mainly Indian and Chinese students. The subject was the growing strength of U.S. imperialism in the Pacific, using the Philippines as a case study. Nearing was on his way home from a trip to China and Southeast Asia (see Smedley to Sanger, February 14, 1928, and Scott Nearing, *The Making of a Radical* [New York, 1972], pp. 140–45). This, the spring of 1928, was the first time Smedley had been able to combine sex and friendship in relationships with American men.

14. What distinguished *Daughter of Earth* (U.S. edition) from autobiography was the following: personal names and many geographical locations were changed; to give the reader a sense of history from an anarchist perspective, the false suggestion is made that Smedley was in the Ludlow, Colorado, area at the time of the massacre and in San Diego participating in the Free Speech Movement; in order to disguise the identity of her Indian comrades and their contacts with the Soviet Union, New York remains the setting for the latter part of the story, which deals with the Indian nationalists. The German translation follows the English original closely except that names of American friends are unchanged, and the opening paragraph of the English text becomes the closing paragraph of the book in the German translation.

15. Interview with Percy Chen. It is worth noting that Smedley did *not* attend the Sixth Congress of the Third Communist International, which met in Moscow in July and August, 1928—as was later alleged (see footnote, pp. 142–43). Smedley spent July and August in Paris visiting Josephine Bennett and making final revisions to *Daughter of Earth*.

16. Jawaharlal Nehru, *Toward Freedom: The Autobiography of Jawaharlal Nehru* (New York, 1942), pp. 128–34.

9. THE SHANGHAI YEARS, 1929–1933

1. Smedley to Brundin, December 24, 1928; Smedley to Sanger, February 22, May 12, June 13, 1929; Smedley to Gilbert Roe, January 14, April 12, June 5, 1929 (Box H8); *Battle Hymn*, p. 43; Smedley to Lennon, February 8, 1929. For British intelligence, see P. C. Joshi Collection, nos. 1929–7, reports of special agent Halland; also British Shanghai police files in F.B.I. 100–68282–1B32 (Exhibits), for more fragmentary references. On Chatto's marriage to a cloistered Irishwoman, see footnote on p. 70. Smedley was also questioned by the American consulate-general in Shanghai.

2. Charlotte L. Beahan, "Feminism and Nationalism in the Chinese Women's Press, 1902–1911," *Modern China* 1, no. 4 (October 1975): 379–416.

3. Smedley's early articles on women for the *Zeitung* and other publications are collected in Jan and Steve MacKinnon, eds., *Portraits of Chinese Women in Revolution* (New York, 1976).

4. Helen F. Snow, *Women in Modern China* (The Hague, 1967), p. 242, and *Inside Red China* (New York, 1939), p. 170. On Xiang Jingyu, see Delia Davin, *Women-Work* (Oxford, 1976), pp. 16–18. The classic work focusing on the left Guomindang and the catastrophe of 1927 is by onetime Smedley associate Harold Isaacs: *The Tragedy of the Chinese Revolution* (New York, 1936), original edition with preface by Leon Trotsky; the second edition (1954) was rewritten with an anticommunist bias.

5. *Battle Hymn*, p. 43; Smedley to Sanger, June 13, 1929. For Smedley's earlier view of Japan see Chapter 4.

6. Smedley to Sanger, March 21, June 13, October 12, November 21, December 6, 1929.

7. Smedley to Roe, April 12; to Lennon, May 6; to Sanger, June 13, 1929. "Nanking" and "Sun Yat-sen's Funeral" in *Modern Review* 46 (August 1929): 137–42, 167–73.

8. Smedley to Lennon, February 8, and to Roe, June 5, 1929; P. C. Joshi Collection, file 1929–7; interview with Sohan Singh Josh; British Intelligence, National Archives, Meerut Conspiracy Case Exhibits, files S1.1871, 1881, and Session Court Judgment, p. 122. For an overview, see Stanley Wolpert, *A New History of India* (New York, 1977), pp. 312–13; *People* 8 (April 13, 1929): 11, for Smedley's tribute to Lajpat Rai.

9. Rhoads Murphey, *Shanghai: Key to Modern China* (Cambridge, Mass., 1953).

10. Interviews with Gertrude Binder; P. C. Joshi Collection, file 1929–7; Smedley to Lennon, July 14, 1929.

11. *China Weekly Review*, May 4, 11, 25, June 1, 15, July 3, 13, 1929; P. C. Joshi Collection, file 1929–7; Smedley to Roe, June 5, 1929; interviews with Rewi Alley.

12. Smedley to Nehru, September 9, 1930, Motilal Nehru papers, series no. 819. On the Missouri group of journalists in Shanghai see Stephen MacKinnon and Oris Friesen, *China Reporting: An Oral History of American Journalism in the 1930s and 1940s* (Berkeley and Los Angeles, 1987), chapter 3; interview with Randall Gould; *Battle Hymn*, p. 96; Smedley to Sanger, June 13, 1929.

13. The Shanghai police (British) focused on Smedley's German connections: see F.B.I. 100–68282–1B32 (Exhibits). German sources include Hede Massing, *This Deception* (New York, 1951), pp. 95–97 and Ruth (Kuczynski) Werner, *Sonjas Rapport* (Berlin, 1977), pp. 42–113.

14. E. H. Carr, *Twilight of the Comintern, 1930–35* (New York, 1982), pp. 356, 358, 360.

15. Smedley's earlier observations about Browder are given in Chapter 5, above.

16. *Battle Hymn*, pp. 50–57; Smedley to Sanger, August 10, October 12, 1929.

17. On Xu, see Jonathan Spence, *Gate of Heavenly Peace: The Chinese and Their Revolution, 1895–1980* (New York, 1981), pp. 188–278. About two years earlier Xu had an affair with Pearl Buck. On his affair with Smedley, see her letters to Sanger, August 10, October 12, 1929.

18. See also her "Chinese Poets and Professors," *New York Herald Tribune*, May 18, 1930, as well as other articles cited in the Bibliography.

19. Interviews: Chen Hansheng; Gertrude Binder. Also *Battle Hymn*, pp. 64ff. On Chen Hansheng's career the best work to date is Xie Baoding and Xing Ruojun, "Chen Hansheng tongzhi zouguo di daolu," in *Shanghai wenshi ziliao xuanji*, vol. 43 (Shanghai, 1983), pp. 133–46.

20. Rewi Alley, *You Banfa* (Beijing, 1952), pp. 15–16, and, more recently, his *Six Americans in China* (Beijing, 1985), pp. 119–66.

21. Chen Hansheng, *Shanghai shaokuang neibao shengzhi di diaocha* (Shanghai, 1929); Smedley to Sanger, October 12, November 21, 1929.

22. MacKinnon and MacKinnon, eds., *Portraits*, pp. 27–39, 103–10.

23. Smedley to Sanger, February 22, March 21, June 13, July 25, August 10, October 12, November 21, December 6, 29, 1929; March 23, April 2, June 30, July 3, 1930; May 4, 6, 29, June 11, July 30, November 19, 1931; January 3, April 1, 1932.

24. Quoted in Richard Drinnon, *Rebel in Paradise: A Biography of Emma Goldman* (Boston, 1961), p. 252.

25. Today something like a "Sorge industry" exists, a quantity of books and articles produced annually about him in various languages around the world. Recent works in English are Gordon W. Prange, *Target Tokyo: The Story of the Sorge Spy Ring* (New York, 1984), and Chapman Pincher, *Too Secret Too Long: The Great Betrayal of Britain's Crucial Secrets and the Cover-up* (London, 1984). The industry is biggest in Japan. Chalmers Johnson's *An Instance of Treason: Ozaki Hotsumi and the Sorge Spy Ring* (Stanford, 1964) remains the best survey of Sorge's China period and the most useful review of Japanese works and sources. By the late 1930s Ozaki Hotsumi emerged as a top Japanese China expert and adviser to Prince Konoye.

26. Massing, *This Deception*, pp. 95–97; Johnson, *An Instance of Treason*, p. 77; interviews with Chen Hansheng.

27. In Guangzhou (Canton) Smedley's mood was blissful despite harassment by Guomindang police, which became so intense at one point that she felt compelled to seek asylum and protection from the U.S. consul, whose chief response was to urge her to leave China. National Archives, Justice Department, RG 60, file 193424, section 2, contains a long memo on Smedley by the U.S. consul in

Guangzhou; see also U.S. Treasury attaché report (Shanghai) on August 10, 1931, in F.B.I. 61–6580–127, pp. 13–14. On Sorge, see Johnson, *An Instance of Treason,* pp. 69–70.

28. Johnson, *An Instance of Treason,* pp. 60–83; Kinoshita Jinji, *Otto to yobareru Nihonjin* (Tokyo, 1963), three acts; first performed in 1962. Reference courtesy of Eric Gangloff.

29. See the Bibliography for articles in *Modern Review* and *New Masses* in 1931.

30. Werner, *Sonjas Rapport,* pp. 108–10. For background on Ruth Kuczynski see Philip Knightly, *The Second Oldest Profession: Spies and Spying in the Twentieth Century* (New York, 1987), pp. 194–209. Ruth Kuczynski used aliases in Shanghai and is known today as Ruth Werner. Pincher in *Too Secret Too Long* relied heavily upon Ruth Werner as a basis for his allegation of a relationship between Smedley and Roger Hollis, future British intelligence chief. We have found no evidence of such a relationship. At this time, Smedley had few, if any, British friends, on the left or otherwise; her suspicion of Oxford- or Cambridge-educated young Englishmen was especially strong. Knightly refutes Pincher on many points but repeats the allegation that Smedley was a Communist.

31. "Agnes Smedley and the Shanghai Die Hards," editorial, *China Weekly Review,* September 19, 1931, pp. 84–85. A large file on the Noulens case collected by the Shanghai Municipal Police (British) is to be found in Army Intelligence, National Archives, Box D, file 2510. On Smedley's involvement see also F.B.I. 100–68282–1B32 (Exhibits). Continuing references to the Noulens case are in *China Weekly Review,* December 26, 1931; January 23, June 25, 1932; January 6, 20, 1934; April 13, 20, June 8, 1935; *China Forum* issues for 1932–33 and Harold Isaacs, *Re-encounters in China* (Armonk, N.Y., 1985), pp. 19–20. Johnson, *An Instance of Treason,* p. 61, erred as to the length of the Noulens' imprisonment.

32. Interview with Mao Dun; Smedley articles from 1930 in *Modern Review* and *Frankfurter Zeitung,* cited in Bibliography.

33. Quotation from a statement read at the memorial meeting for Agnes Smedley held in Beijing on May 31, 1980.

34. *Mengya yuekan* 1, no. 5 (May 1930). A Chinese translation was published in Shanghai in 1934.

35. *Lu Xun riji* (Beijing, 1959); indexed Smedley references begin with an entry for December 17, 1929. In *Battle Hymn,* Smedley misremembered her first meeting with Lu Xun, confusing it with his birthday party in September, 1930. For a detailed chronological record of the Lu Xun–Agnes Smedley relationship, see Ge Baochuan, "Lu Xun he Shimodelai di geming youyi," *Geming wenwu,* no. 3 (May–June, 1976): 15–18; also interview with Ge Baochuan.

36. Smedley articles were in *New Masses, Modern Review,* and *Frankfurter Zeitung* (see Bibliography). The material on the League of Left Wing Writers is abundant: recent articles have appeared in *People's Daily,* April 2, 16, 1980; the book compilation, *Zuolian ziliao* (Beijing, 1980) commemorated its fiftieth anniversary; *Xinwenxue shiliao,* issues for 1980, have much source material, including, in issue no. 3, articles about Smedley by Ge Baochuan. For a solid sur-

vey in English of the life and death of the league and its internal disputes, see Neal Hunter, "The Chinese League of Left Wing Writers, Shanghai, 1930–36," diss., 1973, Australian National University.

37. Malcolm Cowley in New York responded with an impressive petition drive: see "Chinese Ministers," in Cowley papers. "Present Conditions" by Lu Xun was published in part in English in *Voice of China* 2, no. 6 (June 1, 1936): 6, 21; the full English text is to be found in Smedley papers, File VII–24. See also *Battle Hymn*, p. 84; Ge, "Lu Xun"; and interview with Mao Dun. To further publicize the League of Left Wing Writers and repression by Chiang Kaishek, Smedley edited *Short Stories from China* (New York, ca. 1933), which featured the executed writers.

38. Interviews: Chen Hansheng; Randall Gould; Rewi Alley; inscribed copy of *Daughter of Earth* in Mme. Sun's Shanghai residence (information courtesy of Israel Epstein).

39. Johnson, *An Instance of Treason*, pp. 80–81.

40. See Carr, *Twilight of the Comintern*, for Comintern and Chinese Communist Party positions on international issues.

41. Interview with Chen Hansheng, and an article in *Guangming ribao*, May 23, 1981, indicate that Hu Shi was behind her dismissal; see also Smedley to Sanger, January 3, April 1, 1933. Her articles appeared in *New Masses* and *Modern Review* (see Bibliography).

42. Organized around Mme. Sun Yat-sen and a distinguished group of academic intellectuals (members of the Academica Sinica, China's national academy), the League's leaders included Hu Shi, Lin Yutang, Lu Xun, and Cai Yuanpei. The Executive Secretary was Yang Quan (Yang Xingfo), an Academica Sinica economist and one of Smedley's bourgeois "patrician" friends from her first year in Shanghai. Although the League drew public attention to the problem of persecution, including some well-publicized visits to prisons, its achievements were few and fleeting. In the summer of 1933 Yang Quan was brutally assassinated by Guomindang agents, and the League broke up shortly thereafter. See *Zhongguo minquan baochang tongmeng* (Beijing, 1979), and interviews with Chen Hansheng.

43. Isaacs, *Re-encounters in China;* interviews with Frank Glass and Grace Cook, and with Chen Hansheng. Only Isaacs' name appeared on the book.

44. John K. Fairbank, *China Bound: A Fifty-Year Memoir* (New York, 1982), pp. 66–77; also Gywneth Roe papers: Smedley to Roe, April 30, 1931, January 25, 1933.

45. Paul Frillman and Graham Peck, *China: The Remembered Life* (Boston, 1968), p. 22; J. B. Powell editorial, "Agnes Smedley and the Shanghai Diehards," *China Weekly Review*, September 19, 1931, pp. 84–85; Smedley to Lennon, April 4, 1932, and to Sanger, September 20, 1932.

46. Smedley to Sanger, April 1, 1932; *Battle Hymn*, pp. 123–24, 151, 194. Interviews: Chen Hansheng; Rewi Alley; Maude Russell. Otto Braun, *A Comintern Agent in China* (Stanford, 1982), p. 6. See also Mu Xin, *Chen Geng tongzhi zai Shanghai* (Shanghai, 1980). On police surveillance see Shanghai (British) police reports in F.B.I. 100–68282–1B32 (Exhibits); also Isaacs, *Re-encounters in China*, p. 29, and interview with Frank Glass and Grace Cook. The authority on address changes is Ge Baochuan, interviews.

47. For a careful chronological account of Sorge's movements see Prange, *Target Tokyo*.

48. For a note on the curious history of this photo see Isaacs, *Re-encounters in China*, pp. 125–41. Quote is from transcript of Shaw–Lu Xun interview in Smedley papers. Smedley's mood is confirmed in a letter to Roe, January 25, 1933.

49. *Battle Hymn*, pp. 115–20; Spence, *Gate of Heavenly Peace*, p. 288. Interviews: Mao Dun; Ding Ling. Feng Da was still alive in Taibei, Taiwan, in the late 1970s and a source for a book on Ding Ling: Zhou Fenna, *Ding Ling yu Zhonggong wenxue* (Taibei, 1980).

10. MOSCOW, NEW YORK, AND SHANGHAI, 1933–1936

1. *Short Stories from China*. The translator was George Kennedy. This collection preceded by forty years the volume of similar stories (some are duplicates) that Harold Isaacs edited, *Straw Sandals* (Boston, 1974) without acknowledging George Kennedy as translator or Smedley's earlier volume.

2. Smedley to Michaelis, July 12, 31, September 7, October 17, 22, 1933.

3. Interviews: Emile Xiao (Xiao San); and Jack Chen. Smedley was also in contact with the most important Chinese Communist figures in Moscow, such as Wang Ming and Kang Sheng; see Werner, *Sonjas Rapport*, pp. 129–30.

4. Interview, Jack Chen; letters to Michaelis cited in note 2 and November 2, 1933, April 4, 1934. On Phinney, see Marion Gridley, ed., *Indians Today* (Chicago, 1947), pp. 72–73; and Immanuel Gonick diary entries for 1933–34, courtesy of Amy Gonick.

5. Smedley to Lennon, March 17, 1934; to Wilma Fairbank, March 30, 1934, in Fairbank, *China Bound*, pp. 76–77; and to Michaelis, April 4, 1934. On Chatto's last years in Leningrad see G. Adhikari, Introduction to *Documents*, vol. 1, pp. 83–84. In the Soviet Union, see the memoir of his Russian wife, L. E. Karunovskaia, "Vospominaniia L. E. Karunovskoi," in the Archive of the Leningrad Division of the Institute of Oriental Studies, *fond* 138, *opis'* 2 (LOIVAN, Academy of Sciences, U.S.S.R.).

6. Telegram from Paris to Lennon, April 18, 1934, and interview with Florence Lennon.

7. O. E. Clubb, *The Witness and I* (New York, 1974), p. 165; Smedley to Sanger, May 19, 1934, and to Gwyneth Roe, dated only "Sunday."

8. Malcolm Cowley, *Dream of Golden Mountain* (New York, 1980), pp. 224–25. After completing his undergraduate studies at Harvard, which had been interrupted by a stint driving an ambulance during World War I, Cowley moved to New York in 1919. He was an editor of the *New Republic* from 1929 to 1944; his critically acclaimed *Exiles Return* was published in 1934 (New York).

9. *New Republic* 80 (September 19, 1934): 163.

10. Interviews: Elizabeth Smedley; Elinor Brundin; Harry Steinmetz.

11. Johnson, *An Instance of Treason*, p. 64.

12. Clubb, *The Witness and I*, p. 165; Shanghai police files in F.B.I. 100–68282–1B32 (Exhibits); "The Corrupt Press in China," *Nation* 141 (July 3, 1935): 10.

13. For the split within the League of Left Wing Writers, the best work in English is Hunter, "Chinese League of Left Wing Writers"; see also Spence, *Gate of Heavenly Peace,* chapter 9; and for a highly partisan view, Chung Wen, "National Defense Literature," *Chinese Literature,* no. 10 (1971): 91–99. In Chinese the materials are fragmentary but numerous; for recent comments see *Xinwenxue shiliao,* no. 2 (1979): 243–58. The best work treating the complexity and ambiguity of changes in *both* Comintern and Chinese Communist Party policy in 1935 in the direction of a united front is Carr, *Twilight of the Comintern.* By the 1950s Zhou Yang had become a figure of great influence over party literary policy. He used his power as literary czar systematically to purge those who had opposed him—and sided with Lu Xun—in the 1930s. Later, during the Cultural Revolution, Zhou Yang himself was jailed. After 1976 he was returned to power, but as a shell of his former self. He was no longer widely admired, and he knew it. On one occasion the authors saw him choke up in the middle of a speech, unable to continue speaking to an assemblage of intellectuals, many of whom he had once purged. Needless to say, on the subject of Agnes Smedley, Zhou Yang was enthusiastic but not very informative (interview).

14. Interview with Frank Glass and Grace Cook; *China Weekly Review,* August 3, p. 348; August 31, p. 488; and September 7, 1935, p. 2. See *Liening shenghuo* 34 (February 18, 1934): 4 for the changing Chinese Communist view of *China Forum.*

15. Interviews: Rewi Alley, Chen Hansheng; also Alley, *Six Americans in China,* p. 128; and *Shanghai wenshi ziliao xuanji,* p. 140. In 1978 the authors found that Smedley's physical movements in Shanghai could be traced with surprising precision. This was possible because the old French concession area where Smedley lived is still mostly intact and because recent Chinese investigations into Smedley's whereabouts have been meticulous, to the point of uncovering the majority of her old addresses (our source was interviews with Ge Baochuan). The old Bearn complex now houses a giant women's department store at the street level.

16. Interview with Liu Ding. Smedley spent much time and money in 1935 and 1936 helping various fugitives escape Guomindang assassins or firing squads. Another example was Lu Xun's request that Smedley smuggle out a politically progressive painter, Hu Man (Wang Junchu) who was wanted by the Guomindang Blueshirts. Like Chen Hansheng, Hu was smuggled onto a Russian freighter bound for Vladivostok. See Nym Wales Collection, ms. on painters and Lu Xun; also interview with Mao Dun.

17. Interview, George Hatem; see also his "American Childhood, Chinese Maturing," *China Reconstructs* 33, no. 10 (October 1984): 26–29, and note in *Beijing Review* 28, no. 28 (July 1985): 5, and his "On Agnes Smedley," *Voice of Friendship,* no. 12 (August 1985): 11–12. In the 1980s Hatem still lived in Beijing as a grandfather with near-ministerial rank in the Ministry of Health. He has a legendary reputation, especially for his part in the campaign to eradicate venereal disease during the early 1950s.

18. Interviews: F. McCracken Fisher; Ruth Weiss; George Hatem; Rewi Alley; Xiao Qian. For Edgar Snow, see his memoir, *Journey to the Beginning* (New York, 1958), and Snow to Nym Wales, June 4, 1939, in Nym Wales's per-

sonal possession. On the December Ninth movement a standard work in Chinese is *Yier jiu yundong shi* (Beijing, 1980); see pp. 16–17 for reference to Smedley. Xiao Qian remembers meeting Smedley as "Mrs. Brown" at the Snows' apartment.

19. Interviews: Rewi Alley; Trudy Rosenberg, 1980.

20. *Dangdai shilang* (1934), pp. 170–71. Interviews: Chen Hansheng; Ruth Weiss; Rewi Alley. See the *Nation,* May 1, 1937, p. 520, for the announcement that Smedley had never been Mme. Sun's secretary. Grace Granich's side provided from her partially completed Shanghai diary ms., references courtesy of Tom Grunefeld.

21. Interviews: Liu Ding; Rewi Alley. Also, Alley, *Six Americans in China,* p. 131; *Battle Hymn,* pp. 133–34.

11. SMEDLEY AS "WHITE EMPRESS": THE XI'AN INCIDENT, 1936–1937

1. Interview with Liu Ding. The Xi'an Incident has been much studied. The chief sources for background on the Incident are Tien-wei Wu, *Sian Incident: A Pivotal Point in Modern Chinese History* (Ann Arbor, 1976), pp. 1–74, and his 1984 review article, "New Materials on the Xi'an Incident," *Modern China* 10, no. 1 (January 1984): 115–41. See also Lyman P. Van Slyke, *Enemies and Friends: The United Front in China* (Stanford, 1967), and Mi Zanchen, *Yang Hucheng zhuan* (Shaanxi, 1979).

2. Interview with Liu Ding.

3. *Battle Hymn,* p. 135. In absentia Smedley was made a member of Lu Xun's funeral committee—the only foreigner to be so named. Later Smedley published two articles in Chinese about Lu Xun in *Wenhua yuekan,* no. 3 (October 27, 1939) and *Wenxue* 9, no. 4 (November 10, 1937), reproduced in *Xinwenxue shiliao,* no. 3 (1980): 125–28. Authors' interview with Mao Dun about the funeral; see also his memoir in *Lu Xun huiyilu* (Beijing, 1978), pp. 3–5, 257–59; and Ge, "Lu Xun."

4. Ding Ling memoir in *Guangming ribao,* June 4, 1980, p. 4; on Dr. Wunsch, interview with Rewi Alley.

5. Wu, *Sian Incident;* idem, "Xi'an Incident"; on Chiang Kai-shek and the Germans, see William C. Kirby, *Germany and Republican China* (Stanford, 1984).

6. Wu, *Sian Incident,* pp. 75–82; James Bertram, *First Act in China: The Story of the Sian Mutiny* (New York, 1938), pp. 111–23.

7. Interview with Wang Bingnan. After the Xi'an Incident, Wang Bingnan moved to Yan'an and later Chongqing, where he worked closely with Zhou Enlai in foreign affairs. During the early 1960s, as China's ambassador to Poland, Wang conducted quiet talks with the Kennedy administration about the possibilities of improving United States-China relations. These talks were suspended in 1964 by the escalating Vietnam War. During the Cultural Revolution of 1966–76, Wang was attacked for his association with Chiang Kai-shek and Yang Hucheng in 1936. His second wife committed suicide. In the 1980s Wang Bingnan remained one of China's most senior, respected diplomats.

8. Interview with Liu Ding. After proving himself in the Xi'an Incident, Liu Ding joined the Red Army at the new capital of Yan'an. He thereafter played a crucial role in the development of a guerrilla-based munitions industry during World War II and in the civil war period that culminated in communist victory in 1949. In the 1950s Liu advanced to the vice-ministerial level in China's munitions industry. His career was interrupted by the 1966–69 Cultural Revolution, of which he became a major target, ironically enough because of his role in the Xi'an Incident. He was imprisoned and condemned for his association with Chiang Kai-shek and Zhang Xueliang in 1936. In 1981, in his mid-seventies and recently retired, Liu Ding told us that he finally had time to reminisce a bit and take charge of a new party history project concerning the Xi'an Incident. The Chinese Communist Party, it appears, is preparing to reveal much more by way of documents and memoir accounts about the Incident and the communist role in it. Warlord generals Yang Hucheng and Zhang Xueliang—and even, to some degree, Chiang Kai-shek—are to be portrayed in a more positive light. It is hoped that this will help clear the air for a reconciliation with Chiang Kai-shek's son on Taiwan. Ironically, the now not-so-young Zhang Xueliang, whom Chiang Kai-shek detained for the Xi'an kidnapping, is still under house arrest in Taiwan. Liu Ding died in 1986.

9. Anna Wang, *Ich kampfte für Mao* (Hamburg, 1973), and Luo Ruiqing, Lu Chengsao, Wang Bingnan, *Xi'an shibian yu Zhou Enlai tongzhi* (Beijing, 1978), pp. 1–44.

10. Associated Press release, January 7, 1937; *Kansas City Star,* January 9, 1937; *New York Post,* January 7, 1937; see also *New York Herald Tribune,* January 8, 1937; *New York Times,* January 10, 1937.

11. Associated Press release, January 8, 1937; *Liberty* 14 (March 13, 1937): 19–20; *Daily Worker,* January 29, 1937, p. 1.

12. See Wu, *Sian Incident,* for detailed analysis.

13. Bertram, *First Act in China,* p. 157; Wang, *Ich kampfte für Mao,* pp. 87–92; Smedley to Gould, May 19, 1937 (Gould papers); British missionaries claimed that she had led peasant uprisings in India in the 1920s: *New York Post,* January 7, 1937.

14. John Henle (Vanguard Press) to Florence Rose (Sanger's secretary), October 25 and November 3, 1937 (Sanger papers). See also Smedley to Gould, May 19, 1937, and Sanger to Smedley, October 29, 1937, as well as *San Diego Sun,* May 22, 1937, based on United Press dispatch of May 19.

15. Bertram, *First Act in China,* pp. 1–85.

16. Ibid., pp. 156–57.

17. Ibid., p. 176.

18. Ibid., pp. 214–15.

12. YAN'AN, 1937

1. Edgar Snow, *Red Star over China* (New York, 1938; repr. 1968), p. 56.

2. Smedley, *China Fights Back: An American Woman with the Eighth Route Army* (New York, 1938), pp. 15, 19–20.

3. R. H. Tawney, *Land and Labour in China* (London, 1936), p. 76; China

International Famine Relief Commission, *Annual Reports, 1928–33;* in Chinese see *Shaanxi sheng nongcun diaocha* (Nanjing, 1934), a survey by the Nationalist government.

4. During World War II, He Long and Peng Dehuai were among the half-dozen key field commanders of the Eighth Route Army operating in northern China. Between 1946 and 1949 they played a pivotal role in the undoing of Chiang Kai-shek on the battlefield. During the 1950s Peng became defense minister and probably the most important military figure in China. He oversaw Chinese operations in Korea and directed the push toward modernization of the People's Liberation Army along Russian lines. Then dramatically, in 1959, Peng fell from power after an open clash at Lushan with Mao over policy. He Long, the former bandit, did not join the Communist Party until 1945. After 1949 he took up civilian posts at the rank of vice-premier, fading slowly into retirement in the 1960s. Both soldiers of the revolution were arrested and died in prison during the Cultural Revolution of the late 1960s.

5. *Guangming ribao,* June 4, 1980; interview with Ding Ling; *Xibei tequ texie* (Shanghai, 1938), pp. 44–52. For one of the many recent portraits of Ding Ling in English, see Spence, *Gate of Heavenly Peace,* and, in translation, her own appreciation of Smedley, "Memories of American Journalist Agnes Smedley," *China Reconstructs* 34, no. 4 (April 1985): 41–43.

6. *Xibei tequ texie,* pp. 49–51; interview with Huang Hua, who was the translator.

7. Interviews: George Hatem; Ding Ling; Liu Ding. Also see Wang, *Ich kampfte für Mao,* pp. 115–79.

8. Smedley, "Chinese Red Army Goes to Town," *Modern Review* 62, no. 5 (November 1937): 486.

9. Smedley's major interview, on March 1, 1937, with Chairman Mao was published and widely distributed in Chinese as *Zhong-Ri wenti yu Xi'an shibian* (Yan'an, 1937).

10. On Lily Wu, see Nym Wales (Helen F. Snow), "Autobiographical Profile and Biographical Sketches," Book 2 in Wales, *The Chinese Communists* (Westport, Conn., 1952; repr. 1972), pp. 250–61; also Smedley, "Chinese Theatre in the Trenches," *Daily Worker,* October 28, 1937.

11. Interviews: Huang Hua; George Hatem. The Chinese title of *The Great Road: The Life and Times of Chu Teh* (New York, 1956) is *Weidadi dalu* (Beijing, 1981); the translator is Hu Ji'an, who added a separate introduction.

12. Smedley's own account is given in *Battle Hymn,* pp. 171–72; see also letters to Sanger, September 19, 23, 1937. Interviews: Randall Gould; Earl Leaf.

13. Mark Selden, *The Yenan Way* (Boston, 1971), chapter 4.

14. So Lu Dingyi told his cousin, Chen Hansheng, who repeated it to the authors in an interview; confirmed in Hatem, "On Agnes Smedley." Interview with Ding Ling.

15. Edgar Snow, "Mō Takutō no renai," artfully rendered into Japanese by Matsuoka Yoko and published in *Chūo Kōron* 69, no. 7 (July 1954): 55. The authors are much in debt to Susan Chambers for the help with the translations from the Japanese which follow. An original English-language text evidently still exists in Mrs. Lois W. Snow's private collection of Snow papers, but it was un-

available to the authors; see Ross Terrill, *The White-Boned Demon* (New York, 1984), p. 413, for his summary of the text with Lois Snow.

16. Edgar Snow, "Mō Takutō no renai."

17. Wales, *Chinese Communists,* Book 2, pp. 250–54.

18. On the Jiangxi experience, see Chi-hsi Hu, "The Sexual Revolution in the Kiangsi Soviet," *China Quarterly* 59 (July–September 1974): 477–90.

19. Smedley's depression over the Party rejection is confirmed in interviews: with Chen Hansheng; Rewi Alley; and in Hatem, "On Agnes Smedley"; as well as memoirs of Nym Wales, see chapter 13, note 2.

20. Smedley's words were recalled by Jacques Marcuse, *The Peking Papers: Leaves from the Notebook of a China Correspondent* (New York, 1967), p. 286.

13. THE EIGHTH ROUTE ARMY AND THE MAGIC OF HANKOU, 1937–1938

1. *China Fights Back,* pp. 17–18.

2. This is clear from an interview with Nym Wales in June 1975; from her *Chinese Communists,* pp. 252–54; and her memoir, *My China Years* (New York, 1984), pp. 264–87.

3. The Eighth Route Army headquarters at Xi'an is today a museum.

4. Interviews: Zhou Libo; Zhou Yang.

5. See, for example, Ross Terrill, *Mao* (New York, 1980), p. 159.

6. Jawaharlal Nehru, *Bunch of Old Letters* (Delhi, 1958), pp. 260–62; and the Basu diaries, read in the handwritten original in New Delhi, November, 1977, along with an interview with Dr. B. K. Basu, who was a member of the five-man mission. Further details in Congress Party and Nehru papers, Nehru Library, New Delhi, files for 1937–38.

7. Today there is a Kotnis memorial hospital in central Hebei province, as well as many commemorative volumes put out by both sides. A recent example is *Jinian Ketihua* (Beijing, 1982), which has on p. 129 a photo of Smedley with the mission in Hankou. In English, see Sheng Xiangong, *An Indian Freedom Fighter in China* (Beijing, 1983).

8. *Battle Hymn,* p. 198.

9. Michael Blankfort, *Big Yankee: The Life of Carlson of the Raiders* (Boston, 1947), p. 205, citing an undated Smedley letter to the author.

10. Excerpts from Carlson's diary are quoted by Blankfort, *Big Yankee,* pp. 205–7.

11. *Battle Hymn,* p. 199.

12. Diary entries from Blankfort, *Big Yankee,* pp. 211–12.

13. Ibid., p. 209; interview with Kang Keqing.

14. On Smedley the celebrity see *New York Times* for 1938: January 13, February 5, March 28.

15. Howard Boorman, ed., *Dictionary of Republican China* (New York, 1967–71), vol. 3, pp. 373–74; interview with Zhang Wenjin; also "Red Cross Society Recuperates from Heavy War Losses," *China Weekly Review,* April 9, 1938, p. 166.

16. *Battle Hymn,* pp. 212–31, focuses on medical work. Interviews: Randall Gould; F. McCracken Fisher; A. T. Steele; Israel Epstein. Also see John P. Davies, *Dragon by the Tail* (New York, 1972), p. 195. Two contemporary press accounts are *New York Times,* March 28, 1938, and Smedley's own "Help Needed for Eighth Route Army and Partisans of Northwest" (see Bibliography).

17. Tracy Strong and Helene Keyssar, *Right in Her Soul: The Life of Anna L. Strong* (New York, 1983), pp. 180–81.

18. Frank Dorn, *The Sino-Japanese War* (New York, 1974), p. 190; confirmed in interview.

19. Freda Utley, *Odyssey of a Liberal* (Washington, D.C., 1970), pp. 200–201. Utley became an ultra-rightist, propagandist for the China lobby, and participant in the McCarthy attacks on China experts from government, academia, and the press in the early 1950s. Hence this flattering portrait of Smedley in her memoirs is all the more remarkable and a testimony to their special personal relationship; confirmed by interview with Utley.

20. The "formal charges" set forth at the dinner are to be found in the F. McCracken Fisher papers; the presiding judge was A. T. Steele: interviews with A. T. Steele, and F. McCracken Fisher. Smedley's affectionate letter and the "formal charges" are reproduced and discussed in MacKinnon and Friesen, *China Reporting,* chapter 4, devoted to the Hankou press corps.

21. *Xinhua ribao,* January 15, 1938; *Kangzhan wenyi,* August 13, 1938. Guo Moruo, *Hong boqu* (Tianjin, 1959); *Renmin ribao,* March 18, 1979; interviews with Kong Loushun and Ge Baochuan; see vol. 1 of *Guo Moruo nianpu* (Beijing, 1983), for Hankou activities.

22. *Shimodelai Zhongguo renmin zhi you* (Beijing, 1950), pp. 40–44.

23. Utley, *Odyssey of a Liberal,* pp. 206–7; Tillman Durdin was a *New York Times* correspondent at the time; Jack Belden worked for United Press and is considered by many today to have been the best Asian war correspondent of his generation. For more on both men, see MacKinnon and Friesen, *China Reporting.*

14. AT THE FRONT, 1939–1941

1. Gregor Benton, "The South Anhui Incident," *Journal of Asian Studies* 45, no. 4 (August 1986): 681–720, is the definitive work in English; see also Anhui Sheng Junqu, eds., *Xinsijun zai Anhui* (Hefei, 1982), for greater detail.

2. Interview with Shen Jizhen; photo exhibit, National Military Museum, Beijing, 1978. Also Anhui Sheng Junqu, eds., *Xinsijun zai Anhui,* pp. 230–35, and Shen Chi-chen (Shen Jizhen), "In Memory of Agnes Smedley," *China Reconstructs* (December 1960): 27–29.

3. In addition to Smedley articles cited in the Bibliography, see Smedley to Brundin, March 9, 1939, and to Mildred Price and Jean Chang, June 29 and July 25, 1939 (Smedley papers). Interview with Shen Jizhen.

4. Interview with Shen Jizhen.

5. Wu Jiang, "Shimodelai zai Huinan," *Yibao zhoukan* (1939); for Wu's later career, see *Beijing wanbao,* June 23, 1980.

6. Interview with Wu Jiang.

7. Quote from Wu Yunduo, *Bayijie xianjidang* (Beijing, 1953), pp. 26–27; story confirmed by interview with Shen Jizhen.

8. Asiaticus, "Critique and Responses to Snow," *Pacific Affairs* 11, no. 2 (June 1938): 237–52.

9. Edgar Snow, *Random Notes on Red China* (Cambridge, Mass., 1957), pp. 20–22.

10. For subtleties of the split, see Benton, "South Anhui Incident," pp. 684–85. The specific issue in the spring of 1939 was whether to position substantial numbers of troops north of the Yangzi. Clearly Smedley sided with Chen Yi, who wanted to go north despite Guomindang objections. Chen Yi was Smedley's favorite New Fourth Army commander and in the summer she would follow his units north. Interview with Dr. Shen Jizhen, Wang Huo, "Hansi Xibo," *Geming wenwu*, no. 4 (July–August 1979): 38–41.

11. Edgar Snow to Peg (Helen Foster) Snow, June 4, 1939, from Hong Kong (in Nym Wales's private possession). The authors are indebted to John M. Hamilton for the reference.

12. On the Guangxi warlords, see Diana Lary, *Region and Nation: The Kwangsi Clique in Chinese Politics, 1925–37* (London, 1974). Also see Smedley to Mildred Price (two letters) of China Aid Council (New York), dated October 19, 1939 (courtesy of Ayako Ishigaki); *Manchester Guardian*, April 13, 1940; and *Battle Hymn*, Book 7.

13. Nehru correspondence, nos. 5594–95, 5610–12 and Hutheesing papers, vol. 33, pp. 55–56; both located in the Nehru Memorial Library, New Delhi, India. See also *Battle Hymn*, p. 299.

14. *Renmin ribao* (People's Daily), memoir biography of Smedley by Li Lou, March 11, 18, 1979.

15. Smedley to China Aid Council, November 8, 1939, from Henan. On bandit–secret-society collaboration with New Fourth Army guerrilla units, see Elizabeth Perry, *Rebels and Revolutionaries in North China, 1845–1945* (Stanford, 1981).

16. *Battle Hymn*, Book 9; photos in Museum of Chinese History, Beijing, and University Archives, Arizona State University.

17. Source material on Big Sister Chen is scarce; for a portrait see *Beijing wanbao*, January 1, 1981; also *Battle Hymn*, p. 460. Big Sister Chen, who became a general and held high military positions into the 1970s, never married. In China in 1980 this fact still seemed a point of embarrassment and may help to explain the lack of attention to her in contemporary histories. Discussions at National Military Museum, Beijing, 1978, and with Li Zongyi, Modern History Institute, March, 1984.

18. For an academic study of General Dai Li's historical role see Lloyd Eastman, *The Abortive Revolution: China under Nationalist Rule* (Cambridge, Mass., 1974), chapter 2. For a more informal, sympathetic portrait of Dai Li in Chongqing, see H. O. Yardley's memoir references to "Hatchet Man" in *The Chinese Black Chamber: An Adventure in Espionage* (Boston, 1983).

19. "Agnes Smedley Addresses Club," *China at War* 4, no. 5 (June 1940): 36–40; *New York Times*, April 17, 1940; *Battle Hymn*, pp. 499–500. Inter-

views with Hugh Deane, and T. H. White, as well as Hugh Deane, "Meeting Agnes Smedley," *China and U.S.* 3, no. 2 (March—April 1974): 9.

20. Interviews with Lu Yunming, and Zhang Wenjin; also Zhang Wenjin's letter to the authors, April 14, 1985. Some underground Communists worked for Dr. Lin. One of them was Zhang Wenjin, who in the 1980s became vice-minister of Foreign Affairs and ambassador to Washington, D.C. Zhang joined Dr. Lin in 1939 after graduating from Qinghua University. He left Guiyang as soon as the Guomindang agent, Wang Zhong, arrived. Zhang proceeded to Chongqing and worked for the rest of the decade for Zhou Enlai.

21. *South China Morning Post,* August 27, 29, 1940.

22. Many memoir accounts depict the liveliness of Chinese intellectual life at the time. Besides those of Zou Taofen and Mao Dun cited earlier, see Xu Zijian's memoir in *Wenhuibao* (Hong Kong), November 22, 1978, p. 10.

23. *South China Morning Post,* September 21, 26, 27, 28, 1940. Smedley's observations on Hong Kong were revised and published in the *Clipper* (Los Angeles) as "The Light of East Asia" 2, no. 7 (September 1941): 11—16.

24. *Lih Pao,* December 11, 1940; *Sing Tao Jih Pao,* October 21, 1940; *Hong Kong Daily Press,* November 12, 15, 1940.

25. Interviews: Rewi Alley; Elsie Cholmeley; Israel Epstein; Chen Hansheng. See also oblique references in medical relief records, Public Records Office (London), FO 676, file 301.

26. Benton, "South Anhui Incident," is the definitive study.

27. Strong and Keyssar, *Right in Her Soul,* pp. 196—99; Anna Louise Strong, "The Kuomintang-Communist Crisis in China," *Amerasia* 5, no. 1 (March 1941): 11—23.

28. *South China Morning Post,* January 14, 1941; interview with Rewi Alley, and Harry Steinmetz; Emily Hahn, *China to Me* (New York, 1944), p. 245.

29. *Battle Hymn,* p. 523; William White, ed., *ByLine: Ernest Hemingway* (New York, 1967), pp. 303—39; interview with Rosie Tan; *Hong Kong Sunday Herald,* March 9, 1941.

30. Hahn, *China to Me,* pp. 243—44; confirmed by interview with Emily Hahn.

31. *Battle Hymn,* p. 524; Mao Dun, Preface to *Hulan he zhuan* (Guilin, 1942), pp. 27—28; also Lo Binji, *Xiao Hong xiaozhuan* (Shanghai, 1947), p. 142. For an excellent treatment in English see Howard Goldblatt, *Hsiao Hong* (Boston, 1976).

15. CALIFORNIA REVISITED, 1941—1942

1. Interviews: Freda Utley; Harry Steinmetz. Josephine Bennett Brooks was another "angel."

2. See Michael Schaller, *The United States and China in the Twentieth Century* (New York, 1979), pp. 60—61, for a sophisticated summary of the specialized works by Dorothy Borg, himself, and others.

3. On the group of those with hands-on experience with Chinese Commu-

nists, see Kenneth E. Shewmaker, *Americans and Chinese Communists, 1927–45: A Persuading Encounter* (Ithaca, N.Y., 1971).

4. Interview with Elinor Brundin.

5. *San Diego Union,* June 11, 1941. On the list also was J. B. Powell. See F.B.I. 100–1541–5 for report on San Diego Smedley-Carlson talk dated July 8, 1941.

6. Carlson to Smedley, March 26, 1943, in Smedley papers.

7. Publicity in Smedley papers; also *New Republic,* September 22, 1941, Smedley's letter to the editor. Smedley debated on more than one occasion a Mr. Carroll Lunt, who took Japan's side in the Sino-Japanese War and downplayed the threat to the United States.

8. Interviews: Aino Taylor; Harry Steinmetz.

9. Smedley diary fragments in Smedley papers. See also *Los Angeles Times* for December 9, 1941, plus Smedley papers for more reports on talks.

10. Speech summarized in "China, Front Door to Freedom," *California Arts and Architecture,* see Bibliography.

11. Quotes from "China, Front Door to Freedom."

12. Interview with Mamie Weston McCullough.

16. BITTERSWEET HOMECOMING: NEW YORK, 1942–1943

1. On Anna L. Strong's role as spokesperson, see Strong and Keyssar, *Right in Her Soul,* pp. 196–99.

2. For Emily Hahn's whereabouts at the time, see her memoir, *China to Me.*

3. Two letters to Taylor, dated only en route to and from Chicago; interview with Emily Hahn.

4. To Taylor, en route from Chicago to New York, 1942.

5. Two letters to Taylor, dated only October and November, 1942.

6. Alfred Kazin, *New York Jew* (New York, 1978), pp. 58–64.

7. See John Hersey's comments in chapter 2, "Henry Luce and the Gordian Knot," in MacKinnon and Friesen, *China Reporting.*

8. Cited in Barbara Tuchman, *Stilwell and the American Experience in China* (New York, 1970), p. 238.

9. Kazin, *New York Jew,* p. 61; letter to Taylor, January 24, 1943.

10. Letters to Taylor, February 7, 27, 1943, and letter dated only October, 1942.

11. Letter to Taylor, January 27, 1943.

12. Letter to Taylor, November 20, 1942.

13. Letter to Taylor dated October, 1942. Dr. Liu had been a close associate of Dr. Robert K. Lin's and a high Guomindang medical official since 1930; for Liu's views in 1943 on China's medical needs, see his contribution in Harley F. MacNair, ed., *Voices from Unoccupied China* (Chicago, 1944), pp. 36–45.

14. Letter to Taylor, January 27, 1943.

15. For Smedley's sympathetic interest in these events and meetings, see letters to Taylor, November 11 and December 8, 1942, and January 13, 1943.

16. Letters to Taylor, December 12, 1942, and January 13, 1943.

17. Letter to Taylor, October, 1942.

18. Letter to Taylor, January 3, 1943; interview with William Powell (J. B. Powell's son).

19. Letter to Taylor, January 3, 1943.

20. Letters to Taylor, March 17, 25, 31, 1943; and interview with William Powell.

21. *St. Louis Daily Globe Democrat,* April 21, 1943, noted Smedley's Press Club appearance. In social situations like the one at the Magruder home, Smedley, as she had in the 1920s, was proving unwilling to play Eliza Doolittle, even a middle-class version: "I met a descendant of Thomas Jefferson. . . . Almost no chin, an old-maid face, and she wore a stiff sailor hat with stiff feathers sticking straight up in front. . . . She is the wife of a Colonel and she looks like one of those Daughters of the American Revolution. . . . The only value I could see in her was that she was a descendant of Jefferson; and all that he was had been washed out of her. I told her that were I a descendant of Jefferson, I would be a flaming torch" (letter to Taylor, April 24, 1943).

22. Tuchman, *Stilwell,* pp. 452–53.

23. T. H. White, *In Search of History* (New York, 1972), pp. 144–56.

24. Whittaker Chambers, *Witness* (New York, 1952), pp. 86–87, 503.

17. RIDING HIGH: YADDO AND THE LECTURE CIRCUIT, 1943–1944

1. Smedley to Malcolm Cowley, June 20, 1943; on Elizabeth Ames, see the obituary in the *New York Times,* March 30, 1977.

2. Virginia Spencer Carr, *The Lonely Hunter: A Biography of Carson Mc-Cullers* (New York, 1975), p. 233.

3. F.B.I. 61–6580–127, p. 58.

4. Smedley to Elviira Taylor, August 17, 1943; J. B. Powell to Elviira Taylor, November 22, 1943. The reviews appeared in *New York Herald Tribune,* September 5; *New York Times Book Review,* September 5; *Newsweek,* September 6, pp. 109–10; and *New York Times,* September 18.

5. Louisville *Courier-Journal,* October 10; Kansas City *Star,* September 11; *Saturday Review of Literature,* September 18; *Nation,* October 2; *New Yorker,* September 11; *Christian Register* (February 1944).

6. Field quote from *New Masses,* November 30, 1943; also *Asia* (October 1943); *New York Post,* September 8, 1943.

7. *Shanghai Evening Post and Mercury* (American ed., New York), October 1, 1943.

8. She wrote to Aino Taylor on September 8, 1943: "I'm working on my play. Buried in the pines, in a little wooden bungalow; all but two guests have gone, and we alone inhabit the great mansion. A snake got into the huge reception room and made its home under a statue—we chased it out. It was a poor garter snake living on mosquitoes and flies and bugs. Poor things! . . . I dread going on lecture tour."

9. *Skidmore News,* September 29, 1943; *Publisher's Weekly,* October 16, 1943, p. 1529.

10. Smedley to A. Taylor, October 11, 1943; *Boston Traveler,* October 21, and *New York Herald-Tribune,* October 27, 1943.

11. Smedley's account of tour in letter to A. Taylor, December 17, 1943.

12. Smedley to A. Taylor, June 11, 1944; for clippings from the tour, see Smedley papers, file VI–73D–5, 12, 13, 14, 16, 18, 65, 67, 68, 70, and 73E–5; Smedley's account in letters to A. Taylor, February 4, May 8, 15, 1944.

13. *Chicago Daily News,* March 17, 1944.

14. Smedley papers, file VI–73D–5, 12, 16, 18, 67, and 73E–5.

15. *Los Angeles Tribune,* February 21, 1944, and Smedley papers, file VI–73D–64, 65, 67, 71; see also *Afro-American,* July 29, 1944.

16. Gibson, August 29, 1944, in *Congressional Record,* vol. 90, part 12, pp. 7378–80 and appendix 3906.

17. F.B.I. 61–6580–332, pp. 12, 13; 100–9125–1–5 (Albany); Malcolm Cowley papers, Yaddo Box, second folder marked "1949, Yaddo—The Affair." The name of the secretary was Mary Townsend, whose personal relations with Smedley were, needless to say, never good.

18. Carr, *Lonely Hunter,* p. 248.

19. Interview with Katherine A. Porter; Joan Givner, *Katherine Anne Porter: A Life* (New York, 1982), references to the Habermans on pp. 151, 152, 157, 209, 217, and chapter 7 on the Greenwich Village and Mexico City network.

20. Interview with Xie Hegeng; Xie, Introduction to *Liangzhong Meiguoren* (Beijing, 1980); Smedley to Wang Yong: June 15, 1944, and three datable by context between May and July, 1944; also Wang Yong to Smedley, June 20, 1944, February 28, 1945.

21. Smedley to A. Taylor, August 9, 1944.

18. FRIENDS BECOME ENEMIES: THE DEBATE OVER CHINA POLICY, 1944–1945

1. See Dick Wilson, *When Tigers Fight* (New York, 1982), pp. 223–46, on the military situation; Tuchman, *Stilwell,* and Michael Schaller, *The United States Crusade in China, 1938–1945* (New York, 1979), are authoritative background works on F.D.R.'s decision.

2. The most readable accounts of this famous episode are probably Tuchman, *Stilwell,* pp. 581–670, and White, *In Search of History,* pp. 132–79. See also Schaller, *United States Crusade,* for a deeper exploration of American motives.

3. *Time,* November 13, 1944; White, *In Search of History,* pp. 209–10. See also Schaller's comments on press coverage of Stilwell's recall in chapter 8 of MacKinnon and Friesen, *China Reporting.*

4. Hahn, *China to Me,* pp. 199–200; Carlson to Smedley, December 22, 1944; and F.B.I. 61–6580–9, p. 19.

5. Carlson to Smedley, March 26, 1943. For a detailed discussion of the agrarian reformer idea see E. J. Kahn, Jr., *The China Hands: America's Foreign*

Service Officers and What Befell Them (New York, 1975), pp. 112–14, and Shewmaker, *American and Chinese Communists*. For Freda Utley's relationship with the China Lobby and Guomindang see Ross Y. Koen, *The China Lobby in American Politics* (2d ed. New York, 1974).

6. Carlson to Smedley, May 26, 1943.

7. For Carlson's career see Blankfort, *Big Yankee*.

8. Smedley to A. Taylor, November 6, 1943.

9. Smedley to Anna Wang, October, 1945.

10. The rise of Alfred Kohlberg is a remarkable story, told with much sympathy by Joseph Keeley in *The China Lobby Man* (New York, 1969). Coincidentally, Kohlberg and Smedley shared an admiration for Dr. Robert K. Lin, whom Kohlberg had first met while raising funds for medical aid to China during the early 1940s.

11. F.B.I. 61–6580–2, 3 and 127, p. 197.

12. See *Fries Deutschland* and other German press clippings in Smedley papers; Smedley, "What Chinese Soldiers Asked Me to Tell," *German-American*, October 19, 1943; F.B.I. 61–6580–6, 9 and 127, p. 163.

13. See also White, *In Search of History*, pp. 176–79.

14. F.B.I. 61–6580–9, p. 38; Smedley to A. Taylor, December 11, 1944.

15. F.B.I. 61–6580–9, pp. 32–34, and clippings in Smedley papers, file V–73D–79.

16. F.B.I. 100–9125–12 and 61–6580–222, p. 4; clippings in Smedley papers, files V–72–10 and VI–73D–82; Smedley to A. Taylor, January 8, 1944.

17. *New York Times*, January 28, 1945; Smedley to A. Taylor, January 24, 1945. Sun Fo was the son of Dr. Sun Yat-sen's first wife and a favorite alternative to Chiang Kai-shek.

18. Smedley to A. Taylor, March 7, 1943.

19. F.B.I. 61–6580–7.

20. F.B.I. 61–6580–5, 9, and 100–9125–5.

21. F.B.I. 61–6580–127, p. 134.

22. F.B.I. 100–68282–464 and 61–6580–127, p. 137.

23. F.B.I. 61–6580–20. The Amerasia case centered on the discovery by government agents in March, 1945, of classified (O.S.S.) documents in the offices of the allegedly pro-Communist *Amerasia* monthly. In June six people, including Gayn, were arrested under the Espionage Act; eventually three were indicted, two of whom were found guilty and fined. Historically the case is important as one of the first internal subversion or spy cases leading to the House Un-American Activities Committee and McCarthy-McCarran hearings of the late 1940s and early 1950s. On the case and its echoes, see Kahn, Jr., *China Hands*, pp. 163–71.

24. F.B.I. 100–9125–27.

25. Smedley to A. Taylor, June 1, 1945; *Saratogian*, August 8, 1945.

26. Donald Klein and Ann Clark, eds., *Biographical Dictionary of Chinese Communism* (Cambridge, Mass., 1971), pp. 341–45.

27. Smedley to A. Taylor, August 12, 1945, as well as Smedley's published work from this period.

28. Full texts of Round Table papers in Smedley papers; Smedley's comments had been published in *PM,* August 19, 1945.

29. F.B.I. 61–6580–14, p. 4.

19. THE COLD WAR BEGINS, 1945–1948

1. Smedley to Karin Michaelis, July 21, 1947.

2. F.B.I. 100–9125–42; 61–6580–20, 21, 127, p. 168 (included in *Weekly Intelligence Summary,* no. 204, Army Services, Boston). See also 100–1541–5.

3. F.B.I. 61–6580–20, 29, p. 8, 117, p. 11. In the 1940s *Daughter of Earth* was out of print but available in libraries.

4. F.B.I. 100–9125–49.

5. F.B.I. 61–6580–27.

6. Kenneth O'Reilly, *Hoover and the UnAmericans* (Philadelphia, 1983), chapter 3, especially pp. 76–77; on the Security Index, see Athan G. Theoharis, "In-house Cover-up: Researching FBI Files," in Theoharis, ed., *Beyond the Hiss Case* (Philadelphia, 1982), pp. 31–32.

7. F.B.I. 61–6580–127, p. 208. Writer Ralph Bates and Mrs. Ames's secretary (Mary Townsend) appear to be the informants.

8. In China in 1934–35 and 1940, Smedley had befriended Berislav Borcic and other Yugoslav doctors. In 1946 she was alarmed by American news reports criticizing the independent nationalist challenge of Tito. She wrote to Anna Wang in China on February 29: "I have just read a clipping from a Shanghai paper—an interview with Dr. Borcic. My heart was deeply moved when I read of his activities in Yugoslavia during the war and his tribute to Tito. How deeply I was moved you cannot know! The reaction in this country is so very great, and smart alec newspaper men have been 'exposing' Tito as a tyrant who kills all who do not agree with his personal political viewpoint."

9. Kenneth Chern, "Politics of American China Policy, 1945: Roots of the Cold War in Asia," *Political Science Quarterly* 91, no. 4 (Winter 1976–77): 631–47.

10. Fairbank, *China Bound;* on Wen Yiduo, see Spence, *Gate of Heavenly Peace,* pp. 228–33, 249–54, 313–17, 337–44; *New York Times,* March 7, 1946; F.B.I. 61–6580–223, p. 73; Smedley, "Voice from the Grave," *New Republic,* May 28, 1945; Smedley to A. Taylor, February 29, 1946; to Wang, August 31, 1946; Smedley, "We're Building a Fascist China," *Nation,* August 31, 1946, p. 236.

11. F.B.I. 61–6580–127, p. 189. On the China Lobby at this time, see Koen, *China Lobby,* pp. 27–78, and, for Kohlberg as an individual, Keeley, *China Lobby Man.* On the Truman administration, Greece, the Marshall Plan, and the Red Scare, see Richard M. Freeland, *The Truman Doctrine and the Origins of McCarthyism* (New York, 1972).

12. F.B.I. 65–56402–1862, p. 281, and 61–6580–127, p. 182.

13. F.B.I. 100–9125–64, 102, p. 10, and 61–6580–31.

14. On Yang Gang see *Yang Gang wenji* (Beijing, 1984); *Meiguo zhaji* (Beijing, 1950); Gao Ji, "Yang Gang he tadi Meiguo," *Xinwen zhanxian,* no. 2

(1980): 30–33; and Fairbank, *China Bound*, pp. 273–77; interview with writer Xiao Qian.

15. Interviews, Chen Hansheng; *Shanghai wenshi ziliao xuanji*, vol. 43 (Shanghai, 1983), pp. 133–46.

16. Interview with Lao She's widow, Hu Xieqing. In Chinese, the key biographical work is Hu Xieqing, *Lao She shenghuo* (Hong Kong, 1980); in English, with emphasis on the American years, see Spence, *Gate of Heavenly Peace*, esp. p. 394.

17. Smedley to Israel Epstein, October 16, 1946; F.B.I. 61–6580–30 and 100–9125–65. For an example of a Stilwell letter to Smedley at about this time, see Alley, *Six Americans in China*, p. 197.

18. Zhu De to Smedley, July 1, 1946, and Smedley to Zhu De, December 17, 1946.

19. Karen Kerpen, "The Committee for a Democratic Far Eastern Policy," *U.S.-China Review* 6, no. 3 (May 1982): 23–24, and no. 4 (August 1982): 22–24. Interview with Elsie Cholmeley and Israel Epstein. See also Chen Hansheng, "In Memory of a Dear Old Friend," *China Reconstructs* 33, no. 12 (December 1984): 30–32. *Newsletter* (China Aid Council) 7, nos. 1–8 (January–August 1945) in Smedley papers.

20. Smedley to Epstein, October 16, 1946; F.B.I. 61–6580–30 and 100–9125–65.

21. Smedley to Epstein, October 6, 1946, and to Elsie Cholmeley, October 30, 1946. One of Stilwell's letters to Smedley, dated April 6, 1946, was leaked to the *Daily Worker* and published on January 26, 1947. It was miscaptioned "Stilwell Itched to Fight in Chu Teh's Army"; the letter itself says it was Zhu De who had agreed to fight under Stilwell. The whereabouts of most of the letters remains a mystery; for a few see Alley, *Six Americans in China;* see also Tuchman, *Stilwell*, pp. 673–74.

22. T. H. White, ed., *The Stilwell Papers* (New York, 1948).

23. Smedley, "In Memoriam—Evans Carlson," eulogy delivered on January 25, 1948, and published in *Social Questions Bulletin* 38, no. 4 (May 1948). See also Blankfort, *Big Yankee*.

24. F.B.I. 61–6580–57, pp. 1–2 and 127, p. 210.

25. F.B.I. 61–6580–34 and 100–68282–36.

26. F.B.I. 61–6580–32, with appendix 1B32 including the full statement of charges, is the key document; see also 61–6580–127, p. 202, and 100–9125–68.

27. Smedley to A. Taylor, November 13, 1947. F.B.I. 100–9125–70; 100–68282–464; 61–6580–127, pp. 194–95.

28. The *Tribune* articles were written from a narrow Cold War perspective and did not note that the United States had been an ally of the Russians and at war with Japan at the time Sorge was caught and executed (1941, 1944). Simmons seemed to equate the two men with Tojo and other Japanese war criminals. Moreover, Simmons accused a leading figure in the Japanese Communist Party, Itō Ritsu, of being the key figure who had been indirectly responsible for the cracking of the spy ring by the Japanese authorities. The evidence later made

public was not conclusive, but the leak about Itō managed to split the Japanese Communist Party into two factions, those who believed Itō was innocent and those who did not. This, of course, was exactly what General Willoughby, Mac-Arthur's intelligence chief, had hoped for. On Itō Ritsu and the Sorge case in general, see Johnson, *An Instance of Treason*.

29. F.B.I. 100–9125–105 and 61–6580–103, p. 15; Smedley to A. Taylor, September 13, 1948; transcript of February 26, 1949, Yaddo Board of Directors meeting in Malcolm Cowley papers, Yaddo Box, folder 2; Elizabeth Ames to Cowley, April 16, 1948, and dated only "Wednesday"; *Skidmore News*, October 27, 1947.

20. THE LAST ACT, 1948–1950

1. *Plain Talk* (May 1948): 1.

2. F.B.I. 100–9125–83; 100–68282–1B32 (Exhibits) includes Willoughby documents in toto.

3. F.B.I. 61–6580–31, 38.

4. *New York Herald Tribune*, April 6, 1948, and James Sheridan, *Chinese Warlord: The Career of Feng Yu-hsiang* (Stanford, 1966).

5. F.B.I. 100–68282–137.

6. Ayako Ishigaki, *Kaiso no Sumedore* (Tokyo, 1967), pp. 180, 192; and Smedley to Zhu De, October, 1949.

7. F.B.I. 100–9125–78.

8. *New York Mirror*, February 11, 1949; F.B.I. 100–68282–137.

9. *New York Mirror*, December 21, 1948.

10. Koen, *China Lobby*.

11. F.B.I. 100–68282–137; *Time*, January 31, 1949, p. 53. Smedley remained on bad terms with the editors of the *Daily Worker* and thus never contributed articles, but she had been mentioned as a speaker, and parts of articles published elsewhere had been reprinted there.

12. F.B.I. 61–6580–48 and 127, pp. 243–44.

13. U.S. Army, Far East Command, Military Intelligence Section (G-2), *Sorge Espionage Case,* dated December 15, 1947, to be found in the F.B.I. Exhibits cited in note 2; the report was slightly revised and privately printed for the House Committee by Willoughby in 1951.

14. Press release for February 10, 1949, Smedley papers; on Rogge, see, for example, his *Our Vanishing Civil Liberties* (New York, 1949).

15. Copy of radio statement, February 10, Smedley papers; published as "J'accuse," *China Digest* (Hong Kong), March 8, 1949, pp. 8–9; see also *New York Herald Tribune*, February 11, 1949.

16. *New York Times*, February 12, 1949.

17. *New York Times*, February 16, 1949.

18. *New York Times*, February 19, 1949.

19. F.B.I. 100–68282–93; *New York Mirror*, February 22, 1949; *New York Times*, February 22, 1949; *New York Post*, March 19, 1949.

20. Johnson, *An Instance of Treason;* Francis X. Gannon (John Birch Society), *Biographical Dictionary of the Left* (Boston, 1969–73), pp. 583–88;

Arizona Republic, February 23, 1975. Recent works drawing on Willoughby are Pincher, *Too Secret Too Long*, and Prange, *Target Tokyo*.

21. *New York World Telegram*, February 10, 1949. Willoughby wrote his report in 1947. At that time he was also using Kohlberg's allegations about the Institute of Pacific Relations to investigate and purge American occupation government figures like the scholarly T. A. Bisson. See Howard Schonberger, "T. A. Bisson and the Limits of Reform in Occupied Japan," *Bulletin of Concerned Asian Scholars* 12, no. 4 (December 1980): 26–37.

22. *New York Times*, February 20, 1949.

23. *Plain Talk* (March–April 1949); reproduced in Willoughby, *Sorge Espionage Case* (note 13). *New York World Telegram*, February 10, and *New York Mirror*, February 11, 1949. *Daily Worker*, February 11, 1949. *Nation*, February 19, 1949, pp. 202–3; *Washington Star*, February 11; *Washington Post*, March 3, p. 12; *New York Post and Home News*, February 11.

24. Transcript of meeting in Cowley papers, Yaddo Box, dated February 26, 1949, typescript; F.B.I. 61–6580–103, pp. 21–22.

25. Robert Fitzgerald, summarizing Lowell's view in an Open Letter, May 26, 1949, Cowley papers.

26. Ian Hamilton, *Robert Lowell: A Biography* (New York, 1982), pp. 145–46, quoting February 26 transcript (cited in note 24).

27. February 26, 1949, transcript; see also F.B.I. comments in 61–6580–103, pp. 21–22.

28. F.B.I. 61–6580–103, pp. 21–22; confirmed by February 26 transcript.

29. Cowley to Louis Kronenberger, March 8, 1949, in Cowley papers, Yaddo Box.

30. Carr, *Lonely Hunter*, p. 326; petition in Cowley papers, Yaddo Box; *New York Herald Tribune*, March 27, 1949, for press coverage.

31. F.B.I. 100–68282–130, 134.

32. F.B.I. 61–6580–61.

33. F.B.I. 61–6580–52, 61, 100, 127, and 100–68282–129, 163.

34. F.B.I. 100–9125–102.

35. F.B.I. 61–6580–52.

36. F.B.I. 100–68282–129, 130, 132.

37. F.B.I. 100–68282–103, p. 14, and 61–6580–127, p. 254; for 1945 interview see 61–6580–61; also sources in the footnote on p. 325.

38. F.B.I. 61–6580–89, 94, 121, 127, 135, 142, 164, 180, 223; 100–68282–130, 190.

39. Excerpt from T. H. White letter quoted in Smedley to Harold Ickes, March 6, 1949, in Ickes papers.

40. *New York Post*, March 16, 19, 1949; Charles A. Willoughby, *Shanghai Conspiracy* (New York, 1952); the secondary literature on Harold Ickes (1874–1952), progressive politician and journalist, and secretary of the interior from 1933 to 1946, is voluminous. For a recent popular portrait see T. H. Watkins, "The Terrible-Tempered Mr. Ickes," *Audubon* 86, no. 2 (March 1984): 94–111. Relevant Smedley to Ickes correspondence, dated February 25, 26, March 6, and March 28, 1949, is in Ickes papers.

41. F.B.I. 61–6580–127, p. 278. On the conference see Dwight Macdon-

ald, "Waldorf Conference," *Politics* (Winter 1949): 37A–D. Freda Kirchway, "Battle of the Waldorf," *Nation*, April 2, 1949, pp. 377–78; Margaret Marshal, "Notes by the Way," *Nation*, April 9, 1949, pp. 419–20; Joseph Lash, "Weekend at the Waldorf," *New Republic*, April 18, 1949, pp. 10–14; William Barrett, "Culture Conference of the Waldorf," *Commentary* (May 1949):487–93.

42. *New York Times*, March 28, 1949; MacDonald, *Politics*, p. 32C.

43. William L. O'Neill, *A Better World, the Great Schism: Stalinism and the American Intellectuals* (New York, 1982), pp. 129, 163–69, 186–88, 259, 290.

44. Marjia Vilfan, "Agnes Smedley," *Review of International Affairs* (Belgrade) 1, no. 1 (June 7, 1958): 16 (reference courtesy of Mark Seldon).

45. F.B.I. 100–68282–173; *Daily Worker*, June 12, 1949.

46. Strong and Keyssar, *Right in Her Soul*, pp. 233–65. It was because of this split in the Committee for Democratic Far Eastern Policy over the Strong matter that two (rival) memorial meetings were held in New York after Smedley's death in May, 1950. One was organized by Snow; the other by the committee.

47. Smedley to Raymond Robins, February 12, 1949, in Robins papers.

48. Ishigaki, *Kaiso no Sumedore*, pp. 190–96; interview with David Loth; Smedley to Ickes, August 23, 1949, in Ickes papers.

49. Private communication, Lois W. Snow, May, 1984; interview with Loth.

50. Ishigaki, *Kaiso no Sumedore*, pp. 190–92; Smedley to Zhu De, October, 1949; F.B.I. 61–6580–181.

51. Smedley to Zhu De, October, 1949; Ishigaki, *Kaiso no Sumedore*, p. 193.

52. Smedley to Zhu De, October, 1949; Ishigaki, *Kaiso no Sumedore*, pp. 192–93; Smedley to Raymond Robins, August 23, September 6, 1949.

53. Smedley to Ickes, August 25, 29, 30, September 6, 12, 22, 30, October 20, 31, November 4, 1949; also Ickes, "Death by Assassination," *New Republic*, May 29, 1950; Ishigaki, *Kaiso no Sumedore*, p. 200; Smedley to Zhu De, October, 1949; F.B.I. 61–6580–168, 328, p. 60.

54. Ishigaki, *Kaiso no Sumedore*, pp. 196–200; Smedley to Ickes, October 20, 1949; Ambassador Vijaya L. Pandit to Ickes, June 26, 1950; interview with Tang Mingqiao; Ickes, "Death by Assassination," pp. 16–17.

55. Interview with Chen Hansheng.

56. Ishigaki, *Kaiso no Sumedore*, pp. 194–95.

57. Circular letter beginning "Dear family," undated but clearly late November, 1949 (courtesy of A. Ishigaki). See also letters to A. Taylor, December, 1949, January 23, February 11, 1950.

58. Circular letter to "Dear family," undated but clearly late November, 1949.

59. Circular letter dated December 2, 1949.

60. Interview with Hu Ji'an.

61. Smedley to Chris Rand, undated (courtesy of Peter Rand); interview with Hu Ji'an; Smedley to Wang, March 18, 1950.

62. "Agnes Smedley's Last Plea," *Korean Handbook* (London, 1950), pp. 9–12; and "Terror Bombing in China," *Labour Monthly* (July 1950): 302–4. Quote from the latter.

63. January 9, 1950, letter, quoted by Snow at May 18, 1950, memorial service for Smedley in New York City. Copy of remarks with Elinor Brundin.

64. Hilda Selwyn-Clarke to Mildred Price, May 9, 1950 (courtesy of A. Ishigaki).

65. Hilda Selwyn-Clarke to Mildred Price, May 9, 1950. Margaret Watson Sloss was a nurse and had known Smedley in Hong Kong.

66. Letter to Brooks quoted by Snow at memorial service (May 18) for Smedley; see also Smedley to Aino Taylor, April 28, 1950.

67. Copy courtesy of Ayako Ishigaki.

CONCLUSION

1. Velde, in *New York Times,* June 13, 1950; *Journal-American* (New York), June 14, 1950, based on Associated Press wire story. *Shimodelai* (Beijing, 1950). See the very interesting eulogy by Yang Gang, in which she mixes praise with criticism of Smedley's bourgeois "individualism": *People's China* 3, no. 10 (May 16, 1953): 13–14; Wilfred Burchett, *At the Barricades* (New York, 1981), p. 155; also Strong and Keyssar, *Right in Her Soul,* p. 264.

2. Alfred Kohlberg, American China Policy Association press release of May 28, 1951; in F.B.I. 61–6580–324.

3. F.B.I. 61–6580–343, 345.

4. F.B.I. 61–6580–346.

5. Hahn, *China to Me,* pp. 243–44.

6. Interview with Harry Steinmetz.

Bibliography of Primary Sources

The bibliography is intended for use as a reference tool on Smedley as well as an explanation of the primary sources cited in the notes. The first two parts consist of chronological lists of Smedley's published work, beginning with her books and pamphlets, with information added about those items that are still in print. An inventory of her articles in three languages has heretofore never been attempted, and the one offered here is probably incomplete. The next two parts provide detail about the government intelligence archives and collections of Smedley letters cited in the text, giving their locations around the world. At the end, listed in alphabetical order with locations and dates, are the names of Smedley contemporaries whom the authors interviewed over a fourteen-year period. These interviews were usually in depth and often involved multiple sessions.

BOOKS AND PAMPHLETS BY AGNES SMEDLEY

India and the Next War, Amritsar, India: Sohan S. Josh, 1928 (pamphlet).

Daughter of Earth. New York: Coward-McCann, 1929. Reprinted in a shortened version with an introduction by Malcolm Cowley, New York: Coward-McCann, 1935. 1929 edition reprinted New York: Feminist Press, 1973 and 1986 (paper).

(Co-editor), *Five Years of Kuomintang Reaction*. Shanghai: China Forum, 1932.

(Editor), *Short Stories from China*. Trans. Cze Ming-Ting (George Kennedy), with an introduction by Agnes Smedley. New York: International Publishers, ca. 1933.

Chinese Destinies: Sketches of Present-Day China. New York: Vanguard Press, 1933. Reprinted Westport, Conn.: Hyperion, 1977.

China's Red Army Marches. New York: Vanguard Press, 1934. Also published as *Red Flood over China,* Moscow and Leningrad: Co-operative Publishing Society of Foreign Workers in the U.S.S.R., 1934. Reprinted Westport, Conn.: Hyperion, 1977.

(Co-editor), *Banhua Xuanji: Kaisui kelehuizhi* (Selected Prints of Käthe Kollwitz). Shanghai: Sanxian shuwu, 1936.

Zhong-Ri wenti yu Xi'an shibian (The Sino-Japanese Question and the Xi'an Incident). Interview with Mao Zedong. Yan'an: n.p., 1937 (pamphlet).

China Fights Back: An American Woman with the Eighth Route Army. New York: Vanguard Press, 1938. Reprinted Westport, Conn.: Hyperion, 1977.

Stories of the Wounded: An Appeal for Orthopaedic Centres of the Chinese Red Cross. Hong Kong: n.p., 1941 (pamphlet).

Battle Hymn of China. New York: Knopf, 1943. Reprinted as *China Correspondent,* London: Methuen, 1984 (paper).

The Great Road: The Life and Times of Chu Teh. New York: Monthly Review Press, 1956. Paper ed., 1972, still in print.

Portraits of Chinese Women in Revolution. Edited by Jan and Steve MacKinnon, with an introduction. New York: Feminist Press, 1976, in print (paper).

ARTICLES BY AGNES SMEDLEY

"Tascosa." *Tempe Normal Student,* January 19, 1912.

"The Valentine." *Tempe Normal Student,* February 16, 1912.

"The Magazine Agent." *Tempe Normal Student,* March 22, 1912.

Editorial. *Tempe Normal Student,* March 29, 1912.

Review. *Tempe Normal Student,* April 12, 1912.

"The Romance." *Tempe Normal Student,* April 12, 1912.

"The Yellow Man." *Tempe Normal Student,* February 28, 1913.

"All India Revolts against Rule of Briton: Mass Meeting." *Fresno Morning Republican,* September 25, 1916.

Book review (as Alice Bird). *Modern Review* (Calcutta) 27, no. 3 (March 1919): 271–73.

"Sidelights on Women of India." *The Call,* March 16, 1919.

"Babies and Imperialism in Japan." *Birth Control Review* 3, no. 6 (June 1919): 6–8.

"The Spirit of Revolt in Hindu Poetry." *The Call,* June 22, 1919.

"Trinity of Starvation, Disease, and Executions Bringing 'Peace' to India." *The Call,* September 16, 1919.

"The Awakening of Japan." *Birth Control Review* 4, no. 2 (February 1920): 6–8.

"Britain Trembles for Fear of Losing East." *The Call,* February 3, 1920.

"Britain Seeks to Expand Empire by Control of Air." *The Call,* February 8, 1920.

"Cell Mate, Nos. 1–4." *The Call,* February 15, 22, 29, March 14, 1920.

"Modern Drama in Teaching." *The Call,* February 20, 1920.

"Indians Mark Sepoy Revolt by Continued Demand for Liberty." *The Call,* May 10, 1920.

"Garbage Scows Poison Entire Section of City." *The Call,* July 23, 1920.

"176 Ex-Soldiers in Sing-Sing, Quashed Prison Papers Shows." *The Call,* August 19, 1920.

Book review. *Modern Review* 28, no. 6 (December 1920): 626–28.

"Letter on Question of Indian Home Rule." *Modern Review* 29, no. 1 (January 1921): 108.

Book review (as Alice Bird). *Modern Review* 30, no. 1 (July 1921): 41–46.

"The Parliament of Man." *The Liberator* 4 (October 1921): 13–15.

Book review (as Alice Bird). *Modern Review* 31, no. 1 (January 1922): 75–77.

Book review (as Alice Bird). *Modern Review* 31, no. 3 (March 1922): 291–93.

"Jodh Singh." *Nation* 114 (March 22, 1922): 341–42.

Book review (as Alice Bird). *Modern Review* 33, no. 1 (January 1923): 44–46.

Book review (as Alice Bird). *Modern Review* 33, no. 6 (June 1923): 680–84.

"Starving Germany." *Nation* 117 (November 28, 1923): 601–2.

"Die indische Frau von gestern und heute." *Frau: Monatsschrift für das Gesampte Frauenleben unserer Zeit* 32 (1924): 239–44, 279–83.

"Akali Movement: An Heroic Epic." *Nation* 119 (July 2, 1924): 15–17.

"Die Inderin von heute." *Neue Generation: Zeitschrift für Mutterschutz und Sexuelle Reform* (1925): 95–100.

"Der kommende Krieg gegen Asien." *International Arbeiter-Assoziation* 2, no. 64 (1925): 22–28.

"India's Role in World Politics." *Modern Review* 37, no. 5 (May 1925): 530–41.

"Indien als entscheidender Faktor der Weltpolitik." *Zeitschrift für Geopolitik* 2, no. 6 (June 1925): 385–403.

"Germany's Artist of Social Misery." *Modern Review* 38, no. 2 (August 1925): 148–55.

"Die Frau in Indien." *Neue Zürcher Zeitung,* August 12, 1925.

"Käthe Kollwitz: Germany's Artist of the Masses." *Industrial Pioneers* 2 (September 1925): 4–9.

"Freiwilliger Opfertod bei den Hindus." *Neue Zürcher Zeitung,* December 24, 1925.

"Indiens nationale Führerin," *Deutsche Allgemeine Zeitung,* December 31, 1925.

"Indiens Führerin (Sarojini Naidu)." *Frau im Staat: Eine Monatsschrift* 8, no. 4 (1926): 2–5.

"Adult Education in Czechoslovakia." *Modern Review* 39, no. 1 (January 1926): 8–13.

"Prague—The City of the Czechs." *Modern Review* 39, no. 4 (April 1926): 378–82.

"Cultural Film in Germany." *Modern Review* 40, no. 1 (July 1926): 61–66.

"Denmark's Creative Women. I: Karin Michaelis." *Modern Review* 40, no. 2 (August 1926): 149–53.

"Denmark's Creative Women. II: Betty Nansen." *Modern Review* 40, no. 3 (September 1926): 265–68.

"Indiens Dichterin." *Berliner Tageblatt,* September 4, 1926.

"Indians in European Zoological Gardens." *The People* 3, no. 10 (September 5, 1926): 202–4.

"Denmark's Creative Women. III: Ingrid Jespersen." *Modern Review* 40, no. 4 (October 1926): 366–71.

"The Negro Renaissance." *Modern Review* 40, no. 6 (December 1926): 657–61.

"The Salzburg Festival Plays." *Modern Review* 41, no. 1 (January 1927): 40–56.

"Indonesia's Struggle for Freedom." *The People* 4, no. 1 (January 2, 1927): 11–13.

"Indonesia's Struggle for Freedom" (Part II). *The People* 4, no. 2 (January 9, 1927): 28–30.

"Indians in the Zoo." *The People* 4, no. 12 (March 20, 1927): 220–22, and Correspondence, p. 224.

"China and the Indian Press." *The People* 4, no. 16 (April 19, 1927): 307–8.

"Dr. Helena Lange." *Modern Review* 41, no. 5 (May 1927): 566–72.

"Chinese Peasant Movement 1926" (trans. Agnes Smedley). *The People* 4, no. 21 (May 29, 1927): 426–27.

"Factory Life in China" (trans. A. Smedley). *The People* 4, no. 26 (June 26, 1927): 504–6.

"The Chinese Woman Today: An Interview with Madame Sun Yat Sen." *Modern Review* 42, no. 1 (July 1927): 31–33.

"One Is Not Made of Wood." *New Masses* (August 1927): 5–7.

"A Last Word About 'Female.'" *The People* 5, no. 3 (August 4, 1927): 88–89.

"Indian Revolutionary Movement Abroad: An Historical Sketch." *The People* 5, no. 6 (August 11, 1927): 110–11.

"Indian Revolutionary Movement Abroad: An Historical Sketch" (Part II). *The People* 5, no. 7 (August 18, 1927): 129–31.

"Who Is Putnam Weale?" *The People* 5, no. 7 (August 18, 1927): 136–37.

"England's War Plans against Asia: India and the Next War." *The People* 5, no. 8 (August 25, 1927): 148–51; no. 9 (September 1, 1927): 169–70; no. 12 (September 22, 1927): 223–25; no. 15 (October 13, 1927): 278–80.

"Mother India" (review). *Modern Review* 42, no. 3 (September 1927): 296–99.

"Britain's Agents in Russia." *The People* 5, no. 10 (September 8, 1927): 189.

"Mother India" (review). *New Masses* (November 1927): 26–27.

"A Woman Young Turk." *The People* 5, no. 21 (November 24, 1927): 378–79.

"Letter to Lajpat Rai." *Forward* (Calcutta, India), January 29, 1928.

"Margaret Sanger Comes to Berlin." *Birth Control Review* 7, no. 2 (February 1928): 50–51, 54, 66.

"Die Neger-Renaissance." *Der Philologe* 3, no. 6 (March 15, 1928): 1–2.

"A Berlin Birth Control Clinic." *Birth Control Review* 7, no. 6 (June 1928): 179.

"Theatre in Revolutionary Russia." *Modern Review* 44, no. 2 (August 1928): 177–83, and Reviews, 165–67.

"Germany's Red Front." *Nation* 127 (August 1, 1928): 116–17.

Reviews. *Modern Review* 44, no. 5 (November 1928): 545–47.

"German Literature since the War" (co-author, with Julian Gumperz). *Modern Review* 45, no. 2 (February 1929): 171–74.

"Writing since the War" (co-author, with Julian Gumperz). *Survey* 61 (February 1, 1929): 596.

"Birth Control in Germany." *Birth Control Review* 8, no. 3 (March 1929): 77–78.

"The Wild Children of Russia." *Nation* 128 (April 10, 1929): 436–37.

"Lajpat Rai." *The People* 8 (April 13, 1929): 11 (special issue).

Review (as M. R.). *China Weekly Review* (July 6, 1929): 260–61.

Review. *China Weekly Review* (July 27, 1929): 392.

"Nanking" and "Sun Yat-sen's Funeral." *Modern Review* 46, no. 2 (August 1929): 137–42, 167–73.

Review. *China Weekly Review* (August 10, 1929): 484–86.

Review. *China Weekly Review* (August 24, 1929): 566.

Review (as M. R.). *China Weekly Review* (August 31, 1929): 628.

Review. *China Weekly Review* (September 14, 1929): 102–4.

Review. *China Weekly Review* (September 21, 1929): 142–43.

Review. *China Weekly Review* (September 28, 1929): 175–76.

Review. *China Weekly Review* (October 5, 1929): 212.

Review. *China Weekly Review* (October 19, 1929): 282.

"Creative Woman of Germany: Dr. Alice Salomon." *Modern Review* 46, no. 5 (November 1929): 513–18.

"Die 'Amerikanisierung' Chinas." *Frankfurter Zeitung*, November 3, 1929 (second morning edition).

"Eine Frau allein." *Frankfurter Zeitung*, November 6, 1929, through December 12, 1929; 32 installments (second morning edition).

"Die Zensur in China." *Frankfurter Zeitung*, November 14, 1929 (evening edition).

"Küssen ist keine Sünde—aber in China." *Frankfurter Zeitung*, November 16, 1929 (first morning edition).

"Chinesische Generale." *Frankfurter Zeitung*, November 22, 1929 (first morning edition).

"Schanghai, die unruhige Stadt." *Frankfurter Zeitung*, November 27, 1929 (second morning edition).

"Immer noch kein Ausweg in China." *Frankfurter Zeitung*, December 8, 1929 (second morning edition).

"Chinesische Hochzeiten." *Frankfurter Zeitung*, December 12, 1929 (first morning edition).

"Exterritorialität und Aussenhandel in China." *Frankfurter Zeitung*, December 18, 1929 (second morning edition).

"Wenn in Schanghai 'Verbrecher' verfolgt werden." *Frankfurter Zeitung*, December 24, 1929 (Christmas Eve edition).

"Das Schicksal von Hsu Mei-ling." *Frankfurter Zeitung*, December 25, 1929 (second morning edition).

"Währungsreform in China?" *Frankfurter Zeitung*, December 28, 1929 (second morning edition).

"Wird die Exterritorialität in China wirklich aufgehoben?" *Frankfurter Zeitung*, January 8, 1930 (second morning edition).

"Berlin-Schanghai—Eine deutsche Fluglinie nach China." *Frankfurter Zeitung*, January 12, 1930.

"Die kühne Piratin." *Frankfurter Zeitung*, January 28, 1930 (first morning edition).

"Die Bürgerkriege in China—und was weiter?" *Frankfurter Zeitung*, February 5, 1930.

"Amerikanische Studenten 'erforschen' China." *Frankfurter Zeitung*, February 11, 1930.

"300.000 Ausländer in China." *Frankfurter Zeitung*, February 18, 1930.

"Wissenschaftliche Forschung in China." *Frankfurter Zeitung*, March 16, 1930.

"Theater—Eine revolutionäre Anstalt." *Frankfurter Zeitung*, March 24, 1930.

"Tendencies in Modern Chinese Literature." *Modern Review* 47, no. 4 (April 1930): 431–38.

"Hsu Mei-Ling." *New Republic* 62 (April 9, 1930): 219.

"Eine grosszügige Aktion in China." *Frankfurter Zeitung*, April 17, 1930.

"Zhongguo nongcun shenghuo jiduan." *Mengya yuekan* 1, no. 5 (May 1930): 175–81.

"Dchiang Kai-Schek rechnet ab." *Frankfurter Zeitung*, May 1, 1930.

"Chinese Poets and Professors." *New York Herald Tribune*, May 18, 1930.

"Die Chinesin treibt Sport." *Frankfurter Zeitung*, May 31, 1930.

"Chinese Athletes." *Modern Review* 47, no. 6 (June 1930): 739–41.

"Five Women of Mukden." *New Republic* 63 (June 11, 1930): 99–101.

"Revolte in Korea." *Frankfurter Zeitung*, June 13, 1930.

"Cinéma aus Schanghai." *Frankfurter Zeitung*, June 15, 1930.

"Gegen die Zensur in China." *Frankfurter Zeitung*, July 23, 1930.

"China in der Wirtschaftskrise." *Frankfurter Zeitung*, August 3, 1930.

"Russische Weissgardisten im britischen Dienst." *Frankfurter Zeitung*, August 10, 1930.

"Für die chinesische Gerichtsbarkeit." *Frankfurter Zeitung*, August 13, 1930.

"Die Memoiren des 'christlichen' Generals." *Frankfurter Zeitung*, August 25, 1930.

"Von einem toten General." *Frankfurter Zeitung*, August 26, 1930.

"Revolutionary Theatre in China." *New Masses* (September 1930): 9–10.

"War and Revolution in China." *Modern Review* 48, no. 3 (September 1930): 245–49.

"Peasants and Lords in China." *New Republic* 64 (September 3, 1930): 69–71.

"Mui Tsai." *Frankfurter Zeitung*, September 10, 1930.

"Opfer des Opiums und eine allgemeine Enquete in China?" *Frankfurter Zeitung*, September 14, 1930.

"Gefängmisse in China." *Frankfurter Zeitung*, September 15, 1930.

"Die Verschiebung der Fronten in China." *Frankfurter Zeitung*, October 24, 1930.

"Bei den Bauern von Kwangtung." *Frankfurter Zeitung*, November 28, 1930.

"Amongst the Peasants of Kwangtung." *Modern Review* 48, no. 6 (December 1930): 683–88.

"A Chinese Red Army." *New Masses* (January 1931): 8–9.

"Students and Communism in China." *Modern Review* 49, no. 2 (February 1931): 158–61.

"Thru Darkness in China." *New Masses* (February 1931): 10–11.

"Women in the Philippines." *Modern Review* 49, no. 4 (April 1931): 456–61.

"Portraits from the Philippines." *Modern Review* 49, no. 5 (May 1931): 577–79.

"Shan-Fei, Communist." *New Masses* (May 1931): 3–5, and Smedley bio. and picture, p. 23.

"Philippine Sketches." *New Masses* (June 1931): 12–13.

"Wars of Rival Generals Continue in China." *Modern Review* 50, no. 3 (September 1931): 315–17.

"Death Comes to China." *Modern Review* 50, no. 5 (November 1931): 513–18.

"Birth Control Not Enough for China." *Nation* 134 (March 9, 1932): 282–83.

"Horrors at Shanghai." *Nation* 134 (March 30, 1932): 369–71.

"Japanese at Shanghai." *Modern Review* 51, no. 4 (April 1932): 402–6.

"Shanghai Thermopylae." *Modern Review* 51, no. 5 (May 1932): 501–6.

"The 19th Route Army Speaks" (presumed author). *New Masses* (June 1932): 6.

"Li Dschen-Sung—Chinese Revolutionist" (presumed author). *New Masses* (February 1933): 15–18.

"Extracts from Letters—Dr. Yang Chien Assassinated." *New Republic* 75 (July 26, 1933): 291.

"Dirge for a Dead Hero." *Asia* 34 (March 1934): 144–47.

"A White Episode." *International Literature* (June 1934): 20–24.

"Shanghai Episode." *New Republic* 79 (June 13, 1934): 122–24.

"China's 'Renaissance'—A Review of *The Chinese Renaissance* by Hu Shih." *Nation* 139 (August 29, 1934): 250.

"Day with China's Red Army." *Travel* 63 (September 1934): 18–21.

"Soldiers for China." *Golden Book Magazine* 20 (September 1934): 251–57.

"The Puppet Emperor—A Review of *Twilight in the Forbidden City* by Sir Reginald Johnson." *Nation* 139 (September 19, 1934): 332.

"Truth about the Chinese Reds." *American Mercury* 33 (October 1934): 200–210.

" 'Peace and Order' in China—A Review of Problems in the Pacific, 1933. Proceedings of the 5th Conference of the Institute of Pacific Relations, 1933." *Nation* 140 (January 2, 1935): 24.

Letter by A.S. attacking Tang Leangli (editor of the *People's Tribune*). *China Today* 1, no. 6 (March 1935): 110.

"China Betrayed." *China Today* 1, no. 8 (May 1935): 144–55.

"Corrupt Press in China." *Nation* 141 (July 3, 1935): 8–10.

"When the Radicals Quarrel—Agnes Smedley's Reply." *China Weekly Review* (August 31, 1935): 488.

"A Day Passes." *Voice of Youth*, December 5, 1935.

"Brief aus China." *AIZ Das Illustrierte Volksblatt* 15, no. 4 (January 23, 1936): 50–52.

"The Students Fight" (as R. Knailes). *Voice of China* 1, no. 1 (March 15, 1936): 3–6.

"The Northern Front" (as R. Knailes). *Voice of China* 2, no. 2 (April 1, 1936): 3–4.

"Peace, Order, and Banditry" (as R. Knailes). *Voice of China* 2, no. 3 (April 15, 1936): 12–13.

"China's Rulers Ride the Tiger." *China Today* 2, no. 8 (May 1936): 148–50.

"We Shall Drive All China . . ." (as R. Knailes). *Voice of China* 2, no. 4 (May 1, 1936): 4–5, 18, 22.

"Vignettes from China." *Partisan Review* 3, no. 6 (October 1936): 26–28.

"Bei der Volks-Armee in Shensi." *Die Volks-Illustrierte*, no date [1937–38].

"How Chiang Was Captured." *Nation* 144 (February 13, 1937): 180–82.

"Hundred White Horses." *Nation* 144 (April 3, 1937): 377–78.

"China wehrt sich." *Die Volks-Illustrierte*, no. 31 (August 1937): n.p.

"Chinese Theatre in the Trenches." *Daily Worker,* October 28, 1937.

"Chinese Red Army Goes to Town." *Modern Review* 62, no. 5 (November 1937): 486–88.

"China's Silent Heroes—Wounded Soldiers of Shansi." *China Weekly Review* (November 6, 1937): 214–15.

"Zhuinian Lu Xun." *Wenxue* 9, no. 4 (November 10, 1937): 139–44.

"We Start for the Front." *Modern Review* 62, no. 6 (December 1937): 606–14.

"Interview with Chu Teh." *Modern Review* 63, no. 1 (January 1938): 9–11.

"China's Silent Heroes." *New Masses* (January 4, 1938): 5.

"Chinese People Arm Themselves." *Modern Review* 63, no. 2 (February 1938): 133–40.

"Help Needed for Eighth Route Army and Partisans of Northwest." *China Weekly Review* (March 5, 1938): 12–13.

Letter to Editor: "Aid for Chinese Fighters." *Nation* 146 (June 11, 1938): 682.

"Bombing in Canton." *Manchester Guardian,* July 1, 1938.

"Japanese Bomb Treaty Port." *Manchester Guardian,* July 2, 1938.

"Swatou Bombed and Shelled." *Manchester Guardian,* July 4, 1938.

"Fifty Japanese Planes." *Manchester Guardian,* July 5, 1938.

"Fresh General Offensive." *Manchester Guardian,* July 6, 1938.

"Three Japanese Warships Sunk." *Manchester Guardian,* July 11, 1938.

"Japanese to Bomb." *Manchester Guardian,* July 12, 1938.

"Advance on Hankow." *Manchester Guardian,* July 20, 1938.

"Yangtze Port's Fate." *Manchester Guardian,* July 26, 1938.

"Japan's Next Moves." *Manchester Guardian,* July 30, 1938.

"Another Crisis." *Manchester Guardian,* August 2, 1938.

"Japanese Drive on Hankow." *Manchester Guardian,* August 2, 1938.

"Shanghai to Hankow." *Manchester Guardian,* August 3, 1938.

"The Guerrilla War in China." *Manchester Guardian,* August 4, 1938.

"Japanese Give Up on Advance." *Manchester Guardian,* August 6, 1938.

"Japanese Held on the Yangtze." *Manchester Guardian,* August 10, 1938.

"Fu lu." *Kangzhan wenyi* 3, no. 4 (August 13, 1938): 56.

"Hankow's Worst Air Raid." *Manchester Guardian,* August 13, 1938.

"Japanese Bomb *Four* Cities." *Manchester Guardian,* August 17, 1938.

"Japanese Checked." *Manchester Guardian,* August 18, 1938.

"Japan Attacks Again." *Manchester Guardian,* August 23, 1938.

"The Wounded in China." *Manchester Guardian,* August 24, 1938.

"Japan Using Poison Gas." *Manchester Guardian,* September 1, 1938.

"Chinese Claim Big Victory." *Manchester Guardian,* September 2, 1938.

"Chinese Effort to Save Railway." *Manchester Guardian,* September 3, 1938.

"Chinese Fight Back." *Manchester Guardian,* September 6, 1938.

"Setback of Chinese." *Manchester Guardian,* September 7, 1938.

"Defenders of Hankow Falling Back." *Manchester Guardian,* September 9, 1938.

"Two Japanese Forces Retreat." *Manchester Guardian,* September 10, 1938.

"The Soldiers of China." *Manchester Guardian,* September 13, 1938.

"Chinese Defend Kwangchow." *Manchester Guardian,* September 20, 1938.

"Chinese Hold Key Town." *Manchester Guardian,* September 22, 1938.

"Chinese Soldier." *Modern Review* 64, no. 4 (October 1938): 426–28.

"Japanese Push on the Yangtze." *Manchester Guardian,* October 7, 1938.

"Chinese Resist Advance." *Manchester Guardian,* October 8, 1938.

"Japanese Advances in North and South China." *Manchester Guardian,* October 10, 1938.

"Struggle for Railway North of Hankow." *Manchester Guardian,* October 10, 1938.

"Japanese Landings in South China." *Manchester Guardian,* October 13, 1938.

"The Advance on Hankow." *Manchester Guardian,* October 17, 1938.

"Japan Costs Again" (editorial). *Manchester Guardian,* October 19, 1938.

"Fall of Canton" (editorial). *Manchester Guardian,* October 22, 1938.

"Japanese Advance on Canton." *Manchester Guardian,* October 22, 1938.

"Chinese Stunned." *Manchester Guardian,* October 24, 1938.

"Last Stages of Fight for Hankow." *Manchester Guardian,* October 25, 1938.

"Refugees Still Pouring out of Hankow." *Manchester Guardian,* October 25, 1938.

"After Hankow." *Manchester Guardian,* October 26, 1938.

"Great Fires in Hankow as Japanese Enter." *Manchester Guardian,* October 26, 1938.

"British Move in China." *Manchester Guardian,* October 27, 1938.

"Japan Still Determined to Crush China." *Manchester Guardian,* October 28, 1938.

"The Last Days of Hankow." *Manchester Guardian,* October 28, 1938.

"China Will Resist Till Japan Is Exhausted." *Manchester Guardian,* November 4, 1938.

"China's Wounded." *Nation* 147 (November 5, 1938): 477–79.

"Pictures of Fall of Hankow." *Manchester Guardian,* November 18, 1938.

Letter to Editor: "Response to 'China's Wounded' article by William H. Talbot." *Nation* 147 (November 19, 1938): 548.

"Pictures of Japanese Advance in Hankow." *Manchester Guardian,* November 21, 1938.

"After Hankow—Changsha, Hunan." *Manchester Guardian,* December 2, 1938.

"North China—Japan's Endless Struggle." *Manchester Guardian,* December 13, 1938.

"North China." *Manchester Guardian,* December 14, 1938.

"New Fourth Army Springs into Limelight as Leading Guerilla Force." *China Weekly Review* (December 17, 1938): 76–78.

"The Wounded." *Manchester Guardian,* December 24, 1938.

"The Wounded—The Problem of Women." *Manchester Guardian,* December 27, 1938.

"Rival Governments in North China." *Manchester Guardian,* December 29, 1938.

"Hospitals in China." *Manchester Guardian,* January 17, 1939.

"The Peasants of China." *Manchester Guardian,* February 9, 1939.

"A Japanese Soldier's Diary." *China Weekly Review* (February 18, 1939): 372.

"The Japanese in China." *Manchester Guardian,* March 9, 1939.

"China Shall Arise Again" (ghost-written for Mme. Chiang Kai-shek). *China Weekly Review* (March 11, 1939): 45.

"Sources of Sadism in the China War." *China Weekly Review* (March 18, 1939): 67–68.

"China's Unknown Soldier." *China Weekly Review* (April 8, 1939): 177.

"Takemasu Enyu's Diary." *New Masses* (April 18, 1939): 7.

"Guerrilla War in China." *Manchester Guardian,* April 26, 1939.

"China's Refugee Millions Stricken by Hunger and Disease." *China Weekly Review* (May 20, 1939): 378–80.

"Sadism in China." *New Masses* (May 23, 1939): 3–4.

"China's Guerrilla Warfare." Reprint from *Manchester Guardian,* April 26, 1939, in *Shanghai Evening Post and Mercury,* May 25, 1939.

"Sad Plight of China's War Refugees, Told by Prominent American Writer." *China Weekly Review* (September 9, 1939): 55–58.

"Lu Xun shi yiba baojian," *Wenhua yuekan,* no. 3 (October 27, 1939): 1–2.

"Agnes Smedley Addresses Club." *China at War* 4, no. 5 (June 1940): 36–40.

"The Other Great War: Resistance or Surrender in China?" *Manchester Guardian,* August 30, 1940.

"Conditions in Hong Kong." *South China Morning Post,* September 21, 1940.

Correspondence. *South China Morning Post,* September 27, 1940.

Correspondence. *South China Morning Post,* September 28, 1940.

"The People in China." *The Clipper* 2, no. 6 (August 1941): 4–10.

"The Light of East Asia—Observations in England's Colony of Hong Kong." *The Clipper* 2, no. 7 (September 1941): 11–16.

Letter to Editor: "Declare War on Axis!" *New Republic* 105 (September 22, 1941): 375.

"What China's Fighters Are Thinking." *Asia* 41 (December 1941): 680–85.

"After the Final Victory." *Men at War,* ed. Ernest Hemingway. New York: Crown, 1942, pp. 768–74.

"After the Final Victory." *Asia* 42 (February 1942): 119–23.

"China—Front Door to Freedom." *California Arts and Architecture* 59 (April 1942): 17, 38.

"Guerrilla Court Martial." *Town and Country* 97 (April 1942): 41.

"No Sacrifice—No Victory." *Vogue* (April 15, 1942): 48, 49, 87.

"Memories after Midnight." *Asia* 42 (September 1942): 510–13.

"Imperialistic Sins in Burma—A Review of *Retreat with Stilwell* by Jack Belden." *The Progressive* 7 (March 29, 1943): 7.

"With the Chinese Guerrillas." *New Republic* 108 (April 12, 1943): 471–73.

"The Mind of China's Ruling Class—A Review of *All We Are And All We Have* by Chiang Kai-shek." *The Progressive* 7 (May 10, 1943): 5.

"Jefferson: Still 50 Years Ahead—A Review of *Jefferson: The Road to Glory* by Marie Kimball; *Thomas Jefferson* by Hendrik Willem Van Loon; and *Jefferson Himself* by Bernard Mayo." *The Progressive* 7 (August 23, 1943): 9.

Letter to Editor. *New York Herald-Tribune,* September 6, 1943.

"Lin Yutang Scolds and Warns—A Review of *Between Tears and Laughter* by Dr. Lin Yutang," *The Progressive* 7 (September 13, 1943): 8.

"Tell Your Countrymen." *New Republic* 109 (September 13, 1943): 366.

"Smedley Lecture at Skidmore College." *Publishers Weekly* 144 (October 16, 1943): 1529.

"What Chinese Soldiers Asked Me to Tell—A Message to the German People." *The German American,* October 19, 1943.

"Answer to Grace Cook." *Shanghai Evening Post and Mercury* (New York), October 29, 1943.

"Review of *A Short History of Chinese Civilization,* by Tsiu Chi." *Nation* 157 (November 13, 1943): 558–59.

"A Few Things You Should Know about China," *Red Book* 82 (March 1944): 56–57, 80–82.

"Plain Talk about China—A Review of *Shark's Fins and Millet* by Ralf Sues." *Nation* 158 (April 15, 1944): 452.

"China's Great Past—A Review of L. Carrington Goodrich's *A Short History of the Chinese People.*" *Nation* 159 (July 8, 1944): 246.

"God Damned Those White Southerners." *Afro-American,* July 29, 1944.

"His Majesty's Opposition—A Review of Sun Fo's *China Looks Forward.*" *New Republic* 111 (August 21, 1944): 224.

"The Generalissimo—A Review of *Chiang Kai-shek: Asia's Man of Destiny* by Dr. H. H. Chang." *Nation* 159 (August 26, 1944): 755.

"Essence of Modern War—A Review of Jack Belden's *Still Time to Die.*" *New Republic* 111 (October 2, 1944): 433.

"Crisis in China: Defeat and Disunity." *PM,* October 22, 1944.

"Stilwell Scapegoat for China's Defeats." *PM,* October 30, 1944.

"Nehru and Jefferson." *Voice of India* (November 1944): 42–45.

"The City of Peter and Lenin—A Review of Alexander Werth's *Leningrad.*" *New Republic* 111 (November 13, 1944): 636–37.

"Chinese Shakeup Strictly Ersatz." *PM,* November 21, 1944.

"Behind the News in China—A Review of Laurence K. Rosinger's *China's Wartime Politics 1937–1944.*" *New Republic* 111 (November 27, 1944): 697.

Speech. *Skidmore News,* December 7, 1944.

"Agnes Smedley's Open Letter to Henry R. Luce—Challenging *Time Life* articles on China." *PM,* December 10, 1944.

Letters to Editor: "A Few Remarks" (response to A. S.'s review of his *Chiang Kai-shek* by Dr. H. H. Chang, with Smedley's reply). *Nation* 159 (December 16, 1944): 755.

"War Without End—Reviews of *The Art of War* by Sun Tzu; *Winter Cherry* by Keith West; *The Phoenix and the Dwarf* by George E. Taylor and George M. Savage." *New Republic* 111 (December 18, 1944): 844.

"Voice from the Grave" (editor). *New Republic* 112 (May 28, 1945): 747–49.

"China Political Strife Heads to Showdown." *PM,* August 19, 1945.

Letter to Editor: "A Tokyo Rose." *PM,* September 15, 1945.

"J. B. Powell's China—A Review of *My Twenty-Five Years in China.*" *New Republic* 113 (November 26, 1945): 717–18.

"Pertinent Poetry." *Nation* 161 (December 29, 1945): 161.

"The Social Revolution." *China,* ed. H. F. MacNair. Berkeley and Los Angeles: University of California Press, 1946, pp. 167–99.

"Sun Yat Sen: A Partial Portrait—A Review of *Sun Yat Sen: A Portrait* by Stephen Chen and Robert Payne." *Nation* 163 (August 17, 1946): 187.

"We're Building a Fascist China." *Nation* 163 (August 31, 1946): 236–38.

Letter to Editor: "Arms and the Chinese." *Knickerbocker News,* September 23, 1946.

"The Real China—A Review of Theodore H. White and Annalee Jacoby's *Thunder Out of China.*" *Nation* 163 (November 30, 1946): 619.

"In Memoriam—Evans Carlson." *Social Questions Bulletin* 38, no. 4 (May 1948): 64–66, 74–75.

"General Stilwell Speaks." *Far East Spotlight* (June 1948): 15.

"Tokyo Martyrs." *Far East Spotlight* (March 1949): 3–5.

"J'accuse." *China Digest* (Hong Kong) (March 8, 1949): 8–9.

"From Sun Yat-sen to Chinese People's Republic." *National Guardian,* October 10, 1949.

"Terror Bombing in China." *Labour Monthly* (July 1950): 302–4.

"Agnes Smedley's Last Plea." *Korean Handbook,* ed. Labour Monthly. London: Trinity Trust, 1950, pp. 9–12.

GOVERNMENT INTELLIGENCE COLLECTIONS, BY LOCATION

British Police and Army Intelligence (Indian Colonial Service)
    India Library, London, England.
    Jawaharlal Nehru University, New Delhi: P. C. Joshi Collection.
    National Archives, New Delhi: Meerut Conspiracy Case Exhibits and Session Court Judgement.

U.S. Government
    Federal Bureau of Investigation, Washington, D.C. Relevant files: 100–68282; 61–6580; 100–9125 (100–68282–1B32 [Exhibits] contains Willoughby and British Shanghai police materials).
    National Archives, Washington, D.C.: General Records of the Justice Department, Immigration, RG 60, 118; U.S. Army Intelligence Division, RG 165, and Shanghai Municipal Police (British) files on other matters besides Smedley in Box D.
    U.S. Army, Far East Command, Military Intelligence Section (G–2), *Sorge Espionage Case,* dated December 15, 1947 (confidential printing by House Un-American Activities Committee, U.S. Congress, 1951).

SMEDLEY LETTERS AND ARCHIVAL SOURCES, BY LOCATION

Arizona State University, Hayden Library, Tempe
    F. McCracken Fisher papers (letters to Fisher)
    Smedley papers (includes letters to Zhu De and Evans Carlson, as well as Smedley's personal files and photographs in her possession in 1949)

Archibald T. Steele papers
See also Private collections
Chinese History Museum, Beijing, China
    Smedley papers (includes photographs, letters to and from Zhu De, and mementos from memorial meetings)
Det Kongelige Bibliotek, Copenhagen, Denmark
    Karin Michaelis papers (letters to Michaelis)
Dwarka Das Library, Chandigarh, Punjab, India
    Lajpat Rai's personal library
Jawaharlal Nehru Memorial Library, Teen Mooti House, New Delhi, India
    All India Congress Committee (A.I.C.C.) papers
    Ramanand Chatterjee papers
    Dr. N. S. Hardiker papers
    Raja Hutheesing papers
    Motilal Nehru papers
    Jawaharlal Nehru papers (letters to and from Nehru; oral histories)
London, England
    Public Records Office, Foreign Office files, 676 series (concerning medical aid to China)
National Archives, Manuscript Collections, Washington, D.C.
    Margaret Sanger papers (letters to and from Sanger and Josephine Bennett)
    Harold Ickes papers (letters to and from Ickes, Mme. Vijaya Pandit)
    Gilbert Roe papers (Boxes H7 and H8 of LaFollette family papers: letters to and from Roe, legal briefs, and Friends of Freedom for India materials)
Newberry Library, Chicago, Ill.
    Malcolm Cowley papers (letters to Cowley, Yaddo records)
Princeton University, Firestone Library, Princeton, N.J.
    Roger Baldwin papers (Boxes 4, 5, and 26)
Private collections of Smedley correspondence
(copies now housed at Arizona State University, Hayden Library)
    Ernest and Elinor Brundin (includes notes from Snow memorial talk, May 18, 1950)
    Israel Epstein and Elsie Cholmeley
    John and Wilma Fairbank
    Randall Gould
    Ayako Ishigaki
    Anna Wang Martens
    Mildred Price
    Margaret Sloss, Hilda Selwyn-Clarke, and circular letters (courtesy of Ayako Ishigaki)
    Aino and Elviira Taylor
    Wang Yong (courtesy of Xie Hegeng)
Stanford University, Hoover Library, Stanford, Calif.
    Randall Gould papers
    Nym Wales Collection
University of California, Berkeley, South and Southeast Asia Library
    Friends of Freedom for India Collection (letters to and from San Francisco office, Ed Gammons)

University of Colorado Library, Boulder
    Florence Lennon papers (letters to Lennon)
University of Indiana, Lilly Library, Bloomington
    Upton Sinclair papers
Wisconsin State Historical Society, Madison
    Raymond Robins papers (letters to Robins)
    Gwyneth Roe papers (letters to G. Roe)

INTERVIEWS WITH SMEDLEY'S CONTEMPORARIES
(only initial date given for multiple sessions)

Adhikari, Gangadhar. October 16, 1977, New Delhi.
Alley, Rewi. March 15, 1978, Beijing (multiple).
An Gang. November 17, 1979, Beijing.
Basu, B. K. February 6, 1978, Calcutta (multiple).
Binder, Gertrude. January 1, 1976, New York (multiple).
Brundin, Elinor. September 7, 1975, Carmel, Calif.
Brundin, Thorberg (Haberman Ellison). January 2, 1975, Islamorada, Fl.
    (multiple).
Chattopadhyaya, Kamaladevi. November 10, 1977, New Delhi.
Chattopadhyaya, Ram. November 10, 1977, New Delhi.
Chen Hansheng. March 17, 1978, Beijing (multiple).
Chen, Jack. April 1, 1979, San Francisco.
Chen, Percy. November 24, 1978, Hong Kong.
Cholmeley, Elsie. March 19, 1978, Beijing (multiple).
Clubb, O. Edmund. December 30, 1975, New York.
Cook, Grace. August 9, 1975, Los Angeles.
Deane, Hugh. November 18, 1982, Scottsdale, Ariz. (multiple).
Ding Ling. November 10, 1979, Beijing.
Dorn, Frank. January 2, 1976, Washington, D.C.
Epstein, Israel. March 19, 1978, Beijing (multiple).
Fairbank, John. November 18, 1982, Scottsdale, Ariz.
Fairbank, Wilma. November 18, 1982, Scottsdale, Ariz.
Fisher, F. McCracken. November 18, 1982, Scottsdale, Ariz. (multiple).
Fisher, Ruth Ralls. September 10, 1976, Osgood, Mo.
Ge Baochuan. March 21, 1978, Beijing (multiple).
Gerlach, Telitha. August 6, 1977, Shanghai (multiple).
Glass, Frank. August 9, 1975, Los Angeles.
Gong Loushun. April 4, 1978, Shanghai.
Gould, Randall. July 13, 1975, Mill Valley, Calif.
Hahn, Emily. April 19, 1975, Tucson, Ariz.
Hatem, George. March 29, 1978, Beijing (multiple).
Hu Ji'an. March 21, 1978, Beijing (multiple).
Hu Xieqing. September 10, 1979, Beijing.
Huang Hua. October 3, 1984, Beijing (multiple).
Huang Shaoxiang. March 22, 1979, Beijing (multiple).
Ishigaki, Ayako. August 15, 1975, Berkeley, Calif. (multiple).

Josh, Sohan Singh. October 16, 1977, New Delhi.
Judd, Walter. March 17, 1979, by telephone.
Kang Keqing. March 30, 1978, Beijing.
Kawai Teikichi. December 23, 1978, Tokyo.
Lang, Olga. December 31, 1975, New York.
Leaf, Earl. August 12, 1975, Los Angeles.
Lennon, Florence. June 10, 1977, Boulder, Colo. (multiple).
Liu Ding. May 15, 1981, Beijing.
Liu Liangmo. April 2, 1978, Shanghai.
Loth, David. January 21, 1985, Scottsdale, Ariz.
Loth, Helen. January 21, 1985, Scottsdale, Ariz.
Lu Yunming. June 6, 1980, Beijing.
McCullough, Mamie Weston. August 14, 1975, Osgood, Mo. (multiple).
Mao Dun. March 29, 1978, Beijing.
Massing, Hede. January 1, 1976, New York.
Meng Bo. April 5, 1978, Shanghai.
Nambiar, A. C. N. July 23, 1981, Zurich.
Osaki Hotsuki. December 23, 1978, Tokyo.
Porter, Katherine A. January 2, 1976, by telephone.
Powell, Sylvia. July 12, 1975, San Francisco (multiple).
Powell, William. July 12, 1975, San Francisco (multiple).
Pruitt, Ida. September 5, 1976, Philadelphia.
Qian Junrui. February 6, 1980, Beijing (multiple).
Roots, Francis. February 13, 1976, by telephone.
Rosenberg, Trudy. October 17, 1979, Beijing (multiple).
Russell, Maude. December 10, 1974, Tempe, Ariz. (multiple).
Shen Jizhen. March 27, 1978, Beijing.
Smedley, Elizabeth. November 15, 1976, Chula Vista, Calif.
Snow, Lois W. May 10, 1984, San Francisco (multiple).
Steele, A. T. January 15, 1974, Tempe, Ariz. (multiple).
Steinmetz, Harry. November 13, 1976, San Diego, Calif. (multiple).
Tan, Rosie. November 3, 1978, Hong Kong (multiple).
Tang Mingqiao. October 3, 1984, Beijing.
Taylor, Aino. June 16, 1975, Ojai, Calif. (multiple).
Taylor, Elviira. June 16, 1975, Ojai, Calif.
Utley, Freda. June 10, 1974, Washington, D.C.
Wales, Nym. June 12, 1974, Madison, Conn.
Walker, Margaret. June 3, 1986, by telephone.
Wang Bingnan. March 30, 1978, Beijing.
Weiss, Ruth. March 18, 1978, Beijing (multiple).
White, T. H. April 21, 1979, by telephone.
Willison, Toni. June 17, 1974, Ballston Spa, N.Y. (multiple).
Wu Jiang. April 4, 1978, Shanghai.
Xia Yan. May 28, 1980, Beijing.
Xiao Qian. July 10, 1985, Beijing.
Xiao San (Emile). February 20, 1980, Beijing.
Xie Hegeng. June 4, 1981, Beijing.

Xu, Frank. June 4, 1981, Beijing (multiple).
Xu Ming. September 15, 1979, Beijing.
Xu Xizuan. May 30, 1982, Beijing.
Zhang Wenjin. November 10, 1983, Phoenix, Ariz.
Zhou Libo. March 16, 1978, Beijing.
Zhou Yang. February 6, 1980, Beijing.

INDEX